车辆动力学建模与仿真

王孝鹏 吴 龙 ◎ 著

西南交通大学出版社
·成 都·

图书在版编目（CIP）数据

车辆动力学建模与仿真 / 王孝鹏，吴龙著. —成都：西南交通大学出版社，2020.5
ISBN 978-7-5643-7411-2

Ⅰ. ①车… Ⅱ. ①王… ②吴… Ⅲ. ①车辆动力学 – 系统建模②车辆动力学 – 系统仿真 Ⅳ. ① U270.1

中国版本图书馆 CIP 数据核字（2020）第 059439 号

Cheliang Donglixue Jianmo yu Fangzhen
车辆动力学建模与仿真
王孝鹏　吴　龙　著

责 任 编 辑	刘　昕
封 面 设 计	何东琳设计工作室
出 版 发 行	西南交通大学出版社 （四川省成都市金牛区二环路北一段 111 号 西南交通大学创新大厦 21 楼）
发行部电话	028-87600564　028-87600533
邮 政 编 码	610031
网　　　址	http://www.xnjdcbs.com
印　　　刷	四川森林印务有限责任公司
成 品 尺 寸	185 mm × 260 mm
印　　　张	35
字　　　数	874 千
版　　　次	2020 年 5 月第 1 版
印　　　次	2020 年 5 月第 1 次
书　　　号	ISBN 978-7-5643-7411-2
定　　　价	280.00 元

课件咨询　81435775
图书如有印装质量问题　本社负责退换
版权所有　盗版必究　举报电话：028-87600562

序

车辆动力学是研究车辆运行过程中的动态特性，关系到整车的操纵稳定性、平顺性等性能指标，同时也可以为整车及零部件分析提供各种工况下的精确载荷谱，是研究疲劳耐久特性的前提。整车模型下研究车辆的局部子系统是一种较好的方法，此种方法在研究过程中需要建立整车模型，真实地考虑整车运行工况下局部子系统的动态特性；联合仿真模型需要同时考虑车辆子系统（或整车平台下子系统）与控制系统的结合。因此车辆模型的精确建立是研究车辆系统动力学的前提与基础。

车辆动力学研究目前主要采用两种方法：① 基于子系统或整车系统建立基本的框架数学模型，此种方法在研究过程中模型较为粗糙，忽略较多实际因素，只考虑车辆的基本动态特性；② 采用多体动力学平台建立子系统或整车平台，此种方法可以考虑部件间不同柔性衬套约束、车辆的不同轮胎特性，最明显的优势是在结构框架下建立系统级的中大及超大规模集成及耦合模型，同时在研究过程中可以与有限元结合研究多柔体系统动力学，缺点是针对系统模型计算速度较慢。

本书内容主要包含五部分。① 悬架：针对不同类型的悬架系统描述其建模过程及对应的变量参数与通信器特性，横置板簧悬架模型建模过程中引入多柔体系统动力学特性，非独立悬架模型建模过程中介绍多簧片板簧间的接触特性，复杂耦合悬架模型的引入对于大学方程式赛车设计具有指导意义，商用车平衡悬架模型介绍了模型间的合并关系及平衡悬架与推杆角度与整车稳定性关系，随动转向介绍了 FSAE 赛车后悬架结构及衬套特性对瞬时转向的影响。② 传动模型：系统介绍了发动机、变速器、传动轴、齿轮、皮带、链条、电动机、转向模型的建立及不同传动模型之间的组合，例如皮带链条电动组合传动模型，摩托车整车模型考虑链条传动、同步皮带传动。③ 整车模型：通过 CAR 与 VIEW 建立不同种类的整车平台，包括基于非独立悬架的整车模型，基于独立悬架的 FSAE 赛车模型，基于通用 VIEW 模块建立的三轮车模型、"逆"三轮车模型、摩托车模型。④ 联合仿真模型：基于 VIEW 模块建立麦弗逊联合仿真模型，通过 Control 插件把多体模型与控制系统协同为耦合模型；基于整车平台下驾驶室联合仿真模型，此模型在 6×4 商用车整车平台下研究驾驶室的振动特性，整车共包含 977 个自由度。⑤ 通过悬架、运载火箭案例介绍了在 INSIGHT 模块下工程案例的研究、优化策略，提升产品的质量、缩短研究周期。

本书是作者近些年在技术服务与课题研究中的心得，以工程案例的计算建模与仿真分析为主，在机械工程重点学科和省部级科技平台的支持下，着重探讨了整车系统的动力学仿真特性。书中的案例凝聚作者的心血，对工程设计与仿真验证具有指导意义，适合汽车工程研究院设计研发人员及高等院所高年级本科生、研究生学习车辆系统动力学之用。

王孝鹏
2020 年 1 月于三明学院

仿真模型资源包

目录 CONTENTS

第1章 绪 论 ··· 1
- 1.1 ADAMS/VIEW ··· 1
- 1.2 ADAMS/CAR ·· 2
- 1.3 ADAMS/DRIVELINE ·· 2
- 1.4 ADAMS/CONTROLS ·· 4
- 1.5 ADAMS/VIEWFLEX ··· 4

第2章 横置板簧悬架 ·· 6
- 2.1 横置板簧前处理 ·· 6
- 2.2 横置板簧MNF ·· 11
- 2.3 横置板簧双A臂悬架模型 ·· 11
- 2.4 横置板簧悬架约束 ··· 27
- 2.5 横置板簧悬架变量参数 ··· 37
- 2.6 横置板簧悬架通信器 ·· 38
- 2.7 横置板簧悬架驱动轴显示组建 ·· 43
- 2.8 单轮振动测试仿真 ··· 45

第3章 非独立悬架模型 ··· 48
- 3.1 板簧悬架模型 ··· 49
- 3.2 非独立悬架安装部件 ·· 60
- 3.3 钢板弹簧 ··· 61
- 3.4 非独立悬架约束 ·· 68
- 3.5 非独立悬架变量参数 ·· 70
- 3.6 非独立悬架通信器 ··· 72
- 3.7 非独立悬架驱动轴显示组建 ··· 78
- 3.8 双轮反向激振仿真 ··· 80
- 3.9 整车模型 ··· 82
- 3.10 Fish-Hook 仿真 ··· 83

第4章 路面模型 ·· 87
- 4.1 路面类型简介 ··· 87
- 4.2 对开路面 ··· 89
- 4.3 对接路面 ··· 91

	4.4	减速带路面 ················	93
	4.5	单线移仿真 ················	95
	4.6	连续障碍路面 ··············	96
	4.7	匀速直线行驶仿真 ············	98
	4.8	直线制动系统仿真 ············	99
	4.9	分离轮胎路面设置 ············	101
	4.10	分离轮胎路面直线制动仿真 ········	103
	4.11	弯道制动系统仿真 ············	104

第 5 章 发动机模型 ································ 106
    5.1　发动机机体 ································ 107
    5.2　曲　轴 ···································· 110
    5.3　飞　轮 ···································· 113
    5.4　安装部件 body ······························ 114
    5.5　发动机约束 ································ 115
    5.6　发动机变量参数 ······························ 118
    5.7　曲轴动力元素 ······························ 118
    5.8　发动机状态变量 ······························ 119
    5.9　发动机系统单元 ······························ 120
    5.10　复合弹簧 Complex Spring ······················ 122
    5.11　发动机通信器 ······························ 125
    5.12　速度保持仿真 ······························ 130

第 6 章 变速器 ···································· 138
    6.1　变速器输入轴 ······························ 139
    6.2　变速器输出轴 ······························ 141
    6.3　变速器齿轮副 ······························ 142
    6.4　变速器轴承连接 ······························ 151
    6.5　变速器动力元 ······························ 155
    6.7　纵向变速器 ································ 159
    6.8　半车台架仿真（传动轴与后悬架）·············· 171

第 7 轴 传动轴 ···································· 175
    7.1　前轴差速器 ································ 176
    7.2　限滑差速器 ································ 178
    7.3　传动轴 ···································· 180
    7.4　后差速器 ·································· 184
    7.5　差速器壳 ·································· 187
    7.6　滑叉部件与连接 ······························ 199
    7.7　动力传动系统-底盘连接 ······················ 201

7.8　差速器动力元·················203
7.9　阶跃扭矩仿真···············205

第8章　齿轮传动···············209
8.1　直齿轮传动···················209
8.2　锥齿轮传动···················216
8.3　蜗轮蜗杆齿轮传动··········217
8.4　齿轮齿条传动···············218
8.5　准双曲面齿轮传动··········220
8.6　行星齿轮传动···············221

第9章　皮带传动···············225
9.1　滑　轮························226
9.2　皮　带························231
9.3　皮带驱动元···················233
9.4　五轴皮带轮传动·············235

第10章　链条传动·············239
10.1　链　轮······················240
10.2　链　条······················244
10.3　链条驱动元·················246

第11章　电动机················249
11.1　电动机——Curve Based···249
11.2　连杆驱动仿真··············254
11.3　电动机——Analytical·····255
11.4　电动-链条-皮带耦合传动···258

第12章　三轮车Ⅰ··············261
12.1　车架系统···················262
12.2　前单轮转向系统···········272
12.3　转向轴减震器··············275
12.4　三轮车约束·················276
12.5　轮胎与路面·················279
12.6　转弯仿真···················285
12.7　后非独立悬架避震器·····288

第13章　三轮车Ⅱ··············291
13.1　双A臂悬架·················292
13.2　双A臂悬架约束···········296
13.3　后单轮拖拽悬架···········300

- 13.4 后单轮拖拽臂架约束 ·················· 302
- 13.5 三轮车右舵转向系统 ·················· 303
- 13.6 三轮车右舵转向系统约束 ·············· 304
- 13.7 三轮车轮胎 ·························· 307
- 13.8 漂移仿真 ···························· 310
- 13.9 约束关系讨论 ························ 314
- 13.10 "逆"三轮车衬套约束 ················ 318

第14章 摩托车 ·································· 325
- 14.1 摩托车身 ···························· 326
- 14.2 前双避震器转向系统 ·················· 326
- 14.3 后驱动悬架系统 ······················ 330
- 14.4 摩托车约束 ·························· 332
- 14.5 摩托车轮胎 ·························· 335
- 14.6 摩托车驱动 ·························· 339
- 14.7 摩托车加速仿真 ······················ 340
- 14.8 摩托车同步带传动 ···················· 342
- 14.9 电动机驱动同步带传动 ················ 353

第15章 双轴转向系统 ···························· 356
- 15.1 双轴转向模型 ························ 357
- 15.2 双轴转向系统约束 ···················· 376
- 15.3 减速齿轮 ···························· 384
- 15.4 双轴转向变量参数 ···················· 385
- 15.5 双轴转向通信器 ······················ 386
- 15.6 TASA 转向仿真 ······················· 389
- 15.7 单轴右舵转向系统 ···················· 394

第16章 麦弗逊悬架联合仿真 ······················ 401
- 16.1 麦弗逊悬架模型建立 ·················· 402
- 16.2 路面模型 ···························· 412
- 16.3 路面驱动方案 A ······················ 413
- 16.4 路面驱动方案 B ······················ 419
- 16.5 PID 控制器设计 ······················ 420
- 16.6 半主动悬架联合仿真 ·················· 421
- 16.7 时频域、功率谱密度变换程序 ·········· 429

第17章 驾驶室隔振联合仿真 ······················ 431
- 17.1 驾驶模型 ···························· 432
- 17.2 前横向稳定杆 ························ 442

17.3 驾驶室弹簧与避震器 443
17.4 驾驶室约束关系 446
17.5 主动驾驶室函数设定 459
17.6 整车平台 463
17.7 ADAMS\CONTROLS 设置 465
17.8 匀速直线仿真 466
17.9 ADAMS 与 MATLAB 协同 467
17.10 模糊 PID-D 耦合算法 474
17.11 驾驶室机控联合仿真 475

第 18 章 FSAE 整车变刚度悬架特性研究 479
18.1 横置板簧悬架 480
18.2 定常半径弯道仿真 482
18.3 板簧优化 484
18.4 总 结 488

第 19 章 FSAE 赛车后轮随动转向 489
19.1 随动转向数学模型 490
19.2 随动转向物理模型 492
19.3 柔性扭转梁 493
19.4 反向激振仿真 494
19.5 弯道仿真 494
19.6 扭力梁位置因素 496
19.7 衬套安装角度 497
19.8 总 结 499

第 20 章 平衡悬架与推杆特性研究 500
20.1 平衡悬架模型 501
20.2 白双驱动轴程序 502
20.3 振动台模型 502
20.4 垂向刚度测试 503
20.5 扭转刚度测试 504
20.6 推杆传力模型 504
20.7 稳定性仿真 505
20.8 总 结 508

第 21 章 复杂耦合式悬架模型 509
21.1 耦合悬架模型 510
21.2 耦合悬架变量参数 523
21.3 耦合悬架通信器 524

21.4 耦合悬架车轮反向激振仿真 ··· 525

第 22 章 优化设计实验——INSIGHT ··· 529
  22.1 双 A 臂悬架前束角优化——AVIEW ·· 529
  22.2 运载火箭模型优化 ·· 538
  22.3 推杆式悬架外倾角优化——ACAR ··· 543

参考文献 ··· 548

第 1 章　绪　论

车辆系统动力学是研究整车及子系统运动（动态）特性的一门学科。整车及其子系统的动态特性极为复杂，在研究过程中，需要建立其不同系统及整车模型。建模是较为烦琐的过程，目前研究建模方法主要包含三种方法：① 通过将整车简化为弹簧与质量系统研究其动态特性；② 通过专业级系统仿真软件建立整车及子系统模型，考虑部件之间的结构、柔性约束、轮胎等特性，例如 ADAMS；③ 以 14 自由度整车架构为基础（包含轮胎特性），通过不考虑整车结构的参数化仿真软件建立而成，例如 Car-sim。目前国内高校及科研院所多采用 ADAMS 动力学软件建立整车及子系统模型对其特性进行研究。

1.1　ADAMS/VIEW

ADAMS 为机械系统动力学仿真软件，核心模块包括通用模块 VIEW、求解器模块 SOLVE 及后处理模型。通用模块理论上可以建立任何复杂的机械系统，其他专业插件中的模块依然可以在通用模块中建立，如图 1-1 所示为通用模块中建立的"逆"三轮车模型，包含前双 A 臂悬架、转向系统、车身、后单轮拖拽悬架及轮胎。专业模块与通用模块的区别在于专业模块集成度更高，专业的系统模型可以更快建立其子系统及整车，子系统可以通过不同的组合装配为不同的车辆模型。建模过程中，专业模块与通用模块相互结合可以大大提升建立的效率及质量，如图 1-2 所示为非独立悬架模型，簧片之间的接触是通过通用模块 VIEW 建立的，而整个非独立悬架在 ADAMS/CAR 模块中建立，可以通过在 CAR 模块中插件切换到 VIEW 模块。

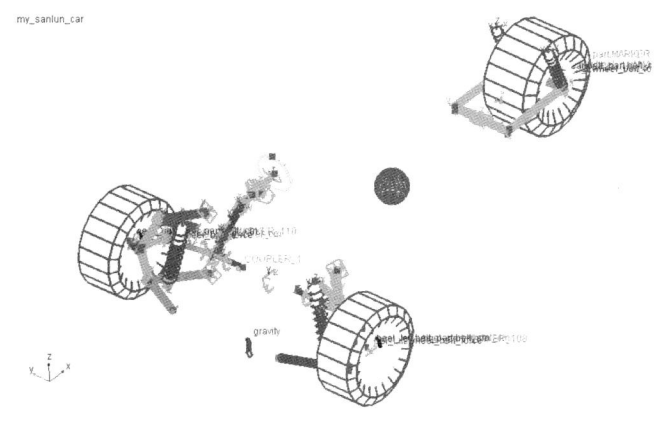

图 1-1　"逆"三轮车模型

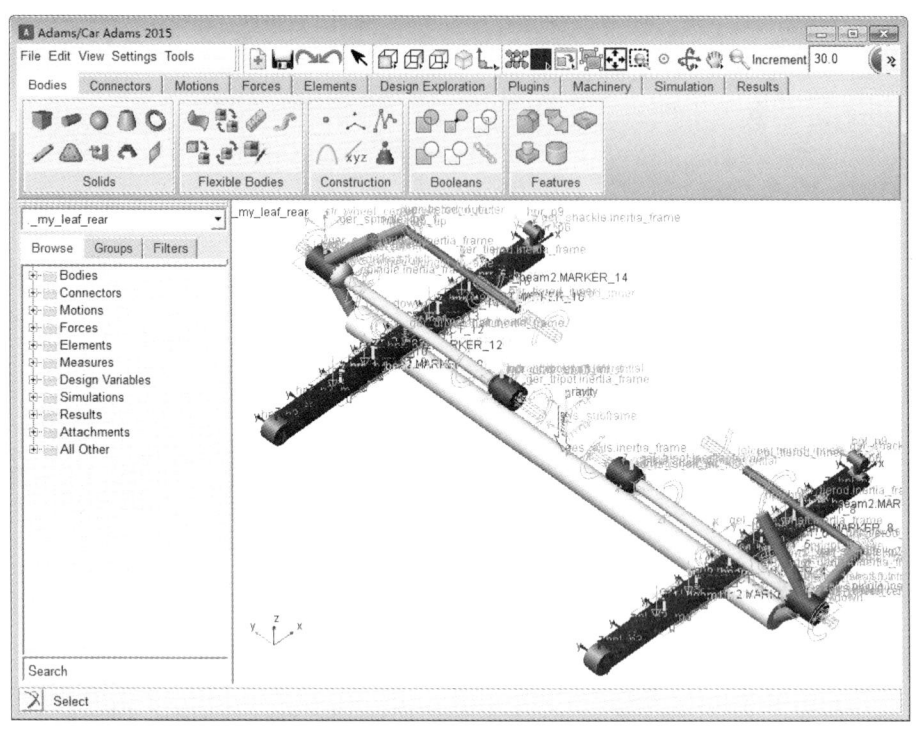

图 1-2 非独立悬架模型（VIEW)

1.2 ADAMS/CAR

ACAR 是 ADAMS 软件中车辆系统动力学仿真插件，最大的优势是悬架系统的快速设计与优化，通过测量真实车辆悬挂的关键点参数，可以快速建立其包含简化物理结构（硬点之间通过简化的连杆连接）的悬架模型，模型建立好之后可以测试同向、反向及单个车轮的激振仿真，后处理可以快速处理车轮定位参数与车轮激振行程之间的关系；2015 版软件可以测试在整车平台下悬架的特性，整车平台下测试子系统更符合真实车辆动态行为，同时整车之间子系统匹配更加真实。

1.3 ADAMS/DRIVELINE

ADRIVELINE 提供给工程师和分析专家进行传动系统部件建模和仿真的专用工具，可以用来研究整个传动系在各种工作条件下的动力学性能。利用 DRIVELINE 模块，可以快速创建完整的、参数化的传动系统，建立包含传动系统的功能化数字样机可集成到 ADAMS/CAR 中分析整车（如前轮驱动、后轮驱动以及全轮驱动）的动力学性能。如图 1-3 所示为 DRIVELINE 模块下建立的整车模型，包含自建发动机、变速器、传动轴、差速器等；如图 1-4 所示为简化的后轮驱动半车平台，通过在发动机曲轴处施加动力元扭矩，可以通过传动系统驱动后车轮转动。

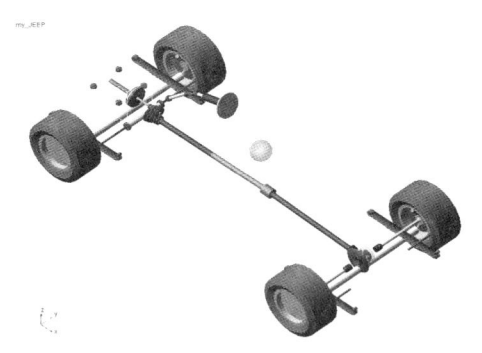

图 1-3　整车模型

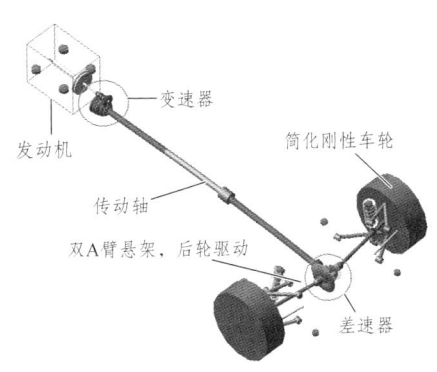

图 1-4　半车模型

传动系模块提供了应用范围很广的强有力工具，支持操稳分析中的前轮驱动、后轮驱动及四轮驱动，力矩转移、分配、陀螺效应和平衡效应、轴承动力学和弹性，以及部件级的噪声和振动激励。用户只需输入参数，差速器、驱动轴、分动器和变速器的模型将自动创建。齿轮力、自由行程、黏性联轴器和防滑差速器则来自详尽的单元库。部件可以很容易地激活或失效以研究其对整个系统行为的影响。同时提供了丰富的标准试验，用户也可以高效地创建自己的试验。如图 1-5 所示为自建的纵向变速器模型，图 1-6 所示为自建的传动轴模型，图 1-7 为差速器模型，图 1-8 为简化发动机模型。

图 1-5　变速器模型（5 挡）

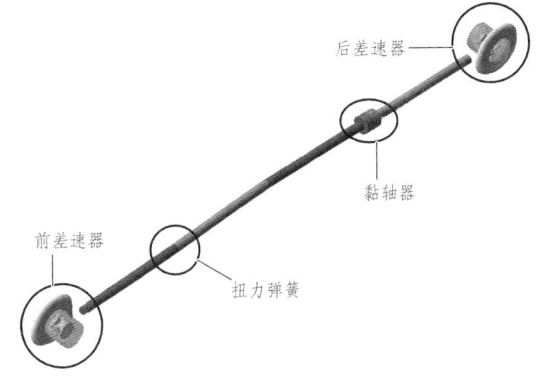

图 1-6　四轮驱动传动系统

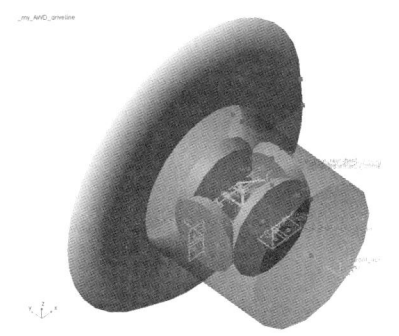

图 1-7　差速器模型

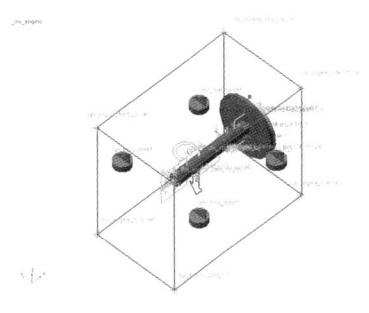

图 1-8　发动机模型

1.4 ADAMS/CONTROLS

近年来,多学科联合仿真是整个 CAE 行业发展的方向,只有对关键学科之间复杂交互作用的准确表述才能保证真实的模拟物理现象。如何通过使用一个模型实现不同学科之间的交互作用和耦合、优化不确定因素和利用高性能处理器提高计算速度是目前仿真领域亟待解决的问题。机电产品通常是由液压、电子、机械与控制等子系统共同协作发挥功能的,复合系统仿真问题不可以局限在某单一专业学科。ADAMS/CONTROLS 插件可以很方便地在相应的物理领域及恰当的仿真工具中对各子系统建立仿真模型,通过 TCP/IP 等方式实现不同仿真工具之间的数据交换和调用,完成复杂物理模型的仿真。ADAMS 控制系统设计是对复杂机械系统进行建模和仿真分析的基本环节之一。ADAMS 控制系统的设计主要有两个途径:对于一般的控制环节可以使用自带的控制工具箱进行处理;对于复杂的控制装置的机械系统则必须利用 ADAMS\CONTROL 模块进行设计和建模。在数据的传递过程中,ADAMS 的输出变量为 MATLAB 控制系统的输入变量,MATLAB 的输出变量为 ADAMS 的输入变量。如图 1-9 所示为自建的主动商用车驾驶室模型,具体建模及联合仿真过程请参考后文对应章节。

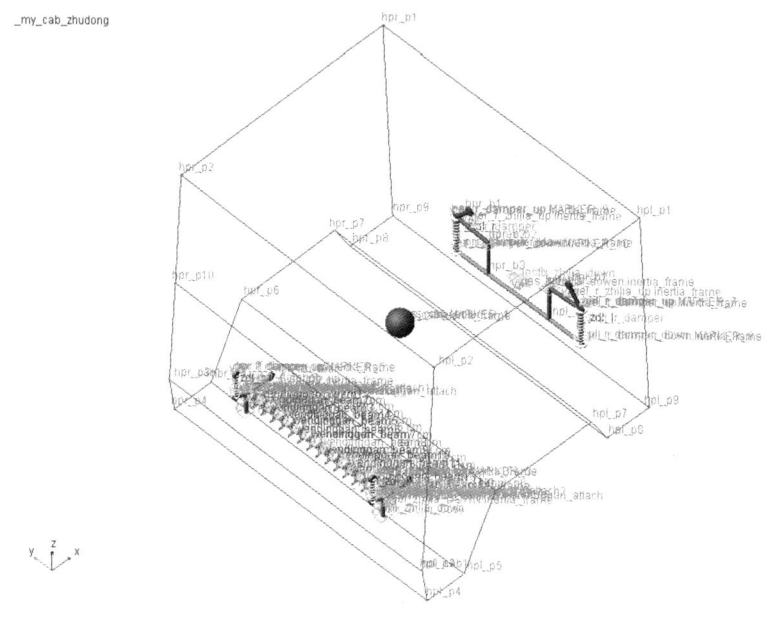

图 1-9 商用车主动驾驶室模型

1.5 ADAMS/VIEWFLEX

VIEWFLEX 是集成在 ADAMS/VIEW 及 ADAMS/CAR 中的自动柔性体生成工具,它使得不必离开 ADAMS 环境即可创建柔性体,并且不需要借助任何其他有限元软件,VIEWFLEX 模块让有关柔性体的仿真分析比传统方式更流畅、更高效。VIEWFLEX 可以通过外部环境(ABAQUS、ANSYS、NASTRAN、HYPERMESH 等软件)导入模态中性文件对系统部件进行柔性化处理。通过 ABAQUS 软件导入横置板簧建立悬架模型如图 1-10 所示。其功能特色

如下:
(1)在 ADAMS 环境下自动直接生成弹性体。
(2)后台完成网格划分,求解,MNF 文件生成。
(3)由内置的 NASTRAN 求解。
(4)高效、流畅的流程。
(5)高精确度。

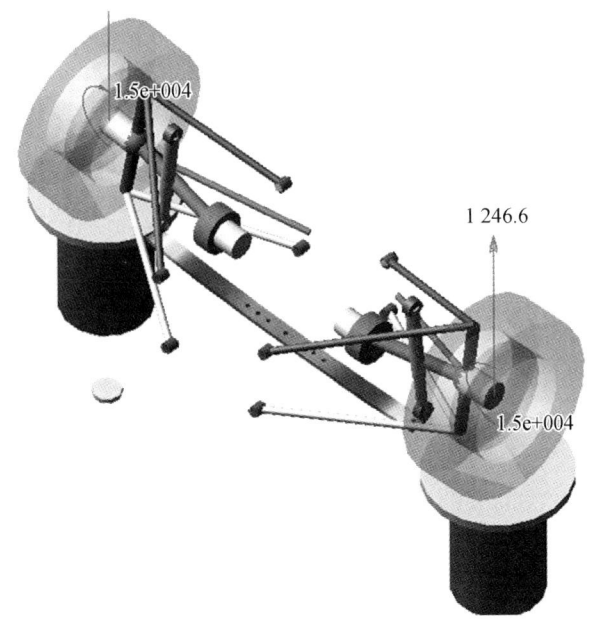

图 1-10　板簧柔性体 MNF

第 2 章　横置板簧悬架

横置板簧悬架较为少见，目前克尔维特跑车前后悬架以及沃尔沃后悬架采用此类悬架，横置板簧上有不同距离的螺孔，固定不同的螺孔位置，可以改变板簧的刚度，进而调整整车底盘的特性。横置板簧同时相当于一根横拉杆，对整车的稳定性起到提升作用。安装横置板簧后，螺旋弹簧可以省去，增大悬架系统的空间，降低非簧载质量。非簧载质量减小，车辆的制动特性改善明显。建立好的横置板簧双 A 臂悬架模型如图 2-1 所示。

图 2-1　横置板簧双 A 臂悬架模型

学习目标

- ◇ 横置板簧前处理。
- ◇ 横置板簧 MNF。
- ◇ 横置板簧双 A 臂悬架模型。
- ◇ 通信器。
- ◇ 单轮激振仿真。

2.1　横置板簧前处理

- 启动 ABAQUS/CAE，切换到 PART 模块，创建草图绘制后通过拉伸厚度为 5 mm 完成几何体的创建，如图 2-2 所示。

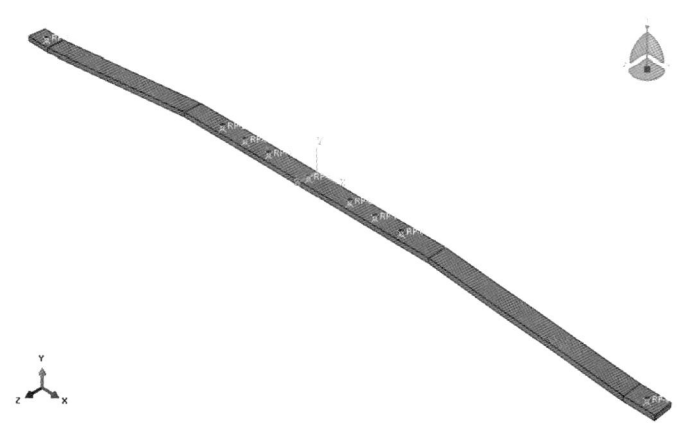

图 2-2　板簧三维模型（20×5）

● 切换到 Property 界面，创建材料属性。弹性模量：2.1E5，泊松比：0.3，密度：7.9E－9。材料属性参数一定要保持正确，要注意不同软件的单位制不同，否则会导致计算出的模态出错。材料通过界面属性赋予三维模型上，赋予成功后，板簧几何体颜色变为浅绿色，界面属性如图 2-3 所示。

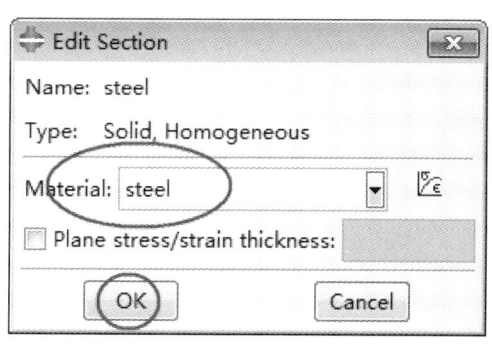

图 2-3　材料界面属性—steel

● 切换到 Assembly 界面，单击装配完成单体部件装配。
● 切换到分析部 Step 界面，完成 2 个分析部创建，如图 2-4 所示，Step-1 为模态分析步，设置提取前 20 阶模态；Step-2 为子结构生成，子结构即把整个连杆作为一个单一部件。Step-2 子结构在 Basic 选项卡设置子结构标示（Substructure identifier:Z101），点选 Whole model，在后续方框中选择整个模型；切换到 Options 选项卡：勾选 Specify retained eigenmodes by，点选 Mode range，在 Date 方框中输入 1,20,1。Step-2 设置如图 2-5、图 2-6 所示。

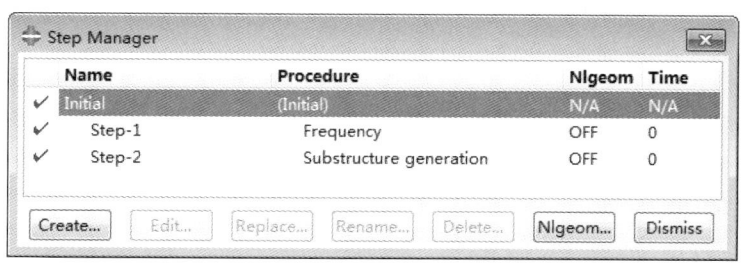

图 2-4　分析步设置

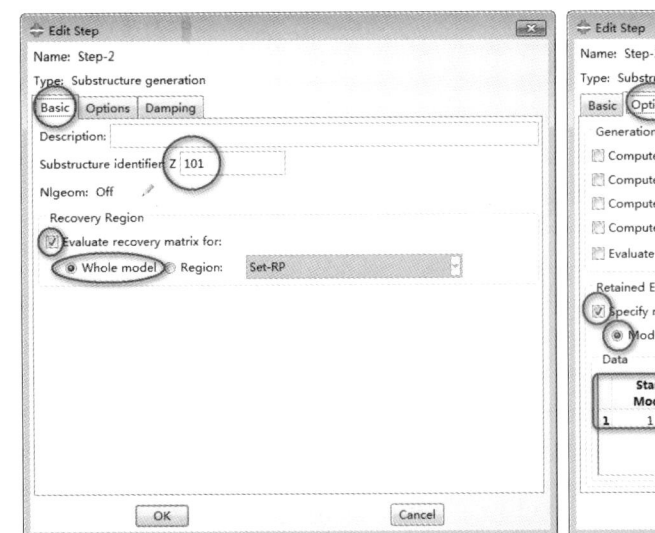 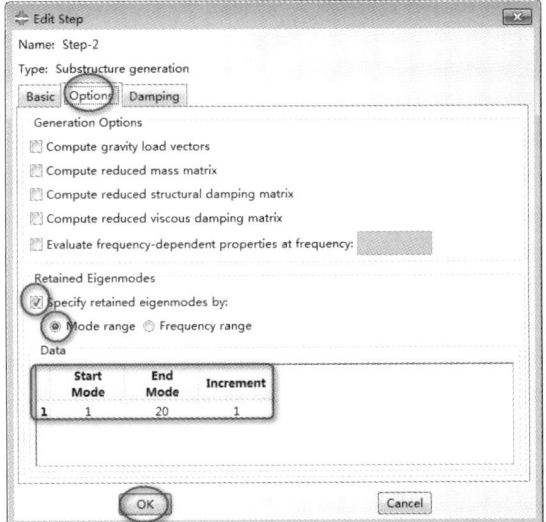

图 2-5 Basic 选项卡设置　　　　　　图 2-6 Options 选项卡设置

• 切换到相互作用 Interaction 界面，在连杆两圆孔中心创建 RP 参考点，建立 RP 点与孔内表面的 MPC 多点约束，如图 2-7 所示。

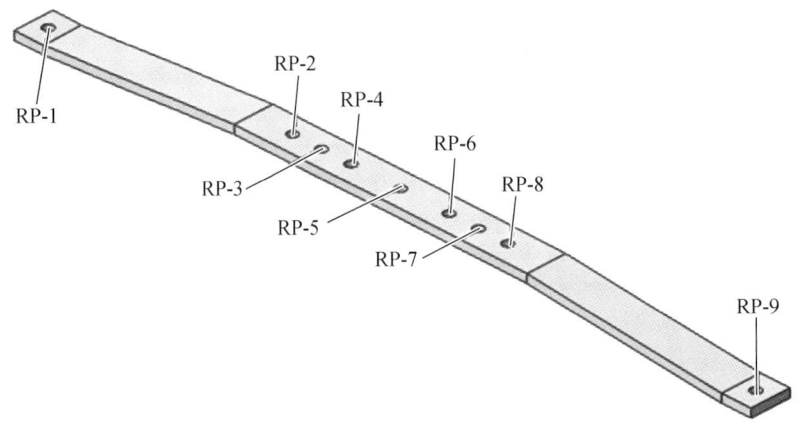

图 2-7 RP 点约束

板簧长度中心线上设计出 9 个孔，孔直径为 5 mm，此板簧有 4 种刚度：RP-5 为板簧长度的中心，固定 RP-5 时，单侧臂 RP-5 与 RP-1 之间的刚度为 A，单侧臂 RP-5 与 RP-9 之间的刚度为 A；RP-4 与 RP-6 关于 RP-5 对称，固定 RP-4 与 RP-6 时，单侧臂 RP-4 与 RP-1 之间的刚度为 B，单侧臂 RP-6 与 RP-9 之间的刚度为 B；RP-3 与 RP-7 关于 RP-5 对称，固定 RP-4 与 RP-6 时，单侧臂 RP-3 与 RP-1 之间的刚度为 C，单侧臂 RP-7 与 RP-9 之间的刚度为 C；RP-2 与 RP-8 关于 RP-5 对称，固定 RP-2 与 RP-8 时，单侧臂 RP-2 与 RP-1 之间的刚度为 D，单侧臂 RP-8 与 RP-9 之间的刚度为 D；RP-1、RP-9 与下控制臂刚性固定连接。

• 切换到网格划分 Mesh 界面，设置网格全局尺寸为 2 mm，网格划分完成后如图 2-8 所示，共包含 5 488 个六面体单元，经检查，网格全部符合要求。

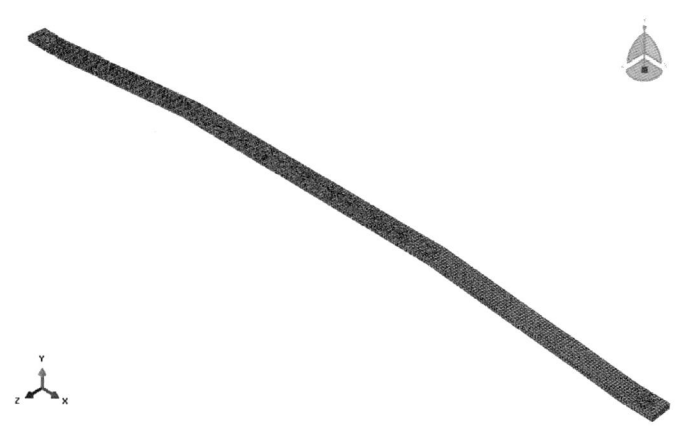

图 2-8 板簧网格划分——六面体

- 切换到 Load 界面，在 Step-1 分析步下约束 RP-1、RP-2 两个参考点完全固定。
- Step-2 分析步下选择 Retained nodal dofs，点击继续弹出编辑界面对话框如图 2-9 所示，勾选全部约束。
- 切换到 Job 界面，在模型下点击编辑关键字，弹出关键字命令窗口如图 2-10 所示。

在图片位置处添加关键字符如下：

MASS MATRIX=YES　　　%质量矩阵

*FLEXIBLE BODY, TYPE=ADAMS　　　%转换为 ADAMS 关键字；

*ELEMENT RECOVERY MATRIX, POSITION=AVERAGED AT NODES　　　%计算结果中显示应力应变

S,

E,

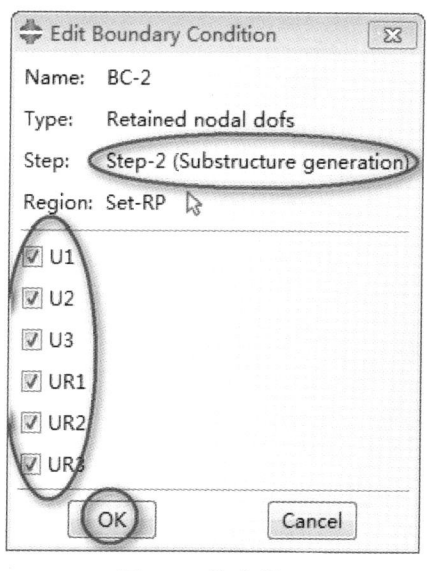

图 2-9 约束设置

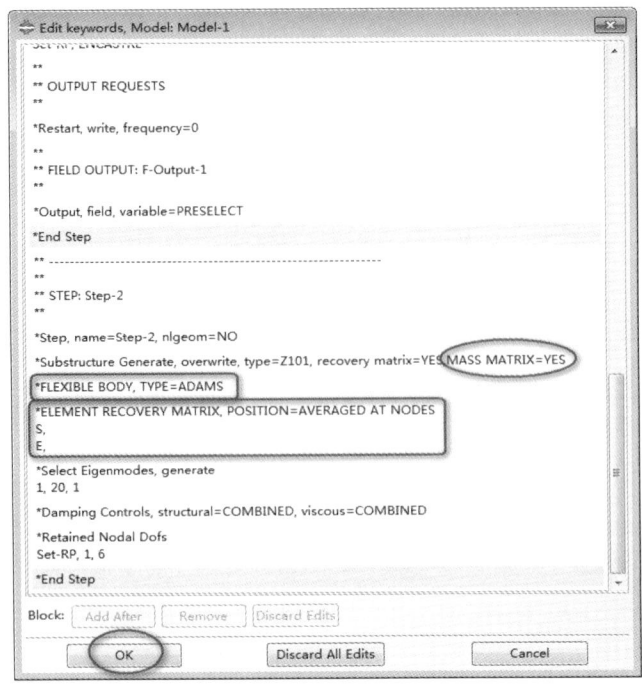

图 2-10 模型关键字编辑

- 创建 fsae_leaf_20p5 分析作业并提交运算，运算完成后可以在后处理模块中显示连杆的模态变形及对应的频率。前 4 阶模态变形如图 2-11~图 2-14 所示。

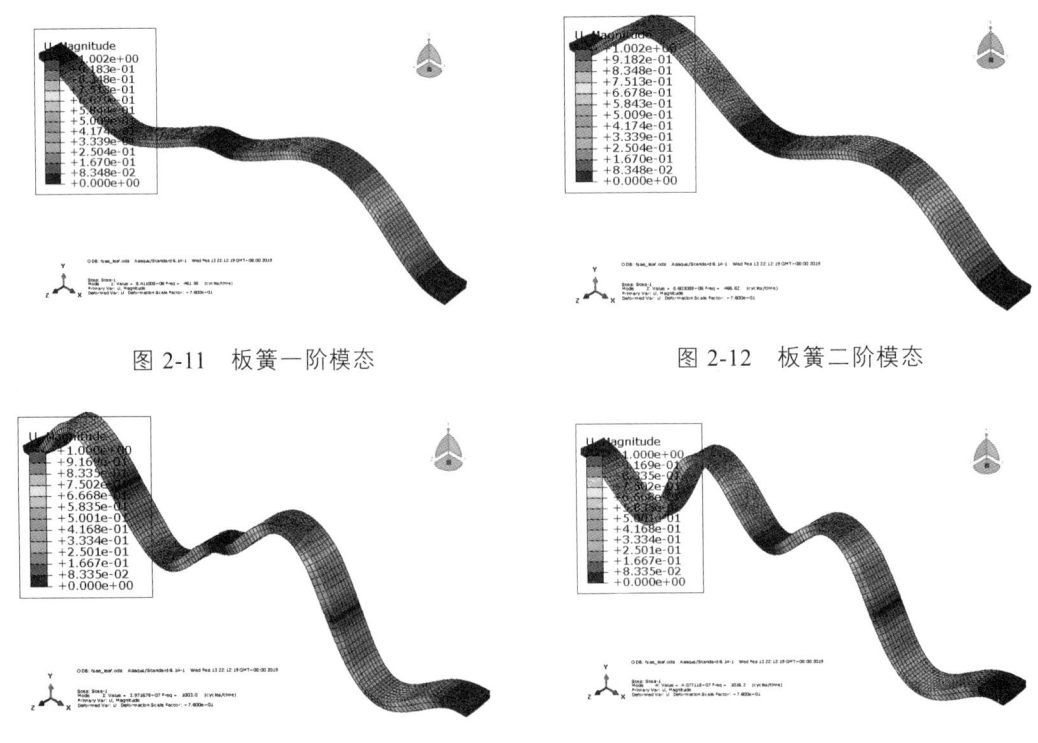

图 2-11 板簧一阶模态　　　　　　　　图 2-12 板簧二阶模态

图 2-13 板簧三阶模态　　　　　　　　图 2-14 板簧四阶模态

- 10 -

2.2 横置板簧 MNF

· 打开 ABAQUS COMMAND，输入 cd D:\ADAMS_MNF，切换命令至 ADAMS_MNF 文件夹。

· 继续输入以下命令：abaqus adams job= fsae_leaf_20p5 substructure_sim=fsae_leaf_20p5_Z101 model_odb= fsae_leaf_20p5 length=mm mass=tonne time=sec force=N，命令输入完成后，ABAQUS COMMAND 完成提交并运算产生 fsae_leaf_20p5.mnf 中性文件。

· 板簧子数据块完成计算后通过转换命令生成板簧中性文件 MNF，在 ADAMS 中导入中性文件添加约束、驱动计算板簧刚度，单侧臂刚度测试过程如下：RP-9 处添加与 Y 轴平行的移动副，在移动副上添加驱动位移，运动速度为 20 mm/s，分别固定约束 RP-5、RP-6、RP-7、RP-8 计算出刚度 A、B、C、D 如图 2-15 所示；刚度 A 为 26.10 N/mm、刚度 B 为 56.04 N/mm、刚度 C 为 107.54 N/mm、刚度 D 为 232.55 N/mm。从计算结果可以看出，同一片钢板弹簧，通过改变力臂大小，刚度实现了 9 倍范围内变化。

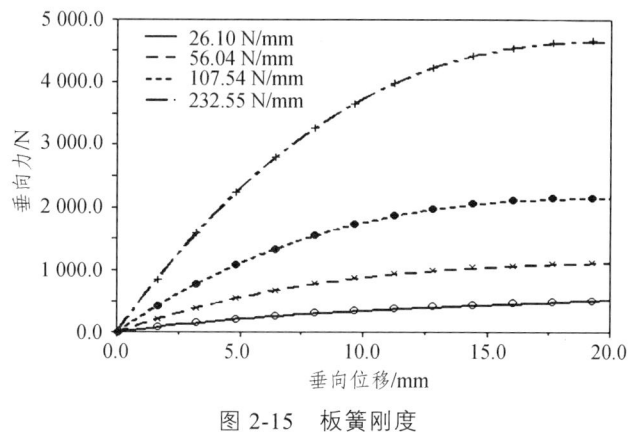

图 2-15 板簧刚度

2.3 横置板簧双 A 臂悬架模型

· 启动 ADAMS/CAR，选择专家模块进入建模界面。

· 单击 File > New 命令，弹出建模对话框如图 2-16 所示，在模板名称输入 fsae_suspension_rear_axle，主特征选择 suspension，单击 OK。

· 单击 Build > Hardpoint > New 命令，弹出创建硬点对话框如图 2-17 所示。

· 在硬点名称里输入 drive_shaft_inr,类型选择 left；在位置文本框输入 1 500,－200.0, 225.0。

· 单击 Apply，完成 drive_shaft_inr 硬点的创建。此时在屏幕上显示出左右对称的两个硬点。以此类推，重复上述步骤完成如图 2-18 中硬点的创建，创建完成后单击 OK。

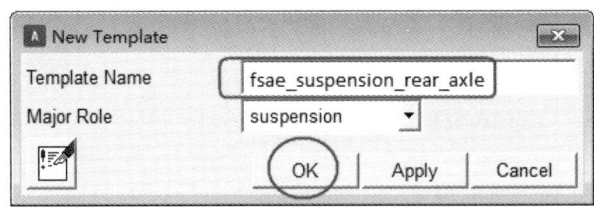

图 2-16 模板框

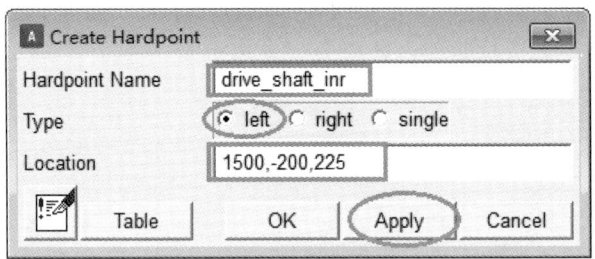

图 2-17 硬点对话框

	loc_x	loc_y	loc_z
hpl_arb_bushing_mount	1651.0	-127.0	101.6
hpl_drive_shaft_inr	1500.0	-200.0	225.0
hpl_lca_front	1270.0	-127.0	127.0
hpl_lca_outer	1498.6	-482.6	101.6
hpl_lca_rear	1651.0	-127.0	127.0
hpl_strut_low	1498.6	-375.0	101.6
hpl_strut_low_ref	1498.6	-375.0	1.6
hpl_strut_up	1498.6	-345.0	401.6
hpl_strut_up_ref	1498.6	-345.0	501.6
hpl_tierod_inner	1676.4	-127.0	152.4
hpl_tierod_outer	1574.8	-457.2	152.4
hpl_uca_front	1270.0	-152.4	304.8
hpl_uca_outer	1549.4	-482.6	355.6
hpl_uca_rear	1625.6	-152.4	304.8
hpl_wheel_center	1524.0	-558.8	228.6
hps_global	1524.0	0.0	0.0

图 2-18 后推力杆式双横臂悬架硬点数据

2.3.1 上控制臂部件 UCA

- 单击 Build > Part > General Part > New 命令，弹出创建部件对话框如图 2-19 所示，其为已经创建好的横置板簧悬架模型，通过右击._fsae_suspension_rear_axle.gel_uca 部件，在弹出的快捷菜单中单击 Modify 而弹出对话框；

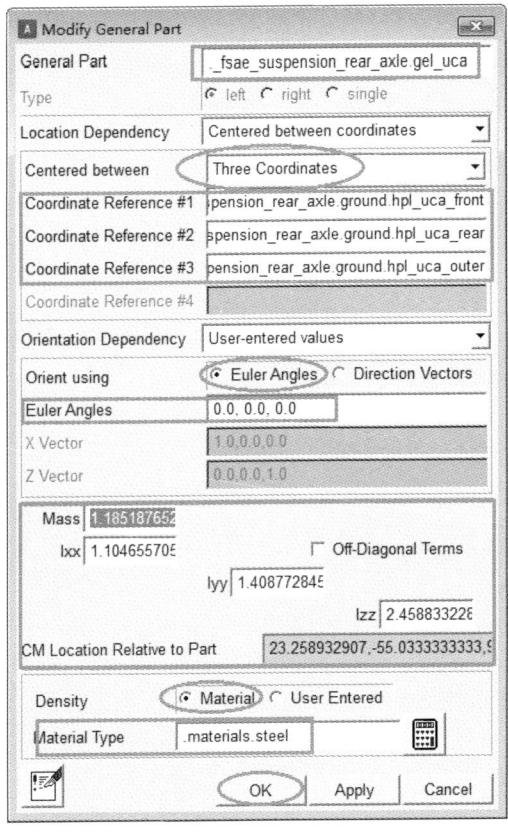

图 2-19 控制臂 UCA 部件创建对话框

- General Part 输入 uca；
- Location Dependency：Centered between coordinates；
- Centered between：Three Coordinates，即上控制臂部件 uca 位于三点坐标的中心位置；
- Coordinate Reference #1(参考坐标)：._fsae_suspension_rear_axle.ground.hpl_uca_front；
- Coordinate Reference #2(参考坐标)：._fsae_suspension_rear_axle.ground.hpl_uca_rear；
- Coordinate Reference #3(参考坐标)：._fsae_suspension_rear_axle.ground.hpl_uca_outer；
- Orient using：Euler Angles，即部件定向采用欧拉角模式；
- Euler Angles：0,0,0；
- Mass：1；
- Ixx：1；
- Iyy：1；
- Izz：1；
- Density：Material；
- Material Type：.materials.steel；
- 单击 OK，完成部件._fsae_suspension_rear_axle.gel_uca 创建。
- 单击 Build > Geometry > Link > New 命令，弹出创建连杆几何体对话框如图 2-20 所示；
- Link Name (连杆名称) 输入几何名称：uca_link_front；

- General Part 输入._fsae_suspension_rear_axle.gel_uca；
- Coordinate Reference #1(参考坐标)：._fsae_suspension_rear_axle.ground.hpl_uca_front；
- Coordinate Reference #2(参考坐标)：._fsae_suspension_rear_axle.ground.hpl_uca_outer；
- Radius(半径): 8；
- Color：dark gray；
- 选择 Calculate Mass Properties of General Part 复选框，当几何建立好之后会更新对应部件的质量和惯量参数；
- Density：Material；
- Material Type：steel；
- 单击 Apply,完成 uca_link_front 几何体的创建；
- Link Name (连杆名称)输入几何名称：uca_link_rear；
- General Part 输入._fsae_suspension_rear_axle.gel_uca；
- Coordinate Reference #1(参考坐标)：._fsae_suspension_rear_axle.ground.hpl_uca_rear；
- Coordinate Reference #2(参考坐标)：._fsae_suspension_rear_axle.ground.hpl_uca_outer；
- Radius(半径): 8；
- Color：dark gray；
- 勾选 Calculate Mass Properties of General Part 复选框；
- Density：Material；
- Material Type：steel；
- 单击 OK，完成 uca_link_rear 几何体的创建。

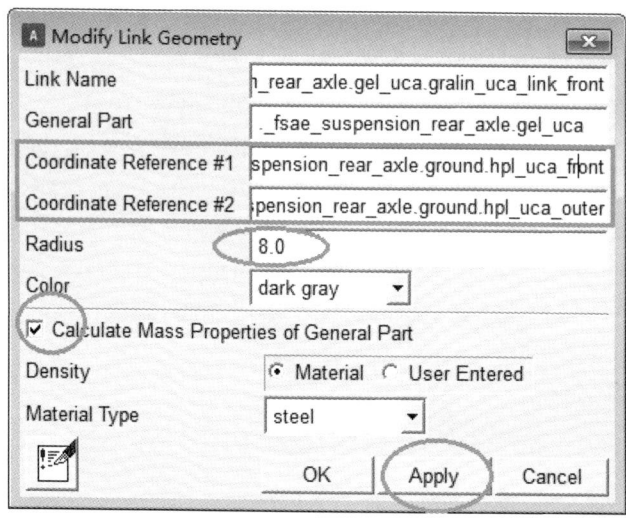

图 2-20 控制臂 UCA 几何体创建对话框

2.3.2 下控制臂部件 LCA

- 单击 Build > Part > General Part > New 命令，弹出创建部件对话框可参考如图 2-19 所示；

- General Part 输入 lca；
- Location Dependency：Centered between coordinates；
- Centered between：Three Coordinates；
- Coordinate Reference #1(参考坐标)：._fsae_suspension_rear_axle.ground.hpl_lca_front；
- Coordinate Reference #2(参考坐标)：._fsae_suspension_rear_axle.ground.hpl_lca_rear；
- Coordinate Reference #3(参考坐标)：._fsae_suspension_rear_axle.ground.hpl_lca_outer；
- Orient using：Euler Angles；
- Euler Angles：0,0,0；
- Mass：1；
- Ixx：1；
- Iyy：1；
- Izz：1；
- Density：Material；
- Material Type：.materials.steel；
- 单击 OK，完成部件._fsae_suspension_rear_axle.gel_lca 创建。
- 单击 Build > Geometry > Link > New 命令；
- Link Name (连杆名称) 输入几何名称：lca_link_front；
- General Part 输入._fsae_suspension_rear_axle.gel_lca；
- Coordinate Reference #1(参考坐标)：._fsae_suspension_rear_axle.ground.hpl_lca_front；
- Coordinate Reference #2(参考坐标)：._fsae_suspension_rear_axle.ground.hpl_lca_outer；
- Radius(半径): 8；
- Color：yellow；
- 选择 Calculate Mass Properties of General Part 复选框，当几何建立好之后会更新对应部件的质量和惯量参数；
- Density：Material；
- Material Type：steel；
- 单击 Apply,完成 lca_link_front 几何体的创建；
- Link Name (连杆名称) 输入几何名称：lca_link_rear；
- General Part 输入：._fsae_suspension_rear_axle.gel_lca；
- Coordinate Reference #1（参考坐标）：._fsae_suspension_rear_axle.ground.hpl_lca_rear；
- Coordinate Reference #2（参考坐标）：._fsae_suspension_rear_axle.ground.hpl_lca_outer；
- Radius(半径): 8；
- Color：yellow；
- 勾选 Calculate Mass Properties of General Part 复选框；
- Density：Material；
- Material Type：steel；
- 单击 OK，完成 lca_link_rear 几何体的创建。

2.3.3 转向节 upright 部件

- 单击 Build > Part > General Part > New 命令，弹出创建部件对话框可参考如图 2-19 所示；
- General Part 输入 upright；
- Location Dependency：Centered between coordinates；
- Centered between：Two Coordinates；
- Coordinate Reference #1(参考坐标)：._fsae_suspension_rear_axle.ground.hpl_uca_outer；
- Coordinate Reference #2(参考坐标)：._fsae_suspension_rear_axle.ground.hpl_lca_outer；
- Orient using：Euler Angles；
- Euler Angles：0,0,0；
- Mass：1；
- Ixx：1；
- Iyy：1；
- Izz：1；
- Density：Material；
- Material Type：.materials.steel；
- 单击 OK，完成部件._fsae_suspension_rear_axle.gel_upright 创建。
- 单击 Build > Geometry > Link > New 命令；
- Link Name (连杆名称) 输入几何名称：upright；
- General Part 输入._fsae_suspension_rear_axle.gel_upright；
- Coordinate Reference #1(参考坐标)：._fsae_suspension_rear_axle.ground.hpl_uca_outer；
- Coordinate Reference #2(参考坐标)：._fsae_suspension_rear_axle.ground.hpl_lca_outer；
- Radius(半径): 13；
- Color（杆件几何体颜色）：blue；
- 选择 Calculate Mass Properties of General Part 复选框，当几何建立好之后会更新对应部件的质量和惯量参数；
- Density：Material；
- Material Type：steel；
- 单击 OK，完成 upright 几何体的创建。

2.3.4 转向横拉杆 tierod 部件

- 单击 Build > Part > General Part > New 命令，弹出创建部件对话框可参考如图 2-19 所示；
- General Part 输入 tierod；
- Location Dependency：Centered between coordinates；
- Centered between：Two Coordinates；
- Coordinate Reference #1(参考坐标)：._fsae_suspension_rear_axle.ground.hpl_tierod_inner；

- Coordinate Reference #2(参考坐标)：._fsae_suspension_rear_axle.ground.hpl_tierod_outer；
- Orientation Dependency：User-entered values；
- Orient using：Euler Angles；
- Euler Angles：0,0,0；
- Mass：1；
- Ixx：1；
- Iyy：1；
- Izz：1；
- Density：Material；
- Material Type：.materials.steel；
- 单击 OK，完成部件._fsae_suspension_rear_axle.gel_tierod 创建。
- 单击 Build > Geometry > Link > New 命令；
- Link Name (连杆名称) 输入几何名称：tierod；
- General Part 输入._fsae_suspension_rear_axle.gel_tierod；
- Coordinate Reference #1(参考坐标)：._fsae_suspension_rear_axle.ground.hpl_tierod_innerr；
- Coordinate Reference #2(参考坐标)：._fsae_suspension_rear_axle.ground.hpl_tierod_outer；
- Radius(半径): 7；
- Color（杆件几何体颜色）：magenta；
- 选择 Calculate Mass Properties of General Part 复选框，当几何建立好之后会更新对应部件的质量和惯量参数；
- Density：Material；
- Material Type：steel；
- 单击 OK，完成横拉杆._fsae_suspension_rear_axle.gel_tierod.gralin_tierod 几何体的创建。

2.3.5 部件 strut_up

- 单击 Build > Part > General Part > New 命令，弹出创建部件对话框可参考如图 2-19 所示；
- General Part 输入 strut_up；
- Location Dependency：Delta location from coordinate；
- Coordinate Reference (参考坐标)：._fsae_suspension_rear_axle.ground.hpl_strut_up；
- Location：0,0,0；
- Location in：local；
- Orientation Dependency：User-entered values；
- Orient using：Euler Angles；
- Euler Angles：0,0,0；
- Mass：1；
- Ixx：1；
- Iyy：1；

- Izz：1；
- Density：Material；
- Material Type：.materials.steel；
- 单击 OK，完成部件._fsae_suspension_rear_axle.gel_strut_up 创建。

2.3.6 部件 strut_low

- 单击 Build > Part > General Part > New 命令，弹出创建部件对话框可参考如图 2-19 所示；
- General Part 输入 strut_low；
- Location Dependency：Delta location from coordinate；
- Coordinate Reference（参考坐标）：._fsae_suspension_rear_axle.ground.hpl_strut_low；
- Location：0,0,0；
- Location in：local；
- Orientation Dependency：User-entered values；
- Orient using：Euler Angles；
- Euler Angles：0,0,0；
- Mass：1；
- Ixx：1；
- Iyy：1；
- Izz：1；
- Density：Material；
- Material Type：.materials.steel；
- 单击 OK，完成部件._fsae_suspension_rear_axle.gel_strut_low 创建。

2.3.7 轮毂 spindle 部件

- 单击 Build > Suspension Parameters > Toe/Camber Values> Set 命令，弹出悬架参数对话框如图 2-21 所示。前束角输入 0；外倾角输入 –1.5；单击 OK，完成参数创建。与此同时系统自动建立两个输出通信器：col[r]_toe_angle、col[r]_camber_angle。

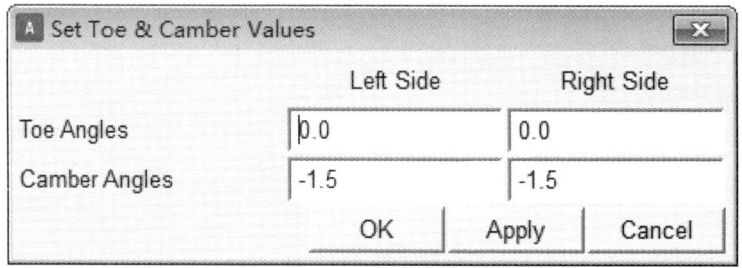

图 2-21 悬架参数

- 单击 Build > Construction Frame > New 命令，弹出创建结构框如图 2-22 所示；
- Construction Frame（结构框名称）：wheel_center；
- Coordinate Reference（参考坐标）：_fsae_suspension_rear_axle.ground.hpl_wheel_center；
- Location：0,0,0；
- Location in：local；
- Orientation Dependency：User-entered values；
- Variable Type（变量类型）:Parameter Variable(参数变量)；
- Toe Parameter Values（前束变量值）：._fsae_suspension_rear_axle.pvl_toe_angle；
- Camber Parameter Values（外倾变量值）：._fsae_suspension_rear_axle.pvl_camber_angle；
- 单击 OK，完成._fsae_suspension_rear_axle.ground.cfl_wheel_center 结构框的创建。
- 单击 Build > Construction Frame > New 命令；
- Construction Frame（结构框名称）：wheel_center；
- Coordinate Reference（参考坐标）：_fsae_suspension_rear_axle.ground.hpl_wheel_center；
- Location：0,0,0；
- Location in：local；
- Orientation Dependency：User-entered values；
- Variable Type（变量类型）:Parameter Variable(参数变量)；
- Toe Parameter Values（前束变量值）：._fsae_suspension_rear_axle.pvl_toe_angle；
- Camber Parameter Values（外倾变量值）：._fsae_suspension_rear_axle. pvl_camber_angle；
- 单击 OK，完成._fsae_suspension_rear_axle.ground.cfl_wheel_center 结构框的创建。

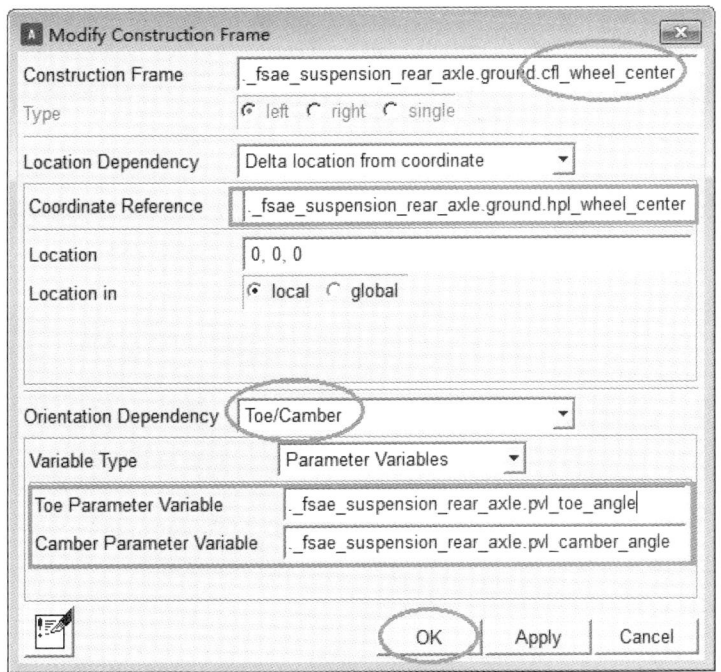

图 2-22 wheel_center 结构框

- 单击 Build > Part > General Part > New 命令，弹出创建部件对话框可参考如图 2-19 所示；
- General Part 输入 spindle；
- Location Dependency：Delta location from coordinate；
- Coordinate Reference（参考坐标）：._fsae_suspension_rear_axle.ground.cfl_wheel_center；
- Location：0,0,0；
- Location in：local；
- Orientation Dependency：Delta orientation from coordinate；
- Construction Frame：._fsae_suspension_rear_axle.ground.cfl_wheel_center；
- Orientation：0,0,0；
- Mass：1；
- Ixx：1；
- Iyy：1；
- Izz：1；
- Density：Material；
- Material Type：.materials.steel；
- 单击 OK，完成部件._fsae_suspension_rear_axle.gel_spindle 创建。
- 单击 Build > Geometry > Cylinder（圆柱体）> New 命令，弹出创建圆柱几何体对话框如图 2-23 所示；

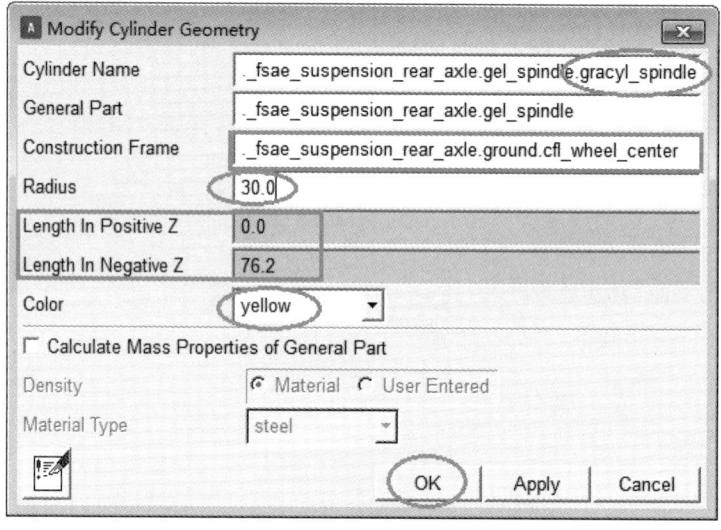

图 2-23 轮毂几何体创建对话框

- Cylinder Name（连杆名称）输入几何名称：spindle；
- General Part 输入._fsae_suspension_rear_axle.gel_spindle；
- Radius(半径): 30；
- Length In Postive Z（Z 轴正方向长度）：0；
- Length In Negative Z（Z 轴负方向长度）：76.2；

- Color（圆柱体几何体颜色）：yellow；
- 选择 Calculate Mass Properties of General Part 复选框；
- 单击 OK，完成轮毂圆柱体._fsae_suspension_rear_axle.gel_spindle.gracyl_spindle 几何体的创建。

2.3.8 驱动轴 drive_shaft 部件

- 单击 Build > Parameter Variable > New 命令，弹出参数变量对话框如图 2-24 所示；

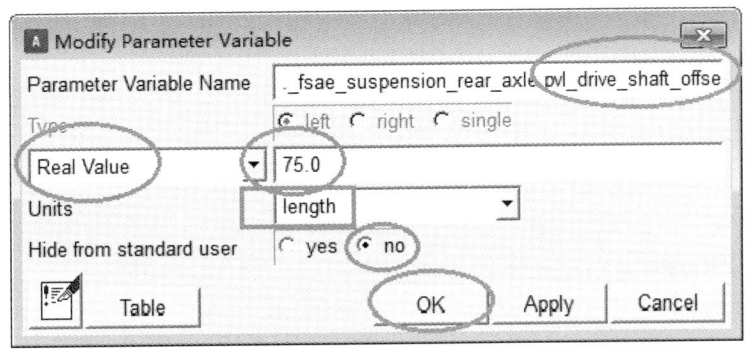

图 2-24 drive_shaft_offset 变量

- Parameter Variable Name: drive_shaft_offset；
- 参数类型：Real Value（实数值），数值为 75；
- Units：length；
- Hide from standard user(是否从标准界面隐藏)：no；
- 单击 OK，完成变量._fsae_suspension_rear_axle.pvl_drive_shaft_offset 的创建；
- 单击 Build > Construction Frame > New 命令；
- Construction Frame（结构框名称）：drive_shaft_otr；
- Location Dependency：Delta location from coordinate；
- Coordinate Reference（参考坐标）：._fsae_suspension_rear_axle.ground.cfl_wheel_center；
- Location：0.0, 0.0,（-1.0 * ._fsae_suspension_rear_axle.pvl_drive_shaft_offset）；
- Location in：local；
- Orientation Dependency：Orient axis to point；
- Coordinate Reference（参考坐标）：._fsae_suspension_rear_axle.ground.hpl_wheel_center；:
- Axis：Z；
- 单击 OK，完成._fsae_suspension_rear_axle.ground.cfl_drive_shaft_otr 结构框的创建。
- 单击 Build > Part > General Part > New 命令；
- General Part 输入 drive_shaft；
- Location Dependency：Delta location from coordinate；
- Coordinate Reference（参考坐标）：._fsae_suspension_rear_axle.ground.hpl_drive_shaft_inr；
- Location：0, 0, 0；
- Location in：local；

- Orientation Dependency：Orient in plane；
- Coordinate Reference #1(参考坐标)：._fsae_suspension_rear_axle.ground.cfl_drive_shaft_otr；
- Coordinate Reference #2(参考坐标)：._fsae_suspension_rear_axle.ground.hpl_drive_shaft_inr；
- Coordinate Reference#3 (参考坐标)：._fsae_suspension_rear_axle.ground.hpl_wheel_center；
- Axis：ZX；
- Mass：1；
- Ixx：1；
- Iyy：1；
- Izz：1；
- Density：Material；
- Material Type：.materials.steel；
- 单击 OK，完成部件._fsae_suspension_rear_axle.gel_drive_shaft 创建。
- 单击 Build > Geometry > Link > New 命令；
- Link Name (连杆名称) 输入几何名称：drive_shaft；
- General Part 输入._fsae_suspension_rear_axle.gel_drive_shaft；
- Coordinate Reference #1(参考坐标)：._fsae_suspension_rear_axle.ground.hpl_drive_shaft_inr；
- Coordinate Reference #2(参考坐标)：._fsae_suspension_rear_axle.ground.cfl_drive_shaft_otr；
- Radius（半径）：15；
- Color（杆件几何体颜色）：red；
- 选择 Calculate Mass Properties of General Part 复选框，当几何建立好之后会更新对应部件的质量和惯量参数；
- Density：Material；
- Material Type：steel；
- 单击 OK，完成._fsae_suspension_rear_axle.gel_drive_shaft.gralin_drive_shaft 几何体的创建。

- 单击 Build > Geometry > Ellipsoid > New 命令；
- Ellipsoid Name (连杆名称) 输入几何名称：otr_cv_housing；
- Coordinate Reference (参考坐标)：._fsae_suspension_rear_axle.ground.cfl_drive_shaft_otr；
- Link：._fsae_suspension_rear_axle.gel_drive_shaft.gralin_drive_shaft；
- X Scale：2；
- Y Scale：2；
- Z Scale：2；
- Color（杆件几何体颜色）：red；
- 选择 Calculate Mass Properties of General Part 复选框，当几何建立好之后会更新对应部件的质量和惯量参数；
- Density：Material；
- Material Type：steel；
- 单击 Apply，完成._fsae_suspension_rear_axle.gel_drive_shaft.graell_otr_cv_housing 几何体的创建；

- Ellipsoid Name（连杆名称）输入几何名称：tripot_housing；
- Coordinate Reference（参考坐标）：._fsae_suspension_rear_axle.ground.hpl_drive_shaft_inr；
- Link：._fsae_suspension_rear_axle.gel_drive_shaft.gralin_drive_shaft；
- X Scale：2；
- Y Scale：2；
- Z Scale：2；
- Color（杆件几何体颜色）：yellow；
- 选择 Calculate Mass Properties of General Part 复选框；
- Density：Material；
- Material Type：steel；
- 单击 OK，完成._fsae_suspension_rear_axle.gel_drive_shaft.graell_tripot_housing 几何体的创建；

2.3.9 等速万向节 tripot 部件

- 单击 Build > Construction Frame > New 命令；
- Construction Frame（结构框名称）：drive_shaft_inr；
- Location Dependency：Delta location from coordinate；
- Coordinate Reference（参考坐标）：._fsae_suspension_rear_axle.ground.hpl_drive_shaft_inr；
- Location：0,0,0；
- Location in：local；
- Orientation Dependency：Orient in plane；
- Coordinate Reference #1（参考坐标）：._fsae_suspension_rear_axle.ground.hpl_drive_shaft_inr；
- Coordinate Reference #2（参考坐标）：._fsae_suspension_rear_axle.ground.hpr_drive_shaft_inr；
- Coordinate Reference#3（参考坐标）：._fsae_suspension_rear_axle.ground.cfl_drive_shaft_otr；
- Axis：ZX；
- 单击 OK，完成._fsae_suspension_rear_axle.ground.cfl_drive_shaft_inr 结构框的创建。
- 单击 Build > Part > General Part > New 命令，弹出创建部件对话框可参考如图 2-19 所示；
- General Part 输入 tripot；
- Location Dependency：Delta location from coordinate；
- Coordinate Reference (参考坐标)：._fsae_suspension_rear_axle.ground.hpl_drive_shaft_inr；
- Location：0,0,0；
- Location in：local；
- Orientation Dependency：Delta orientation from coordinate；
- Construction Frame：._fsae_suspension_rear_axle.ground.cfl_drive_shaft_inr；
- Orientation：0,0,0；
- Mass：1；
- Ixx：1；

- Iyy：1；
- Izz：1；
- Density：Material；
- Material Type：.materials.steel；
- 单击 OK，完成部件._fsae_suspension_rear_axle.gel_tripot 创建；
- 单击 Build > Geometry > Cylinder (圆柱体) > New 命令；
- Cylinder Name (连杆名称) 输入几何名称：tripot_housing_extention；
- General Part 输入._fsae_suspension_rear_axle.gel_tripot；
- Radius(半径): 30；
- Length In Postive Z（Z轴正方向长度）:50；
- Length In Negative Z（Z轴负方向长度）: 0；
- Color（圆柱体几何体颜色）：yellow；
- 选择 Calculate Mass Properties of General Part 复选框；
- 单击 OK，完成轮毂圆柱体._fsae_suspension_rear_axle.gel_tripot.gracyl_tripot_housing_extention 几何体的创建。

2.3.10 柔性板簧部件

- 单击 Build > Part > Flexible Body > New 命令；
- General Part 输入_fsae_leaf；
- Location Dependency：Centered between coordinates；
- Centered between：Two Coordinates；
- Coordinate Reference #1（参考坐标）：._fsae_suspension_rear_axle.ground.hpr_strut_low；
- Coordinate Reference #2（参考坐标）：._fsae_suspension_rear_axle.ground.hpl_strut_low；
- Orientation Dependency：User entered values
- Orient using：Euler Angles；
- Euler Angles：–90, 90, 0；
- MNF File: file://D:/ADAMS_MNF/fsae_leaf_20p5.mnf；
- Sprung Mass：100；
- Color：.peach；
- 单击 OK，完成板簧柔性部件._fsae_suspension_rear_axle.fbs_fsae_leaf 创建。

2.3.11 避震器

- 单击 Build > Force > Damper > New 命令，弹出避震器创建对话框如图 2-25 所示；
- Damper Name(减震器名称)：damper ；
- I Part :._fsae_suspension_rear_axle.gel_strut_up；
- J Part：._fsae_suspension_rear_axle.gel_strut_low；
- I Coordinate Reference(参考坐标)：._fsae_suspension_rear_axle.ground.hpl_strut_up；

- J Coordinate Reference（参考坐标）：._fsae_suspension_rear_axle.ground.hpl_strut_low；
- Property File（属性文件）：mdids://FASE/dampers.tbl/msc_0001.dpr，避震器系数曲线如图 2-26 所示，具体数据如下列避震器信息。
- Damper Diameter(避震器直径)：拖动滑块选择 15 mm；
- Color：maize；
- 单击 OK，完成避震器._fsae_suspension_rear_axle.dal_damper 的创建。

```
避震器属性文件信息：
$--------------------------------------------------------MDI_HEADER
[MDI_HEADER]
FILE_TYPE      =   'dpr'
FILE_VERSION   =   4.0
FILE_FORMAT    =   'ASCII'
$--------------------------------------------------------UNITS
[UNITS]
LENGTH  =  'mm'
ANGLE   =  'degrees'
FORCE   =  'newton'
MASS    =  'kg'
TIME    =  'second'
$--------------------------------------------------------  CURVE
[CURVE]
{   vel                     force}
-4916.935               -8.889
-1000.0                 -3.0
-500.0                  -1.5
-250.0                  -0.75
-100.0                  -0.3
0.0                     0.0
100.0                   0.3
250.0                   0.75
500.0                   1.5
1000.0                  3.0
4914.298                9.0416
```

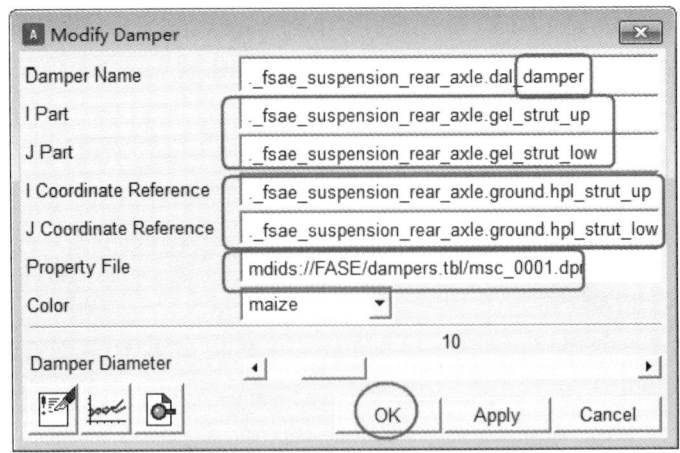

图 2-25 damper 避震器创建对话框

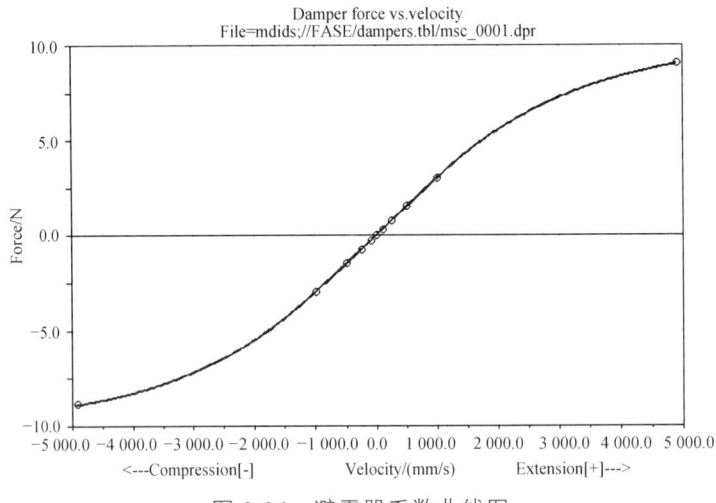

图 2-26 避震器系数曲线图

2.3.12 安装部件

- 单击 Build > Part > Mount > New 命令，弹出创建部件对话框如图 2-27 所示；
- Mount name（安装件名称）：suspension_to_chassis；
- Coordinate Reference （参考坐标）：._fsae_suspension_rear_axle.ground.hps_global；
- 安装件特征选择：inherit(继承特性)；
- 单击单击 Apply,完成._fsae_suspension_rear_axle.mts_suspension_to_chassis 安装部件的创建；
- Mount name（安装件名称）：tierod_to_steering；
- Coordinate Reference （参考坐标）：._fsae_suspension_rear_axle.ground.hpl_tierod_inner；
- 安装件特征选择：inherit（继承特性）；
- 单击单击 Apply，完成._fsae_suspension_rear_axle.mtl_tierod_to_steering 安装部件的创建；

- Mount name（安装件名称）：tripot_to_differential；
- Coordinate Reference（参考坐标）：._fsae_suspension_rear_axle.ground.hpl_drive_shaft_inr；
- 安装件特征选择：inherit(继承特性)；
- 单击 OK，完成._fsae_suspension_rear_axle.mtl_tripot_to_differential 安装部件的创建。

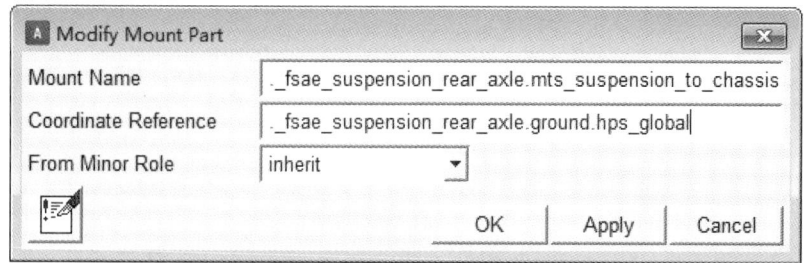

图 2-27　安装部件对话框

2.4 横置板簧悬架约束

2.4.1 刚性约束

单击 Build > Attachments > Joint > New 命令，弹出创约束件对话框如图 2-28 所示。
（1）部件 uca 与安装件 suspension_to_chassis 之间 revolute 约束。
- Joint Name（约束副名称）：uca_mid；
- I　Part：._fsae_suspension_rear_axle.gel_uca；
- J　Part：._fsae_suspension_rear_axle.mts_suspension_to_chassis；
- Joint Type（约束副类型）：revolute，转动副，约束 5 个自由度；
- Active(激活)：kinematic mode（运动学模式）；
- Location Dependency：Centered between coordinates；
- Centered between：Two Coordinates；
- Coordinate Reference #1（参考坐标）：._fsae_suspension_rear_axle.ground.hpl_uca_rear；
- Coordinate Reference #2（参考坐标）：._fsae_suspension_rear_axle.ground.hpl_uca_front；
- Orientation Dependency：Orient axis along line；
- Coordinate Reference #1（参考坐标）：._fsae_suspension_rear_axle.ground.hpl_uca_rear；
- Coordinate Reference #2（参考坐标）：._fsae_suspension_rear_axle.ground.hpl_uca_front；
- 单击 Apply，完成._fsae_suspension_rear_axle.jklrev_uca_mid 转动副的创建。

（2）部件 uca 与 upright 之间 spherical 约束。
- Joint Name（约束副名称）：uca_outer；
- I　Part：._fsae_suspension_rear_axle.gel_uca；
- J　Part：._fsae_suspension_rear_axle.gel_upright；
- Joint Type（约束副类型）：spherical，转动副，约束 3 个自由度；
- Active(激活)：always；

- Location Dependency：Delta location from coordinate；
- Coordinate Reference（参考坐标）：._fsae_suspension_rear_axle.ground.hpl_uca_outer；
- Location: 0,0,0；
- Location in：local；
- Orientation：None；
- 单击 Apply，完成约束副._fsae_suspension_rear_axle.jolsph_uca_outer 的创建。

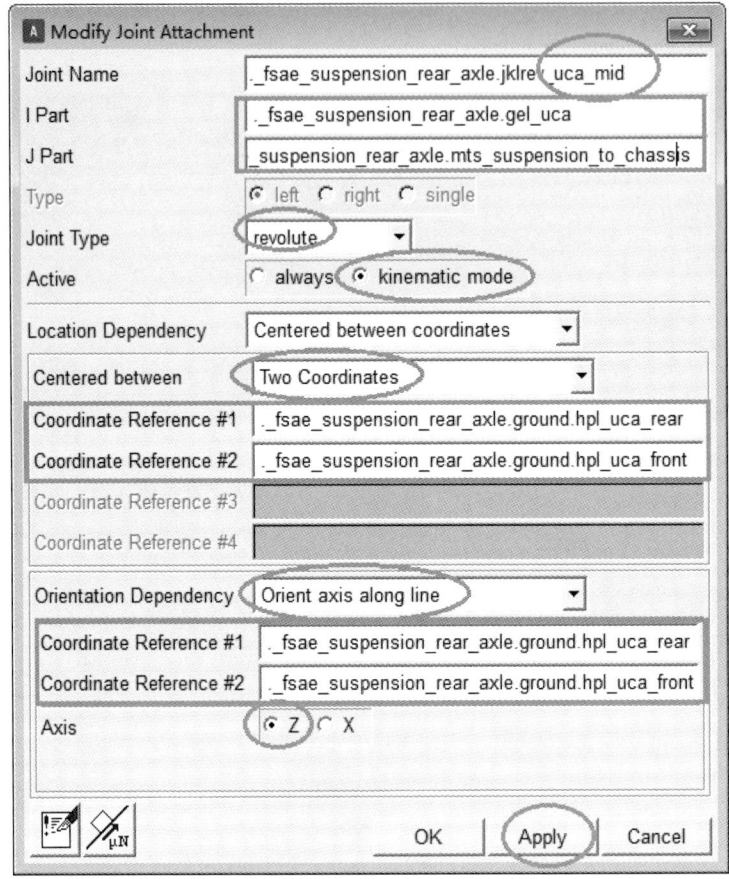

图 2-28　刚性约束对话框-revolute

（3）部件 spindle 与 upright 之间 revolute 约束。
- Joint Name（约束副名称）：spindle；
- I　Part：._fsae_suspension_rear_axle.gel_spindle；
- J　Part：._fsae_suspension_rear_axle.gel_upright；
- Joint Type（约束副类型）：revolute；
- Active(激活)：always；
- Location Dependency：Delta location from coordinate；
- Coordinate Reference（参考坐标）：._fsae_suspension_rear_axle.ground.hpl_wheel_center；
- Location: 0,0,0；
- Location in：local；

- Orientation Dependency：Delta orientation from coordinate；
- Construction Frame：._fsae_suspension_rear_axle.ground.cfl_wheel_center；
- 单击 Apply，完成约束副._fsae_suspension_rear_axle.jolrev_spindle 的创建。

（4）部件 strut_up 与安装件 suspension_to_chassis 之间 hooke 约束。
- Joint Name（约束副名称）：strut_up；
- I　Part：._fsae_suspension_rear_axle.gel_strut_up；
- J　Part：._fsae_suspension_rear_axle.mts_suspension_to_chassis；
- Joint Type（约束副类型）：hooke；
- Active(激活)：kinematic mode；
- Location Dependency：Delta location from coordinate；
- Coordinate Reference（参考坐标）：._fsae_suspension_rear_axle.ground.hpl_strut_up；
- Location: 0,0,0；
- Location in：local；
- I-Part　Axis：._fsae_suspension_rear_axle.ground.hpl_strut_up_ref；
- J-Part　Axis：._fsae_suspension_rear_axle.ground.hpl_strut_low；
- 单击 Apply，完成约束副._fsae_suspension_rear_axle.jolhoo_strut_up 的创建。

（5）部件 strut_lower 与安装件 lca 之间 hooke 约束。
- Joint Name（约束副名称）：strut_lower；
- I　Part：._fsae_suspension_rear_axle.gel_strut_low；
- J　Part：._fsae_suspension_rear_axle.gel_lca；
- Joint Type（约束副类型）：hooke；
- Active(激活)：kinematic mode；
- Location Dependency：Delta location from coordinate；
- Coordinate Reference（参考坐标）：._fsae_suspension_rear_axle.ground.hpl_strut_low；
- Location: 0,0,0；
- Location in：local；
- I-Part　Axis：._fsae_suspension_rear_axle.ground.hpl_strut_up；
- J-Part　Axis：._fsae_suspension_rear_axle.ground.hpl_strut_low_ref；
- 单击 Apply，完成约束副._fsae_suspension_rear_axle.jklhoo_strut_lower 的创建。

（6）部件 lca 与安装件 suspension_to_chassis 之间 revolute 约束。
- Joint Name（约束副名称）：lca_inner_mid；
- I　Part：._fsae_suspension_rear_axle.gel_lca；
- J　Part：._fsae_suspension_rear_axle.mts_suspension_to_chassis；
- Joint Type（约束副类型）：revolute，转动副，约束 5 个自由度；
- Active(激活)：kinematic mode(运动学模式)；
- Location Dependency：Centered between coordinates；
- Centered between：Two Coordinates；
- Coordinate Reference #1（参考坐标）：._fsae_suspension_rear_axle.ground.hpl_lca_rear；
- Coordinate Reference #2（参考坐标）：._fsae_suspension_rear_axle.ground.hpl_lca_front；

- Orientation Dependency：Orient axis along line；
- Coordinate Reference #1（参考坐标）：._fsae_suspension_rear_axle.ground.hpl_lca_rear；
- Coordinate Reference #2（参考坐标）：._fsae_suspension_rear_axle.ground.hpl_lca_front；
- Axis：Z；
- 单击 Apply，完成._fsae_suspension_rear_axle.jklrev_lca_inner_mid 铰接副的创建。

（7）部件 tierod 与安装件 tierod_to_steering 之间 convel 约束。
- Joint Name（约束副名称）：tierod_inner；
- I Part：._fsae_suspension_rear_axle.gel_tierod；
- J Part：._fsae_suspension_rear_axle.mtl_tierod_to_steering；
- Joint Type（约束副类型）：convel，恒速副；
- Active(激活)：always；
- Location Dependency：Delta location from coordinate；
- Coordinate Reference（参考坐标）：._fsae_suspension_rear_axle.ground.hpl_tierod_inner；
- Location：0，0，0；
- Location in：local；
- I-Part Axis：._fsae_suspension_rear_axle.ground.hpl_tierod_outer；
- J-Part Axis：._fsae_suspension_rear_axle.ground.hpr_tierod_inner；
- 单击 Apply，完成约束副._fsae_suspension_rear_axle.jolcon_tierod_inner 的创建。

（8）部件 tierod 与 upright 之间 spherical 约束。
- Joint Name（约束副名称）：tierod_outer；
- I Part：._fsae_suspension_rear_axle.gel_tierod；
- J Part：._fsae_suspension_rear_axle.gel_upright；
- Joint Type（约束副类型）：spherical，约束 3 个自由度；
- Active(激活)：always；
- Location Dependency：Delta location from coordinate；
- Coordinate Reference（参考坐标）：._fsae_suspension_rear_axle.ground.hpl_tierod_outer；
- Location：0,0,0；
- Location in：local；
- Orientation：None；
- 单击 Apply，完成约束副._fsae_suspension_rear_axle.jolsph_tierod_outer 的创建。

（9）部件 lca 与 upright 之间 spherical 约束。
- Joint Name（约束副名称）：lca_outer；
- I Part：._fsae_suspension_rear_axle.gel_lca；
- J Part：._fsae_suspension_rear_axle.gel_upright；
- Joint Type（约束副类型）：spherical，约束 3 个自由度；
- Active(激活)：always；
- Location Dependency：Delta location from coordinate；
- Coordinate Reference（参考坐标）：._fsae_suspension_rear_axle.ground.hpl_lca_outer；
- Location：0,0,0；

- Location in：local；
- Orientation：None；
- 单击 Apply，完成约束副._fsae_suspension_rear_axle.jolsph_lca_outer 的创建。

（10）部件 strut_up 与 strut_low 之间 cylindrical 约束。
- Joint Name（约束副名称）：strut_mid；
- I   Part：._fsae_suspension_rear_axle.gel_strut_low；
- J   Part：._fsae_suspension_rear_axle.gel_strut_up；
- Joint Type（约束副类型）：cylindrical；
- Active(激活）：always；
- Location Dependency：Centered between coordinates；
- Centered between：Two Coordinates；
- Coordinate Reference #1（参考坐标）：._fsae_suspension_rear_axle.ground.hpl_strut_low；
- Coordinate Reference #2（参考坐标）：._fsae_suspension_rear_axle.ground.hpl_strut_up；
- Orientation Dependency：Orient axis along line；
- Coordinate Reference #1（参考坐标）：._fsae_suspension_rear_axle.ground.hpl_strut_low；
- Coordinate Reference #2（参考坐标）：._fsae_suspension_rear_axle.ground.hpl_strut_up；
- Axis：Z；
- 单击 Apply，完成._fsae_suspension_rear_axle.jolcyl_strut_mid 约束副的创建。

（11）部件 tripot 与 drive_shaft 之间 convel 约束。
- Joint Name（约束副名称）：drive_sft_int_jt；
- I   Part：._fsae_suspension_rear_axle.gel_tripot；
- J   Part：._fsae_suspension_rear_axle.gel_drive_shaft；
- Joint Type（约束副类型）：convel，恒速副；
- Active(激活）：always；
- Location Dependency：Delta location from coordinate；
- Coordinate Reference（参考坐标）：._fsae_suspension_rear_axle.ground.hpl_drive_shaft_inr；
- Location：0，0，0；
- Location in：local；
- I-Part   Axis：._fsae_suspension_rear_axle.ground.hpr_drive_shaft_inr；
- J-Part   Axis：._fsae_suspension_rear_axle.ground.cfl_drive_shaft_otr；
- 单击 Apply，完成约束副._fsae_suspension_rear_axle.jolcon_drive_sft_int_jt 的创建。

（12）部件 spindle 与 drive_shaft 之间 convel 约束。
- 单击 Build > Construction Frame > New 命令；
- Construction Frame（结构框名称）：drive_shaft_otr；
- Location Dependency：Delta location from coordinate；
- Coordinate Reference （参考坐标）：._fsae_suspension_rear_axle.ground.cfl_wheel_center；
- Location：0.0, 0.0, (－1.0 * ._fsae_suspension_rear_axle.pvl_drive_shaft_offset)；
- Location in：local；
- Orientation Dependency：Orient axie to point；

- Coordinate Reference（参考坐标）：._fsae_suspension_rear_axle.ground.hpl_wheel_center；
- Axis：Z；
- 单击OK，完成._fsae_suspension_rear_axle.ground.cfl_drive_shaft_otr结构框的创建。
- Joint Name（约束副名称）：drive_sft_otr；
- I Part：._fsae_suspension_rear_axle.gel_drive_shaft；
- J Part：._fsae_suspension_rear_axle.gel_spindle；
- Joint Type（约束副类型）：convel，恒速副；
- Active（激活）：always；
- Location Dependency：Delta location from coordinate；
- Coordinate Reference（参考坐标）：._fsae_suspension_rear_axle.ground.cfl_drive_shaft_otr；
- Location：0，0，0；
- Location in：local；
- I-Part Axis：._fsae_suspension_rear_axle.ground.hpl_drive_shaft_inr；
- J-Part Axis：._fsae_suspension_rear_axle.ground.hpl_wheel_center；
- 单击Apply，完成约束副_fsae_suspension_rear_axle.jolcon_drive_sft_otr的创建。。

（13）部件tripot与安装件tripot_to_differential之间translational约束。
- Joint Name（约束副名称）：tripot_to_differential；
- I Part：._fsae_suspension_rear_axle.gel_tripot；
- J Part：._fsae_suspension_rear_axle.mtl_tripot_to_differential；
- Joint Type（约束副类型）：translational；
- Active(激活)：always；
- Location Dependency：Delta location from coordinate；
- Coordinate Reference #1(参考坐标)：._fsae_suspension_rear_axle.ground.hpl_drive_shaft_inr；
- Orientation Dependency：Orient to zpoint-xpoint；
- Coordinate Reference #1(参考坐标)：._fsae_suspension_rear_axle.ground.hpr_drive_shaft_inr；
- Coordinate Reference #2(参考坐标)：._fsae_suspension_rear_axle.ground.cfl_drive_shaft_otr；
- Axis：ZX；
- 单击OK，完成约束副._fsae_suspension_rear_axle.joltra_tripot_to_differential的创建。

（14）柔性部件fbs_fsae_leaf与部件lca之间Fixed约束。
- Tools > Adams/View > Interface，切换到View模块；
- 单击固定副约束快捷方式：
- 选择柔性部件fbs_fsae_leaf与部件._fsae_suspension_rear_axle.gel_lca，创建左侧固定副约束；
- 选择柔性部件fbs_fsae_leaf与部件._fsae_suspension_rear_axle.ger_lca，创建右侧固定副约束。

2.4.2 柔性约束

单击Build > Attachments > Bushing > New命令，弹出创衬套件对话框如图2-29所示。

（1）部件 uca 与 suspension_to_chassis 之间 bushing 约束。
- Bushing Name（约束副名称）：uca_front；
- I Part：._fsae_suspension_rear_axle.gel_uca；
- J Part：._fsae_suspension_rear_axle.mts_suspension_to_chassis；
- Inactive（抑制）：kinematic mode（运动学模式）；
- Preload：0，0，0；
- Tpreload:0，0，0；
- Offset：0，0，0；
- Roffset：0，0，0；
- Geometry Length：25.4；
- Geometry Radius：12.7；

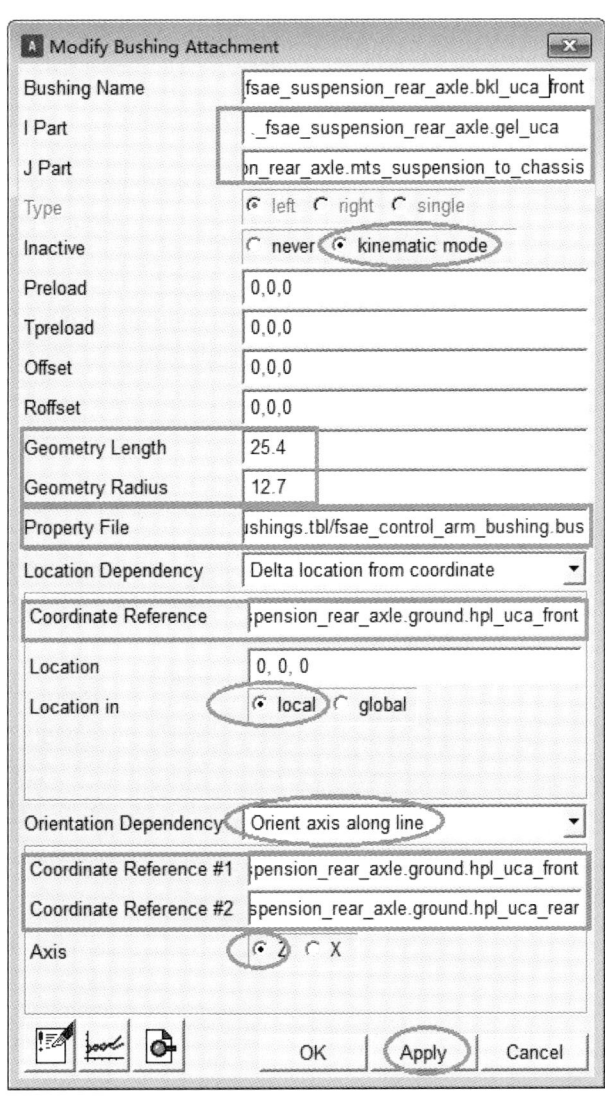

图 2-29 衬套约束对话框-bushing

- Property File：mdids://FASE/bushings.tbl/fsae_control_arm_bushing.bus；用记事本文件打开衬套属性文件，用 MATLAB 软件绘制在 X、Y、Z 方向的垂向刚度及扭转刚度，如图 2-30、图 2-31 所示；
- Location Dependency：Delta location from coordinate；
- Coordinate Reference（参考坐标）：._fsae_suspension_rear_axle.ground.hpl_uca_front；
- Location：0，0，0；
- Location in：local；
- Orientation Dependency：Orient axis along line；
- Coordinate Reference #1（参考坐标）：._fsae_suspension_rear_axle.ground.hpl_uca_front；
- Coordinate Reference #2（参考坐标）：._fsae_suspension_rear_axle.ground.hpl_uca_rear；
- Axis：Z；
- 单击 Apply，完成轴套._fsae_suspension_rear_axle.bkl_uca_front 的创建；
- Bushing Name（约束副名称）：uca_rear；
- I Part：._fsae_suspension_rear_axle.gel_uca；
- J Part：._fsae_suspension_rear_axle.mts_suspension_to_chassis；
- Inactive（抑制）：kinematic mode（运动学模式）；
- Preload：0，0，0；
- Tpreload：0，0，0；
- Offset：0，0，0；
- Roffset：0，0，0；
- Geometry Length：25.4；
- Geometry Radius：12.7；
- Property File：mdids://FASE/bushings.tbl/fsae_control_arm_bushing.bus；
- Location Dependency：Delta location from coordinate；
- Coordinate Reference（参考坐标）：._fsae_suspension_rear_axle.ground.hpl_uca_rear；
- Location：0，0，0；
- Location in：local；
- Orientation Dependency：Orient axis along line；
- Coordinate Reference #1（参考坐标）：._fsae_suspension_rear_axle.ground.hpl_uca_front；
- Coordinate Reference #2（参考坐标）：._fsae_suspension_rear_axle.ground.hpl_uca_rear；
- Axis：Z；
- 单击 Apply，完成轴套._fsae_suspension_rear_axle.bkl_uca_rear 的创建；
- Bushing Name（约束副名称）：uca_rear；
- I Part：._fsae_suspension_rear_axle.gel_uca；
- J Part：._fsae_suspension_rear_axle.mts_suspension_to_chassis；
- Inactive（抑制）：kinematic mode（运动学模式）；
- Preload：0，0，0；
- Tpreload：0，0，0；
- Offset：0，0，0；
- Roffset：0，0，0；

- Geometry Length：25.4；
- Geometry Radius：12.7；
- Property File：mdids://FASE/bushings.tbl/fsae_control_arm_bushing.bus；
- Location Dependency：Delta location from coordinate；
- Coordinate Reference（参考坐标）：._fsae_suspension_rear_axle.ground.hpl_uca_rear；
- Location: 0，0，0；
- Location in：local；
- Orientation Dependency：Orient axis along line；
- Coordinate Reference #1（参考坐标）：._fsae_suspension_rear_axle.ground.hpl_uca_front；
- Coordinate Reference #2（参考坐标）：._fsae_suspension_rear_axle.ground.hpl_uca_rear；
- Axis：Z；
- 单击 Apply，完成轴套._fsae_suspension_rear_axle.bkl_uca_rear 的创建。

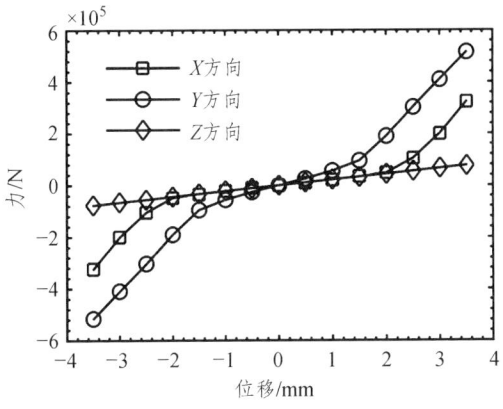

图 2-30　衬套垂向刚度　　　　图 2-31　衬套扭转刚度

（2）部件 lca 与 suspension_to_chassis 之间 bushing 约束。

- Bushing Name（约束副名称）：lca_front；
- I　Part：._fsae_suspension_rear_axle.gel_lca；
- J　Part：._fsae_suspension_rear_axle.mts_suspension_to_chassis；
- Inactive（抑制）：kinematic mode（运动学模式）；
- Preload：0，0，0；
- Tpreload：0，0，0；
- Offset：0，0，0；
- Roffset：0，0，0；
- Geometry Length：25.4；
- Geometry Radius：12.7；
- Property File：mdids://FASE/bushings.tbl/fsae_control_arm_bushing.bus；
- Location Dependency：Delta location from coordinate；
- Coordinate Reference（参考坐标）：._fsae_suspension_rear_axle.ground.hpl_lca_front；
- Location: 0，0，0；

- Location in：local；
- Orientation Dependency：Orient axis along line；
- Coordinate Reference #1（参考坐标）：._fsae_suspension_rear_axle.ground.hpl_lca_front；
- Coordinate Reference #2（参考坐标）：._fsae_suspension_rear_axle.ground.hpl_lca_rear；
- Axis：Z；
- 单击 Apply，完成轴套._fsae_suspension_rear_axle.bkl_lca_front 的创建；
- Bushing Name（约束副名称）：lca_rear；
- I Part：._fsae_suspension_rear_axle.gel_lca；
- J Part：._fsae_suspension_rear_axle.mts_suspension_to_chassis；
- Inactive（抑制）：kinematic mode（运动学模式）；
- Preload：0，0，0；
- Tpreload：0，0，0；
- Offset：0，0，0；
- Roffset：0，0，0；
- Geometry Length：25.4；
- Geometry Radius：12.7；
- Property File：mdids://FASE/bushings.tbl/fsae_control_arm_bushing.bus；
- Location Dependency：Delta location from coordinate；
- Coordinate Reference（参考坐标）：._fsae_suspension_rear_axle.ground.hpl_lca_rear；
- Location：0，0，0；
- Location in：local；
- Orientation Dependency：Orient axis along line；
- Coordinate Reference #1（参考坐标）：._fsae_suspension_rear_axle.ground.hpl_lca_front；
- Coordinate Reference #2（参考坐标）：._fsae_suspension_rear_axle.ground.hpl_lca_rear；
- Axis：Z；
- 单击 OK，完成轴套._fsae_suspension_rear_axle.bkl_lca_rear 的创建。

（3）避震器与 suspension_to_chassis 之间 bushing 约束。

- Bushing Name（约束副名称）：strut_up；
- I Part：._fsae_suspension_rear_axle.gel_strut_up；
- J Part：._fsae_suspension_rear_axle.mts_suspension_to_chassis；
- Inactive（抑制）：kinematic mode（运动学模式）；
- Preload：0，0，0；
- Tpreload：0，0，0；
- Offset：0，0，0；
- Roffset：0，0，0；
- Geometry Length：25.4；
- Geometry Radius：12.7；
- Property File：mdids://acar_shared/bushings.tbl/mdi_0001.bus；

- Location Dependency：Delta location from coordinate；
- Coordinate Reference（参考坐标）：._fsae_suspension_rear_axle.ground.hpl_strut_up；
- Location：0，0，0；
- Location in：local；
- Orientation Dependency：Orient axis to point；
- Coordinate Reference #1（参考坐标）：._fsae_suspension_rear_axle.ground.hpr_strut_up；
- Axis：Z；
- 单击 Apply，完成轴套._fsae_suspension_rear_axle.bkl_strut_up 的创建。
- Bushing Name（约束副名称）：strut_lower；
- I　Part：._fsae_suspension_rear_axle.gel_strut_low；
- J　Part：._fsae_suspension_rear_axle.gel_lca；
- Inactive（抑制）：kinematic mode（运动学模式）；
- Preload：0，0，0；
- Tpreload：0，0，0；
- Offset：0，0，0；
- Roffset：0，0，0；
- Geometry Length：25.4；
- Geometry Radius：12.7；
- Property File：mdids://acar_shared/bushings.tbl/mdi_0004.bus；
- Location Dependency：Delta location from coordinate；
- Coordinate Reference（参考坐标）：._fsae_suspension_rear_axle.ground.hpl_strut_low；
- Location：0，0，0；
- Location in：local；
- Orientation Dependency：Orient axis to point；
- Coordinate Reference #1（参考坐标）：._fsae_suspension_rear_axle.ground.hpr_strut_low；
- Axis：Z；
- 单击 OK，完成轴套._fsae_suspension_rear_axle.bkl_strut_lower 的创建。

2.5　横置板簧悬架变量参数

- 单击 Build > Parameter Variable > New 命令；
- Parameter Variable Name: driveline_active；
- Integer　Value（实数值）：1；
- Units：length；
- Hide from standard user（是否从标准界面隐藏）：yes；
- 单击单击 Apply，完成变量._fsae_suspension_rear_axle.phs_driveline_active 的创建；
- Parameter Variable Name：　kinematic_flag；

- Integer Value（实数值）：1；
- Units：length；
- Hide from standard user（是否从标准界面隐藏）：yes；
- 单击 OK，完成变量._fsae_suspension_rear_axle.phs_kinematic_flag 的创建。
- 单击 Build > Suspension Parameters > Characteristics Arrary > Set 命令，此设置主要用于设置悬架的转向主销，如图 2-32 所示；
- Steer Axis Caculation：Geometric；
- Suspension Type：Independent，非独立悬架；
- I Part：._fsae_suspension_rear_axle.gel_uca；
- J Part：._fsae_suspension_rear_axle.gel_lca；
- I Coordinate Reference：._fsae_suspension_rear_axle.ground.hpl_uca_outer；
- J Coordinate Reference：._fsae_suspension_rear_axle.ground.hpl_lca_outer；
- 单击 OK，完成悬架参数变量设置。

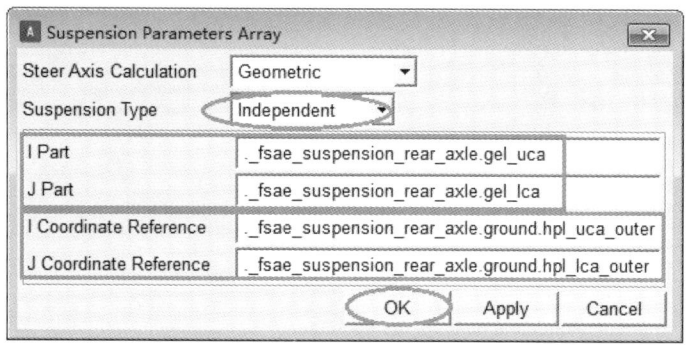

图 2-32　悬架参数变量设置

2.6　横置板簧悬架通信器

2.6.1　通信器建立

- 单击 Build > Communicator > Output > New 命令，弹出输出通信器对话框；
- Output Communicator Name（输出通信器名称）：driveline_active；
- Matching Name(s)：driveline_active；
- Type：single；
- Entity：parameter integer；
- To Minor Role：inherit；
- Parameter Variable Name：._fsae_suspension_rear_axle.phs_driveline_active；
- 单击单击 Apply，完成通信器._fsae_suspension_rear_axle.cos_driveline_active 的创建；
- Output Communicator Name（输出通信器名称）：tripot_to_differential；
- Matching Name(s)：tripot_to_differential；

- Type：left；
- Entity：Location；
- To Minor Role：inherit；
- Coordinate Reference Name：._fsae_suspension_rear_axle.ground.hpl_drive_shaft_inr；
- 单击 Apply，完成通信器._fsae_suspension_rear_axle.col_tripot_to_differential 的创建；
- Output Communicator Name（输出通信器名称）：arb_pickup；
- Matching Name(s)：arb_pickup；
- Type：left；
- Entity：mount；
- To Minor Role：inherit；
- Part Name：._fsae_suspension_rear_axle.gel_upright；
- 单击 Apply，完成通信器._fsae_suspension_rear_axle.col_arb_pickup 的创建；
- Output Communicator Name（输出通信器名称）：suspension_mount；
- Matching Name(s)：suspension_mount；
- Type：left；
- Entity：mount；
- To Minor Role：inherit；
- Part Name：._fsae_suspension_rear_axle.gel_spindle；
- 单击 Apply，完成通信器._fsae_suspension_rear_axle.col_suspension_mount 的创建；
- Output Communicator Name（输出通信器名称）：wheel_center；
- Matching Name(s)：wheel_center；
- Type：left；
- Entity：Location；
- To Minor Role：inherit；
- Coordinate Reference Name：._fsae_suspension_rear_axle.ground.hpl_wheel_center；
- 单击 Apply，完成通信器._fsae_suspension_rear_axle.col_wheel_center 的创建；
- Output Communicator Name（输出通信器名称）：suspension_upright；
- Matching Name(s)：suspension_upright；
- Type：left；
- Entity：mount；
- To Minor Role：inherit；
- Part　Name：._fsae_suspension_rear_axle.gel_upright；
- 单击 OK，完成通信器._fsae_suspension_rear_axle.col_suspension_upright 的创建。

2.6.2　通信器测试

- 单击 Build > Communicator > Test 命令，弹出输出通信器测试对话框，如图 2-33 所示；

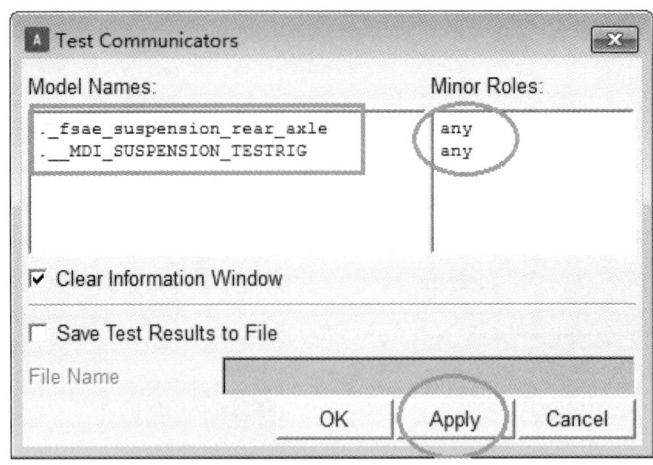

图 2-33　通信器测试对话框设置

- Model Names：._fsae_suspension_rear_axle 与.__MDI_SUSPENSION_TESTRIGG；
- Minor Roles：并列两排输入特征 any，也可以并排输入特征 front，在此两个都可以；
- 单击 OK，完成推杆式双叉臂悬架和悬架试验台._fsae_suspension_rear_axle 与.__MDI_SUSPENSION_TESTRIGG 的匹配测试；测试结果如下列信息所示。

通信器匹配信息如下：

!--- -- Matched communicators: --------!　%以下为匹配的通信器

Communicator Matching Name: tripot_to_differential
Input Communicator Name: ci[lr]_tripot_to_differential
Located in: _fsae_suspension_rear_axle
Output Communicator Name: co[lr]_tripot_to_differential
Output from: __MDI_SUSPENSION_TESTRIG

Communicator Matching Name: camber_angle
Input Communicator Name: ci[lr]_camber_angle
Located in: __MDI_SUSPENSION_TESTRIG
Output Communicator Name: co[lr]_camber_angle
Output from: _fsae_suspension_rear_axle

Communicator Matching Name: toe_angle
Input Communicator Name: ci[lr]_toe_angle
Located in: __MDI_SUSPENSION_TESTRIG
Output Communicator Name: co[lr]_toe_angle
Output from: _fsae_suspension_rear_axle

Communicator Matching Name: wheel_center
Input Communicator Name: ci[lr]_wheel_center
Located in: __MDI_SUSPENSION_TESTRIG
Output Communicator Name: co[lr]_wheel_center

Output from: _fsae_suspension_rear_axle

Communicator Matching Name: suspension_mount
Input Communicator Name: ci[lr]_suspension_mount
Located in: __MDI_SUSPENSION_TESTRIG
Output Communicator Name: co[lr]_suspension_mount
Output from: _fsae_suspension_rear_axle

Communicator Matching Name: driveline_active
Input Communicator Name: cis_driveline_active
Located in: __MDI_SUSPENSION_TESTRIG
Output Communicator Name: cos_driveline_active
Output from: _fsae_suspension_rear_axle

Communicator Matching Name: suspension_parameters_array
Input Communicator Name: cis_suspension_parameters_ARRAY
Located in: __MDI_SUSPENSION_TESTRIG
Output Communicator Name: cos_suspension_parameters_ARRAY
Output from: _fsae_suspension_rear_axle

Communicator Matching Name: tripot_to_differential
Input Communicator Name: ci[lr]_diff_tripot
Located in: __MDI_SUSPENSION_TESTRIG
Output Communicator Name: co[lr]_tripot_to_differential
Output from: _fsae_suspension_rear_axle

Communicator Matching Name: suspension_upright
Input Communicator Name: ci[lr]_suspension_upright
Located in: __MDI_SUSPENSION_TESTRIG
Output Communicator Name: co[lr]_suspension_upright
Output from: _fsae_suspension_rear_axle

!----------Unmatched input communicators: ----------!   %以下为不匹配的输入通信器
Input Communicator Name: cis_suspension_to_chassis
Class: mount
From Minor Role: any
Matching Name(s): suspension_to_chassis
In Template: _fsae_suspension_rear_axle

Input Communicator Name: ci[lr]_tierod_to_steering
Class: mount
From Minor Role: any
Matching Name(s): tierod_to_steering

In Template: _fsae_suspension_rear_axle

Input Communicator Name: ci[lr]_jack_frame
Class: mount
From Minor Role: any
Matching Name(s): jack_frame
In Template: __MDI_SUSPENSION_TESTRIG

Input Communicator Name: cis_leaf_adjustment_steps
Class: parameter_integer
From Minor Role: any
Matching Name(s): leaf_adjustment_steps
In Template: __MDI_SUSPENSION_TESTRIG

Input Communicator Name: cis_powertrain_to_body
Class: mount
From Minor Role: any
Matching Name(s): powertrain_to_body
In Template: __MDI_SUSPENSION_TESTRIG

Input Communicator Name: cis_steering_rack_joint
Class: joint_for_motion
From Minor Role: any
Matching Name(s): steering_rack_joint
In Template: __MDI_SUSPENSION_TESTRIG

Input Communicator Name: cis_steering_wheel_joint
Class: joint_for_motion
From Minor Role: any
Matching Name(s): steering_wheel_joint
In Template: __MDI_SUSPENSION_TESTRIG

!----------Unmatched output communicators: -----------! %以下为不匹配的输出通信器
Output Communicator Name: cos_leaf_adjustment_multiplier
Class: array
To Minor Role: any
Matching Name(s): leaf_adjustment_multiplier
In Template: __MDI_SUSPENSION_TESTRIG

Output Communicator Name: cos_characteristics_input_ARRAY
Class: array
To Minor Role: any
Matching Name(s): characteristics_input_array

In Template: __MDI_SUSPENSION_TESTRIG

2.7 横置板簧悬架驱动轴显示组建

- 在模型树栏，点击 Group 菜单，在模型树栏右击鼠标 New Group，弹出创建组件对话框，如图 2-34 所示；
- Group Name：driveline_active；

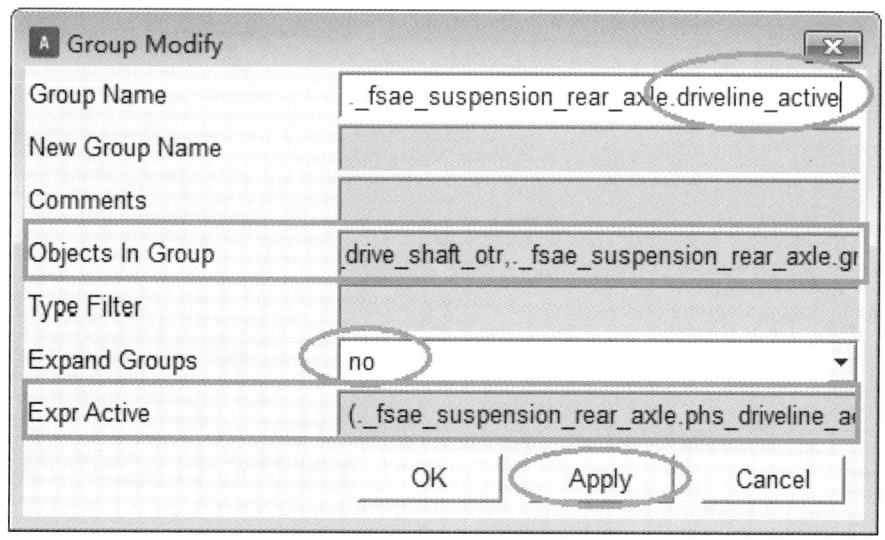

图 2-34 驱动轴显示组件对话框

- Object In Group（显示组件包括的部件、几何体、约束等对象），顺序输入①~㉖对象，如下信息所示：

① ._fsae_suspension_rear_axle.gel_drive_shaft,
② ._fsae_suspension_rear_axle.ger_drive_shaft,
③ ._fsae_suspension_rear_axle.gel_tripot,
④ ._fsae_suspension_rear_axle.ger_tripot,
⑤ ._fsae_suspension_rear_axle.ground.cfl_drive_shaft_otr,
⑥ ._fsae_suspension_rear_axle.ground.cfr_drive_shaft_otr,
⑦ ._fsae_suspension_rear_axle.ground.cfl_drive_shaft_inr,
⑧ ._fsae_suspension_rear_axle.ground.cfr_drive_shaft_inr,
⑨ ._fsae_suspension_rear_axle.mtl_tripot_to_differential,
⑩ ._fsae_suspension_rear_axle.mtr_tripot_to_differential,
⑪._fsae_suspension_rear_axle.jolcon_drive_sft_int_jt,
⑫._fsae_suspension_rear_axle.jorcon_drive_sft_int_jt,
⑬._fsae_suspension_rear_axle.jolcon_drive_sft_otr,
⑭._fsae_suspension_rear_axle.jorcon_drive_sft_otr,

⑮._fsae_suspension_rear_axle.joltra_tripot_to_differential,
⑯._fsae_suspension_rear_axle.jortra_tripot_to_differential,
⑰._fsae_suspension_rear_axle.gel_drive_shaft.gralin_drive_shaft,
⑱._fsae_suspension_rear_axle.gel_drive_shaft.graell_otr_cv_housing,
⑲._fsae_suspension_rear_axle.gel_drive_shaft.graell_tripot_housing,
⑳._fsae_suspension_rear_axle.gel_tripot.gracyl_tripot_housing_extention,
㉑._fsae_suspension_rear_axle.ger_drive_shaft.gralin_drive_shaft,
㉒._fsae_suspension_rear_axle.ger_drive_shaft.graell_otr_cv_housing,
㉓._fsae_suspension_rear_axle.ger_drive_shaft.graell_tripot_housing,
㉔._fsae_suspension_rear_axle.ger_tripot.gracyl_tripot_housing_extention,
㉕._fsae_suspension_rear_axle.mtl_fixed_2,
㉖._fsae_suspension_rear_axle.mtr_fixed_2。

- Expr Active：(._fsae_suspension_rear_axle.phs_driveline_active || ._fsae_suspension_rear_axle.model_class == "template" ? 1 : 0);
- 单击 Apply，完成组件 driveline_active 的创建；
- Group Name：driveline_inactive；
- Expr Active：(! ._fsae_suspension_rear_axle.phs_driveline_active || ._fsae_suspension_rear_axle.model_class == "template" ? 1 : 0);
- 单击 OK，完成组件 driveline_inactive 的创建。
- 单击 File > Save As 命令，弹出保存模板对话框，如图 2-35 所示；
- Major Role(主特征)：suspension；
- File Format：Binary；
- Target：Directory；
- 单击 Select，选择存储路径为 D:/fsae_MD_2010.cdb/templates.tbl；
- 单击 OK，完成横置板簧式悬架模型._fsae_suspension_rear_axle 的保存。

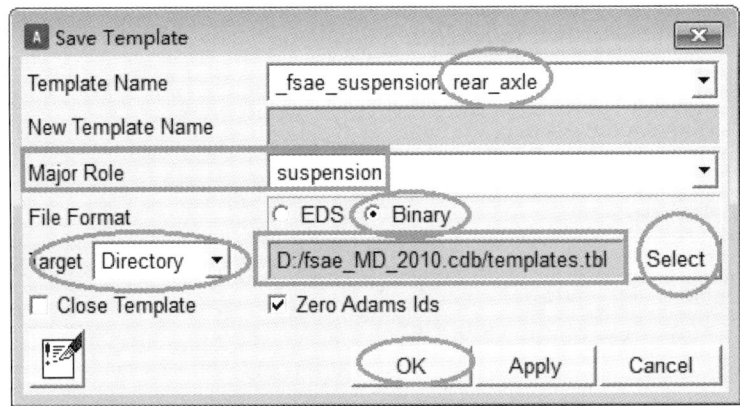

图 2-35　横置板簧悬架模型保存

2.8 单轮振动测试仿真

2.8.1 横置板簧式悬架子系统

- 按 F9，把专家模板转换到标准模式，单击 File > New > Suspension 命令，弹出子系统对话框，如图 2-36 所示；
- Subsystem Name(系统名称)：fsae_suspension_rear_axle；
- Minor Role（副特征）：rear（指悬架为后悬架）；
- Template Name(模板路径)：mdids://FASE/templates.tbl/_fsae_suspension_rear_axle.tpl；
- 单击 OK，完成推杆式悬架子系统 fsae_suspension_rear_axle 的创建。

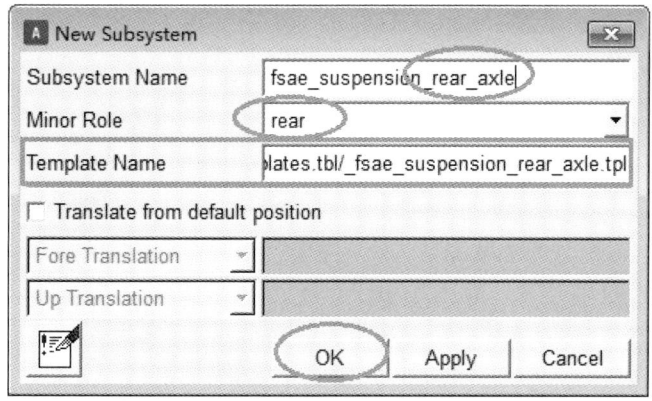

图 2-36 横置板簧式悬架子系统创建对话框

2.8.2 单轮激振设置

- 单击 Simulate > Suspension Analysis > Single Wheel Travel 命令，弹出双轮同向激振对话框，如图 2-37 所示；
- Output Prefix：single traavel；
- Number of Steps（仿真步数）：100；
- Mode of Simulation：interactive；
- Vertical Setup Mode：Wheel Center；
- Bump Travel：50；
- Rebound Travel：-50；
- Side：Left；
- Travel Relative To：Wheel Center；
- Control Mode：Absolute；
- Coordinate System：Vehicle；
- 单击 Apply，完成横置板簧悬架在 C 模式下的仿真；
- 菜单栏单击 Review > Animation Controls，开始动画观看，动画结束后悬架模型变化如图 2-38 所示；

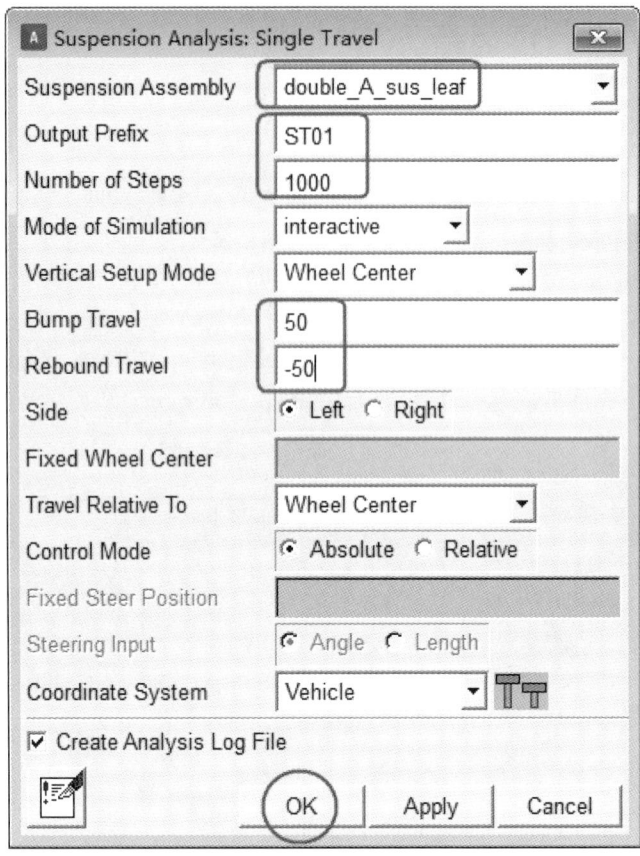

图 2-37　左单轮激振仿真设置

- 按 F8，界面转换到后处理模块；
- Filter：user defined；

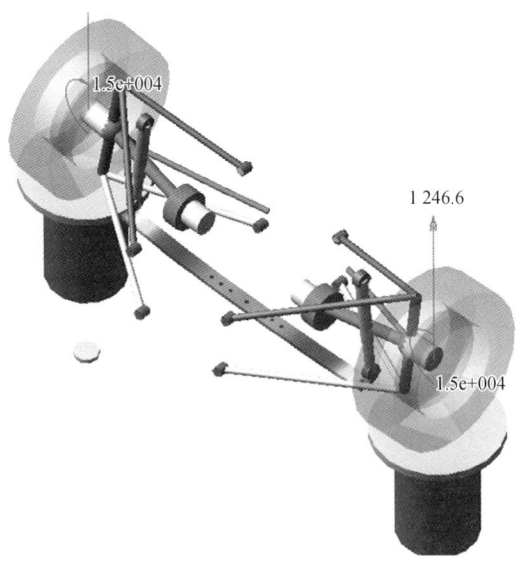

图 2-38　单轮跳动仿真

- Request：选择左前轮 toe_angle；
- Component：left；
- 单击 Add Curves，完成相关参数曲线绘制，如图 2-39 ~ 图 2-43 所示。

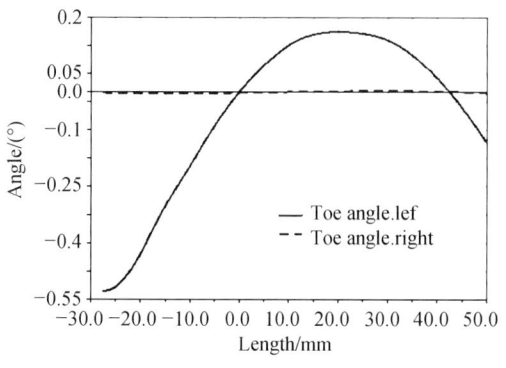

图 2-39　前束角

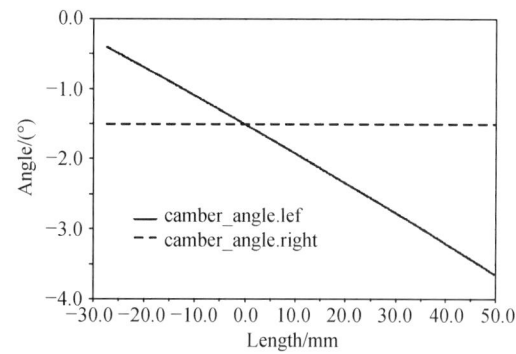

图 2-40　外倾角

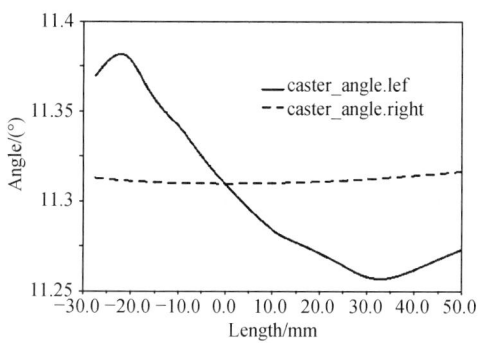

图 2-41　主销后倾角

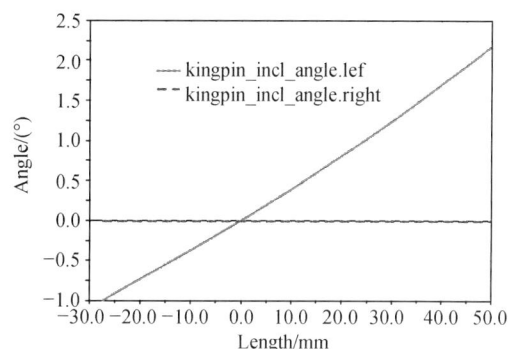

图 2-42　主销内倾角

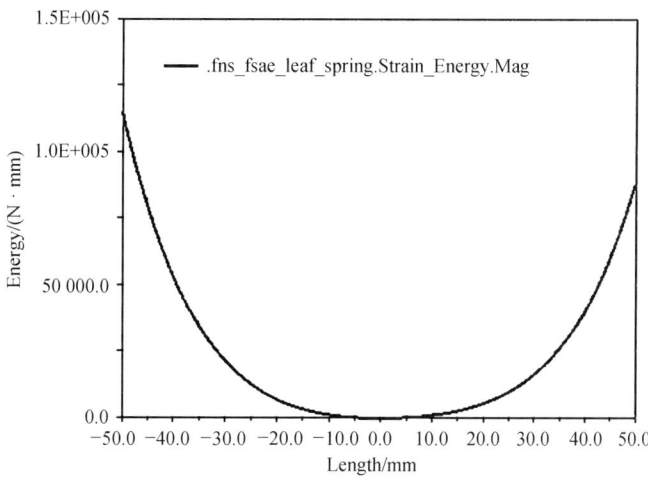

图 2-43　板簧能量变化特性

第 3 章　非独立悬架模型

钢板弹簧由于其特殊性在工、农等行业均有应用，农业三轮车后悬架以及商用牵引车、挂车、工程车辆等均采用钢板弹簧。悬架系统的优劣不在于采用何种悬架类型，关键在于悬架与车身等的参数匹配与调教，调教参数包含连接位置、衬套刚度、弹簧与阻尼器参数等，采用同一个底盘的不同车辆并不能得到相同的性能原因主要在此。例如克尔维特跑车、沃尔沃依然采用横置板簧悬架系统，横置板簧可以节省安装空间，同时起到拉杆的作用（见图3-1），其特性表现均衡。牵引车及工程车辆后驱动轴采用平衡悬架在较差的路面依然极具优势。本章介绍皮卡类车辆或小工具车采用的非独立悬架系统，建立悬架模型并装配到整车上验证其动态特性。

图 3-1　板簧悬架

学习目标

- ◇ 板簧悬架模型。
- ◇ 驱动轴部件。
- ◇ 变量参数。
- ◇ 通信器匹配。
- ◇ 半车模型装配。
- ◇ 车轮激振分析。
- ◇ 整车模型装配。
- ◇ Fish-Hook 仿真。

3.1 板簧悬架模型

- 启动 ADAMS/Car、选择专家模块 Expert 进入建模界面；
- 单击 File > New 命令，弹出建模对话框如图 3-2 所示；
- 在模板名称力输入 my_leaf_rear,主特征选择 suspension，单击 OK。

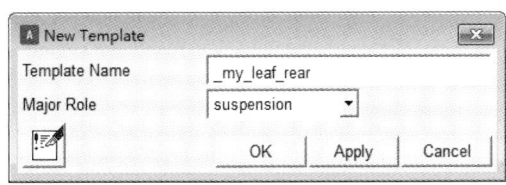

图 3-2　模板框

3.1.1 板簧悬架硬点

- 单击 Build > Hardpoint > New 命令，弹出创建硬点对话框如图 3-3 所示；
- 在硬点名称里输入 wheel_center，类型选择 left；在位置文本框输入 0.0，–750.0，–75.0；
- 单击 Apply,完成 wheel_center 硬点的创建，此时在屏幕上显示出左右对称的两个硬点；
- 重复上述步骤完成如图 3-4 所示硬点的创建。

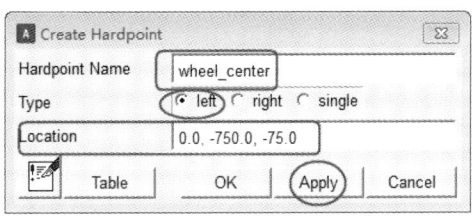

图 3-3　硬点对话框

	loc_x	loc_y	loc_z
hpl_drive_shaft_in	0.0	-200.0	-70.0
hpl_hub_down	0.0	-650.0	-175.0
hpl_hub_up	0.0	-600.0	105.0
hpl_p1	0.0	-500.0	-130.0
hpl_p11	0.0	-500.0	-140.0
hpl_p3	-400.0	-500.0	-130.0
hpl_p3_m	-300.0	-500.0	-130.0
hpl_p4	-200.0	-500.0	-130.0
hpl_p41	-200.0	-500.0	-140.0
hpl_p41_m	-100.0	-500.0	-140.0
hpl_p4_m	-100.0	-500.0	-130.0
hpl_p6	400.0	-500.0	-130.0
hpl_p7	300.0	-500.0	-130.0
hpl_p8	200.0	-500.0	-130.0
hpl_p81	200.0	-500.0	-140.0
hpl_p81_m	100.0	-500.0	-140.0
hpl_p8_m	100.0	-500.0	-130.0
hpl_p9	400.0	-500.0	-80.0
hpl_tierod_inner	200.0	-350.0	-75.0
hpl_tierod_outer	200.0	-700.0	-75.0
hpl_wheel_center	0.0	-750.0	-75.0

图 3-4　板簧硬点参数

3.1.2 横梁部件

- 单击 Build > Part > General Part > New 命令，弹出创建横梁部件对话框如图 3-5 所示，其为已经建立好的板簧非独立悬架模型，通过右击._my_leaf_rear.ges_axis 部件，在弹出的快捷菜单中单击 Modify 而弹出对话框，修改对话框与新建对话框完全一致；
  - General Part 输入 axis；
  - Location Dependency：Centered between coordinates；
  - Centered between：two Coordinates；
  - Coordinate Reference #1(参考坐标)：._my_leaf_rear.ground.hpl_wheel_center；
  - Coordinate Reference #2(参考坐标)：._my_leaf_rear.ground.hpr_wheel_center；
  - Orient using：Euler Angles，即部件定向采用欧拉角模式；
  - Euler Angles：0,0,0；
  - Mass：1；Ixx：1；Iyy：1；Izz：1；
  - Density：Material；
  - Material Type：.materials.steel；
  - 单击 OK，完成部件._my_leaf_rear.ges_axis 创建。

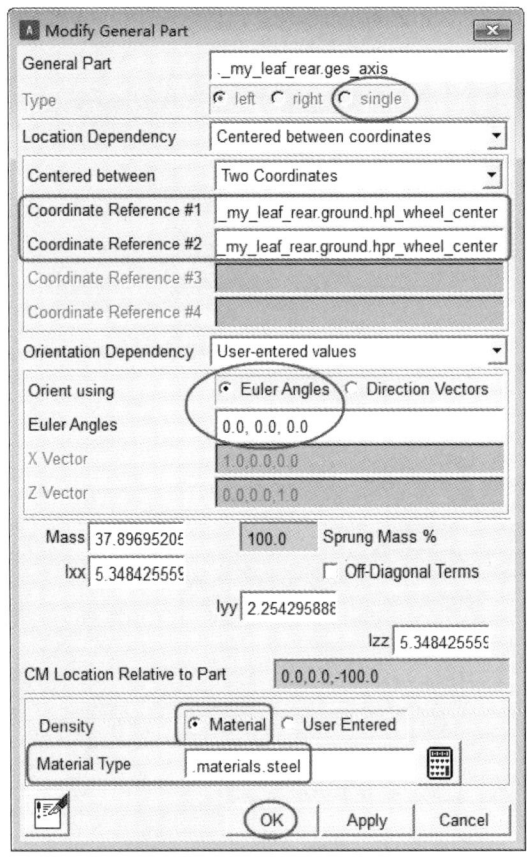

图 3-5 横梁部件

- 单击 Build > Geometry > Link > New 命令（见图 3-6）；
- Link Name (连杆名称) 输入几何名称：axis；
- General Part 输入._my_leaf_rear.ges_axis；
- Coordinate Reference #1(参考坐标)：._my_leaf_rear.ground.hpl_hub_down；
- Coordinate Reference #2(参考坐标)：._my_leaf_rear.ground.hpr_hub_down；
- Radius(半径): 35；
- Color：white；
- 勾选 Calculate Mass Properties of General Part 复选框，当几何建立好之后会更新对应部件的质量和惯量参数；
- Density：Material；
- Material Type：steel；
- 单击 OK，完成._my_leaf_rear.ges_axis.gralin_axis 几何体的创建。

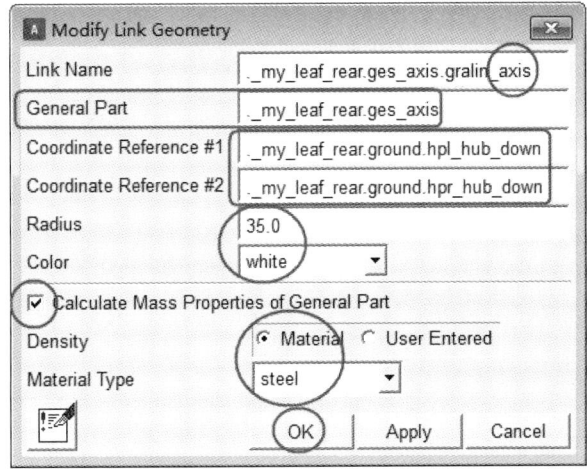

图 3-6　横梁部件连杆几何体创建对话框

3.1.3　轮毂 spindle

- 单击 Build > Suspension Parameters > Toe/Camber Values> Set 命令，弹出悬架参数对话框如图 3-7 所示，前束角输入 0；外倾角输入 0；单击 OK,完成前束与外倾参数创建。创建悬架参数同时系统自动建立两个输出通信器：col[r]_toe_angle、col[r]_camber_angle。

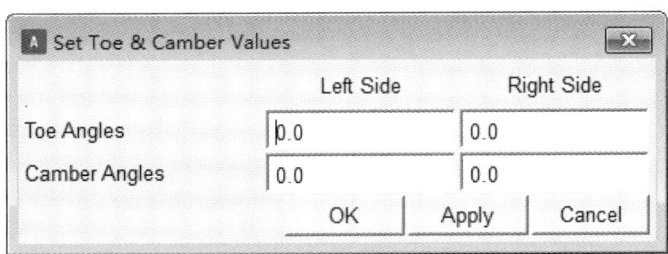

图 3-7　悬架参数对话框

- 单击 Build > Construction Frame > New 命令，弹出创建结构框如图 3-8 所示；
- Construction Frame（结构框名称）：wheel_center；
- Coordinate Reference（参考坐标）：._my_leaf_rear.ground.hpl_wheel_center；
- Location：0,0,0；
- Location in：local；
- Orientation Dependency：Toe/Camber；
- Variable Type（变量类型）:Parameter Variable(参数变量）；
- Toe Parameter Values（前束变量值）：._my_leaf_rear.pvl_toe_angle；
- Camber Parameter Values（外倾变量值）：._my_leaf_rear.pvl_camber_angle；
- 单击 OK,完成._my_leaf_rear.ground.cfl_wheel_center 结构框的创建。

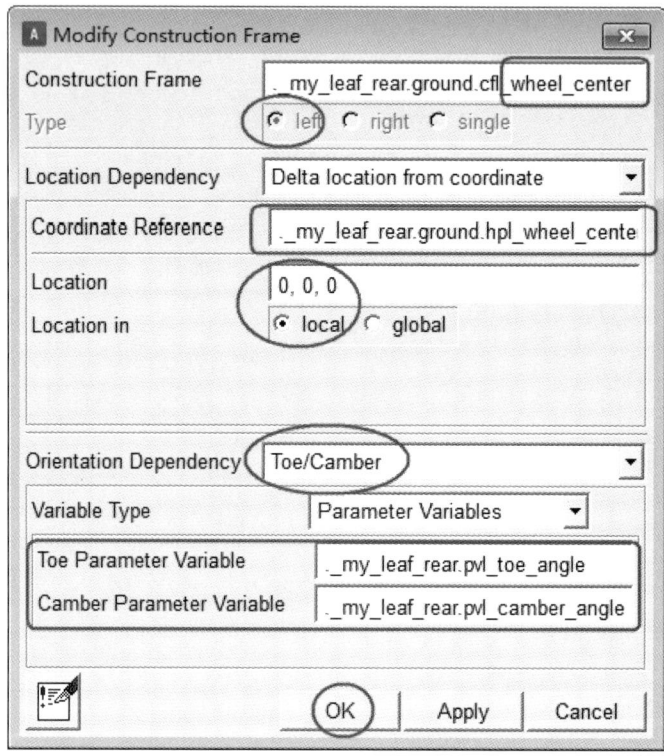

图 3-8　wheel_center 结构框

- 单击 Build > Part > General Part > New 命令，弹出创建部件对话框参考如图 3-5 所示；
- General Part 输入 spindle；
- Location Dependency：Delta location from coordinate；
- Coordinate Reference (参考坐标）：._my_leaf_rear.ground.hpl_wheel_center；
- Location：0,0,0；
- Location in：local；
- Orientation Dependency：Delta orientation from coordinate；
- Construction Frame：._my_leaf_rear.ground.cfl_wheel_center；
- Orientation：0,0,0；

- Mass：1；
- Ixx：1；
- Iyy：1；
- Izz：1；
- Density：Material；
- Material Type：.materials.steel；
- 单击 OK，完成部件._my_leaf_rear.gel_spindle 创建。
- 单击 Build > Geometry > Cylinder (圆柱体)> New 命令，弹出创建部件对话框如图 3-9 所示；
- Cylinder Name（连杆名称）输入几何名称：spindle；
- General Part 输入._my_leaf_rear.gel_spindle；
- Construction Frame：._my_leaf_rear.ground.cfl_wheel_center；
- Radius(半径): 30；
- Length In Postive Z（Z 轴正方向长度）：30；
- Length In Negative Z（Z 轴负方向长度）：50；
- Color（圆柱体几何体颜色）：blue；
- 选择 Calculate Mass Properties of General Part 复选框；
- 单击 OK，完成轮毂圆柱体._my_leaf_rear.gel_spindle.gracyl_spindle 几何体的创建。

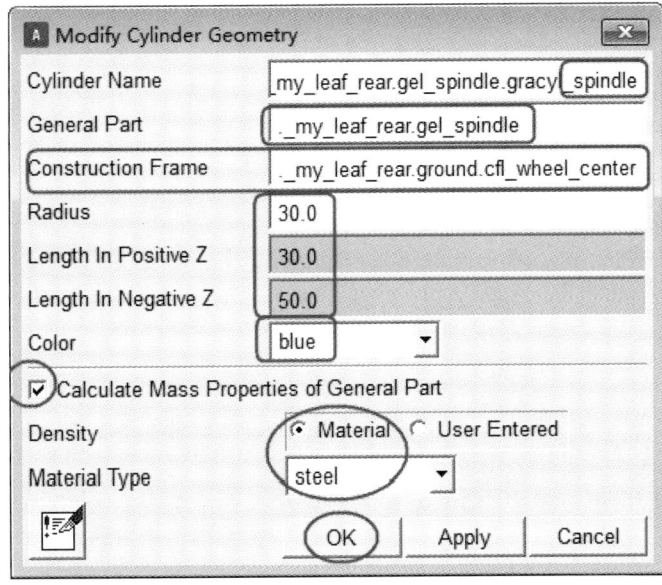

图 3-9 轮毂几何体创建对话框

3.1.4 转向节 upright

- 单击 Build > Part > General Part > New 命令，弹出创建部件对话框参考如图 3-5 所示；
- General Part 输入 upright；

- ocation Dependency：Delta location from coordinate；
- Coordinate Reference (参考坐标)：._my_leaf_rear.ground.cfl_wheel_center；
- Location：0,0,0；
- Location in：local；
- Orient using：Euler Angles；
- Euler Angles：0,0,0；
- Mass：1；
- Ixx：1；
- Iyy：1；
- Izz：1；
- Density：Material；
- Material Type：.materials.steel；
- 单击 OK，完成部件._my_leaf_rear.gel_upright 创建。
- 单击 Build > Geometry > Link > New 命令；
- Link Name (连杆名称）输入几何名称：link1；
- General Part 输入._my_leaf_rear.gel_upright；
- Coordinate Reference #1(参考坐标)：._my_leaf_rear.ground.hpl_hub_down；
- Coordinate Reference #2(参考坐标)：._my_leaf_rear.ground.cfl_wheel_center；
- Radius(半径): 15；
- Color（杆件几何体颜色）：green；
- 选择 Calculate Mass Properties of General Part 复选框，当几何建立好之后会更新对应部件的质量和惯量参数；
- Density：Material；
- Material Type：steel；
- 单击 Apply,完成._my_leaf_rear.gel_upright.gralin_link1 几何体的创建；
- Link Name (连杆名称）输入几何名称：link2；
- General Part 输入._my_leaf_rear.gel_upright；
- Coordinate Reference #1(参考坐标)：._my_leaf_rear.ground.hpl_hub_up；
- Coordinate Reference #2(参考坐标)：._my_leaf_rear.ground.cfl_wheel_center；
- Radius(半径): 15；
- Color（杆件几何体颜色）：green；
- 选择 Calculate Mass Properties of General Part 复选框，当几何建立好之后会更新对应部件的质量和惯量参数；
- Density：Material；
- Material Type：steel；
- 单击 Apply,完成._my_leaf_rear.gel_upright.gralin_link2 几何体的创建；
- Link Name (连杆名称）输入几何名称：link3；
- General Part 输入._my_leaf_rear.gel_upright；
- Coordinate Reference #1(参考坐标)：._my_leaf_rear.ground.hpl_tierod_outer；

- Coordinate Reference #2(参考坐标)：._my_leaf_rear.ground.cfl_wheel_center；
- Radius(半径): 15；
- Color（杆件几何体颜色）：green；
- 选择 Calculate Mass Properties of General Part 复选框，当几何建立好之后会更新对应部件的质量和惯量参数；
- Density：Material；
- Material Type：steel；
- 单击 OK，完成._my_leaf_rear.gel_upright.gralin_link3 几何体的创建。

3.1.5 转向横拉杆

- 单击 Build > Part > General Part > New 命令，弹出创建部件对话框可参考如图 3-5 所示；
- General Part 输入 tierod；
- Location Dependency：Centered between coordinates；
- Centered between：Two Coordinates；
- Coordinate Reference #1(参考坐标)：._my_leaf_rear.ground.hpl_tierod_outer；
- Coordinate Reference #2(参考坐标)：._my_leaf_rear.ground.hpl_tierod_inner；
- Orientation Dependency：User-entered values；
- Orient using：Euler Angles；
- Euler Angles：0,0,0；
- Mass：1；
- Ixx：1；
- Iyy：1；
- Izz：1；
- Density：Material；
- Material Type：.materials.steel；
- 单击 OK，完成部件._my_leaf_rear.gel_tierod 创建。
- 单击 Build > Geometry > Link > New 命令；
- Link Name (连杆名称）输入几何名称：tierod；
- General Part 输入._my_leaf_rear.gel_tierod；
- Coordinate Reference #1(参考坐标)：._my_leaf_rear.ground.hpl_tierod_outer；
- Coordinate Reference #2(参考坐标)：._my_leaf_rear.ground.hpl_tierod_inner；
- Radius(半径): 10；
- Color（杆件几何体颜色）：red；
- 选择 Calculate Mass Properties of General Part 复选框，当几何建立好之后会更新对应部件的质量和惯量参数；
- Density：Material；
- Material Type：steel；
- 单击 OK，完成横拉杆._my_leaf_rear.gel_tierod.gralin_tierod 几何体的创建。

3.1.6 吊耳

- 单击 Build > Part > General Part > New 命令，弹出创建部件对话框可参考如图 3-5 所示；
- General Part 输入 shackle；
- ocation Dependency：Delta location from coordinate；
- Coordinate Reference（参考坐标）：._my_leaf_rear.ground.hpl_p9；
- Location：0,0,0；
- Location in：local；
- Orientation Dependency：User-entered values；
- Orient using：Euler Angles；
- Euler Angles：0,0,0；
- Mass：1；
- Ixx：1；
- Iyy：1；
- Izz：1；
- Density：Material；
- Material Type：materials.steel；
- 单击 OK，完成部件._my_leaf_rear.gel_shackle 创建。
- 单击 Build > Geometry > Link > New 命令；
- Link Name (连杆名称）输入几何名称：shackle；
- General Part 输入._my_leaf_rear.gel_shackle；
- Coordinate Reference #1(参考坐标）：._my_leaf_rear.ground.hpl_p6；
- Coordinate Reference #2(参考坐标）：._my_leaf_rear.ground.hpl_p9；
- Radius(半径): 10；
- Color（杆件几何体颜色）：red；
- 选择 Calculate Mass Properties of General Part 复选框，当几何建立好之后会更新对应部件的质量和惯量参数；
- Density：Material；
- Material Type：steel；
- 单击 OK，完成吊耳._my_leaf_rear.gel_shackle.gralin_shackle 几何体的创建。

3.1.7 驱动轴 drive_shaft 部件

- 单击 Build > Parameter Variable > New 命令，弹出参数变量对话框如图 3-10 所示；
- Parameter Variable Name: drive_shaft_offset;
- 参数类型：Real Value（实数值），数值为 50；
- Units：length；
- Hide from standard user(是否从标准界面隐藏）: no；
- 单击 OK，完成变量._my_leaf_rear.pvl_drive_shaft_offset 的创建。

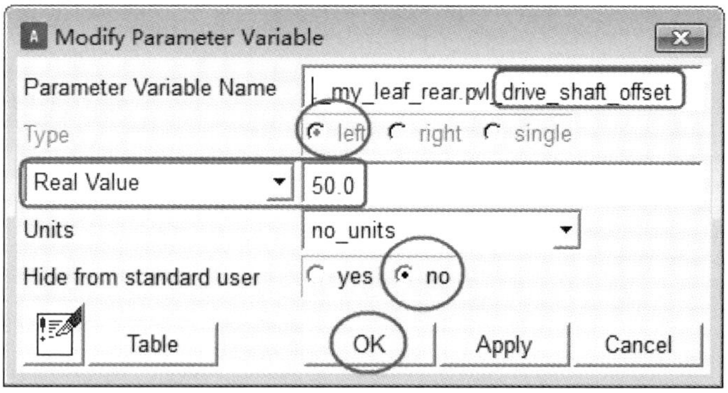

图 3-10 drive_shaft_offset 变量

- 单击 Build > Construction Frame > New 命令；
- Construction Frame（结构框名称）：drive_shaft_otr；
- Location Dependency：Delta location from coordinate；
- Coordinate Reference（参考坐标）：._my_leaf_rear.ground.cfl_wheel_center；
- Location：0.0, 0.0,（ – 1.0 * ._my_leaf_rear.pvl_drive_shaft_offset)；
- Location in：local；
- Orientation Dependency：Orient axis to point；
- Coordinate Reference（参考坐标）：._my_leaf_rear.ground.hpl_wheel_center；
- Axis：Z；
- 单击 OK，完成._my_leaf_rear.ground.cfl_drive_shaft_otr 结构框的创建。
- 单击 Build > Part > General Part > New 命令；
- General Part 输入 drive_shaft；
- Location Dependency：Delta location from coordinate；
- Coordinate Reference（参考坐标）：._my_leaf_rear.ground.hpl_drive_shaft_inr；
- Location：0,0,0；
- Location in：local；
- Orientation Dependency：Oriented in plane；
- Coordinate Reference #1(参考坐标)：._my_leaf_rear.ground.cfl_drive_shaft_otr；
- Coordinate Reference #2(参考坐标)：._my_leaf_rear.ground.hpl_drive_shaft_inr；
- Coordinate Reference#3 (参考坐标)：._my_leaf_rear.ground.hpl_wheel_center；
- Axis：ZX；
- Mass：1；
- Ixx：1；
- Iyy：1；
- Izz：1；
- Density：Material；
- Material Type：.materials.steel；
- 单击 OK，完成部件._my_leaf_rear.gel_drive_shaft 创建。
- 单击 Build > Geometry > Link > New 命令；

- Link Name (连杆名称) 输入几何名称：drive_shaft；
- General Part 输入._my_leaf_rear.gel_drive_shaft；
- Coordinate Reference #1(参考坐标)：._my_leaf_rear.ground.hpl_drive_shaft_inr；
- Coordinate Reference #2(参考坐标)：._my_leaf_rear.ground.cfl_drive_shaft_otr；
- Radius(半径): 15；
- Color（杆件几何体颜色）：yellow；
- 选择 Calculate Mass Properties of General Part 复选框，当几何建立好之后会更新对应部件的质量和惯量参数；
- Density：Material；
- Material Type：steel；
- 单击 OK，完成._my_leaf_rear.gel_drive_shaft.gralin_drive_shaft 几何体的创建。
- 单击 Build > Geometry > Ellipsoid > New 命令；
- Ellipsoid Name (连杆名称) 输入几何名称：cv_housing；
- Coordinate Reference (参考坐标)：._my_leaf_rear.ground.cfl_drive_shaft_otr；
- Link：._my_leaf_rear.gel_drive_shaft.gralin_drive_shaft；
- X   Scale：2；
- Y   Scale：2；
- Z   Scale：2；
- Color（杆件几何体颜色）：yellow；
- 选择 Calculate Mass Properties of General Part 复选框，当几何建立好之后会更新对应部件的质量和惯量参数；
- Density：Material；
- Material Type：steel；
- 单击 Apply，完成._my_leaf_rear.gel_drive_shaft.graell_cv_housing 几何体的创建。
- Ellipsoid Name (连杆名称) 输入几何名称：tripot_housing；
- Coordinate Reference (参考坐标)：._my_leaf_rear.ground.hpl_drive_shaft_inr；
- Link：._fsae_suspension_rear_axle.gel_drive_shaft.gralin_drive_shaft；
- X   Scale：2；
- Y   Scale：2；
- Z   Scale：2；
- Color（杆件几何体颜色）：yellow；
- 选择 Calculate Mass Properties of General Part 复选框；
- Density：Material；
- Material Type：steel；
- 单击 OK，完成._my_leaf_rear.gel_drive_shaft.graell_tripot_housing 几何体的创建。

3.1.8 等速万向节 tripot 部件

- 单击 Build > Construction Frame > New 命令；

- Construction Frame（结构框名称）：drive_shaft_inr；
- Location Dependency：Delta location from coordinate；
- Coordinate Reference（参考坐标）：._my_leaf_rear.ground.hpl_drive_shaft_inr；
- Location：0,0,0；
- Location in：local；
- Orientation Dependency：Orient in plane；
- Coordinate Reference #1(参考坐标)：._my_leaf_rear.ground.hpl_drive_shaft_inr；
- Coordinate Reference #2(参考坐标)：._my_leaf_rear.ground.hpr_drive_shaft_inr；
- Coordinate Reference#3 (参考坐标)：._my_leaf_rear.ground.cfl_drive_shaft_otr；
- Axis：ZX；
- 单击 OK，完成._my_leaf_rear.ground.cfl_drive_shaft_inr 结构框的创建。
- 单击 Build > Part > General Part > New 命令，弹出创建部件对话框可参考如图 3-5 所示；
- General Part 输入 tripot；
- Location Dependency：Delta location from coordinate；
- Coordinate Reference（参考坐标）：._my_leaf_rear.ground.hpl_drive_shaft_inr；
- Location：0,0,0；
- Location in：local；
- Orientation Dependency：Orient to zpoint-xpoint；
- Coordinate Reference #1(参考坐标)：._my_leaf_rear.ground.hpl_drive_shaft_inr；
- Coordinate Reference #2(参考坐标)：._my_leaf_rear.ground.cfl_drive_shaft_otr；
- Axis：ZX；
- Mass：1；
- Ixx：1；
- Iyy：1；
- Izz：1；
- Density：Material；
- Material Type：.materials.steel；
- 单击 OK，完成部件._my_leaf_rear.gel_tripot 创建。
- 单击 Build > Geometry > Cylinder (圆柱体) > New 命令，参考如图 3-9 所示；
- Cylinder Name (连杆名称) 输入几何名称：tripot_housing_extention；
- General Part 输入._my_leaf_rear.gel_tripot；
- Radius(半径): 30；
- Length In Postive Z（Z 轴正方向长度）:50；
- Length In Negative Z（Z 轴负方向长度）：0；
- Color（圆柱体几何体颜色）：blue；
- 选择 Calculate Mass Properties of General Part 复选框；

- 单击 OK，完成圆柱体._my_leaf_rear.gel_tripot.gracyl_tripot_housing_extention 几何体的创建。

3.2 非独立悬架安装部件

- 单击 Build > Construction Frame > New 命令；
- Construction Frame（结构框名称）：subframe；
- Location Dependency：Centered between coordinates；
- Centered between：Two Coordinates；
- Coordinate Reference #1(参考坐标)：._my_leaf_rear.ground.hpl_wheel_center；
- Coordinate Reference #2(参考坐标)：._my_leaf_rear.ground.hpr_wheel_center；
- Orientation Dependency：User-entered values；
- Orient using：Euler Angles；
- Euler Angles：0,0,0；
- 单击 OK，完成._my_leaf_rear.ground.cfs_subframe 结构框的创建。
- 单击 Build > Part > Mount > New 命令，弹出创建部件对话框如图 3-11 所示；
- Mount name（安装件名称）：tierod_to_steering；
- Coordinate Reference（参考坐标）：._my_leaf_rear.ground.hpl_tierod_inner；
- 安装件特征选择：inherit（继承特性）；
- 单击 Apply，完成._my_leaf_rear.mtl_tierod_to_steering 安装部件的创建；
- Mount name（安装件名称）：tripot_to_differential；
- Coordinate Reference（参考坐标）：._my_leaf_rear.ground.hpl_drive_shaft_inr；
- 安装件特征选择：inherit(继承特性)；
- 单击 Apply，完成._my_leaf_rear.mtl_tripot_to_differential 安装部件的创建；
- Mount name（安装件名称）：leafspring_to_body；
- Coordinate Reference（参考坐标）：._my_leaf_rear.ground.cfs_subframe；
- 安装件特征选择：inherit（继承特性）；
- 单击 OK，完成._my_leaf_rear.mts_leafspring_to_body 安装部件的创建。

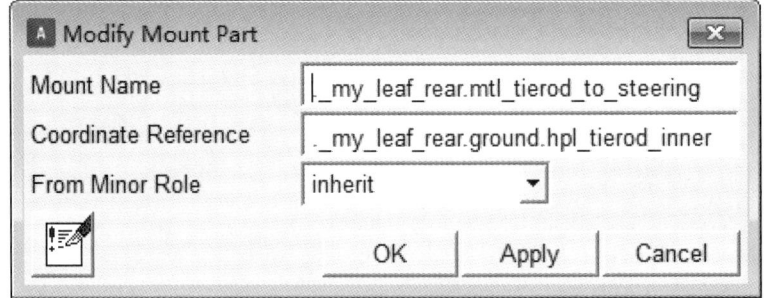

图 3-11 安装部件对话框

3.3 钢板弹簧

3.3.1 线性梁

- 单击 Build > Part > Nonlinear Beam > New 命令，弹出创建非线性梁对话框如图 3-12 所示；
- General Part 输入 beam1；

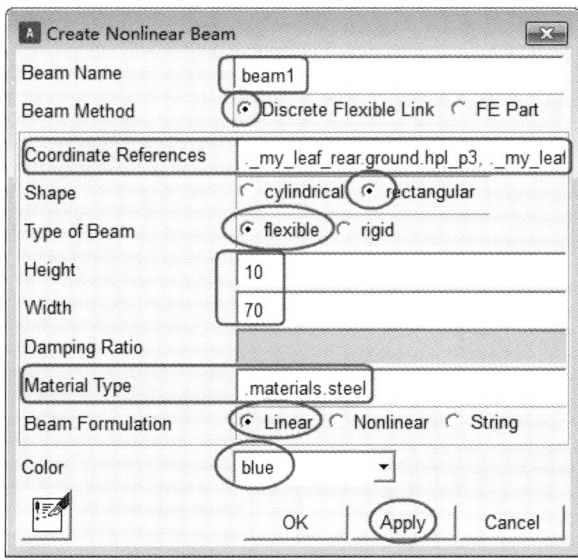

图 3-12 非线性梁部件 Beam1

- Coordinate Reference（参考坐标,依次输入如下硬点信息，硬点信息属性应准确，右击鼠标选择 Pick 选取）：

[1] ._my_leaf_rear.ground.hpl_p3,
[2] ._my_leaf_rear.ground.hpl_p3_m,
[3] ._my_leaf_rear.ground.hpl_p4,
[4] ._my_leaf_rear.ground.hpl_p4_m,
[5] ._my_leaf_rear.ground.hpl_p1,
[6] ._my_leaf_rear.ground.hpl_p8_m,
[7] ._my_leaf_rear.ground.hpl_p8,
[8] ._my_leaf_rear.ground.hpl_p7,
[9] ._my_leaf_rear.ground.hpl_p6。

- Shape（非线性梁形状，包括圆形和矩形两种）：rectangular；
- Height：10；
- Width：70；
- Material Type：steel；
- Type of Beam：flexible；

- Beam Formulation：linear；
- 单击 Apply，完成._my_leaf_rear.nrl_1_beam1 部件的创建；
- General Part 输入 beam2；
- Coordinate Reference（参考坐标,依次输入如下硬点信息，硬点信息属性应准确，右击鼠标选择 Pick 选取）：

[1] ._my_leaf_rear.ground.hpl_p41,
[2] ._my_leaf_rear.ground.hpl_p41_m,
[3] ._my_leaf_rear.ground.hpl_p11,
[4] ._my_leaf_rear.ground.hpl_p81_m,
[5] ._my_leaf_rear.ground.hpl_p81。

- Shape（非线性梁形状，包括圆形和矩形两种）：rectangular；
- Height：10；
- Width：70；
- Material Type：steel；
- Type of Beam：flexible；
- Beam Formulation：linear；
- 单击 OK，完成._my_leaf_rear.nrl_1_beam2 部件的创建。

3.3.2 簧片接触力

- 单击 Tools > Adams/View Interface 命令，切换到 View 通用界面，如图 3-13 所示；

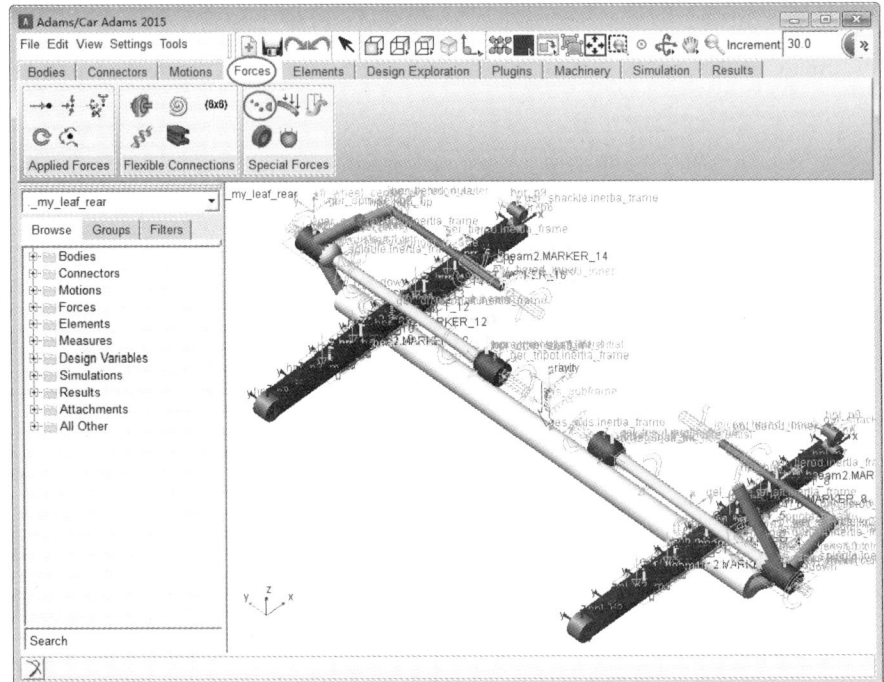

图 3-13　Adams/View 界面

- 单击 Forces > Create a Contact 命令，弹出创建接触对话框如图 3-14 所示；

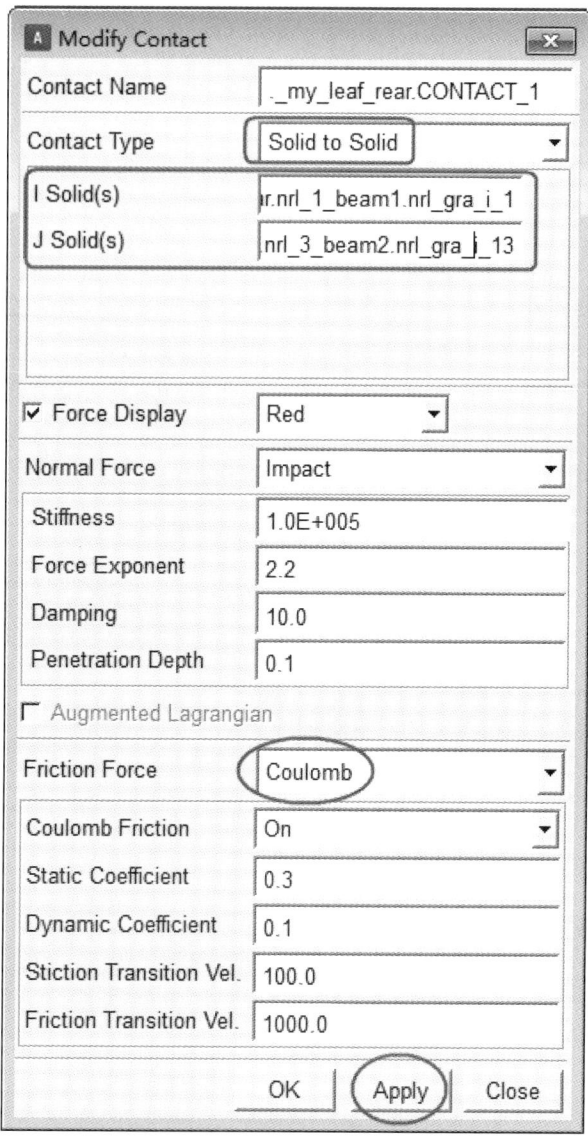

图 3-14 接触力创建对话框

- Contant Type：Solid to Solid；
- I Solid（s）：._my_leaf_rear.nrl_1_beam1.nrl_gra_i_1；
- J Solid（s）：._my_leaf_rear.nrl_3_beam2.nrl_gra_i_13；
- Force Display：Red；
- Normal Force：Impact；
- Force Exponent：2.2；
- Damping：10；
- Coulomb Force：Coulomb；
- Coulomb Coulomb：On；

- Static Coefficient：0.3；
- Dynamic Coefficient：0.3；

● 其余参数保持默认，单击 Apply，完成._my_leaf_rear.CONTACT_1 接触设置，重复上述步骤，完成所有对应接触面的是接触力设置，特别强调的是接触面要一一对应，此模型包含 16 个接触。

3.3.3 弹簧夹

钢板弹簧夹的主要作用是保障弹簧在上下运动过程中装配（模型中为接触）的两簧片不产生分离，通过约束关系中的点面约束抽象为弹簧夹。当钢板弹簧长度较大时，在板簧接触的端部和大概中间部位约束。在大载荷冲击下，点面约束是保证整车静平衡或者板簧计算模型收敛的必要条件。

- 单击 Connectors > Primitives> Create an inplane Joint Primitive 命令；
- Construction：2 Bodies-1 Location；
- Normal To Grid；
- 用鼠标分别选择钢板弹簧部件._my_leaf_rear.nrl_1_beam1、._my_leaf_rear.nrl_3_beam2 及._my_leaf_rear.ground.hpl_p4 点，完成._my_leaf_rear.JPRIM_1 点面约束的创建；
- 在模型树上右击点面约束._my_leaf_rear.JPRIM_1，点击 Modify 或者双击点面约束._my_leaf_rear.JPRIM_1，弹出约束对话框如图 3-15 所示。此模型建立过程中共包含 8 个点面约束。

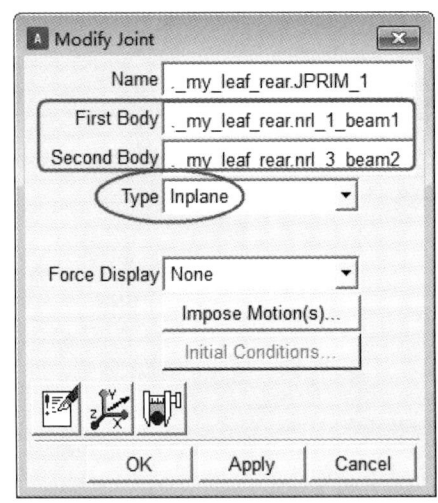

图 3-15 点面约束对话框

3.3.4 板簧约束

- 单击 Tools > Select Mode > Switch To A/Car Template Biulder 命令，切换到 ADAMS/CAR 专家模块；

（1）部件 axle 与 nrl_3_beam1 之间 fixed 约束。
- Joint Name（约束副名称）：beam1_and_axis；
- I Part：._my_leaf_rear.nrl_3_beam1；
- J Part：._my_leaf_rear.ges_axis；
- Joint Type：fixed；
- Active(激活)：always；
- Location Dependency：Delta location from coordinate；
- Coordinate Reference（参考坐标）：._my_leaf_rear.ground.hpl_p11；
- Location: 0,0,0；
- Location in：local；
- 单击 Apply，完成约束副._my_leaf_rear.jolfix_beam1_and_axis 的创建，如图 3-16 所示。

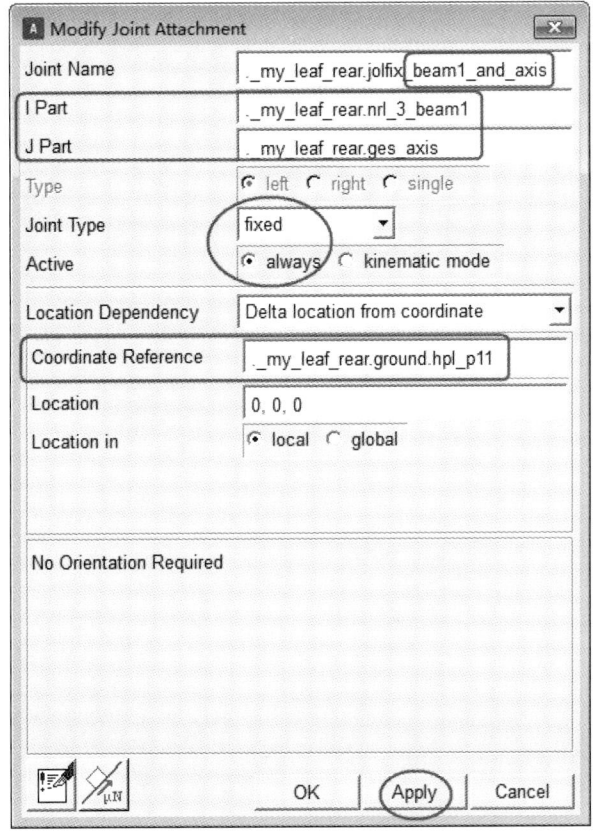

图 3-16　刚性约束对话框——fixed

（2）部件 beam1 与 beam2 之间 fixed 约束。
- Joint Name（约束副名称）：beam2_and_beam1；
- I Part：._my_leaf_rear.nrl_3_beam1；
- J Part：._my_leaf_rear.nrl_5_beam2；
- Joint Type：fixed；
- Active(激活)：always；

- Location Dependency：Delta location from coordinate；
- Coordinate Reference（参考坐标）：._my_leaf_rear.ground.hpl_p1；
- Location: 0,0,0；
- Location in：local；
- 单击 Apply，完成约束副._my_leaf_rear.jolfix_beam2_and_beam1 的创建。

（3）部件 nrl_1_beam2 与 leafspring_to_body 之间 bushing 约束。
- 单击 Build > Attachments > Bushing > New 命令，弹出创衬套件对话框如图 3-17 所示；

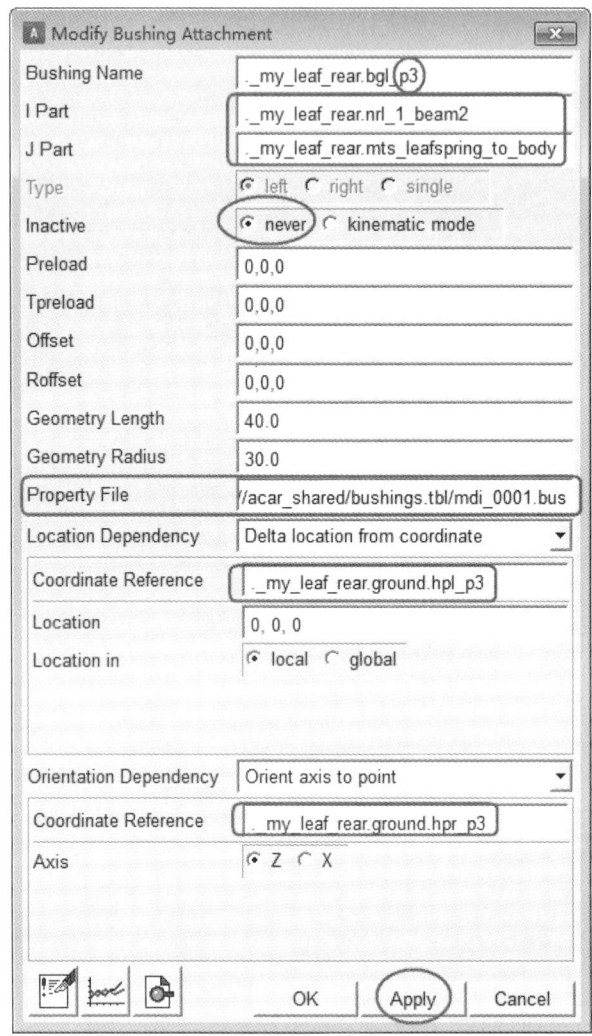

图 3-17　柔性衬套约束对话框——bushing

- Bushing Name（约束副名称）：p3；
- I Part：._my_leaf_rear.nrl_1_beam2；
- J Part：._my_leaf_rear.mts_leafspring_to_body；
- Inactive（抑制）：never；
- Preload：0,0,0；

- Tpreload:0，0，0；
- Offset：0，0，0；
- Roffset：0，0，0；
- Geometry Length：40；
- Geometry Radius：30；
- Property File：mdids://acar_shared/bushings.tbl/mdi_0001.bus；
- Location Dependency：Delta location from coordinate；
- Coordinate Reference（参考坐标）：._my_leaf_rear.ground.hpl_p3；
- Location: 0，0，0；
- Location in：local；
- Orientation Dependency：Orient axis to point；
- Construction Frame：._my_leaf_rear.ground.hpr_p3；
- Axis: Z；
- 单击 Apply，完成轴套._my_leaf_rear.bgl_p3 的创建。

（4）部件 nrl_9_beam2 与 shackle 之间 bushing 约束。
- Bushing Name（约束副名称）：p6；
- I Part：._my_leaf_rear.nrl_9_beam2；
- J Part：._my_leaf_rear.gel_shackle；
- Inactive（抑制）：never；
- Preload：0，0，0；
- Tpreload：0，0，0；
- Offset：0，0，0；
- Roffset：0，0，0；
- Geometry Length：40；
- Geometry Radius：15；
- Property File：mdids://acar_shared/bushings.tbl/mdi_0001.bus；
- Location Dependency：Delta location from coordinate；
- Coordinate Reference（参考坐标）：._my_leaf_rear.ground.hpl_p6；
- Location: 0，0，0；
- Location in：local；
- Orientation Dependency：Orient axis to point；
- Construction Frame：._my_leaf_rear.ground.hpr_p6；
- Axis: Z；
- 单击 Apply，完成轴套._my_leaf_rear.bgl_p6 的创建。

（5）部件 leafspring_to_body 与 shackle 之间 bushing 约束。
- Bushing Name（约束副名称）：p9；
- I Part：._my_leaf_rear.gel_shackle；
- J Part：._my_leaf_rear.mts_leafspring_to_body；
- Inactive（抑制）：never；

- Preload：0，0，0；
- Tpreload：0，0，0；
- Offset：0，0，0；
- Roffset：0，0，0；
- Geometry Length：40；
- Geometry Radius：15；
- Property File：mdids://acar_shared/bushings.tbl/mdi_0001.bus；
- Location Dependency：Delta location from coordinate；
- Coordinate Reference（参考坐标）：._my_leaf_rear.ground.hpl_p9；
- Location：0，0，0；
- Location in：local；
- Orientation Dependency：Orient axis to point；
- Construction Frame：._my_leaf_rear.ground.hpr_p9；
- Axis：Z；
- 单击 Apply，完成轴套._my_leaf_rear.bgl_p9 的创建。

3.4 非独立悬架约束

（1）部件 tripot 与安装件 tripot_to_differential 之间 translational 约束。
- Joint Name（约束副名称）：tripot_to_differential；
- I Part：._my_leaf_rear.gel_tripot；
- J Part：._my_leaf_rear.mtl_tripot_to_differential；
- Joint Type（约束副类型）：translational；
- Active（激活）：always；
- Location Dependency：Delta location from coordinate；
- Coordinate Reference #1（参考坐标）：._my_leaf_rear.ground.hpl_drive_shaft_inr；
- Orientation Dependency：Orient to zpoint-xpoint；
- Coordinate Reference #1（参考坐标）：._my_leaf_rear.ground.hpr_drive_shaft_inr；
- Coordinate Reference #2（参考坐标）：._my_leaf_rear.ground.cfl_drive_shaft_otr；
- Axis：ZX；
- 单击 Apply，完成约束副._my_leaf_rear.joltra_tripot_to_differential 的创建。

（2）部件 tripot 与 drive_shaft 之间 convel 约束。
- Joint Name（约束副名称）：drive_sft_otr；
- I Part：._my_leaf_rear.gel_tripot；
- J Part：._my_leaf_rear.gel_drive_shaft；
- Joint Type（约束副类型）：convel，恒速副；
- Active（激活）：always；
- Location Dependency：Delta location from coordinate；

- Coordinate Reference（参考坐标）：._my_leaf_rear.ground.hpl_drive_shaft_inr；
- Location：0，0，0；
- Location in：local；
- I-Part　Axis：._my_leaf_rear.ground.hpr_drive_shaft_inr；
- J-Part　Axis：._my_leaf_rear.ground.cfl_drive_shaft_otr r；
- 单击 Apply，完成约束副._my_leaf_rear.jolcon_drive_sft_int_jt 的创建。

（3）部件 spindle 与 drive_shaft 之间 convel 约束。
- Joint Name（约束副名称）：drive_sft_otr；
- I　Part：._my_leaf_rear.gel_drive_shaft；
- J　Part：._my_leaf_rear.gel_spindle；
- Joint Type（约束副类型）：convel，恒速副；
- Active（激活）：always；
- Location Dependency：Delta location from coordinate；
- Coordinate Reference（参考坐标）：._my_leaf_rear.ground.cfl_drive_shaft_otr；
- Location：0，0，0；
- Location in：local；
- I-Part　Axis：._my_leaf_rear.ground.hpr_drive_shaft_inr；
- J-Part　Axis：._my_leaf_rear.ground.hpl_wheel_center；
- 单击 Apply，完成约束副._my_leaf_rear.jolcon_drive_sft_otr 的创建。

（4）部件 spindle 与安装件 upright 之间 revolute 约束。
- Joint Name（约束副名称）：spindle_upright；
- I　Part：._my_leaf_rear.gel_spindle；
- J　Part：._my_leaf_rear.gel_upright；
- Joint Type（约束副类型）：revolute；
- Active（激活）：always；
- Location Dependency：Delta location from coordinate；
- Coordinate Reference（参考坐标）：._my_leaf_rear.ground.hpl_wheel_center；
- Location：0，0，0；
- Location in：local；
- Orientation Dependency：Delta orientation from coordinate；
- Construction Frame：._my_leaf_rear.ground.cfl_wheel_center；
- Orientation：0，0，0；
- 单击 Apply，完成约束副._my_leaf_rear.jolrev_spindle_upright 的创建。

（5）部件 upright 与安装件 axis 之间 revolute 约束。
- Joint Name（约束副名称）：spindle_upright；
- I　Part：._my_leaf_rear.gel_upright；
- J　Part：._my_leaf_rear.ges_axis；
- Joint Type（约束副类型）：revolute；
- Active（激活）：always；

- Location Dependency：Centered between coordinate；
- Coordinate Reference #1（参考坐标1）：._my_leaf_rear.ground.hpl_hub_up；
- Coordinate Reference #2（参考坐标2）：._my_leaf_rear.ground.hpl_hub_down；
- Orientation Dependency：Orient axis to point；
- Construction Frame：._my_leaf_rear.ground.hpl_hub_up；
- Axis：Z；
- 单击 Apply，完成约束副._my_leaf_rear.jolrev_upright_to_axle 的创建。

（6）部件 tierod 与 upright 之间 spherical 约束。
- Joint Name（约束副名称）：tierod_outer；
- I   Part：._my_leaf_rear.gel_tierod；
- J   Part：._my_leaf_rear.gel_upright；
- Joint Type（约束副类型）：spherical，转动副，约束3个自由度；
- Active（激活）：always；
- Location Dependency：Delta location from coordinate；
- Coordinate Reference（参考坐标）：._my_leaf_rear.ground.hpl_tierod_outer；
- Location: 0,0,0；
- Location in：local；
- Orientation：None；
- 单击 Apply，完成约束副._my_leaf_rear.jolsph_tierod_outer 的创建。

（7）部件 tierod 与安装部件 tierod_to_steering 之间 convel 约束。
- Joint Name（约束副名称）：tierod_inner；
- I   Part：._my_leaf_rear.gel_tierod；
- J   Part：._my_leaf_rear.mtl_tierod_to_steering；
- Joint Type（约束副类型）：convel，恒速副；
- Active（激活）：always；
- Location Dependency：Delta location from coordinate；
- Coordinate Reference（参考坐标）：._my_leaf_rear.ground.hpl_tierod_inner；
- Location: 0，0，0；
- Location in：local；
- I-Part   Axis：._my_leaf_rear.ground.hpl_tierod_outer；
- J-Part   Axis：._my_leaf_rear.ground.hpr_tierod_inner；
- 单击 OK，完成约束副._my_leaf_rear.jolcon_tierod_inner 的创建；

3.5　非独立悬架变量参数

- 单击 Build > Parameter Variable > New 命令，弹出参数变量对话框如图3-18所示；
- Parameter Variable Name：driveline_active；
- Integer   Value（实数值）：0；

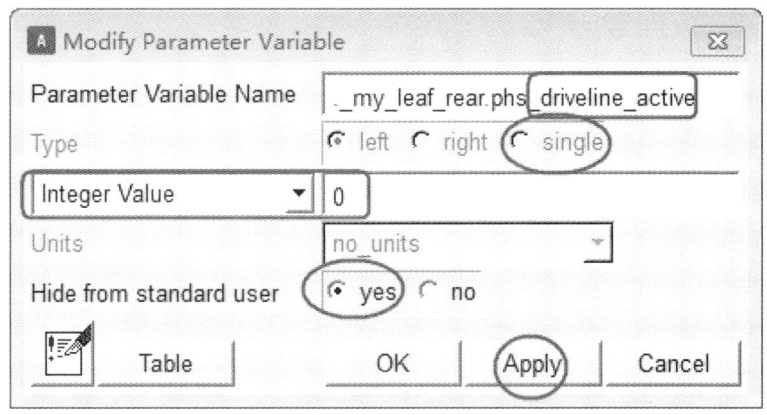

图 3-18 参数变量——driveline_active

- Units：no_units；
- Hide from standard user（是否从标准界面隐藏）：yes；
- 单击 Apply，完成变量._my_leaf_rear.phs_driveline_active 的创建；
- Parameter Variable Name：kinematic_flag；
- Integer Value（实数值）：0；
- Units：no_units；
- Hide from standard user（是否从标准界面隐藏）：yes；
- 单击 OK，完成变量._my_leaf_rear.phs_kinematic_flag 的创建。
- 单击 Build > Construction Frame > New 命令；
- Construction Frame（结构框名称）：wheel_center_ref；
- Location Dependency：Delta location from coordinate；
- Coordinate Reference（参考坐标）：._my_leaf_rear.ground.hpl_wheel_center；
- Location：0, 0, 100；
- Location in：local；
- Orientation Dependency：Delta location from coordinate；
- Coordinate Reference（参考坐标）：._my_leaf_rear.ground.cfl_wheel_center；
- Orientation：0，0，0；
- 单击 OK，完成._my_leaf_rear.ground.cfl_wheel_center_ref 结构框的创建。
- 单击 Build > Suspension Parameters > Characteristics Arrary > Set 命令，主要用于设置悬架的转向主销，如图 3-19 所示；
- Steer Axis Caculation：Geometric；
- Suspension Type：dependent，非独立悬架；
- I Part：._my_leaf_rear.ges_axis；
- J Part：._my_leaf_rear.gel_spindle；
- I Coordinate Reference：._my_leaf_rear.ground.cfl_wheel_center；
- J Coordinate Reference：._my_leaf_rear.ground.cfl_wheel_center_ref；
- 单击 OK，完成悬架参数变量设置。

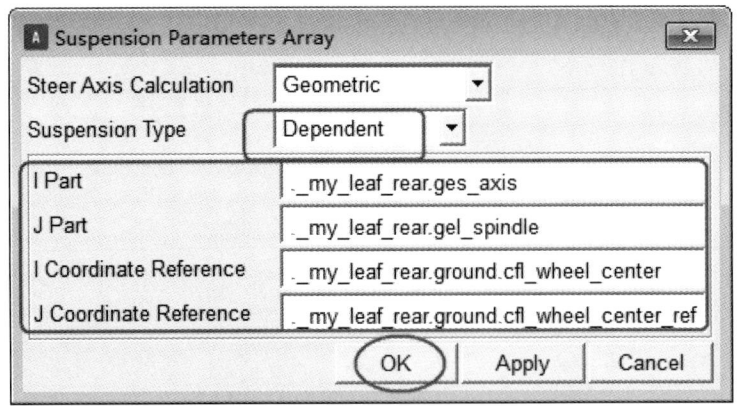

图 3-19 悬架参数变量设置

3.6 非独立悬架通信器

3.6.1 通信器建立

- 单击 Build > Communicator > Output > New 命令,弹出输出通信器对话框如图 3-20 所示;
- Output Communicator Name(输出通信器名称):driveline_active;
- Matching Name(s):driveline_active;
- Type:single;
- Entity:parameter integer;
- To Minor Role:inherit;
- Parameter Variable Name:._my_leaf_rear.phs_driveline_active;
- 单击 Apply,完成通信器 ._my_leaf_rear.cos_driveline_active 的创建;

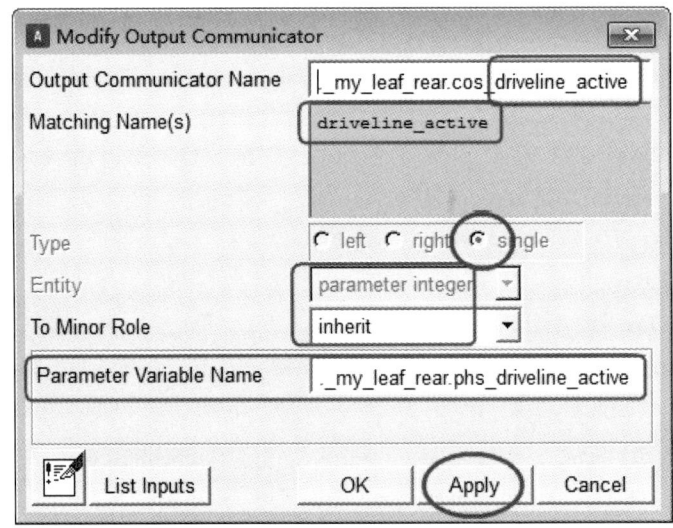

图 3-20 通信器——driveline_active

- Output Communicator Name（输出通信器名称）：tripot_to_differential；
- Matching Name(s)：tripot_to_differential；
- Type：left；
- Entity：Location；
- To Minor Role：inherit；
- Coordinate Reference Name：._my_leaf_rear.ground.hpl_drive_shaft_inr；
- 单击 Apply，完成通信器._my_leaf_rear.col_tripot_to_differential 的创建；
- Output Communicator Name（输出通信器名称）：suspension_mount；
- Matching Name(s)：suspension_mount；
- Type：left；
- Entity：mount；
- To Minor Role：inherit；
- Part Name：._my_leaf_rear.gel_spindle；
- 单击 Apply，完成通信器._my_leaf_rear.col_suspension_mount 的创建；
- Output Communicator Name（输出通信器名称）：wheel_center；
- Matching Name(s)：wheel_center；
- Type：left；
- Entity：Location；
- To Minor Role：inherit；
- Coordinate Reference Name：._my_leaf_rear.ground.hpl_wheel_center；
- 单击 Apply，完成通信器._my_leaf_rear.col_wheel_center 的创建；
- Output Communicator Name（输出通信器名称）：suspension_upright；
- Matching Name(s)：suspension_upright；
- Type：left；
- Entity：mount；
- To Minor Role：inherit；
- Part Name：._my_leaf_rear.ges_axis；
- 单击 Apply，完成通信器._my_leaf_rear.col_suspension_upright 的创建；
- Output Communicator Name（输出通信器名称）：engine_to_subframe；
- Matching Name(s)：engine_to_subframe；
- Type：single；
- Entity：mount；
- To Minor Role：inherit；
- Part Name：._my_leaf_rear.ges_axis；
- 单击 Apply，完成通信器._my_leaf_rear.cos_engine_to_subframe 的创建；
- Output Communicator Name（输出通信器名称）：wheel_joint；
- Matching Name(s)：wheel_joint；
- Type：left；
- Entity：joint for motion；

- To Minor Role：inherit；
- Joint Name：._my_leaf_rear.jolrev_spindle_upright；
- 单击 Apply，完成通信器._my_leaf_rear.col_wheel_joint 的创建；
- Output Communicator Name（输出通信器名称）：rack_housing_to_suspension_subframe；
- Matching Name(s)：rack_housing_to_suspension_subframe；
- Type：single；
- Entity：mount；
- To Minor Role：inherit；
- Part Name：._my_leaf_rear.ges_axis；
- 单击 OK，完成通信器._my_leaf_rear.cos_rack_housing_to_suspension_subframe 的创建。

3.6.2 通信器测试

- 单击 Build > Communicator > Test 命令，弹出输出通信器测试对话框如图 3-21 所示；

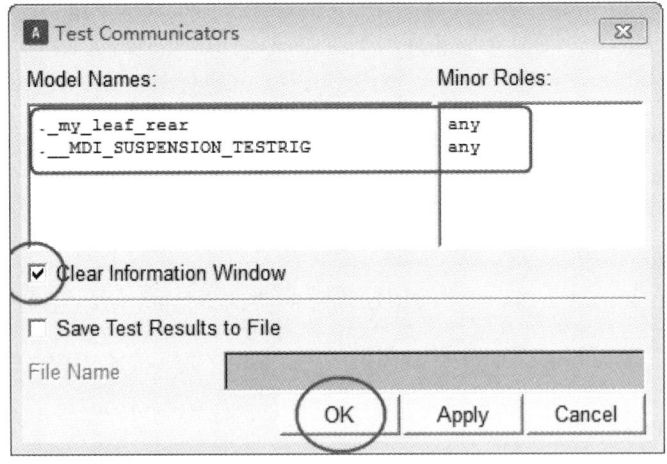

图 3-21 通信器测试对话框设置

- Model Names：

① ._my_leaf_rear；

② .__MDI_SUSPENSION_TESTRIGG。

- Minor Roles：并列两排输入特征 any，也可以并排输入特征 front,在此两个都可以；
- 单击 OK，完成推杆式双叉臂悬架和悬架试验台._my_leaf_rear、.__MDI_SUSPENSION_TESTRIGG 的匹配测试，测试结果如下列信息所示。

通信器匹配信息如下：

!--------------------------- Matched communicators: ---------------------------!
%以下为匹配的通信器

Communicator Matching Name: tripot_to_differential
Input Communicator Name: ci[lr]_tripot_to_differential

Located in: _my_leaf_rear
Output Communicator Name: co[lr]_tripot_to_differential
Output from: __MDI_SUSPENSION_TESTRIG

Communicator Matching Name: camber_angle
Input Communicator Name: ci[lr]_camber_angle
Located in: __MDI_SUSPENSION_TESTRIG
Output Communicator Name: co[lr]_camber_angle
Output from: _my_leaf_rear

Communicator Matching Name: toe_angle
Input Communicator Name: ci[lr]_toe_angle
Located in: __MDI_SUSPENSION_TESTRIG
Output Communicator Name: co[lr]_toe_angle
Output from: _my_leaf_rear

Communicator Matching Name: wheel_center
Input Communicator Name: ci[lr]_wheel_center
Located in: __MDI_SUSPENSION_TESTRIG
Output Communicator Name: co[lr]_wheel_center
Output from: _my_leaf_rear

Communicator Matching Name: suspension_mount
Input Communicator Name: ci[lr]_suspension_mount
Located in: __MDI_SUSPENSION_TESTRIG
Output Communicator Name: co[lr]_suspension_mount
Output from: _my_leaf_rear

Communicator Matching Name: driveline_active
Input Communicator Name: cis_driveline_active
Located in: __MDI_SUSPENSION_TESTRIG
Output Communicator Name: cos_driveline_active
Output from: _my_leaf_rear

Communicator Matching Name: suspension_parameters_array
Input Communicator Name: cis_suspension_parameters_ARRAY
Located in: __MDI_SUSPENSION_TESTRIG
Output Communicator Name: cos_suspension_parameters_ARRAY
Output from: _my_leaf_rear

Communicator Matching Name: tripot_to_differential
Input Communicator Name: ci[lr]_diff_tripot
Located in: _MDI_SUSPENSION_TESTRIG
Output Communicator Name: co[lr]_tripot_to_differential
Output from: _my_leaf_rear

Communicator Matching Name: suspension_upright
Input Communicator Name: ci[lr]_suspension_upright
Located in: _MDI_SUSPENSION_TESTRIG
Output Communicator Name: co[lr]_suspension_upright
Output from: _my_leaf_rear

!---------------------- Unmatched input communicators: ----------------------!
%以下为不匹配的输入通信器

Input Communicator Name: cis_leafspring_to_body
Class: mount
From Minor Role: any
Matching Name(s): leafspring_to_body
In Template: _my_leaf_rear

Input Communicator Name: ci[lr]_tierod_to_steering
Class: mount
From Minor Role: any
Matching Name(s): tierod_to_steering
In Template: _my_leaf_rear

Input Communicator Name: ci[lr]_jack_frame
Class: mount
From Minor Role: any
Matching Name(s): jack_frame
In Template: _MDI_SUSPENSION_TESTRIG

Input Communicator Name: cis_leaf_adjustment_steps
Class: parameter_integer
From Minor Role: any
Matching Name(s): leaf_adjustment_steps
In Template: _MDI_SUSPENSION_TESTRIG

Input Communicator Name: cis_powertrain_to_body
Class: mount
From Minor Role: any
Matching Name(s): powertrain_to_body
In Template: __MDI_SUSPENSION_TESTRIG

Input Communicator Name: cis_steering_rack_joint
Class: joint_for_motion
From Minor Role: any
Matching Name(s): steering_rack_joint
In Template: __MDI_SUSPENSION_TESTRIG

Input Communicator Name: cis_steering_wheel_joint
Class: joint_for_motion
From Minor Role: any
Matching Name(s): steering_wheel_joint
In Template: __MDI_SUSPENSION_TESTRIG

!---------------------- Unmatched output communicators: ----------------------!
%以下为不匹配的输出通信器

Output Communicator Name: cos_engine_to_subframe
Class: mount
To Minor Role: any
Matching Name(s): engine_to_subframe
In Template: _my_leaf_rear

Output Communicator Name: co[lr]_wheel_joint
Class: joint_for_motion
To Minor Role: any
Matching Name(s): wheel_joint
In Template: _my_leaf_rear

Output Communicator Name: cos_rack_housing_to_suspension_subframe
Class: mount
To Minor Role: any
Matching Name(s): rack_housing_to_suspension_subframe
In Template: _my_leaf_rear

Output Communicator Name: cos_leaf_adjustment_multiplier
Class: array
To Minor Role: any
Matching Name(s): leaf_adjustment_multiplier
In Template: __MDI_SUSPENSION_TESTRIG

Output Communicator Name: cos_characteristics_input_ARRAY
Class: array
To Minor Role: any
Matching Name(s): characteristics_input_array
In Template: __MDI_SUSPENSION_TESTRIG

3.7　非独立悬架驱动轴显示组建

- 在模型树栏，点击 Group 菜单，在模型树栏右击鼠标 New Group，弹出创建组件对话框如图 3-22 所示；

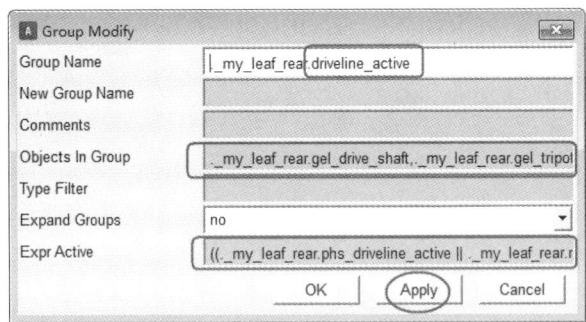

图 3-22　驱动轴显示组件对话框

- Group Name：driveline_active；
- Object In Group（显示组件包括的部件、几何体、约束等对象），顺序输入①～㉖对象如下信息所示：

① ._my_leaf_rear.gel_drive_shaft,
② ._my_leaf_rear.gel_tripot,
③ ._my_leaf_rear.ger_drive_shaft,
④ ._my_leaf_rear.ger_tripot,
⑤ ._my_leaf_rear.mtl_tripot_to_differential,
⑥ ._my_leaf_rear.mtr_tripot_to_differential,
⑦ ._my_leaf_rear.gel_drive_shaft.gralin_drive_shaft,
⑧ ._my_leaf_rear.gel_drive_shaft.graell_cv_housing,
⑨ ._my_leaf_rear.gel_drive_shaft.graell_tripot_housing,

⑩._my_leaf_rear.ger_drive_shaft.gralin_drive_shaft,
⑪._my_leaf_rear.ger_drive_shaft.graell_cv_housing,
⑫._my_leaf_rear.ger_drive_shaft.graell_tripot_housing,
⑬._my_leaf_rear.gel_tripot.gracyl_tripot_housing_extention,
⑭._my_leaf_rear.ger_tripot.gracyl_tripot_housing_extention,
⑮._my_leaf_rear.jolcon_drive_sft_int_jt,
⑯._my_leaf_rear.jolcon_drive_sft_otr,
⑰._my_leaf_rear.joltra_tripot_to_differential,
⑱._my_leaf_rear.jorcon_drive_sft_int_jt,
⑲._my_leaf_rear.jorcon_drive_sft_otr,
⑳._my_leaf_rear.jortra_tripot_to_differential,
㉑._my_leaf_rear.mtl_fixed_2,
㉒._my_leaf_rear.mtr_fixed_2,
㉓._my_leaf_rear.cil_tripot_to_differential,
㉔._my_leaf_rear.cir_tripot_to_differential,
㉕._my_leaf_rear.col_tripot_to_differential,
㉖._my_leaf_rear.cor_tripot_to_differential。

- Expr Active：((._my_leaf_rear.phs_driveline_active || ._my_leaf_rear.model_class == "template" ? 1 : 0) && DB_ACTIVE(._my_leaf_rear));
- 单击 Apply，完成组件 driveline_active 的创建；
- Group Name：driveline_inactive；
- Expr Active：((! ._my_leaf_rear.phs_driveline_active || ._my_leaf_rear.model_class == "template" ? 1 : 0) && DB_ACTIVE(._my_leaf_rear));
- 单击 OK，完成组件 driveline_inactive 的创建。
- 单击 File > Save As 命令，弹出保存模板对话框如图 3-23 所示；
- Major Role(主特征)：suspension；
- File Format：Binary；
- Target：Database \ my_driveline；
- 单击 OK，完成推杆式悬架模型模板_my_leaf_rear 的保存。

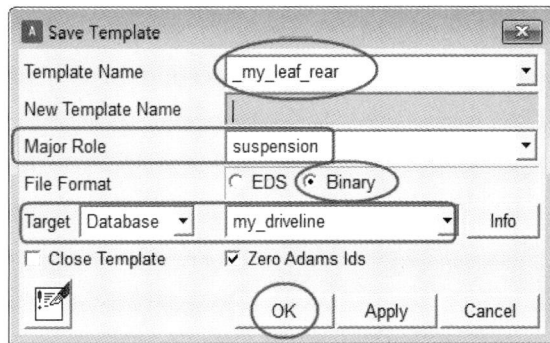

图 3-23　板簧悬架模型保存

3.8 双轮反向激振仿真

3.8.1 非独立悬架子系统

- 按 F9，把专家模板转换到标准模式，单击 File > New > Suspension 命令，弹出子系统对话框如图 3-24 所示；

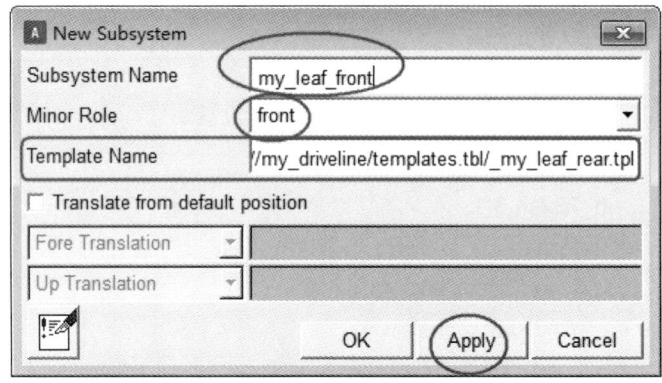

图 3-24 板簧悬架子系统（前）

- Subsystem Name(系统名称)：my_leaf_front；
- Minor Role（副特征）：front（指悬架为前悬架）；
- Template Name（模板路径）：mdids://my_driveline/templates.tbl/_my_leaf_rear.tpl；
- 单击 Apply，完成推杆式悬架子系统 my_leaf_front 的创建；
- Subsystem Name(系统名称)：my_leaf_rear_jeep；
- Minor Role（副特征）：rear（指悬架为后悬架）；
- Template Name（模板路径）：mdids://my_driveline/templates.tbl/_my_leaf_rear.tpl；
- Aft Translation：2 800；
- 单击 OK，完成推杆式悬架子系统 my_leaf_rear_jeep 的创建。

3.8.2 双轮反向激振设置

- 单击 Simulate > Suspension Analysis > Parallel Wheel Travel 命令，弹出双轮同向激振对话框如图 3-25 所示；
  - Output Prefix：OT；
  - Number of Steps（仿真步数）：1 000；
  - Mode of Simulation：interactive；
  - Vertical Setup Mode：Wheel Center；
  - Bump Travel：50；
  - Rebound Travel：−50；
  - Side：Left；

- Travel Relative To：Wheel Center；
- Control Mode：Absolute；
- Coordinate System：Vehicle；
- 单击 OK，完成板簧悬架在 C 模式下的仿真。

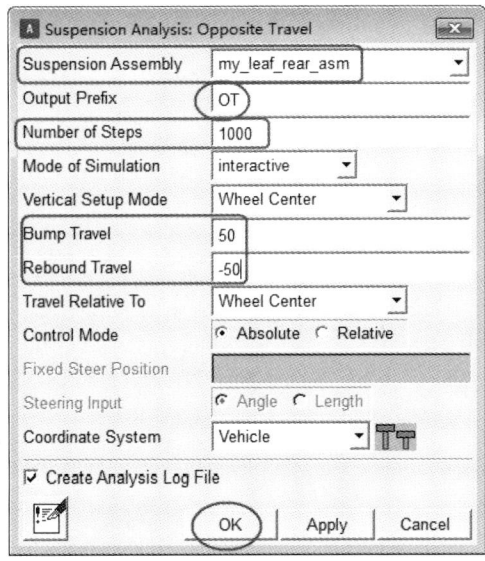

图 3-25　车辆反向激振仿真设置

- 菜单栏单击 Review > Animation Controls，开始动画观看，动画结束后悬架模型变化如图 3-26 所示；
- 按 F8，界面转换到后处理模块；车轮四轮定位参数如图 3-27 ~ 图 3-30 所示。

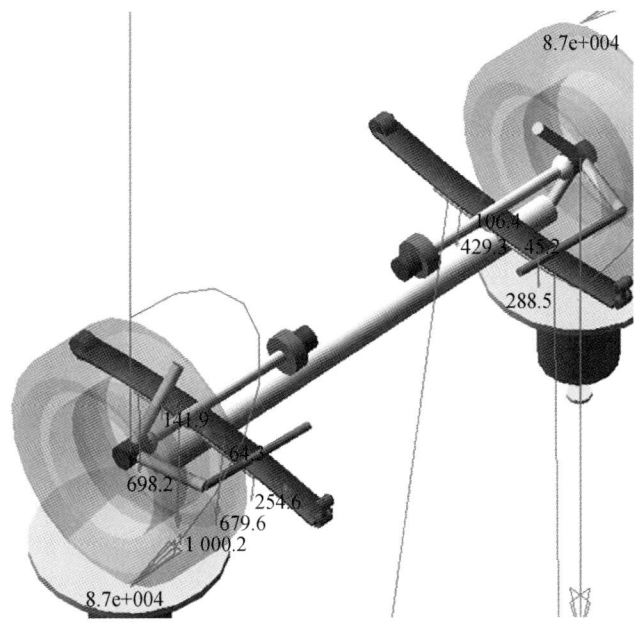

图 3-26　板簧悬架双轮反向跳动

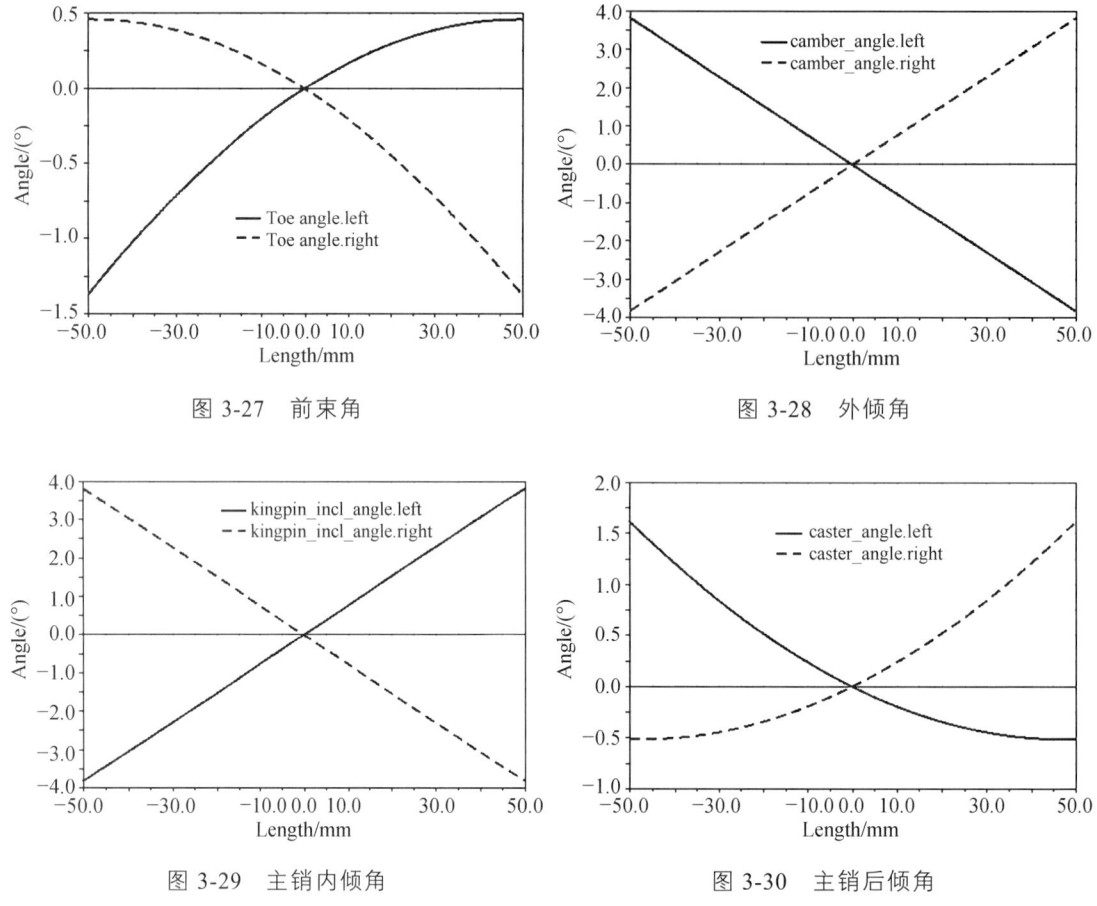

图 3-27 前束角　　　　　　　　　图 3-28 外倾角

图 3-29 主销内倾角　　　　　　　图 3-30 主销后倾角

3.9 整车模型

- 单击 File > Assembly 命令;
- Assembly Name: mdids://acar_shared/assemblies.tbl/MDI_Demo_Vehicle_lt.asy;
- 单击 OK, 完成公版数据库中整车模型的导入。
- 前后悬架分别替换为如下子系统与转向系统:

① mdids://my_driveline/subsystems.tbl/my_leaf_front.sub;
② mdids://my_driveline/subsystems.tbl/my_leaf_rear_jeep.sub;
③ mdids://my_driveline/subsystems.tbl/my_steering_right.sub。

- 修改轮胎属性文件中胎面宽度为 235, 其余参数保持不变;
- 替换完成后整车模型另存为 my_car, 整车模型如图 3-31 所示。

图 3-31 整车模型（前后为建立的板簧悬架模型）

3.10 Fish-Hook 仿真

- 单击 Simulate > Full-Vehicle Analysis > Open-loop Steering Events > Fish Hook 命令，弹出蛇形绕桩仿真对话框如图 3-32 所示；
- Output Prefix：FH；
- Output Step Size（仿真步数）：0.01；
- Mode of Simulation：interactive；
- Road Date File：mdids://FASE/roads.tbl/2d_flat.rdf，在仿真过程中，由于路面场地过小，可能导致整车运行中驶出场地，但不影响仿真的正常运行，可以打开路面属性文件，对路面的长度与宽度参数进行修改，本路面长 × 宽为 500 000 × 400 000，单位为 mm；
- Initial Velocity：50；
- First Turn Direction：right；
- First Steer Angle：200；
- Duration of First Turn：5；
- Second Turn Direction：left；
- Second Steer Angle：400；
- Duration of First Turn：5；
- 勾选 Quasi-Static Straight-Line Setup；
- 单击 OK，完成蛇形绕桩仿真设置并提交运算。

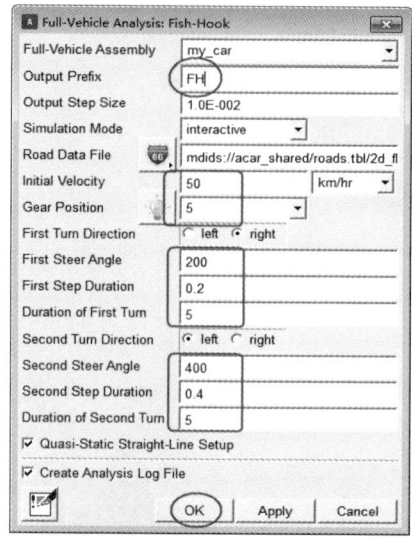

图 3-32 Fish-Hook 仿真设置

仿真结束后,整车的运行轨迹如图 3-33 所示,在运行过程中,计算参数如图 3-34~图 3-45 所示。

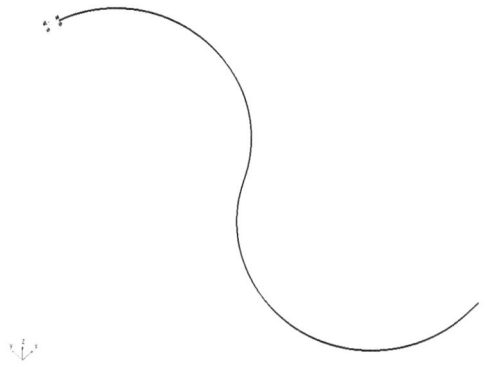

图 3-33 整车运行轨迹

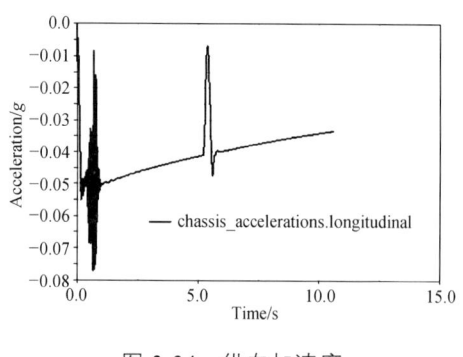

图 3-34 纵向加速度

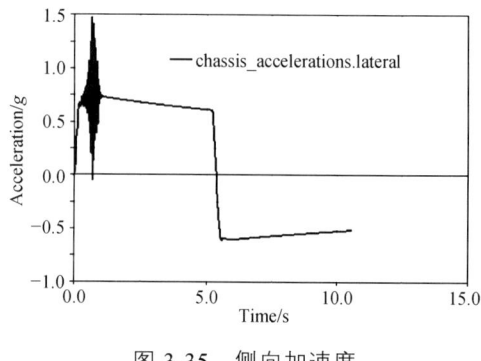

图 3-35 侧向加速度

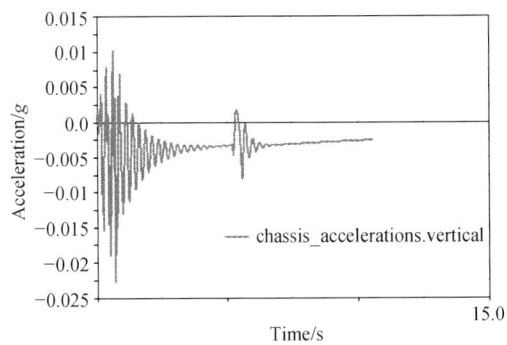

图 3-36 垂向加速度

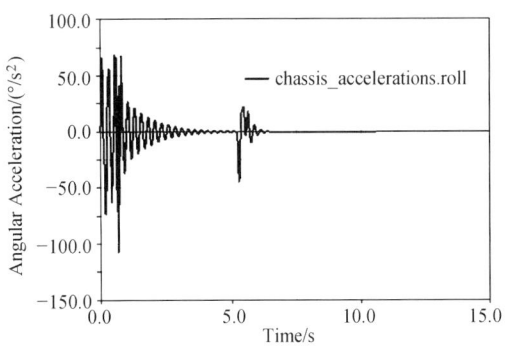

图 3-37 俯仰角加速度

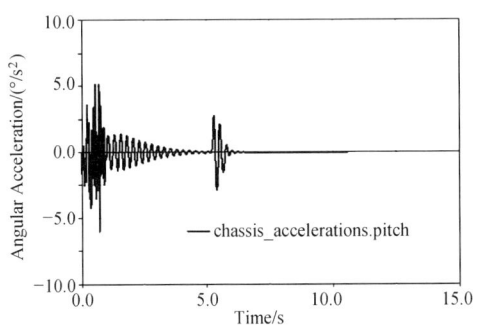

图 3-38 侧倾角加速度

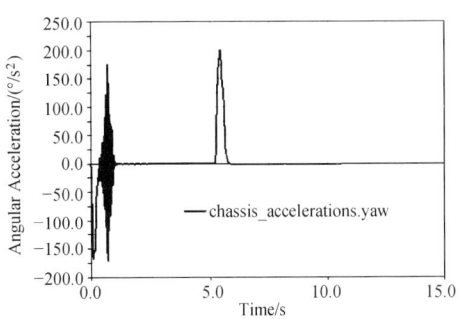

图 3-39 横摆角加速度

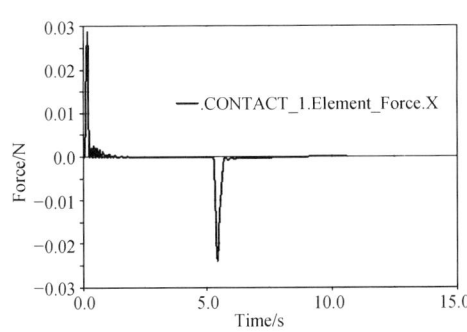

图 3-40 X 方向接触力

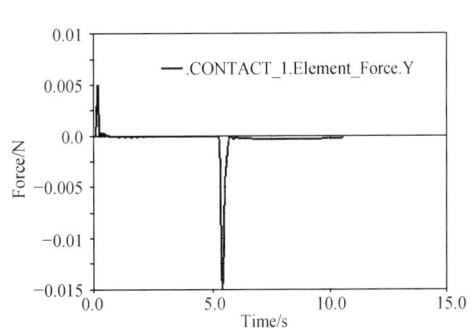

图 3-41 Y 方向接触力

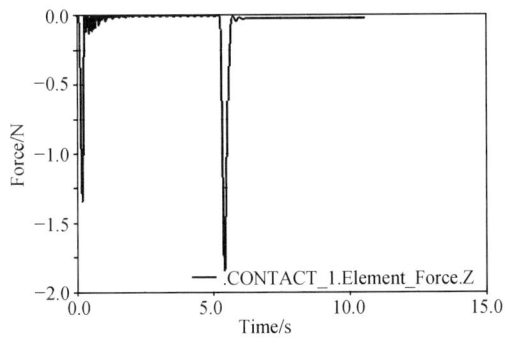

图 3-42 Z 方向接触力

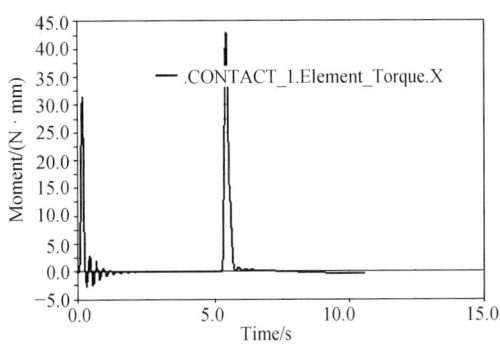

图 3-43 X 方向接触力矩

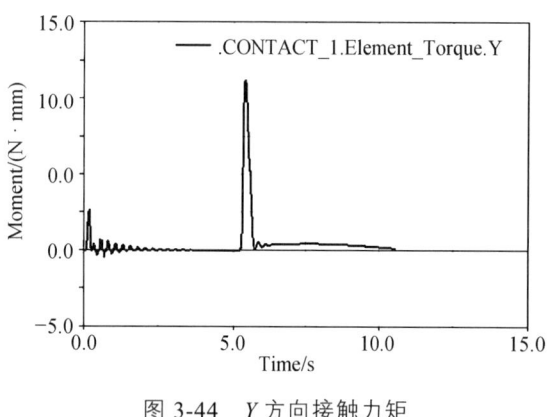

图 3-44　Y 方向接触力矩

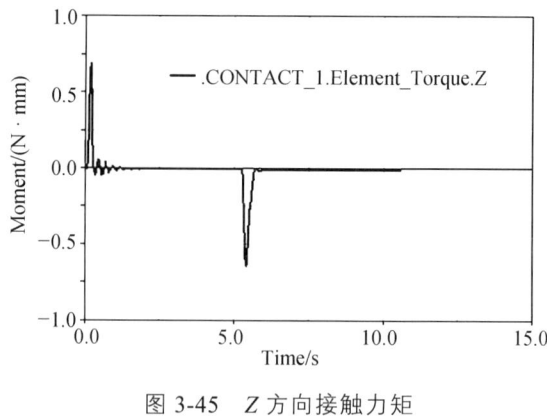

图 3-45　Z 方向接触力矩

第 4 章 路面模型

整车模型计算仿真的前提是必须在路面上进行。路面的状态设置类型较为多样，以满足不同计算工况的需要。对整车制动系统评估时，需要设置对开及对接路面；对整车的平顺性计算仿真时需要不同等级的路面及通过减速带、连续坑洼路面等。ADAMS\CAR 模块共享数据库中 ROAD 文件夹提供的路面文件足以满足日常所需工况仿真要求，但对于一些特殊工况仍需要读者自己建立相应路面。

学习目标

- ✧ 路面类型简介。
- ✧ 对开路面。
- ✧ 对接路面。
- ✧ 减速带路面。
- ✧ 连续障碍路面。
- ✧ 直线制动系统仿真。
- ✧ 分离轮胎路面设置。
- ✧ 弯道制动系统仿真。

4.1 路面类型简介

路面模型可以分为 2D 与 3D 模型。2D 路面接触通常采用点式跟踪法；3D 路面模型为三维轮胎-路面接触模型，用以计算路面和轮胎之间交叉体积，路面采用一系列离散三角形面表示，而轮胎用一系列的圆柱表示。采用 3D 路面模型（或者称 3D 等效体积路面模型），可以模拟车辆在运动过程中碰到路边台阶、凹坑、粗糙路面及其在不规则路面上运动的情形。3D 等效体积路面模型如图 4-1 所示，此路面由 6 个节点构成 4 个三角形单元，每个三角形单元的单位法向矢量与有限元网格中定义较为相似。ADAMS/TIRE 在定义路面时需要首先指定每个节点在路面参考坐标系下的坐标,再按顺序指定三个节点构成三角形单元,对应每个单元,可以指定不同的摩擦系数。除此之外还有 3D 光滑路面,用于定义停车场和赛道路面等,3D 光滑路面一般指路面的曲率小于轮胎的曲率。

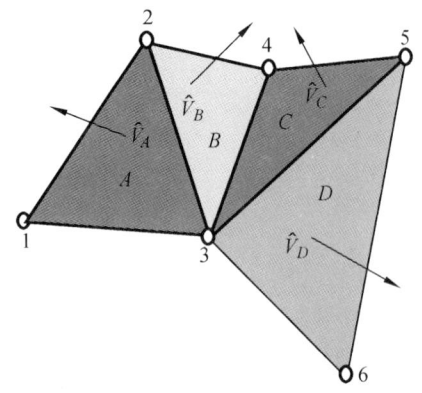

图 4-1　3D 等效体积路面模型

路面模型存储于共享数据库的文件夹中,路径为 D:\MSC.Software\Adams_x64\2014\acar\shared_car_database.cdb\roads.tbl。2D 路面模型除平整路面 FLAT 外其他路面在仿真时均不能显示几何图形。

① DRUM:测试轮胎用转股试验台。
② FLAT:平整路面。
③ PLANK:矩形凸块路面。
④ POLY_LINE:折线路面。
⑤ POT_HOLE:凹坑路面。
⑥ RAMP:斜坡路面。
⑦ ROOF:三角形凸块路面。
⑧ SINE:正弦波路面。
⑨ SINE_SWEEP:正弦波波纹路面。
⑩ STOCHASTIC_UNEVEN:随即不平路面。

- 单击 Simulate > Component Analysis > consin/tiretlls 命令,弹出 consin2014-3 插件对话框如图 4-2 所示;
- 单击 File > Open road 命令,弹出选择路面文件对话框,选择正弦波波纹路面 2d_sine_sweep.rdf;
- 单击"打开"按钮,弹出 roadtools 工具对话框(见图 4-3);
- 单击显示按钮快捷方式,显示正弦波波纹路面如图 4-4 所示,其余不同类型路面形状读者可自行尝试打开观看。

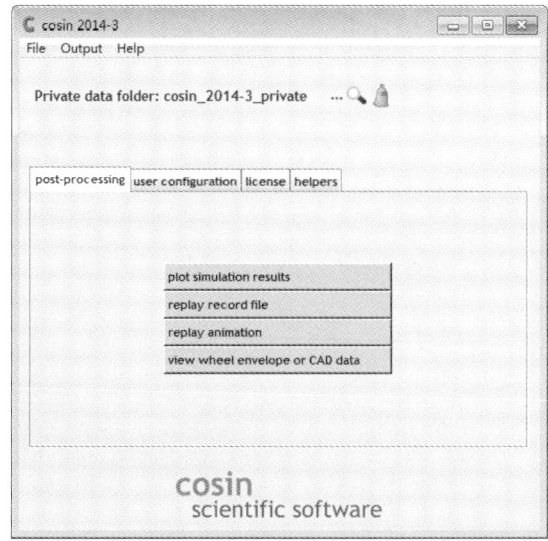
图 4-2 consin2014-3 插件

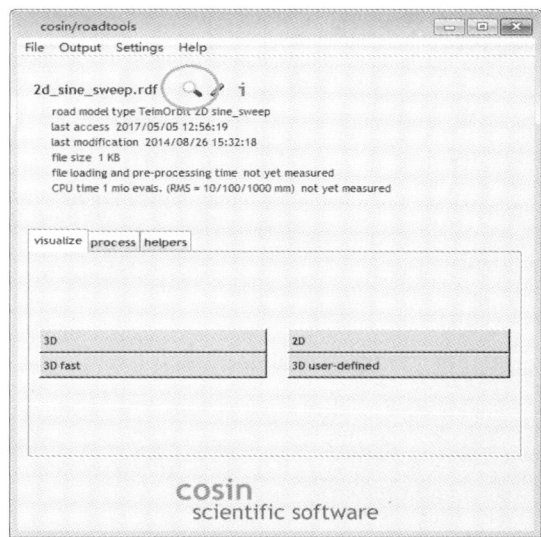
图 4-3 roadtools 工具对话框

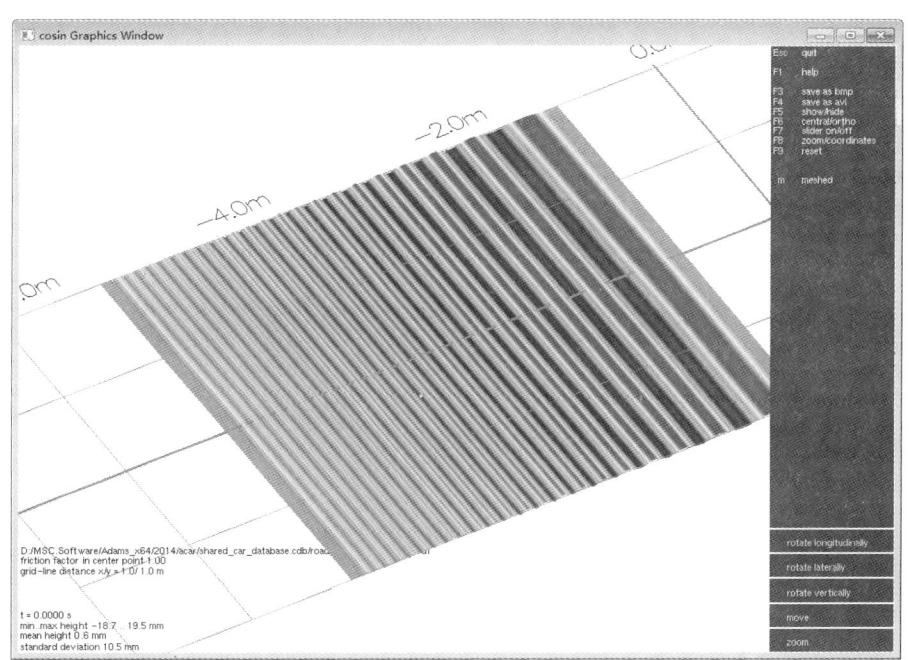
图 4-4 正弦波波纹路面图

4.2 对开路面

真实车辆在制动过程中,左右两侧车轮可能处在不同的路面上,对开路面主要用于车辆 ABS 制动状态下系统的仿真,或者模拟车辆在失控状态下整车的稳定性能。对开路面编辑以

3D 样条路面 mdi_3d_smooth_road.rdf 为模板，对路面左侧摩擦系数 MU_LEFT 与右侧路面摩擦系数 MU_RIGHT 进行更改；高、低附路面以摩擦系数 0.5 为中间值，大于 0.5 为高附路面，小于 0.5 为低附路面，同时要求高、低附路面摩擦系数比值大于等于 2。对 3D 样条路面 mdi_3d_smooth_road.rdf 进行局部修改，修改部分用斜体加下划线标注。修改好的路面另存为 mdi_3d_smooth_road_DK.rdf，文件存放于章节文件夹中。

```
对开路面信息按如下方式修改：
$--------------------------------------------------------------MDI_HEADER
[MDI_HEADER]
FILE_TYPE       =  'rdf'
FILE_VERSION    =   5.00
FILE_FORMAT     =  'ASCII'
(COMMENTS)
( comment_string)
'3d smooth road'
$--------------------------------------------------------------UNITS
[UNITS]
LENGTH              = 'meter'
FORCE               = 'newton'
ANGLE               = 'radians'
MASS                = 'kg'
TIME                = 'sec'
$--------------------------------------------------------------DEFINITION
[MODEL]
METHOD              = '3D_SPLINE'
FUNCTION_NAME       = 'ARC903'
VERSION             = 1.00
$--------------------------------------------------------------ROAD_PARAMETERS
[GLOBAL_PARAMETERS]
CLOSED_ROAD         = 'nO'
SEARCH_ALGORITHM    = 'FaSt'
ROAD_VERTICAL       = '0.0 0.0 1.0'
FORWARD_DIR         =  'NORMAL'
MU_LEFT             =   1.0
MU_RIGHT            =   1.0
WIDTH               =   7.000
BANK                =   0.0
```

```
$------------------------------------------------------------DATA_POINTS
[DATA_POINTS]
{     X              Y              Z            WIDTH   BANK    MU_LEFT   MU_RIGHT }
 12.50000E+00    0.00000E-00    0.00000E-00     7.000   0.000    0.800     0.400
 10.50000E+00    0.00000E-00    0.00000E-00     7.000   0.000    0.800     0.400
  5.50000E+00    0.00000E-00    0.00000E-00     7.000   0.000    0.800     0.400
  0.50000E+00    0.00000E-00    0.00000E-00     7.000   0.000    0.800     0.400
  0.00000E+00    0.00000E-00    0.00000E-00     7.000   0.000    0.800     0.400
 -2.50000E+00    0.00000E-00    0.00000E-00     7.000   0.000    0.800     0.400
 -5.00000E+00    0.00000E-00    0.00000E-00     7.000   0.000    0.800     0.400
 -1.00000E+01    0.00000E-00    0.00000E-00     7.000   0.000    0.800     0.400
 -2.00000E+01    0.00000E-00    0.10000E-00     7.000   0.000    0.800     0.400
 -3.00000E+01    0.00000E-00    0.20000E-00     7.000   0.000    0.800     0.400
 -4.00000E+01    0.00000E-00    0.30000E-00     7.000   0.000    0.800     0.400
 -5.00000E+01    0.00000E-00    0.40000E-00     7.000   0.000    0.800     0.400
 -6.00000E+01    0.00000E-00    0.50000E-00     7.000   0.000    0.800     0.400
 -7.00000E+01    0.00000E-00    0.60000E-00     7.000   0.000    0.800     0.400
 -8.00000E+01    0.00000E-00    0.70000E-00     7.000   0.000    0.800     0.400
 -9.00000E+01    0.00000E-00    0.80000E-00     7.000   0.000    0.800     0.400
 -1.00000E+02    0.00000E-00    0.90000E-00     7.000   0.000    0.800     0.400
 -1.10000E+02    0.00000E-00    1.00000E+00     7.000   0.000    0.800     0.400
 -1.20000E+02    0.00000E-00    1.10000E-00     7.000   0.000    0.800     0.400
 -1.30000E+02    0.00000E-00    1.20000E-00     7.000   0.000    0.800     0.400
$------------------------------------------------------------END_DATA_POINTS
```

4.3 对接路面

对接路面同样用于车辆 ABS 制动状态下系统的仿真，对接路面以长度为单位划分为各小整体，每个整体路面摩擦系数不同，以路面中轴线为界，对接路面编辑以 3D 样条路面 mdi_3d_smooth_road.rdf 为模板，经过某一个长度后（长度的大小可以对整车进行直线制动仿真进行估计）路面左右侧的摩擦系数同时变更，一般情况下变小；高、低附路面以摩擦系数 0.5 为中间值，大于 0.5 为高附路面，小于 0.5 为低附路面，同时要求高、低附路面摩擦系数比值大于等于 2；对 3D 样条路面 mdi_3d_smooth_road.rdf 进行局部修改，修改部分用斜体加下划线标注。修改好的路面另存为 mdi_3d_smooth_road_DJ.rdf，文件存放于章节文件夹中。

对接路面信息按如下方式修改：

```
$------------------------------------------------------MDI_HEADER
[MDI_HEADER]
FILE_TYPE         = 'rdf'
FILE_VERSION      = 5.00
FILE_FORMAT       = 'ASCII'
(COMMENTS)
(comment_string)
'3d smooth road'
$------------------------------------------------------UNITS
[UNITS]
LENGTH            = 'meter'
FORCE             = 'newton'
ANGLE             = 'radians'
MASS              = 'kg'
TIME              = 'sec'
$------------------------------------------------------DEFINITION
[MODEL]
METHOD            = '3D_SPLINE'
FUNCTION_NAME     = 'ARC903'
VERSION           = 1.00
$------------------------------------------------------ROAD_PARAMETERS
[GLOBAL_PARAMETERS]
CLOSED_ROAD       = 'nO'
SEARCH_ALGORITHM  = 'FaSt'
ROAD_VERTICAL     = '0.0 0.0 1.0'
FORWARD_DIR       =  'NORMAL'
MU_LEFT           = 1.0
MU_RIGHT          = 1.0
WIDTH             = 7.000
BANK              = 0.0


$------------------------------------------------------DATA_POINTS
[DATA_POINTS]
{     X          Y            Z         WIDTH  BANK   MU_LEFT   MU_RIGHT }
12.50000E+00  0.00000E-00  0.00000E-00  3.000  0.000   0.900     0.900
```

10.50000E+00	0.00000E – 00	0.00000E – 00	3.000 0.000	0.900	0.900
5.50000E+00	0.00000E – 00	0.00000E – 00	3.000 0.000	0.900	0.900
0.50000E+00	0.00000E – 00	0.00000E – 00	3.000 0.000	0.900	0.900
0.00000E+00	0.00000E – 00	0.00000E – 00	3.000 0.000	0.900	0.900
-2.50000E+00	0.00000E – 00	0.00000E – 00	3.000 0.000	0.900	0.900
-5.00000E+00	0.00000E – 00	0.00000E – 00	3.000 0.000	0.900	0.900
-1.00000E+01	0.00000E – 00	0.00000E – 00	3.000 0.000	*0.300*	*0.300*
-2.00000E+01	0.00000E – 00	0.10000E – 00	3.000 0.000	*0.300*	*0.300*
-3.00000E+01	0.00000E – 00	0.20000E – 00	3.000 0.000	*0.300*	*0.300*
-4.00000E+01	0.00000E – 00	0.30000E – 00	3.000 0.000	*0.300*	*0.300*
-5.00000E+01	0.00000E – 00	0.40000E – 00	3.000 0.000	*0.300*	*0.300*
-6.00000E+01	0.00000E – 00	0.50000E – 00	3.000 0.000	*0.300*	*0.300*
-7.00000E+01	0.00000E – 00	0.60000E – 00	3.000 0.000	*0.300*	*0.300*
-8.00000E+01	0.00000E – 00	0.70000E – 00	3.000 0.000	*0.300*	*0.300*
-9.00000E+01	0.00000E – 00	0.80000E – 00	3.000 0.000	*0.300*	*0.300*
-1.00000E+02	0.00000E – 00	0.90000E – 00	3.000 0.000	*0.300*	*0.300*
-1.10000E+02	0.00000E – 00	1.00000E+00	3.000 0.000	*0.300*	*0.300*
-1.20000E+02	0.00000E – 00	1.10000E – 00	3.000 0.000	*0.300*	*0.300*
-1.30000E+02	0.00000E – 00	1.20000E – 00	3.000 0.000	*0.300*	*0.300*
$--END\_DATA\_POINTS$					

4.4 减速带路面

减速带主要设置在路口、学校、小区门口等车流量较多、人口较为密集的地方，提示车辆减速慢行，注意安全。减速带规格类型较多，此案例采用的减速带规格为 250×350×50（长×宽×高），其中减速带断面参数为 350×50。通过 ADAMS\CAR 建立减速带模型，模拟 FSAE 赛车通过减速整车的运动状态。

- 单击 Simulate > Full-Vehicle Analyses > Road builder 命令，弹出路面构建对话框如图 4-5 所示，对话框主要包含四部分：路面文件、标题栏、路面文件版本信息、路面单位信息。
- Road File：D:\MSC.Software\Adams_x64\2014\acar\shared_car_database.cdb\roads.tbl\road_3d_sine_example.xml；
- 路面文件中输入上述路径，路面建模器打开后默认存在，也可以点击后面的文件快捷方式输入其他路面文件；界面其余设置均保持默认；
- 单击 Obstacle（障碍物，包括凸块路面、凹坑路面、三角形凸台路面等），此时图 4-5 转换成障碍物路面设置界面，如图 4-6 所示；

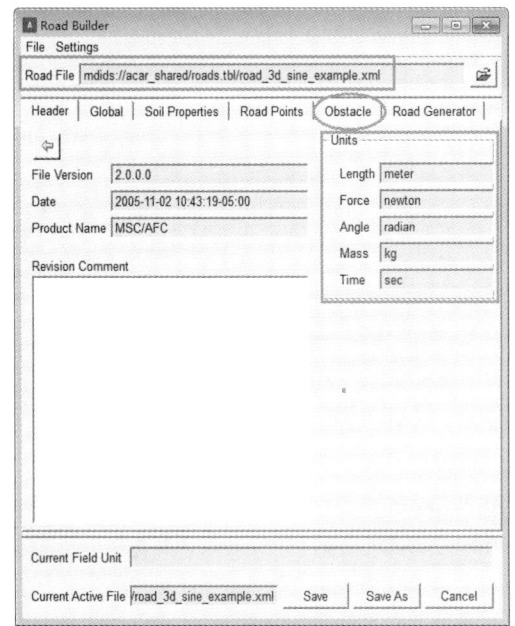 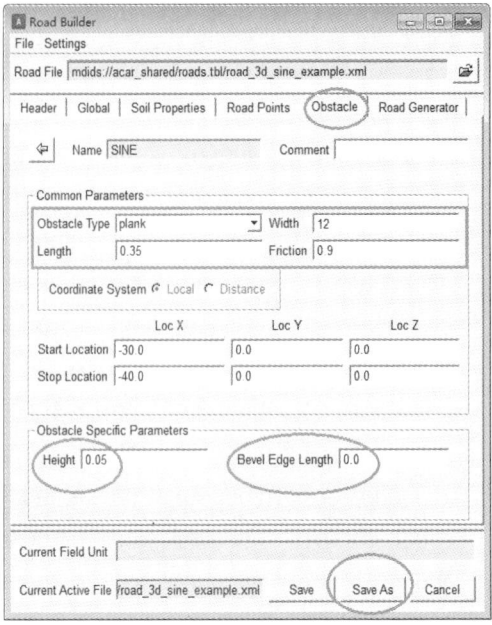

图 4-5　路面构建对话框　　　　　图 4-6　路面障碍对话框

- Obstacle Type：plank，即障碍物选择凸块路面；
- Width（路面宽度）：12，单位 m（减速带宽度与路面宽度相同，路面宽度可以用记事本打开 road_3d_sine_example.xml 查询）；
- Length（减速带断面宽度）：0.35，单位 m；
- Friction（摩擦系数）：0.9；
- Height（减速带高度）0.05，单位 m；
- Bevel Edge Length（凸块倒角变长度，默认角度为 45°）：0，单位 m；
- 其余保持默认设置，单击 Save As 标签，另存为 road_3d_sine_example_JIANSUDAI.xml；存储路径为 D:\fsae_MD_2010.cdb\roads.tbl\ road_3d_sine_example_JIANSUDAI.xml。减速带路面模型如图 4-7 所示。

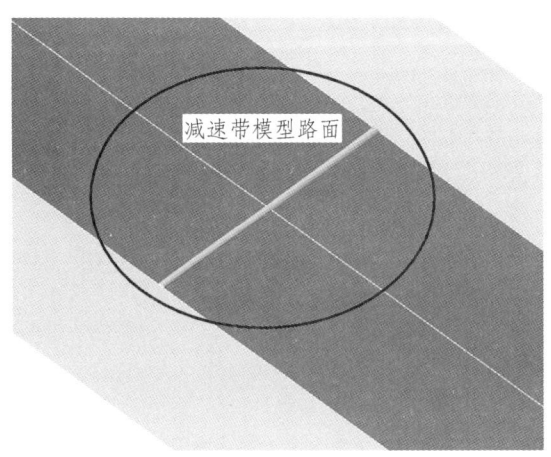

图 4-7　减速带路面模型

4.5 单线移仿真

- 单击 Simulate > Full-Vehicle Analysis > Open-Loop Steering Events > Single Lane Change 命令，弹出单线移仿真对话框，如图 4-8 所示；
- Output Prefix（输出别名）：FSAE_single_lane；
- End Time：10；
- Number Of Steps：1 000；
- Simulation Mode（仿真类型）：interactive；
- Road Date File: mdids://FASE/roads.tbl/road_3d_sine_example_JIANSUDAI.xml；
- Initial Velocity（初始速度）：50；
- Gear Position（挡位）：4 挡；
- Maximum Steer Value（方向盘输入最大角度）：90，单位：度；
- Start Time：2；
- Cycle length（转向时间）：1；
- Steering Input（转向输入）：Angle；
- 其余设置保持默认，单击 OK，完成单线移仿真设置并提交软件进行计算。

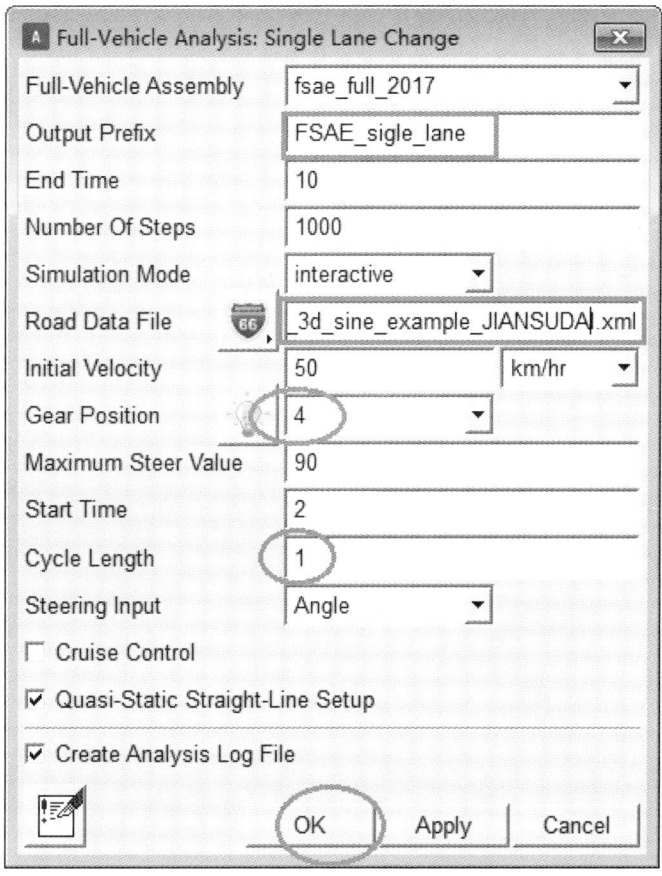

图 4-8　单线移仿真设置对话框

仿真正确且结束后,查看车身的垂向加速度与侧向加速度,根据数据评估 FSAE 整车运行状态及稳定性。查看数据有两种方法:一种是直接在后处理模块中查询,另一种是直接在标准窗口界面建立测量函数测量。

- 标准窗口界面右击选择.fsae_full_2017.FSAE_Body_2017.ges_chassis > Measure,弹出测量对话框;
- Measure Name:chassis_acc_Z;
- Characteristic:CM acceleration;
- Component:Z;
- 单击 Apply,完成 FSAE 赛车的垂向加速度的测量,如图 4-9 所示;
- Measure Name:chassis_acc_Y;
- Component:Y;
- 其余保持默认,单击 OK,完成 FSAE 赛车的侧向加速度的测量,如图 4-10 所示。

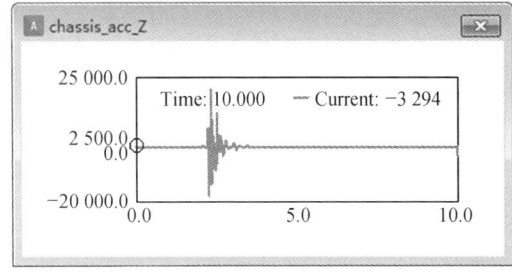
图 4-9 车身垂向加速度

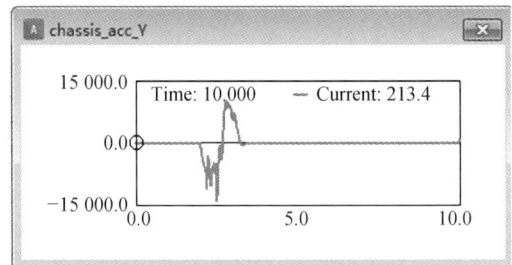
图 4-10 车身侧向加速度

从仿真结果中可以看出,FSAE 赛车在经过减速度瞬间,车身垂直方向产生剧烈振动,最大值接近 2.5g;车身侧向加速度最大值接近 1.5g,在负方向伴有高频振动趋势(线条变化并不光滑)。

> 单线移仿真注意事项:
> 单线移在仿真时可能出现错误,但能仿真完成。出现此种问题的原因主要有转向时间 Cycle length 设置过大、整车在转向过程中方向盘转向时间过长、整车行驶出宽度为 12 m 的路面跌落到空中。解决此问题① 需要多次尝试设置不同 Cycle length 值进行仿真,并根据整车运行的动画进行评估确定合适值;② 更换平整路面 FLAT,平整路面的长宽值可以在路面文件中进行修改;③ 也可以多次尝试使 FSAE 赛车从不同的角度四个车轮先后通过减速带,Cycle length 设置为 1 可以满足要求。

4.6 连续障碍路面

整车在高速路上行驶时,会存在多个连续减速带提示驾驶员与前车保持合适的车距。在整车设计量产之前,需要对整车的性能进行评估,也需要整车在随即不平路面上或者连续障碍路面上行驶。连续 3 个减速带路面创建如下,其他障碍路面创建也可参考。

- 单击 Simulate > Full-Vehicle Analyses > Road builder 命令，弹出路面构建对话框如图 4-5 所示；
- Road File：D:\fsae_MD_2010.cdb\roads.tbl\ road_3d_sine_example_JIANSUDAI.xml；
- 单击 Obstacle；
- 单击 Display table view，显示出连续障碍路面设置对话框，如图 4-11 所示；

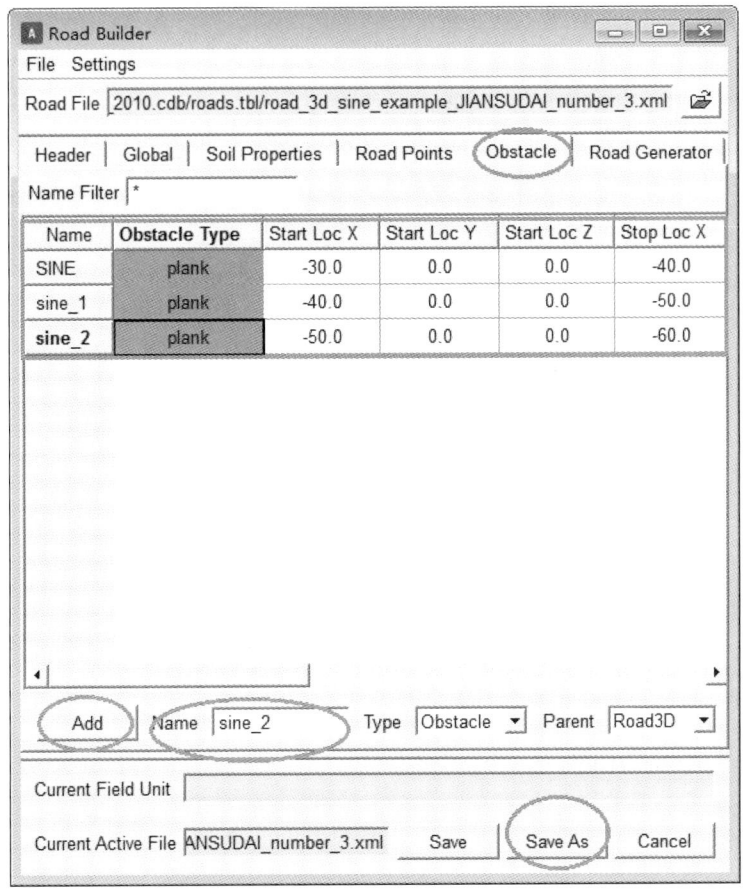

图 4-11　路面连续障碍设置对话框

- Name：sine_1；
- 单击 Add，双击列表中的 sine_1 界面转换成如图 4-6 所示；
- Obstacle Type：plank，即障碍物选择凸块路面；
- Width（路面宽度）：12，单位 m；减速带宽度与路面宽度相同，路面宽度可以用记事本打开 road_3d_sine_example.xml 查询；
- Length（减速带断面宽度）：0.35，单位 m；
- Friction（摩擦系数）：0.9；
- Height（减速带高度）：0.05，单位 m；
- Start Location：Loc X 下列方框输入 – 40；
- Stop Location：Loc X 下列方框输入 – 50；
- 单击 Display table view，重复一次上述过程；

- Name：sine_2；
- Start Location：Loc X 下列方框输入 – 50；
- Stop Location：Loc X 下列方框输入 – 60；

• 其余保持默认设置，单击 Save As 标签，另存为 road_3d_sine_example_JIANSUDAI_number_3.xml；存储路径为 D:\fsae_MD_2010.cdb\roads.tbl\ road_3d_sine_example_JIANSUDAI_number_3.xml。连续减速带路面模型如图 4-12 所示。

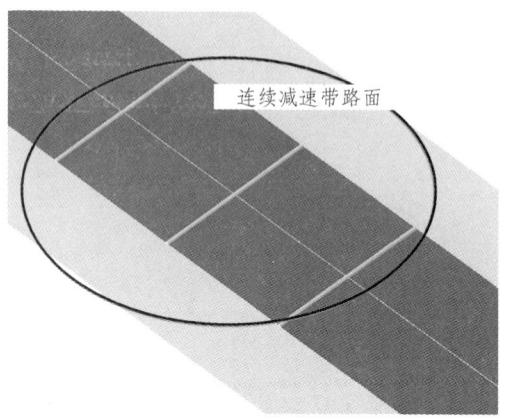

图 4-12　连续减速带路面模型

4.7　匀速直线行驶仿真

• 单击 Simulate > Full-Vehicle Analysis > Straight-Line Events > Maintain 命令，弹出匀速直线行驶仿真对话框如图 4-13 所示；

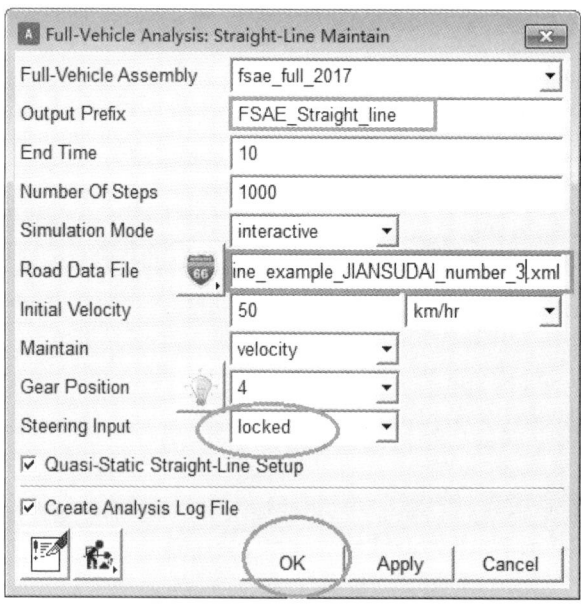

图 4-13　匀速行驶仿真对话框

- Output Prefix（输出别名）：FSAE_Straight_Line；
- End Time：10；
- Number Of Steps：1 000；
- Simulation Mode（仿真类型）：interactive；
- Road Date File: mdids://FASE/roads.tbl/road_3d_sine_example_JIANSUDAI_number_3.xml；
- Initial Velocity（初始速度）：50；
- Gear Position（挡位）：4 挡；
- Steering Input（转向输入）：Locked；
- 其余设置保持默认，单击 OK，完成匀速直线行驶仿真设置并提交软件进行计算。
- 标准窗口界面右击选择.fsae_full_2017.FSAE_Body_2017.ges_chassis > Measure，弹出测量对话框；
- Measure Name：Maintain_chassis_acc_Z；
- Characteristic：CM acceleration；
- Component：Z；
- 单击 OK，完成 FSAE 赛车在匀速仿真下垂向加速度的测量，如图 4-14 所示。

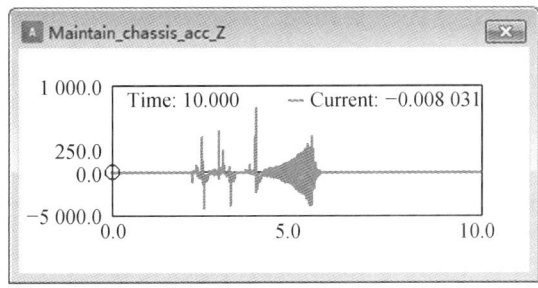

图 4-14　车身垂向加速度_Maintain

4.8　直线制动系统仿真

- 启动 ADAMS/CAR，选择 Standard 标准模块进入界面；
- 单击 File > Open > Assembly 命令，弹出装配打开对话框；
- Assembly Name：mdids://FASE/assemblies.tbl/fsae_full_2017.asy；
- 单击 OK，完成方程式赛车整车模型的打开。
- 单击 Simulate > Full-Vehicle Analysis > Straight-Line Event > Braking 命令，弹出制动仿真对话框如图 4-15 所示；
- Output Prefix（输出别名）：brake_line；
- End Time：10；
- Number Of Steps：1 000；
- Simulation Mode（仿真类型）：interactive；

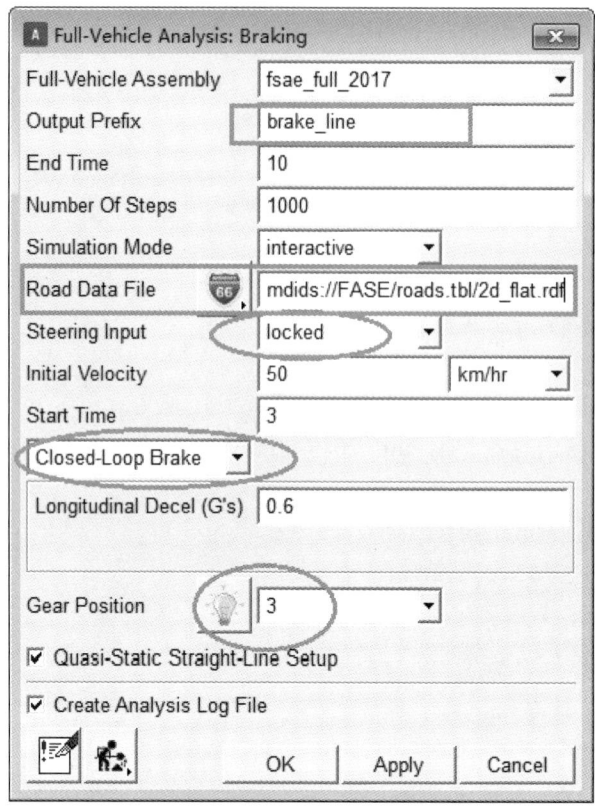

图 4-15 直线制动仿真对话框

- Road Date File: mdids://FASE/roads.tbl/2d_flat.rdf，此处导入 CAR 模块中共享数据库中的路面 mdids://acar_shared/roads.tbl/2d_flat.rdf 也可以，路面文件是相同的，为方程式赛车建模方便，把共享数据库中的 ROAD 文件复制到方程式赛车数据库中即可；
- Steering Input（转向输入）：lock，即转向时保持转向锁定；
- Start Time：3；
- 选择闭环制动模式：Closed-Loop Bbrake；
- Longitudinal Decel(G's)（制动时侧向加速度）：0.6；
- Gear Position（挡位）：3 挡；
- 单击 OK，完成直线制动仿真设置并提交软件进行计算。
- 计算提示完成后，右击选择 General Part：FSAE_Body_2017.ges_chassis > Measure，弹出部件测量对话框；
- Characteristic：CM position；
- Component：Y；
- 单击 OK，完成车身制动过程中侧向偏移量：.fsae_full_2017.ges_chassis_MEA_1。方程赛车制动过程中，车身侧向滑移量小，说明在制动过程中车身稳定性较好，直线制动车身侧向滑移率计算经过如图 4-16 所示。

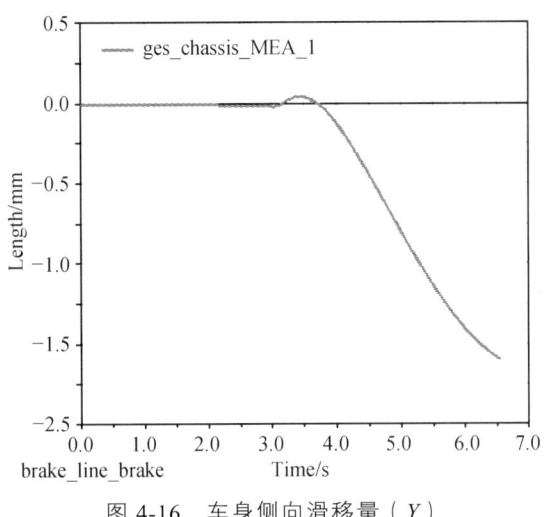

图 4-16 车身侧向滑移量（Y）

4.9 分离轮胎路面设置

整车在行驶过程中，四个轮胎接触的路面不可能完全相同，即使是在良好的一级路面上，也会存在微小差异。针对整车的制动特性，在一些特殊路面，如雨地、雪地、坑洼泥泞路面，四个车轮（或者多个车轮）与路面接触不可能具有相同的摩擦系数。因此有必要在虚拟仿真时设置分离路面，左右车轮或者四个车轮设置不同的摩擦系数。

根据文件夹路径 D:\fsae_MD_2010.cdb\roads.tbl，用记事本格式打开平整路面文件 2d_flat.rdf 如以下信息所示，在 PARAMETERS 栏修改 MU=0.5，保存文件重命名为 2d_flat_mu_0.5.rdf；

```
平整路面信息如下：
$---------------------------------------------------------------MDI_HEADER
[MDI_HEADER]
FILE_TYPE        =   'rdf'
FILE_VERSION     =   5.00
FILE_FORMAT      =   'ASCII'
(COMMENTS)
{comment_string}
'flat 2d contact road for testing purposes'
$---------------------------------------------------------------UNITS
[UNITS]
LENGTH                   = 'mm'
FORCE                    = 'newton'
ANGLE                    = 'radians'
MASS                     = 'kg'
```

```
TIME                    = 'sec'
$------------------------------------------------------------------MODEL
[MODEL]
METHOD                  = '2D'
FUNCTION_NAME           = 'ARC901'
ROAD_TYPE               = 'flat'
$------------------------------------------------------------------GRAPHICS
[GRAPHICS]
LENGTH                  = 160 000.0
WIDTH                   = 80 000.0
NUM_LENGTH_GRIDS        = 16
NUM_WIDTH_GRIDS         = 8
LENGTH_SHIFT            = 10 000.0
WIDTH_SHIFT             = 0.0              %此栏参数也可以修改,用以改变路面
的大小
$------------------------------------------------------------------PARAMETERS
[PARAMETERS]
MU                      =   0.5       %可修改的轮胎与路面的接触摩擦系数,范围在0
到1之间
$------------------------------------------------------------------REFSYS
[REFSYS]
OFFSET                  =   0.0 0.0 0.0
ROTATION_ANGLE_XY_PLANE =   0.0
```

- 单击 Simulate > Full-Vehicle Analyses > Vehicle Set-Up > Set Road for individual Tires 命令,弹出分离轮胎路面数据文件对话框如图 4-17 所示;
- Wheel:.fsae_full_2017.front_tire.whl_wheel,方框中右击 Wheel > Pick 选择;
- 不勾选使用路面默认文件:Use default road date file;
- Road Date File:mdids://FASE/roads.tbl/2d_flat_mu_0.5.rdf;

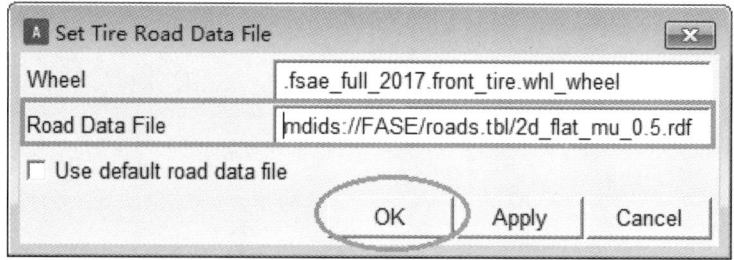

图 4-17 分离轮胎路面设置对话框

- 单击 Apply，完成左前轮轮胎路面设置；
- Wheel：.fsae_full_2017.rear_tire.whl_wheel，方框中右击 Wheel > Pick 选择；
- 不勾选使用路面默认文件：Use default road date file；
- Road Date File：mdids://FASE/roads.tbl/2d_flat_mu_0.5.rdf；
- 单击 OK，完成左后轮轮胎路面设置。

4.10 分离轮胎路面直线制动仿真

- 单击 Simulate > Full-Vehicle > Straight-Line Event > Braking 命令，弹出制动仿真对话框；
- Output Prefix（输出别名）：brake_line_individual；
- 其余选项保持默认；
- 单击 OK，完成分离轮胎路面直线制动仿真设置并提交软件进行计算。
- 计算提示完成后，右击选择 General Part：FSAE_Body_2017.ges_chassis > Measure，弹出部件测量对话框；
- Characteristic：CM position；
- Component：Y；
- 单击 OK，完成分离轮胎路面直线制动车身侧向偏移量：.fsae_full_2017.ges_chassis_MEA_2，偏移量如图 4-18 所示，把.fsae_full_2017.ges_ chassis_ MEA_1 与.fsae_full_2017.ges_chassis_MEA_2 在同一张图中显示，可以看出分离轮胎路面制动时，车身已经产生严重的侧向滑移，制动稳定性丧失，如图 4-19 所示。

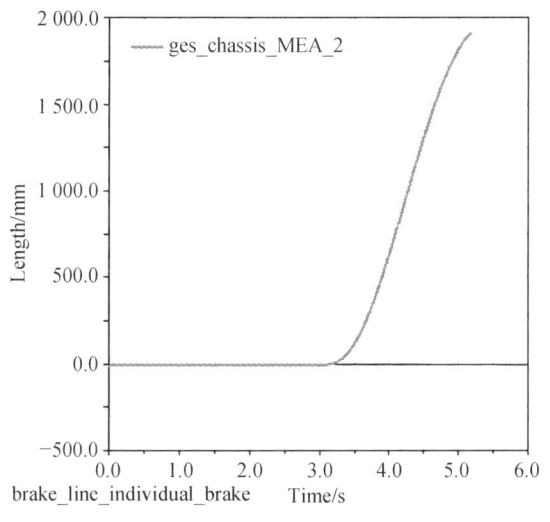
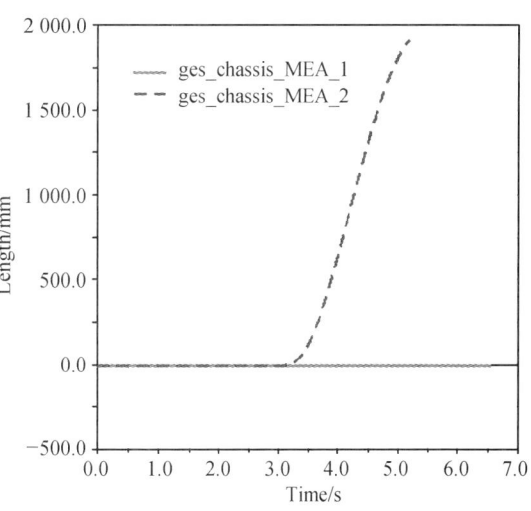

图 4-18 分离轮胎路面制动时车身侧向滑移量（Y）　　图 4-19 车身侧向滑移量对比图（Y）

4.11 弯道制动系统仿真

- 单击 Simulate > Full-Vehicle > Cornering Event >Braking-In-Turn 命令，弹出弯道制动仿真对话框如图 4-20 所示；

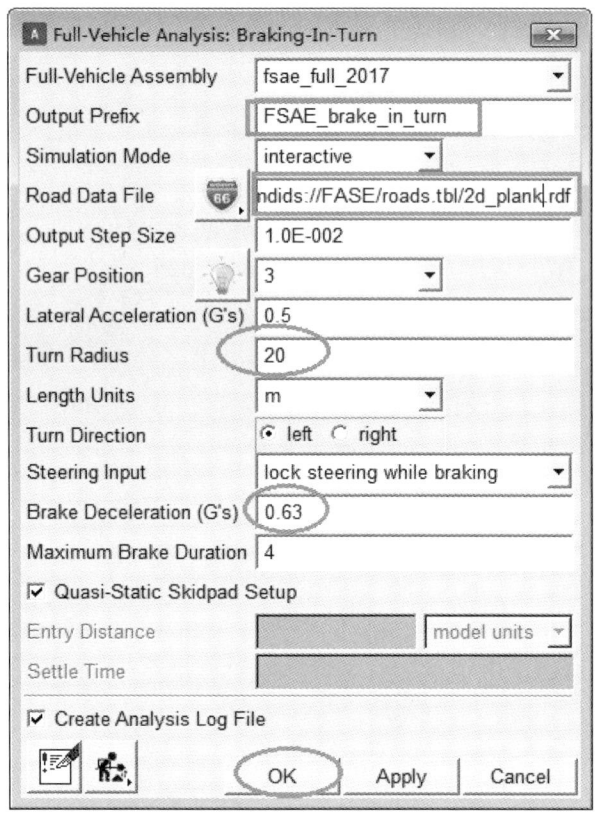

图 4-20 弯道制动仿真设置

- Prefix（输出别名）：abs_consimulation；
- Simulation Mode（仿真类型）：files_only；
- Road Date File: mdids://acar_shared/roads.tbl/2d_flat.rdf；路面为共享数据库中路面，此处可以选择其他路面模型或者自编的路面模型，包括对开路面、对接路面等；
- Output Step Size（计算步长）：5.0E – 002；
- Gear Position（挡位）：3 挡；
- Lateral Acceleration(G's)（制动时侧向加速度）：0.5；
- Turn Radiud（转弯半径）：15；
- Length Units（长度单位）：m；
- Steering Input（转向输入）：lock steering while braking，即转向时保持转向锁定；
- Brake Decelaeration(G's)（制动时减速度）：0.63；
- Maximum Brake Duration(制动时间)：4；
- 单击 OK，完成弯道制动设置并提交软件进行计算。

- 按F8进入后处理模块,显示弯道制动模式下车身侧向加速度、垂向加速度,如图4-21、图4-22所示;左前轮、右后轮滑移率如图4-23、图4-24所示,从滑移率可以看出,左前轮产生抱死现象,右后轮也会产生滑移,车辆失去稳定性。

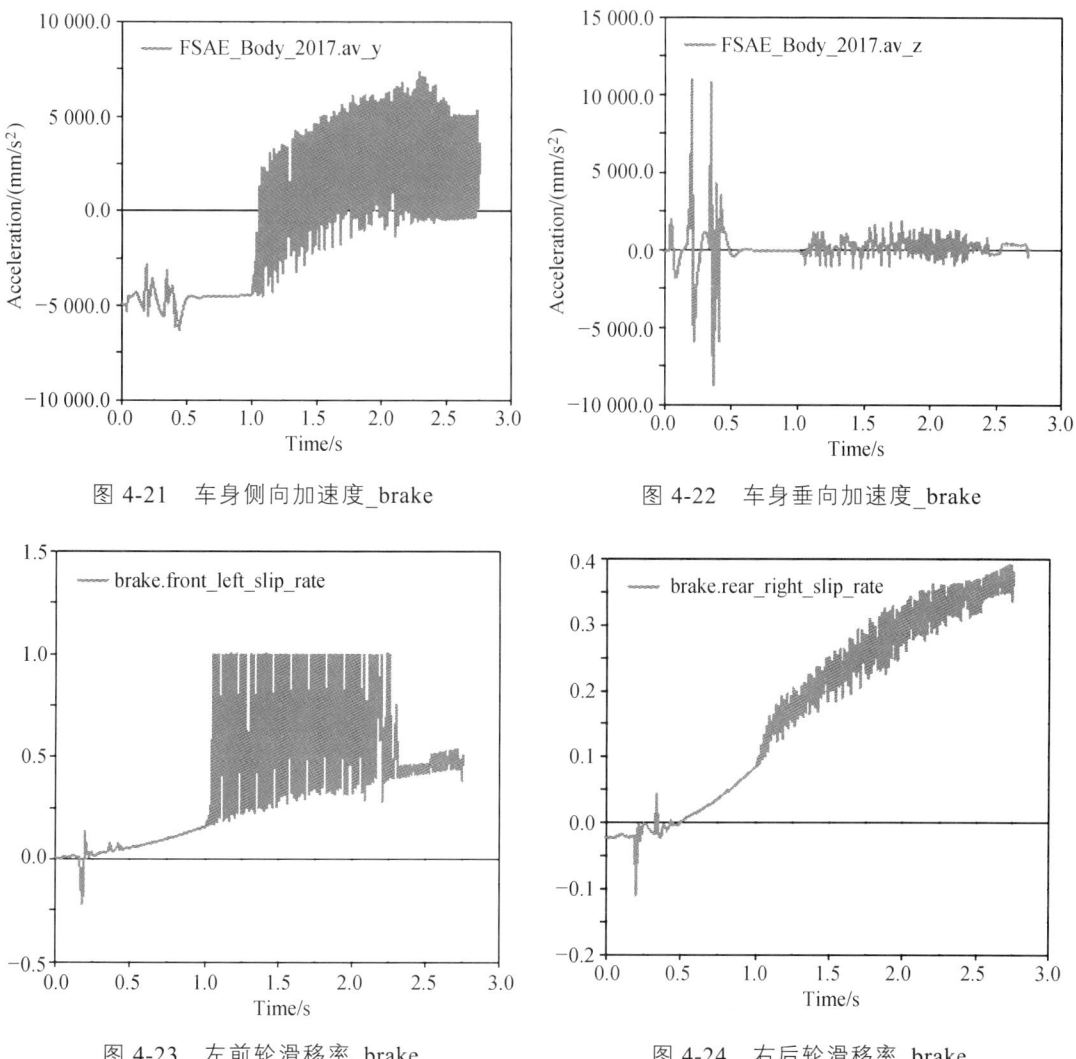

图 4-21　车身侧向加速度_brake　　　　　图 4-22　车身垂向加速度_brake

图 4-23　左前轮滑移率_brake　　　　　　图 4-24　右后轮滑移率_brake

第 5 章　发动机模型

发动机的主要功能是提供动力源,经过变速器及传动系统把动力源输出传递到车轮上驱动车轮运动,动力源模型可有不同的形式,在 CAR 模块中是通过函数把发动机、变速器及主减速器整合在一起,整车动力单元并不需要真实的传动系统驱动,集成度较高;DRIVELINE 模块中发动机模型为简化模型,主要由简化机体和曲轴组成,曲轴绕机体产生旋转驱动后续的传动部件,曲轴旋转运动由动力元驱动,驱动元可以是固定参数,也可以是编制的发动机真实工况特性文件。简化发动机模型避免了复杂函数的整合,更容易直观理解,但必须与传动系统相配合驱动整车,同时传动系统可以拓展到多轴系车辆驱动。简化发动机通过衬套与车身或者前后悬架系统机械匹配安装,建立好的简化发动机模型如图 5-1 所示。

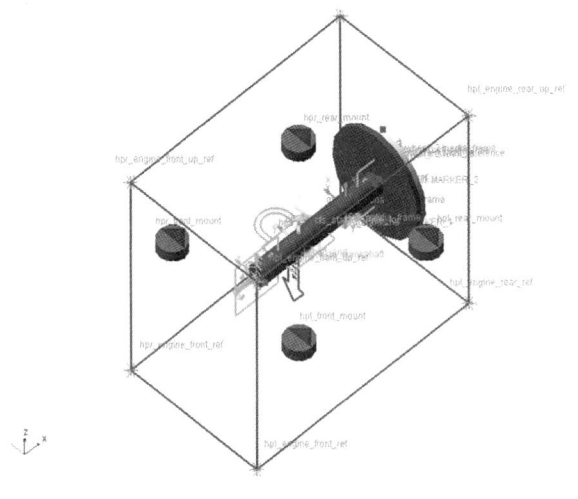

图 5-1　发动机模型

学习目标

- ◆ 机体。
- ◆ 曲轴。
- ◆ 飞轮。
- ◆ 驱动元。
- ◆ 发动机调试。
- ◆ 直线仿真。

- 启动 ADAMS/DRIVELINE，选择专家模块进入建模界面；
- 单击 File > New 命令，弹出建模对话框如图 5-2 所示；在模板名称里输入 my_engine，主特征选择 poweertrain，单击 OK；

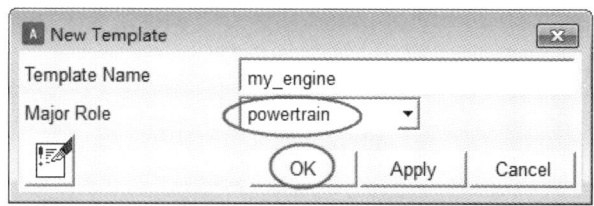

图 5-2　发动机模板框

- 单击 Build > Hardpoint > New 命令，弹出创建硬点对话框如图 5-3 所示；
- 在硬点名称里输入 engine_CM，类型选择 single；在位置文本框输入 0.0, 0.0, 0.0；
- 单击 Apply，完成 engine_CM 硬点的创建。此时在屏幕上显示出左右对称的单个硬点；以此类推，重复上述步骤完成如图 5-4 所示硬点的创建，完成后单击 OK。

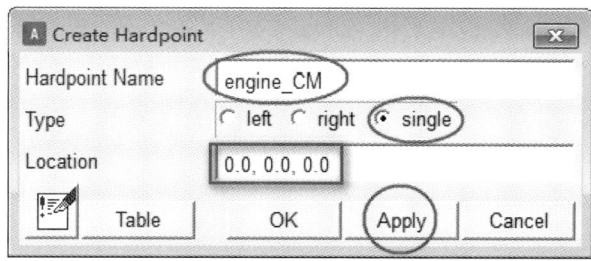

图 5-3　硬点对话框

	loc_x	loc_y	loc_z
hpl_engine_front_ref	-250.0	-150.0	-200.0
hpl_engine_front_up_ref	-250.0	-150.0	200.0
hpl_engine_rear_ref	250.0	-150.0	-200.0
hpl_engine_rear_up_ref	250.0	-150.0	200.0
hpl_front_mount	-150.0	-150.0	0.0
hpl_rear_mount	150.0	-150.0	0.0
hps_crankshaft_reference	200.0	0.0	0.0
hps_engine_CM	0.0	0.0	0.0
hps_static_torque_loc	0.0	0.0	0.0

图 5-4　发动机硬点数据

5.1　发动机机体

- 单击 Build > Part > General Part > New 命令，弹出创建发动机机体部件对话框如图 5-5

所示；
- General Part 输入 engine_block；
- Location Dependency：Delta location from coordinate；
- Coordinate Reference (参考坐标)：._my_engine.ground.hps_engine_CM；
- Location：0,0,0；
- Location in：local；
- Orientation Dependency：User-entered values；
- Orient using：Euler Angles；
- Euler Angles：0,0,0；
- Mass：100；
- Ixx：1 000；
- Iyy：1 000；
- Izz：1 000；
- Density：Material；
- Material Type：.materials.steel；
- 单击 OK，完成部件._my_engine.ges_engine_block 创建。

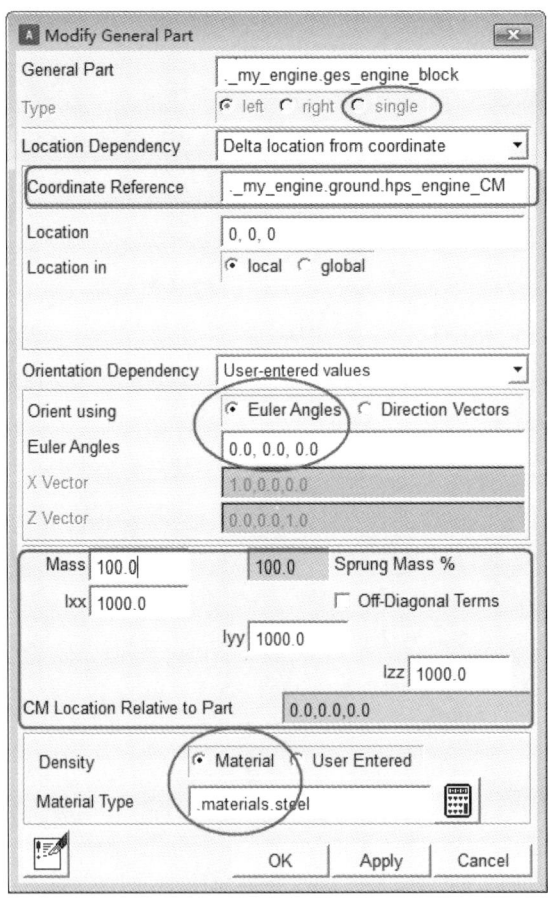

图 5-5　发动机机体部件创建对话框

- 单击 Build > Geometry > Outline > New 命令，轮廓线建立如图 5-6 所示；

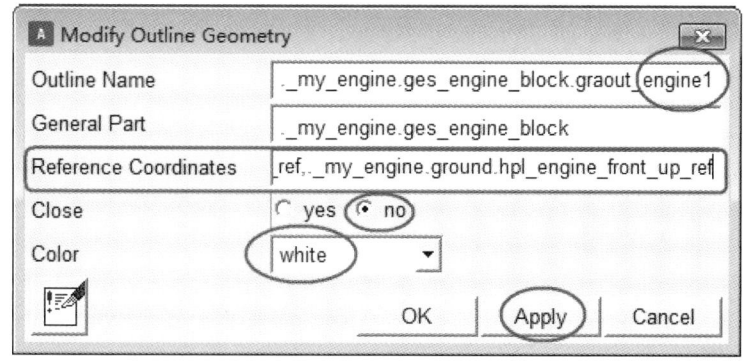

图 5-6　发动机轮廓

- Outline Name (轮廓线名称) 输入几何名称：engine1；
- General Part 输入._my_engine.ges_engine_block；
- Reference Coordinates (参考坐标点，顺序不能乱)：
① ._my_engine.ground.hpr_engine_front_up_ref；
② ._my_engine.ground.hpr_engine_front_ref；
③ ._my_engine.ground.hpl_engine_front_ref；
④ ._my_engine.ground.hpl_engine_front_up_ref。
- Close(轮廓线是否封闭)：no；
- Color (杆件几何体颜色)：white；
- 单击 Apply，完成轮廓线._my_engine.ges_engine_block.graout_engine1 的创建；
- Outline Name (轮廓线名称) 输入几何名称：engine2；
- General Part 输入._my_engine.ges_engine_block；
- Reference Coordinates (参考坐标点，顺序不能乱)：
① ._my_engine.ground.hpl_engine_front_up_ref；
② ._my_engine.ground.hpl_engine_rear_up_ref；
③ ._my_engine.ground.hpl_engine_rear_ref；
④ ._my_engine.ground.hpl_engine_front_ref。
- Close(轮廓线是否封闭)：no；
- Color (杆件几何体颜色)：white；
- 单击 Apply，完成轮廓线._my_engine.ges_engine_block.graout_engine2 的创建；
- Outline Name (轮廓线名称) 输入几何名称：engine3；
- General Part 输入._my_engine.ges_engine_block；
- Reference Coordinates (参考坐标点，顺序不能乱)：
① ._my_engine.ground.hpr_engine_front_up_ref；
② ._my_engine.ground.hpr_engine_rear_up_ref；
③ ._my_engine.ground.hpl_engine_rear_up_ref；

④ ._my_engine.ground.hpl_engine_front_up_ref。
- Close(轮廓线是否封闭)：no；
- Color（杆件几何体颜色）：white；
- 单击 Apply，完成轮廓线._my_engine.ges_engine_block.graout_engine3 的创建；
- Outline Name (轮廓线名称）输入几何名称：engine4；
- General Part 输入._my_engine.ges_engine_block；
- Reference Coordinates (参考坐标点，顺序不能乱)：

① ._my_engine.ground.hpr_engine_front_ref；
② ._my_engine.ground.hpr_engine_rear_ref；
③ ._my_engine.ground.hpl_engine_rear_ref。
- Close(轮廓线是否封闭)：no；
- Color（杆件几何体颜色）：white；
- 单击 Apply，完成轮廓线._my_engine.ges_engine_block.graout_engine4 的创建；
- Outline Name (轮廓线名称）输入几何名称：engine5；
- General Part 输入._my_engine.ges_engine_block；
- Reference Coordinates (参考坐标点，顺序不能乱)：

① ._my_engine.ground.hpr_engine_rear_ref；
② ._my_engine.ground.hpr_engine_rear_up_ref。
- Close(轮廓线是否封闭)：no；
- Color（杆件几何体颜色）：white；
- 单击 Apply，完成轮廓线._my_engine.ges_engine_block.graout_engine5 的创建；
- Outline Name (轮廓线名称）输入几何名称：engine6；
- General Part 输入._my_engine.ges_engine_block；
- Reference Coordinates (参考坐标点，顺序不能乱)：

① ._my_engine.ground.hpr_engine_front_up_ref；
② ._my_engine.ground.hpl_engine_front_up_ref。
- Close(轮廓线是否封闭)：no；
- Color（杆件几何体颜色）：white；
- 单击 OK，完成轮廓线._my_engine.ges_engine_block.graout_engine6 的创建。

5.2 曲 轴

- 单击 Build > Construction Frame > New 命令，结构框创建如图 5-7 所示；
- Construction Frame（结构框名称）：crankshaft_reference；
- Location Dependency：Delta location from coordinate；

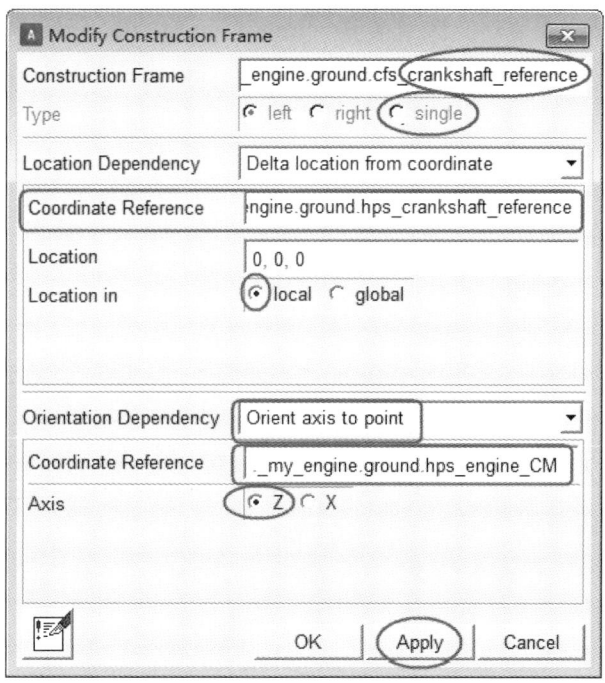

图 5-7 结构框

- Coordinate Reference（参考坐标）：._my_engine.ground.hps_crankshaft_reference；
- Location：0，0，0；
- Location in：local；
- Orientation Dependency：Orient axis to point；
- Coordinate Reference（参考坐标）：._my_engine.ground.hps_engine_CM；
- Axis：Z；
- 单击 Apply，完成 ._my_engine.ground.cfs_crankshaft_reference 结构框的创建；
- Construction Frame（结构框名称）：crankshaft_end；
- Location Dependency：Delta location from coordinate；
- Coordinate Reference（参考坐标）：._my_engine.ground.cfs_crankshaft_reference；
- Location：0，0，0；
- Location in：local；
- Orientation Dependency：Delta orientation from coordinate；
- Construction Frame：._my_engine.ground.cfs_crankshaft_reference；
- Orientation：0，0，0；
- 单击 OK，完成 ._my_engine.ground.cfs_crankshaft_end 结构框的创建。
- 单击 Build > Part > General Part > New 命令，弹出创建部件对话框可参考如图 5-5 所示；
- General Part 输入 crankshaft；
- Location Dependency：Centered between coordinates；
- Centered between：Two Coordinates；

- Coordinate Reference #1(参考坐标)：._my_engine.ground.cfs_crankshaft_end；
- Coordinate Reference #2(参考坐标)：._my_engine.ground.hps_crankshaft_reference；
- Orientation Dependency（部件坐标轴方向）：Orient to zpoint-xpoint；
- Coordinate Reference #1(参考坐标)：._my_engine.ground.cfs_crankshaft_end；
- Coordinate Reference #2(参考坐标)：._my_engine.ground.hps_crankshaft_reference；
- Axes：ZX；
- Mass：1；
- Ixx：1；
- Iyy：1；
- Izz：1；
- Density：Material；
- Material Type：.materials.steel；
- 单击 OK，完成部件._my_engine.ges_crankshaft 创建。
- 单击 Build > Geometry > Link > New 命令，创建曲轴连杆几何体如图 5-8 所示；
- Link Name (连杆名称) 输入几何名称：crankshaft；
- General Part 输入._my_engine.ges_crankshaft；
- Coordinate Reference #1(参考坐标)：._my_engine.ground.cfs_crankshaft_end；
- Coordinate Reference #2(参考坐标)：._my_engine.ground.hps_crankshaft_reference；
- Radius(半径): 20；
- Color（杆件几何体颜色）：red；
- 选择 Calculate Mass Properties of General Part 复选框，当几何体建立好之后会更新对应部件的质量和惯量参数；
- Density：Material；
- Material Type：steel；
- 单击 OK，完成._my_engine.ges_crankshaft.gralin_crankshaft 几何体的创建。

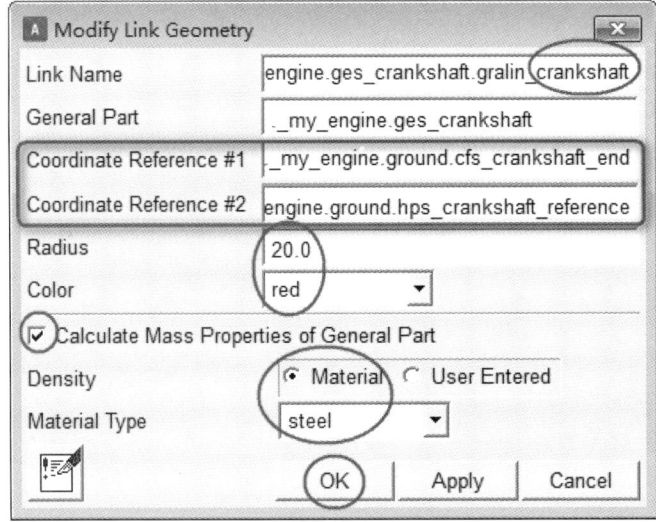

图 5-8 曲轴连杆几何体

- 单击 Build > Geometry > Cylinder (圆柱体) > New 命令，弹出创建曲轴圆柱几何体如图 5-9 所示；

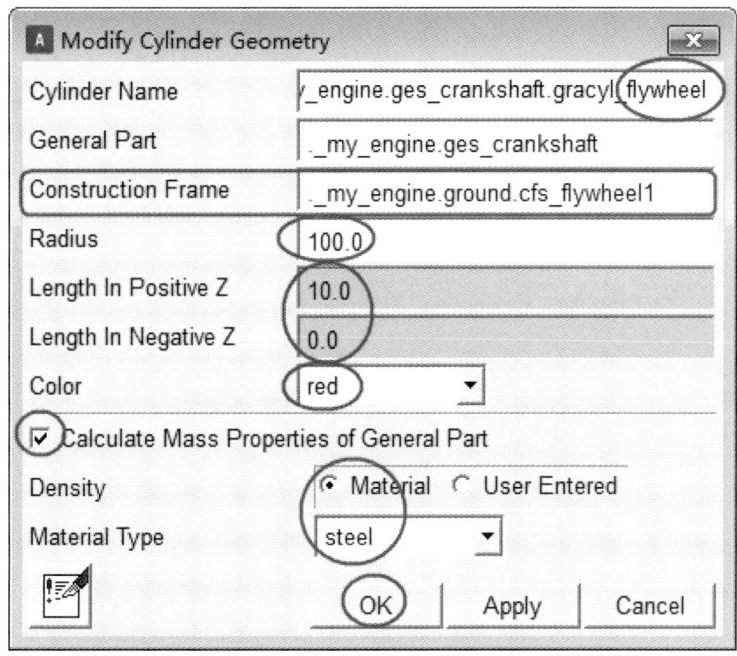

图 5-9 曲轴圆柱几何体

- Cylinder Name（连杆名称）输入几何名称：flywheel；
- General Part 输入._my_engine.ges_crankshaft；
- Radius(半径): 100；
- Length In Postive Z（Z 轴正方向长度）：10；
- Length In Negative Z（Z 轴负方向长度）：0；
- Color（圆柱体几何体颜色）：red；
- 选择 Calculate Mass Properties of General Part 复选框；
- 单击 OK，完成曲轴圆柱体._my_engine.ges_crankshaft.gracyl_flywheel 几何体的创建。

5.3 飞 轮

- 单击 Build > Part > General Part > New 命令，弹出创建部件对话参考如图 5-5 所示；
- General Part 输入 flywheel_2；
- Location Dependency：Delta location from coordinate；
- Coordinate Reference (参考坐标)：._my_engine.ground.hps_crankshaft_reference；
- Location：0,0,0；
- Location in：local；
- Orientation Dependency：Delta orientation from coordinate；

- Construction Frame：._my_engine.ground.cfs_crankshaft_reference；
- Orientation：0,0,0；
- Mass：1；
- Ixx：1；
- Iyy：1；
- Izz：1；
- Density：Material；
- Material Type：.materials.steel；
- 单击 OK，完成部件._my_engine.ges_flywheel_2 创建。
- 单击 Build > Geometry > Cylinder（圆柱体）> New 命令，弹出创建飞轮圆柱体参考如图 5-9 所示；
- Cylinder Name（连杆名称）输入几何名称：flywheel；
- General Part 输入._my_engine.ges_flywheel_2；
- Radius(半径): 100；
- Length In Postive Z（Z 轴正方向长度）：10；
- Length In Negative Z（Z 轴负方向长度）：0；
- Color（圆柱体几何体颜色）：white；
- 选择 Calculate Mass Properties of General Part 复选框；
- 单击 OK，完成曲轴飞轮圆柱体._my_engine.ges_flywheel_2.gracyl_flywheel 几何体的创建。

5.4 安装部件 body

- 单击 Build > Part > Mount > New 命令，安装部件对话框如图 5-10 所示；
- Mount name（安装件名称）：body；
- Coordinate Reference（参考坐标）：._my_engine.ground.hps_engine_CM；
- 安装件此特征选择：inherit(继承特性)；
- 单击 OK，完成._my_engine.mts_body 安装部件的创建。

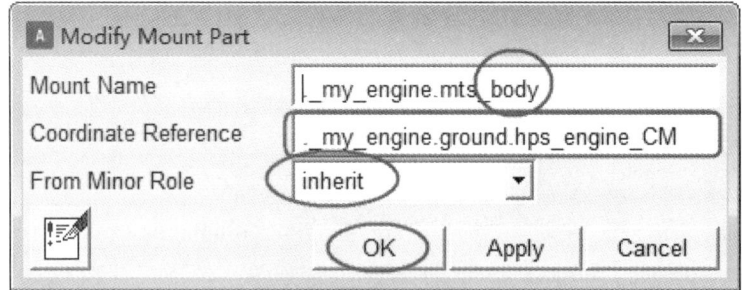

图 5-10 车身部件安装

5.5 发动机约束

5.5.1 刚性约束

- 单击 Build > Attachments > Joint > New 命令，弹出创约束件对话框如图 5-11 所示。

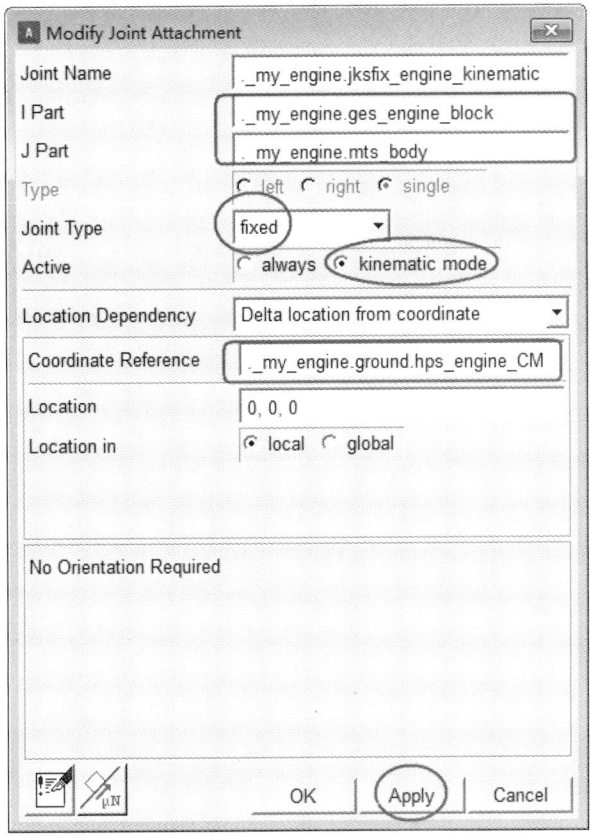

图 5-11 固定副约束

（1）部件 engine_block 与安装件 body 之间 fixed 约束。
- Joint Name（约束副名称）：engine_kinematic；
- I Part：._my_engine.ges_engine_block；
- J Part：._my_engine.mts_body；
- Joint Type（约束副类型）：fixed，即转动副，约束 6 个自由度；
- Active（激活）：kinematic mode（运动学模式）；
- Location Dependency：Delta location from coordinate；
- Coordinate Reference（参考坐标）：._my_engine.ground.hps_engine_CM；
- Location: 0,0,0；
- Location in：local；
- 单击 Apply，完成约束副._my_engine.jksfix_engine_kinematic 的创建。

（2）部件 engine_block 与 crankshaft 之间 revolute 约束。

- Joint Name（约束副名称）：block_to_crankshaft；
- I Part：._my_engine.ges_crankshaft；
- J Part：._my_engine.ges_engine_block；
- Joint Type（约束副类型）：revolute；
- Active（激活）：always；
- Location Dependency：Delta location from coordinate；
- Coordinate Reference（参考坐标）：._my_engine.ground.cfs_crankshaft_end；
- Location：0,0,0；
- Location in：local；
- Orientation Dependency：Delta orientation from coordinate；
- Construction Frame：._my_engine.ground.cfs_crankshaft_end；
- 单击 OK，完成约束副._my_engine.josrev_block_to_crankshaft 的创建。

5.5.2 柔性约束

- 单击 Build > Attachments > Bushing > New 命令，弹出衬套件对话框如图 5-12 所示；
- Bushing Name（约束副名称）：front_mount；
- I Part：._my_engine.ges_engine_block；
- J Part：._my_engine.mts_body；
- Inactive（抑制）：勾选 kinematic mode（运动学模式）；
- Preload：0，0，0；
- Tpreload：0，0，0；
- Offset：0，0，0；
- Roffset：0，0，0；
- Geometry Length：20；
- Geometry Radius：30；
- Property File：mdids://adriveline_shared/bushings.tbl/MDI_engine_mount.bus；
- Location Dependency：Delta location from coordinate；
- Coordinate Reference（参考坐标）：._my_engine.ground.hpl_front_mount；
- Location：0，0，0；
- Location in：local；
- Orientation Dependency：User entered values；
- Orient using：Euler Angles；
- Euler Angles：0,0,0；
- 单击 Apply，完成轴套._my_engine.bkl_front_mount 的创建；

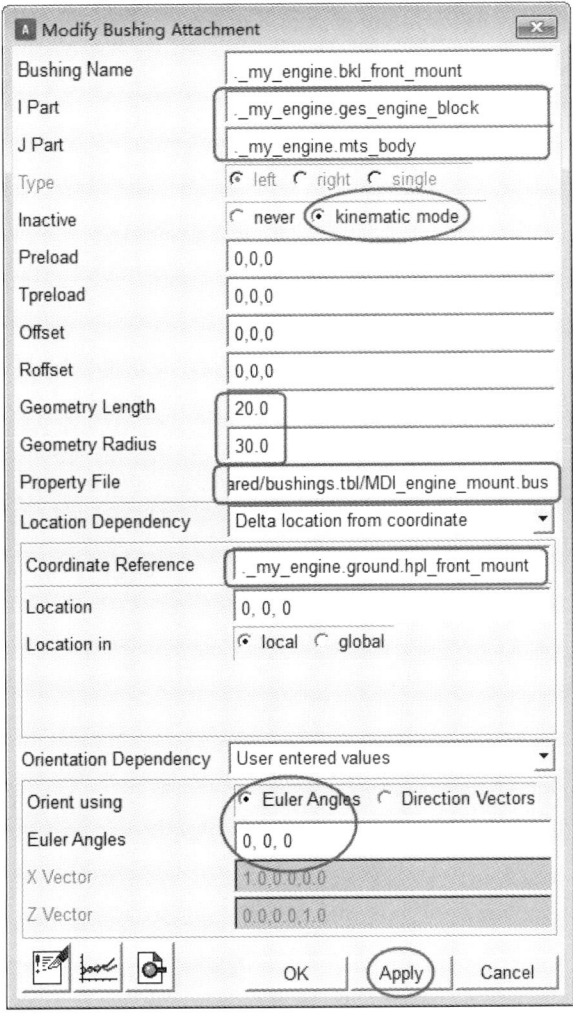

图 5-12 Bushing 衬套柔性约束

- Bushing Name（约束副名称）：rear_mount；
- I Part：._my_engine.ges_engine_block；
- J Part：._my_engine.mts_body；
- Inactive（抑制）：勾选 kinematic mode（运动学模式）；
- Preload：0，0，0；
- Tpreload：0，0，0；
- Offset：0，0，0；
- Roffset：0，0，0；
- Geometry Length：20；
- Geometry Radius：30；
- Property File：mdids://adriveline_shared/bushings.tbl/MDI_engine_mount.bus；
- Location Dependency：Delta location from coordinate；
- Coordinate Reference（参考坐标）：._my_engine.ground.hpl_rear_mount；

- Location: 0，0，0；
- Location in：local；
- Orientation Dependency：User entered values；
- Orient using：Euler Angles；
- Euler Angles：0，0，0；
- 单击 OK，完成轴套._my_engine.bkl_rear_mount 的创建。

5.6 发动机变量参数

- 单击 Build > Parameter Variable > New 命令，弹出参数变量对话框如图 5-13 所示；

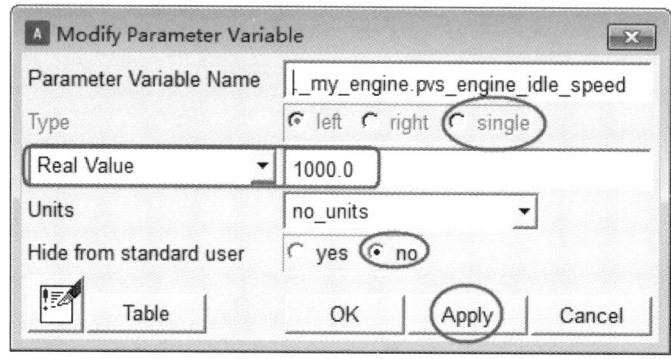

图 5-13 变量参数

- Parameter Variable Name: engine_idle_speed；
- Integer Value（实数值）：1 000；
- Units：no_units；
- Hide from standard user（是否从标准界面隐藏）：no；
- 单击 Apply，完成变量._my_engine.pvs_engine_idle_speed 的创建；
- Parameter Variable Name：：engine_rev_limit；
- Integer Value（实数值）：6 000；
- Units：no_units；
- Hide from standard user（是否从标准界面隐藏）：no；
- 单击 OK，完成变量._my_engine.pvs_engine_rev_limit 的创建。

5.7 曲轴动力元素

动力元素用来传递扭矩或者旋转运动，用以驱动传动系统，此功能可以在没有发动机和变速箱装配的整车工况下使用。
- 切换到 ADAMS/VIEW；

- 在部件 crankshaft 上添加参考点 MARKER_1，在部件 engine_block 上添加参考点 MARKER_2；
- 切换到 ADAMS/DRIVELINE；
- 单击 Driveline Components > Dyno > New 命令，弹出动力元素对话框如图 5-14 所示；

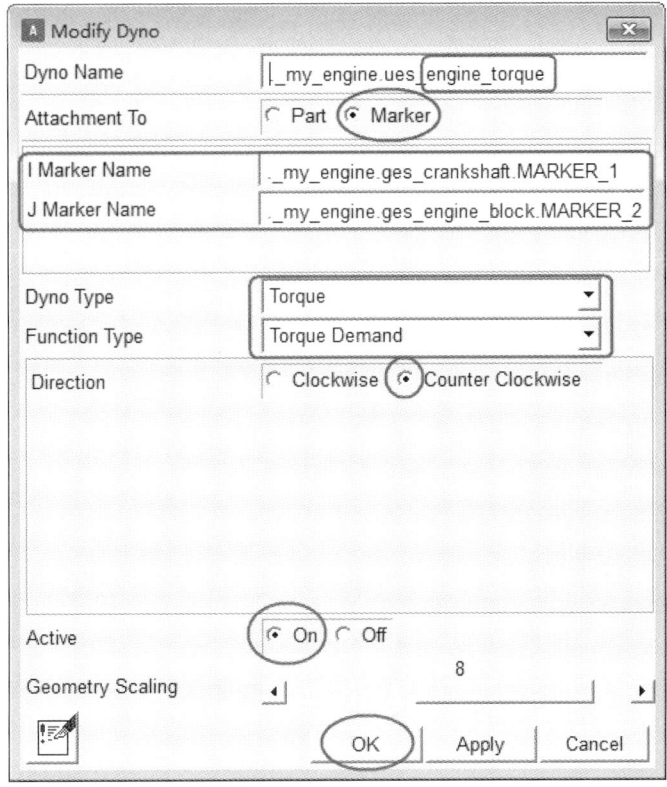

图 5-14 动力元素

- Dyno Name: engine_torque；
- Attachment To:勾选 Marker；
- I Marker Name: ._my_engine.ges_crankshaft.MARKER_1；
- J Marker Name: ._my_engine.ges_engine_block.MARKER_2；
- Dyno Type:Torque；
- Function Type: Torque Demand；
- Direction: Counter Clockwise；
- Active: On；
- 单击 OK，完成动力元素._my_engine.ues_engine_torque 创建。

5.8 发动机状态变量

- 切换到 Adams/view 界面，创建设计变量如图 5-15 所示；

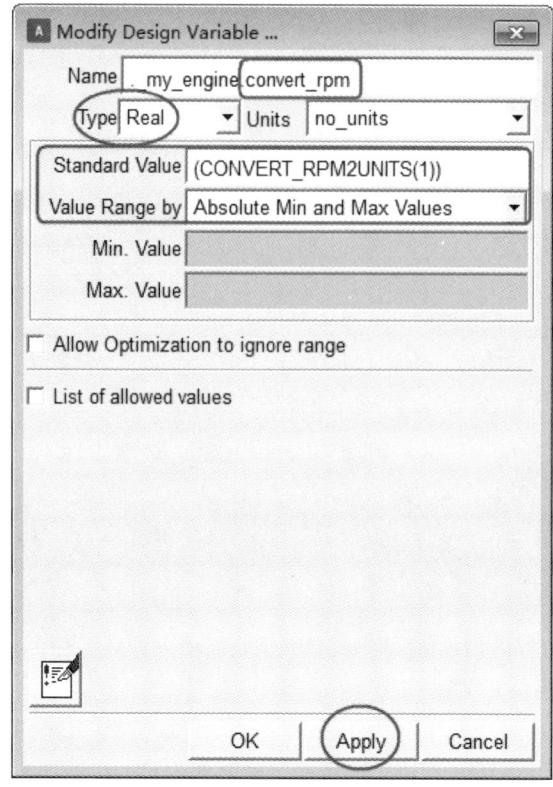

图 5-15 设计变量

- Name: convert_rpm；
- Type: Real;
- Units: no_units；
- Standard Value: (CONVERT_RPM2UNITS(1))；
- Value Range by: Absolute Min and Max Values；
- 单击 Apply，完成设计变量._my_engine.convert_rpm 创建；
- Name: conv_angle；
- Type: Real;
- Units: no_units；
- Standard Value: (CONVERT_FROM_UNITS("radian", 1))；
- Value Range by: Absolute Min and Max Values；
- 单击 OK，完成设计变量._my_engine.conv_angle 创建。

5.9 发动机系统单元

- 单击 Build >System Elements > State variable > New 命令，弹出创建状态变量对话框如图 5-16 所示；

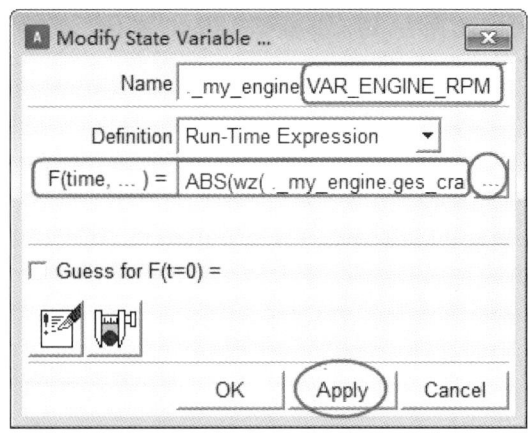

图 5-16 状态变量

- Name (状态变量名称): VAR_ENGINE_RPM;
- Definition: Run-Time Expression;
- F(time=0): ABS(wz(._my_engine.ges_crankshaft.jxs_joint_i_1,._my_engine.ges_engine_block.jxs_joint_j_1, ._my_engine.ges_engine_block.jxs_joint_j_1)*60/(2*PI));状态变量函数的创建如图 5-17 所示,函数中所需的参数通过数据库 Database Navigator 在对应的部件下寻找,状态变量编写完成后单击 Verify 判定函数的正确性,如果正确单击 OK 完成函数编写返回状态变量创建对话框;

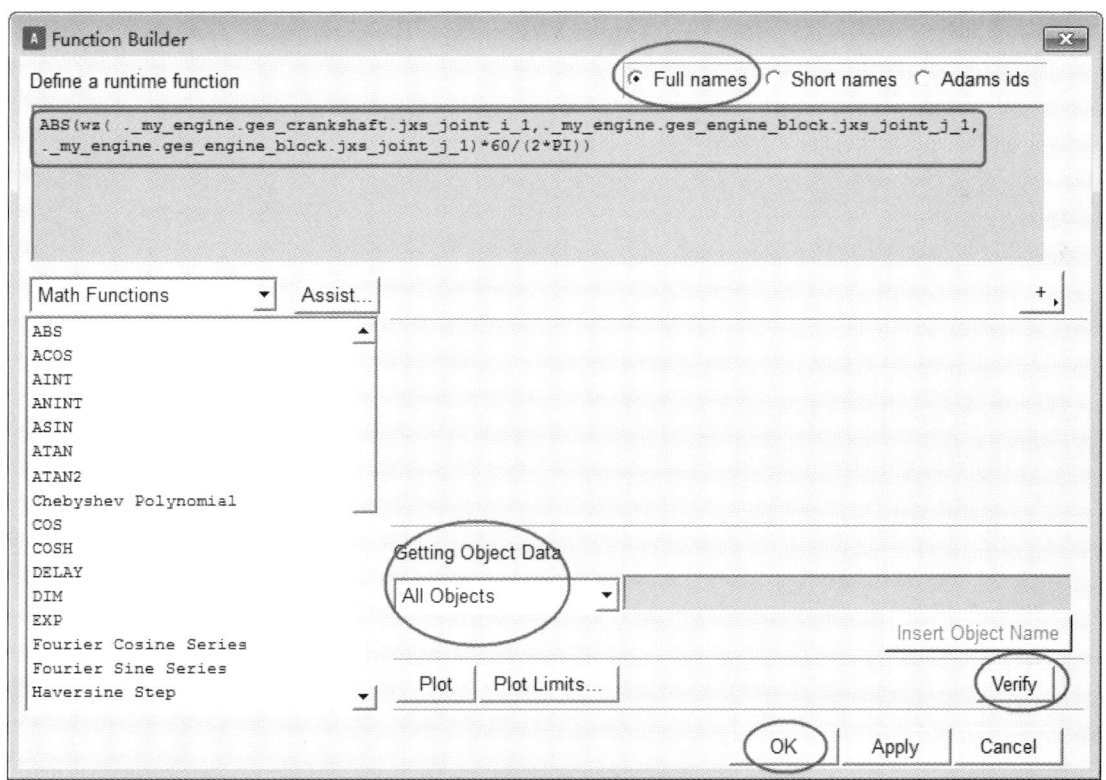

图 5-17 状态变量函数

- 单击 Apply，完成状态变量 ._my_engine.VAR_ENGINE_RPM 的创建；
- Name（状态变量名称）：VAR_ENGINE_OMEGA；
- Definition: Run-Time Expression；
- F(time=0)：VARVAL(._my_engine.VAR_ENGINE_RPM)*PI/30；
- 单击 Apply，完成状态变量 ._my_engine.VAR_ENGINE_OMEGA 的创建；
- Name（状态变量名称）：VAR_max_driving_torque；
- Definition: Run-Time Expression；
- F(time=0)：AKISPL(MAX(0,(._my_engine.convert_rpm)*VARVAL(._my_engine.ues_engine_torque.rpm_input)),1,._my_engine.ues_engine_torque.gss_spline)；
- 单击 Apply，完成状态变量 ._my_engine.VAR_max_driving_torque 的创建。
- Name（状态变量名称）：VAR_ENGINE_RPM_SSE；
- Definition: Run-Time Expression；
- F(time=0)：VARVAL(._my_engine.cis_transmission_output_omega_sse_adams_id)*._my_engine.cis_gear_ratio*30/PI；
- 单击 Apply，完成状态变量 ._my_engine.VAR_ENGINE_RPM_SSE 的创建；
- Name（状态变量名称）：VAR_max_braking_torque；
- Definition: Run-Time Expression；
- F(time=0)：AKISPL(MAX(0,(._my_engine.convert_rpm)*VARVAL(._my_engine.ues_engine_torque.rpm_input)),0,._my_engine.ues_engine_torque.gss_spline)；
- 单击 OK，完成状态变量 ._my_engine.VAR_max_braking_torque 的创建。

5.10 复合弹簧 Complex Spring

旋转弹簧主要用来模拟离合器摩擦片中弹簧及其滞后特性。
- 单击 Driveline Components > Complex（Torsional）Spring > New 命令，弹出旋转弹簧对话框如图 5-18 所示；
- Complex Spring Name（约束副名称）：flywheel_12；
- I Part：._my_engine.ges_crankshaft；
- J Part：._my_engine.ges_flywheel_2；
- Construction Frame：._my_engine.ground.cfs_flywheel1；
- Property File: mdids://adriveline_shared/complex_springs.tbl/mdi_0001.csp；
- RPM Solver Variable：._my_engine.VAR_ENGINE_RPM；
- Hysteresis Activity（滞后特性是否激活）：yes；
- 单击 OK，完成复合弹簧 ._my_engine.ues_flywheel_12 的创建。

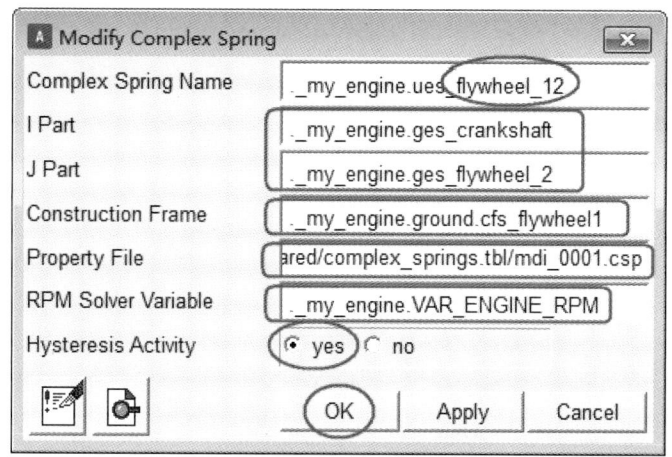

图 5-18 复合弹簧

旋转弹簧参数及信息如下:

$----------------------------------MDI_HEADER

[MDI_HEADER]

FILE_TYPE   = 'csp'

FILE_VERSION   = 4.0

FILE_FORMAT   = 'ASCII'

$--UNITS

[UNITS]

LENGTH = 'mm'

ANGLE = 'degree'

FORCE = 'newton'

MASS   = 'kg'

TIME   = 'second'

$--------------------------------SPRING_PARAMETERS

[SPRING_PARAMETERS]

TRANSITION_VELOCITY   = 1.000

DAMPING   = 10000

$----------------------------------LOADING_SPLINE

[LOADING_SPLINE]

(Z_DATA)

{rpm}

0.0

1000.0

4000.0

(XY_DATA)

x	y
−60	−400000 −400000 −400000
−50	−200000 −200000 −200000
−40	−150000 −150000 −150000
−30	−110000 −110000 −110000
−20	−70000 −70000 −70000
−10	−25000 −25000 −25000
0	0 0 0
10	50000 50000 50000
20	110000 110000 110000
30	180000 180000 180000
40	220000 220000 220000
50	300000 300000 300000
60	400000 400000 400000

$---UNLOADING_SPLINE

[UNLOADING_SPLINE]

(Z_DATA)

{rpm}

0.0

1000.0

4000.0

(XY_DATA)

x	y
−60	−400000 −400000 −400000
−50	−300000 −300000 −300000
−40	−220000 −220000 −220000
−30	−175000 −175000 −175000
−20	−115000 −115000 −115000
−10	−50000 −50000 −50000
0	0 0 0
10	30000 30000 30000
20	50000 50000 50000
30	100000 100000 100000
40	160000 160000 160000
50	200000 200000 200000
60	400000 400000 400000

5.11 发动机通信器

- 单击 Build > Communicator > Input >New 命令，弹出输出通信器对话框如图 5-19 所示；
- Input Communicator Name（输入通信器名称）：torque_demand；
- Matching Name(s)：torque_demand；
- Type：single；
- Entity：solver variable；
- From Minor Role：inherit；
- 单击 Apply，完成通信器._my_engine.cis_torque_demand 的创建；
- Input Communicator Name（输入通信器名称）：throttle_demand；
- Matching Name(s)：throttle_demand；
- Type：single；
- Entity：solver variable；
- From Minor Role：inherit；
- 单击 Apply，完成通信器._my_engine.cis_throttle_demand 的创建；

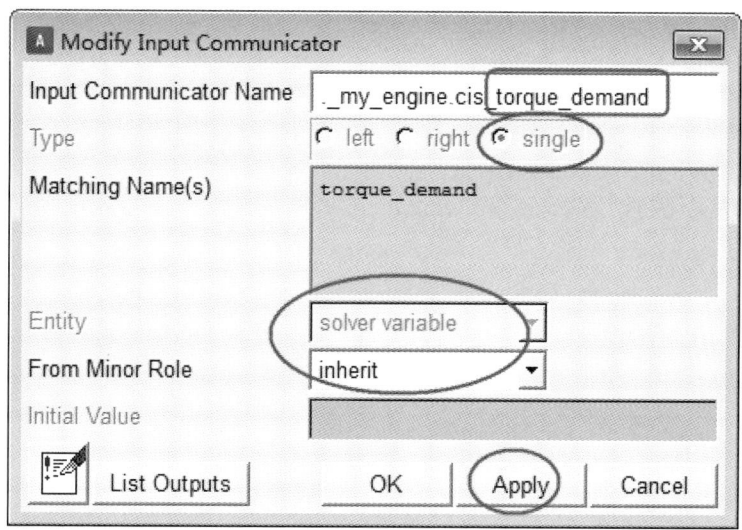

图 5-19 通信器

- Input Communicator Name（输入通信器名称）：gear_ratio；
- Matching Name(s)：gear_ratio；
- Type：single；
- Entity：parameter real；
- From Minor Role：inherit；
- Initial Value：1；
- 单击 Apply，完成通信器._my_engine.cis_gear_ratio 的创建；
- Input Communicator Name（输入通信器名称）：transmission_output_omega_sse；
- Matching Name(s)：transmission_output_omega_sse；

- Type：single；
- Entity：solver variable；
- From Minor Role：inherit；
- 单击 Apply，完成通信器._my_engine.cis_transmission_output_omega_sse 的创建；
- Input Communicator Name（输入通信器名称）：transmission_output_omega_sse_adams_id；
- Matching Name(s)：transmission_output_omega_sse_adams_id；
- Type：single；
- Entity：solver variable；
- From Minor Role：inherit；
- 单击 OK，完成通信器._my_engine.cis_transmission_output_omega_sse_adams_id 的创建。
- 单击 Build > Construction Frame > New 命令；
- Construction Frame（结构框名称）：flywheel1；
- Location Dependency：Delta location from coordinate；
- Coordinate Reference（参考坐标）：._my_engine.ground.cfs_crankshaft_reference；
- Location：0，0，10；
- Location in：local；
- Orientation Dependency：Delta location from coordinate；
- Coordinate Reference（参考坐标）：._my_engine.ground.cfs_crankshaft_reference；
- Orientation：0,0,0；
- 单击 Apply，完成._my_engine.ground.cfs_flywheel1 结构框的创建；
- Construction Frame（结构框名称）：engine_CM；
- Location Dependency：Delta location from coordinate；
- Coordinate Reference（参考坐标）：._my_engine.ground.hps_engine_CM；
- Location：0，0，0；
- Location in：local；
- Orientation Dependency：User entered values；
- Orient using：Euler Angles；
- Euler Angles：0,0,0；
- 单击 Apply，完成._my_engine.ground.cfs_engine_CM 结构框的创建。
- Construction Frame（结构框名称）：static_torque_loc；
- Location Dependency：Delta location from coordinate；
- Coordinate Reference（参考坐标）：._my_engine.ground.hps_static_torque_loc；
- Location：0，0，0；
- Location in：local；
- Orientation Dependency：User entered values；
- Orient using：Euler Angles；
- Euler Angles：0,0,0；
- 单击 OK，完成._my_engine.ground.cfs_static_torque_loc 结构框的创建。

- 单击 Build > Communicator > Output >New 命令，参考如图 5-19 所示；
- Output Communicator Name（输出通信器名称）：flywheel；
- Matching Name(s)：flywheel；
- Type：single；
- Entity：mount；
- To Minor Role：inherit；
- Part Name：._my_engine.ges_flywheel_2；
- 单击 Apply，完成通信器._my_engine.cos_flywheel 的创建；
- Output Communicator Name（输出通信器名称）：static_torque_marker；
- Matching Name(s)：static_torque_marker；
- Type：single；
- Entity：mark；
- To Minor Role：inherit；
- Construction Frame Name: ._my_engine.ground.cfs_static_torque_loc；
- Part Name：._my_engine.ges_engine_block；
- 单击 Apply，完成通信器._my_engine.cos_static_torque_marker 的创建；
- Output Communicator Name（输出通信器名称）：engine_map；
- Matching Name(s)：engine_map；
- Type：single；
- Entity：spline；
- To Minor Role：inherit；
- Spline Name:._my_engine.ues_engine_torque.gss_spline，此样条函数在数据 Database Navigator 中查找选取：

发动机扭曲样条数据信息如下。

Object Name : ._my_engine.ues_engine_torque.gss_spline

Object Type : Spline

Parent Type : ac_dyno

Adams ID : 0

Active : NO_OPINION

Units : NO UNITS

Endpoints : Linear Interpolation

Spline Points:

(X = 1.0, Y = 1.0)

(X = 2.0, Y = 2.0)

(X = 3.0, Y = 3.0)

(X = 4.0, Y = 4.0)

(X = 5.0, Y = 5.0)

- 单击 Apply，完成通信器._my_engine.cos_engine_map 的创建；
- Output Communicator Name（输出通信器名称）：engine_rpm；
- Matching Name(s)：engine_rpm；
- Type：single；
- Entity：solver variable；
- To Minor Role：inherit；
- Solver Variable Name：._my_engine.VAR_ENGINE_RPM；
- 单击 Apply，完成通信器._my_engine.cos_engine_rpm 的创建；
- Output Communicator Name（输出通信器名称）：engine_speed；
- Matching Name(s)：engine_speed；
- Type：single；
- Entity：solver variable；
- To Minor Role：inherit；
- Solver Variable Name：._my_engine.VAR_ENGINE_OMEGA；
- 单击 Apply，完成通信器._my_engine.cos_engine_speed 的创建；
- Output Communicator Name（输出通信器名称）：default_downshift_rpm；
- Matching Name(s)：min_engine_speed；
- Type：single；
- Entity：parameter real；
- To Minor Role：inherit；
- Parameter Variable Name：._my_engine.pvs_engine_idle_speed；
- 单击 Apply，完成通信器._my_engine.cos_default_downshift_rpm 的创建；
- Output Communicator Name（输出通信器名称）：engine_idle_rpm；
- Matching Name(s)：engine_idle_rpm；
- Type：single；
- Entity：parameter real；
- To Minor Role：inherit；
- Parameter Variable Name：._my_engine.pvs_engine_idle_speed；
- 单击 Apply，完成通信器._my_engine.pvs_engine_idle_speed 的创建；
- Output Communicator Name（输出通信器名称）：default_upshift_rpm；
- Matching Name(s)：max_engine_speed；
- Type：single；
- Entity：parameter real；
- To Minor Role：inherit；
- Parameter Variable Name：._my_engine.pvs_engine_rev_limit；
- 单击 Apply，完成通信器._my_engine.cos_default_upshift_rpm 的创建；
- Output Communicator Name（输出通信器名称）：engine_max_rpm；
- Matching Name(s)：engine_revlimit_rpm；
- Type：single；

- Entity：parameter real；
- To Minor Role：inherit；
- Parameter Variable Name：._my_engine.pvs_engine_rev_limit；
- 单击 Apply，完成通信器._my_engine.cos_engine_max_rpm 的创建；
- Output Communicator Name（输出通信器名称）：max_engine_braking_torque；
- Matching Name(s)：engine_maximum_braking_torque；
- Type：single；
- Entity：solver variable；
- To Minor Role：inherit；
- Solver Variable Name：._my_engine.VAR_max_braking_torque；
- 单击 Apply，完成通信器._my_engine.cos_max_engine_braking_torque 的创建；
- Output Communicator Name（输出通信器名称）：max_engine_driving_torque；
- Matching Name(s)：engine_maximum_driving_torque；
- Type：single；
- Entity：solver variable；
- To Minor Role：inherit；
- Solver Variable Name：._my_engine.VAR_max_driving_torque；
- 单击 Apply，完成通信器._my_engine.cos_max_engine_driving_torque 的创建；
- Output Communicator Name（输出通信器名称）：engine_rpm_sse；
- Matching Name(s)：engine_rpm_sse；
- Type：single；
- Entity：solver variable；
- To Minor Role：inherit；
- Solver Variable Name：._my_engine.VAR_ENGINE_RPM_SSE；
- 单击 Apply，完成通信器._my_engine.cos_engine_rpm_sse 的创建；
- 单击 File > Save As 命令，弹出保存模板对话框如图 5-20 所示；

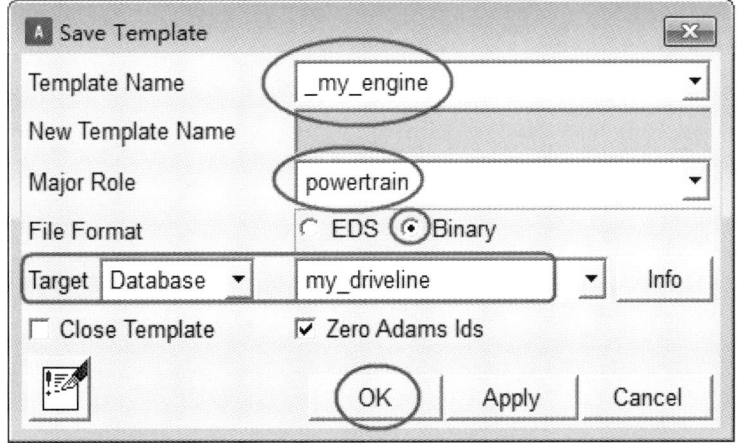

图 5-20　保存发动机模型

- Major Role(主特征)：powertrain；
- File Format：Binary；
- Target：Database，my_driveline；
- 单击 OK，完成发动机模板_my_engine.tpl 的保存。

5.12 速度保持仿真

5.12.1 发动机子系统

- 按 F9，把专家模板转换到标准模式，单击 File > New > Suspension 命令，弹出子系统对话框如图 5-21 所示；
- Subsystem Name(系统名称)：my_engine；
- Minor Role（副特征）:front（指发动机位于前轴）；
- Template Name（模板路径）：mdids://my_driveline/templates.tbl/_my_engine.tpl；
- 单击 OK，完成发动机子系统 my_engine 的创建。

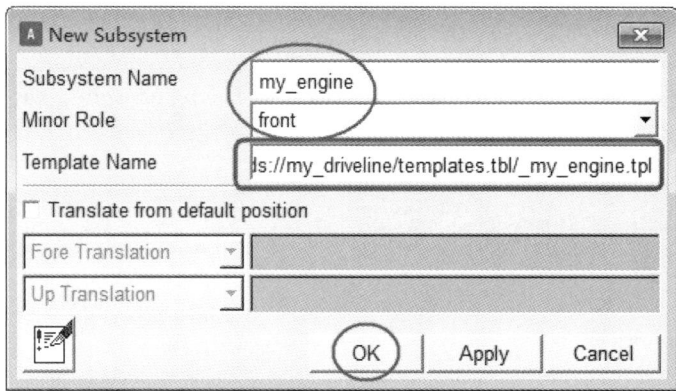

图 5-21 发动机子系统创建

5.12.2 发动机调试

- 单击 File > Open > Assembly 命令，如图 5-22 所示；

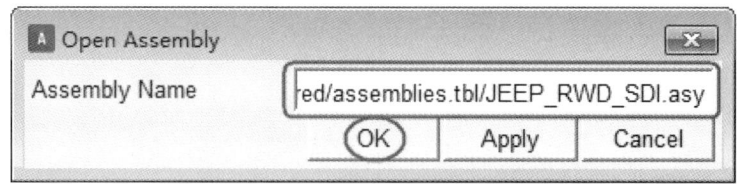

图 5-22 整车模型打开对话框

- Assembly Name：mdids://adriveline_shared/assemblies.tbl/JEEP_RWD_SDI.asy；
- 单击 OK，完成后轴驱动整车 JEEP_RWD_SDI 打开。

- 右击车身.JEEP_RWD_SDI.JEEP_body.ges_graph_ref > Hide，隐藏车身，此时整车模型如图 5-23 所示。

图 5-23　整车模型（共享数据库）

- 单击 File > Manage Assembly > Replace Subsystem 命令；
- Subsystem(S) to remove：勾选 engine_02，表明替换发动机 engine_02 子系统；
- Subsystem(S) toadd：mdids://my_driveline/subsystems.tbl/my_engine.sub，发动机子系统替换设置如图 5-24 所示；

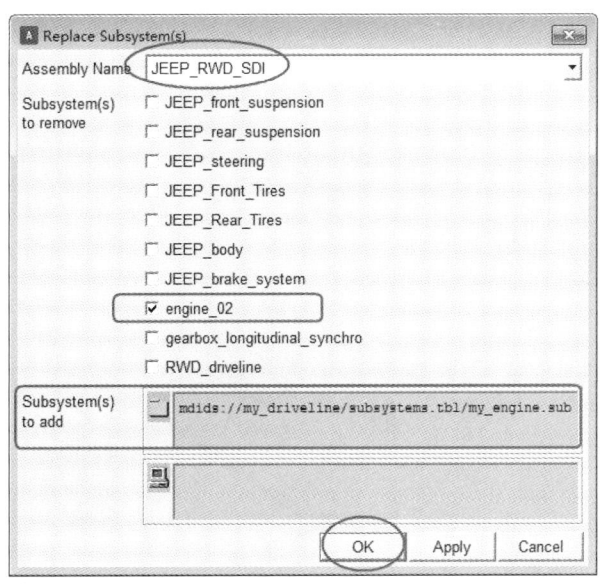

图 5-24　发动机子系统替换设置

- 单击 OK，完成发动机子系统 my_engine.sub 的替换。替换发动机子系统后的整车模型如图 5-25 所示，可以看出发动机与变速器并没有正确对接，因此需要对发动机的位置进移动。

图 5-25　整车模型（替换为自建发动机模型）

- 切换到整车装配体子系统，.my_JEEP.my_engine.ground.hps_engine_CM 硬点位置为 0,0,0；
- .my_JEEP.gearbox_longitudinal_synchro.ground.hps_gearbox_reference 硬点位置为 200.0, 0.0, 490.0；
- 通过对比两个系统的硬点位置，在 Z 轴上需要把发动机子系统向上移动 490 mm；
- 单击 Adjust > Shift 命令，弹出移动对话框如图 5-26 所示；
- Up Translation 对话框中输入 490；
- 单击 OK，完成发动机子系统 my_engine.sub 在 Z 方向上的平移，此时整车装配如图 5-27 所示，发动机子系统与变速器精准对接。

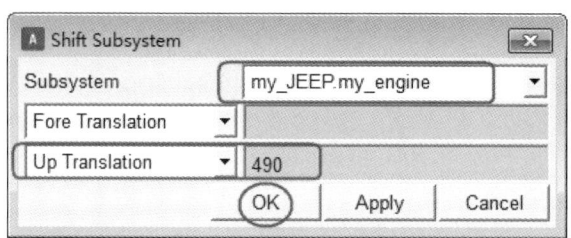

图 5-26　子系统移动设置

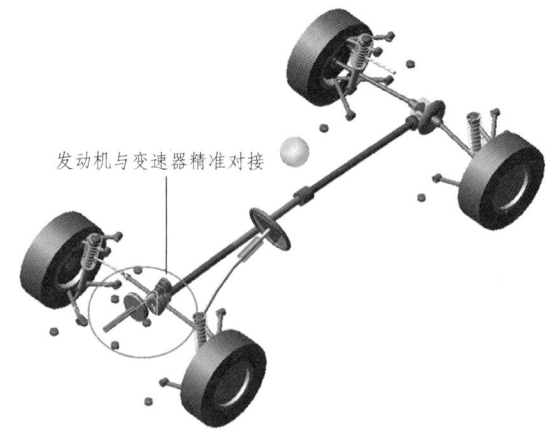

图 5-27　整车模型（发动机精准对接）

5.12.3 速度保持仿真设置

对整车进行直线速度保持（匀速直线）仿真，设置如下：
- 单击 Simulate > Full-Vehicle Analysis > Straight-line Events > Straight-line Maintain 命令；
- Output Prefix：SLM_1；
- End Time：10；
- Output Step Size（仿真步数）：1 000；
- Mode of Simulation：interactive；
- Road Date File：mdids://acar_shared/roads.tbl/2d_flat.rdf；
- Initial Velocity：20；
- Gear Position：1；
- Steering Input：locked；
- Quasi-Static Straight-Line Setup：勾选，整车模型包含发动机能运行准静态平衡；
- 单击 OK，完成速度保持仿真设置并提交运算，如图 5-28 所示。

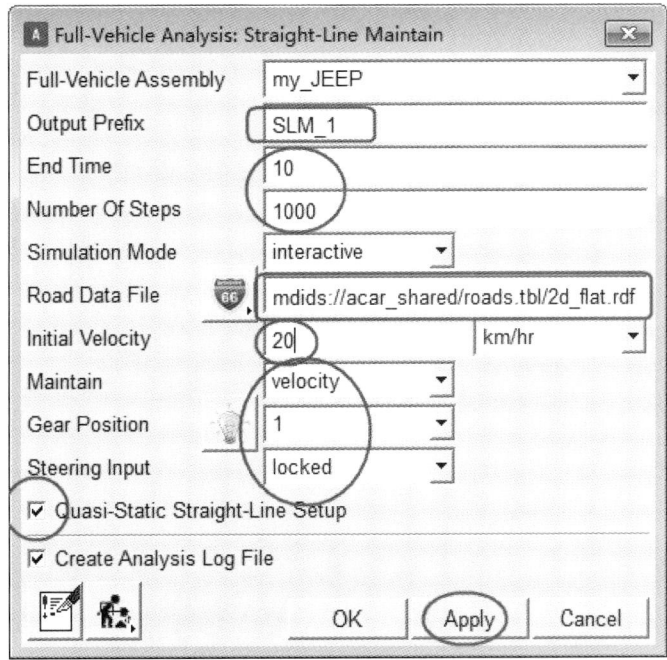

图 5-28　速度保持仿真

提交运算后命令窗口提示速度保持仿真并不能提交,经分析发现问题在于发动机子系统，发动机的动力元设置存在问题，命令窗口信息如下：

速度保持仿真命令窗口提示信息，下划线为发动机子系统存在的问题：
Reading in property files...
Reading of property files completed.
Setting up the vehicle assembly for Driving Machine maneuver...

> Transmission data spline only 2D, using fixed shift points.
> Setup of vehicle assembly completed.
> In Adams/Car SDI analyses, the active dyno (ues_engine_torque)
> is required to be setup as per below:
> *<u>Dyno type = Torque</u>*
> *<u>Function type = Throttle Demand</u>*
> *<u>Please change to the settings above.</u>*
> Hence, Quasi-Static Straight-Line Setup is not supported.
> Analysis is not submitted!

切换到整车装配下对应的子系统：.my_JEEP.my_engine；

右击动力元素：.my_JEEP.my_engine.ues_engine_torque > Modify，更改设置如图 5-29 所示：

- Dyno Type:Torque；
- Function Type: Throttle Demand；
- Engine Map：mdids://adriveline_shared/powertrains.tbl/V12_engine_map.pwr
- Direction: Counter Clockwise；
- Active: On；
- 单击 OK，完成动力元素._my_engine.ues_engine_torque 的修改。

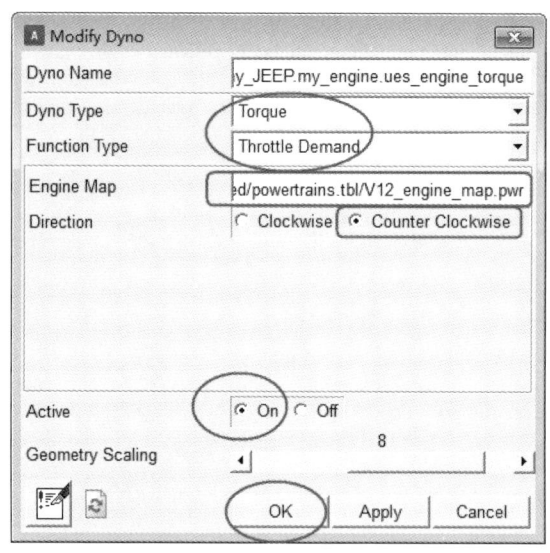

图 5-29　动力元素修改设置

V12_engine 发动机特性曲线图，此问题可以通过实验数据编写真实的发动机参数，此处为共享数据库中发动机模板数据：

$--MDI_HEADER
[MDI_HEADER]
FILE_TYPE   = 'pwr'

```
FILE_VERSION  =  1.0
FILE_FORMAT   =  'ASCII'
$------------------------------------------------UNITS
[UNITS]
(BASE)
{length    force     angle       mass      time}
'mm'       'newton'  'degrees'   'kg'      'sec'
(USER)
{unit_type   length    force    angle    mass    time    conversion}
'rpm'          0         0        1        0      -1        6.0
'torque'       1         1        0        0       0        1.0
$-----------------------ENGINE
```

%可以通过测功机获取发动机速度特性、负荷特性、万有特性数据替换以下数据

```
[ENGINE]
(Z_DATA)
{throttle}
0.0
1.00
(XY_DATA)
{engine_speed <rpm>    torque@throttle <torque>}
   0                 0                 0
 500             -20000             80000
1000             -42000            135000
1500             -44000            200000
2000             -46000            245000
2500             -48000            263000
3000             -50000            310000
3500             -50000            358000
4000             -50000            404000
4500             -50000            455000
5000             -50000            475000
5500             -50000            485000
6000             -50000            468000
6250             -50000            462000
6500             -52000            455000
6750             -56000            427000
7000             -60000            370000
7500             -64000            259000
```

修改完成后，速度保持仿真设置不变，重新提交，整车顺利完成仿真，切换到后处理模块，计算结果如图 5-30～图 5-38 所示。从计算结果中可以看出，在 1 s 之前，发动机与离合器接触的瞬间各参数的振动幅值都较大，随着时间的推移，各参数进入平稳工作状态。

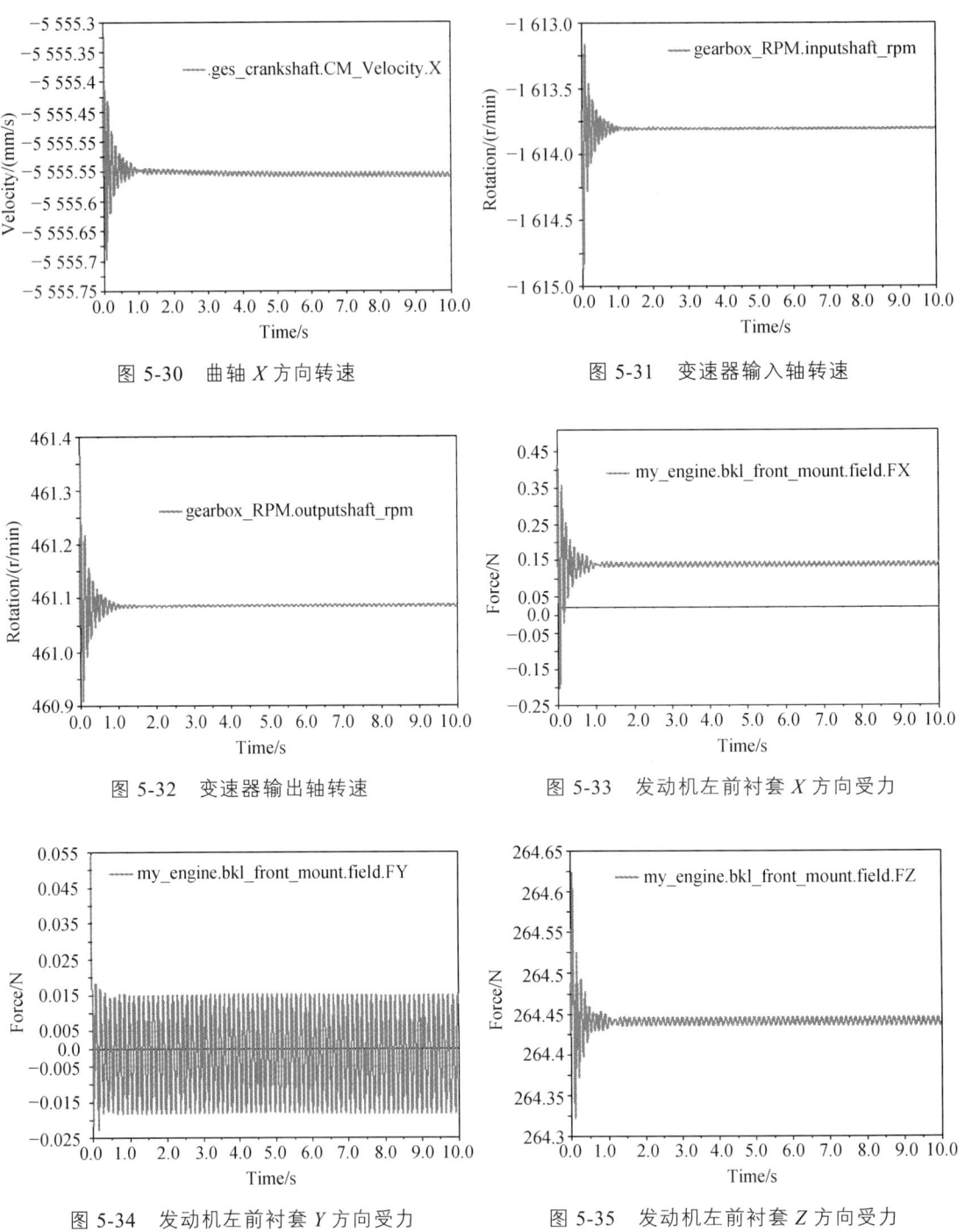

图 5-30　曲轴 X 方向转速

图 5-31　变速器输入轴转速

图 5-32　变速器输出轴转速

图 5-33　发动机左前衬套 X 方向受力

图 5-34　发动机左前衬套 Y 方向受力

图 5-35　发动机左前衬套 Z 方向受力

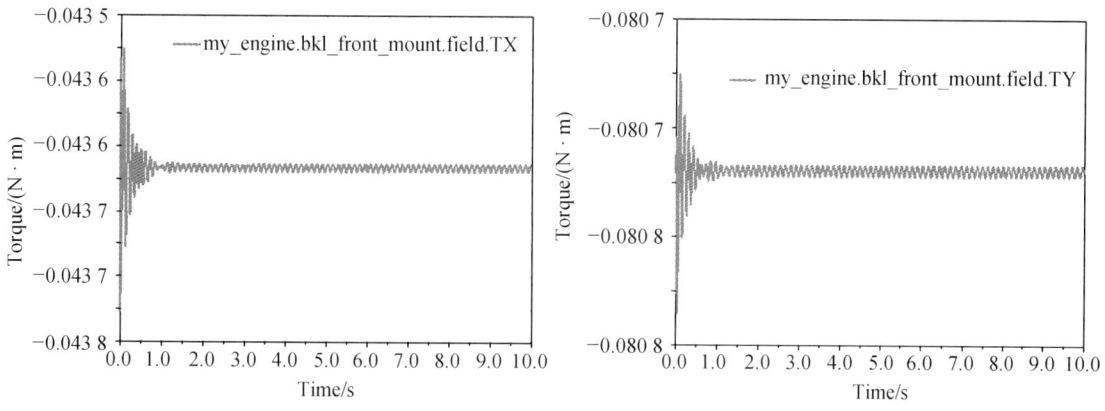

图 5-36 发动机左前衬套 X 方向扭矩　　图 5-37 发动机左前衬套 Y 方向扭矩

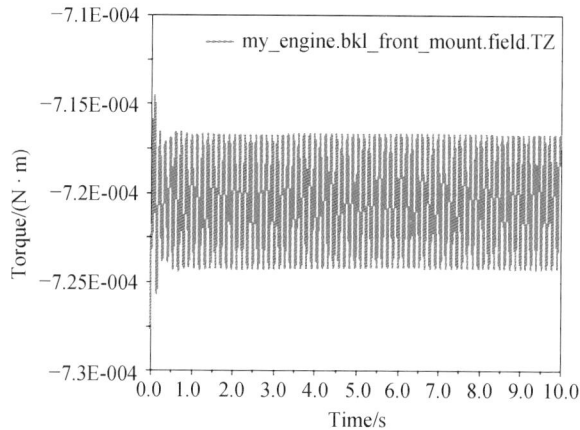

图 5-38 发动机左前衬套 Z 方向扭矩

第 6 章 变速器

变速器（见图 6-1）是用来改变来自发动机的转速和转矩的机构，它能固定或分挡改变输出轴和输入轴传动比，又称变速箱。变速器由变速传动机构和操纵机构组成，变速器的功用如下：① 改变传动比，以满足不同行驶条件对牵引力的需要，使发动机尽可能工作在有利的工况下，满足不同行驶速度要求，也可以在较大范围内改变汽车行驶速度的大小和汽车驱动轮上扭矩的大小；② 实现倒车行驶，用来满足汽车倒退行驶的需要；③ 中断动力传递，在发动机启动、怠速运转、汽车换挡或需要停车进行动力输出时，中断向驱动轮的动力传递；④ 实现空挡，当离合器接合时，变速箱可以不输出动力，例如，可以保证驾驶员在发动机不熄火时松开离合器踏板离开驾驶员座位。

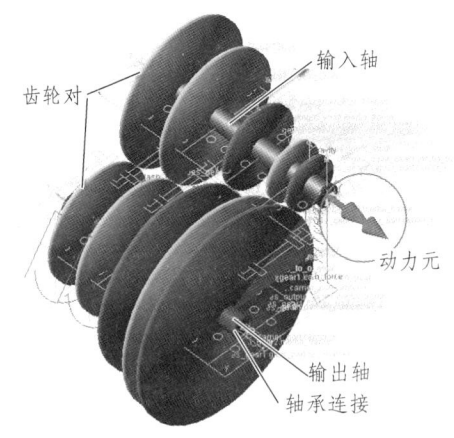

图 6-1 变速器模型（横向）

学习目标

- ◆ 横向变速器。
- ◆ 纵向变速器。
- ◆ 输入轴。
- ◆ 输出轴。
- ◆ 齿轮接触对。
- ◆ 轴承连接。
- ◆ 变速箱动力元。
- ◆ 同步器。

- 启动 ADAMS/DRIVERLINE；
- 单击 File > New 命令，弹出新建模板如图 6-2 所示；

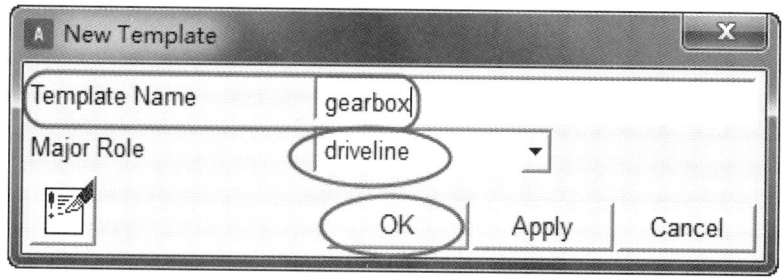

图 6-2 变速器模板

- Template Name：gearbox；
- Major Role：driveline；
- 单击 OK，完成变速器模板建立，进入建模界面。

6.1 变速器输入轴

- 单击 Build > Hardpoint > New 命令，弹出创建硬点对话框如图 6-3 所示；
- Hardpoint Name: input_shaft；
- Type：single；
- Location ：0，0，0；
- 单击 OK，完成 input_shaft 硬点的创建。

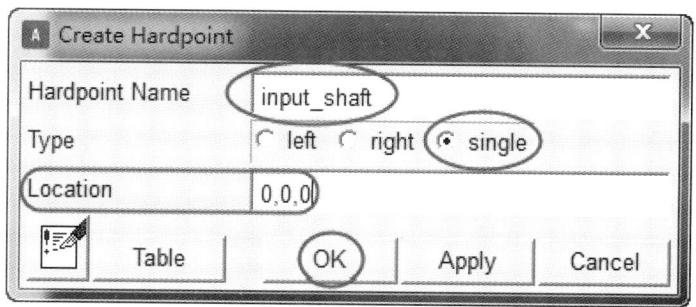

图 6-3 硬点创建——input_shaft

- 单击 Build > Construction Frame > New 命令，如图 6-4 所示；
- Construction Frame: input_shaft；
- Type: single；
- Location Dependency: Delta location from coordinate；

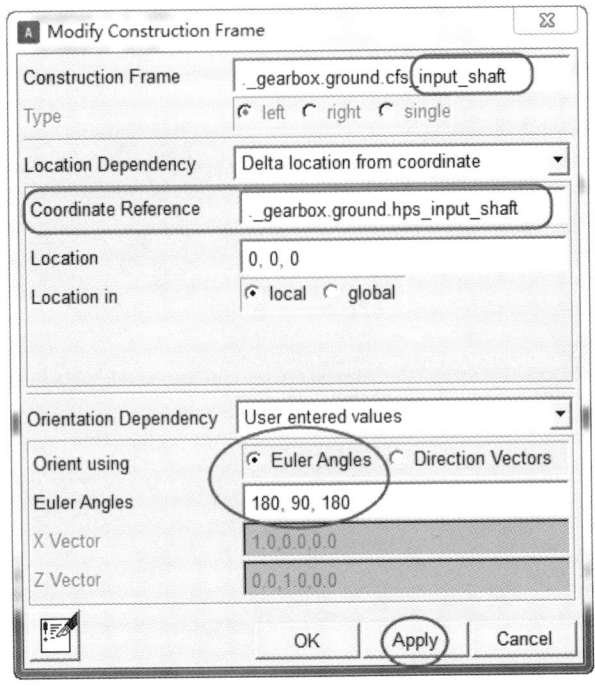

图 6-4 结构框——input_shaft

- Coordinate Reference: hps_input_shaft;
- Location: 0, 0, 0;
- Location in: local;
- Orientation Dependency: User entered values;
- Orient using: Euler Angles;
- Euler Angles: 0, -90, 0;
- 单击 Apply, 完成 ._gearbox.ground.cfs_input_shaft 结构框的创建;
- Construction Frame: input_shaft_end;
- Type: single;
- Location Dependency: Delta location from coordinate;
- Coordinate Reference: cfs_input_shaft;
- Location: 0, 0, 200;
- Location in: local;
- Orientation Dependency: Orient axis to point;
- Coordinate Reference: cfs_input_shaft;
- Axis: Z;
- 单击 OK, 完成._gearbox.ground.cfs_input_shaft_end 结构框的创建。
- 单击 Build > Part > General Part > Wizard 命令, 如图 6-5 所示;
- General Part Name: input_shaft;
- Type: single;
- Geometry Type: Link;

- Coordinate Reference # 1: cfs_input_shaft；
- Coordinate Reference # 2: cfs_input_shaft_end；
- Radius: 10；
- Color: dark gray；
- 单击 OK，完成部件._gearbox.ges_input_shaft 创建。

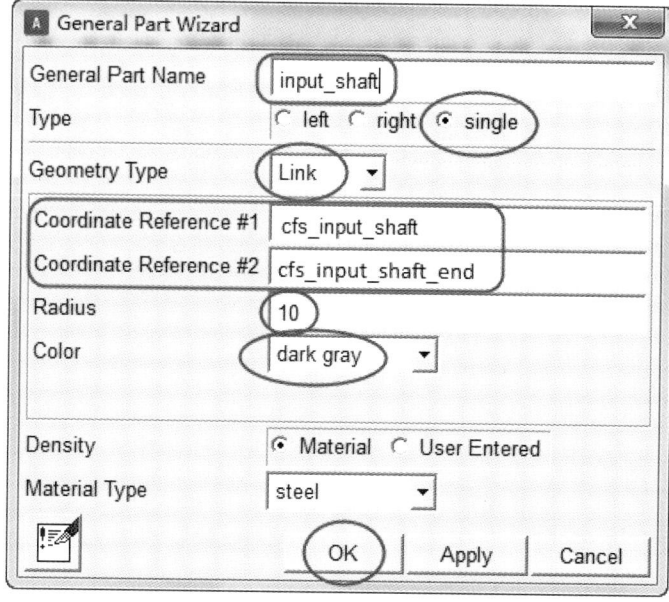

图 6-5　部件——input_shaft

6.2　变速器输出轴

- 单击 Build > Construction Frame > New 命令，参考如图 6-4 所示；
- Construction Frame: output_shaft；
- Type: single；
- Location Dependency: Delta location from coordinate；
- Coordinate Reference: cfs_input_shaft；
- Location: -100, 80, 0；
- Location in: local；
- Orientation Dependency: Delta orientation from coordinate；
- Construction Frame: cfs_input_shaft；
- Orientation: 0, 0, 0；
- 单击 Apply，完成._gearbox.ground.cfs_output_shaft 结构框的创建；
- Construction Frame: output_shaft_end；
- Type: single；
- Location Dependency: Delta location from coordinate；

- Coordinate Reference: cfs_output_shaft；
- Location: 0, 0, 200；
- Location in: local；
- Orientation Dependency: Delta orientation from coordinate；
- Construction Frame: cfs_output_shaft；
- Axis: Z；
- 单击 OK，完成._gearbox.ground.cfs_output_shaft 结构框的创建。
- 单击 Build > Part > General Part > Wizard 命令，参考如图 6-5 所示；
- General Part Name: output_shaft；
- Type: single；
- Geometry Type: Link；
- Coordinate Reference # 1: cfs_output_shaft；
- Coordinate Reference # 2: cfs_output_shaft_end；
- Radius: 10；
- Color: dark blue；
- 单击 OK，完成部件._gearbox.ges_output_shaft 创建。

6.3 变速器齿轮副

- 单击 Build > Construction Frame > New 命令，参考如图 6-4 所示；
- Construction Frame: input_gear1；
- Type: single；
- Location Dependency: Delta location from coordinate；
- Coordinate Reference: cfs_input_shaft；
- Location: 0, 0, 20；
- Location in: local；
- Orientation Dependency: Delta orientation from coordinate；
- Construction Frame: cfs_input_shaft；
- Orientation: 0, 0, 0；
- 单击 Apply，完成._gearbox.ground.cfs_input_gear1 结构框的创建；
- Construction Frame: input_gear2；
- Type: single；
- Location Dependency: Delta location from coordinate；
- Coordinate Reference: cfs_input_shaft；
- Location: 0, 0, 40；
- Location in: local；
- Orientation Dependency: Delta orientation from coordinate；
- Construction Frame: cfs_input_shaft；

- Orientation: 0, 0, 0；
- 单击 Apply，完成._gearbox.ground.cfs_input_gear2 结构框的创建；
- Construction Frame: input_gear3；
- Type: single；
- Location Dependency: Delta location from coordinate；
- Coordinate Reference: cfs_input_shaft；
- Location: 0, 0, 80；
- Location in: local；
- Orientation Dependency: Delta orientation from coordinate；
- Construction Frame: cfs_input_shaft；
- Orientation: 0, 0, 0；
- 单击 Apply，完成._gearbox.ground.cfs_input_gear3 结构框的创建；
- Construction Frame: input_gear4；
- Type: single；
- Location Dependency: Delta location from coordinate；
- Coordinate Reference: cfs_input_shaft；
- Location: 0, 0, 130；
- Location in: local；
- Orientation Dependency: Delta orientation from coordinate；
- Construction Frame: cfs_input_shaft；
- Orientation: 0, 0, 0；
- 单击 Apply，完成._gearbox.ground.cfs_input_gear4 结构框的创建；
- Construction Frame: input_gear5；
- Type: single；
- Location Dependency: Delta location from coordinate；
- Coordinate Reference: cfs_input_shaft；
- Location: 0, 0, 170；
- Location in: local；
- Orientation Dependency: Delta orientation from coordinate；
- Construction Frame: cfs_input_shaft；
- Orientation: 0, 0, 0；
- 单击 Apply，完成._gearbox.ground.cfs_input_gear5 结构框的创建；
- Construction Frame: output_gear1；
- Type: single；
- Location Dependency: Delta location from coordinate；
- Coordinate Reference: cfs_output_shaft；
- Location: 0, 0, 20；
- Location in: local；
- Orientation Dependency: Delta orientation from coordinate；

- Construction Frame: cfs_output_shaft；
- Orientation: 0, 0, 0；
- 单击 Apply，完成._gearbox.ground.cfs_output_gear1 结构框的创建；
- Construction Frame: output_gear2；
- Type: single；
- Location Dependency: Delta location from coordinate；
- Coordinate Reference: cfs_output_shaft；
- Location: 0, 0, 40；
- Location in: local；
- Orientation Dependency: Delta orientation from coordinate；
- Construction Frame: cfs_output_shaft；
- Orientation: 0, 0, 0；
- 单击 Apply，完成._gearbox.ground.cfs_output_gear2 结构框的创建；
- Construction Frame: output_gear3；
- Type: single；
- Location Dependency: Delta location from coordinate；
- Coordinate Reference: cfs_output_shaft；
- Location: 0, 0, 80；
- Location in: local；
- Orientation Dependency: Delta orientation from coordinate；
- Construction Frame: cfs_output_shaft；
- Orientation: 0, 0, 0；
- 单击 Apply，完成._gearbox.ground.cfs_output_gear3 结构框的创建；
- Construction Frame: output_gear4；
- Type: single；
- Location Dependency: Delta location from coordinate；
- Coordinate Reference: cfs_output_shaft；
- Location: 0, 0, 130；
- Location in: local；
- Orientation Dependency: Delta orientation from coordinate；
- Construction Frame: cfs_output_shaft；
- Orientation: 0, 0, 0；
- 单击 Apply，完成._gearbox.ground.cfs_output_gear4 结构框的创建；
- Construction Frame: output_gear5；
- Type: single；
- Location Dependency: Delta location from coordinate；
- Coordinate Reference: cfs_output_shaft；
- Location: 0, 0, 170；
- Location in: local；

- Orientation Dependency: Delta orientation from coordinate;
- Construction Frame: cfs_output_shaft;
- Orientation: 0, 0, 0;
- 单击 OK，完成._gearbox.ground.cfs_output_gear5 结构框的创建。
- 单击 Build > Part > General Part > Wizard 命令，如图 6-6 所示；

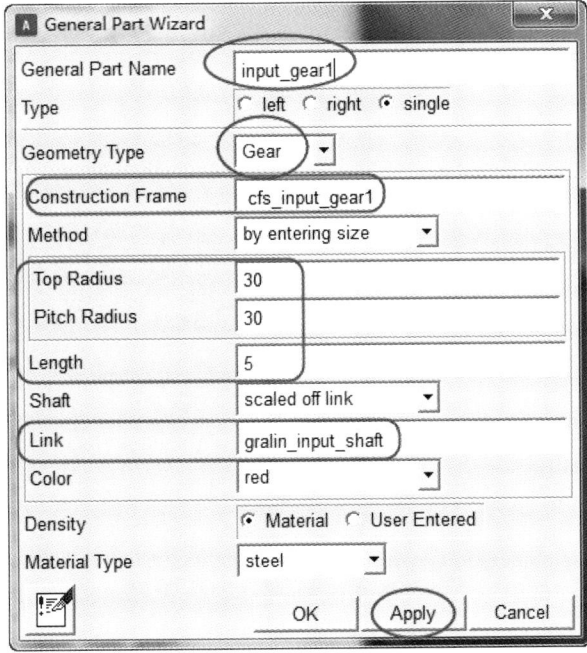

图 6-6 齿轮部件

- General Part Name: input_gear1;
- Type: single;
- Geometry Type: Gear;
- Construction Frame: cfs_input_gear1;
- Method: by entering size;
- Top Radius: 30;
- Pitch Radius: 30;
- Length: 5;
- Shaft: scaled off link;
- Link: gralin_input_shaft;
- Color: red;
- 单击 Appiy，完成部件._gearbox.ges_input_gear1 创建；
- General Part Name: input_gear2;
- Type: single;
- Geometry Type: Gear;
- Construction Frame: cfs_input_gear2;

- Method: by entering size;
- Top Radius: 30;
- Pitch Radius: 30;
- Length: 5;
- Shaft: scaled off link;
- Link: gralin_input_shaft;
- Color: green;
- 单击 Apply，完成部件._gearbox.ges_input_gear2 创建;
- General Part Name: input_gear3;
- Type: single;
- Geometry Type: Gear;
- Construction Frame: cfs_input_gear3;
- Method: by entering size;
- Top Radius: 30;
- Pitch Radius: 30;
- Length: 5;
- Shaft: scaled off link;
- Link: gralin_input_shaft;
- Color:magenta;
- 单击 Apply，完成部件._gearbox.ges_input_gear3 创建;
- General Part Name: input_gear4;
- Type: single;
- Geometry Type: Gear;
- Construction Frame: cfs_input_gear4;
- Method: by entering size;
- Top Radius: 30;
- Pitch Radius: 30;
- Length: 5;
- Shaft: scaled off link;
- Link: gralin_input_shaft;
- Color: cyan;
- 单击 Apply，完成部件._gearbox.ges_input_gear4 创建;
- General Part Name: input_gear5;
- Type: single;
- Geometry Type: Gear;
- Construction Frame: cfs_input_gear5;
- Method: by entering size;
- Top Radius: 30;
- Pitch Radius: 30;

- Length: 5;
- Shaft: scaled off link;
- Link: gralin_input_shaft;
- Color: skyblue;
- 单击 Apply，完成部件._gearbox.ges_input_gear5 创建;
- General Part Name: output_gear1;
- Type: single;
- Geometry Type: Gear;
- Construction Frame: cfs_output_gear1;
- Method: by entering size;
- Top Radius: 30;
- Pitch Radius: 30;
- Length: 5;
- Shaft: scaled off link;
- Link: gralin_ouput_shaft;
- Color: red;
- 单击 Apply，完成部件._gearbox.ges_ouput_gear1 创建;
- General Part Name: output_gear2;
- Type: single;
- Geometry Type: Gear;
- Construction Frame: cfs_output_gear2;
- Method: by entering size;
- Top Radius: 30;
- Pitch Radius: 30;
- Length: 5;
- Shaft: scaled off link;
- Link: gralin_ouput_shaft;
- Color: green;
- 单击 Apply，完成部件._gearbox.ges_ouput_gear2 创建;
- General Part Name: output_gear3;
- Type: single;
- Geometry Type: Gear;
- Construction Frame: cfs_output_gear3;
- Method: by entering size;
- Top Radius: 30;
- Pitch Radius: 30;
- Length: 5;
- Shaft: scaled off link;
- Link: gralin_ouput_shaft;

- Color: magenta；
- 单击 Apply，完成部件._gearbox.ges_ouput_gear3 创建；
- General Part Name: output_gear4；
- Type: single；
- Geometry Type: Gear；
- Construction Frame: cfs_output_gear4；
- Method: by entering size；
- Top Radius: 30；
- Pitch Radius: 30；
- Length: 5；
- Shaft: scaled off link；
- Link: gralin_ouput_shaft；
- Color: cyan；
- 单击 Apply，完成部件._gearbox.ges_ouput_gear4 创建；
- General Part Name: output_gear5；
- Type: single；
- Geometry Type: Gear；
- Construction Frame: cfs_output_gear5；
- Method: by entering size；
- Top Radius: 30；
- Pitch Radius: 30；
- Length: 5；
- Shaft: scaled off link；
- Link: gralin_ouput_shaft；
- Color: skyblue；
- 单击 OK，完成部件._gearbox.ges_ouput_gear5 创建。
- 单击 Driveline Components > Gear Pair > New 命令，如图 6-7 所示；
- Gear Pair Name: gear1；
- Input Shaft: ges_input_shaft；
- Output Shaft: ges_output_shaft；
- Input Reference Frame: cfs_input_gear1；
- Output Reference Frame: cfs_output_gear1；
- Gear Number: 1；
- Configuration: Input Gear to Shaft；
- Backlash: 0.0 deg；
- Contact Stiffness: 1e7；
- Contact Damping: 1e3；
- Sharpness Factor: 1e4；
- 勾选 Invert output direction from input direction: selected；

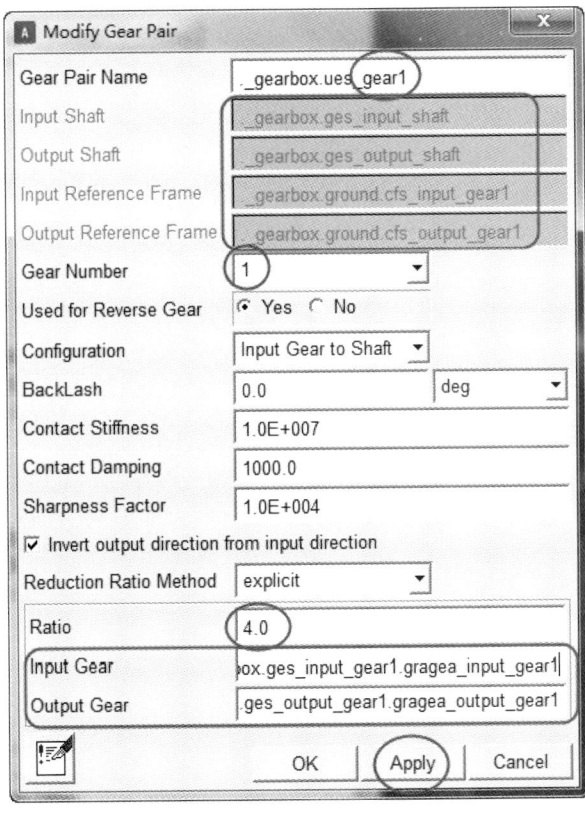

图 6-7 齿轮副

- Reduction Ratio Method: explicit；
- Ratio: 4；
- Input Gear: gragea_input_gear1；
- Output Gear: gragea_output_gear1；
- 单击 Apply，完成齿轮副._gearbox.ues_gear1 创建；
- Gear Pair Name: gear2；
- Input Shaft: ges_input_shaft；
- Output Shaft: ges_output_shaft；
- Input Reference Frame: cfs_input_gear2；
- Output Reference Frame: cfs_output_gear2；
- Gear Number: 2；
- Configuration: Input Gear to Shaft；
- Backlash: 0.0 deg；
- Contact Stiffness: 1e7；
- Contact Damping: 1e3；
- Sharpness Factor: 1e4；
- 勾选 Invert output direction from input direction: selected；
- Reduction Ratio Method: explicit；

- Ratio: 3.5；
- Input Gear: gragea_input_gear2；
- Output Gear: gragea_output_gear2；
- 单击 Apply，完成齿轮副._gearbox.ues_gear2 创建；
- Gear Pair Name: gear3；
- Input Shaft: ges_input_shaft；
- Output Shaft: ges_output_shaft；
- Input Reference Frame: cfs_input_gear3；
- Output Reference Frame: cfs_output_gear3；
- Gear Number:3；
- Configuration: Input Gear to Shaft；
- Backlash: 0.0 deg；
- Contact Stiffness: 1e7；
- Contact Damping: 1e3；
- Sharpness Factor: 1e4；
- 勾选 Invert output direction from input direction: selected；
- Reduction Ratio Method: explicit；
- Ratio: 2.2；
- Input Gear: gragea_input_gear3；
- Output Gear: gragea_output_gear3；
- 单击 Apply，完成齿轮副._gearbox.ues_gear3 创建；
- Gear Pair Name: gear4；
- Input Shaft: ges_input_shaft；
- Output Shaft: ges_output_shaft；
- Input Reference Frame: cfs_input_gear4；
- Output Reference Frame: cfs_output_gear4；
- Gear Number: 4；
- Configuration: Input Gear to Shaft；
- Backlash: 0.0 deg；
- Contact Stiffness: 1e7；
- Contact Damping: 1e3；
- Sharpness Factor: 1e4；
- 勾选 Invert output direction from input direction: selected；
- Reduction Ratio Method: explicit；
- Ratio: 1；
- Input Gear: gragea_input_gear4；
- Output Gear: gragea_output_gear4；
- 单击 Apply，完成齿轮副._gearbox.ues_gear4 创建；
- Gear Pair Name: gear5；

- Input Shaft: ges_input_shaft；
- Output Shaft: ges_output_shaft；
- Input Reference Frame: cfs_input_gear5；
- Output Reference Frame: cfs_output_gear5；
- Gear Number: 5；
- Configuration: Input Gear to Shaft；
- Backlash: 0.0 deg；
- Contact Stiffness: 1e7；
- Contact Damping: 1e3；
- Sharpness Factor: 1e4；
- 勾选 Invert output direction from input direction: selected；
- Reduction Ratio Method: explicit；
- Ratio: 0.8；
- Input Gear: gragea_input_gear5；
- Output Gear: gragea_output_gear5；
- 单击 OK，完成齿轮副._gearbox.ues_gear5 创建。

6.4 变速器轴承连接

- 单击 Driveline Components > Bearing > New 命令，如图 6-8 所示；
- Bearing Name:input_shaft_1；
- I Part:ges_input_shaft；
- J Part:._gearbox.ground；
- Type:single；
- Bearing Type:Axial_Radial；
- Contact Stiffness:1e7；
- Contact Damping:1e4；
- Sharpness Factor:1e4
- Axial Backlash:0.0；
- Radial Backlash:0.0；
- Diameter:20；
- Property File: mdids://adriveline_shared/bearings.tbl/mdi_0001.bea；
- Location:Delta location from coordinate；
- Coordinate Reference:cfs_input_shaft；
- Location:0, 0, 0；
- Location in:local；
- Orientation:Delta orientation from coordinate；
- Construction Frame:cfs_input_shaft；

图 6-8　轴承连接——input_shaft_1

- Orientation:0, 0, 0；
- 单击 Apply，完成轴承._gearbox.ues_input_shaft_1 的创建；

轴承特性参数信息：

$---MDI_HEADER

[MDI_HEADER]

FILE_TYPE   =   'bea'

FILE_VERSION   =   4.0

FILE_FORMAT   =   'ASCII'

$---UNITS

[UNITS]

LENGTH   =   'mm'

ANGLE   =   'degrees'

FORCE   =   'newton'

MASS   =   'kg'

TIME   =   'second'

$---BEARING_PARAMETERS

[BEARING_PARAMETERS]

G1   =   1000

```
   MU        =   10
   K_FACTOR  =   1
$------------------------------------------------------------BEARING_SPLINE
[BEARING_SPLINE]
{   x          y}
  -100.0    6.0E-02
  -50.0     6.0E-02
   0.0      6.0E-02
   50.0     6.0E-02
   100.0    6.0E-02
```

- Bearing Name:input_shaft_2;
- I Part:ges_input_shaft;
- J Part:._gearbox.ground;
- Type:single;
- Bearing Type:Axial_Radial;
- Contact Stiffness:1e7;
- Contact Damping:1e4;
- Sharpness Factor:1e4
- Axial Backlash:0.0;
- Radial Backlash:0.0;
- Diameter:20;
- Property File: mdids://adriveline_shared/bearings.tbl/mdi_0001.bea;
- Location:Delta location from coordinate;
- Coordinate Reference:cfs_input_shaft_end;
- Location:0, 0, 0;
- Location in:local;
- Orientation:Delta orientation from coordinate;
- Construction Frame:cfs_input_shaft_end;
- Orientation:0, 0, 0;
- 单击 Apply，完成轴承._gearbox.ues_input_shaft_2 的创建；
- Bearing Name:output_shaft_1;
- I Part:ges_output_shaft;
- J Part:._gearbox.ground;
- Type:single;
- Bearing Type:Axial_Radial;

- Contact Stiffness:1e7;
- Contact Damping:1e4;
- Sharpness Factor:1e4
- Axial Backlash:0.0;
- Radial Backlash:0.0;
- Diameter:20;
- Property File: mdids://adriveline_shared/bearings.tbl/mdi_0001.bea;
- Location:Delta location from coordinate;
- Coordinate Reference:cfs_output_shaft;
- Location:0, 0, 0;
- Location in:local;
- Orientation:Delta orientation from coordinate;
- Construction Frame:cfs_output_shaft;
- Orientation:0, 0, 0;
- 单击 Apply ，完成轴承._gearbox.ues_output_shaft_1 的创建;
- Bearing Name:output_shaft_2;
- I Part:ges_output_shaft;
- J Part:._gearbox.ground;
- Type:single;
- Bearing Type:Axial_Radial;
- Contact Stiffness:1e7;
- Contact Damping:1e4;
- Sharpness Factor:1e4
- Axial Backlash:0.0;
- Radial Backlash:0.0;
- Diameter:20;
- Property File: mdids://adriveline_shared/bearings.tbl/mdi_0001.bea;
- Location:Delta location from coordinate;
- Coordinate Reference:cfs_output_shaft_end;
- Location:0, 0, 0;
- Location in:local;
- Orientation:Delta orientation from coordinate;
- Construction Frame:cfs_output_shaft_end;
- Orientation:0, 0, 0;
- 单击 OK，完成轴承._gearbox.ues_output_shaft_2 的创建。

6.5 变速器动力元

- 单击 Driveline Components > Dyno > New 命令，弹出动力元对话框如图 6-9 所示；

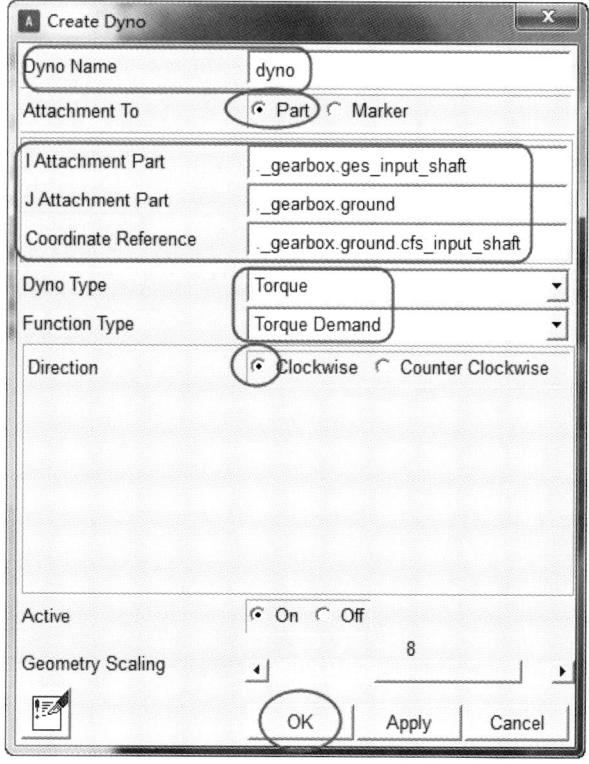

图 6-9 变速器动力元

- Dyno Name: dyno；
- Attachment To: Part；
- I Attachment Part: ges_input_shaft；
- I Attachment Part: ground；
- Coordinate Reference: cfs_input_shaft；
- Dyno Type: Torque；
- Function Type: Torque Demand；
- Direction: Clockwise；
- Active: On；
- Geometry Scaling: 8；
- 单击 OK，完成动力元._gearbox.ues_dyno 的创建，此时变速器模型如图 6-1 所示。
- 单击 File > Save As 命令，弹出保存模板对话框，如图 6-10 所示；
- Major Role（主特征）：driveline；；
- File Format：Binary；
- Target：Datebase/my_driveline

- 单击 OK，完成推杆式悬架模型模板_gearbox 的保存。

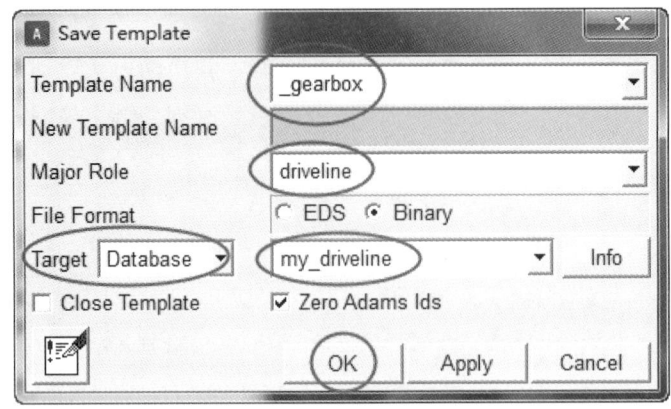

图 6-10　变速器保存

6.6　变速器测试

- 按 F9，专家模板转换到标准模式；
- 单击 File > New > Suspension 命令，弹出子系统对话框如图 6-11 所示；

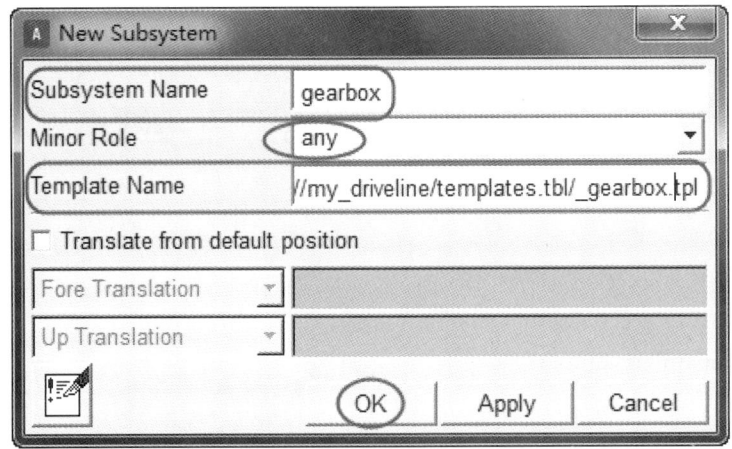

图 6-11　变速器子系统

- Subsystem Name(系统名称)：gearbox；
- Minor Role（副特征）：any；
- Template Name（模板路径）：mdids://my_driveline/templates.tbl/_gearbox.tpl；
- 单击 OK，完成子系统_gearbox 的创建。
- 单击 File > New > Bench Test Assembly 命令，如图 6-12 所示；
- Assembly Name: gearbox_tester；
- Subsystems: mdids://my_driveline/subsystems.tbl/gearbox.sub；
- 单击 OK，完成变速器测试平台建立。

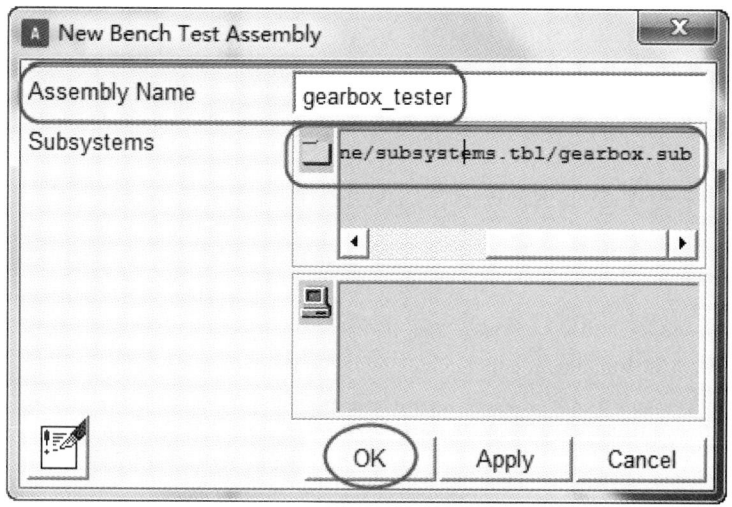

图 6-12 变速器测试平台

变速器平台创建过程信息如下。

Creating the full vehicle assembly: 'gearbox_tester'...
Opening the driveline subsystem: 'gearbox'...
Assembling subsystems...
Assigning communicators...
WARNING: The following input communicators were not assigned during assembly:
testrig.cis_steering_wheel_joint
testrig.cis_steering_rack_joint
testrig.cis_measure_for_distance
testrig.cil_steer_reference
testrig.cir_steer_reference
testrig.cis_chassis_path_reference
testrig.cis_body_subsystem (attached to ground)
testrig.cis_driver_reference
testrig.cis_engine_rpm
testrig.cil_front_suspension_mount (attached to ground)
testrig.cir_front_suspension_mount (attached to ground)
testrig.cil_rear_suspension_mount (attached to ground)
testrig.cir_rear_suspension_mount (attached to ground)
testrig.cil_tire_force_front
testrig.cir_tire_force_front
testrig.cil_tire_force_rear
testrig.cir_tire_force_rear
testrig.cis_body_cg
testrig.cis_static_torque_marker

```
Assignment of communicators completed.
Assembly of subsystems completed.
Full vehicle assembly ready.           %变速器测试平台创建成功
```

- Simulate > Full-Vehicle Analysis > Driveline Tests > Step Torque；
- Output Prefix: gearbox；
- End Time: 2；
- Number Of Steps: 400；
- Mode of Simulation: interactive；
- Road Data File: mdids://acar_shared/roads.tbl/2d_flat.rdf；
- Gear Position: 1；
- Initial Torque Value: 0；
- Final Torque Value: 1e4；
- Step Start Time: 0.5；
- Duration of Step: 1；
- Engine Dyno: gearbox.ues_dyno；
- 单击 OK，完成阶跃扭矩设置并提交计算，变速器各计算参数如图 6-13 ~ 图 6-18 所示。

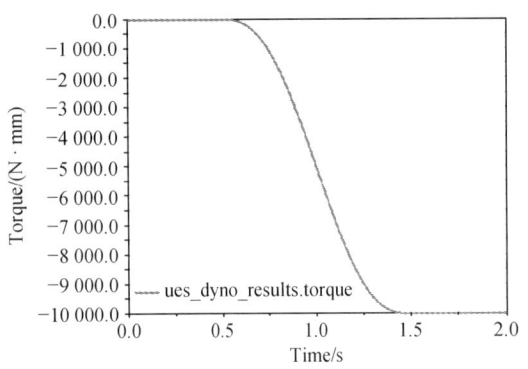

图 6-13 动力元输入扭矩

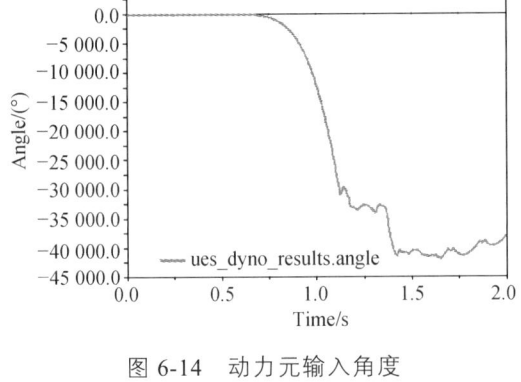

图 6-14 动力元输入角度

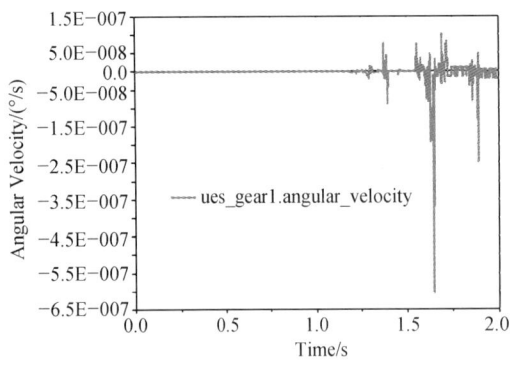

图 6-15 齿轮 1 输入角速度

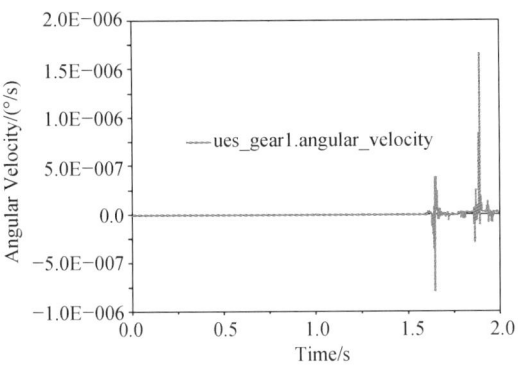

图 6-16 齿轮 1 输出角速度

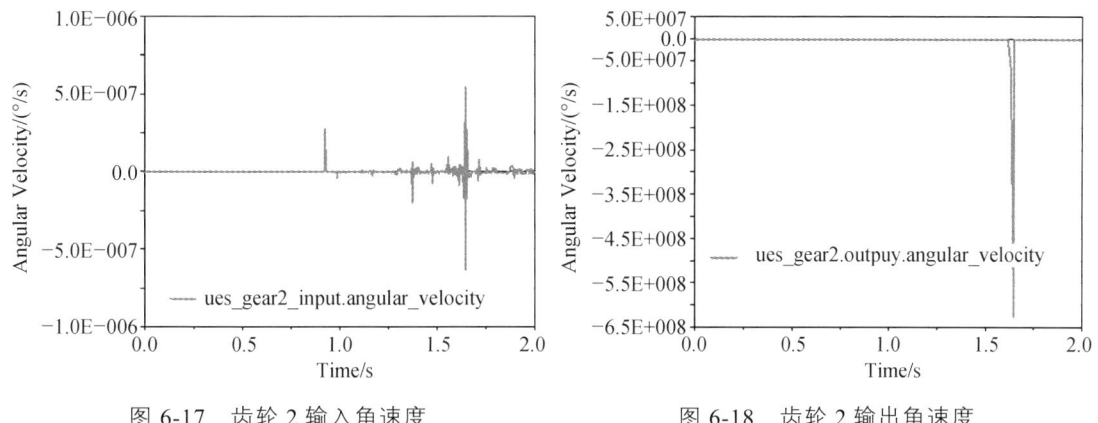

图 6-17 齿轮 2 输入角速度　　　　图 6-18 齿轮 2 输出角速度

6.7 纵向变速器

变速器在车辆上安装分为横置式和纵置式，横置式主要装在前置前轮驱动的车辆上，纵置式主要安装在后轮驱动或四轮驱动车辆上。纵置式变速器建模与横置式相似，此节在纵置变速器的基础上继续创建离合器飞轮等部件，创建好的纵置变速器可以与发动机传动轴对接，完成半车、整车及相关台架的仿真。建模过程可参考公版数据库中的变速器模型建立，建立模型的难点列举如下。

（1）速率样条曲线：._my_gearbox_longitudinal_synchro.gear_ratio_spline，如图 6-19 所示。

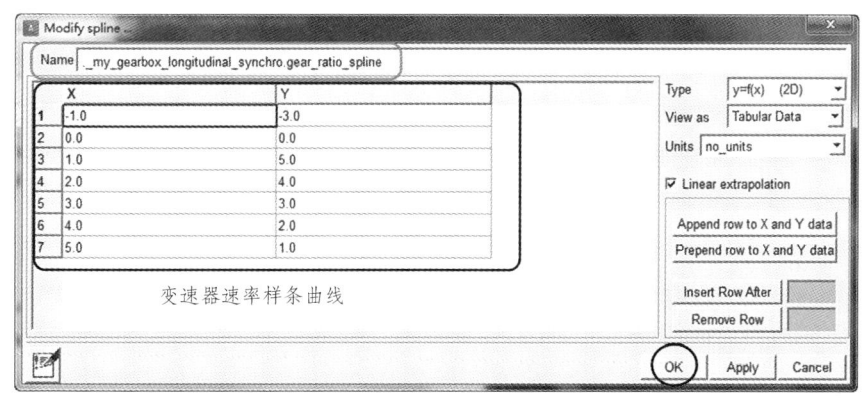

图 6-19 速率样条曲线

（2）解算器变量：._my_gearbox_longitudinal_synchro.VAR_transmission_input_omega，如图 6-20 所示。

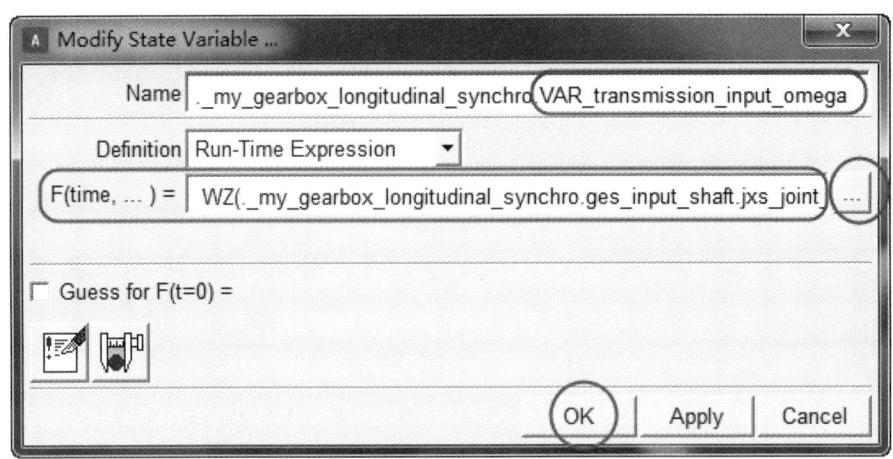

图 6-20 状态变量

状态变量函数：

WZ(._my_gearbox_longitudinal_synchro.ges_input_shaft.jxs_joint_i_1,._my_gearbox_longitudinal_synchro.mts_body.jxs_joint_j_1,._my_gearbox_longitudinal_synchro.mts_body.jxs_joint_j_1)。

（3）设计变量._my_gearbox_longitudinal_synchro.gear_ratio，如图 6-21 所示。

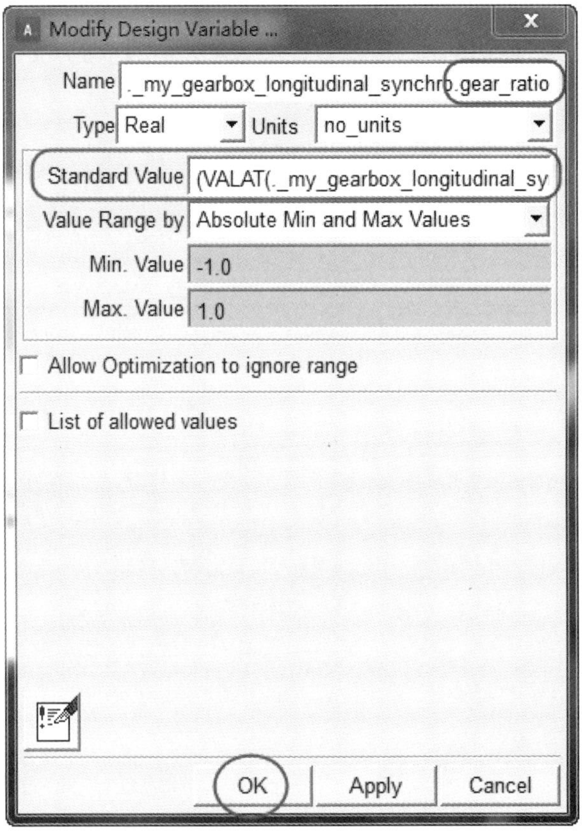

图 6-21 设计变量

设计变量标准值函数：

(VALAT(._my_gearbox_longitudinal_synchro.gear_ratio_spline.xs, ._my_gearbox_longitudinal_synchro.gear_ratio_spline.ys, ._my_gearbox_longitudinal_synchro.cis_transmission_demand.object_value.initial_condition))。

纵向变速器的建模过程不再详细叙述，此处给出纵向变速器子系统信息，读者可以参考信息模型建立变速器，建好的如图6-22所示，变速器模型存储在章节文件中。

图 6-22 纵置式变速器

```
    Info for subsystem:    my_gearbox_longitudinal_synchro    包含同步器的纵置式变速器信息

    File Name    :   <my_driveline>/subsystems.tbl/my_gearbox_longitudinal_synchro.sub
    Template     :   mdids://my_driveline/templates.tbl/_my_gearbox_longitudinal_synchro. tpl
    Comments     :   *no comments found*
    Major Role   :   driveline
    Minor Role   :   any

    HARDPOINTS:              %      硬点信息

    hardpoint name           symmetry          x_value        y_value        z_value
    --------------           --------          -------        -------        -------
    gearbox_reference        single            200.0          0.0            490.0


    PARTS:                          %      部件信息
```

friction_disk1

symmetry	:	single
mass	:	1.9037715316
sprung_percentage	:	100.0
location (dependent)	:	200.0, 0.0, 490.0
orientation (dependent)	:	zp_vector=1.0, 0.0, 0.0
	:	xp_vector=0.0, 0.0, −1.0
cm_location_from_part	:	0.0, 0.0, 4.0
Ixx, Iyy, Izz	:	4632.42419669 , 4632.42419669 , 9244.5414970432
Ixy, Izx, Iyz	:	0.0 , 0.0 , 0.0

friction_disk_hub_1

symmetry	:	single
mass	:	5.0E − 002
sprung_percentage	:	100.0
location (dependent)	:	200.0, 0.0, 490.0
orientation (dependent)	:	zp_vector=1.0, 0.0, 0.0
	:	xp_vector=0.0, 0.0, −1.0
cm_location_from_part	:	0.0, 0.0, 0.0
Ixx, Iyy, Izz	:	50.0 , 50.0 , 500.0
Ixy, Izx, Iyz	:	0.0 , 0.0 , 0.0

input_shaft

symmetry	:	single
mass	:	0.7139143243
sprung_percentage	:	100.0
location (dependent)	:	350.0, 0.0, 490.0
orientation (dependent)	:	zp_vector=1.0, 0.0, 0.0
: xp_vector=0.0, 0.0, -1.0		
cm_location_from_part	:	0.0, 0.0, 0.0
Ixx, Iyy, Izz	:	5371.6909478774 , 5371.6909478774 , 34.6670306139
Ixy, Izx, Iyz	:	0.0 , 0.0 , 0.0

input_shaft link geometry

name	:	input_shaft
symmetry	:	single
radius	:	10.0

inp_gear1
symmetry	:	single
mass	:	0.5851999155
sprung_percentage	:	100.0
location (dependent)	:	370.0, 0.0, 490.0
orientation (dependent)	:	zp_vector=1.0, 0.0, 0.0
	:	xp_vector=0.0, 0.0, −1.0
cm_location_from_part	:	0.0, 0.0, 0.0
Ixx, Iyy, Izz	:	383.3303356656 , 383.3303356656 , 756.9073394066
Ixy, Izx, Iyz	:	0.0 , 0.0 , 0.0

inp_gear2
symmetry	:	single
mass	:	0.5851999155
sprung_percentage	:	100.0
location (dependent)	:	400.0, 0.0, 490.0
orientation (dependent)	:	zp_vector=1.0, 0.0, 0.0
	:	xp_vector=0.0, 0.0, −1.0
cm_location_from_part	:	0.0, 0.0, 0.0
Ixx, Iyy, Izz	:	383.3303356656 , 383.3303356656 , 756.9073394066
Ixy, Izx, Iyz	:	0.0 , 0.0 , 0.0

inp_gear3
symmetry	:	single
mass	:	0.5851999155
sprung_percentage	:	100.0
location (dependent)	:	425.0, 0.0, 490.0
orientation (dependent)	:	zp_vector=1.0, 0.0, 0.0
	:	xp_vector=0.0, 0.0, −1.0
cm_location_from_part	:	0.0, 0.0, 0.0
Ixx, Iyy, Izz	:	383.3303356656 , 383.3303356656 , 756.9073394066
Ixy, Izx, Iyz	:	0.0 , 0.0 , 0.0

inp_gear4
symmetry	:	single
mass	:	0.5851999155
sprung_percentage	:	100.0
location (dependent)	:	460.0, 0.0, 490.0

orientation (dependent)	:	zp_vector=1.0, 0.0, 0.0
	:	xp_vector=0.0, 0.0, −1.0
cm_location_from_part	:	0.0, 0.0, 0.0
Ixx, Iyy, Izz	:	383.3303356656 , 383.3303356656 , 756.9073394066
Ixy, Izx, Iyz	:	0.0 , 0.0 , 0.0

inp_gear5

symmetry	:	single
mass	:	0.5851999155
sprung_percentage	:	100.0
location (dependent)	:	485.0, 0.0, 490.0
orientation (dependent)	:	zp_vector=1.0, 0.0, 0.0
	:	xp_vector=0.0, 0.0, −1.0
cm_location_from_part	:	0.0, 0.0, 0.0
Ixx, Iyy, Izz	:	383.3303356656 , 383.3303356656 , 756.9073394066
Ixy, Izx, Iyz	:	0.0 , 0.0 , 0.0

output_shaft

symmetry	:	single
mass	:	0.3569571622
sprung_percentage	:	100.0
location (dependent)	:	425.0, 0.0, 390.0
orientation (dependent)	:	zp_vector=1.0, 0.0, 0.0
	:	xp_vector=0.0, 0.0, −1.0
cm_location_from_part	:	0.0, 0.0, 0.0
Ixx, Iyy, Izz	:	677.9614367248 , 677.9614367248 , 17.333515307
Ixy, Izx, Iyz	:	0.0 , 0.0 , 0.0

output_shaft link geometry

name	:	output_shaft
symmetry	:	single
radius	:	10.0

out_gear1

symmetry	:	single
mass	:	0.5851999155
sprung_percentage	:	100.0
location (dependent)	:	370.0, 0.0, 390.0

orientation (dependent)	: zp_vector=1.0, 0.0, 0.0
	: xp_vector=0.0, 0.0, − 1.0
cm_location_from_part	: 0.0, 0.0, 0.0
Ixx, Iyy, Izz	: 383.3303356656 , 383.3303356656 , 756.9073394066
Ixy, Izx, Iyz	: 0.0 , 0.0 , 0.0

out_gear2
symmetry	: single
mass	: 0.5851999155
sprung_percentage	: 100.0
location (dependent)	: 400.0, 0.0, 390.0
orientation (dependent)	: zp_vector=1.0, 0.0, 0.0
	: xp_vector=0.0, 0.0, − 1.0
cm_location_from_part	: 0.0, 0.0, 0.0
Ixx, Iyy, Izz	: 383.3303356656 , 383.3303356656 , 756.9073394066
Ixy, Izx, Iyz	: 0.0 , 0.0 , 0.0

out_gear3
symmetry	: single
mass	: 0.5851999155
sprung_percentage	: 100.0
location (dependent)	: 425.0, 0.0, 390.0
orientation (dependent)	: zp_vector=1.0, 0.0, 0.0
	: xp_vector=0.0, 0.0, − 1.0
cm_location_from_part	: 0.0, 0.0, 0.0
Ixx, Iyy, Izz	: 383.3303356656 , 383.3303356656 , 756.9073394066
Ixy, Izx, Iyz	: 0.0 , 0.0 , 0.0

out_gear4
symmetry	: single
mass	: 0.5851999155
sprung_percentage	: 100.0
location (dependent)	: 460.0, 0.0, 390.0
orientation (dependent)	: zp_vector=1.0, 0.0, 0.0
	: xp_vector=0.0, 0.0, − 1.0
cm_location_from_part	: 0.0, 0.0, 0.0
Ixx, Iyy, Izz	: 383.3303356656 , 383.3303356656 , 756.9073394066
Ixy, Izx, Iyz	: 0.0 , 0.0 , 0.0

out_gear5
   symmetry : single
   mass : 0.5851999155
   sprung_percentage : 100.0
   location (dependent) : 485.0, 0.0, 390.0
   orientation (dependent) : zp_vector=1.0, 0.0, 0.0
   : xp_vector=0.0, 0.0, −1.0
   cm_location_from_part : 0.0, 0.0, 0.0
   Ixx, Iyy, Izz : 383.3303356656 , 383.3303356656 , 756.9073394066
   Ixy, Izx, Iyz : 0.0 , 0.0 , 0.0

pressure_plate
   symmetry : single
   mass : 2.3797144145
   sprung_percentage : 100.0
   location (dependent) : 209.0, 0.0, 490.0
   orientation (dependent) : zp_vector=1.0, 0.0, 0.0
   : xp_vector=0.0, 0.0, −1.0
   cm_location_from_part : 0.0, 0.0, 5.0
   Ixx, Iyy, Izz : 5797.669389106 , 5797.669389106 , 1.1555676871E+004
   Ixy, Izx, Iyz : 0.0 , 0.0 , 0.0

NSPRINGS: % 离合器弹簧信息
   clutch_spring
   definition : .ACAR.forces.ac_spring
   symmetry : single
   property file : mdids://adriveline_shared/springs.tbl/MDI_125_300.spr
   value type : 'preload'
   user value : 1000.0

USER_ENTITIES:
   flywheel_2_friction_disk1_1
   definition : .ADRIVELINE.forces.ac_clutch_force
   symmetry : single
   property file : mdids://adriveline_shared/clutch_forces.tbl/mdi_0001.clu
   mu static : 0.9
   mu dynamic : 0.7

```
    static velocity   :   1.0
    dynamic velocity :   2.0
    clearance         :   2.0
    effective radius :   100.0

friction_disk1_2_pressure_plate_1
    definition        :   .ADRIVELINE.forces.ac_clutch_force
    symmetry          :   single
    property file     :   mdids://adriveline_shared/clutch_forces.tbl/mdi_0001.clu
    mu static         :   0.9
    mu dynamic        :   0.7
    static velocity   :   1.0
    dynamic velocity :   2.0
    clearance         :   2.0
    effective radius :   100.0

friction_disk_torsion_spring_1
    definition        :   .ADRIVELINE.forces.ac_torsion_spring
    symmetry          :   single
    spring type       :   'linear'
    property file     :   mdids://adriveline_shared/complex_springs.tbl/mdi_0001.tsf
    stiffness         :   10000.0
    damping           :   10000.0
    hysteresis        :   0.0
    lock              :   'no'

gear1
definition            :   .ADRIVELINE.forces.ac_gear_pair
    symmetry          :   single
    gear number       :   1
    ratio             :   5.0
    backlash          :   0.0
    stiffness         :   1.00E+07
    damping           :   10000.0
    sharpness         :   10000.0
    i2shaft           :   1
    o2shaft           :   0
    invert input      :   1
```

  synchronizer active : 1

 gear2
  definition   : .ADRIVELINE.forces.ac_gear_pair
  symmetry   : single
  gear number   : 2
  ratio   : 4.0
  backlash   : 0.0
  stiffness   : 1.00E+07
  damping   : 10000.0
  sharpness   : 10000.0
  i2shaft   : 1
  o2shaft   : 0
  invert input   : 1
  synchronizer active : 1

 gear3
  definition   : .ADRIVELINE.forces.ac_gear_pair
  symmetry   : single
  gear number   : 3
  ratio   : 3.0
  backlash   : 0.0
  stiffness   : 1.00E+07
  damping   : 10000.0
  sharpness   : 10000.0
  i2shaft   : 1
  o2shaft   : 0
  invert input   : 1
  synchronizer active : 1

 gear4
  definition   : .ADRIVELINE.forces.ac_gear_pair
  symmetry   : single
  gear number   : 4
  ratio   : 2.0
  backlash   : 0.0
  stiffness   : 1.00E+07
  damping   : 10000.0

sharpness : 10000.0
i2shaft : 1
o2shaft : 0
invert input : 1
synchronizer active : 1

gear5
   definition : .ADRIVELINE.forces.ac_gear_pair
   symmetry : single
   gear number : 5
   ratio : 1.0
   backlash : 0.0
   stiffness : 1.00E+07
   damping : 10000.0
   sharpness : 10000.0
   i2shaft : 1
   o2shaft : 0
   invert input : 1
   synchronizer active : 1

sync1
   definition : .ADRIVELINE.forces.ac_synchronizer
   symmetry : single
   gear numbers explicit : 0
   friction ring : 1
   frictional torque max : 50000.0
   frictional torque max vlimit : 2.0
   frictional torque start time : 0.0
   frictional torque step time : 0.05
   dog clutch stiffness : 1.00E+06
   dog clutch damping : 1000.0
   dog clutch step time : 0.05
   dog clutch vlimit : 1.0
   geo length : 20.0
   geo radius : 40.0

sync2
   definition : .ADRIVELINE.forces.ac_synchronizer

symmetry	:	single
gear numbers explicit	:	0
friction ring	:	1
frictional torque max	:	50000.0
frictional torque max vlimit	:	2.0
frictional torque start time	:	0.0
frictional torque step time	:	0.05
dog clutch stiffness	:	1.00E+06
dog clutch damping	:	1000.0
dog clutch step time	:	0.05
dog clutch vlimit	:	1.0
geo length	:	20.0
geo radius	:	40.0

sync3

definition	:	.ADRIVELINE.forces.ac_synchronizer
symmetry	:	single
gear numbers explicit	:	0
friction ring	:	1
frictional torque max	:	50000.0
frictional torque max vlimit	:	2.0
frictional torque start time	:	0.0
frictional torque step time	:	0.05
dog clutch stiffness	:	1.00E+06
dog clutch damping	:	1000.0
dog clutch step time	:	0.05
dog clutch vlimit	:	1.0
geo length	:	20.0
geo radius	:	40.0

sync4

definition	:	.ADRIVELINE.forces.ac_synchronizer
symmetry	:	single
gear numbers explicit	:	0
friction ring	:	1
frictional torque max	:	50000.0
frictional torque max vlimit	:	2.0
frictional torque start time	:	0.0

```
    frictional torque step time       :   0.05
    dog clutch stiffness              :   1.00E+06
    dog clutch damping                :   1000.0
    dog clutch step time              :   0.05
    dog clutch vlimit                 :   1.0
    geo length                        :   20.0
    geo radius                        :   40.0

sync5
    definition                        :   .ADRIVELINE.forces.ac_synchronizer
    symmetry                          :   single
    gear numbers explicit             :   0
    friction ring                     :   1
    frictional torque max             :   50000.0
    frictional torque max vlimit      :   2.0
    frictional torque start time      :   0.0
    frictional torque step time       :   0.05
    dog clutch stiffness              :   1.00E+06
    dog clutch damping                :   1000.0
    dog clutch step time              :   0.05
    dog clutch vlimit                 :   1.0
    geo length                        :   20.0
    geo radius                        :   40.0

PARAMETERS:                    %   变量参数信息
parameter name              symmetry        type        value
--------------              --------        ----        -----
kinematic_flag              single          integer     0
deattaching_force           single          real        7500.0
max_gears                   single          integer     5
transmission_efficiency     single          real        1.0
```

6.8 半车台架仿真（传动轴与后悬架）

- 单击 File > Open > Assembly 命令，对话框如图 6-23 所示；

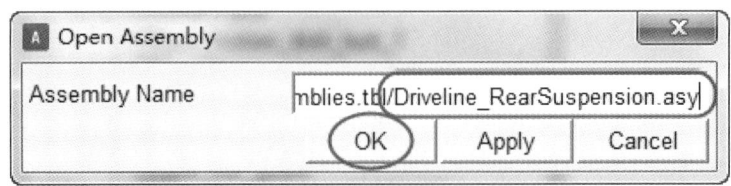

图 6-23 半车台架

- Assembly Name：mdids://adriveline_shared/assemblies.tbl/Driveline_RearSuspension.asy；
- 单击 OK，完成半车台架 Driveline_RearSuspension 打开。
- 单击 File > Manqge Assembly > Replace Subsystem 命令，如图 6-24 所示；
- Subsystem(S) to remove：勾选 gearbox_longitudinal；
- Subsystem(S) to add：mdids://my_driveline/subsystems.tbl/my_gearbox_longitudinal.sub；

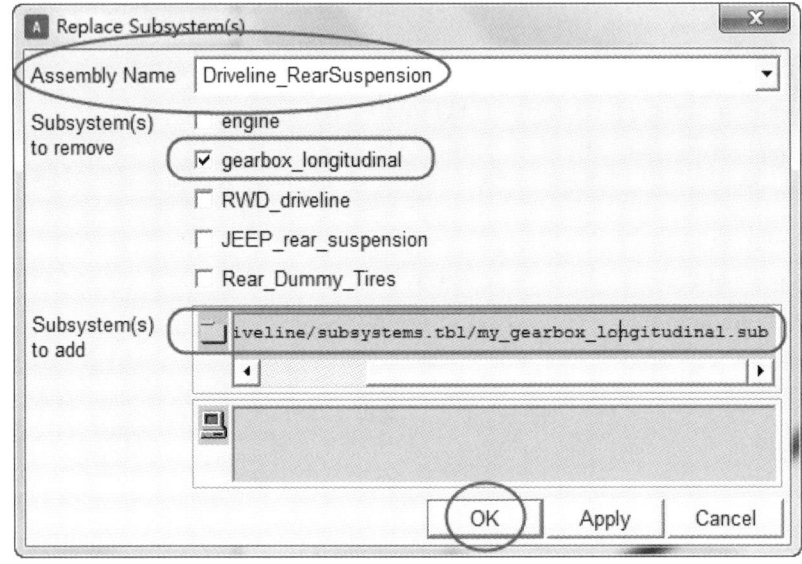

图 6-24 纵置式变速器子系统替换设置

- 单击 OK，完成变速器子系统 my_gearbox_longitudinal.sub 的替换，替换变速器子系统后的半车模型如图 6-25 所示。
- 单击 File > Save As > Assembly 命令；
- New Assembly Name：my_gearbox_longitudinal_synchro_test；
- 单击 OK，完成半车台架装配体的保存。
- 单击 Simulate > Full-Vehicle Analysis > Driveline Tests > Bench Test 命令，如图 6-26 所示；
- Assembly：my_gearbox_longitudinal_synchro_test；
- Output Prefix：BT；
- End Time：5；
- Number of Steps:500；
- Mode of Simulation：interactive；

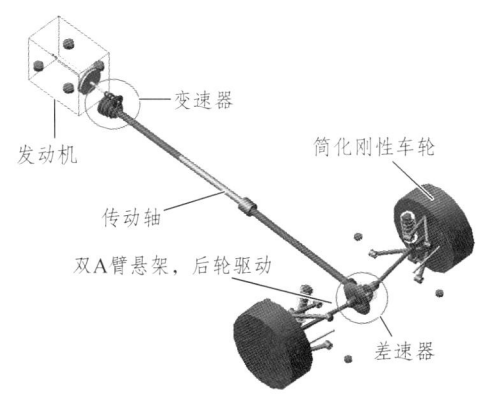

图 6-25 半车台架模型（已替换变速器）

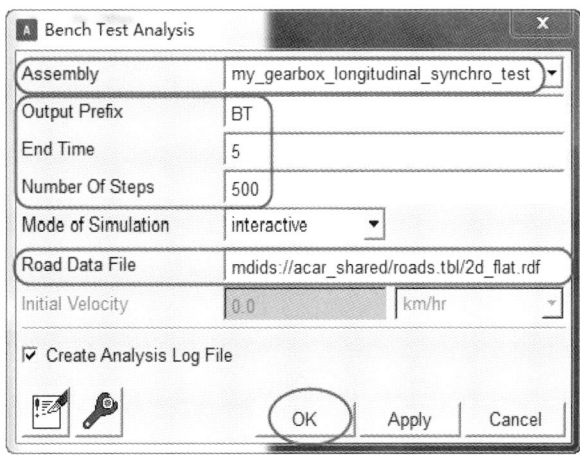

图 6-26 台架测试分析

- Road Date File：mdids://acar_shared/roads.tbl/2d_flat.rdf；
- 单击 OK，完成半车台架测试分析设置并提交计算，计算结果如图 6-27～图 6-34 所示。

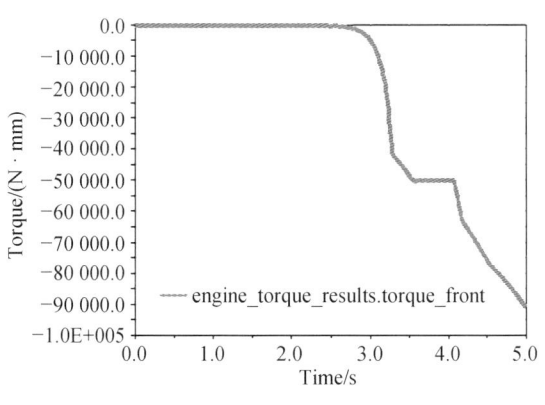

图 6-27 发动机扭矩输出

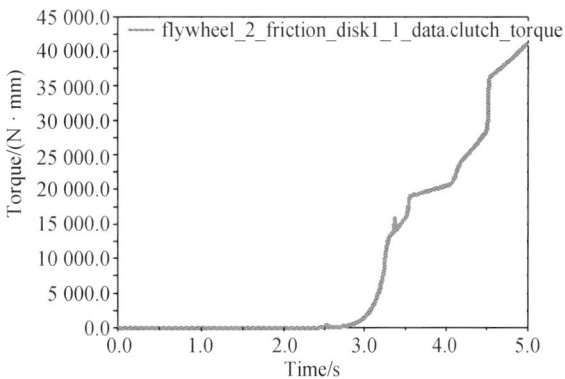

图 6-28 离合器摩擦盘扭矩

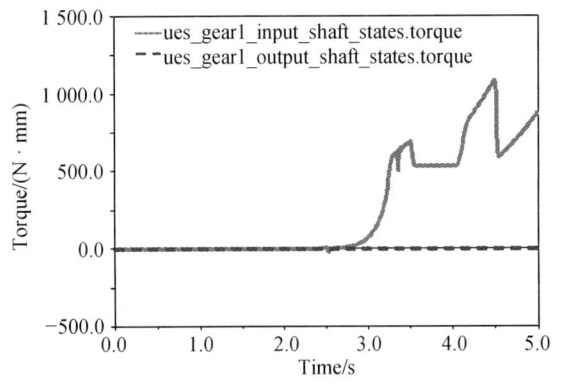

图 6-29 齿轮副 1 输入输出轴扭矩

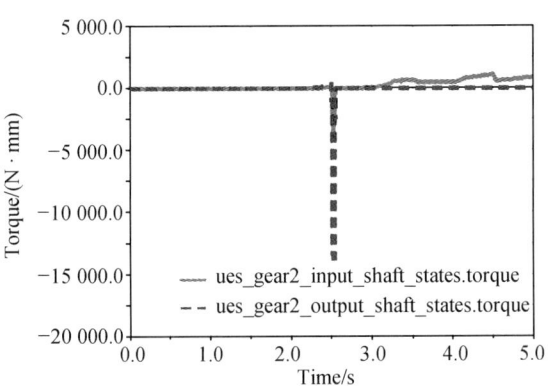

图 6-30 齿轮副 2 输入输出轴扭矩

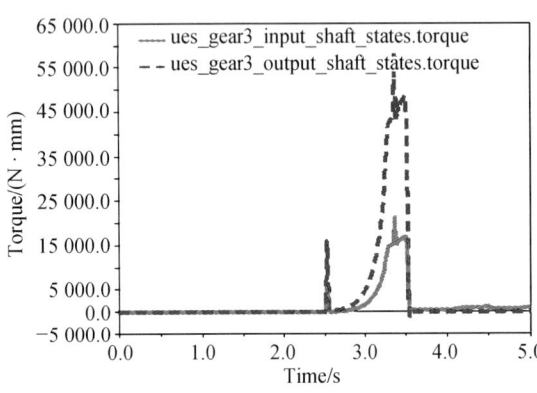

图 6-31 齿轮副 3 输入输出轴扭矩

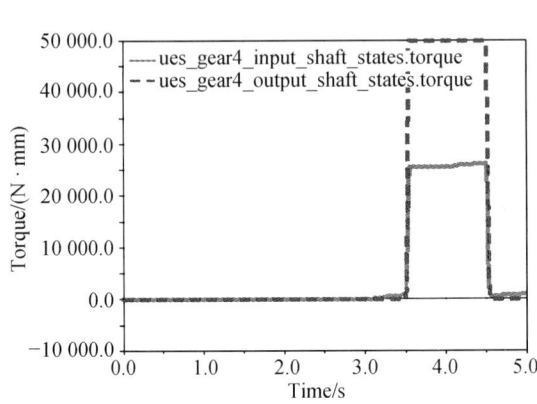

图 6-32 齿轮副 4 输入输出轴扭矩

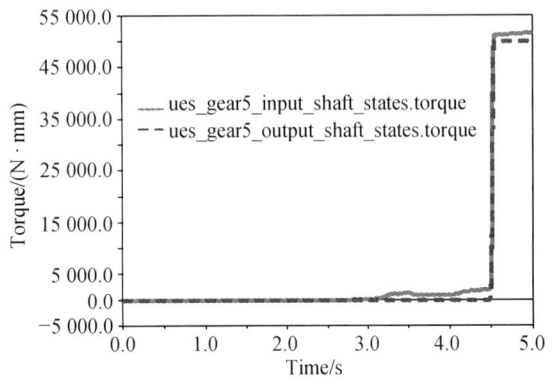

图 6-33 齿轮副 5 输入输出轴扭矩

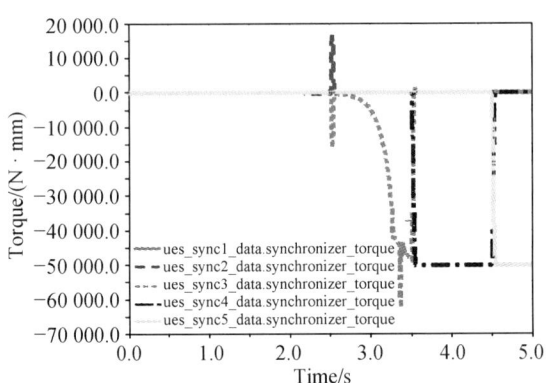

图 6-34 各同步器输出扭矩

第 7 章 传动轴

传动轴是汽车传动系统中传递动力的重要部件，传动轴与变速器、差速器共同作用将发动机输出的扭矩传递到车轮，驱动车辆行驶。如图 7-1 所示为四轮驱动系统的传动轴模型，包含前后差速器、中间传动轴及连接部件。删除前差速器及前半段传动轴，此时模型转换为后轮驱动系统。建模过程中，差速器可以逐个建立完成，亦可通过插件 ADAMS/DRIVERLINE 提供的差速器整体建模方法快速建立整体式前后差速器，这里推荐采用整体方法建立差速器、变速器及离合器模型。模型建立完成后，在前差速器上施加动力源，并建立测试平台仿真，测试传动轴模型的特性。

图 7-1 四轮驱动传动模型

学习目标

- ✧ 差速器。
- ✧ 限滑差速器。
- ✧ 前后传动轴。
- ✧ 连接器。
- ✧ 滑叉部件。
- ✧ 差速器动力元。

7.1 前轴差速器

(1) 前轴差速器参考硬点、结构框。

- 启动 ADAMS/DRIVERLINE；
- 单击 File > New 命令，弹出建模对话框如图 7-2 所示；

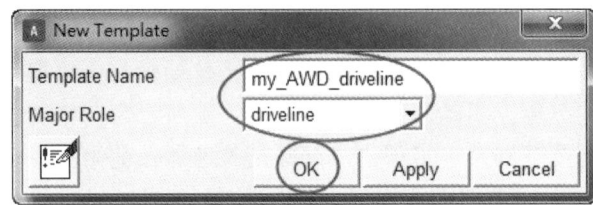

图 7-2 传动系统模板

- Template Name：my_AWD_driveline；
- Major Role：driveline；
- 单击 OK，完成驱动轴模板建立。
- 单击 Build > Hardpoint > New 命令，弹出创建硬点对话框如图 7-3 所示；

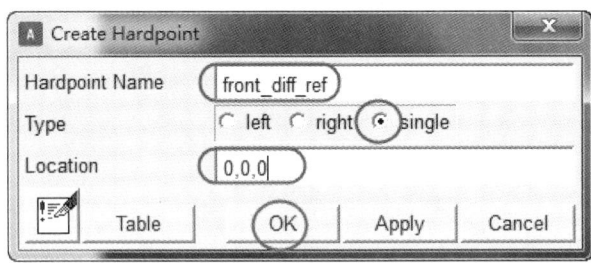

图 7-3 前差速器参考点

- Hardpoint Name：front_diff_ref；
- Type：single；
- Location：1 500，-200.0，225.0；
- 单击 OK，完成 ._my_AWD_driveline.ground.hps_front_diff_ref 硬点的创建。
- 单击 Build > Construction Frame > New 命令；
- Construction Frame（结构框名称）：front_diff_ref，如图 7-4 所示；
- Location Dependency：Delta location from coordinate；
- Coordinate Reference（参考坐标）：._my_AWD_driveline.ground.hps_front_diff_ref；
- Location：0，0，0；
- Location in：local；
- Orientation Dependency：User entered values；
- Orient using：Euler Angles；
- Euler Angles：0，90，0；

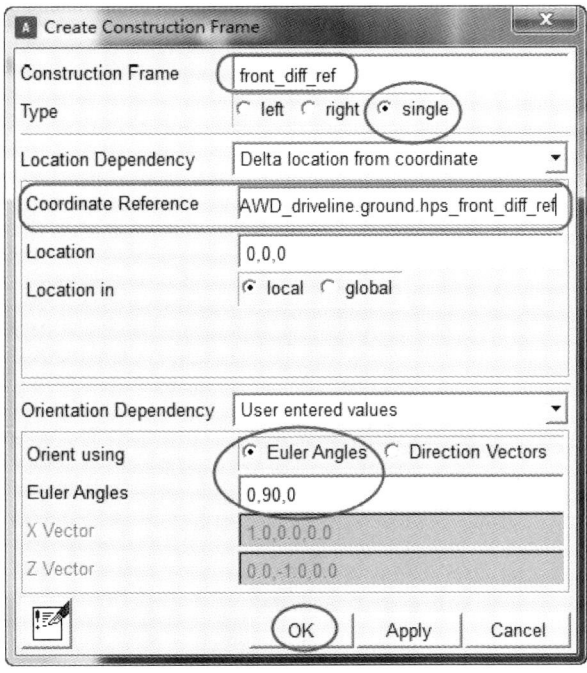

图 7-4 前差速器结构框——front_diff_ref

- 单击 OK，完成 ._my_AWD_driveline.ground.cfs_front_diff_ref 结构框的创建。

（2）前轴差速器整体部件。

- 单击 Driveline Components > COMPLEX COMPONENTS > Entire Differential Unit 命令，如图 7-5 所示；

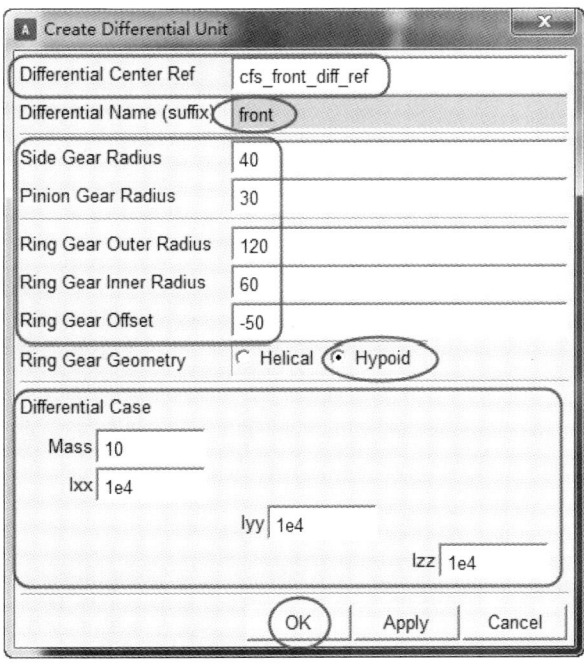

图 7-5 前差速器部件

- 177 -

- Differential Center Reference：Delta location from coordinate；
- Differential Name（变速器名称）：front；
- Side Gear Radius（行星齿轮左右两侧齿轮半径）：40；
- Pinion Gear Radius（行星齿轮前后两侧齿轮半径）：30；
- Ring Gear Outer Radius（从动齿轮外径）：120；
- Ring Gear Inner Radius（从动齿轮内径）：60；
- Ring Gear Offset（从动齿轮偏移量）：-50；
- Ring Gear Geometry（准双曲面齿轮）：Hypoid；
- Mass: 10；
- Ixx: 1e4；
- Iyy: 1e4；
- Izz: 1e4；
- 单击 OK，完成前差速器整体部件的创建，如图 7-6 所示。

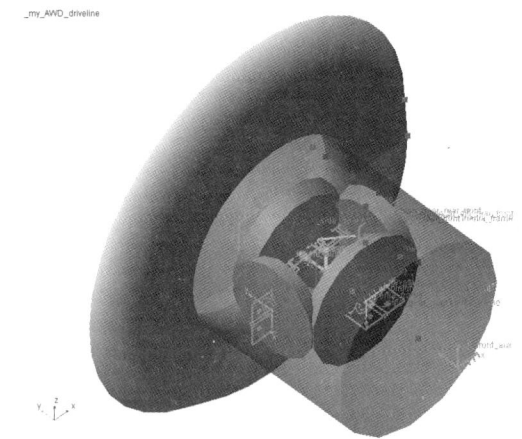

图 7-6　前差速器

7.2　限滑差速器

在前差速器上创建限滑差速器，限滑差速器行为是指通过感应左和右角速度差的扭矩定义，根据属性文件中指定的特性旋转并传递扭矩。

- 单击 Driveline Components > Limited Slip Differential > New 命令，如图 7-7 所示；
- Limited Slip Differential Name：front_lsd；
- First Gear Part: ._my_AWD_driveline.gel_side_gear_front；
- Second Gear Part: ._my_AWD_driveline.ger_side_gear_front；
- Differential Case Part: ._my_AWD_driveline.ger_side_gear_front；
- First Coordinate Reference: ._my_AWD_driveline.ground.cfl_side_gear_front；
- Second Coordinate Reference: ._my_AWD_driveline.ground.cfr_side_gear_front；

- Type：Viscous，黏性耦合，用属性文件确定黏性特性，黏性耦合由作用在两个部件之间的旋转力组成，该旋转力具有位置和方向，当相对角速度为零时，不传递转矩；
- Property File（黏性属性文件）：mdids://adriveline_shared/differentials.tbl/MDI_viscous.dif；
- 单击 OK，完成限滑差速器的创建。

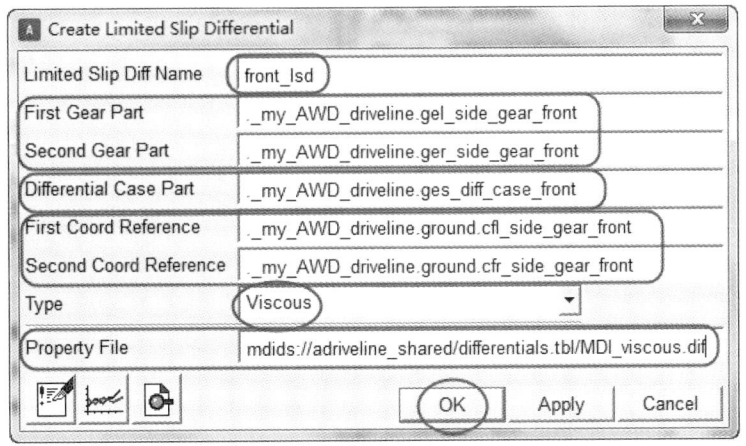

图 7-7　限滑差速器参数设置

```
限滑差速器黏性属性信息：
$-----------------------------------------------------------MDI_HEADER
[MDI_HEADER]
FILE_TYPE      =   'dif'
FILE_VERSION   =   4.0
FILE_FORMAT    =   'ASCII'
$-----------------------------------------------------------UNITS
[UNITS]
LENGTH   =   'mm'
ANGLE    =   'degrees'
FORCE    =   'newton'
MASS     =   'kg'
TIME     =   'second'
$-----------------------------------------------------------DIFFERENTIAL
[DIFFERENTIAL]
(XY_DATA)
{slip_speed        torque}
0.0                0.0
4.1666             868.0556
8.3333             3472.2222
12.5               7812.5
```

16.6667	13888.8889
20.8333	21701.3889
25.0	31250.0
29.1667	42534.7222
33.3333	55555.5556
37.5	70312.5
41.6667	86805.5556
45.8333	105034.7222
50.0	125000.0
54.1667	146701.3889
58.3333	170138.8889
62.5	195312.5
66.6667	222222.2222
70.8333	250868.0556
75.0	281250.0
79.1667	313368.0556
83.3333	347222.2222
87.5	382812.5
91.6667	420138.8889
95.8333	459201.3889
100.0	500000.0

7.3 传动轴

（1）传动轴应点。
- 单击 Build > Hardpoint > New 命令，弹出创建硬点对话框参考如图 7-3 所示；
- Hardpoint Name：propshaft_to_diffcase_front；
- Type：single；
- Location：120.0, 0.0, 0.0；
- 单击 Apply，完成._my_AWD_driveline.ground.hps_propshaft_to_diffcase_front 硬点的创建；
- Hardpoint Name：propshaft_intermediate；
- Type：single；
- Location：1 200.0, 0.0, －50.0；
- 单击 Apply，完成._my_AWD_driveline.ground.hps_propshaft_intermediate 硬点的创建；
- Hardpoint Name：propshaft_to_diffcase_rear；
- Type：single；

- Location：2 400.0, 0.0, -200.0；
- 单击 OK，完成._my_AWD_driveline.ground.hps_propshaft_to_diffcase_rear 硬点的创建。

（2）传动轴结构框。
- 单击 Build > Construction Frame > New 命令；
- Construction Frame（结构框名称）：mid_front_propshaft（见图 7-8）；

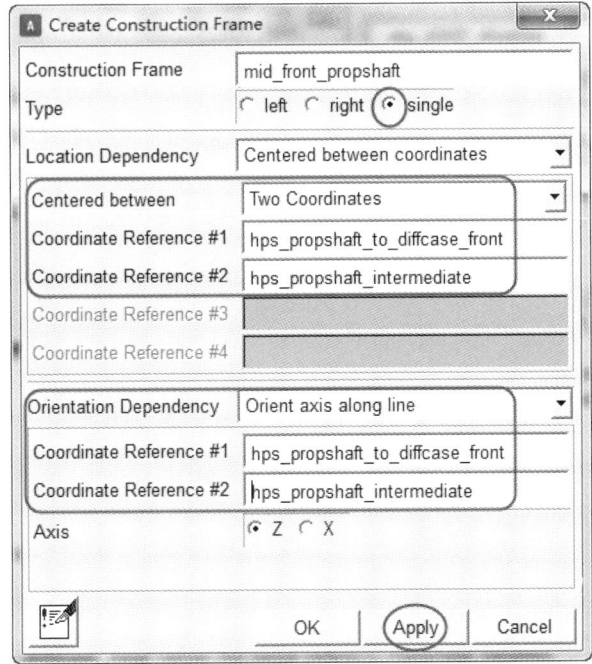

图 7-8 结构框——mid_front_propshaft

- Location Dependency：Center between coordinates；
- Centered between：Two Coordinates；
- Coordinate Reference #1（参考坐标）._my_AWD_driveline.ground.hps_propshaft_to_diffcase_front；
- Coordinate Reference #2（参考坐标）：._my_AWD_driveline.ground.hps_propshaft_intermediate；
- Orientation Dependency：Orient axis along line；
- Coordinate Reference #1（参考坐标）._my_AWD_driveline.ground.hps_propshaft_to_diffcase_front；
- Coordinate Reference #2（参考坐标）：._my_AWD_driveline.ground.hps_propshaft_intermediate；
- Axis：Z；
- 单击 Apply，完成._my_AWD_driveline.ground.cfs_mid_front_propshaft 结构框的创建；
- Construction Frame（结构框名称）：mid_rear_propshaft；
- Location Dependency：Center between coordinates；
- Centered between：Two Coordinates；

- Coordinate Reference #1（参考坐标）._my_AWD_driveline.ground.hps_propshaft_to_diffcase_rear；
- Coordinate Reference #2（参考坐标）：._my_AWD_driveline.ground.hps_propshaft_intermediate；
- Orientation Dependency：Orient axis along line；
- Coordinate Reference #1（参考坐标）._my_AWD_driveline.ground.hps_propshaft_to_diffcase_rear；
- Coordinate Reference #2（参考坐标）：._my_AWD_driveline.ground.hps_propshaft_intermediate；
- Axis：Z；
- 单击 OK，完成._my_AWD_driveline.ground.cfs_mid_rear_propshaft 结构框的创建。

（2）传动轴部件。
- 单击 Build > Part > General Part > Wizard 命令；
- General Part 输入 front_propshaft_1（见图 7-9）；
- Type: single；
- Geometry Type: Link；
- Coordinate Reference #1: cfs_mid_front_propshaft；
- Coordinate Reference #2: hps_propshaft_to_diffcase_front；
- Radius: 20；
- Color: blue；
- 单击 Apply，完成部件._my_AWD_driveline.ges_front_propshaft_1 创建；

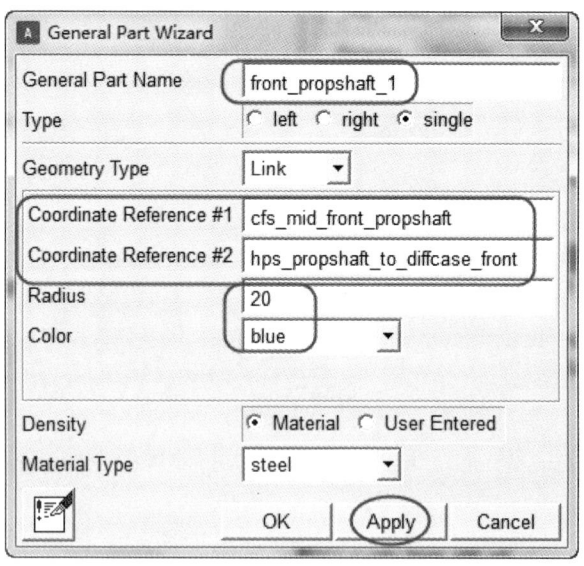

图 7-9　部件——front_propshaft_1

- General Part 输入 front_propshaft_2；
- Type: single；

- Geometry Type: Link；
- Coordinate Reference＃1: cfs_mid_front_propshaft；
- Coordinate Reference＃2: hps_propshaft_intermediate；
- Radius: 20；
- Color: red；
- 单击 Apply，完成部件._my_AWD_driveline.ges_front_propshaft_2 创建；
- General Part 输入 rear_propshaft_1；
- Type: single；
- Geometry Type: Link；
- Coordinate Reference＃1: cfs_mid_rear_propshaft；
- Coordinate Reference＃2: hps_propshaft_intermediate；
- Radius: 20；
- Color: blue；
- 单击 Apply，完成部件._my_AWD_driveline.ges_rear_propshaft_1 创建；
- General Part 输入 rear_propshaft_2；
- Type: single；
- Geometry Type: Link；
- Coordinate Reference＃1: cfs_mid_rear_propshaft；
- Coordinate Reference＃2: hps_propshaft_to_diffcase_rear；
- Radius: 20；
- Color: red；
- 单击 OK，完成部件._my_AWD_driveline.ges_rear_propshaft_2 创建。

（3）扭转弹簧。
- 单击 Driveline Components > Limited Slip Differential > New 命令，如图 7-10 所示；

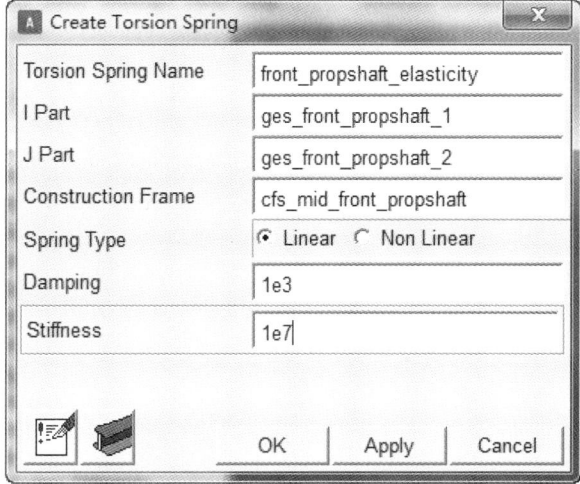

图 7-10　扭力弹簧——front_propshaft_elasticity

- Torsion Spring Name: front_propshaft_elasticity；

- I Part: ges_front_propshaft_1;
- J Part: ges_front_propshaft_2;
- Construction Frame: cfs_mid_front_propshaft;
- Spring Type: Linear;
- Damping: 1e3;
- Stiffness: 1e7;
- 单击 OK，完成扭转弹簧._my_AWD_driveline.ues_front_propshaft_elasticity 创建。

（4）黏性联轴器。
- 单击 Driveline Components > Viscous Coupling > New 命令，如图 7-11 所示；
- Viscous Coupling Name:rear_viscous_coupling;
- I Part: ._my_AWD_driveline.ges_rear_propshaft_1;
- J Part: ._my_AWD_driveline.ges_rear_propshaft_2;
- Construction Frame: ._my_AWD_driveline.ground.cfs_mid_rear_propshaft;
- Property File: mdids://adriveline_shared/differentials.tbl/viscous_coupling.dif;
- 单击 OK，完成黏性联轴器._my_AWD_driveline.ues_rear_viscous_coupling 创建。

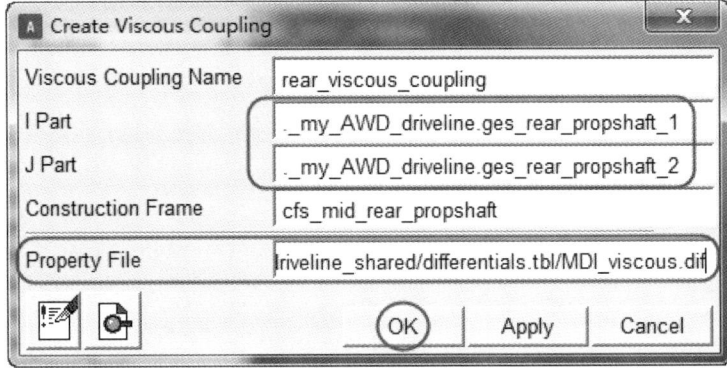

图 7-11 黏性联轴器

7.4 后差速器

（1）后轴差速器参考硬点、结构框。
- 单击 Build > Hardpoint> New 命令，弹出创建硬点对话框参考如图 7-3 所示；
- Hardpoint Name：rear_diff_ref;
- Type：single;
- Location：2 520, 0.0, -200.0;
- 单击 OK，完成._my_AWD_driveline.ground.hps_rear_diff_ref 硬点的创建。
- 单击 Build > Construction Frame > New 命令；
- Construction Frame（结构框名称）：rear_diff_ref;
- Location Dependency：Delta location from coordinate;

- Coordinate Reference (参考坐标)：hps_rear_diff_ref；
- Location：0, 0, 0；
- Location in：local；
- Orientation Dependency：User entered values；
- Orient using：Euler Angles；
- Euler Angles：0, 90, 0；
- 单击 OK，完成 ._my_AWD_driveline.ground.cfs_rear_diff_ref 结构框的创建。

（2）后轴差速器整体部件。
- 单击 Driveline Components > Complex Components > Entire Differential Unit 命令，参考如图 7-5 所示；
  - Differential Center Reference：Delta location from coordinate；
  - Differential Name（变速器名称）：rear；
  - Side Gear Radius（行星齿轮左右两侧齿轮半径）：40；
  - Pinion Gear Radius（行星齿轮前后两侧齿轮半径）：30；
  - Ring Gear Outer Radius（从动齿轮外径）：120；
  - Ring Gear Inner Radius（从动齿轮内径）：60；
  - Ring Gear Offset（从动齿轮偏移量）：50；
  - Ring Gear Geometry（准双曲面齿轮）：Hypoid；
  - Mass: 10；
  - Ixx: 1e4；
  - Iyy: 1e4；
  - Izz: 1e4；
- 单击 OK，完成后轴差速器整体部件的创建，此时传动轴整体模型如图 7-12 所示。

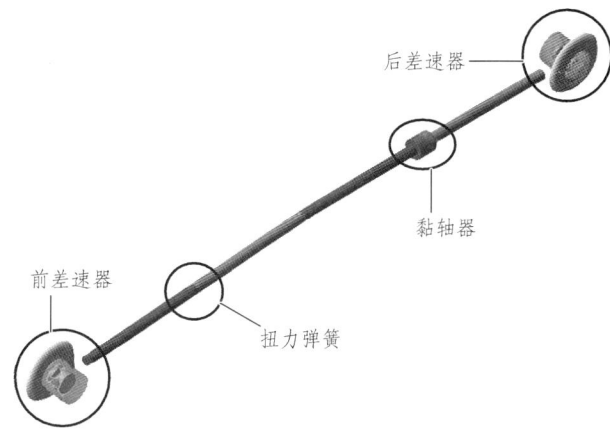

图 7-12 传动轴模型

（3）主动齿轮几何体。
- 单击 Build > Construction Frame > New 命令；
- Construction Frame（结构框名称）：propshaft_to_diffcase_front；

- Location Dependency：Delta location from coordinate；
- Coordinate Reference（参考坐标）：hps_propshaft_to_diffcase_front；
- Location：0, 0, 0；
- Location in：local；
- Orientation Dependency: Orient axis along line；
- Coordinate Reference # 1: cfs_mid_front_propshaft；
- Coordinate Reference # 2: hps_propshaft_to_diffcase_front；
- Axis: Z；
- 单击 Apply，完成 ._my_AWD_driveline.ground.cfs_propshaft_to_diffcase_front 结构框的创建；
- Construction Frame（结构框名称）：propshaft_to_diffcase_rear；
- Location Dependency：Delta location from coordinate；
- Coordinate Reference（参考坐标）：hps_propshaft_to_diffcase_rear；
- Location：0, 0, 0；
- Location in：local；
- Orientation Dependency: Orient axis along line；
- Coordinate Reference # 1: cfs_mid_ rear _propshaft；
- Coordinate Reference # 2: hps_propshaft_to_diffcase_rear；
- Axis: Z；
- 单击 OK，完成 ._my_AWD_driveline.ground.cfs_propshaft_to_diffcase_rear 结构框的创建。
- 单击 Build > Geometry > Frustum（锥形） > New 命令，如图 7-13 所示；

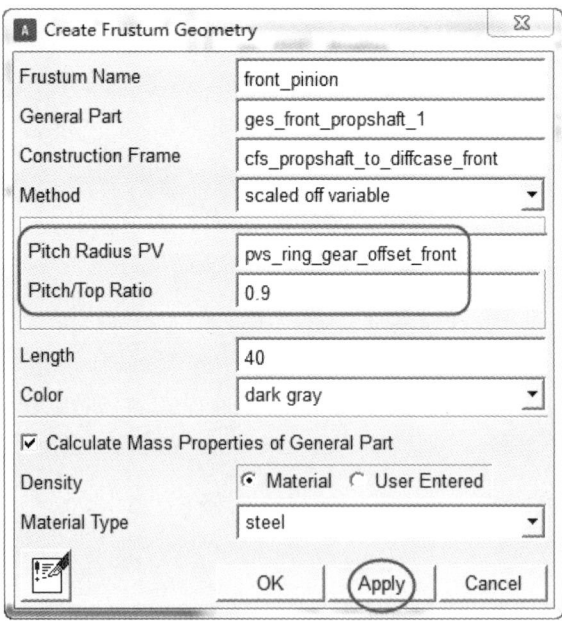

图 7-13 锥形几何体

- Frustum Name: front_pinion;
- General Part: ges_front_propshaft_1;
- Construction Frame: cfs_propshaft_to_diffcase_front;
- Method: scaled off variable;
- Pitch Radius PV: pvs_ring_gear_offset_front;
- Pitch/Top Ratio: 0.9;
- Length: 40;
- Color: dark gray;
- 勾选 Calculate Mass Properties of General Part;
- 单击 Apply，完成前锥形几何体._my_AWD_driveline.ges_front_propshaft_1.grafru_front_pinion 的创建；
- Frustum Name: rear_pinion;
- General Part: ges_ rear _propshaft_1;
- Construction Frame: cfs_propshaft_to_diffcase_ rear;
- Method: scaled off variable;
- Pitch Radius PV: pvs_ring_gear_offset_ rear;
- Pitch/Top Ratio: 0.9;
- Length: 40;
- Color: dark gray;
- 勾选 Calculate Mass Properties of General Part;
- 单击 OK，完成前锥形几何体._my_AWD_driveline.ges_front_propshaft_1.grafru_ rear _pinion 的创建。

7.5 差速器壳

（1）安装部件。
- 单击 Build > Part > Mount > New 命令，弹出创建部件对话框如图 7-14 所示；

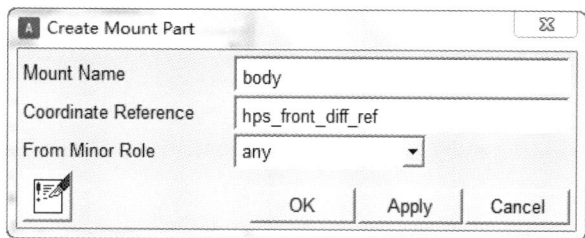

图 7-14 安装部件——body

- Mount name（安装件名称）：body;
- Coordinate Reference（参考坐标）：._my_AWD_driveline.ground.hps_front_diff_ref;
- From Minor Role：any;

- 单击 OK，完成 ._my_AWD_driveline.mts_body 安装部件的创建。

（2）差速器壳部件。
- 单击 Build > Part > General Part > New 命令，如果 7-15 所示；
- General Part：front_diff_housing；
- Type: single；
- Location Dependency: Delta location from coordinate；
- Coordinate Reference: cfs_front_diff_ref；
- Location: 0, 0, 0；
- Orientation Dependency: Delta orientation from coordinate；
- Construction Frame: cfs_front_diff_ref；
- Orientation: 0, 0, 0；
- Mass: 1；
- Ixx: 1；
- Iyy: 1；
- Izz: 1；
- Density：Material；
- Material Type：.materials.steel；
- 单击 Apply，完成部件 ._my_AWD_driveline.ges_front_diff_housing 创建；

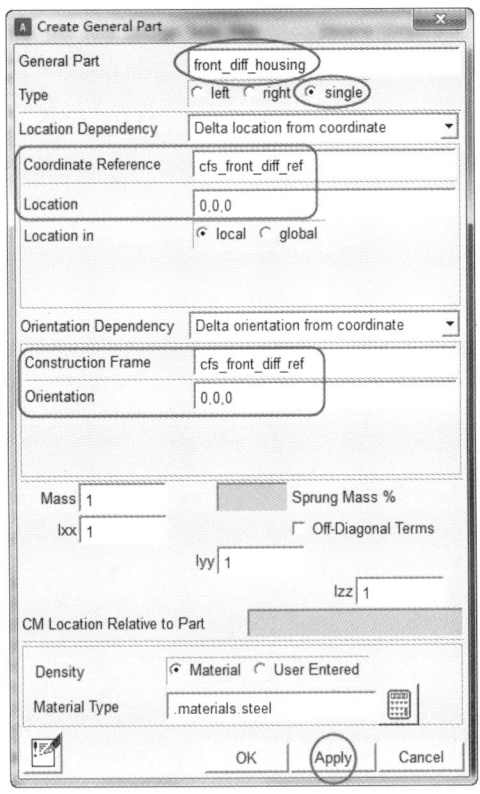

图 7-15　前差速器壳部件

- 单击 Build > Part > General Part > New 命令；
- General Part：rear_diff_housing；
- Type: single；
- Location Dependency: Delta location from coordinate；
- Coordinate Reference: cfs_rear_diff_ref；
- Location: 0, 0, 0 ；
- Orientation Dependency: Delta orientation from coordinate；
- Construction Frame: cfs_ rear _diff_ref；
- Orientation: 0, 0, 0；
- Mass: 1；
- Ixx: 1；
- Iyy: 1；
- Izz: 1；
- Density：Material；
- Material Type：.materials.steel；
- 单击 OK，完成部件._my_AWD_driveline.ges_ rear _diff_housing 创建。

（3）差速器壳约束。
- 单击 Build > Attachments > Joint > New 命令，弹出创约束件对话框如图 7-16 所示；

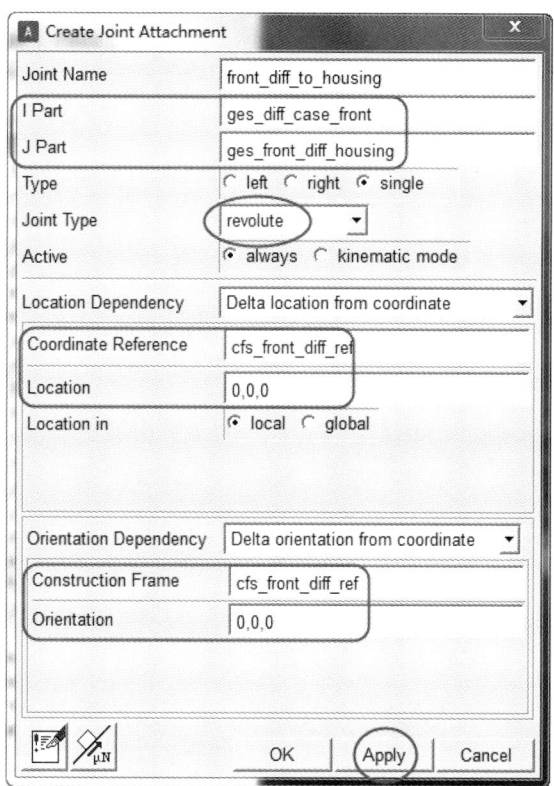

图 7-16　差速器壳约束

- Joint Name: front_diff_to_housing；
- I Part: ges_diff_case_front；
- J Part: ges_front_diff_housing；
- Type: single；
- Joint Type: revolute；
- Active: always；
- Location Dependency: Delta location from coordinate；
- Coordinate Reference: cfs_front_diff_ref；
- Location: 0, 0, 0；
- Orientation Dependency: Delta orientation from coordinate；
- Construction Frame: cfs_front_diff_ref；
- Orientation: 0, 0, 0；
- 单击 Apply，完成约束副._my_AWD_driveline.josrev_front_diff_to_housing 的创建；
- Joint Name: rear_diff_to_housing；
- I Part: ges_diff_case_ rear；
- J Part: ges_ rear _diff_housing；
- Type: single；
- Joint Type: revolute；
- Active: always；
- Location Dependency: Delta location from coordinate；
- Coordinate Reference: cfs_rear_diff_ref；
- Location: 0, 0, 0；
- Orientation Dependency: Delta orientation from coordinate；
- Construction Frame: cfs_rear_diff_ref；
- Orientation: 0, 0, 0；
- 单击 Apply，完成约束副._my_AWD_driveline.josrev_rear_diff_to_housing 的创建；
- Joint Name: front_pinion_to_housing；
- I Part: ges_front_propshaft_1；
- J Part: ges_front_diff_housing；
- Type: single；
- Joint Type: revolute；
- Active: always；
- Location Dependency: Delta location from coordinate；
- Coordinate Reference: cfs_propshaft_to_diffcase_front；
- Location: 0, 0, 0；
- Orientation Dependency: Delta orientation from coordinate；
- Construction Frame: cfs_propshaft_to_diffcase_front；
- Orientation: 0, 0, 0；
- 单击 Apply，完成约束副._my_AWD_driveline.josrev_front_pinion_to_housing 的创建；

- Joint Name: rear_pinion_to_housing;
- I Part: ges_ rear _propshaft_1;
- J Part: ges_ rear_diff_housing;
- Type: single;
- Joint Type: revolute;
- Active: always;
- Location Dependency: Delta location from coordinate;
- Coordinate Reference: cfs_propshaft_to_diffcase_ rear;
- Location: 0, 0, 0;
- Orientation Dependency: Delta orientation from coordinate;
- Construction Frame: cfs_propshaft_to_diffcase_rear;
- Orientation: 0, 0, 0;
- 单击 OK，完成约束副._my_AWD_driveline.josrev_rear _pinion_to_housing 的创建。

（4）减速器约束。
- 单击 Build > Attachments > Joint > New 命令，弹出创约束件对话框如图 7-17 所示；
- Reduction Gear Name: front_ringgear_pinion;
- Input Joint Type: Kinematic Joint;
- Input Joint: josrev_front_pinion_to_housing;
- Output Joint Type: Kinematic Joint;
- Output Joint: josrev_front_diff_to_housing;
- Method: explicit;
- Ratio: 4;
- Active: always;
- 单击 Apply，完成减速副._my_AWD_driveline.grsred_front_ringgear_pinion 的创建；

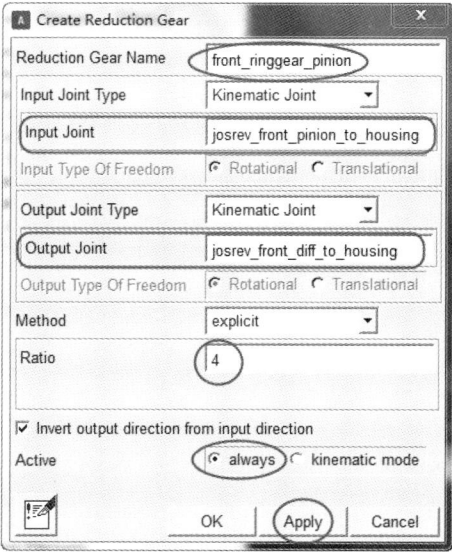

图 7-17　减速器约束

- Reduction Gear Name: rear_ringgear_pinion;
- Input Joint Type: Kinematic Joint;
- Input Joint: josrev_ rear _pinion_to_housing;
- Output Joint Type: Kinematic Joint;
- Output Joint: josrev_rear_diff_to_housing;
- Method: explicit;
- Ratio: 4;
- Active: always;
- 单击 OK，完成_my_AWD_driveline.grsred_ rear _ringgear_pinion 的创建。

（5）前差速器壳几何体。
- 单击 Build > Hardpoint > New 命令，弹出创建硬点对话框参考如图 7-3 所示；
- Hardpoint Name：front_diff_housing_mount_1;
- Type：single;
- Location：150, －100.0, 0.0;
- 单击 Apply，完成._my_AWD_driveline.ground.hps_front_diff_housing_mount_1 硬点的创建；
- Hardpoint Name：front_diff_housing_mount_2;
- Type：single;
- Location：150, 100.0, 0.0;
- 单击 Apply，完成._my_AWD_driveline.ground.hps_front_diff_housing_mount_2 硬点的创建；
- Hardpoint Name：front_diff_housing_mount_3;
- Type：single;
- Location：－200, 0.0, 0.0;
- 单击 OK，完成._my_AWD_driveline.ground.hps_front_diff_housing_mount_3 硬点的创建。
- 单击 Build > Geometry > Link > New 命令如图 7-18 所示；
- Link Name (连杆名称) 输入几何名称：Link_1;
- General Part 输入 ges_front_diff_housing;
- Coordinate Reference #1(参考坐标)：hps_front_diff_housing_mount_1;
- Coordinate Reference #2(参考坐标)：hps_front_diff_housing_mount_2;
- Radius(半径): 15;
- Color（杆件几何体颜色）：yellow;
- 选择 Calculate Mass Properties of General Part;
- Density：Material;
- Material Type：steel;
- 单击 Apply，完成._my_AWD_driveline.ges_front_diff_housing.gralin_link_1 几何体的创建；
- Link Name (连杆名称) 输入几何名称：Link_2;

- Coordinate Reference #1(参考坐标): hps_front_diff_housing_mount_1;
- Coordinate Reference #2(参考坐标): hps_front_diff_housing_mount_3;
- Radius(半径): 15;
- Color（杆件几何体颜色）: yellow;
- 选择 Calculate Mass Properties of General Part;
- Density: Material;
- Material Type: steel;
- 单击 Apply，完成._my_AWD_driveline.ges_front_diff_housing.gralin_link_2 几何体的创建;
- Link Name (连杆名称) 输入几何名称: Link_3;
- Coordinate Reference #1(参考坐标): hps_front_diff_housing_mount_3;
- Coordinate Reference #2(参考坐标): hps_front_diff_housing_mount_2;
- Radius(半径): 15;
- Color（杆件几何体颜色）: yellow;
- 选择 Calculate Mass Properties of General Part;
- Density: Material;
- Material Type: steel;
- 单击 OK，完成._my_AWD_driveline.ges_front_diff_housing.gralin_link_3 几何体的创建。

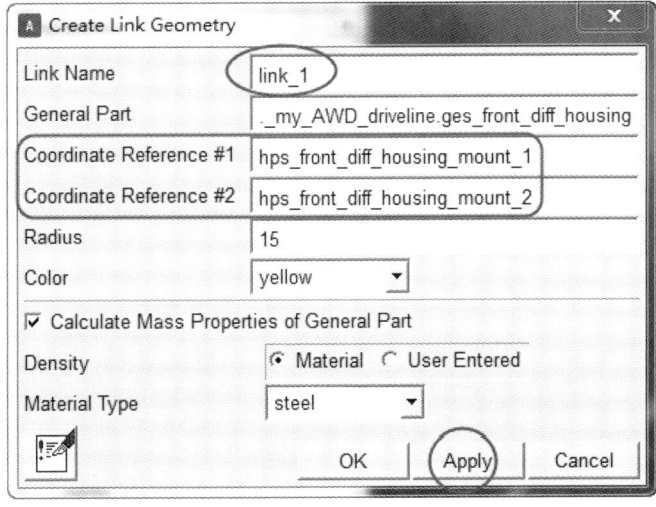

图 7-18　连杆几何体——link_1

（6）前差速器壳 bushing 连接。
- 单击 Build > Attachments > Bushing > New 命令，弹出创衬套件对话框如图 7-19 所示;
- Bushing Name（约束副名称）: front_diff_housing_1;
- I　Part: ges_front_diff_housing;
- J　Part: mts_Body;
- Type: single;

- Inactive（抑制）：never；
- Preload：0，0，0；
- Tpreload: 0，0，0；
- Offset：0，0，0；
- Roffset：0，0，0；
- Geometry Length：20；
- Geometry Radius：30；
- Property File：mdids://acar_shared/bushings.tbl/mdi_0001.bus；
- Location Dependency：Delta location from coordinate；
- Coordinate Reference(参考坐标)：._my_AWD_driveline.ground.hps_front_diff_housing_mount_1；
- Location: 0，0，0；
- Location in：local；
- Orientation Dependency：User entered values；
- Orient using：Euler Angles；
- Euler Angles：0, 90, 0；
- 单击 Apply，完成轴套._my_AWD_driveline.bgs_front_diff_housing_1 的创建；

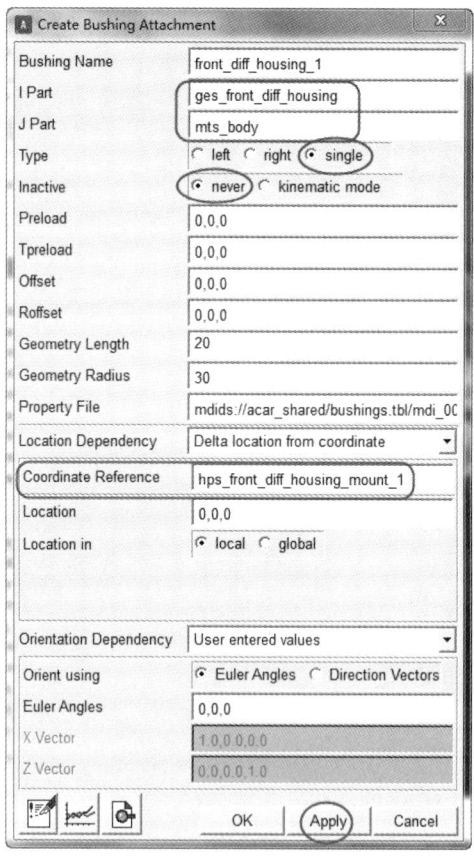

图 7-19 衬套连接——front_diff_housing_1

- Bushing Name（约束副名称）：front_diff_housing_2；
- I   Part：ges_front_diff_housing；
- J   Part：mts_Body；
- Type：single；
- Inactive（抑制）：never；
- Preload：0，0，0；
- Tpreload：0，0，0；
- Offset：0，0，0；
- Roffset：0，0，0；
- Geometry Length：20；
- Geometry Radius：30；
- Property File：mdids://acar_shared/bushings.tbl/mdi_0001.bus；
- Location Dependency：Delta location from coordinate；
- Coordinate Reference（参考坐标）：._my_AWD_driveline.ground.hps_front_diff_ housing_mount_2；
- Location：0，0，0；
- Location in：local；
- Orientation Dependency：User entered values；
- Orient using：Euler Angles；
- Euler Angles：0，90，0；
- 单击 Apply，完成轴套._my_AWD_driveline.bgs_front_diff_housing_2 的创建；
- Bushing Name（约束副名称）：front_diff_housing_3；
- I   Part：ges_front_diff_housing；
- J   Part：mts_Body；
- Type：single；
- Inactive（抑制）：never；
- Preload：0，0，0；
- Tpreload：0，0，0；
- Offset：0，0，0；
- Roffset：0，0，0；
- Geometry Length：20；
- Geometry Radius：30；
- Property File：mdids://acar_shared/bushings.tbl/mdi_0001.bus；
- Location Dependency：Delta location from coordinate；
- Coordinate Reference（参考坐标）：._my_AWD_driveline.ground.hps_front_diff_ housing_mount_3；
- Location：0，0，0；
- Location in：local；
- Orientation Dependency：User entered values；

- Orient using：Euler Angles；
- Euler Angles：0, 90, 0；
- 单击 OK，完成轴套._my_AWD_driveline.bgs_front_diff_housing_3 的创建。

（7）后差速器壳几何体。
- 单击 Build > Hardpoint > New 命令，弹出创建硬点对话框参考如图 7-3 所示；
- Hardpoint Name：rear_diff_housing_mount_1；
- Type：single；
- Location：2650，-100.0，-200.0；
- 单击 Apply，完成._my_AWD_driveline.ground.hps_rear_diff_housing_mount_1 硬点的创建；
- Hardpoint Name：front_diff_housing_mount_2；
- Type：single；
- Location：2 650，100.0，-200.0；
- 单击 Apply，完成._my_AWD_driveline.ground.hps_rear_diff_housing_mount_2 硬点的创建；
- Hardpoint Name：rear_diff_housing_mount_3；
- Type：single；
- Location：2 300，0.0，-200.0；
- 单击 OK，完成._my_AWD_driveline.ground.hps_rear_diff_housing_mount_3 硬点的创建。
- 单击 Build > Geometry > Link > New 命令，如图 7-18 所示；
- Link Name (连杆名称）输入几何名称：Link_1；
- General Part 输入 ges_rear_diff_housing；
- Coordinate Reference #1（参考坐标）：hps_rear_diff_housing_mount_1；
- Coordinate Reference #2（参考坐标）：hps_rear_diff_housing_mount_2；
- Radius(半径): 15；
- Color（杆件几何体颜色）：yellow；
- 选择 Calculate Mass Properties of General Part；
- Density：Material；
- Material Type：steel；
- 单击 Apply，完成._my_AWD_driveline.ges_rear_diff_housing.gralin_link_1 几何体的创建；
- Link Name (连杆名称）输入几何名称：Link_2；
- Coordinate Reference #1(参考坐标）：hps_rear_diff_housing_mount_1；
- Coordinate Reference #2(参考坐标）：hps_rear_diff_housing_mount_3；
- Radius(半径): 15；
- Color（杆件几何体颜色）：yellow；
- 选择 Calculate Mass Properties of General Part；
- Density：Material；
- Material Type：steel；

- 单击 Apply，完成._my_AWD_driveline.ges_rear_diff_housing.gralin_link_2 几何体的创建。
- Link Name (连杆名称) 输入几何名称：Link_3；
- Coordinate Reference #1（参考坐标）：hps_rear_diff_housing_mount_3；
- Coordinate Reference #2（参考坐标）：hps_rear_diff_housing_mount_2；
- Radius(半径)：15；
- Color（杆件几何体颜色）：yellow；
- 选择 Calculate Mass Properties of General Part；
- Density：Material；
- Material Type：steel；
- 单击 OK，完成._my_AWD_driveline.ges_rear_diff_housing.gralin_link_3 几何体的创建。

（8）后差速器壳 bushing 连接。
- 单击 Build > Attachments > Bushing > New 命令，弹出创衬套件对话框参考如图 7-19 所示；
- Bushing Name（约束副名称）：rear_diff_housing_1；
- I   Part : ges_front_diff_housing；
- J   Part : mts_Body；
- Type：single；
- Inactive（抑制）：never；
- Preload：0，0，0；
- Tpreload：0，0，0；
- Offset：0，0，0；
- Roffset：0，0，0；
- Geometry Length：20；
- Geometry Radius：30；
- Property File：mdids://acar_shared/bushings.tbl/mdi_0001.bus；
- Location Dependency：Delta location from coordinate；
- Coordinate Reference(参考坐标)：._my_AWD_driveline.ground.hps_rear_diff_housing_mount_1；
- Location: 0，0，0；
- Location in：local；
- Orientation Dependency：User entered values；
- Orient using：Euler Angles；
- Euler Angles：0, 90, 0；
- 单击 Apply，完成轴套._my_AWD_driveline.bgs_rear_diff_housing_1 的创建；
- Bushing Name（约束副名称）：rear_diff_housing_2；
- I   Part : ges_rear_diff_housing；
- J   Part : mts_Body；
- Type：single；
- Inactive（抑制）：never；

- Preload：0，0，0；
- Tpreload: 0，0，0；
- Offset：0，0，0；
- Roffset：0，0，0；
- Geometry Length：20；
- Geometry Radius：30；
- Property File：mdids://acar_shared/bushings.tbl/mdi_0001.bus；
- Location Dependency：Delta location from coordinate；
- Coordinate Reference（参考坐标）：._my_AWD_driveline.ground.hps_rear_diff_housing_mount_2；
- Location: 0，0，0；
- Location in：local；
- Orientation Dependency：User entered values；
- Orient using：Euler Angles；
- Euler Angles：0，90，0；
- 单击 Apply，完成轴套._my_AWD_driveline.bgs_rear_diff_housing_2 的创建；
- Bushing Name（约束副名称）：front_diff_housing_3；
- I   Part : ges_front_diff_housing；
- J   Part : mts_Body；
- Type：single；
- Inactive（抑制）: never；
- Preload：0，0，0；
- Tpreload: 0，0，0；
- Offset：0，0，0；
- Roffset：0，0，0；
- Geometry Length：20；
- Geometry Radius：30；
- Property File：mdids://acar_shared/bushings.tbl/mdi_0001.bus；
- Location Dependency：Delta location from coordinate；
- Coordinate Reference（参考坐标）：._my_AWD_driveline.ground.hps_rear_diff_housing_mount_3；
- Location: 0，0，0；
- Location in：local；
- Orientation Dependency：User entered values；
- Orient using：Euler Angles；
- Euler Angles：0，90，0；
- 单击 OK，完成轴套._my_AWD_driveline.bgs_rear_diff_housing_3 的创建。

7.6 滑叉部件与连接

（1）结构框 propshaft_intermediate。
- 单击 Build > Construction Frame > New 命令，参考如图 7-4 所示；
- Construction Frame: propshaft_intermediate；
- Type: single；
- Location Dependency: Delta location from coordinate；
- Coordinate Reference: hps_propshaft_intermediate；
- Location: 0,0,0；
- Location in: local；
- Orientation Dependency: Orient axis to point；
- Coordinate Reference: cfs_mid_rear_propshaft；
- Axis: Z；
- 单击 OK，完成._my_AWD_driveline.ground.cfs_propshaft_intermediate 结构框的创建。

（2）滑叉部件。
- 单击 Build > Part > General Part > New 命令，弹出创建部件对话框如图 7-20 所示；

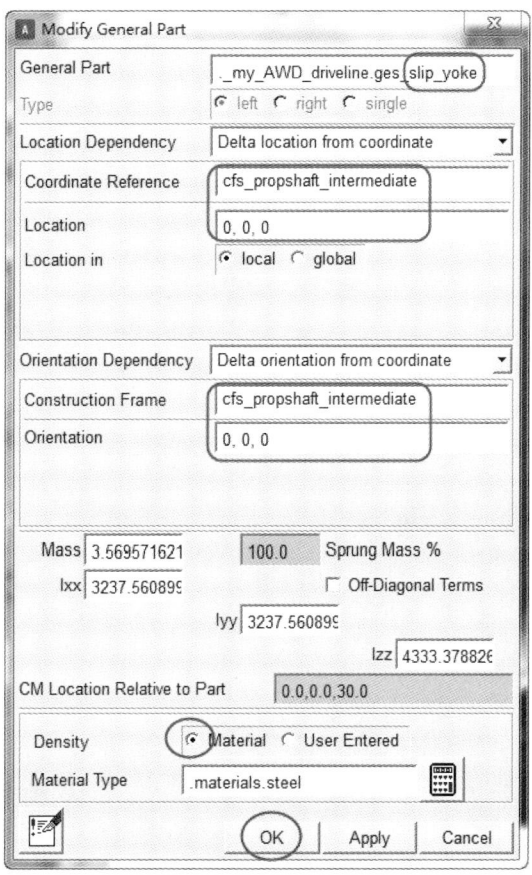

图 7-20　滑叉部件

- General Part: slip_yoke；
- Type: single；
- Location Dependency: Delta location from coordinate；
- Coordinate Reference: cfs_propshaft_intermediate；
- Location: 0,0,0；
- Location Dependency: Delta orientation from coordin；
- Construction Frame: cfs_propshaft_intermediate；
- Orientation: 0,0,0；
- Mass: 1；
- Ixx: 1；
- Iyy: 1；
- Izz: 1；
- Density：Material；
- Material Type：.materials.steel；
- 单击 OK，完成部件._my_AWD_driveline.ges_slip_yoke 创建；

（3）滑叉几何体。
- 单击 Build > Geometry > Cylinder (圆柱体) > New 命令，如图 7-21 所示；
- Cylinder Name （连杆名称）输入几何名称：slip_yoke；
- General Part 输入 ges_slip_yoke；
- Radius（半径）: 50；
- Length In Postive Z（Z 轴正方向长度）: 60；
- Length In Negative Z（Z 轴负方向长度）: 0；
- Color（圆柱体几何体颜色）: yellow；
- 选择 Calculate Mass Properties of General Part 复选框；
- 单击 OK，完成圆柱体._my_AWD_driveline.ges_slip_yoke.gracyl_slip_yoke 几何体的创建。

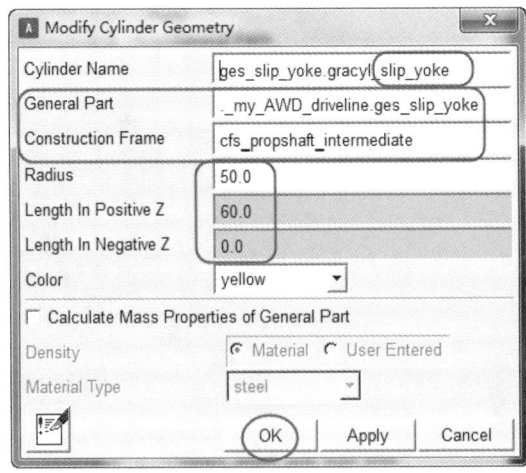

图 7-21　几何体——slip_yoke

（4）滑叉约束。
- 单击 Build > Attachments > Joint > New 命令，弹出创约束件对话框参考如图 7-16 所示；
- Joint Name: slipyoke_to_front_propshaft；
- I Part: ges_slip_yoke；
- J Part: ges_front_propshaft_2；
- Type: single；
- Joint Type: convel；
- Active: always；
- Location Dependency: Delta location from coordina；
- Coordinate Reference: cfs_propshaft_intermediate；
- Location: 0,0,0；
- Part Axis: cfs_mid_front_propshaft；
- J-Part Axis: cfs_mid_rear_propshaft；
- 单击 Apply，完成约束副._my_AWD_driveline.joscon_slipyoke_to_front_propshaft 的创建；
- Joint Name: slipyoke_to_rear_propshaft；
- I Part: ges_slip_yoke；
- J Part: ges_rear_propshaft_1；
- Type: single；
- Joint Type: translational；
- Active: always；
- Location Dependency: Delta location from coordina；
- Coordinate Reference: cfs_propshaft_intermediate；
- Location: 0,0,0；
- Orientation Dependency: Delta orientation from coordinate；
- Construction Frame: cfs_propshaft_intermediate；
- Orientation: 0,0,0；
- 单击 OK，完成约束副._my_AWD_driveline.jostra_slipyoke_to_rear_propshaft 的创建。

7.7 动力传动系统-底盘连接

（1）支撑轴承部件。
- 单击 Build > Part > General Part > New 命令，弹出创建部件对话框如图 7-20 所示；
- General Part: support_bearing；
- Type: single；
- Location Dependency: Delta location from coordinate；
- Coordinate Reference: hps_propshaft_intermediate；
- Location: 0,0,0；

- Orientation Dependency: Delta orientation from coordinate；
- Construction Frame: cfs_propshaft_intermediate；
- Orientation: 0,0,0；
- Mass: 1；
- Ixx: 1；
- Iyy: 1；
- Izz: 1；
- Density：Material；
- Material Type：.materials.steel；
- 单击 OK，完成部件._my_AWD_driveline.ges_support_bearing 创建。

（2）安装部件 propshaft_support_to_body。
- 单击 Build > Part > Mount > New 命令；
- Mount name（安装件名称）：propshaft_support_to_body；
- Coordinate Reference（参考坐标）：._my_AWD_driveline.ground.hps_propshaft_intermediate；
- From Minor Role：any；
- 单击 OK，完成._my_AWD_driveline.mts_propshaft_support_to_body 安装部件的创建。

（3）传动轴连接。
- 单击 Build > Construction Frame > New 命令，参考如图 7-4 所示；
- Construction Frame: propshaft_support_to_bearing；
- Type: single；
- Location Dependency: Located on a line；
- Coordinate Reference # 1: cfs_mid_front_propshaft；
- Coordinate Reference # 2: hps_propshaft_intermediate；
- Relative Location (%): 50；
- Orientation Dependency: Orient to zpoint-xpoint；
- Coordinate Reference # 1: cfs_mid_front_propshaft；
- Coordinate Reference # 2: hps_propshaft_intermediate；
- Axes: ZX；
- 单击 OK,完成._my_AWD_driveline.ground.cfs_propshaft_support_to_bearing 结构框的创建。
- 单击 Build > Attachments > Bushing > New 命令，弹出创衬套件对话框，参考如图 7-19 所示；
- B Bushing Name: support_bearing；
- I Part: ges_support_bearing；
- J Part: mts_propshaft_support_to_body；
- Type: single；
- Inactive: never；
- Preload: 0, 0, 0；
- TPreload: 0, 0, 0；

- Offset: 0, 0, 0；
- Roffset: 0, 0, 0；
- Geometry Length: 20；
- Geometry Radius: 30
- Property File：mdids://acar_shared/bushings.tbl/mdi_0001.bus；
- Location Dependency: Delta location from coordinate；
- Coordinate Reference: cfs_propshaft_support_to_bearing；
- Location: 0, 0, 0
- Location in：local；
- Orientation Dependency: Delta orientation from coordinate；
- Construction Frame: cfs_propshaft_support_to_bearing；
- Orientation: 0, 0, 0；
- 单击 OK，完成轴套._my_AWD_driveline.bgs_support_bearing 的创建。
- 单击 Build > Attachments > Joint > New 命令，弹出创约束件对话框参考如图 7-16 所示；
- Joint Name: support_bearing_to_propshaft_front；
- I Part: ges_support_bearing；
- J Part: ges_front_propshaft_2；
- Type: single；
- Joint Type: inline；
- Active: always；
- Location Dependency: Delta location from coordinate；
- Coordinate Reference: cfs_propshaft_support_to_bearing；
- Location: 0, 0, 0；
- Location in: local；
- Orientation Dependency: Delta orientation from coordinate；
- Construction Frame: cfs_propshaft_support_to_bearing；
- Orientation: 0, 0, 0；
- 单击 OK，完成约束副._my_AWD_driveline.josinl_support_bearing_to_propshaft_front 的创建。

7.8 差速器动力元

- 单击 Driveline Components > Dyno > New 命令，弹出动力元对话框如图 7-22 所示；
- Dyno Name: driveline_input；
- Attachment To: Part；
- I Attachment Part: ges_diff_case_front；
- J Attachment Part: ground；
- Coordinate Reference: cfs_front_diff_ref；

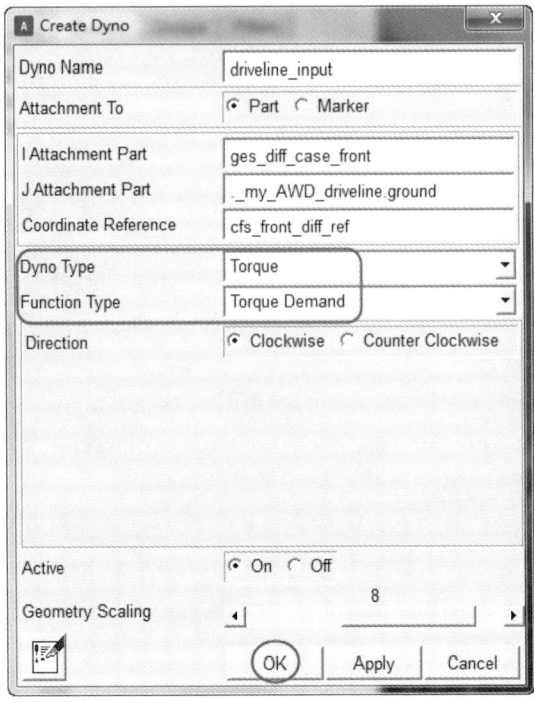

图 7-22 差速器动力元

- Dyno Type: Torque；
- Function Type: Torque Demand；
- Direction: Clockwise；
- Active: On；
- Geometry Scaling: 8；
- 单击 OK，完成动力元 ._my_AWD_driveline.ues_driveline_input 的创建。
- 单击 File > Save As 命令，弹出保存模板对话框如图 7-23 所示；
- Major Role（主特征）：driveline；
- File Format：Binary；
- Target：Datebase/my_driveline；
- 单击 OK，完成推杆式悬架模型模板 my_AWD_driveline 的保存。

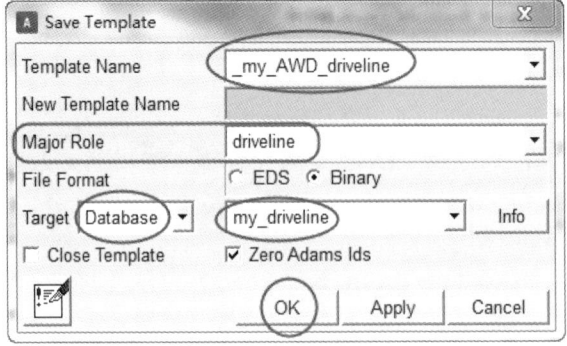

图 7-23 传动轴保存

7.9 阶跃扭矩仿真

（1）传动轴子系统。
- 按 F9，把专家模板转换到标准模式；
- 单击 File > New > Suspension 命令，弹出子系统对话框如图 7-24 所示；

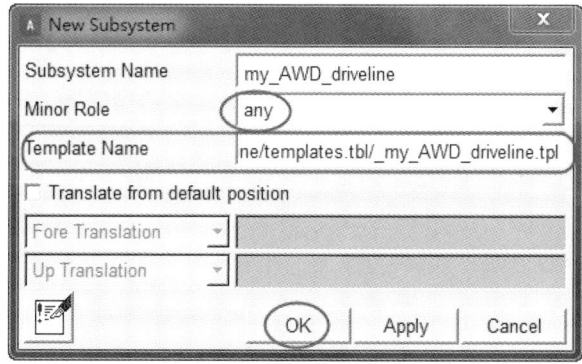

图 7-24 传动轴子系统建立

- Subsystem Name(系统名称)：my_AWD_driveline；
- Minor Role（副特征）：any；
- Template Name（模板路径）：mdids://my_driveline/templates.tbl/_my_AWD_driveline.tpl；
- 单击 OK，完成子系统 my_AWD_driveline 的创建，如图 7-25 所示。

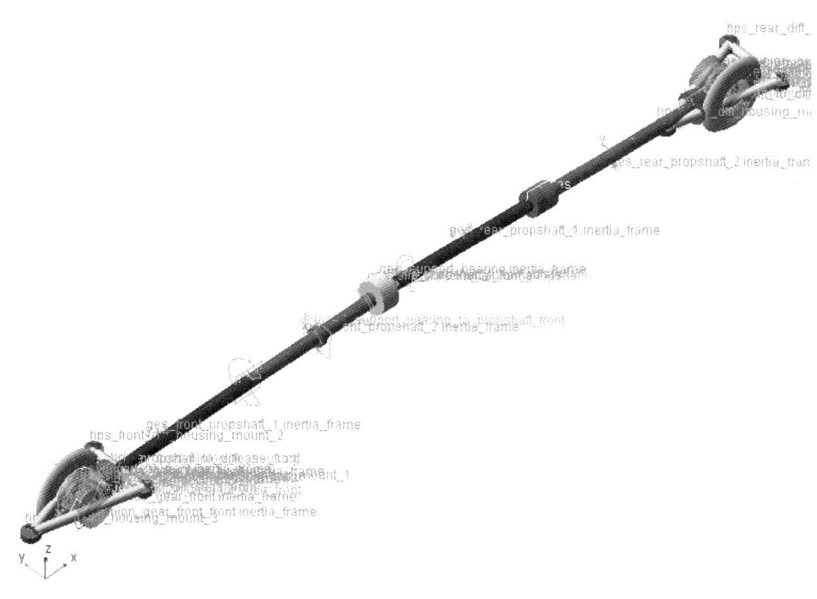

图 7-25 传动轴子系统

(2)传动轴测试平台。
- 单击 File > New > Bench Test Assembly 命令，如图 7-26 所示；

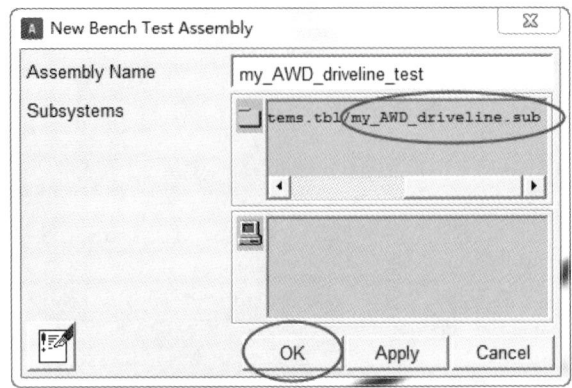

图 7-26　传动轴测试平台

- Assembly Name: my_AWD_driveline_test；
- Subsystems: mdids://my_driveline/subsystems.tbl/my_AWD_driveline.sub；
- 单击 OK，完成传动轴测试平台建立。

(3)阶跃扭矩仿真。
- 单击 Simulate > Full-Vehicle Analysis > Driveline Tests > Step Torque 命令（见图 7-27）；

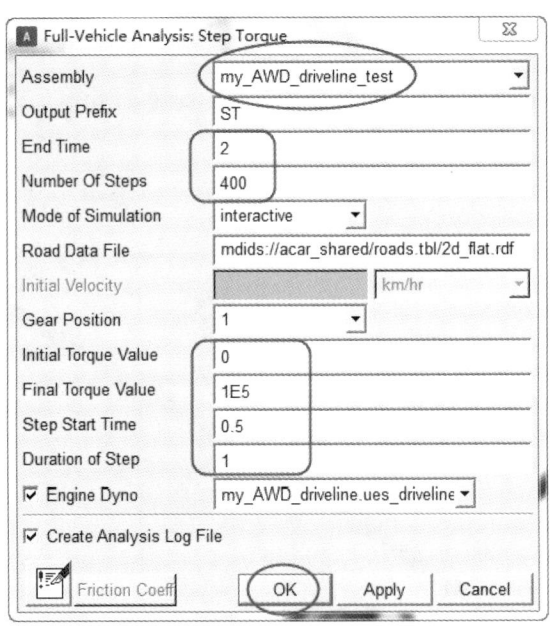

图 7-27　阶跃扭矩仿真

- Output Prefix: AWD_driveline；
- End Time: 2；
- Number Of Steps: 400；
- Mode of Simulation: interactive；

- Road Data File: mdids://acar_shared/roads.tbl/2d_flat.rdf ；
- Gear Position: 1 ；
- Initial Torque Value: 0 ；
- Final Torque Value: 1e5 ；
- Step Start Time: 0.5 ；
- Duration of Step: 1 ；
- Engine Dyno: AWD_driveline.ues_driveline_input；
- 单击 OK，完成阶跃扭矩设置并提交计算，传动轴各计算参数如图 7-28～图 7-39 所示。

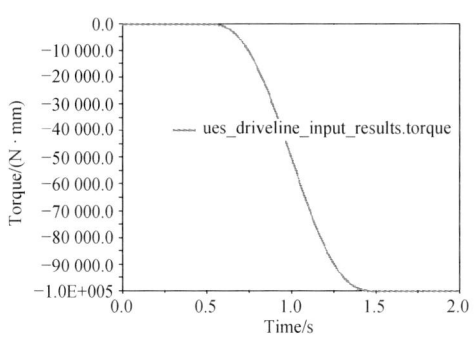

图 7-28　扭矩输入

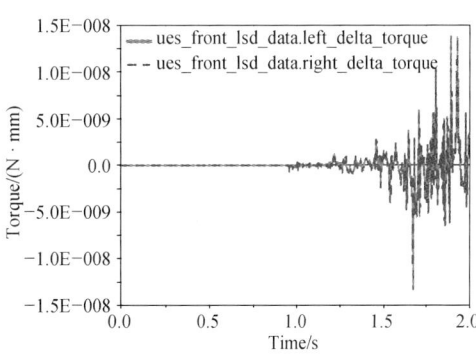

图 7-29　左右限滑差速器扭矩

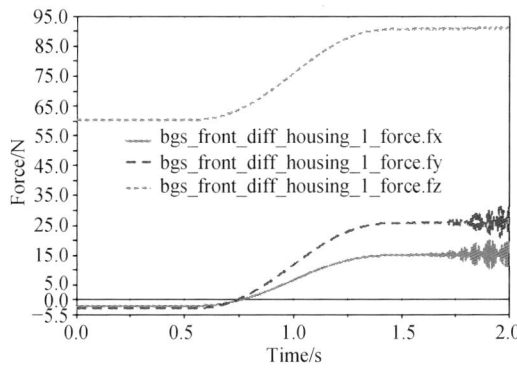

图 7-30　前差速器壳 bushing_1 衬套 X/Y/Z 方向受力　图 7-31　前差速器壳 bushing_2 衬套 X/Y/Z 方向受力

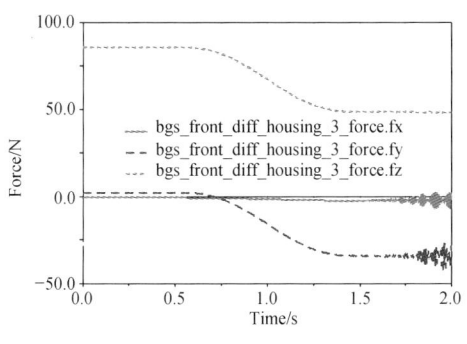

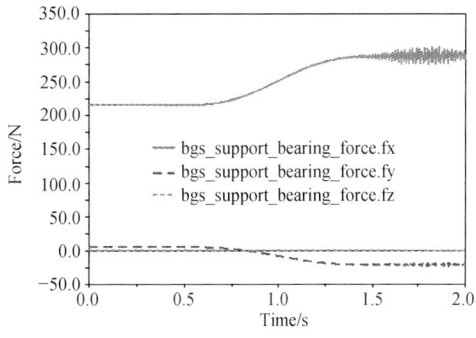

图 7-32　前差速器壳 bushing_3 衬套 X/Y/Z 方向受力　　图 7-33　支撑轴承 X/Y/Z 方向受力

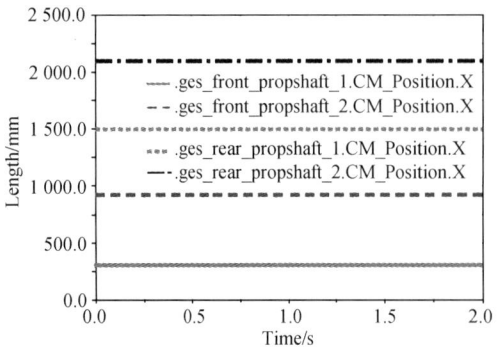

图 7-34 传动轴 X 方向位移

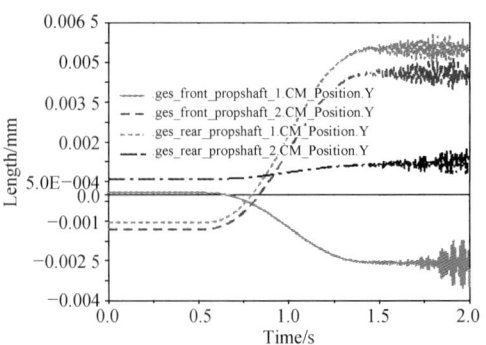

图 7-35 传动轴 Y 方向位移

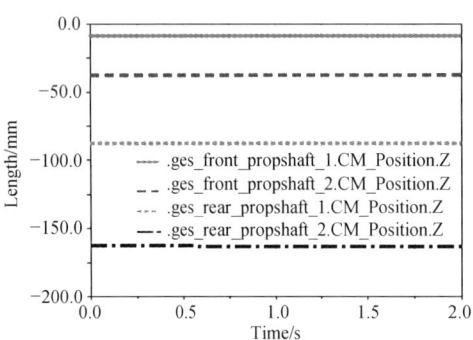

图 7-36 传动轴 Z 方向位移

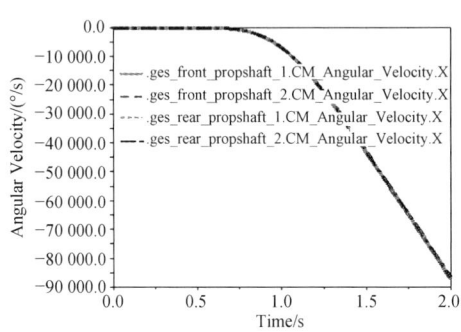

图 7-37 传动轴 X 方向速度

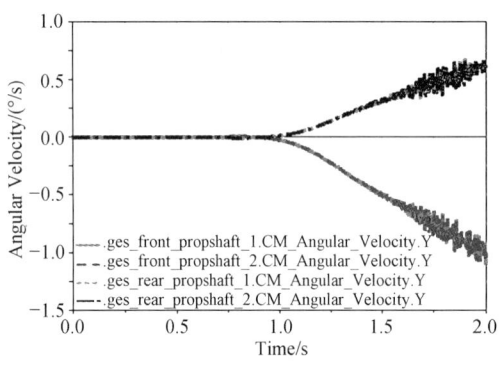

图 7-38 传动轴 Y 方向速度

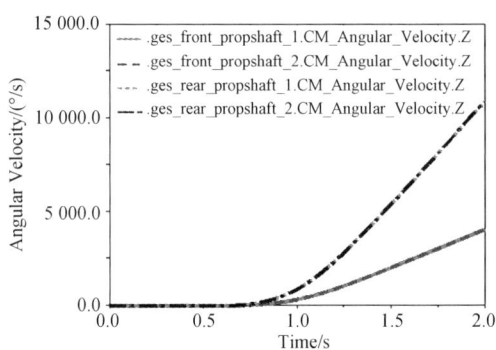

图 7-39 传动轴 Z 方向速度

第 8 章 齿轮传动

ADAMS/MACHINERY 机械传动系统可评估并管理运动、结构、驱动及控制有关的复杂系统部件间的相互作用，以便更好地优化产品设计的性能；ADAMS/MACHINERY 可充分整合到 ADAMS/VIEW 环境中。它包含多个建模模块，与只具备通用标准 ADAMS/VIEW 模型构建功能的软件相比，它能让用户更加快速地创建通用机械部件。ADAMS/MACHINERY 通过几何形状创建、子系统连接等自动化操作来引导用户进行预处理，使用户能够更加高效地创建一些通用的机械部件，同时还为通常所需的输出通道提供自动绘制图形及分析报告提升用户进行后处理效率。机械传动系统包括齿轮、皮带、链条、轴承、缆索、电机、凸轮轴等模块。

学习目标

- ◆ 直齿轮传动。
- ◆ 锥齿轮传动。
- ◆ 蜗轮蜗杆齿轮传动。
- ◆ 齿轮齿条传动。
- ◆ 准双曲面齿轮传动。
- ◆ 行星齿轮组传动。

齿轮模块为预测齿轮副行为（例如齿轮比、齿间隙）对整体系统性能的影响而设计；通过选择正齿轮（内部/外部）、螺旋齿轮（内部/外部）、锥形齿轮（直线和螺旋）、双曲线齿轮、蜗轮齿轮及齿条齿轮来选择齿轮类型；根据实际工作中心距和齿厚，采用接触建模方法来研究齿间隙；通过行星齿轮向导创建行星齿轮组；在后处理器中生成与齿轮有关的输出，采用自动模型参数化作为参考来进行设计探查。

8.1 直齿轮传动

- 启动 ADAMS/VIEW；
- 单击 Machinery > Gear > Create Gear Pair 命令，弹出创建齿轮副对话框如图 8-1 所示；
- 选择 Type；
- Gear Type：Spur（直齿轮）；

Gear Type 下拉菜单包含以下典型齿轮副：

（1）Spur（直齿轮）：正齿轮也是已知的直齿轮。在这个齿轮中，两个轴的轴线是平行的，齿是直的并且平行于两个轴的旋转轴线。

（2）Helical（斜齿轮）：当负载较重，速度较高或噪声必须降低时，主要使用斜齿轮。在斜齿轮中，齿的纵轴相对于轴的轴线倾斜。

（3）Bevel（锥齿轮）：通常在两个轴的轴线相交时使用锥齿轮，它们的俯仰面是锥形，其锥轴与两个旋转轴相匹配。尽管锥齿轮通常在轴之间形成 90°的角度，但它们几乎可以设计成任何角度。

（4）Worm（蜗轮蜗杆传动）：当不交叉的轴之间需要大的减速比时使用蜗轮蜗杆传动，装置由大直径蜗轮组成，蜗杆与蜗轮外齿啮合。

（5）Rack(齿轮齿条传动)：把齿轮的旋转运动转换为齿条的直线运动，齿轮可以为直齿轮或者斜齿轮，例如齿轮齿条转向系统。

（6）Hypoid(准双曲面齿轮)：准双曲面齿轮的特征在于小齿轮轴线偏离齿轮轴线的中心。它比螺旋锥齿轮更平稳，更安静地传递旋转。

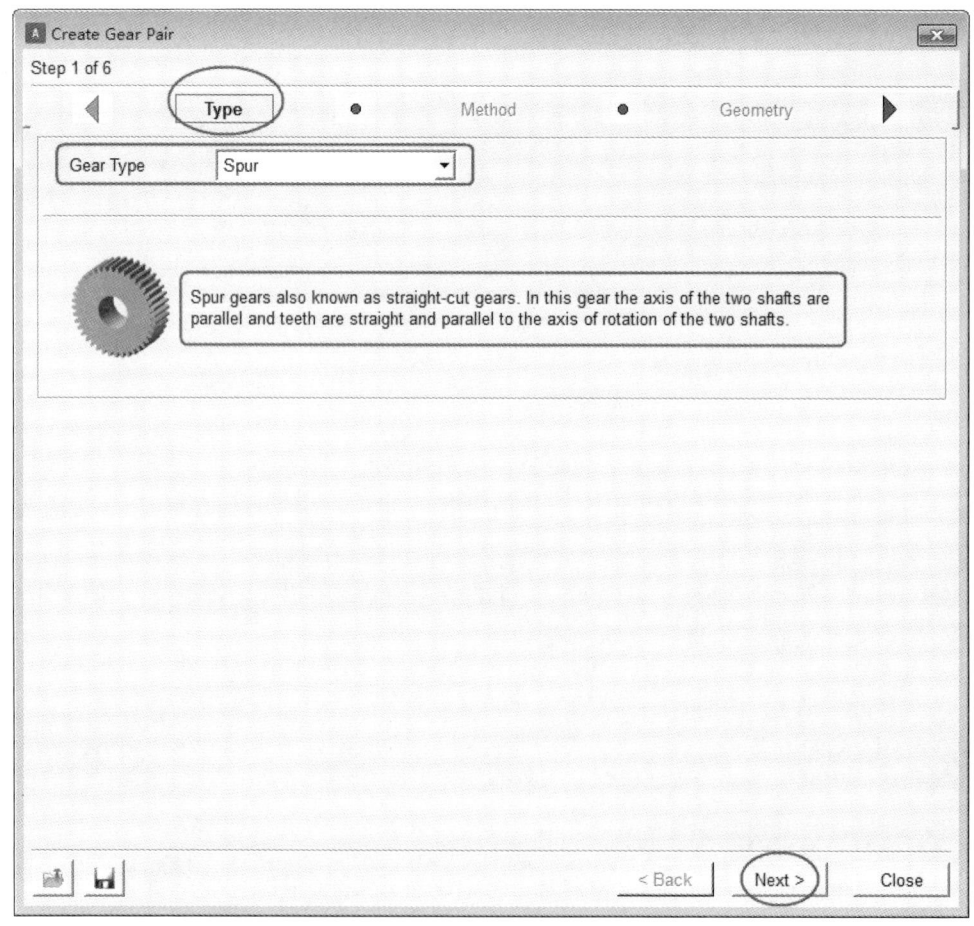

图 8-1　创建直齿轮副对话框/Type

- 完成 Type 界面的设置，单击 Next；
- Method：3D Contact（3D 接触），如图 8-2 所示。

3D Contact：该方法采用基于几何的接触，支持壳-壳三维几何接触，根据实际工作中心距离和齿厚计算出真实齿隙，该方法考虑了齿轮副内的平面外运动；

Simplified:这种方法可以分析计算齿轮副之间的齿轮力和齿隙。忽略摩擦时，这种方法非常有用。由于采用分析方法，接触力计算很快。

- 完成 Methed 界面的设置，单击 Next；

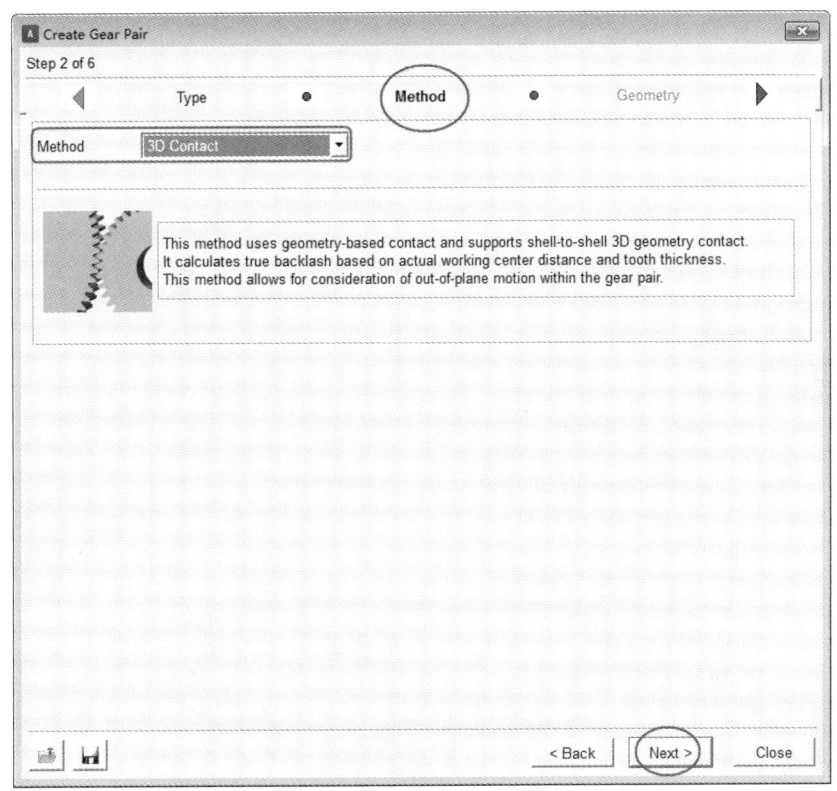

图 8-2　创建直齿轮副对话框/Methed

- Geometry 界面保持默认设置如图 8-3 所示，根据实际需求可以更改几何面板中的参数，单击 Next；
- 切换到 Material 界面如图 8-4 所示，选择 GEAR1：
- Define Mass By：Geometry and Material；
- Material Type：.materials.steel；
- 选择 GEAR2：
- Define Mass By：Geometry and Material；
- Material Type：.materials.steel；
- 完成 Material 界面的设置，单击 Next；
- 切换到 Connection 界面（见图 8-5），齿轮 GEAR1 与齿轮 GEAR2 分别与大地之间用旋转副约束，单击 Next；

- 切换到 Completion 界面，如图 8-6 所示，单击 Finish，完成直齿轮的创建；
- 单击 Motions > Rotational Joint Motion 命令；
- 在图形窗口中选择旋转副：Driver_1.gear_revolute，完成旋转驱动的创建；

图 8-3　创建直齿轮副对话框/Geometry

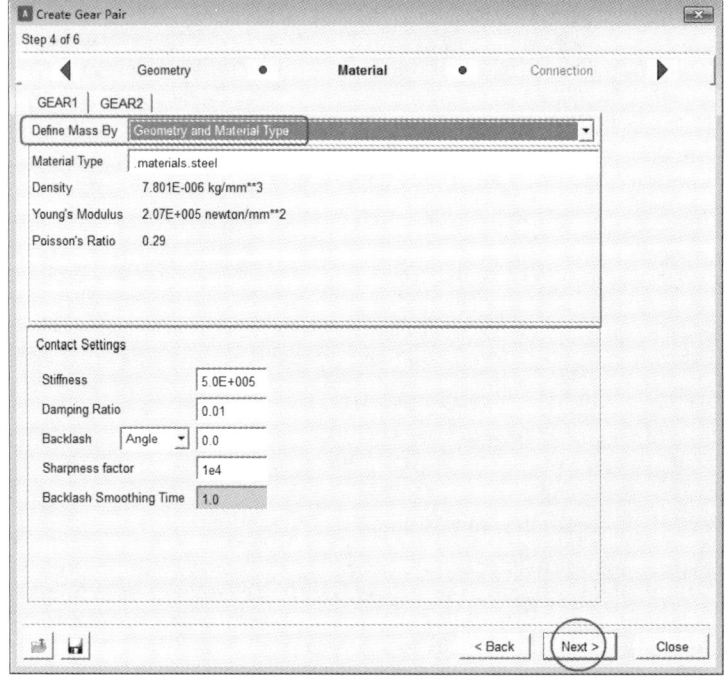

图 8-4　创建直齿轮副对话框/Material

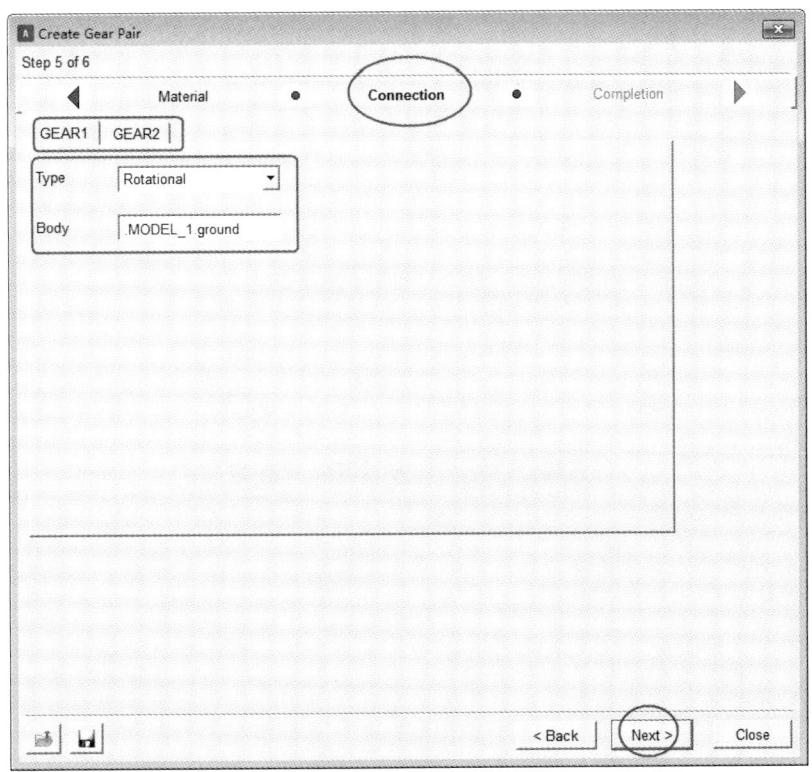

图 8-5 创建直齿轮副对话框/Connection

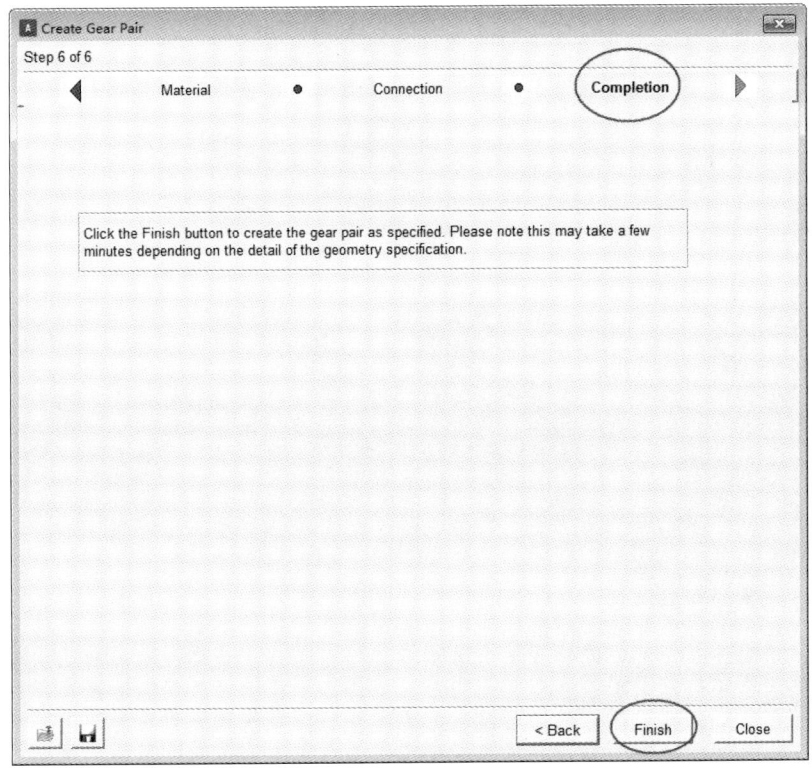

图 8-6 创建直齿轮副对话框/Completion

- 单击 Tools > Database Navigator，弹出数据对话框如图 8-7 所示；
- 单击 Driver_1，选择 gear_revolute；
- 单击 OK，弹出 Information 窗口如图 8-8 所示；
- 单击 Modify 菜单，弹出约束副修改对话框如图 8-9 所示；
- 在约束副修改对话框单击 Joint friction，弹出修改摩擦设置对话框如图 8-10 所示；
- Mu Static：0.2；

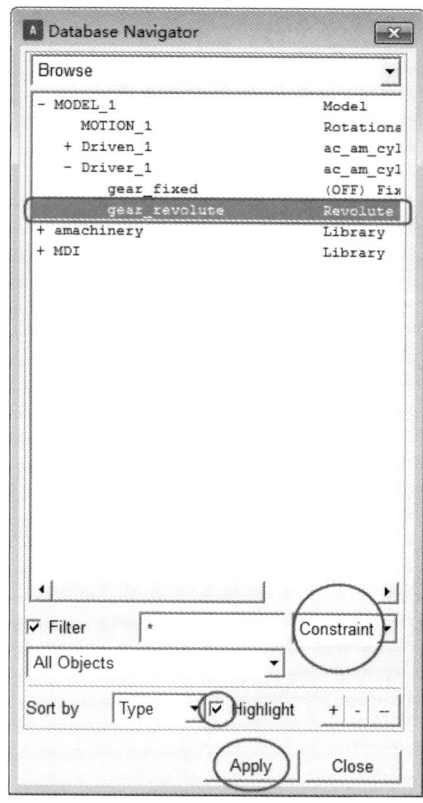

图 8-7 数据库

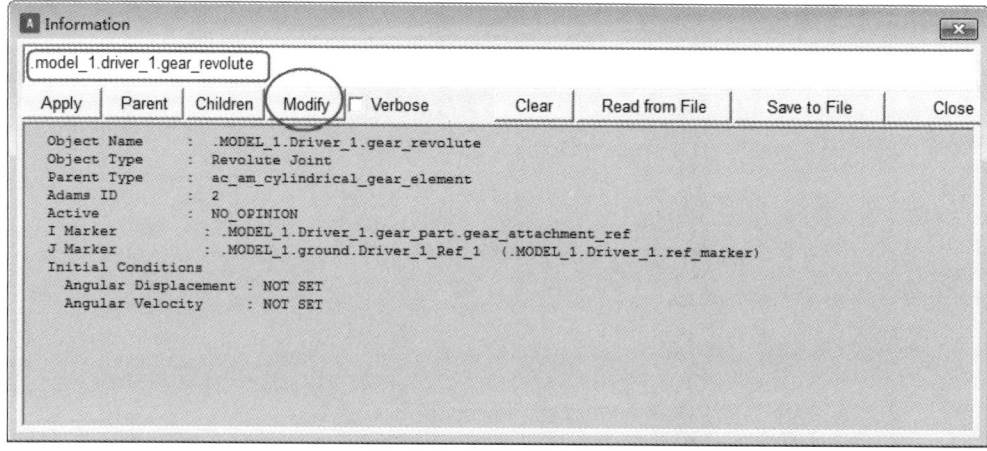

图 8-8 约束副信息窗口

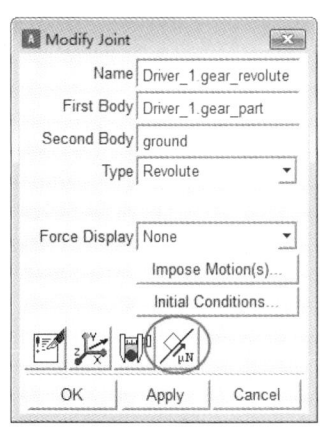

图 8-9　约束副修改窗口　　　　　图 8-10　摩擦系数修改窗口

- Mu Dynamic：0.1；
- Modify Frication 中单击 OK；
- Modify Joint 中单击 OK；此时模型创建并设置完成，创建好的直齿轮副模型如图 8-11 所。
- 单击 Simulation > Simulate 命令；
- End Time：5；
- Steps：500；
- 其余保持默认设置，单击 Start simulation；
- 计算完成后，按 F8 切换到后处理模块。

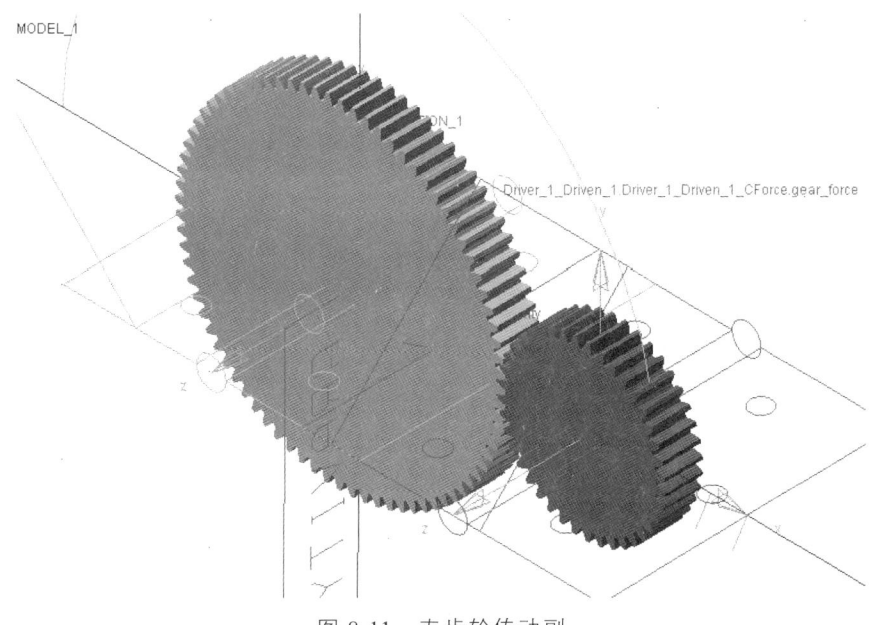

图 8-11　直齿轮传动副

绘制齿轮副在 3 个方向受力及力矩（见图 8-12～图 8-17），从计算结果可以看出，齿轮的受力主要为齿间的接触冲击力，良好的加工精度及动平衡可以有效地抑制齿间的冲击，改善传动的平顺性。

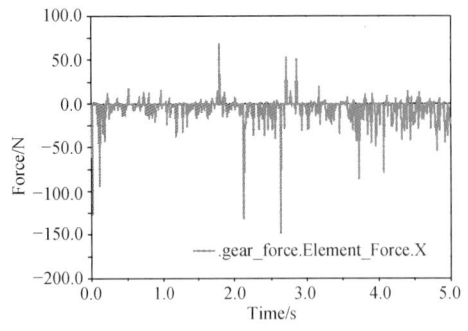

图 8-12　驱动齿轮 X 方向力

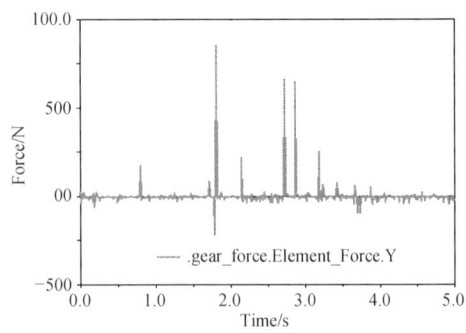

图 8-13　驱动齿轮 Y 方向力

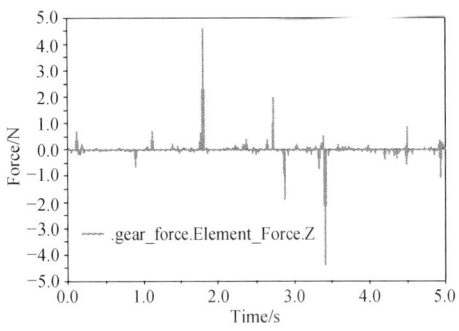

图 8-14　驱动齿轮 Z 方向力

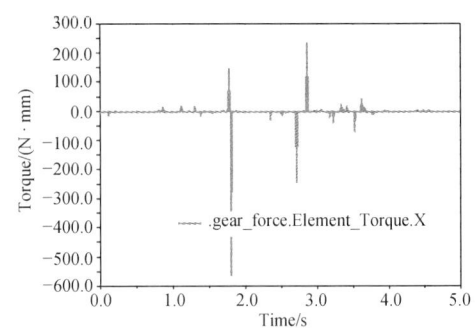

图 8-15　驱动齿轮 X 方向力矩

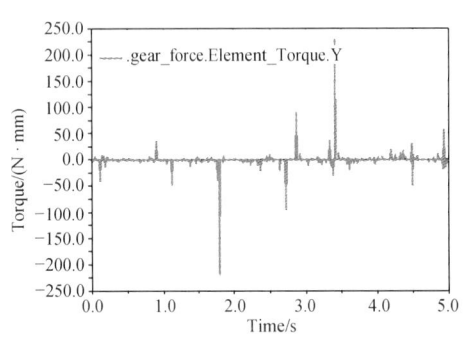

图 8-16　驱动齿轮 Y 方向力矩

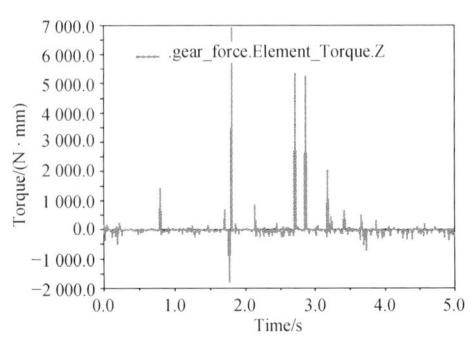

图 8-17　驱动齿轮 Z 方向力矩

8.2　锥齿轮传动

锥齿轮用来传递两相交轴之间的运动和动力，在一般机械中，锥齿轮两轴之间交角等于

90°（可以不等于90度）；与圆柱齿轮类似，锥齿轮有分度圆锥、齿顶圆锥、齿根圆锥和基圆锥；圆锥体有大端和小端，其对应大端的圆分别称为分度圆、齿顶圆、齿根圆和基圆。一对锥齿轮的运动相当于一对节圆锥作纯滚动。锥齿轮的创建方法参考直齿轮，创建好的锥齿轮副如图8-18所示，后处理显示旋转角度如图8-19、图8-20所示。

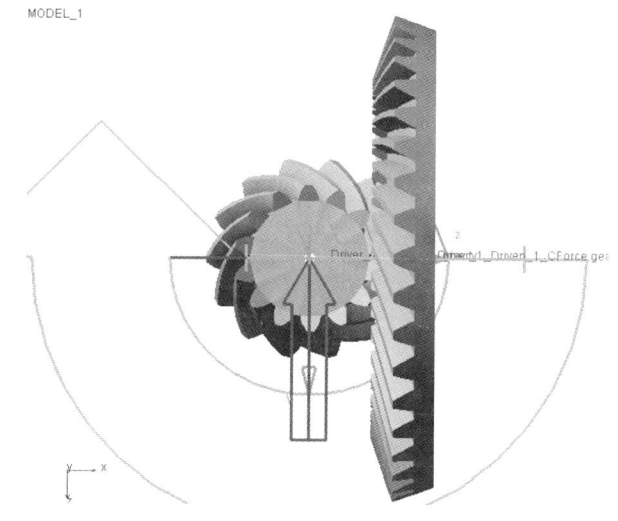

图 8-18　锥齿轮传动副

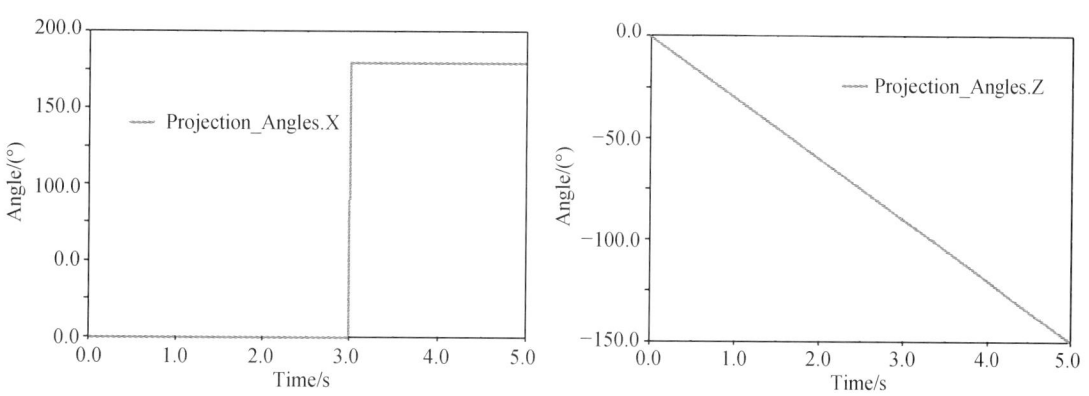

图 8-19　Driver_1 转动副 X 轴旋转投影角度　　图 8-20　Driver_1 转动副 Z 轴旋转投影角度

8.3　蜗轮蜗杆齿轮传动

蜗轮蜗杆机构常用来传递两交错轴之间的运动和动力。蜗轮与蜗杆在其中间平面内相当于齿轮与齿条，蜗杆又与螺杆形状相似。蜗轮蜗杆机构的特点是传动比大，比交错轴斜齿轮机构紧凑；两轮啮合齿面间为线接触，其承载能力大大高于交错轴斜齿轮机构；蜗杆传动相当于螺旋传动，为多齿啮合传动，故传动平稳、噪声很小；具有自锁性。当蜗杆的导程角小于啮合轮齿间的当量摩擦角时，机构具有自锁性，可实现反向自锁，即只能蜗杆带动蜗轮，而不能由蜗轮带动蜗杆，如在起重机械中使用的自锁蜗杆机构，其反向自锁性可起安全保护作用。蜗轮蜗杆啮合传动时，啮合轮齿间的相对滑动速度大，故摩擦损耗大、效率低。蜗轮及蜗杆机构常被用于两轴交错、传动比大、传动功率不大或间歇工作的场合。蜗轮蜗杆传动副的创建方法参考直齿轮，创建好的蜗轮蜗杆传动副如图 8-21 所示，后处理显示力、力矩如图 8-22、图 8-23 所示。

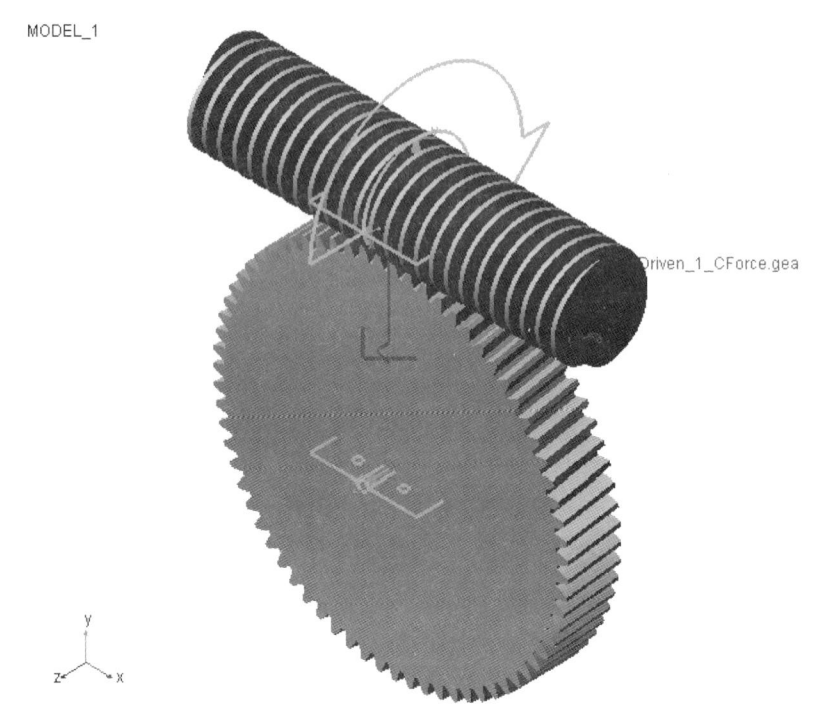

图 8-21　蜗轮蜗杆传动副

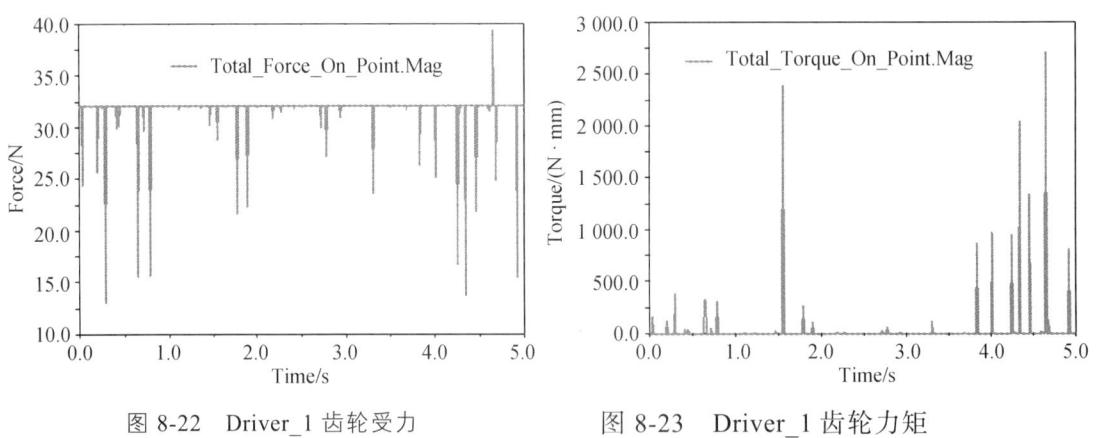

图 8-22　Driver_1 齿轮受力　　　　图 8-23　Driver_1 齿轮力矩

8.4　齿轮齿条传动

齿轮齿条在传动过程中独具运动特点：齿轮传动用来传递任意两轴间的运动和动力，其圆周速度可达到 300 m/s，传递功率可达 105 kW，齿轮直径可从不到 1 mm 至 150 m 以上，是现代机械中应用最广的一种机械传动。丝杆传动的精度高，但是在长距离重负载下，丝杆易导致弯曲，而齿条不存在这些情况。齿轮齿条传动与带传动相比主要有以下优点：① 传递动力大、效率高；② 寿命长，工作平稳，可靠性高；③ 能保证恒定的传动比，能传递任意夹角两轴间的运动。齿轮传动与带传动相比主要缺点：① 制造、安装精度要求较高，因而成本也较高；② 不宜作远距离传动。

齿轮齿条传动副的创建方法参考直齿轮，创建好的齿轮齿条传动副如图 8-24 所示，后处理显示力、力矩如图 8-25、图 8-26 所示。

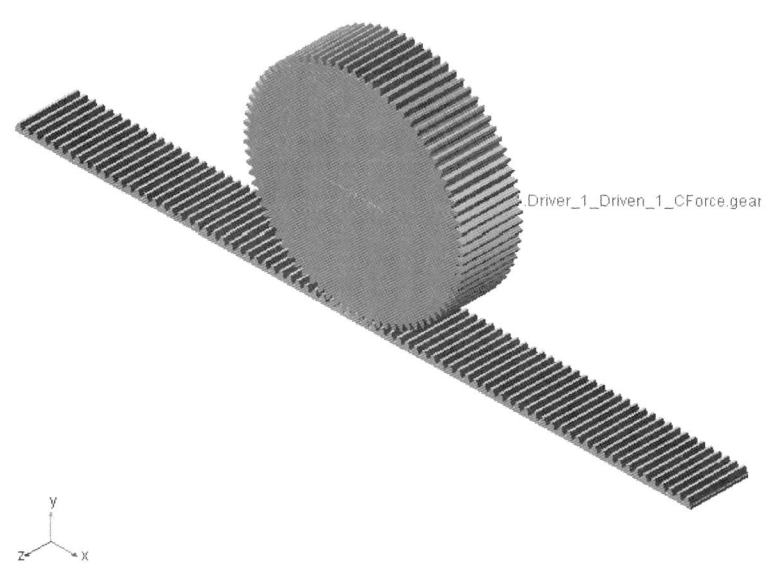

图 8-24　齿轮齿条传动副

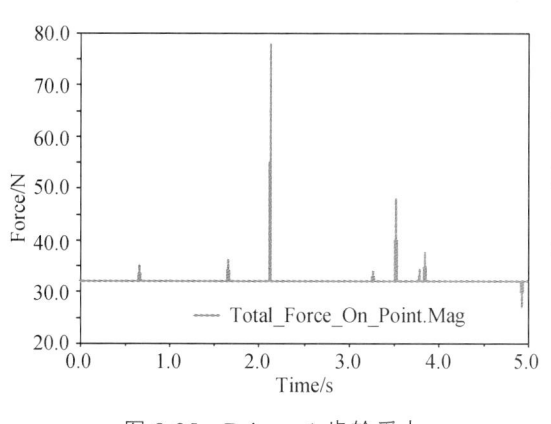

图 8-25　Driven_1 齿轮受力

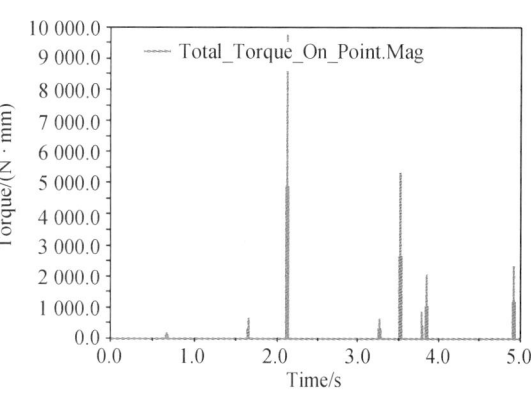

图 8-26　Driven_1 齿轮力矩

8.5 准双曲面齿轮传动

准双曲面齿轮指轴线偏置的锥齿轮,又习惯称"双曲线齿轮"或"准双曲线齿轮"。准双曲面齿轮在汽车后桥总成开发中的重要性越来越受到重视,对齿轮的质量、传动的平稳性、承载能力及寿命方面的要求也越来越高。准双曲面齿轮,由于齿面是复杂的曲面,很难得到比较精确的有限元模型,而要较准确地模拟分析这种复杂的曲面接触过程,对有限元模型的精确性要求是很高的,比较准确的有限元模型有六面体有限元模型。

准双曲面齿轮传动副的创建方法参考直齿轮,创建好的准双曲面齿轮传动副如图8-27所示;后处理显示力、力矩如图8-28、图8-29所示,从计算结果中可知,准双曲面齿轮传动最大的优点是传动过程中平顺性极好,齿间的接触冲击振动小,有利于提升零部件系统的疲劳特性及耐久特性。

图 8-27 准双曲面齿轮传动副

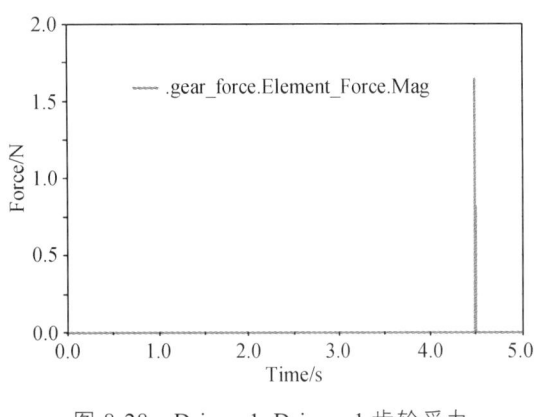

图 8-28 Driver_1_Driven_1 齿轮受力

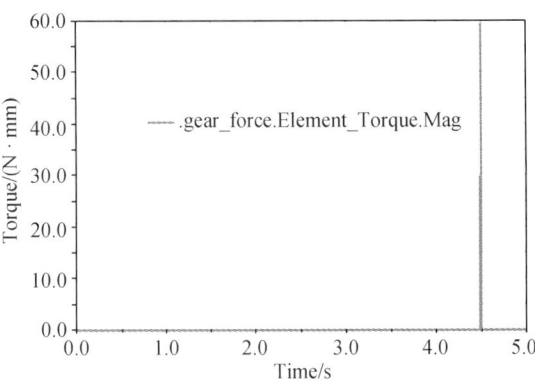

图 8-29 Driver_1_Driven_1 齿轮力矩

8.6 行星齿轮传动

行星齿轮传动与普通齿轮传动相比，具有许多独特优点，最显著的特点是在传递动力时可以进行功率分流，并且输入轴和输出轴处在同一水平线上。行星齿轮传动现已被广泛应用于各种机械传动系统中的减速器、增速器和变速装置，尤其以其具有"高载荷、大传动比"的特点而在飞行器和车辆(特别是重型车辆)中得到大量应用。行星齿轮在发动机的扭矩传递上也发挥了很大的作用。由于发动机的转速扭矩等特性与路面行驶需求大相径庭，要把发动机的功率适当地分配到驱动轮，可以利用行星齿轮的上述特性来进行转换。汽车中的自动变速器，也是利用行星齿轮的这些特性，通过离合器和制动器改变各个构件的相对运动关系而获得不同的传动比。行星齿轮的结构和工作状态复杂，其振动和噪声问题也比较突出，极易发生轮齿疲劳点蚀、齿根裂纹乃至轮齿或轴断裂等失效现象，从而影响到设备的运行精度、传递效率和使用寿命。

在包含行星齿轮的齿轮系统中，传动原理与定轴齿轮不同。由于存在行星架，因此可以有三条转动轴允许动力输入/输出，还可以用离合器或制动器之类的手段，在需要的时候限制其中一条轴的转动，只剩下两条轴进行传动。互相啮合的齿轮之间的关系可以有多种组合：

（1）动力从太阳轮输入，从外齿圈输出，行星架通过机构锁死；
（2）动力从太阳轮输入，从行星架输出，外齿圈锁死；
（3）动力从行星架输入，从太阳轮输出，外齿圈锁死；
（4）动力从行星架输入，从外齿圈输出，太阳轮锁死；
（5）动力从外齿圈输入，从行星架输出，太阳轮锁死；
（6）动力从外齿圈输入，从太阳轮输出，行星架锁死；
（7）两股动力分别从太阳轮和外齿圈输入，合成后从行星架输出；
（8）两股动力分别从行星架和太阳轮输入，合成后从外齿圈输出；
（9）两股动力分别从行星架和外齿圈输入，合成后从太阳轮输出；
（10）动力从太阳轮输入，分两路从外齿圈和行星架输出；
（11）动力从行星架输入，分两路从太阳轮和外齿圈输出；
（12）动力从外齿圈输入，分两路从太阳轮和行星架输出。

行星齿轮传动副的创建方法参考直齿轮，其中创建过程中 Geometry 界面稍有不同，设置如图 3-30 所示。界面分太阳轮、行星架、行星轮三块。

- Sun Gear：下方设置保持默认；
- Ring Gear：下方设置保持默认；
- Planet Gear：默认为 3，更改为 5，即行星齿轮传动副包含 5 个行星轮；
- 单击 Next，其余保持默认直至 Finsh 完成行星齿轮组的创建，如图 8-31 所示；
- 单击 Motions > Rotational Joint Motion 命令；
- 黄色行星轮 planet_1_gear.gear_revolute 添加驱动；
- 单击 Simulation > Simulate 命令；
- End Time：5；
- Steps：500；

- 其余保持默认设置，单击 Start simulation；
- 计算完成后，按 F8 切换到后处理模块，行星齿轮 planet_1、太阳轮、行星架受力及力矩变化特性曲线如图 8-32～图 8-41 所示。

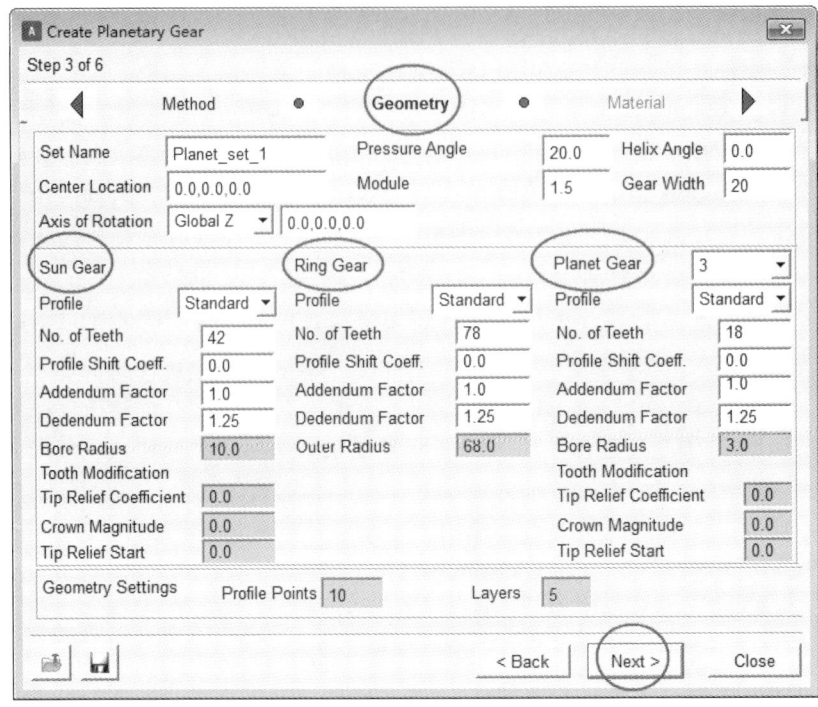

图 8-30　创建行星齿轮副对话框/Geometry

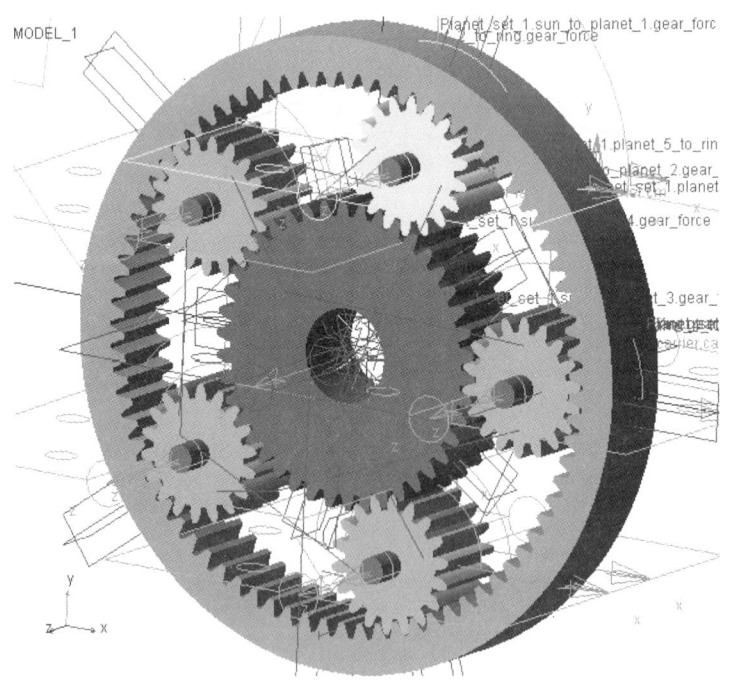

图 8-31　行星齿轮传动副

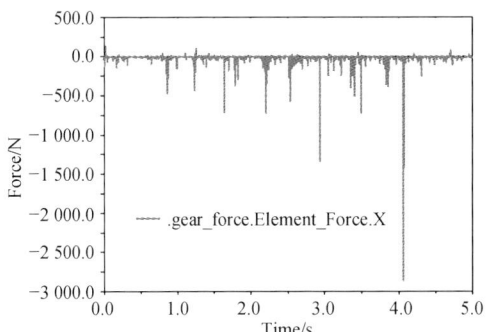

图 8-32 planet_1_to_ring X 方向受力

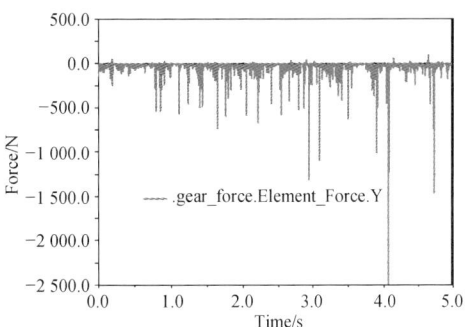

图 8-33 planet_1_to_ring Y 方向受力

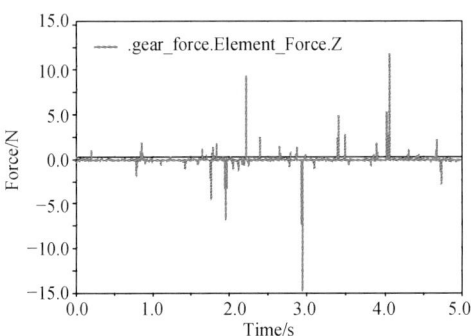

图 8-34 planet_1_to_ring Z 方向受力

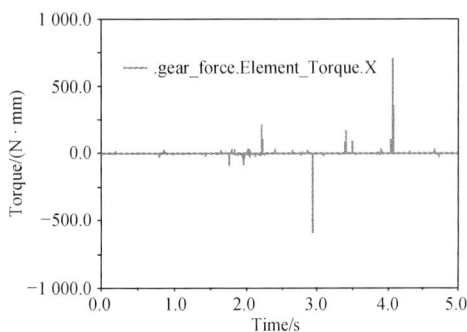

图 8-35 planet_1_to_ring X 方向力矩

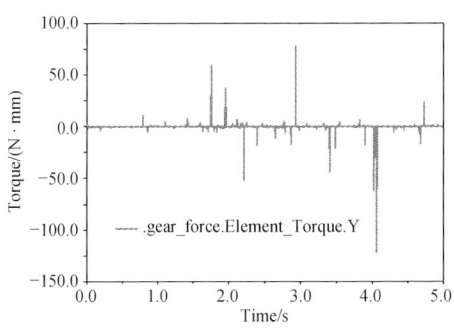

图 8-36 planet_1_to_ring Y 方向力矩

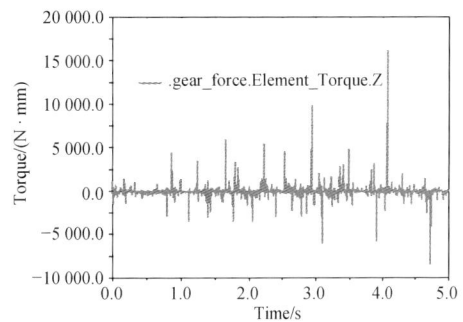

图 8-37 planet_1_to_ring Z 方向力矩

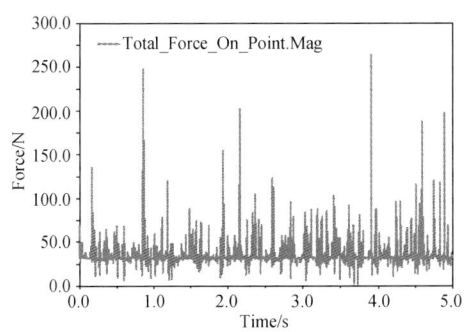

图 8-38 太阳轮合力

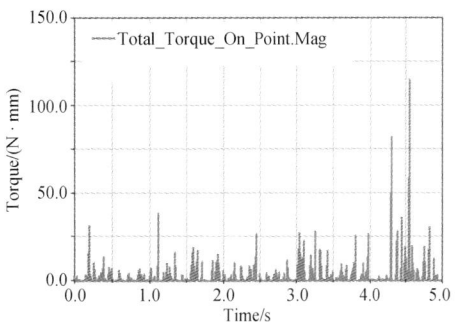

图 8-39 太阳轮合力矩

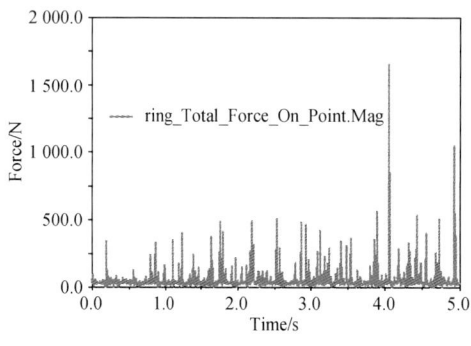 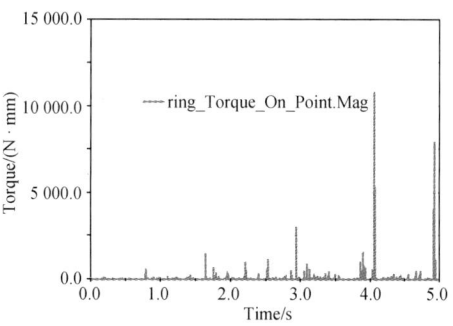

图 8-40　行星架合力　　　　　　　图 8-41　行星架合力矩

第 9 章　皮带传动

皮带模块可以预测皮带轮-皮带系统的设计和动态行为（例如传动比、应变与载荷预测、合规性研究或者履带动力学）。通过选择多 V 形槽皮带、梯形带齿皮带及平滑带来选择皮带类型；采用二维联结建模方法来计算当旋转轴与全局轴（绝对坐标系）之一平行时段节与皮带轮之间的接触力；采用几何形状设置值来定义皮带轮的位置和几何参数；将张紧滑轮应用到皮带系统上，以便张紧额外的松弛度并控制皮带的走行；使用驱动元将作用力或者运动施加到皮带系统的任意皮带轮上。皮带传动是一种依靠摩擦力来传递运动和动力的机械传动。它的特点主要表现在① 皮带有良好的弹性，在工作中能缓和冲击和振动，运动平稳无噪声；② 载荷过大时皮带在轮上打滑，因而可以防止其他零件损坏，起安全保护作用；③ 皮带是中间零件，它可以在一定范围内根据需要来选定长度，以适应中心距要求较大的工作条件；④ 结构简单制造容易，安装和维修方便，成本较低。缺点为① 靠摩擦力传动，不能传递大功率；② 传动中有滑动，不能保持准确的传动比，效率较低；③ 在传递同样大的圆周力时，外廓尺寸和轴上受力都比齿轮传动等啮合传动大，皮带磨损较快，寿命较短，如图 9-1 所示。

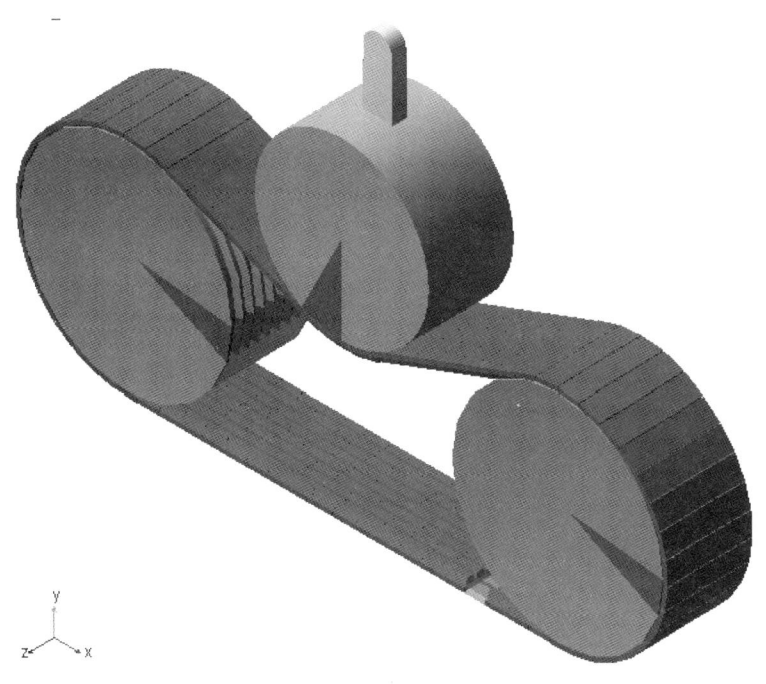

图 9-1　皮带传动

学习目标

- ◇ 滑轮。
- ◇ 张紧轮。
- ◇ 皮带。
- ◇ 驱动元。
- ◇ 双轴皮带轮传动。
- ◇ 五轴皮带轮传动。

9.1 滑　轮

- 启动 ADAMS/VIEW；
- 单击 Machinery > Belt > Create Pulley（创建滑轮），创建滑轮界面如图 9-2 所示，创建滑轮共包含 11 个子菜单界面，此时为 Type 界面；
- Belt System / Name：beltsys_1（默认皮带传动系统名称，可更改）；
- Pully Set / Name：pullyset_1（默认滑轮部件名称，可更改）；
- Type：Poly-V Grooved（多 V 形槽皮带），Trapezoidal Toothed（梯形齿或同步带），Smooth（光滑），此处选择 Poly-V Grooved（V 形槽）；
- 单击 Next，切换到 Method 界面，如图 9-3 所示；
- Method：2D links；

① Constraint：此方法较简单，用于通过一个比率传输速度。当忽略了所涉及的力和分量，只考虑减速或乘法时，使用该方法。因为它是一个理想的模型，所以滑轮只能表示为简单的圆盘。

② 2D links：皮带被约束到平面上。用刚性单元相互连接的平面零件段对皮带进行建模，并分析计算了段与滑轮之间的接触力。这种建模方法比三维链接要快，但旋转轴必须与全局轴之一平行。

③ 3D links：皮带被约束到平面上。皮带采用刚性单元相互连接的三维零件段建模，并通过分析计算段与滑轮之间的接触力。当旋转轴与全局轴不平行时使用此方法。

④ 3D links Nonplanar（非平面三维连接）：皮带采用刚性元件相互连接的三维零件段进行建模，并分析计算段与皮带轮之间的接触力。皮带可以横向穿过皮带轮，并适应皮带轮中的少量平面外偏移和错位。

⑤ 3D Simplified（三维简化）：代替大量的离散元件，皮带由一组具有创造性的零件、约束和力来表示，以重新呈现皮带的轴向柔度、皮带弯曲、滚动和质量运输效果。当皮带质量和阻力的影响可以忽略时使用该方法，因为它比离散化方法求解速度快得多；这种方法不支持连续、不受限制的闭环系统模拟，对于往复系统或某些闭环系统模拟效果更好，其中包括了最大滚子距离不超过几个跨度的带运动。

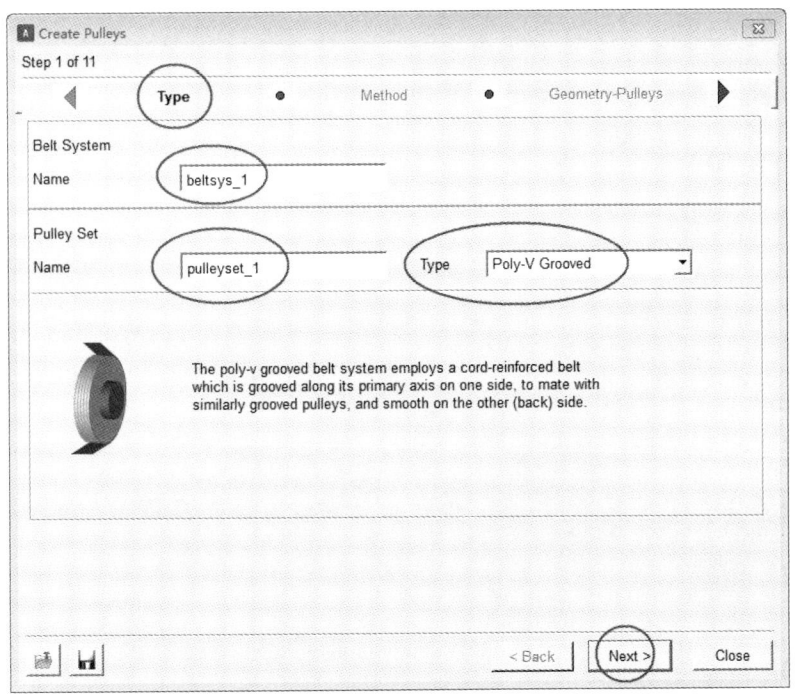

图 9-2 创建滑轮/Type

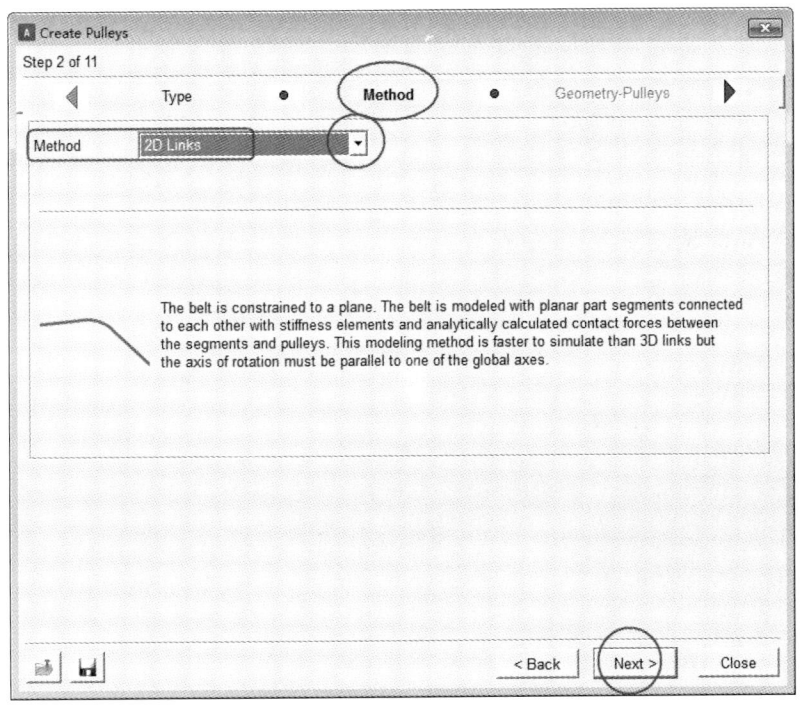

图 9-3 创建滑轮/Method

- 单击 Next，切换到 Gemetry-Pulleys 滑轮几何参数界面，如图 9-4 所示；
- Number of Pulleys（滑轮数量）：2，即皮带轮传动系统中包含两个滑轮，滑轮数量与下面的滑轮几何参数设置保持数量一致；

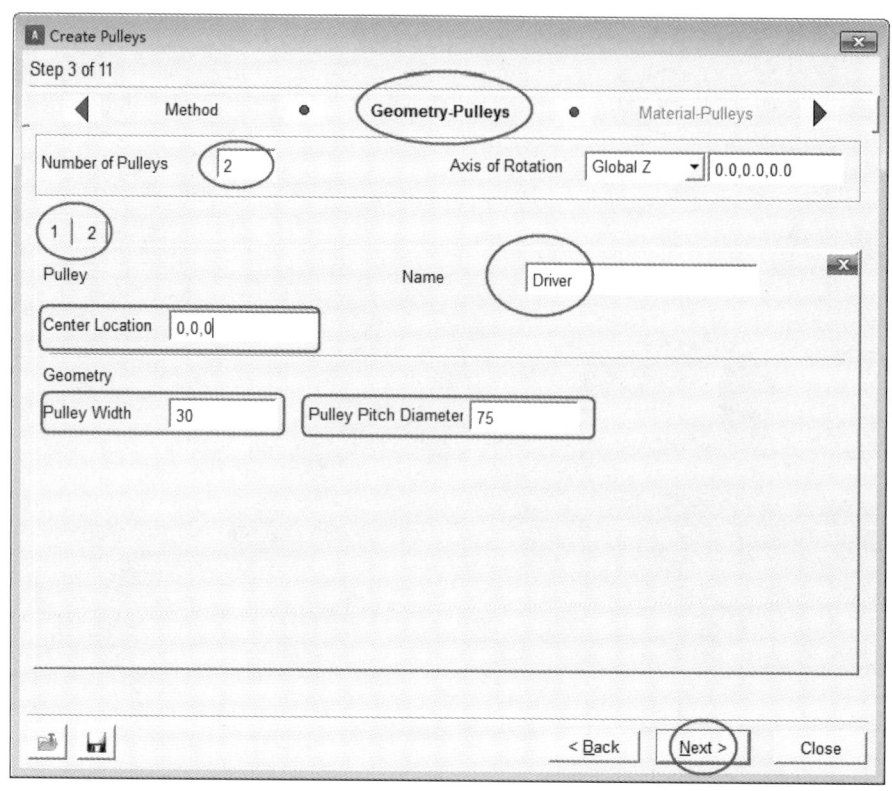

图 9-4　创建滑轮/Gemetry-Pulleys

- 单击 1；
- Name：Driver；
- Center Location：0,0,0，此处可以先建立参考点，然后依次选取；
- Pulley Width（滑轮厚度）：30；
- Pulley Pitch Diameter（滑轮旋转直径）：75；
- 单击 2；
- Name：Driven；
- Center Location：150,0,0；
- Pulley Width（滑轮厚度）：30；
- Pulley Pitch Diameter（滑轮旋转直径）：75；
- 单击 Next，切换到 Material-Pulleys 滑轮材料参数界面，如图 9-5 所示，保持默认设置；
- 单击 Next，切换到 Connection-Pulleys 滑轮约束参数界面；
- 单击 1；
- Type：Rotational；
- Body：.MODEL_1.ground，滑轮与大地之间采用转动副约束；
- 单击 2；
- Type：Rotational；
- Body：.MODEL_1.ground，滑轮与大地之间采用转动副约束；
- 单击 Next，切换到 Output-Pulleys 滑轮输出参数界面，保持默认设置；

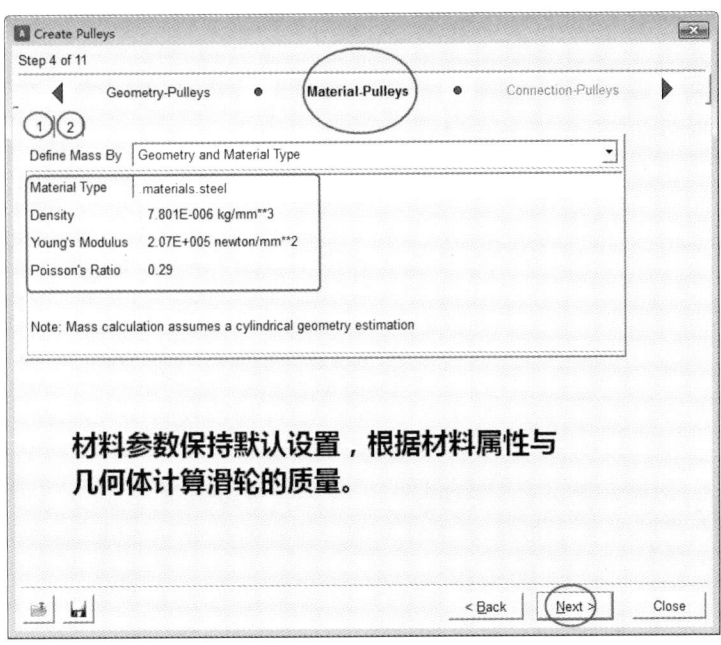

图 9-5 创建滑轮/Material-Pulleys

- 单击 Next，切换到 Completion-Pulleys 滑轮完成参数界面，保持默认设置；
- 单击 Next，切换到 Gemetry-Tensioners 张紧器参数界面，如图 9-6 所示；

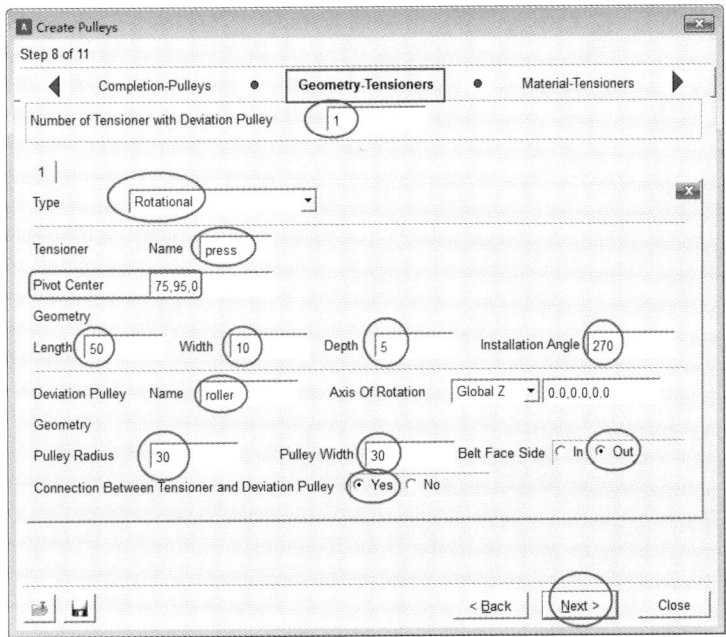

图 9-6 创建张紧轮/ Gemetry- Tensioners

- Number of Tensioners with Deviation Pulley（带偏差滑轮的张紧器数量）：1；
- Type：Rotational；
- Tensioner/Name：press ；

- Pivot Center：75,95,0；
- Length：50；
- Width：10；
- Depth：5；
- Installation Angle：270；
- Deviation Pully/Name：roller；
- Pulley Radius：30；
- Pulley Width：30；
- Belt Face Side（皮带轮与张紧器内侧还是外侧接触）：Out；
- Connection Between Tensioner and Deviation Pulley（是否用转动副连接张紧器与偏心滑轮）：Yes；
- 单击 Next，切换到 Material-Tensioners 张紧器材料参数界面，保持默认设置；
- 单击 Next，切换到 Connection-Tensioners 张紧器约束参数界面，如图 9-7 所示；

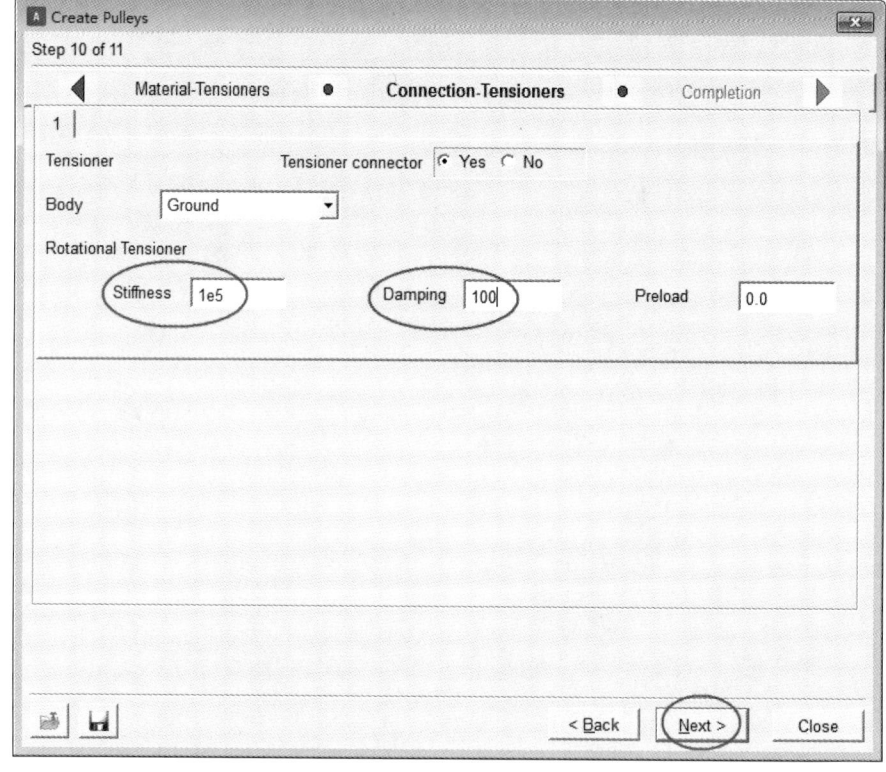

图 9-7 创建张紧轮/ Connection-Tensioners

- Stiffness（刚度）：1E5；
- Damping（阻尼）：100；
- Preload（预载荷）：0；
- 单击 Next，切换到 Completion 参数设置；
- 单击 Finish，完成滑轮、张紧器的建模，如图 9-8 所示。

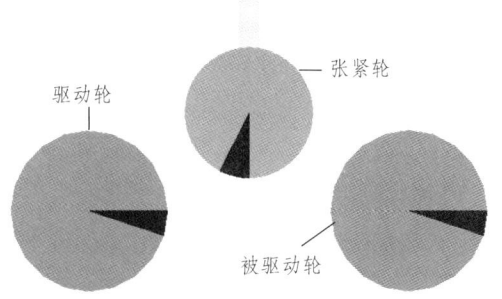

图 9-8 滑轮与张紧轮

9.2 皮 带

- 单击 Machinery > Belt > Create Belt（创建皮带），创建皮带界面如图 9-9 所示，创建皮带共包含 7 个子菜单界面，此时为 Type 界面；

图 9-9 创建皮带/Type

- Pulley Set/Name：pulleyset_1，通过 Pulley Set > Guesses 选取已经创建好的滑轮；
- Belt System/Name：.MODEL_1.beltsys_1，系统自动默认命名；
- 单击 Next，切换到 Method 界面，如图 9-3 所示；
- Method：2D links；
- 单击 Next，切换到 Gemetry 皮带几何参数界面，如图 9-10 所示；
- Belt Width（皮带宽度）：30；

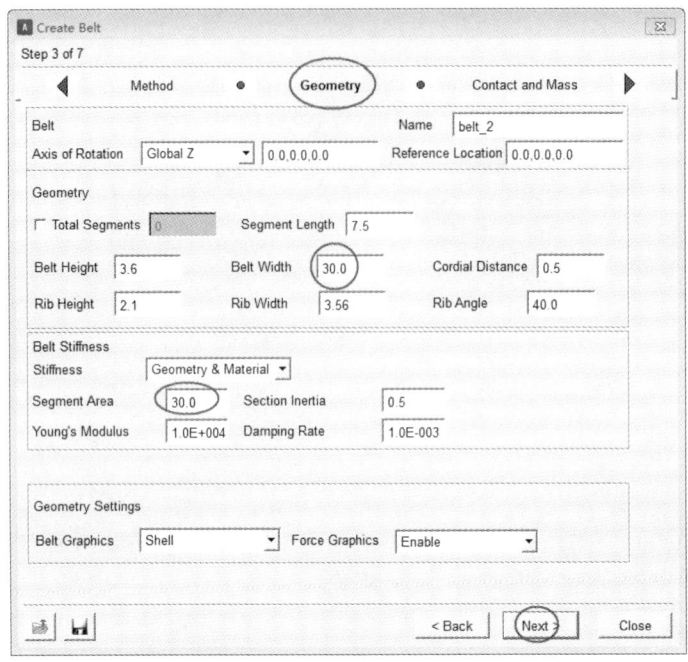

图 9-10 创建皮带/Gemetry

- Segment Area（皮带段块面积）：30；
- 单击 Next，切换到 Contant and Mass 皮带接触与质量参数界面，如图 9-11 所示，所有参数保持默认设置；
- 单击 Next，切换到 Wrapping Order 皮带包裹顺序参数界面；

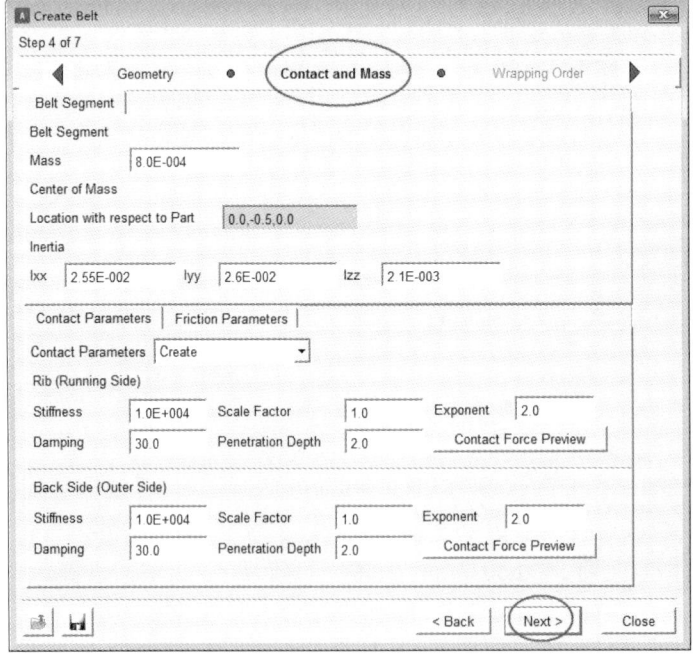

图 9-11 创建皮带/Contant and Mass

- Wrapping Order：① pulleyset_1_Driver；② pulleyset_1dev_roller；③ pulleyset_1_Drven，注意输入顺序不能乱；
- 单击 Next，弹出问题提示框如图 9-12 所示，皮带共包含 72 个段块，单击 Yes，继续包裹皮带；皮带包裹完成后切换到 Output Request 输出请求界面；

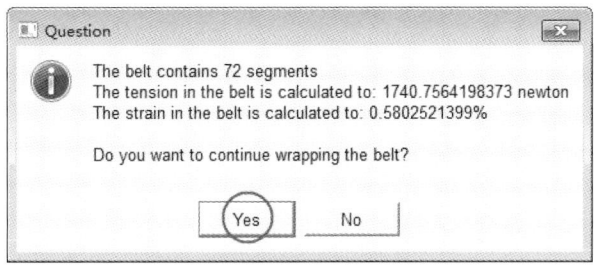

图 9-12　皮带创建问题提示框

- 勾选 Segment Request；
- Link Part(s)：segment_57（皮带中第 57 个段块）；
- 单击 Next，切换到 Completion 参数设置；
- 单击 Finish，完成皮带的建模如图 9-1 所示；

9.3　皮带驱动元

- 单击 Machinery > Belt > Belt Actuation Input（皮带驱动输入或称为动力元），创建动力元界面如图 9-13 所示，创建动力元共包含 5 个子菜单界面，此时为 Actuator 界面；

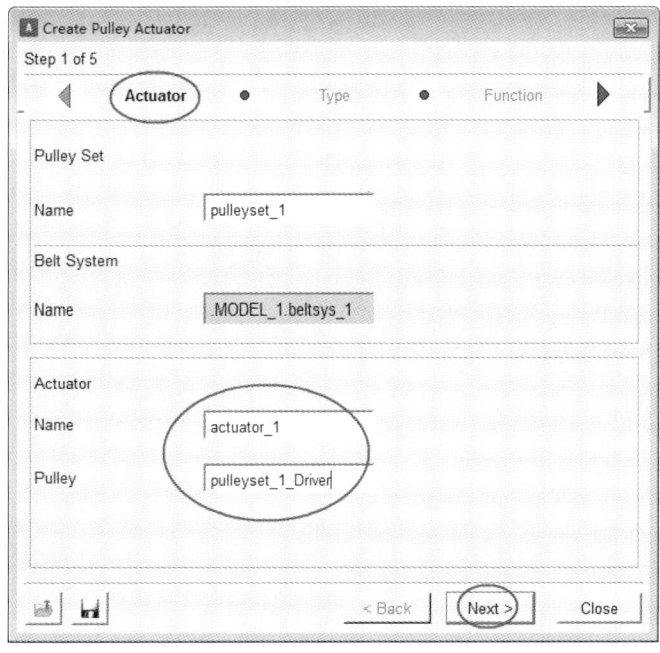

图 9-13　创建驱动元/Actuator

- 233 -

- Actuator / Name：actuator_1；
- Pulley：pulleyset_1_Driver；
- 单击 Next，切换到 Type 参数设置界面；
- Type：Motion；
- 单击 Next，切换到 Function 参数设置界面如图 9-14 所示；

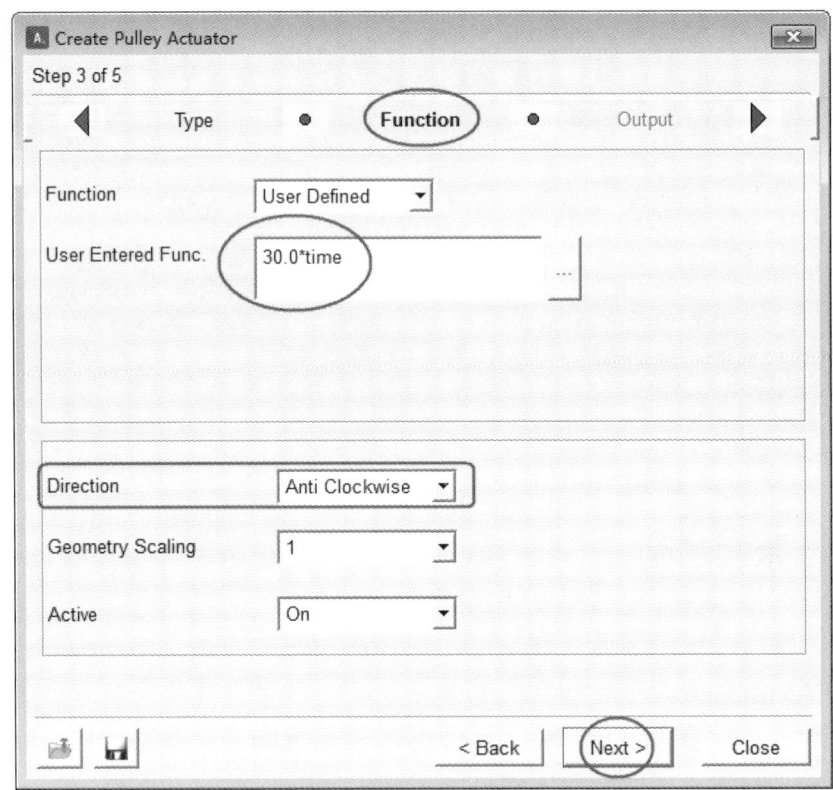

图 9-14　创建驱动元/Function

- Function：User Defined；
- User Entered Func.：30.0*time；
- Direction：Anti Clockwise（动力元为逆时针方向）；
- 单击 Next，切换到 Output 参数设置界面，保持默认设置；
- 单击 Next，切换到 Completion 参数设置；
- 单击 Finish，完成驱动元的创建；
- 单击 Simulation > Simulate 命令；
- End Time：5；
- Steps：500；
- 其余保持默认设置，单击 Start simulation；
- 计算完成后，按 F8 切换到后处理模块，皮带段块 57 所受轴向及法向接触力、驱动元转动角度及角速度如图 9-15 ~ 图 9-18 所示。

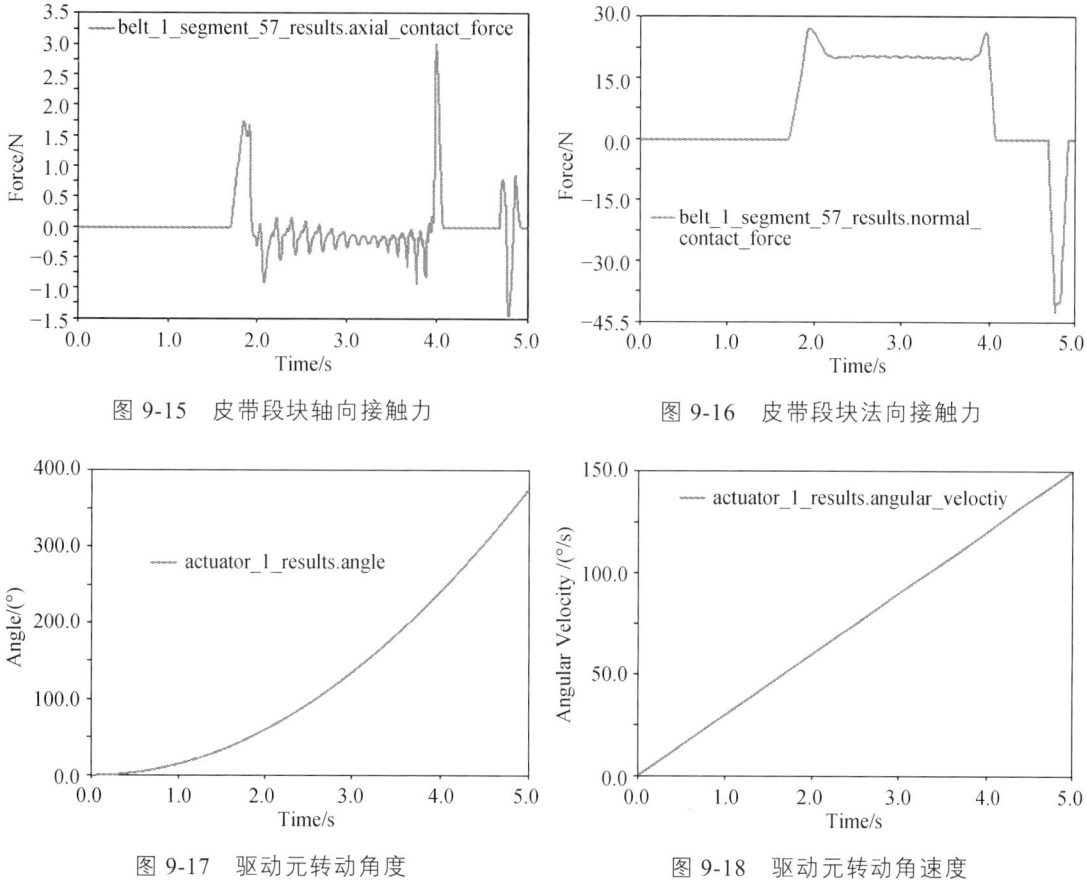

图 9-15 皮带段块轴向接触力　　　　图 9-16 皮带段块法向接触力

图 9-17 驱动元转动角度　　　　图 9-18 驱动元转动角速度

9.4　五轴皮带轮传动

- 工具条中选择参考点创建快捷方式，方向保持默认，创建 6 个参考点：
① 参考点 P1：-1 400.0，550.0，0.0；
② 参考点 P2：-850.0，800.0，0.0；
③ 参考点 P3：-300.0，750.0，0.0；
④ 参考点 P4：0.0，500.0，0.0；
⑤ 参考点 P5：-400.0，150.0，0.0；
⑥ 参考点 T1：-850.0，350.0，0.0。
- 创建滑轮与张紧器共包含 11 个界面，Step 1 of 11、Step 2 of 11 保持默认设置；
- 切换到 Step 3 of 11 界面，如图 9-19 所示：
- Number of Pulleys（滑轮数量）：5，皮带轮传动系统中包含 5 个滑轮，滑轮数量与下面的滑轮几何参数设置保持数量一致；
- 单击 1；
- Name：d1；

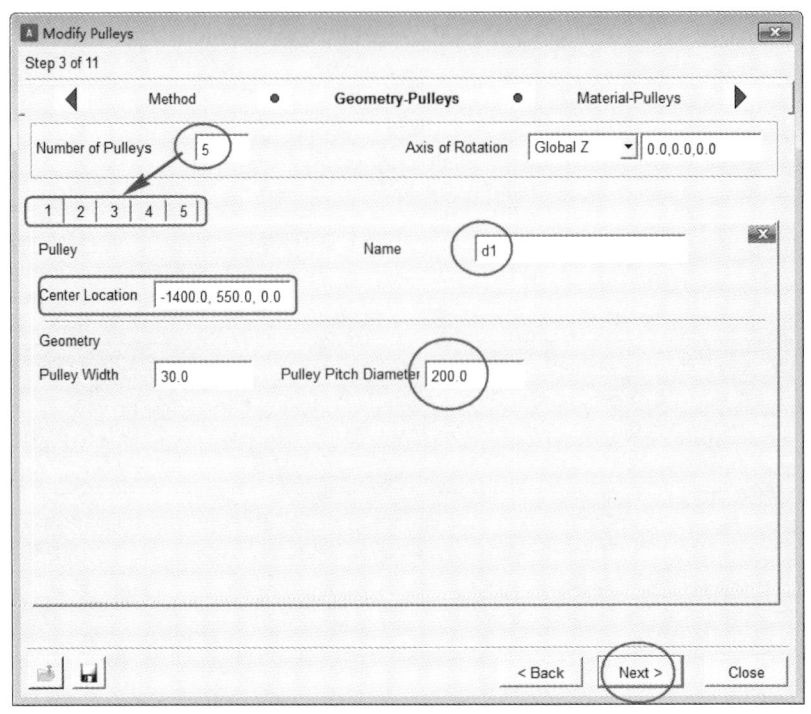

图 9-19　五轴滑轮几何参数设置

- Center Location：-1 400.0, 550.0, 0.0，通过选取图形界面中的 P1 点获取位置信息；
- Pulley Width（滑轮厚度）：30；
- Pulley Pitch Diameter（滑轮旋转直径）：200；
- 单击 2；
- Name：d2；
- Center Location：-850.0, 800.0, 0.0，通过选取图形界面中的 P2 点获取位置信息；
- Pulley Width（滑轮厚度）：30；
- Pulley Pitch Diameter（滑轮旋转直径）：200；
- 单击 3；
- Name：d3；
- Center Location：-300.0, 750.0, 0.0，通过选取图形界面中的 P3 点获取位置信息；
- Pulley Width（滑轮厚度）：30；
- Pulley Pitch Diameter（滑轮旋转直径）：200；
- 单击 4；
- Name：d4；
- Center Location：0.0, 500.0, 0.0，通过选取图形界面中的 P4 点获取位置信息；
- Pulley Width（滑轮厚度）：30；
- Pulley Pitch Diameter（滑轮旋转直径）：300；
- 单击 5；
- Name：d5；

- Center Location：−400.0, 150.0, 0.0，通过选取图形界面中的 P5 点获取位置信息；
- Pulley Width（滑轮厚度）：30；
- Pulley Pitch Diameter（滑轮旋转直径）：250；
- 单击 Next，切换到 Step 8 of 11 参数设置；
- 张紧器与偏心滑轮几何建模参考如图 9-6 所示；
- Pivot Center：−850.0, 350.0, 0.0，通过选取图形界面中的 T1 点获取位置信息；
- Pulley Radius：200；
- 单击 Next，直至完成剩余所有界面默认设置；

皮带与驱动元创建与上述两轴系皮带传动抑制，皮带包裹依次按顺序选取 5 个滑轮和 1 个张紧轮，选择第 20 个皮带段块作为输出，建立好的五轴系皮带传动如图 9-20 所示，段块轴向力与法向力如图 9-21、图 9-22 所示，皮带张力如图 9-23 所示，驱动元转角与力矩如图 9-24、图 9-25 所示。模型存储于章节文件中。

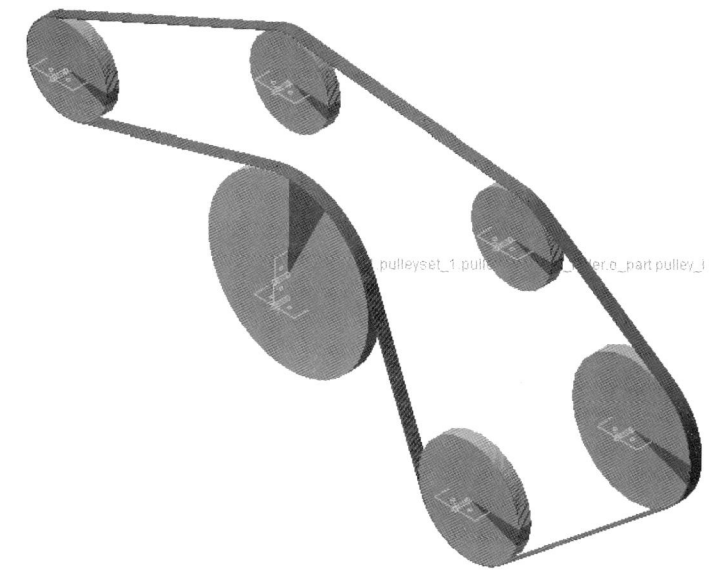

图 9-20　五轴系皮带轮传动

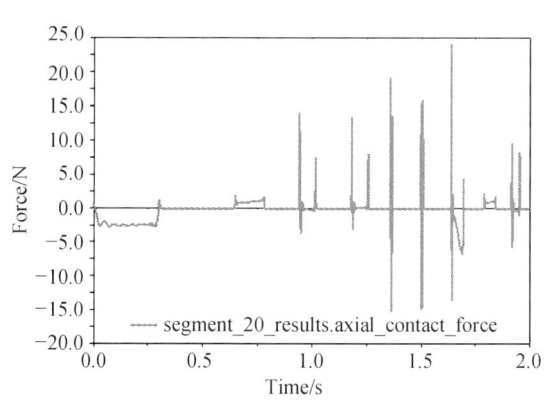

图 9-21　皮带段块轴向接触力

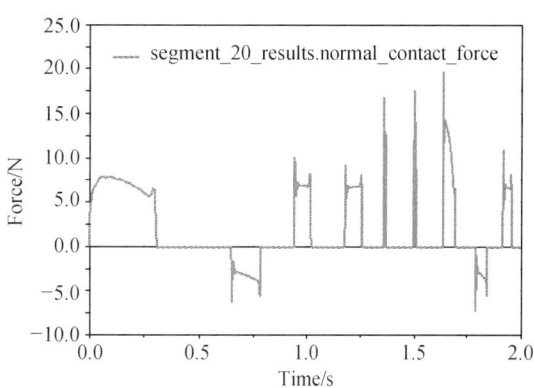

图 9-22　皮带段块法向接触力

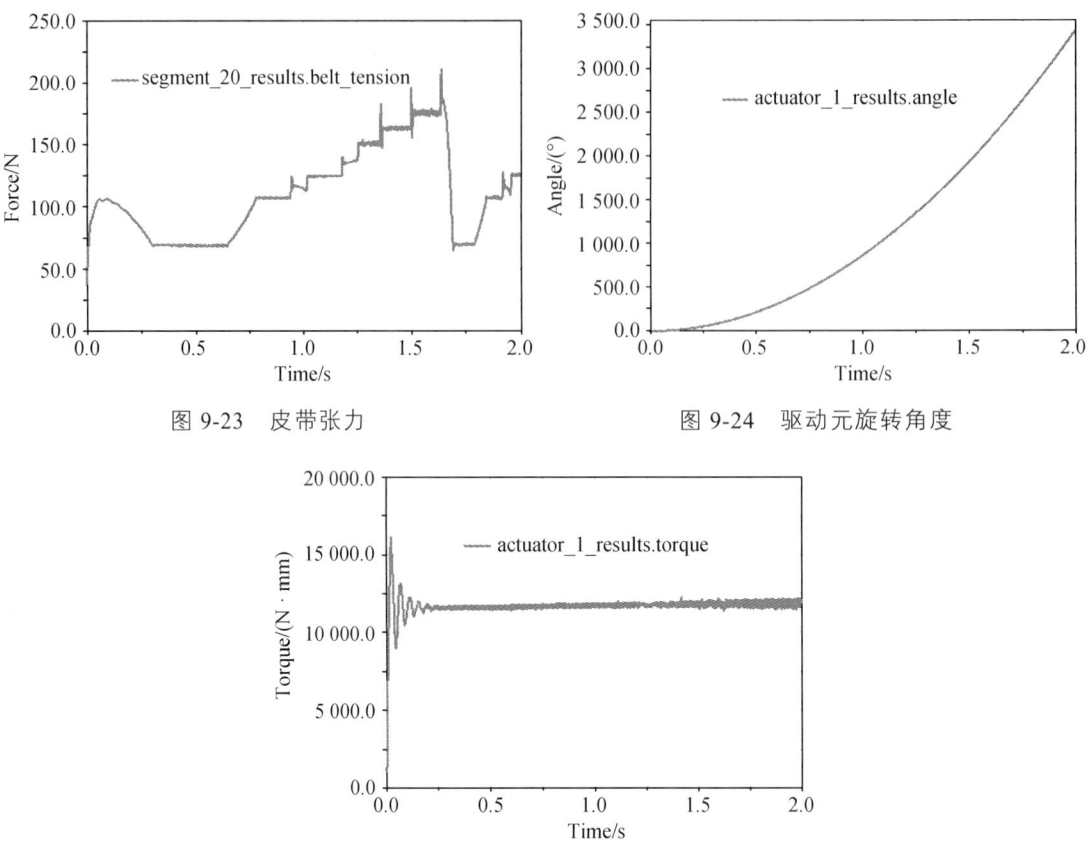

图 9-23 皮带张力

图 9-24 驱动元旋转角度

图 9-25 驱动元旋转力矩

第 10 章 链条传动

链传动是通过链条将具有特殊齿形的主动链轮的运动和动力传递到从动链轮的一种传动方式（见图 10-1）。与带传动相比，链传动无弹性滑动和打滑现象，平均传动比准确，工作可靠，效率高；传递功率大，过载能力强，相同工况下的传动尺寸小；所需张紧力小，作用于轴上的压力小；能在高温、潮湿、多尘、有污染等恶劣环境中工作。缺点是仅能用于两平行轴间的传动；成本高，易磨损，易伸长，传动平稳性差，运转时会产生附加动载荷、振动、冲击和噪声，不宜用在急速反向的传动中。链传动仿真 CHAIN 特点：① 通过选择滚子链和无声链来选择链类型；② 采用二维连结建模方法来计算当旋转轴与全局轴之一平行时链节与链轮之间的接触力；③ 将线性、非线性或高级合规性应用到滚子链上；④ 将枢轴、平移或固定导板应用到链系统上；⑤ 使用作用向导将作用力或者运动施加到链系统的任意链轮上。

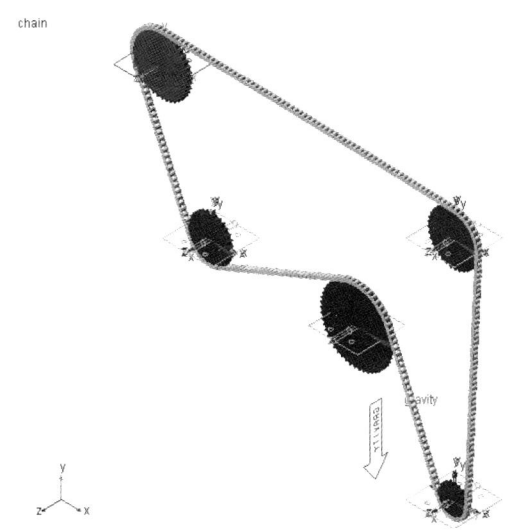

图 10-1 五轴系链传动

学习目标

- ◇ 链轮。
- ◇ 张紧轮。
- ◇ 链条。
- ◇ 驱动元。
- ◇ 五轴链轮传动。

10.1　链　轮

- 启动 ADAMS/VIEW；
- 单击 Machinery > Chain > Create Cloed Loop Sprockets（创建链轮），创建链轮界面如图 10-2 所示，创建链轮共包含 11 个子菜单界面，此时为 Type 界面；
- Chain System / Name：chainsys_1（默认链轮传动系统名称，可更改）；
- Chain Set / Name：pullyset_1（默认链轮部件名称，可更改）；
- Type：Roller Sprocket（滚子链轮），Silent Sprocket（无声链轮），此处选择 Roller Sprocket（滚子链轮）；

（1）Roller Sprocket：滚子链系统采用由圆柱滚子组成的链条，每侧通过连杆相互连接。链条与带齿链轮配合。

（2）Silent Sprocket：无声链条系统，也被称为渐开链，采用由圆柱滚子组成的链条，圆柱滚子通过具有齿形轮廓的每个轴上的链节相互连接。链条与带齿链轮配合。

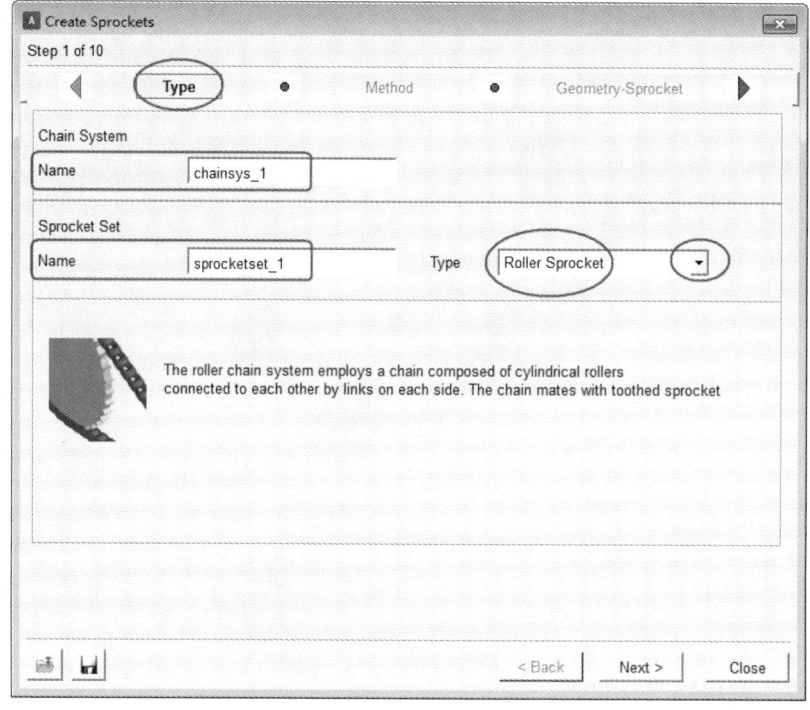

图 10-2　创建链轮/Type

- 单击 Next，切换到 Method 界面，如图 10-3 所示；
- Method：2D links ；

（1）Constraint：这是一种用于通过比率传递速度的简单方法，当忽略所涉及的力和分量并且仅关注减速或乘法时，使用此方法。

（2）2D Links：链被约束到平面，该链条采用刚性单元相互连接的平面零件连杆进行建模，并对连杆、链轮和导轨之间的接触力进行分析计算。这种建模方法比三维链接模拟快，但旋转轴必须与全局轴之一平行。

（3）3D Links：链被约束到平面，该链条采用刚性元件相互连接的三维零件连杆进行建模，并通过分析计算得出连杆、链轮和导轨之间的接触力。当旋转轴与全局轴之一不平行时使用此方法。

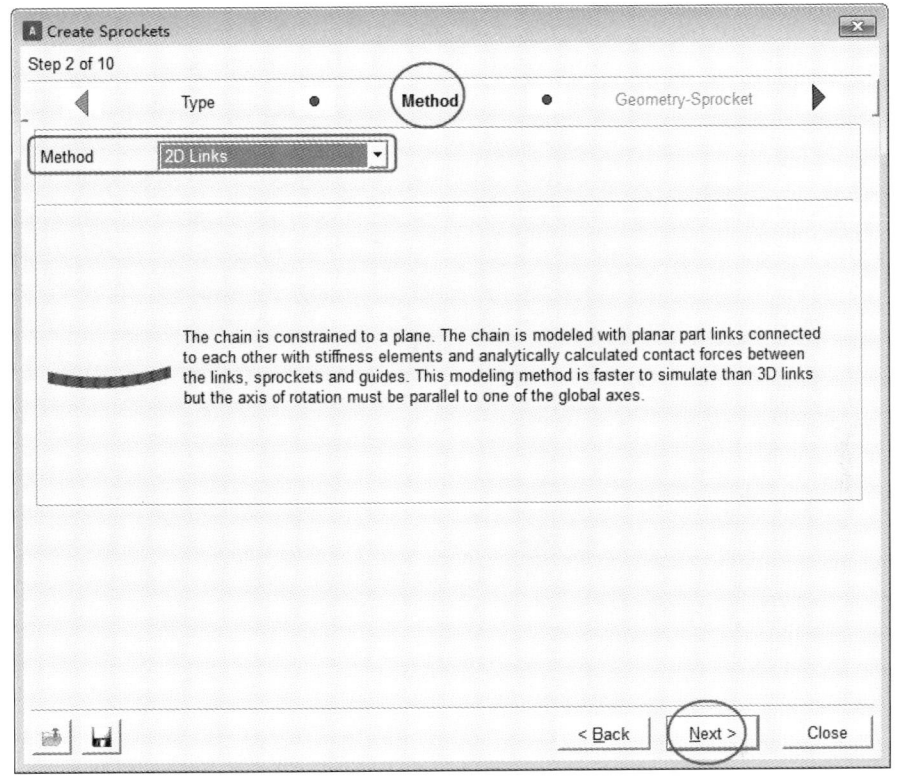

图 10-3　创建链轮/Method

- 单击 Next，切换到 Gemetry-Pulleys 链轮几何参数界面，如图 10-4 所示；
- Number of Pulleys（链轮数量）：5，即链轮传动系统中包含 5 个链轮，链轮数量与下面的链轮几何参数设置保持数量一致；
- 单击 1；
- Name：d1；
- Center Location：－450.0, 350.0, 0.0，此处可以先建立参考点，然后依次选取；
- Sprocket Width：8；
- Number of Teeth：40；
- In/Out Chain：勾选 In，其余参数保持默认设置；
- 单击 2；
- Name：d2；
- Center Location：150.0, 350.0, 0.0；
- Sprocket Width：8；

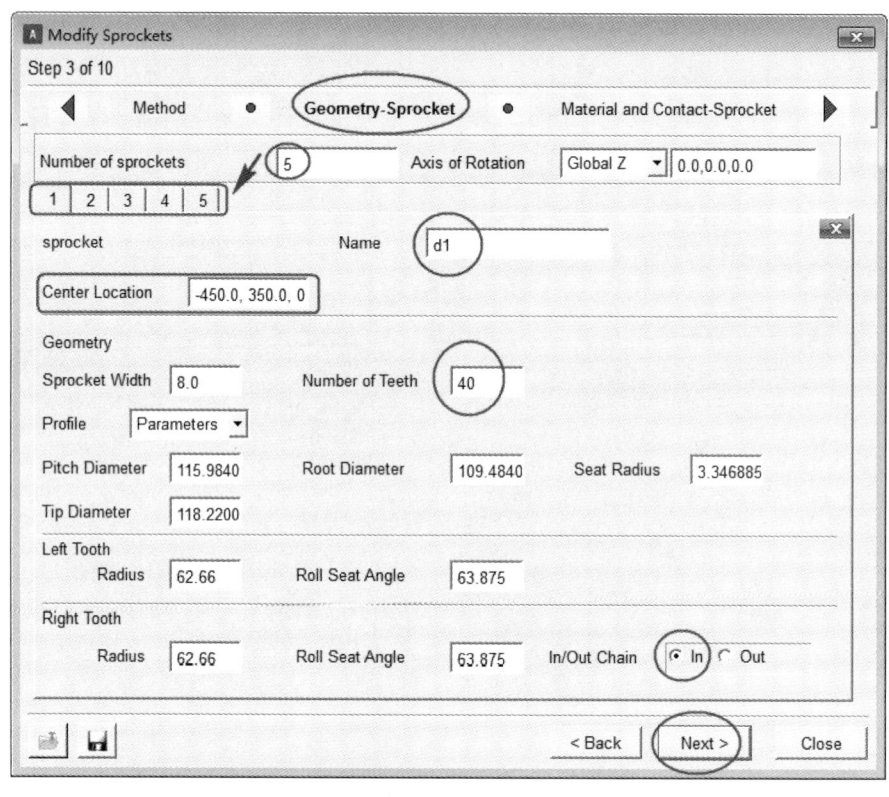

图 10-4 创建链轮/Gemetry-Sprocket

- Number of Teeth：35；
- In/Out Chain：勾选 In，其余参数保持默认设置；
- 单击 3；
- Name：d3；
- Center Location：150.0，－100.0，0.0；
- Sprocket Width：8；
- Number of Teeth：20；
- In/Out Chain：勾选 In，其余参数保持默认设置；
- 单击 4；
- Name：d4；
- Center Location：－50.0，100.0，0.0；
- Sprocket Width：8；
- Number of Teeth：50；
- In/Out Chain：勾选 Out，其余参数保持默认设置；
- 单击 5；
- Name：d5；
- Center Location：－350.0，100.0，0.0；
- Sprocket Width：8；
- Number of Teeth：30；

- In/Out Chain：勾选 In，其余参数保持默认设置；
- 单击 Next，切换到 Material and Contact-Sprocket 链轮材料参数界面，如图 10-5 所示，保持默认设置；

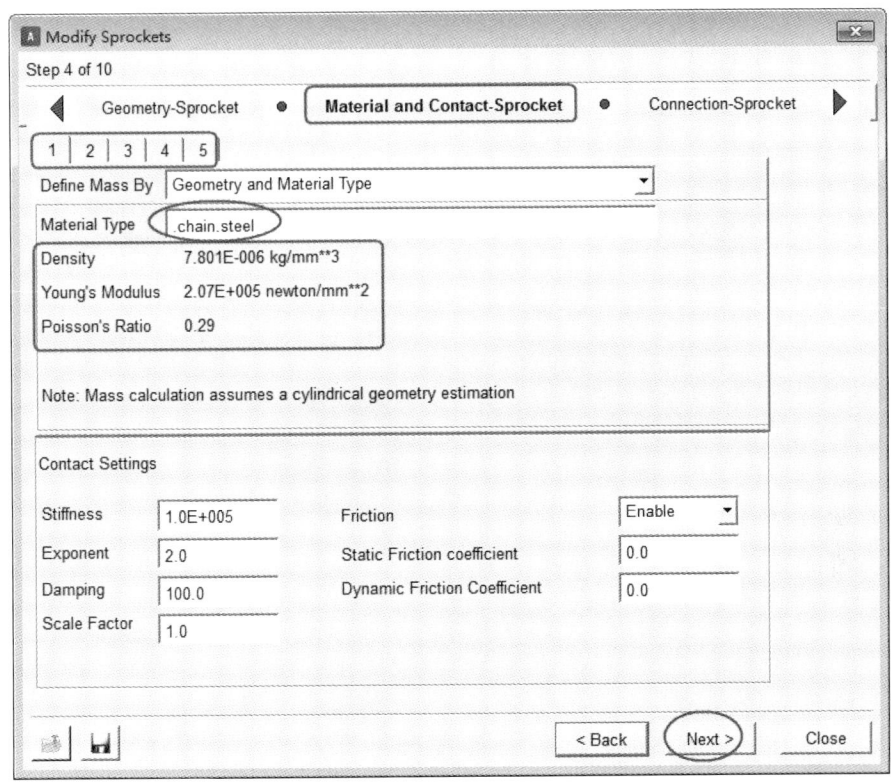

图 10-5　创建链轮/Material and Contact- Sprocket

- 单击 Next，切换到 Connection-Sprocket 链轮约束参数界面；
- 单击 1；
- Type：Rotational；
- Body：.MODEL_1.ground，链轮与大地之间采用转动副约束；
- 单击 2；
- Type：Rotational；
- Body：.MODEL_1.ground；
- 单击 3；
- Type：Rotational；
- Body：.MODEL_1.ground；
- 单击 4；
- Type：Rotational；
- Body：.MODEL_1.ground；
- 单击 5；
- Type：Rotational；

- Body：.MODEL_1.ground；
- 单击 Next，切换到 Output-Sprocket 链轮输出参数界面，保持默认设置；
- 单击 Next，切换到 Completion-Sprocket 链轮完成参数界面，保持默认设置；
- 单击 Next，切换到 Gemetry-Guide 链轮参数界面；
- Number of Guide（链轮导板数量）：0，五轴系链轮传动不需要导链板；
- 依次单击 Next，直至 Finish，完成链轮的建模，如图 10-6 所示。

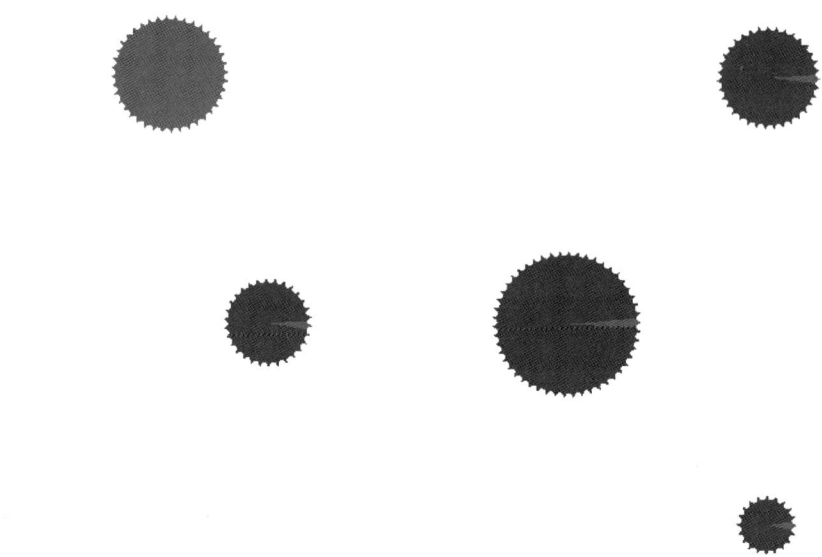

图 10-6　链轮（红色为驱动链轮，可通过参数修改链轮几何体颜色）

10.2　链　条

- 单击 Machinery > Chain > Create Chain（创建链条），创建链条界面如图 10-7 所示，创建链条共包含 8 个子菜单界面，此时为 Type 界面；
- Sprocket Set / Name：sprocketset_1，选取已经创建好的链轮系统名称；
- Chain System / Name：.chain.chainsys_1，系统默认链条名称；
- 单击 Next，切换到 Method 界面；
- Method：2D links；
- 单击 Next，切换到 Geometry 链条几何参数界面（见图 10-8），保持默认设置；
- 单击 Next，切换到 Mass 链条质量参数界面，所有参数保持默认设置；
- 单击 Next，切换到 Wrapping Order 链条包裹链轮顺序参数界面；
- Wrapping Order：① sprocketset_1_d1，② sprocketset_1_d2，③ sprocketset_1_d3，④ sprocketset_1_d4，⑤ sprocketset_1_d5，注意输入顺序不能乱，如图 10-9 所示；
- 单击 Next，弹出问题提示框如图 10-10 所示，链条共包含 257 个链条连接销，单击 Yes，继续包裹链轮，需要注意的是在包裹链轮时可能会出错误，这时候需要调节 Geometry 界面中的 Chain Pitch 参数的大小抑制链条连接时过大的误差所导致的错误；

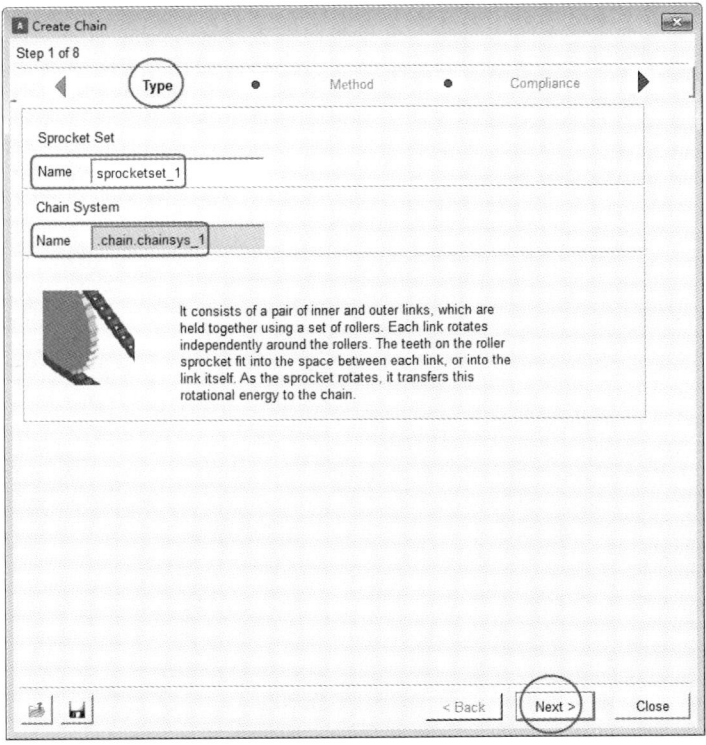

图 10-7 创建链条/Type

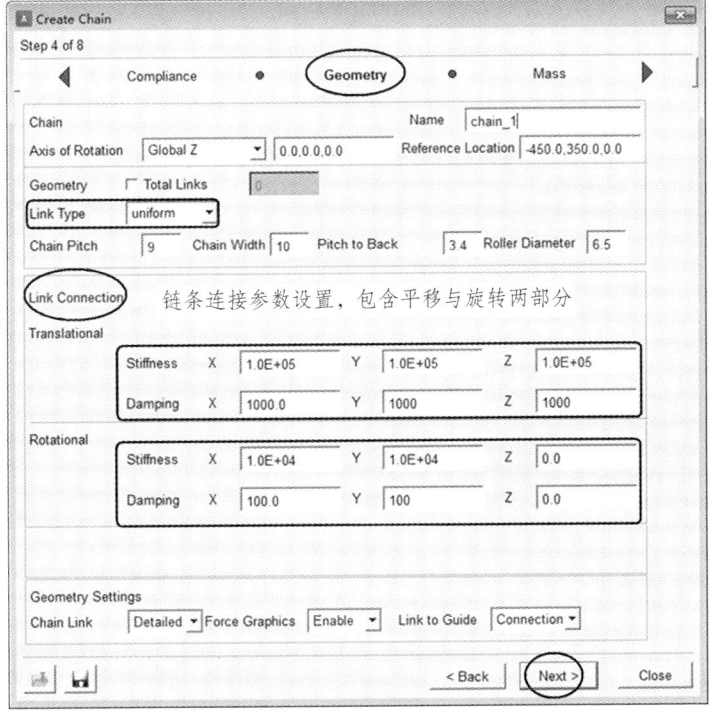

图 10-8 创建链条/Geometry

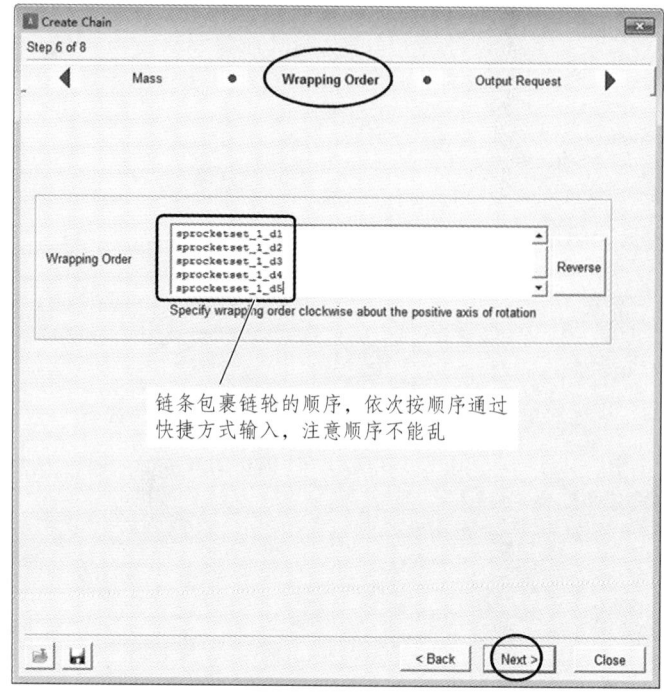

图 10-9 创建链条包裹链轮的顺序（Wrapping Order）

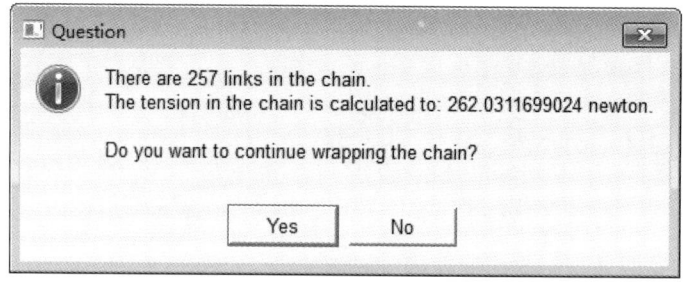

图 10-10 链条创建问题对话框

- 皮带包裹完成后切换到 Output Request 输出请求界面；
- 勾选 Segment Request；
- Link Part(s)：link_1（链条中第 157 连接销）；
- 单击 Next，切换到 Completion 参数设置；
- 单击 Finish，完成链条的建模如图 10-1 所示。

10.3 链条驱动元

- 单击 Machinery > Chain > Create Sproket Actuation Input，创建链条驱动元界面如图 10-11 所示，创建动力元共包含 5 个子菜单界面，此时为 Actuator 界面；
- Actuator / Name：actuator_1；
- Sproket：sprocketset_1_d1；

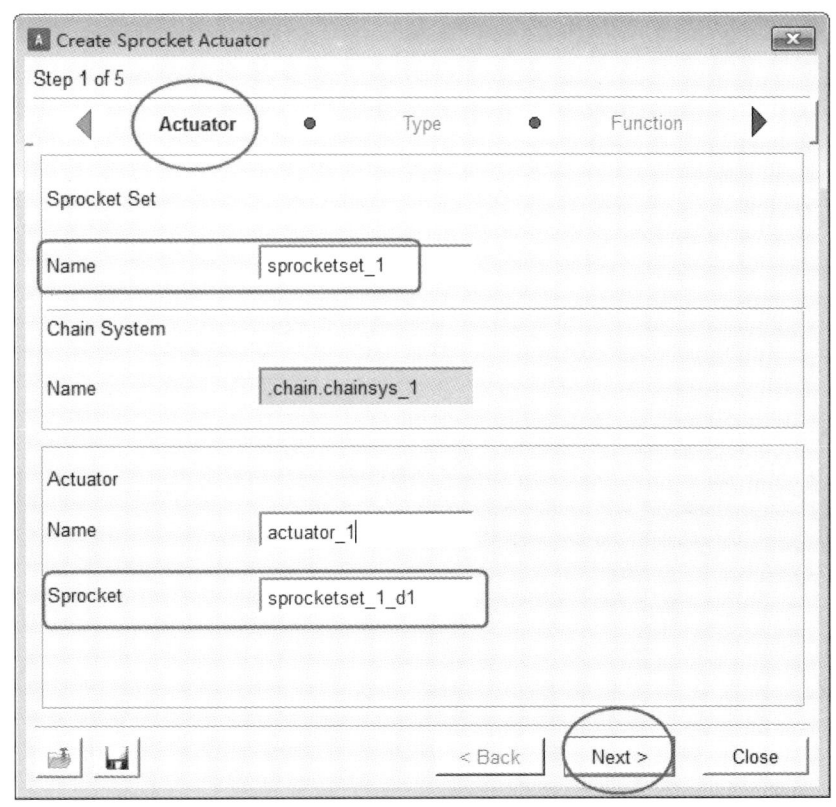

图 10-11 创建驱动元/Actuator

- 单击 Next，切换到 Type 参数设置界面；
- Type：Motion；
- 单击 Next，切换到 Function 参数设置界面如图 10-12 所示；
- Function：User Defined；
- User Entered Func.：30.0*time；
- Direction：Anti Clockwise（动力元为逆时针方向）；
- 单击 Next，切换到 Output 参数设置界面，保持默认设置；
- 单击 Next，切换到 Completion 参数设置；
- 单击 Finish，完成驱动元的创建；
- 单击 Simulation > Simulate 命令；
- End Time：2；
- Steps：2 000；
- 其余保持默认设置，单击 Start simulation；
- 计算完成后（计算时间较长，建议采用服务器运行），按 F8 切换到后处理模块，链条连接销段块 1 所受接触力如图 10-13 所示，张力如图 10-14 所示；链轮受力及旋转参数如图 10-15、图 10-16 所示。

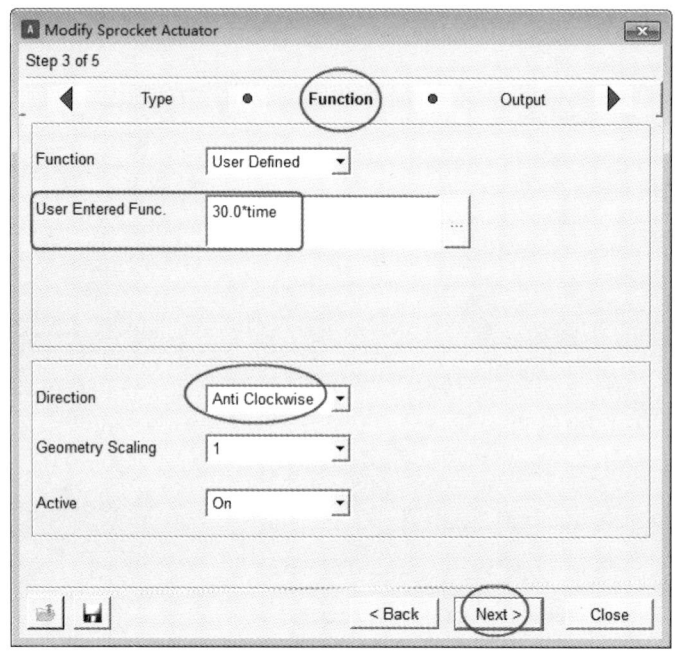

图 10-12　创建驱动元/Function

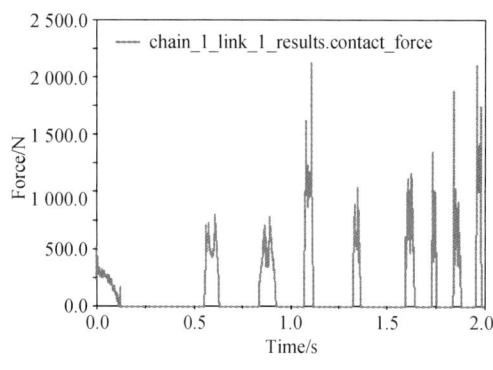

图 10-13　链条 1 段接触力

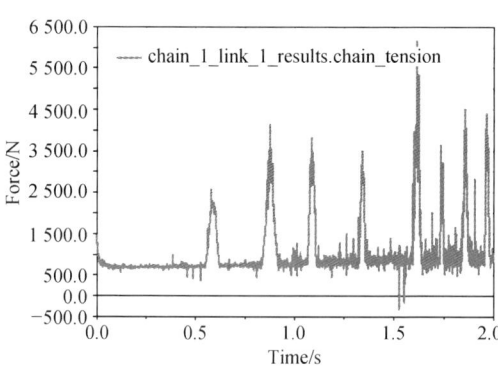

图 10-14　链条 1 段张力

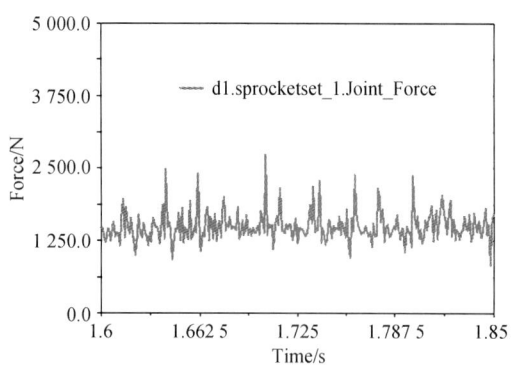

图 10-15　链轮 1 转动约束副受力（放大局部曲线）

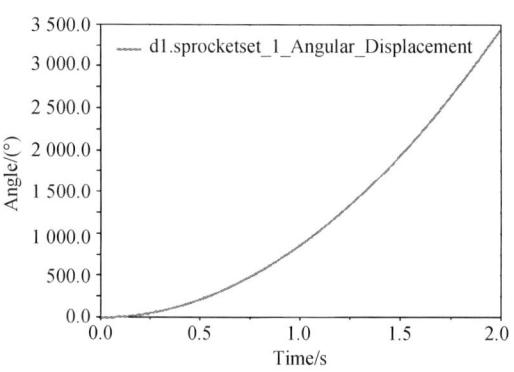

图 10-16　链轮 1 转动角度

第 11 章　电动机

电动机（Motor）是把电能转换成机械能的一种设备，它利用通电线圈（定子绕组）产生旋转磁场并作用于转子形成磁电动力旋转扭矩。电动机按使用电源不同分为直流电动机和交流电动机，电力系统中的电动机大部分是交流电机，可以是同步电机或者异步电机（电机定子磁场转速与转子旋转转速不保持同步）。电动机主要由定子与转子组成，通电导线在磁场中受力运动的方向跟电流方向和磁感线（磁场方向）方向有关。电动机工作原理是磁场对电流受力的作用，使电动机转动。ADAMS/MACHINERY 电机模块使工程师能够更加精密而轻松地表征电机。针对不同的应用选择不同的建模方法；使用分析方法时可从 DDC（并联或串联）、直流无刷电机、步进电机及交流同步电机中进行选择；可采用外部方法，由 Easy5 或 MATLAB Simulink 来定义电机扭矩；计算所需的电机尺寸；预测电机扭矩对系统的影响；进行精密的位置控制；为其他机器部件获取真实驱动信号。

学习目标

- ◆ 电动机——Curve Based。
- ◆ 电动机——AnalyticalF。
- ◆ 连杆传动。
- ◆ 电动-链条-皮带耦合传动。

11.1　电动机——Curve Based

- 启动 ADAMS/VIEW；
- 单击 File > Import...；
- File Type：选择 ADAMS/View Command File（*.cmd）；
- File To Read：D:\MSC.Software\Adams_x64\2015\amachinery\examples\motor\Motor_Start.cmd。Motor_Start.cmd 具体在 ADAMS 软件安装的硬盘目录中，此处采用直接导入，也可以直接在图形窗口中建立相关的连杆机构；建立电动机过程中，首先建立被驱动机构，然后才能建立电动机模型，文件导入如图 11-1 所示，导入后的连杆机构如图 11-2 所示；曲柄一端与大地通过转动副连接，另一端与连杆采用球形副连接；摇臂一端与大地通过转动副连接，另一端与连杆通过万向节连接。

- 单击 Machinery > Motor > Create Motor 命令，弹出创建电动机对话框如图 11-3 所示，创建电动机包含 6 个界面，此时为 Method 界面；
- Method：Curve Based（见图 11-4）；

（1）Curve Based：电机转矩由用户提供的转矩-速度曲线定义。
（2）Analytical：电机扭矩由下一个 PAG 所选电机类型的特定方程式集定义。
（3）External：电机在 ADAMS/CONTROLS 支持的任何软件外部建模。它通过外部系统库（ESL）导入模式或纳入 ADAMS 分析协同仿真模式。

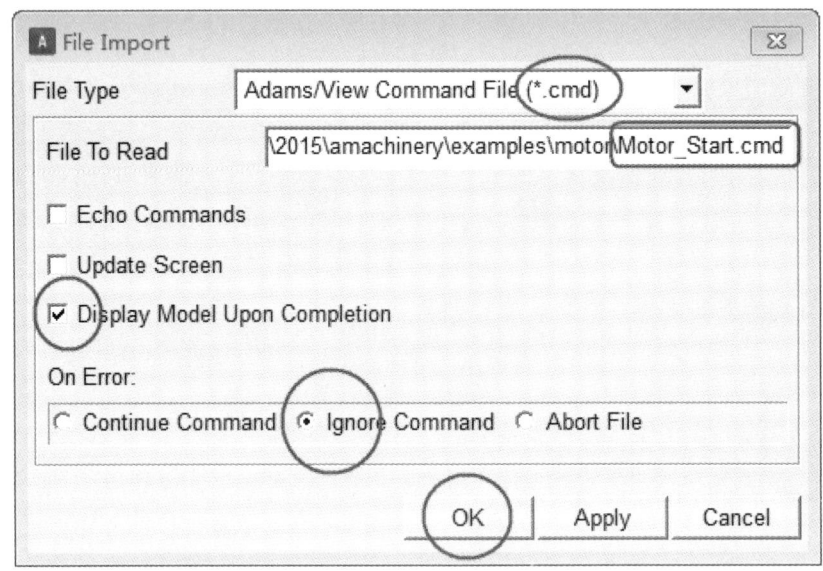

图 11-1 导入四连杆机构

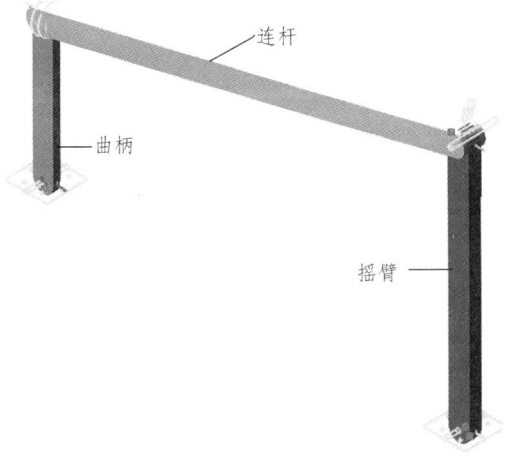

图 11-2 连杆机构

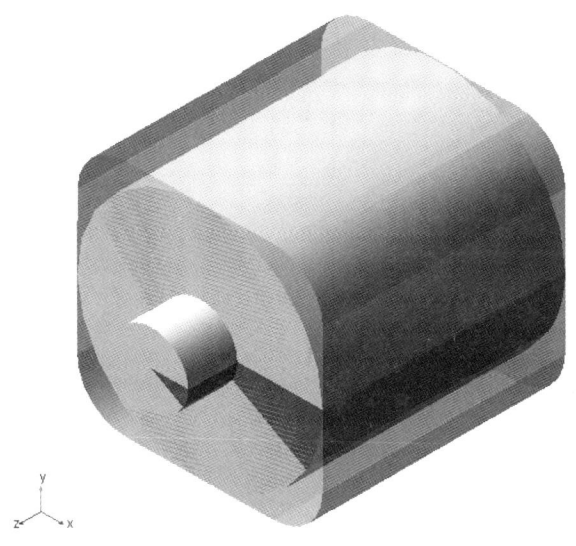

图 11-3 电动机模型

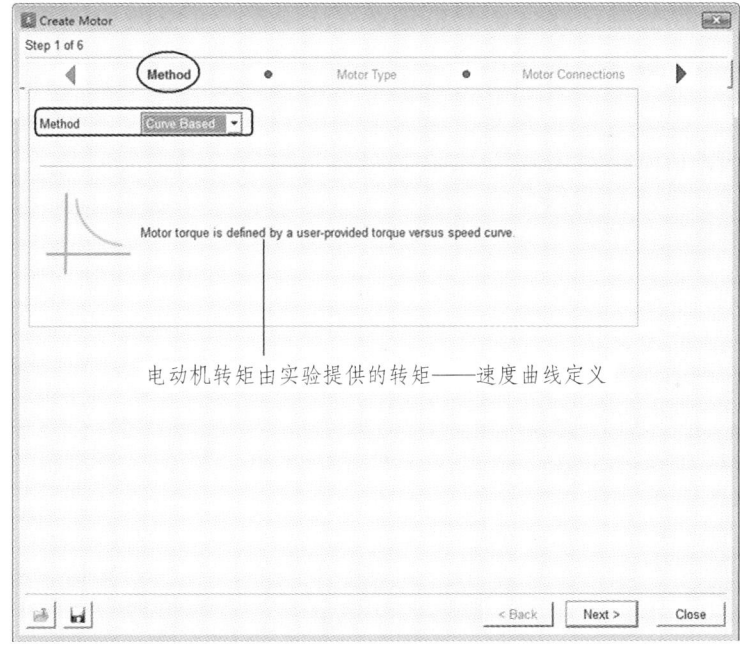

图 11-4 创建电动机（Method）

- 单击 Next，切换到 Motor Type 参数界面，保持默认设置；
- 单击 Next，切换到 Motor Connections 参数界面，如图 11-5 所示；
- Motor：选择 New；
- Location：通过快捷方式选取(LOC_RELATIVE_TO({0,0,0}, POINT_1))，也可以输入 Point1 点坐标 –35, 0, 0；
- Axis of Rotation：Global Z；

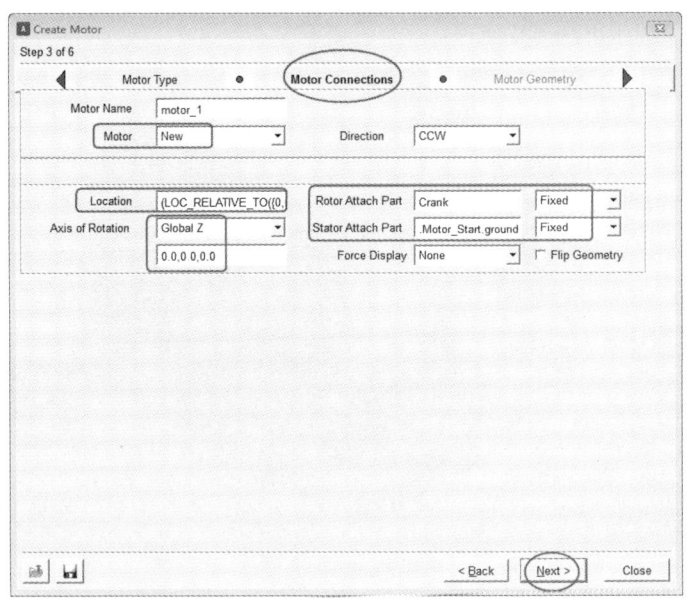

图 11-5 创建电动机/Motor Connections

- Rotor Attach Part：Crank/Fixed，即曲柄与电动机转子通过固定副连接；
- Stator Attach Part：ground/Fixed，定子（即电动机壳体）与大地之间采用固定副连接；
- 单击 Next，切换到 Motor Geometry 电动机几何参数界面，如图 11-6 所示；
- 勾选 Creat Rotor Stator Parts，创建电动机定子与转子几何体；

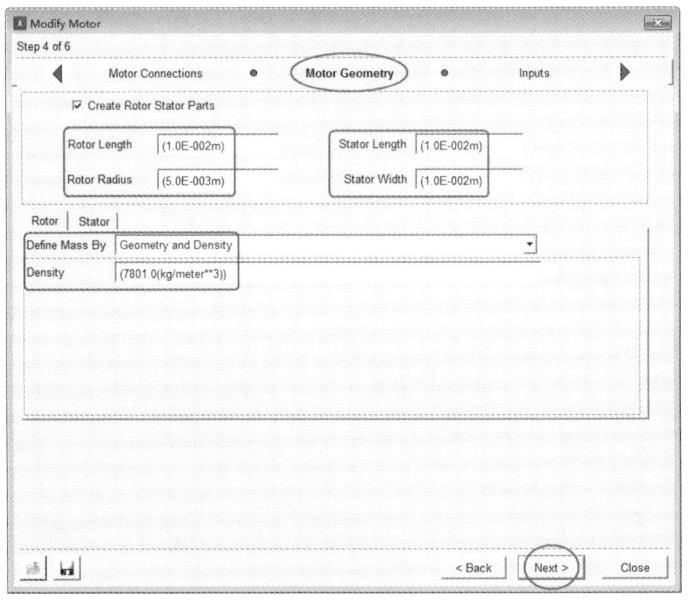

图 11-6 创建电动机/Motor Geometry

- Rotor Length：$1.0E-002$ m；
- Rotor Radius：$5.0E-003$ m；
- Stator Length：$1.0E-002$ m；

- Stator Width：1.0E – 002 m；
- Define Mass By：选择 Geometry and Density；
- 单击 Next，切换到 Inputs 参数界面，如图 11-7（a）所示；
- 选择 Creat Date Points；X、Y 列为默认数据，此数据可以用曲线形式表示，数据可以通过实验获取输入转换为真实的电动机特性；
- View as：Plot，此时 X、Y 列为默认数据转换为曲线图形，如图 11-7（b）所示；

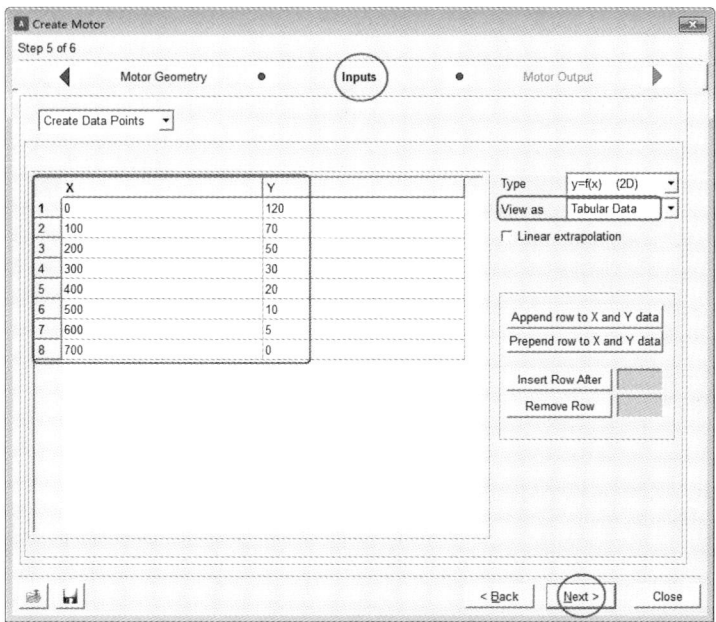

图 11-7（a） 创建电动机/Inputs

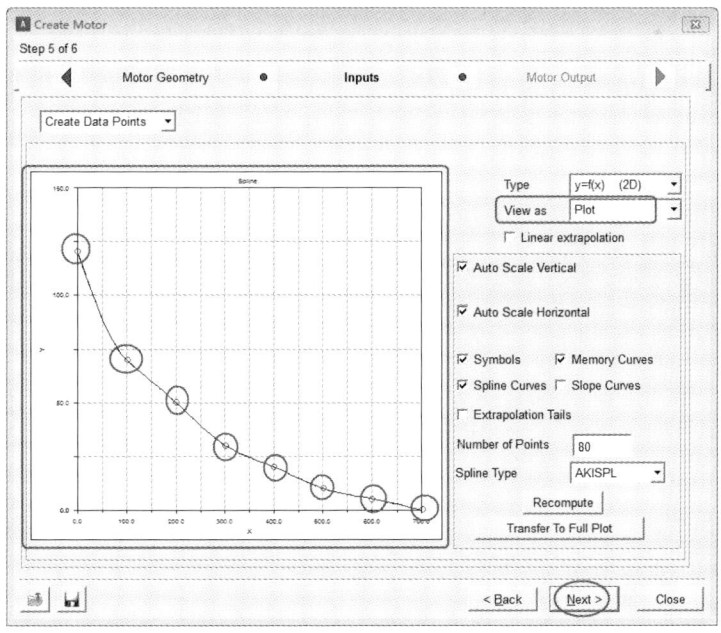

图 11-7（b） 创建电动机/Inputs

- 单击 Next，切换到 Motor Output 参数界面，保持默认设置；
- 单击 Finish，完成电动机创建，创建好的电动机驱动连杆模型如图 11-8 所示。

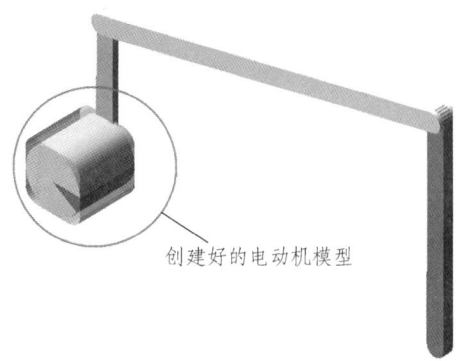

图 11-8　电动机驱动连杆模型

11.2　连杆驱动仿真

- 单击 Simulation > Simulate 命令；
- End Time：25；
- Steps：2 500；
- 其余保持默认设置，单击 Start simulation；
- 计算完成后，按 F8 切换到后处理模块，电动机及约束副计算参数结果如图 11-9 ~ 图 11-16 所示。保存文件为 Motor_Start_link_Curve Based .bin。

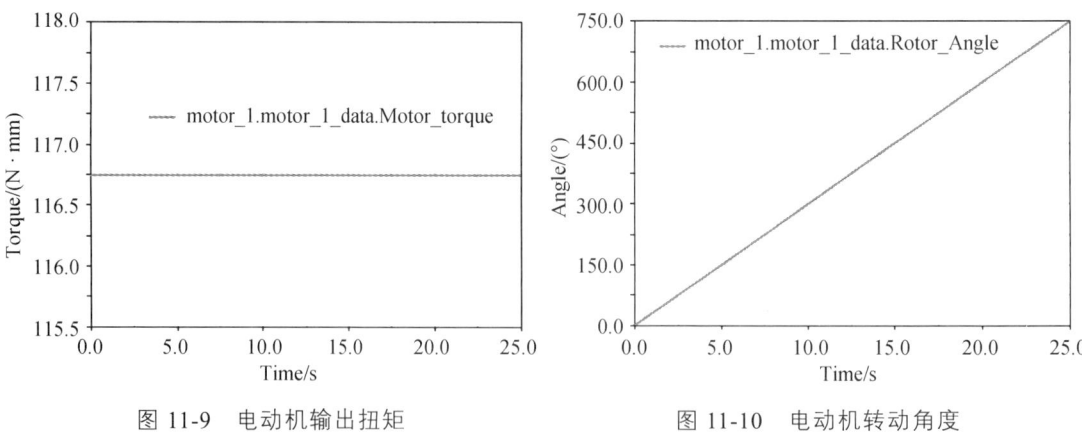

图 11-9　电动机输出扭矩　　　　　　图 11-10　电动机转动角度

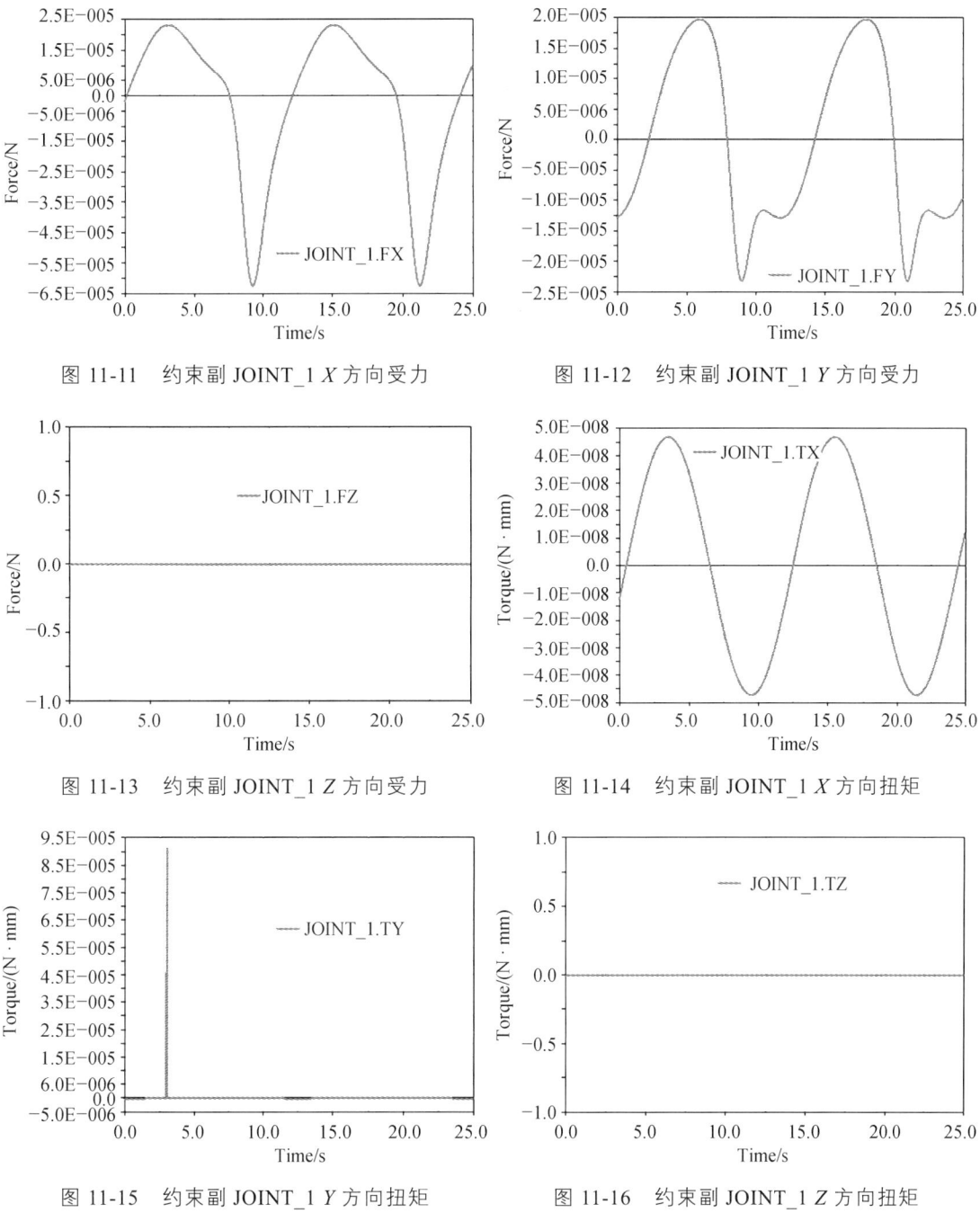

图 11-11　约束副 JOINT_1 X 方向受力

图 11-12　约束副 JOINT_1 Y 方向受力

图 11-13　约束副 JOINT_1 Z 方向受力

图 11-14　约束副 JOINT_1 X 方向扭矩

图 11-15　约束副 JOINT_1 Y 方向扭矩

图 11-16　约束副 JOINT_1 Z 方向扭矩

11.3　电动机——Analytical

- 打开 Motor_Start_link_Curve Based .bin；
- 删除电动机模型，保留连杆机构；

- 单击 Machinery > Motor > Create Motor 命令，弹出创建电动机对话框；
- Method：Analytical；
- 单击 Next，切换到 Motor Type 参数界面，保持默认设置；
- Motor Type：选择 DC 直流电机，如图 11-17 所示；

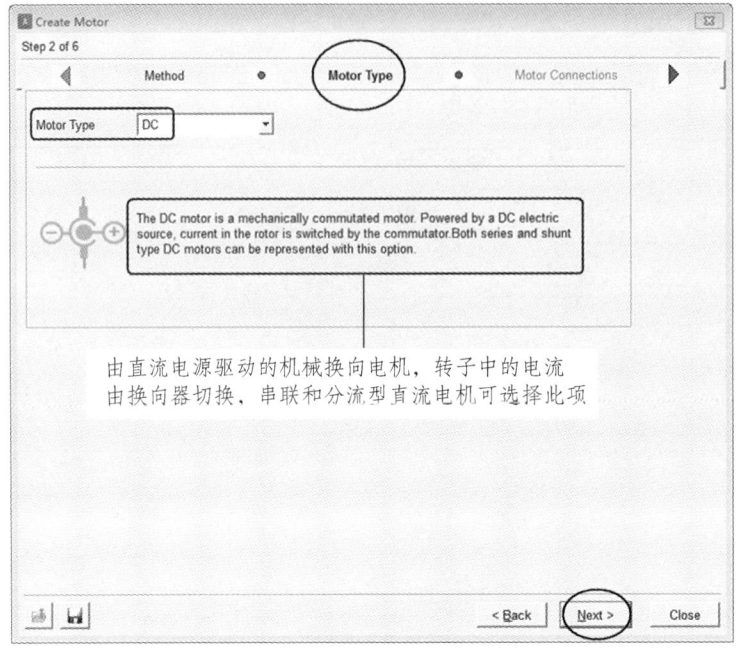

图 11-17 创建 DC 电动机/Motor Type

（1）AC synchronous（交流同步电动机）：交流同步电动机是一种在稳定状态下，轴的旋转与供电电流的频率同步的电动机。旋转周期精确地等于交流循环的整数倍。同步电动机的定子上装有电磁铁，产生一个磁场，该磁场随线电流的振荡而及时旋转。转子与磁场以相同的速度同步转动。

（2）DC（直流电动机）：直流电机是由直流电源驱动的机械换向电机，转子中的电流由换向器切换。串联和分流型直流电机都可以用此选项表示。

（3）Brushless DC（无刷直流电动机）：无刷直流电机也被称为电子换向电机。它们是同步电动机，由直流电源通过集成开关电源供电，产生交流电信号驱动。对于专门设计用于转子经常停止在规定角度位置的模式下运行的电机，使用步进电机选项代替。

（4）Stepper（步进电动机）：步进电机是一种无刷同步电机，它将数字脉冲转换为机械轴旋转。步进电机每转一圈，分成若干步，每转一步，电机必须发出单独的脉冲。步进电机提供了一种不使用反馈传感器的精确定位和速度控制方法。

- 单击 Next，切换到 Motor Connections 参数界面设置，参考如图 11-5 所示；
- 单击 Next，切换到 Motor Connections 参数界面设置，参考如图 11-6 所示；
- 单击 Next，切换到 Motor Geometry 参数界面，保持默认设置；

- 单击 Next，切换到 Input 参数界面设置，参考图 11-18；
- No. of Conuctors（连接器数量）：100；
- Flux Per Pole（每极磁通 Wb）：0.025；
- Source Voltage（电压 V）：110；

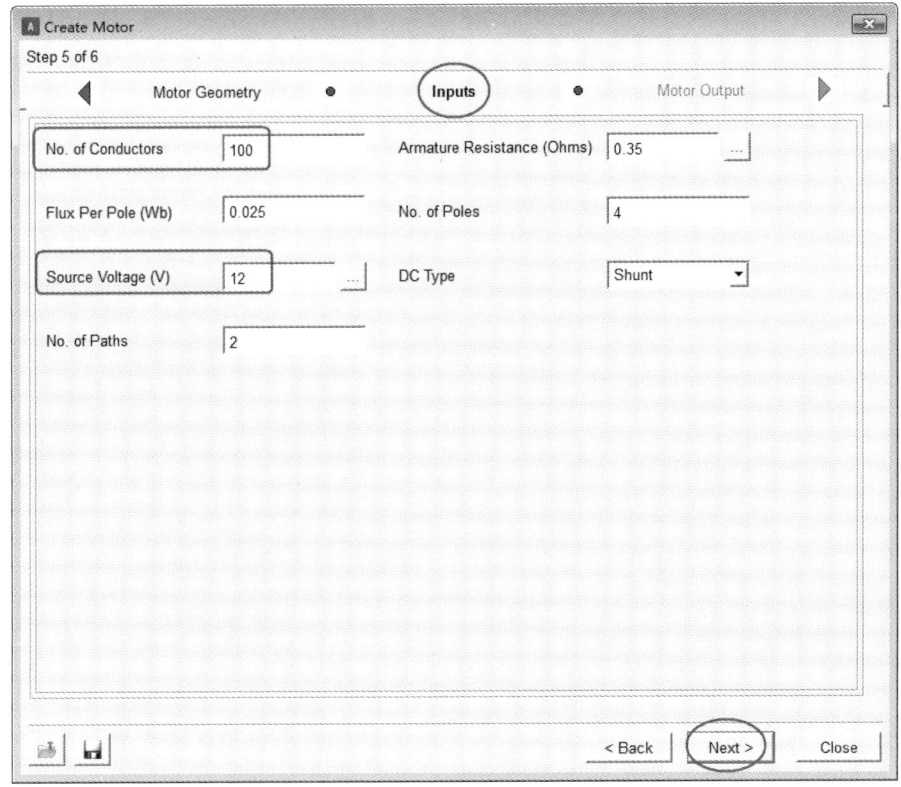

图 11-18　创建 DC 电动机/Input

- No. of Paths：100；
- Armature Resistance（电枢电阻 Ohms）:0.35；
- No. of Poles：4；
- DC Type：Shunt（分流器）；
- 单击 Next，切换到 Motor Output 参数界面，保持默认设置；
- 单击 Finish，完成电动机创建，创建好的电动机（DC）驱动连杆模型参考如图 11-8 所示；
- 单击 Simulation > Simulate 命令；
- End Time：1；
- Steps：1 000；
- 其余保持默认设置，单击 Start simulation；
- 计算完成后，按 F8 切换到后处理模块，电动机计算参数结果如图 11-19 ~ 图 11-22 所示。保存文件为 Motor_Start_link_Analytical_DC .bin。

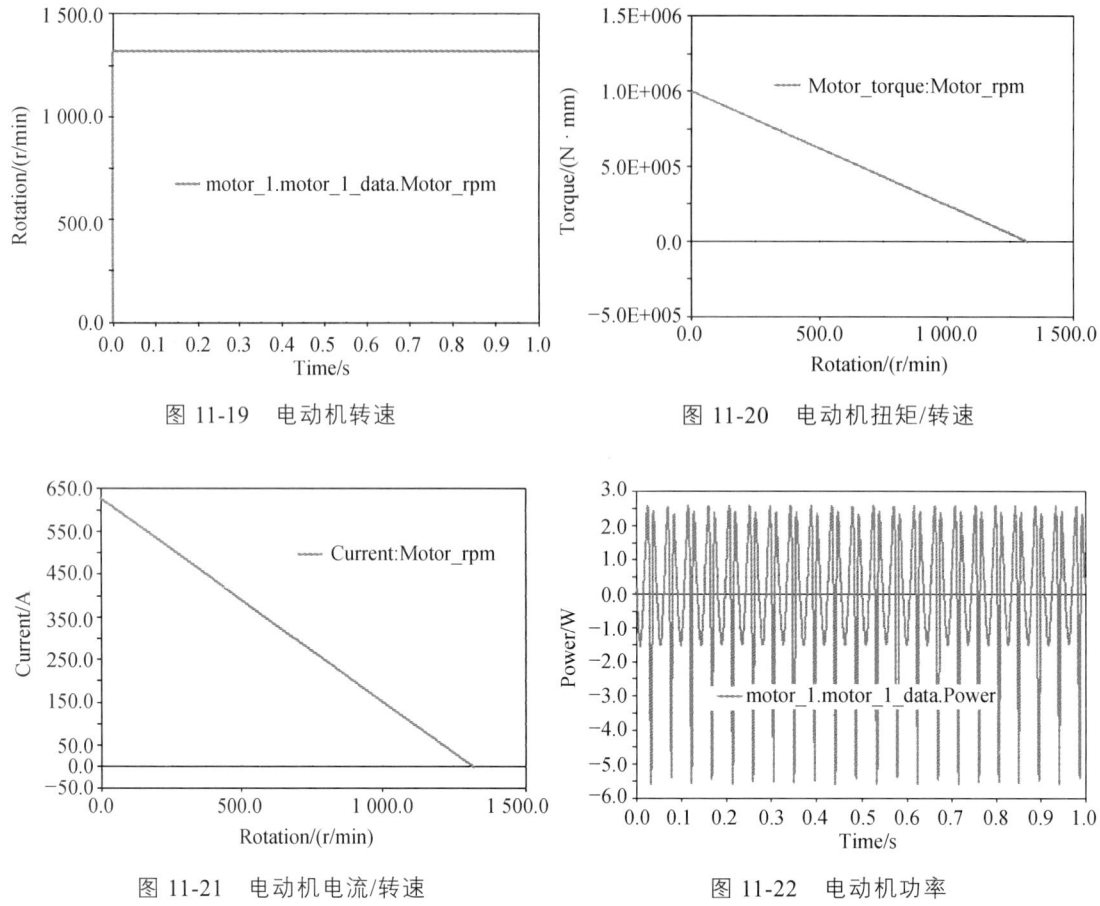

图 11-19 电动机转速

图 11-20 电动机扭矩/转速

图 11-21 电动机电流/转速

图 11-22 电动机功率

11.4 电动-链条-皮带耦合传动

工程上单一传动的案例相对较少，大多是不同传动副之间的耦合，例如链条齿轮、皮带齿轮以及多种传动副之间的耦合。皮带传动与链条传动看似模型简单，其实非常复杂，属于接触范畴；皮带与链条包含多个皮带段块连接、链条销连接，传动距离越大，连接及接触的规模就越大，计算速度极为缓慢，有条件的可使用服务器计算。

电动-链条-皮带耦合传动建立好的模型如图 11-23 所示。建模过程中，先建立链轮、皮带轮及电动机定位的参考点，然后依次通过传动副模型建立链轮传动模型、皮带传动模型；链轮与皮带之间、电动机与链轮之间通过胡可副连接，最终建立电动机模型，仿真设置时长为 1 s，步数为 1 000，仿真结束后切换到后处理模型，链条、皮带、电动机计算参数如图 11-24 ~ 图 11-32 所示，模型文件 ouhechuandong.bin 存储于章节文件中。

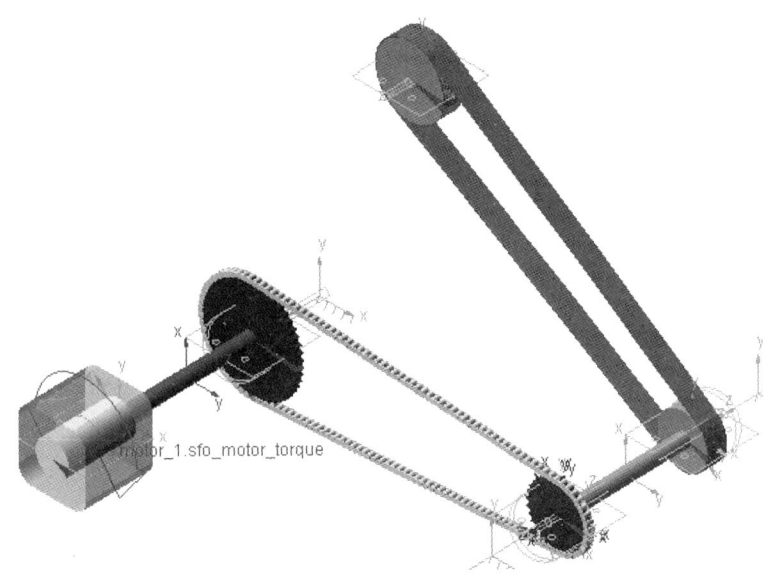

图 11-23 电动机-链条-皮带传动模型

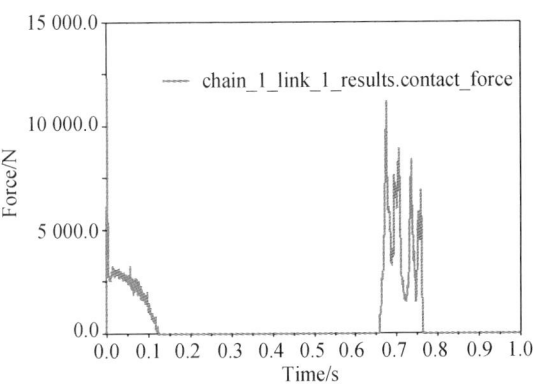

图 11-24 链条连接销接触力

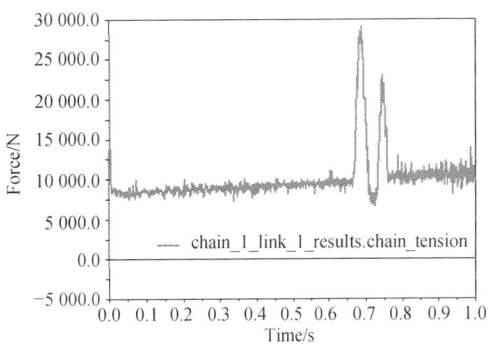

图 11-25 链条连接销张力

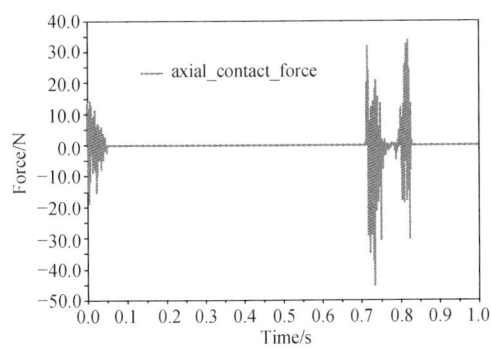

图 11-26 皮带轴向接触力

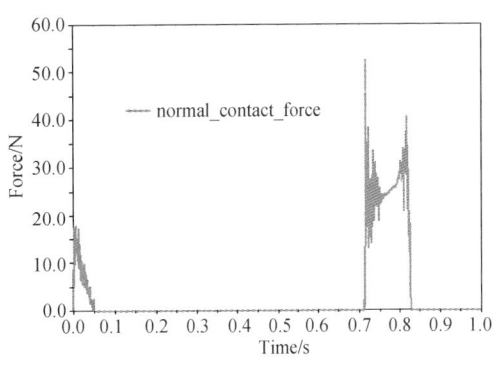

图 11-27 皮带法向接触力

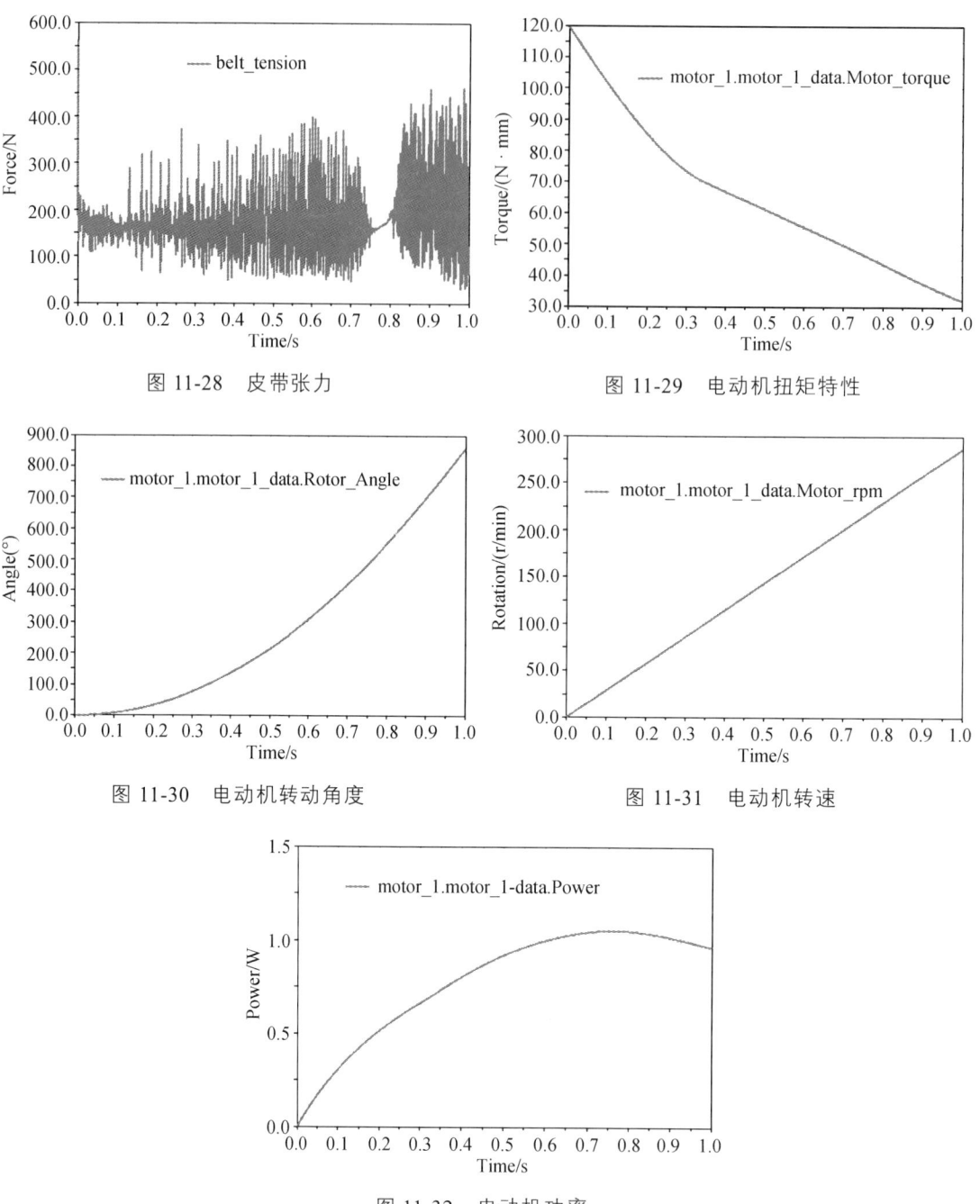

图 11-28　皮带张力

图 11-29　电动机扭矩特性

图 11-30　电动机转动角度

图 11-31　电动机转速

图 11-32　电动机功率

第 12 章　三轴车 I

三轮车由于其结构简单，价格便宜，在城市及农村有广泛的用途，例如城市住宅区的快递输送，田地货物搬运、农药喷洒等。三轮车的主要缺点是由于三个轮胎与地面接触，其稳定性相对于四轮车辆较差，同时货物运输速度低。三轮车后轴一般采用钢板弹簧与车架连接，配置高的后轴与车身之间装有垂向减震器，钢板弹簧的布置一般为纵向式，载重强度过大的话应考虑主副弹簧，少量的三轮车有双纵置板簧布置方式，如图 12-1 所示。

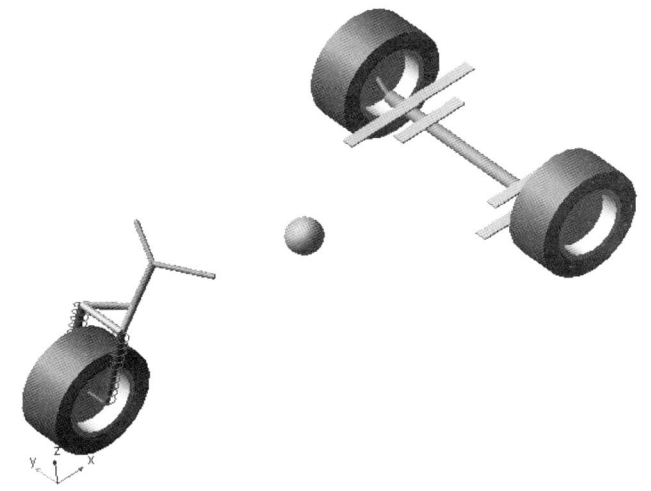

图 12-1　三轮车整车模型

学习目标

- ◇ 非独立悬架。
- ◇ 双纵置钢板弹簧。
- ◇ 衬套。
- ◇ 单轴转向系统。
- ◇ 轮胎模型。
- ◇ 路面模型。
- ◇ 驱动力。
- ◇ 整车约束关系。

12.1 车架系统

12.1.1 工作环境设置

- 启动 ADAMS/VIEW，选择 New Model；
- Model Name: my_sanlunche，其余参数保持默认设置，参考如图 12-2 所示；

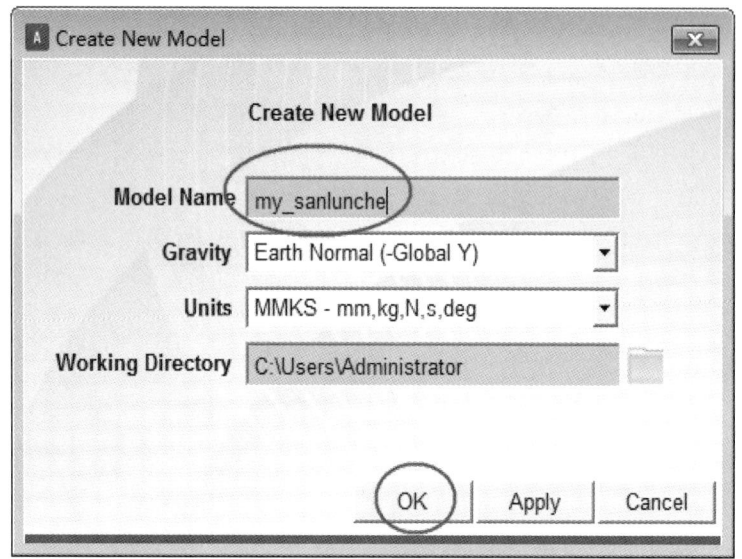

图 12-2 创建模型界面

- 单击 OK，新建模型创建成功，进入工作界面；
- 单击 Setting > Units，弹出单位设置对话框，长度单位为 mm、质量单位为 kg、力单位为 N、时间单击 Setting > Gravity，弹簧重力方向设置对话框如图 12-3 所示，设置重力方向为-Z 方向。

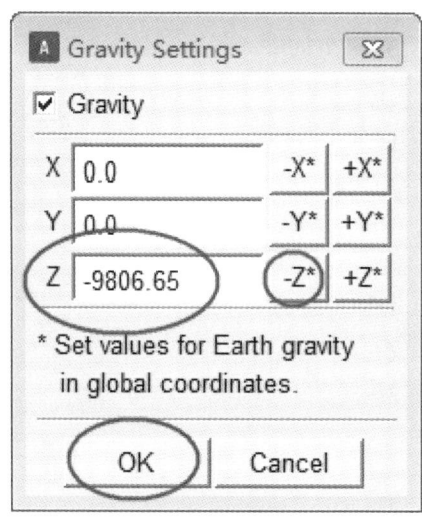

图 11-3 重力方向（-Z）

12.1.2 车身部件

- 单击 Bodies > Construction > Geometry Point 创建硬点；
- Add to Ground；
- Don't Attach；
- 右击鼠标，弹出硬点位置对话框如图 12-4 所示；
- 硬点位置输入 1 700，0，425；
- 单击 Apply，完成硬点创建；
- 右击硬点，选择 Rename，重名为 body_center；

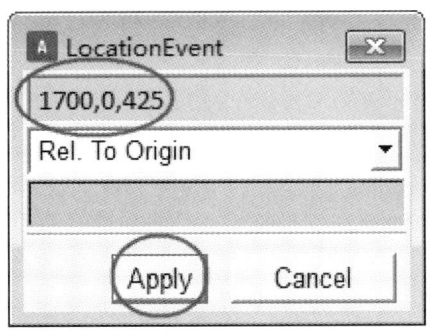

图 12-4　硬点创建对话框

- 单击 Bodies > Geometry Sphere 创建球形几何体；
- 选择 New Part；
- Radius:20；
- 选择硬点：body_center，完成球形部件创建；
- 右击球形部件，选择 Rename，重名为 body。

12.1.3 后轴板簧非独立悬架

- 单击 Bodies > Construction > Geometry Point 创建硬点；
- Add to Ground；
- Don't Attach；
- 右击鼠标，弹出硬点位置对话框，参考如图 12-4 所示；
- 硬点位置输入 2 000，-750，325；
- 单击 Apply，完成硬点创建；
- 右击硬点，选择 Rename，重名为 wheel_center_l；
- 单击 Bodies > Construction > Geometry Point 创建硬点，
- Add to Ground；
- Don't Attach；
- 右击鼠标，弹出硬点位置对话框，参考如图 12-4 所示；
- 硬点位置输入 2 000，750，325；

- 单击 Apply，完成硬点创建；
- 右击硬点，选择 Rename，重名为 wheel_center_r；
- 单击 Bodies > Construction > Geometry Point 创建硬点；
- Add to Ground；
- Don't Attach；
- 右击鼠标，弹出硬点位置对话框，参考如图 12-4 所示；
- 硬点位置输入 2 000，-650，225；
- 单击 Apply，完成硬点创建；
- 右击硬点，选择 Rename，重名为 hub_down_l；
- 单击 Bodies > Construction > Geometry Point 创建硬点；
- Add to Ground；
- Don't Attach；
- 右击鼠标，弹出硬点位置对话框，参考如图 12-4 所示；
- 硬点位置输入 2 000，650，225；
- 单击 Apply，完成硬点创建；
- 右击硬点，选择 Rename，重名为 hub_down_r。

12.1.4 后轴部件 axis

- 单击 Bodies > Geometry Cylinder 创建圆柱几何体；
- 选择 New Part；
- Radius: 35；
- 选择硬点：hub_down_l 与 hub_down_r 完成圆柱形部件创建；
- 右击球形部件，选择 Rename，重名为 axis。

12.1.5 转向节部件 upright

- 单击 Bodies > Geometry Cylinder 创建圆柱几何体；
- 选择 New Part；
- Radius: 15；
- 选择硬点：hub_down_r 与 wheel_center_r 完成圆柱形部件创建；
- 右击球形部件，选择 Rename，重名为 upright_r；
- 单击 Bodies > Geometry Cylinder 创建圆柱几何体；
- 选择 New Part；
- Radius: 15；
- 选择硬点：hub_down_l 与 wheel_center_l 完成圆柱形部件创建；
- 右击球形部件，选择 Rename，重名为 upright_l。

12.1.6 后轮毂部件 hub

- 单击 Setting > Work Grid；
- 网格线设置对话框如图 12-5 所示；

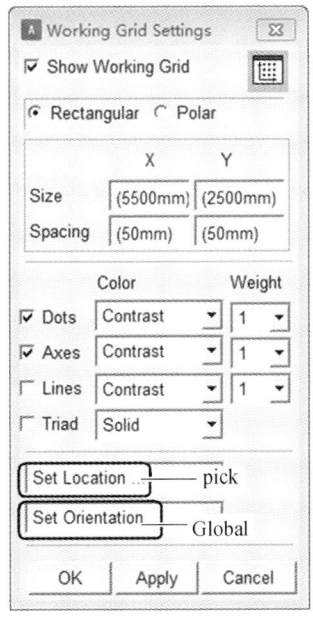

图 12-5 网格位置与方向设置

- 选择 Pick，单击 wheel_center_r 点，网格中心位置平移到 wheel_center_r 处；
- 选择 Global XY，网格方向与 XY 平面方向平行；
- 单击 OK，完成网格线位置与方向设置；
- 单击 Bodies > Geometry Cylinder 创建圆柱几何体；
- 选择 New Part；
- Length：20；
- Radius：30；
- 选择硬点 wheel_center_l，方向与 –Y 方向平行，单击鼠标左键，完成轮毂圆柱几何体部件创建；
- 右击圆柱体形部件，选择 Rename，重名为 bub_l；
- 单击 Bodies > Geometry Cylinder 创建圆柱几何体；
- 选择 New Part；
- Length：20；
- Radius：30；
- 选择硬点 wheel_center_r，方向与 Y 方向平行，单击鼠标左键，完成轮毂圆柱几何体部件创建；
- 右击圆柱体形部件，选择 Rename，重名为 bub_r。

12.1.7 板簧离散梁

- 单击 Bodies > Construction > Geometry Point 创建硬点；
- Add to Ground；
- Don't Attach；
- 右击鼠标，弹出硬点位置对话框参考如图 12-4 所示；
- 硬点位置输入 2 800, -500, 260；
- 单击 Apply，完成硬点创建；
- 右击硬点，选择 Rename，重名为 P1_l；
- 单击 Bodies > Construction > Geometry Point 创建硬点；
- Add to Ground；
- Don't Attach；
- 右击鼠标，弹出硬点位置对话框参考如图 12-4 所示；
- 硬点位置输入 2 800, 500, 260；
- 单击 Apply，完成硬点创建；
- 右击硬点，选择 Rename，重名为 P1_r；
- 单击 Bodies > Construction > Geometry Point 创建硬点；
- Add to Ground；
- Don't Attach；
- 右击鼠标，弹出硬点位置对话框参考如图 12-4 所示；
- 硬点位置输入 2 600, -350, 260；
- 单击 Apply，完成硬点创建；
- 右击硬点，选择 Rename，重名为 P3_l；
- 单击 Bodies > Construction > Geometry Point 创建硬点，
- Add to Ground；
- Don't Attach；
- 右击鼠标，弹出硬点位置对话框参考如图 12-4 所示；
- 硬点位置输入 2 600, 350, 260；
- 单击 Apply，完成硬点创建；
- 右击硬点，选择 Rename，重名为 P3_r；
- 单击 Bodies > Construction > Geometry Point 创建硬点；
- Add to Ground；
- Don't Attach；
- 右击鼠标，弹出硬点位置对话框参考如图 12-4 所示；
- 硬点位置输入 2 400, -500, 270；
- 单击 Apply，完成硬点创建；
- 右击硬点，选择 Rename，重名为 P5_l；
- 单击 Bodies > Construction > Geometry Point 创建硬点；
- Add to Ground；

- Don't Attach；
- 右击鼠标，弹出硬点位置对话框参考如图 12-4 所示；
- 硬点位置输入 2 400，500，270；
- 单击 Apply，完成硬点创建；
- 右击硬点，选择 Rename，重名为 P5_r；
- 单击 Bodies > Construction > Geometry Point 创建硬点；
- Add to Ground；
- Don't Attach；
- 右击鼠标，弹出硬点位置对话框参考如图 12-4 所示；
- 硬点位置输入 3 000，-350，260；
- 单击 Apply，完成硬点创建；
- 右击硬点，选择 Rename，重名为 P7_l；
- 单击 Bodies > Construction > Geometry Point 创建硬点；
- Add to Ground；
- Don't Attach；
- 右击鼠标，弹出硬点位置对话框参考如图 12-4 所示；
- 硬点位置输入 3 000，350，260；
- 单击 Apply，完成硬点创建；
- 右击硬点，选择 Rename，重名为 P7_r；
- 单击 Bodies > Construction > Geometry Point 创建硬点；
- Add to Ground；
- Don't Attach；
- 右击鼠标，弹出硬点位置对话框参考如图 12-4 所示；
- 硬点位置输入 3 200，-500，270；
- 单击 Apply，完成硬点创建；
- 右击硬点，选择 Rename，重名为 P9_l；
- 单击 Bodies > Construction > Geometry Point 创建硬点；
- Add to Ground；
- Don't Attach；
- 右击鼠标，弹出硬点位置对话框参考如图 12-4 所示；
- 硬点位置输入 3 200，500，270；
- 单击 Apply，完成硬点创建；
- 右击硬点，选择 Rename，重名为 P9_r；
- 单击 Bodies > Construction > Marker 创建参考点，参考点与硬点的区别在于参考点包含方向；
- Add to Ground；
- Global XY Plane；
- 选择硬点.my_sanlunche.ground.P5_l；
- 完成 Marker 点的创建，右击参考点，选择 Rename，重名为 M1；

- 单击 Bodies > Construction > Marker；
- Add to Ground；
- Global XY Plane；
- 选择硬点.my_sanlunche.ground.P9_1；
- 完成 Marker 点的创建，右击参考点，选择 Rename，重名为 M2；
- 单击 Bodies > Construction > Marker；
- Add to Ground；
- Global XY Plane；
- 选择硬点.my_sanlunche.ground.P1_1；
- 完成 Marker 点的创建，右击参考点，选择 Rename，重名为 M0_1；
- 单击 Bodies > Flexible Bodies > Discreate Flexible Bodies 创建离散梁如图 12-6 所示；

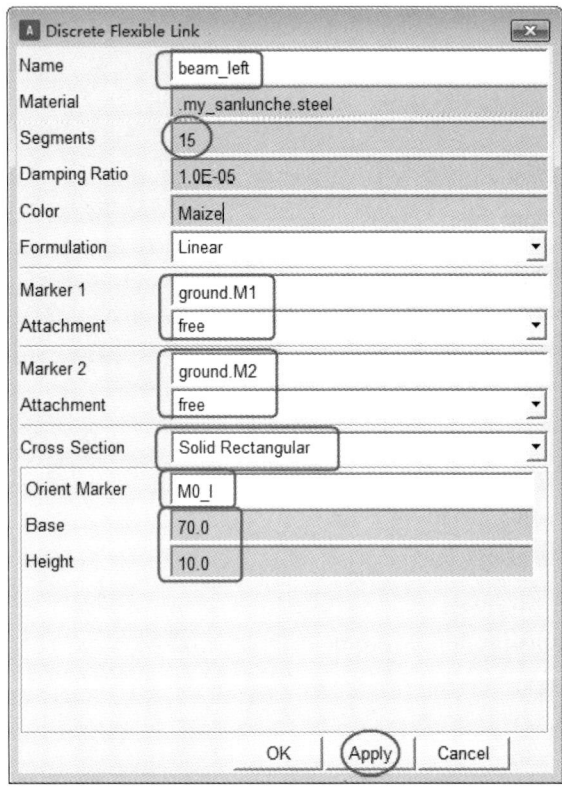

图 12-6　离散梁参数

- Name：beam_left；
- Segments（离散梁段块数量）：15；
- Damping Ratio（阻尼率）：1E－5；
- Color：Maize；
- Formulation：Linear；
- Marker 1：ground.M1；
- Attachment：free；

- Marker 2：ground.M2；
- Attachment：free；
- Cross Section（离散梁截面形状）：Solid Rectangular，即矩形；
- Orient Marker：M0_l；
- Base：70；
- Height：10；
- 单击 OK，完成离散梁 beam_left 的创建。
- 单击 Bodies > Construction > Marker；
- Add to Ground；
- Global XY Plane；
- 选择硬点.my_sanlunche.ground.P5_r；
- 完成 Marker 点的创建，右击参考点，选择 Rename，重名为 M1_r；
- 单击 Bodies > Construction > Marker；
- Add to Ground；
- Global XY Plane；
- 选择硬点.my_sanlunche.ground.P9_r；
- 完成 Marker 点的创建，右击参考点，选择 Rename，重名为 M2_r；
- 单击 Bodies > Construction > Marker；
- Add to Ground；
- Global XY Plane；
- 选择硬点.my_sanlunche.ground.P1_r；
- 完成 Marker 点的创建，右击参考点，选择 Rename，重名为 M0_r；
- 单击 Bodies > Flexible Bodies > Discreate Flexible Bodies 创建离散梁如图 12-6 所示；
- Name：beam_left；
- Segments（离散梁段块数量）：15；
- Damping Ratio（阻尼率）：$1E-5$；
- Color：Maize；
- Formulation：Linear；
- Marker 1：ground.M1_r；
- Attachment：free；
- Marker 2：ground.M2_r；
- Attachment：free；
- Cross Section（离散梁截面形状）：Solid Rectangular，即矩形；
- Orient Marker：M0_r；
- Base：70；
- Height：10；
- 单击 OK，完成离散梁 beam_right 的创建。
- 单击 Bodies > Construction > Marker；
- Add to Ground；

- Global XY Plane；
- 选择硬点.my_sanlunche.ground.P3_l；
- 完成 Marker 点的创建，右击参考点，选择 Rename，重名为 M3_l；
- 单击 Bodies > Construction > Marker；
- Add to Ground；
- Global XY Plane；
- 选择硬点.my_sanlunche.ground.P7_l；
- 完成 Marker 点的创建，右击参考点，选择 Rename，重名为 M4_l；
- 单击 Bodies > Flexible Bodies > Discreate Flexible Bodies 创建离散梁如图 12-6 所示；
- Name：beam_left；
- Segments（离散梁段块数量）：15；
- Damping Ratio（阻尼率）：1E－5；
- Color：Maize；
- Formulation：Linear；
- Marker 1：ground.M3_l；
- Attachment：free；
- Marker 2：ground.M4_l；
- Attachment：free；
- Cross Section（离散梁截面形状）：Solid Rectangular，即矩形；
- Orient Marker：M0_l；
- Base：70；
- Height：10；
- 单击 OK，完成离散梁 beam1_left 的创建。
- 单击 Bodies > Construction > Marker；
- Add to Ground；
- Global XY Plane；
- 选择硬点.my_sanlunche.ground.P3_r；
- 完成 Marker 点的创建，右击参考点，选择 Rename，重名为 M3_r；
- 单击 Bodies > Construction > Marker；
- Add to Ground；
- Global XY Plane；
- 选择硬点.my_sanlunche.ground.P7_r；
- 完成 Marker 点的创建，右击参考点，选择 Rename，重名为 M4_r；
- 单击 Bodies > Flexible Bodies > Discreate Flexible Bodies 创建离散梁如图 12-6 所示；
- Name：beam_left；
- Segments（离散梁段块数量）：15；
- Damping Ratio（阻尼率）：1E－5；
- Color：Maize；
- Formulation：Linear；

- Marker 1：ground.M3_r；
- Attachment：free；
- Marker 2：ground.M4_r；
- Attachment：free；
- Cross Section（离散梁截面形状）：Solid Rectangular，即矩形；
- Orient Marker：M0_r；
- Base：70；
- Height：10；
- 单击 OK，完成离散梁 beam1_right 的创建。

12.1.8 吊耳部件

- 单击 Setting > Work Grid；
- 网格线设置对话参考如图 12-5 所示；
- 选择 Pick，单击.my_sanlunche.ground.P9_1 点，网格中心位置平移到.my_sanlunche.ground.P9_1 处；
- 选择 Global XZ，网格方向与 XZ 平面方向平行；
- 单击 OK，完成网格线位置与方向设置；
- 单击 Bodies > Geometry Cylinder 创建圆柱几何体；
- 选择 New Part；
- Length：50；
- Radius：15；
- 选择硬点.my_sanlunche.ground.P9_1，方向与 –Z 方向平行，单击鼠标左键，完成轮毂圆柱几何体部件创建；
- 右击圆柱体形部件，选择 Rename，重名为 diaoer_left；
- 单击 Setting > Work Grid；
- 网格线设置对话参考如图 12-5 所示；
- 选择 Pick，单击.my_sanlunche.ground.P9_r 点，网格中心位置平移到.my_sanlunche.ground.P9_r 处；
- 选择 Global XZ，网格方向与 XZ 平面方向平行；
- 单击 OK，完成网格线位置与方向设置。
- 单击 Bodies > Geometry Cylinder 创建圆柱几何体；
- 选择 New Part；
- Length：50；
- Radius：15；
- 选择硬点.my_sanlunche.ground.P9_r，方向与 –Z 方向平行，单击鼠标左键，完成轮毂圆柱几何体部件创建；
- 右击圆柱体形部件，选择 Rename，重名为 diaoer_right；
- 单击 Setting > Work Grid；

- 网格线设置对话参考如图 12-5 所示；
- 选择 Pick，单击.my_sanlunche.ground.P7_1 点，网格中心位置平移到.my_sanlunche.ground.P7_1 处；
- 选择 Global XZ，网格方向与 XZ 平面方向平行；
- 单击 OK，完成网格线位置与方向设置。
- 单击 Bodies > Geometry Cylinder 创建圆柱几何体；
- 选择：New Part；
- Length：50；
- Radius： 15；
- 选择硬点.my_sanlunche.ground.P7_1，方向与-Z 方向平行，单击鼠标左键，完成轮毂圆柱几何体部件创建；
- 右击圆柱体形部件，选择 Rename，重名为 diaoer1_left；
- 单击 Setting > Work Grid；
- 网格线设置对话参考如图 12-5 所示；
- 选择 Pick，单击.my_sanlunche.ground.P7_r 点，网格中心位置平移到.my_sanlunche.ground.P7_r 处；
- 选择 Global XZ，网格方向与 XZ 平面方向平行；
- 单击 OK，完成网格线位置与方向设置。
- 单击 Bodies > Geometry Cylinder 创建圆柱几何体；
- 选择 New Part；
- Length：50；
- Radius：15；
- 选择硬点.my_sanlunche.ground.P7_r，方向与 –Z 方向平行，单击鼠标左键，完成轮毂圆柱几何体部件创建；
- 右击圆柱体形部件，选择 Rename，重名为 diaoer1_right。

12.2 前单轮转向系统

- 单击 Bodies > Construction > Geometry Point 创建硬点；
- Add to Ground；
- Don't Attach；
- 右击鼠标，弹出硬点位置对话框参考如图 12-4 所示；
- 硬点位置输入 250，–150，325；
- 单击 Apply，完成硬点创建；
- 右击硬点，选择 Rename，重名为 hub_front_1；
- 单击 Bodies > Construction > Geometry Point 创建硬点；
- Add to Ground；
- Don't Attach；

- 右击鼠标，弹出硬点位置对话框参考如图 12-4 所示；
- 硬点位置输入 250，150，325；
- 单击 Apply，完成硬点创建；
- 右击硬点，选择 Rename，重名为 hub_front_r；
- 单击 Bodies > Construction > Geometry Point 创建硬点；
- Add to Ground；
- Don't Attach；
- 右击鼠标，弹出硬点位置对话框参考如图 12-4 所示；
- 硬点位置输入 400，-150，725；
- 单击 Apply，完成硬点创建；
- 右击硬点，选择 Rename，重名为 damper_l；
- 单击 Bodies > Construction > Geometry Point 创建硬点；
- Add to Ground；
- Don't Attach；
- 右击鼠标，弹出硬点位置对话框参考如图 12-4 所示；
- 硬点位置输入 400，150，725；
- 单击 Apply，完成硬点创建；
- 右击硬点，选择 Rename，重名为 damper_r；
- 单击 Bodies > Construction > Geometry Point 创建硬点，
- Add to Ground；
- Don't Attach；
- 右击鼠标，弹出硬点位置对话框参考如图 12-4 所示；
- 硬点位置输入 600，0，675；
- 单击 Apply，完成硬点创建；
- 右击硬点，选择 Rename，重名为 steer_wheel_low；
- 单击 Bodies > Geometry Cylinder 创建圆柱几何体；
- 选择 New Part；
- Radius: 10；
- 选择硬点：hub_front_l 与 hub_front_r 完成圆柱形部件创建；
- 右击圆柱体部件，选择 Rename，重名为 hub_front；
- 右击硬点，选择 Rename，重名为 steer_wheel_low；
- 单击 Bodies > Geometry Cylinder 创建圆柱几何体；
- 选择 New Part；
- Radius: 20；
- 选择硬点：damper_l 与 damper_r 完成圆柱形部件创建；
- 右击圆柱体部件，选择 Rename，重名为 damper_up；
- 单击 Bodies > Geometry Cylinder 创建圆柱几何体；
- 选择 Add to Part；
- Radius: 20；
- 选择部件 damper_up；

- 选择硬点：damper_l 与 steer_wheel_low 完成圆柱形部件创建；
- 单击 Bodies > Geometry Cylinder 创建圆柱几何体；
- 选择 Add to Part；
- Radius: 20；
- 选择部件 damper_up；
- 选择硬点：damper_r 与 steer_wheel_low 完成圆柱形部件创建；
- 单击 Bodies > Construction > Geometry Point 创建硬点；
- Add to Ground；
- Don't Attach；
- 右击鼠标，弹出硬点位置对话框参考如图 12-4 所示；
- 硬点位置输入 750，0，875；
- 单击 Apply，完成硬点创建；
- 右击硬点，选择 Rename，重名为 steer_wheel_up；
- 单击 Bodies > Construction > Geometry Point 创建硬点；
- Add to Ground；
- Don't Attach；
- 右击鼠标，弹出硬点位置对话框参考如图 12-4 所示；
- 硬点位置输入 900，-300，875；
- 单击 Apply，完成硬点创建；
- 右击硬点，选择 Rename，重名为 steer_wheel_left；
- 单击 Bodies > Construction > Geometry Point 创建硬点；
- Add to Ground；
- Don't Attach；
- 右击鼠标，弹出硬点位置对话框参考如图 12-4 所示；
- 硬点位置输入 900，300，875；
- 单击 Apply，完成硬点创建；
- 右击硬点，选择 Rename，重名为 steer_wheel_right；
- 单击 Bodies > Geometry Cylinder 创建圆柱几何体；
- 选择 New Part；
- Radius: 20;
- 选择硬点：steer_wheel_low 与 steer_wheel_up 完成圆柱形部件创建；
- 右击圆柱体部件，选择 Rename，重名为 steer_wheel；
- 单击 Bodies > Geometry Cylinder 创建圆柱几何体；
- 选择 Add to Part；
- Radius: 20;
- 选择部件 steer_wheel；
- 选择硬点：steer_wheel_up 与 steer_wheel_left 完成圆柱形部件创建；
- 单击 Bodies > Geometry Cylinder 创建圆柱几何体；
- 选择 Add to Part；
- Radius: 20；

- 选择部件 steer_wheel；
- 选择硬点：steer_wheel_up 与 steer_wheel_right 完成圆柱形部件创建。

12.3 转向轴减震器

- 单击 Bodies > Construction > Construction Geometry：Mark 创建参考点；
- Add to Part；
- Don't Attach；
- 选择部件 hub_front；
- 右击鼠标，弹出硬点位置对话框参考如图 12-2 所示；
- 硬点位置输入 250，-150，325；
- 单击 Apply，完成参考点创建；
- 右击参考点，选择 Rename，重名为 M1；
- 单击 Bodies > Construction > Construction Geometry：Mark 创建参考点；
- Add to Part；
- Don't Attach；
- 选择部件 hub_front；
- 右击鼠标，弹出硬点位置对话框参考如图 12-2 所示；
- 硬点位置输入 250，-150，325；
- 单击 Apply，完成参考点创建；
- 右击参考点，选择 Rename，重名为 M2；
- 单击 Bodies > Construction > Construction Geometry：Mark 创建参考点；
- Add to Part；
- Don't Attach；
- 选择部件 damper_up；
- 右击鼠标，弹出硬点位置对话框参考如图 12-2 所示；
- 硬点位置输入 400，-150，725；
- 单击 Apply，完成参考点创建；
- 右击参考点，选择 Rename，重名为 M1；
- 单击 Bodies > Construction > Construction Geometry：Mark 创建参考点；
- Add to Part；
- Don't Attach；
- 选择部件 damper_up；
- 右击鼠标，弹出硬点位置对话框参考如图 12-2 所示；
- 硬点位置输入 400，150，725；
- 单击 Apply，完成参考点创建；
- 右击参考点，选择 Rename，重名为 M2；
- 单击 Forces > Flexible Connections > Spring-Damper；

- K：50；
- C：1 000；
- 选择点.my_sanlunche.hub_front.M1 与.my_sanlunche.damper_up.M1，完成 SPRING_1 的创建；
- 单击 Forces > Flexible Connections >Spring-Damper；
- K：50；
- C：1 000；
- 选择点.my_sanlunche.hub_front.M2 与.my_sanlunche.damper_up.M2，完成 SPRING_2 的创建。

12.4　三轮车约束

（1）部件 axis 与 upright_l 之间 Fixed 约束。
- 单击 Connecton > Joints > Creat a Fixed Joint，固定约束创建（修改）对话框如图 12-7 所示；
- Name：axis_and_upright_l；
- First Body：axis；
- Second Body：upright_l；
- Type：Fixed；
- Force Display：None；
- 单击 OK，完成约束副 axis_and_upright_l 的创建。

（2）部件 axis 与 upright_r 之间 Fixed 约束。
- 单击 Connecton > Joints > Creat a Fixed Joint；
- Name：axis_and_upright_r；
- First Body：axis；
- Second Body：upright_r；
- Type：Fixed；
- Force Display：None；
- 单击 OK，完成约束副 axis_and_upright_r 的创建。

（3）部件 axis 与 beam_left_elem8 之间 Fixed 约束。
- 单击 Connecton > Joints >Creat a Fixed Joint；
- Name：beam_left_elem8_and_axis；
- First Body：axis；
- Second Body：beam_left_elem8；
- Type：Fixed；
- Force Display：None；
- 单击 OK，完成约束副 beam_left_elem8_and_axis 的创建。

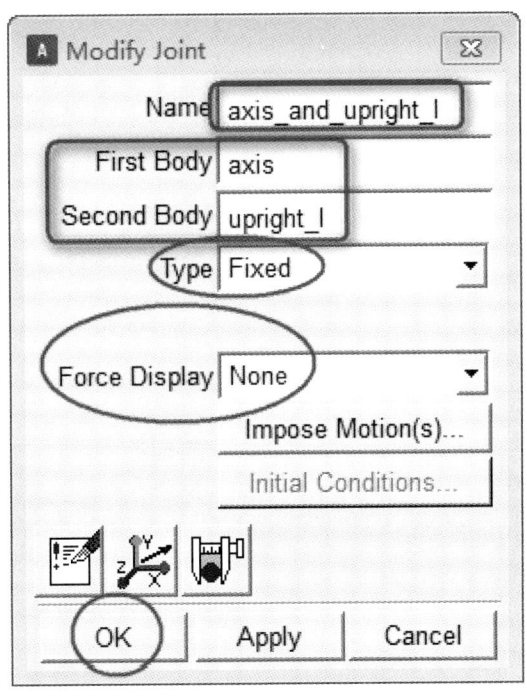

图 12-7 约束——Fixed

（4）部件 axis 与 beam5_left_elem5 之间 Fixed 约束。
- 单击 Connecton > Joints > Creat a Fixed Joint；
- Name：beam1_left_elem5_and_axis；
- First Body：axis；
- Second Body：beam1_left_elem5；
- Type：Fixed；
- Force Display：None；
- 单击 OK，完成约束副 beam1_left_elem5_and_axis 的创建。

（5）部件 axis 与 beam_right_elem8 之间 Fixed 约束。
- 单击 Connecton > Joints > Creat a Fixed Joint；
- Name：beam_right_elem8_and_axis；
- First Body：axis；
- Second Body：beam_right_elem8；
- Type：Fixed；
- Force Display：None；
- 单击 OK，完成约束副 beam_right_elem8_and_axis 的创建。

（6）部件 axis 与 beam1_right_elem5 之间 Fixed 约束。
- 单击 Connecton > Joints > Creat a Fixed Joint；
- Name：beam1_right_elem5_and_axis；
- First Body：axis；
- Second Body：beam1_right_elem5；

- Type：Fixed；
- Force Display：None；
- 单击 OK，完成约束副 beam1_right_elem5_and_axis 的创建。

（7）部件 upright_l 与 hub_l 之间 Fixed 约束。
- 单击 Connecton > Joints >Creat a Fixed Joint；
- Name：upright_l_and_hub_l；
- First Body：upright_l；
- Second Body：hub_l；
- Type：Fixed；
- Force Display：None；
- 单击 OK，完成约束副 upright_l_and_hub_l 的创建。

（8）部件 upright_r 与 hub_r 之间 Fixed 约束。
- 单击 Connecton > Joints >Creat a Fixed Joint；
- Name：upright_r_and_hub_r；
- First Body：upright_r；
- Second Body：hub_r；
- Type：Fixed；
- Force Display：None；
- 单击 OK，完成约束副 upright_l_and_hub_r 的创建。

（9）部件 hub_front 与 damper_up 之间 Cylindrical 约束。
- 单击 Connecton > Joints >Creat a Cylindrical Joint；
- Name：hub_front_and_damper_up_left；
- First Body：hub_front；
- Second Body：damper_up；
- Type：Cylindrical；
- Force Display：None；
- 单击 OK，完成约束副 hub_front_and_damper_up_left 的创建。

（10）部件 hub_front 与 damper_up 之间 Cylindrical 约束。
- 单击 Connecton > Joints > Creat a Cylindrical Joint；
- Name：.hub_front_and_damper_up_right；
- First Body：hub_front；
- Second Body：damper_up；
- Type：Cylindrical；
- Force Display：None；
- 单击 OK，完成约束副.hub_front_and_damper_up_right 的创建。

（11）部件 steer_wheel 与 damper_up 之间 Fixed 约束。
- 单击 Connecton > Joints >Creat a Fixed Joint；
- Name：steer_wheel_and_damper_up；
- First Body：steer_wheel；

- Second Body：damper_up；
- Type：Fixed；
- Force Display：None；
- 单击 OK，完成约束副 steer_wheel_and_damper_up 的创建。

（12）部件 body 与 damper_up 之间 Fixed 约束。
- 单击 Connecton > Joints > Creat a Fixed Joint；
- Name：body_and_damper_up；
- First Body：body；
- Second Body：damper_up；
- Type：Fixed；
- Force Display：None；
- 单击 OK，完成约束副 body_and_damper_up 的创建。

12.5 轮胎与路面

在 ADAMS/VIEW 通用模块中，轮胎模型与路面模型是同时创建的，在创建路面模型时，需要注意路面的方向，否则会导致车辆在仿真过程中跌落到空中。

（1）左后轮胎。
- 单击 Forces > Special Forces > Creat a Tire，创建轮胎（包含路面）模型如图 12-8 所示；

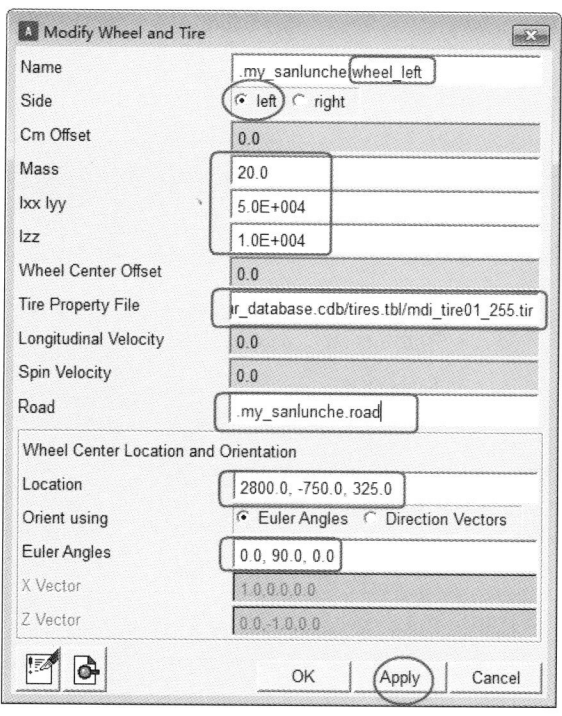

图 12-8　轮胎模型（包含路面）

- Name：wheel_left；
- Side：Left；
- Cm Offset：0；
- Mass：20；
- Ixx Iyy：5e4；
- Izz：1e4；
- Wheel Center Offset：0；
- Tire Property File：D:/MSC.Software/Adams_x64/2015/acar/shared_car_database.cdb/tires.tbl/mdi_tire01_255.tir；轮胎属性文件包含轮胎的一些实验参数及外形参数，轮胎的实验参数获取难度较大，此章节通过改变轮胎的形状，即横截面的宽度改为 255 mm，其余参数保持不变。

```
轮胎属性参数信息：可以通过公版数据库中的轮胎数据进行更改。
$-------------------------------------------------------------MDI_HEADER
[MDI_HEADER]
FILE_TYPE        = 'tir'
FILE_VERSION     = 3.0
FILE_FORMAT      = 'ASCII'
(COMMENTS)
{comment_string}
'Tire      - XXXXXX'
'Pressure  - XXXXXX'
'Test Date - XXXXXX'
'Test tire'
$-------------------------------------------------------------units
[UNITS]
LENGTH               = 'mm'
FORCE                = 'newton'
ANGLE                = 'radians'
MASS                 = 'kg'
TIME                 = 'sec'
$-------------------------------------------------------------model
[MODEL]
! use mode      1    2    3    4    11   12   13   14
! -----------------------------------------------------------------
! smoothing          X    X              X    X
! combined      X         X         X         X
! transient                    X    X    X    X
!
```

```
PROPERTY_FILE_FORMAT    = 'PAC89'
USE_MODE                = 4.0
$----------------------------------------------------------------dimensions
[DIMENSION]
UNLOADED_RADIUS         = 309.9
WIDTH                   = 255.0    %轮胎横街断面宽度参数
ASPECT_RATIO            = 0.50
$----------------------------------------------------------------vertical
[PARAMETER]
VERTICAL_STIFFNESS      = 310.0
VERTICAL_DAMPING        = 3.1
LATERAL_STIFFNESS       = 190.0
ROLLING_RESISTANCE      = 0.0
$----------------------------------------------------------------lateral
[LATERAL_COEFFICIENTS]    %以下参数为实验参数，根据实验获取；
a0  =   1.65000
a1  = – 34.0
a2  =   1250.00
a3  =   3036.00
a4  =   12.80
a5  =   0.00501
a6  = – 0.02103
a7  =   0.77394
a8  =   0.0022890
a9  =   0.013442
a10 =   0.003709
a11 =   19.1656
a12 =   1.21356
a13 =   6.26206
$----------------------------------------------------------------longitudinal
[LONGITUDINAL_COEFFICIENTS]
b0  =   1.67272
b1  = – 9.46000
b2  =   1490.00
b3  =   30.000
b4  =   176.000
b5  =   0.08860
b6  =   0.00402
```

b7 = − 0.06150
b8 = 0.20000
b9 = 0.02990
b10 = − 0.17600

$--aligning

[ALIGNING_COEFFICIENTS]

c_0 = 2.34000
c_1 = 1.4950
c_2 = 6.416654
c_3 = − 3.57403
c_4 = − 0.087737
c_5 = 0.098410
c_6 = 0.0027699
c_7 = − 0.0001151
c_8 = 0.1000
c_9 = − 1.33329
c_{10} = 0.025501
c_{11} = − 0.02357
c_{12} = 0.03027
c_{13} = − 0.0647
c_{14} = 0.0211329
c_{15} = 0.89469
c_{16} = − 0.099443
c_{17} = − 3.336941

$--shape

[SHAPE]
{radial width}
1.0   0.0
1.0   0.2
1.0   0.4
1.0   0.5
1.0   0.6
1.0   0.7
1.0   0.8
1.0   0.85
1.0   0.9
0.9   1.0

$---contact patch parameters

```
! 3D contact can be switched on by deleting the comment ! character
! When no further coefficients are specified, default values will be taken
![CONTACT_COEFFICIENTS]
CONTACT_MODEL                = '3D_ENVELOPING'
```

- Longitudinal Velocity：0；
- Spin Velocity：0；
- Road：.my_sanlunche.road；在 Road 框中右击选择创建路面模型，如图 12-9 所示；

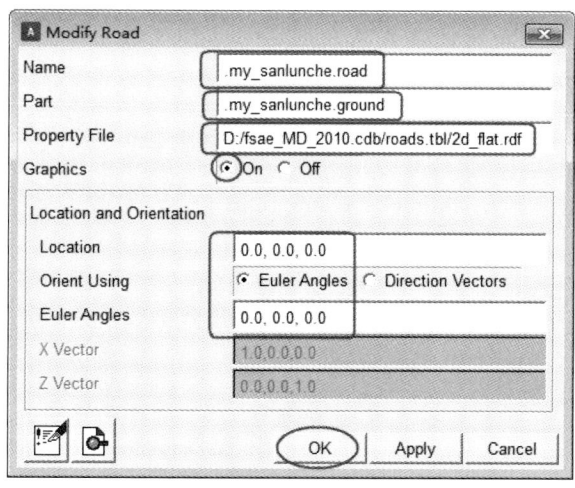

图 12-9　路面模型

① Name：road。

② Part：.my_sanlunche.ground。

③ Property File：D:/fsae_MD_2010.cdb/roads.tbl/2d_flat.rdf，或在共享数据库轮胎文件夹中获取。

④ Location：0.0, 0.0, 0.0。

⑤ Orient using：Euler Angles。

⑥ Euler Angles：0.0, 0.0, 0.0；此处路面角度不用调整，原因在于重力方向在建模初始已经设置为 –Z 方向，如重力方向为系统默认的 –Y 方向，则此处需要调整路面的角度。

⑦ 单击 OK，完成.my_sanlunche.road 路面的创建。

- Location：2800.0, –750.0, 325.0；
- Orient using：Euler Angles；
- Euler Angles：0.0, 90.0, 0.0；
- 单击 Apply，完成.my_sanlunche.wheel_left 轮胎的创建。

（2）右后轮胎。

- 单击 Forces > Special Forces > Creat a Tire；
- Name：wheel_right；
- Side：Right；
- Cm Offset：0；

- Mass：20；
- Ixx Iyy：5e4；
- Izz：1e4；
- Wheel Center Offset：0；
- Tire Property File：D:/MSC.Software/Adams_x64/2015/acar/shared_car_database.cdb/tires.tbl/mdi_tire01_255.tir；
- Longitudinal Velocity：0；
- Spin Velocity：0；
- Road：.my_sanlunche.road；
- Location：2 800.0, 750.0, 325.0；
- Orient using：Euler Angles；
- Euler Angles：0.0, 90.0, 0.0；
- 单击 Apply，完成.my_sanlunche.wheel_right 轮胎的创建。

（3）前轮胎。
- 单击 Forces > Special Forces > Creat a Tire；
- Name：wheel_front；
- Side：Left；
- Cm Offset：0；
- Mass：20；
- Ixx Iyy：5e4；
- Izz：1e4；
- Wheel Center Offset：0；
- Tire Property File：D:/MSC.Software/Adams_x64/2015/acar/shared_car_database.cdb/tires.tbl/mdi_tire01_255.tir；
- Longitudinal Velocity：0；
- Spin Velocity：0；
- Road：.my_sanlunche.road；
- Location：250.0, 0.0, 325.0；
- Orient using：Euler Angles；
- Euler Angles：0.0, 90.0, 0.0；
- 单击 OK，完成.my_sanlunche.wheel_front 轮胎的创建。

（4）部件 wheel_left.wheel_part 与 hub_1 之间 Revolute 约束。
- 单击 Connecton > Joints > Creat a Revolute Joint；
- Name：wheel_left_and_hub；
- First Body：wheel_left.wheel_part；
- Second Body：hub_1；
- Type：Revolute；
- Force Display：None；
- 单击 OK，完成约束副.my_sanlunche.wheel_left_and_hub 的创建。

（5）部件 wheel_right.wheel_part 与 hub_1 之间 Revolute 约束。
- 单击 Connecton > Joints > Creat a Revolute Joint；
- Name：wheel_right_and_hub；
- First Body：wheel_right.wheel_part；
- Second Body：hub_r；
- Type：Revolute；
- Force Display：None；
- 单击 OK，完成约束副.my_sanlunche.wheel_right_and_hub 的创建。

（6）部件 wheel_right.wheel_part 与 hub_1 之间 Revolute 约束。
- 单击 Connecton > Joints > Creat a Revolute Joint；
- Name：wheel_front_and_hub；
- First Body：wheel_front.wheel_part；
- Second Body：hub_front；
- Type：Revolute；
- Force Display：None；
- 单击 OK，完成约束副.my_sanlunche.wheel_front_and_hub 的创建。

12.6 转弯仿真

转弯仿真时，前单轮转向系统需要与车身之间产生转动，创建约束副时，部件 steer_wheel 与 body 之间为固定副，修改固定副为旋转副，并对旋转副添加旋转驱动，使整车在运动时可以产生转向。

- 左侧模型树：单击 Browse > Connectors > body_and_damper_up > Modify（右击），弹出修改约束副如图 12-10 所示；
- Type：Revolute，其余参数项保持默认；
- 单击 OK，完成约束副.my_sanlunche.body_and_damper_up 的修改，此时约束副从固定副转换为旋转副。

（1）部件 steer_wheel 与 body 之间的驱动力。
- 单击 Motions > Joint Motions > Rotational Joint Motion；
- 显示界面选择约束副.my_sanlunche.body_and_damper_up，完成驱动 MOTION_1 的创建；
- 右击 MOTION_1，弹出修改界面如图 12-11 所示；
- Function（time）：1.5d * time；
- 其余参数保持默认，单击 OK 完成 MOTION_1 的修改。

（12）部件 wheel_left_and_hub 与 hub_1 之间的驱动力。
- 单击 Motions > Joint Motions > Rotational Joint Motion；
- 显示界面选择约束副.my_sanlunche.wheel_left_and_hub，完成驱动 MOTION_2 的创建；

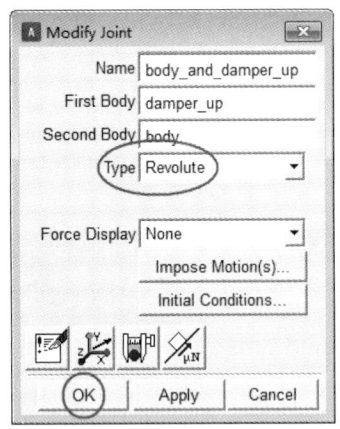　　　　　　　　　　　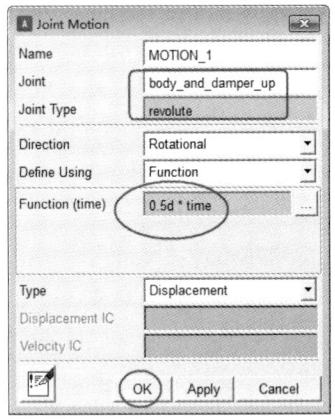

图 12-10　旋转副　　　　　　　　图 12-11　驱动力

- 右击 MOTION_1，弹出修改界面参考如图 12-11 所示；
- Function（time）：–100.0d * time；
- 其余参数保持默认，单击 OK 完成 MOTION_2 的修改。

（3）部件 wheel_right.wheel_part 与 hub_r 之间的驱动力。

- 单击 Motions > Joint Motions > Rotational Joint Motion；
- 显示界面选择约束副.my_sanlunche.wheel_right_and_hub，完成驱动 MOTION_3 的创建；
- 右击 MOTION_1，弹出修改界面参考如图 12-11 所示；
- Function（time）：–100.0d * time；
- 其余参数保持默认，单击 OK 完成 MOTION_3 的修改。

（4）仿真设置：

- 单击 Simulation > Simulate > Run an interative Simulation，仿真参数设置如图 12-12 所示；

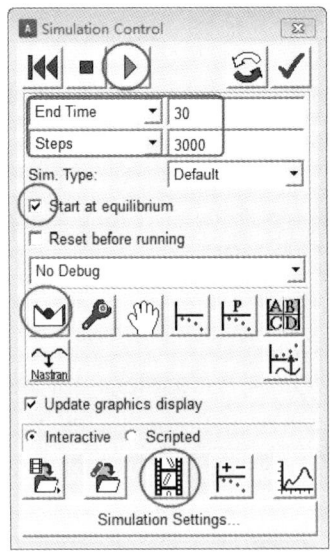

图 12-12　仿真参数设置

- 单击静平衡按钮，检测三轮车整车模型是否能静平衡，静平衡是正确仿真的开始；
- End Time：30；
- Steps：3 000；
- 勾选 Start at equilibrium，从静平衡开始仿真；
- 单击开始完成三轮车转向仿真；
- 切换到后处理模块，计算参数如图 12-13 ~ 图 12-18 所示。

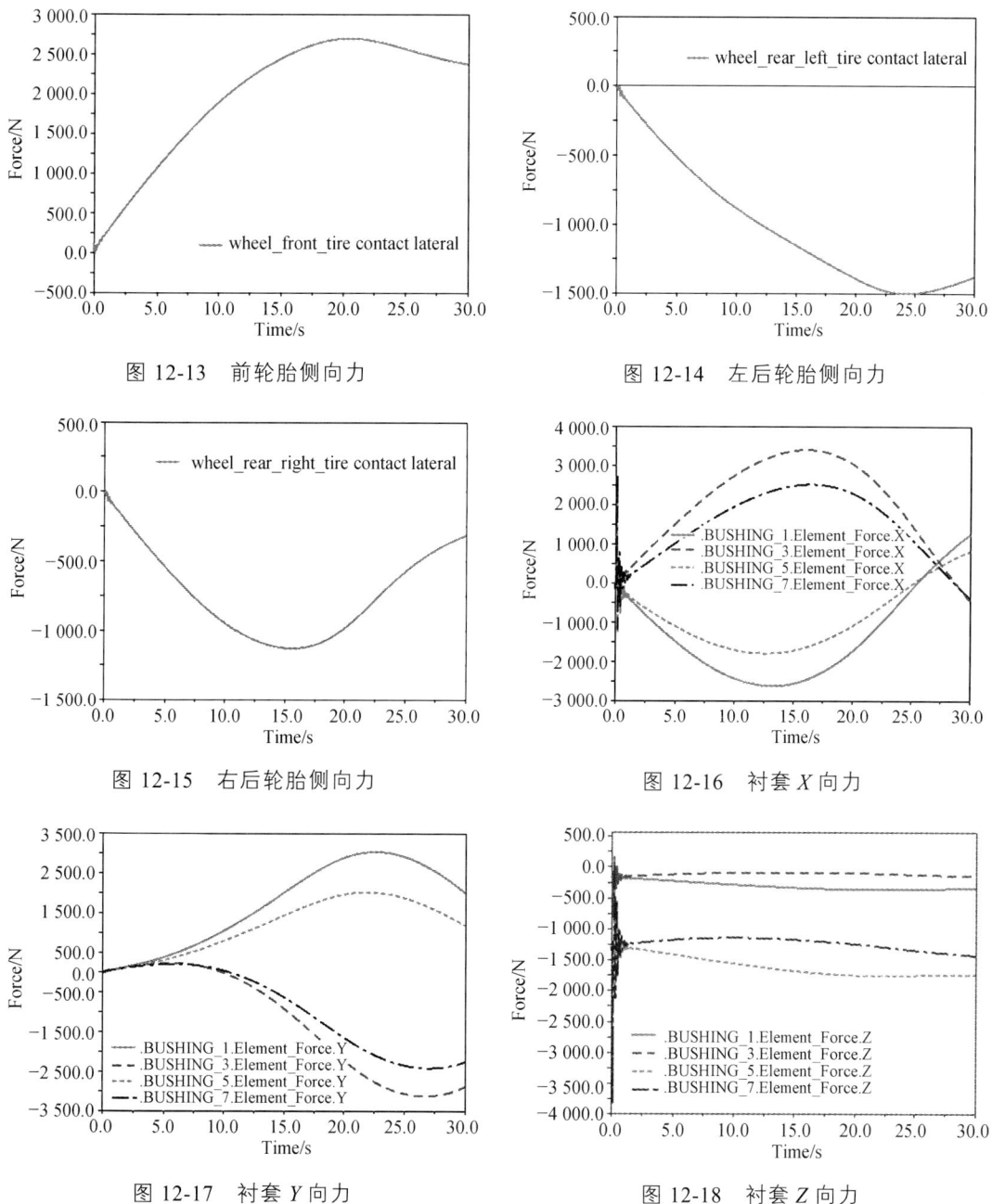

图 12-13　前轮胎侧向力

图 12-14　左后轮胎侧向力

图 12-15　右后轮胎侧向力

图 12-16　衬套 X 向力

图 12-17　衬套 Y 向力

图 12-18　衬套 Z 向力

12.7 后非独立悬架避震器

- 单击 Bodies > Construction > Geometry Point 创建硬点；
- Add to Part；
- Don't Attach；
- 单击部件 axis；
- 右击鼠标，弹出硬点位置对话框如图 12-4 所示；
- 硬点位置输入 2 800，-570，225；
- 单击 Apply，完成硬点创建；
- 右击硬点，选择 Rename，重名为 damper_low_left；
- 单击 Bodies > Construction > Geometry Point 创建硬点；
- Add to Part；
- Don't Attach；
- 单击部件 axis；
- 右击鼠标，弹出硬点位置对话框如图 12-4 所示；
- 硬点位置输入 2 800，570，225；
- 单击 Apply，完成硬点创建；
- 右击硬点，选择 Rename，重名为 damper_low_right；
- 单击 Bodies > Construction > Geometry Point 创建硬点；
- Add to Part；
- Don't Attach；
- 单击部件 body；
- 右击鼠标，弹出硬点位置对话框如图 12-4 所示；
- 硬点位置输入 2 800，-500，625；
- 单击 Apply，完成硬点创建；
- 右击硬点，选择 Rename，重名为 damper_up_left；
- 单击 Bodies > Construction > Geometry Point 创建硬点；
- Add to Part；
- Don't Attach；
- 单击部件 body；
- 右击鼠标，弹出硬点位置对话框如图 12-4 所示；
- 硬点位置输入 2 800，500，625；
- 单击 Apply，完成硬点创建；
- 右击硬点，选择 Rename，重名为 damper_up_right；
- 单击 Forces > Flexible Connections > Spring-Damper；
- K：50；
- C：1 000；
- 选择点 damper_low_left 与 damper_up_left，完成 SPRING_3 的创建；

- 单击 Forces > Flexible Connections > Spring-Damper；
- K：50；
- C：1 000；
- 选择点 damper_low_right 与 damper_up_right，完成 SPRING_4 的创建，减震器创建完成后三轮车模型如图 12-19 所示；

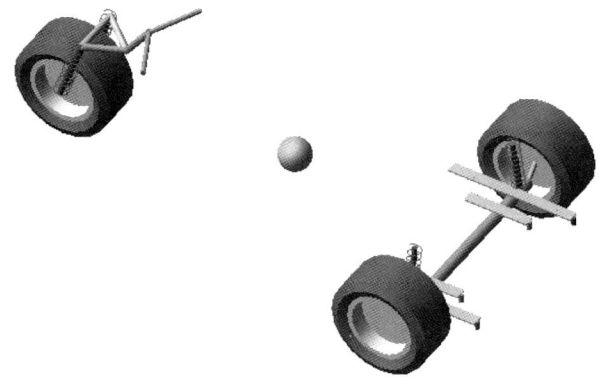

图 12-19　三轮车整车模型（包含后避震器）

- 单击 Simulation > Simulate > Run an interative Simulation，仿真参数设置如图 12-12 所示；
- 单击静平衡按钮，检测三轮车整车模型是否能静平衡，静平衡是正确仿真的开始；
- End Time：30；
- Steps：3 000；
- 勾选 Start at equilibrium，从静平衡开始仿真；
- 单击开始完成三轮车转向仿真；
- 切换到后处理模块，整车运行轨迹如图 12-20 所示，车身垂向与侧向加速度参数如图 12-21、图 12-22 所示。

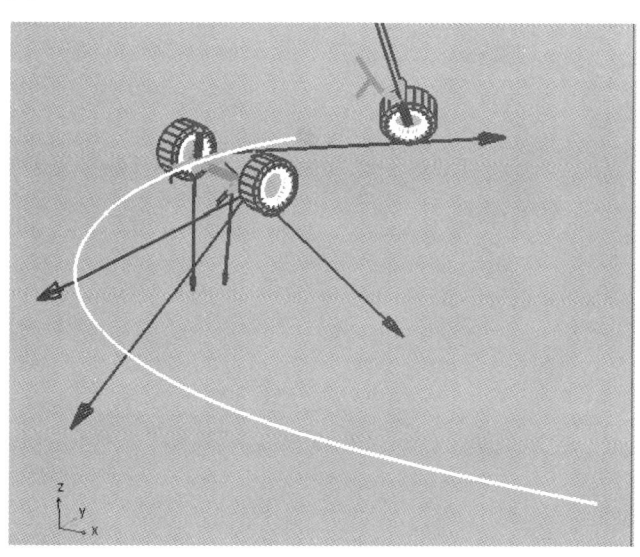

图 12-20　三轮车运行轨迹

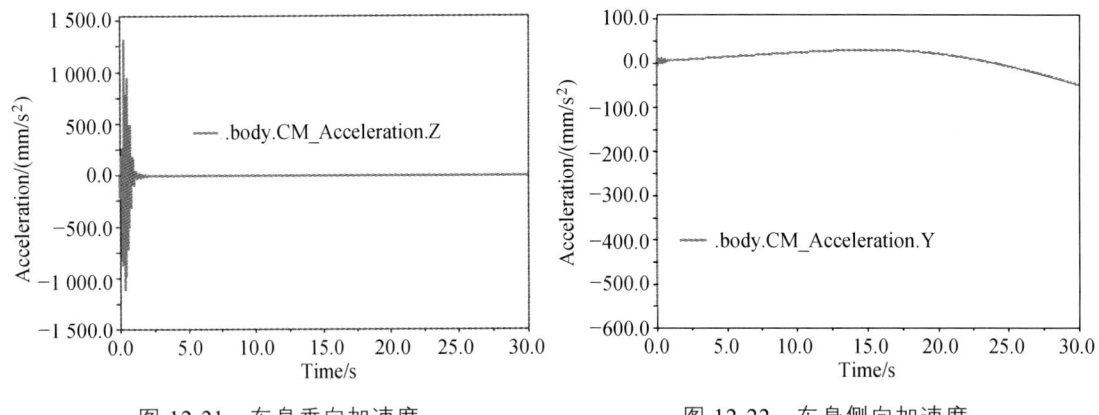

图 12-21 车身垂向加速度　　　　图 12-22 车身侧向加速度

第 13 章　三轮车 II

"逆"三轮车较为特殊，前轴采用双 A 臂独立悬架，后轴采用单轮胎。此三轮车极为少见，在国外一些三轮机车（跑车）上有采用前双后单的布置形式。相对于正三轮车，此种布置形式的三轮车在直线、制动、转弯等工况具有明显的优势，例如制动时抗"点头"特性较好，直线及转弯时车身的稳定性好，缺点是极为不适用、车内空间狭小。"逆"三轮车多采用后轮驱动，传动系统较为简单，发动机排量小，占用空间少；建立好的"逆"三轮车模型（见图 13-1）存在章节文件中。

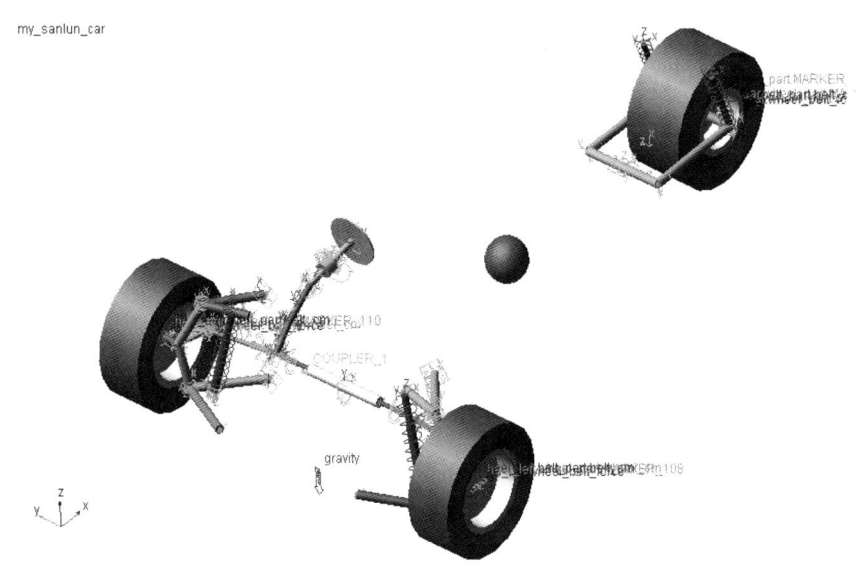

图 13-1　三轮车模型

学习目标

- ◇ 双 A 臂悬架。
- ◇ 后单轮拖拽悬架。
- ◇ 转向系统。
- ◇ 约束关系讨论。
- ◇ 柔性连接。

13.1 双 A 臂悬架

- 单击 Bodies > Construction > Geometry Point 创建硬点；
- Add to Ground；
- Don't Attach；
- 右击鼠标，弹出硬点位置对话框如图 13-2 所示；

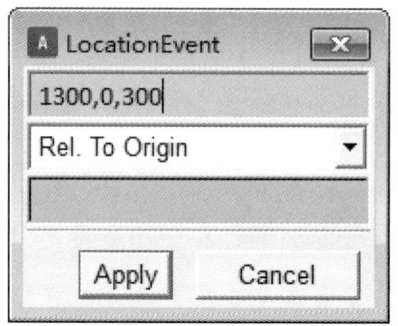

图 13-2　硬点创建对话框

- 硬点位置输入 1 300，0，300；
- 单击 Apply，完成硬点创建；
- 右击硬点，选择 Rename，重名为 body_center；
- 重复上述步骤，完成如图 13-3 所示硬点参数的创建；

	Loc X	Loc Y	Loc Z
wheel_center_left	0.0	-800.0	300.0
wheel_center_right	0.0	800.0	300.0
uca_front_l	100.0	-450.0	525.0
uca_front_r	100.0	450.0	525.0
uca_outer_l	40.0	-675.0	525.0
uca_outer_r	40.0	675.0	525.0
uca_rear_l	250.0	-490.0	530.0
uca_rear_r	250.0	490.0	530.0
tierod_outer_l	150.0	-750.0	300.0
tierod_outer_r	150.0	750.0	300.0
tierod_inner_l	200.0	-400.0	300.0
tierod_inner_r	200.0	400.0	300.0
lca_rear_l	200.0	-450.0	155.0
lca_rear_r	200.0	450.0	155.0
lca_out_l	0.0	-750.0	100.0
lca_out_r	0.0	750.0	100.0
lca_front_l	-200.0	-400.0	150.0
lca_front_r	-200.0	400.0	150.0
hub_l	0.0	-900.0	300.0
hub_r	0.0	900.0	300.0
body_center	1300.0	0.0	300.0

图 13-3　双 A 臂悬架硬点参数

（1）车身部件 body。
- 单击 Bodies > Geometry Sphere 创建球形几何体；
- 选择 New Part；
- Radius：200；
- 选择硬点：body_center，完成球形部件创建；
- 右击球形部件，选择 Rename，重名为 body_center。

（2）左下控制臂部件 lca_l。
- 单击 Bodies > Geometry Cylinder 创建圆柱几何体；
- 选择 New Part；
- Radius: 20；
- 选择硬点：lca_front_l 与 lca_out_l，完成圆柱形几何体创建；
- 右击圆柱体部件，选择 Rename，重名为 lca_l；
- 单击 Bodies > Geometry Cylinder 创建圆柱几何体；
- 选择 Add to Part；
- Radius: 20；
- 选择部件 lca_l；
- 选择硬点：lca_rear_l 与 lca_out_l，完成左下控制臂部件创建。

（3）右下控制臂部件 lca_r。
- 单击 Bodies > Geometry Cylinder 创建圆柱几何体；
- 选择：New Part；
- Radius: 20；
- 选择硬点：lca_front_r 与 lca_out_r，完成圆柱形几何体创建；
- 右击圆柱体部件，选择 Rename，重名为 lca_r；
- 单击 Bodies > Geometry Cylinder 创建圆柱几何体；
- 选择 Add to Part；
- Radius: 20；
- 选择部件 lca_r；
- 选择硬点：lca_rear_r 与 lca_out_r，完成右下控制臂部件创建。

（4）左上控制臂部件 uca_l。
- 单击 Bodies > Geometry Cylinder 创建圆柱几何体；
- 选择 New Part；
- Radius: 20；
- 选择硬点：uca_front_l 与 uca_out_l，完成圆柱形几何体创建；
- 右击圆柱体部件，选择 Rename，重名为 uca_l；
- 单击 Bodies > Geometry Cylinder 创建圆柱几何体；
- 选择 Add to Part；
- Radius: 20；
- 选择部件 uca_l；
- 选择硬点：uca_rear_l 与 uca_out_l，完成左上控制臂部件创建。

(5) 右上控制臂部件 uca_r。
- 单击 Bodies > Geometry Cylinder 创建圆柱几何体；
- 选择 New Part；
- Radius: 20；
- 选择硬点：uca_front_r 与 uca_out_r，完成圆柱形几何体创建；
- 右击圆柱体部件，选择 Rename，重名为 uca_r；
- 单击 Bodies > Geometry Cylinder 创建圆柱几何体；
- 选择 Add to Part；
- Radius: 20；
- 选择部件 uca_r；
- 选择硬点：uca_rear_r 与 uca_out_r，完成右上控制臂部件创建。

(6) 左转向节部件 upright_l。
- 单击 Bodies > Geometry Cylinder 创建圆柱几何体；
- 选择 New Part；
- Radius: 20；
- 选择硬点：wheel_center_left 与 uca_out_l，完成圆柱形几何体创建；
- 右击圆柱体部件，选择 Rename，重名为 upright_l；
- 单击 Bodies > Geometry Cylinder 创建圆柱几何体；
- 选择 Add to Part；
- Radius: 20；
- 选择部件 upright_l；
- 选择硬点：wheel_center_left 与 lca_out_l，完成圆柱形几何体创建；
- 单击 Bodies > Geometry Cylinder 创建圆柱几何体；
- 选择 Add to Part；
- Radius:10；
- 选择部件 upright_l；
- 选择硬点：wheel_center_left 与 tierod_outer_l，完成转向节部件创建。

(7) 右转向节部件 upright_r。
- 单击 Bodies > Geometry Cylinder 创建圆柱几何体；
- 选择 New Part；
- Radius: 20；
- 选择硬点：wheel_center_right 与 uca_out_r，完成圆柱形几何体创建；
- 右击圆柱体部件，选择 Rename，重名为 upright_r；
- 单击 Bodies > Geometry Cylinder 创建圆柱几何体；
- 选择 Add to Part；
- Radius: 20；
- 选择部件 upright_r；
- 选择硬点：wheel_center_right 与 lca_out_r，完成圆柱形几何体创建；
- 单击 Bodies > Geometry Cylinder 创建圆柱几何体；

- 选择 Add to Part；
- Radius:10；
- 选择部件 upright_r；
- 选择硬点：wheel_center_right 与 tierod_outer_l，完成转向节部件创建。

（8）左轮毂部件 hub_left。
- 单击 Bodies > Geometry Cylinder 创建圆柱几何体；
- 选择：New Part；
- Radius: 20；
- 选择硬点：wheel_center_left 与 hub_l，完成圆柱形部件创建；
- 右击圆柱体部件，选择 Rename，重名为 hub_left。

（9）右轮毂部件 hub_right。
- 单击 Bodies > Geometry Cylinder 创建圆柱几何体；
- 选择 New Part；
- Radius: 20；
- 选择硬点：wheel_center_right 与 hub_r，完成圆柱形部件创建；
- 右击圆柱体部件，选择 Rename，重名为 hub_right。

（10）左转向横拉杆部件 tierod_l。
- 单击 Bodies > Geometry Cylinder 创建圆柱几何体；
- 选择 New Part；
- Radius: 20；
- 选择硬点：tierod_outer_l 与 tierod_inner_l，完成圆柱形部件创建；
- 右击圆柱体部件，选择 Rename，重名为 tierod_l。

（11）右转向横拉杆部件 tierod_r。
- 单击 Bodies > Geometry Cylinder 创建圆柱几何体；
- 选择 New Part；
- Radius: 20；
- 选择硬点：tierod_outer_r 与 tierod_inner_r，完成圆柱形部件创建；
- 右击圆柱体部件，选择 Rename，重名为 tierod_r。

（12）双 A 臂悬架弹簧与避震器。
- 单击 Bodies > Construction > Construction Geometry：Mark 创建参考点；
- Add to Part；
- Don't Attach；
- 选择部件 lca_l；
- 右击鼠标，弹出硬点位置对话框参考如图 13-2 所示；
- 硬点位置输入 0，－600，150；
- 单击 Apply，完成参考点创建；
- 右击参考点，选择 Rename，重名为 M1；
- 单击 Bodies > Construction > Construction Geometry：Mark 创建参考点；
- Add to Part；

- Don't Attach;
- 选择部件 lca_r;
- 右击鼠标，弹出硬点位置对话框参考如图 13-2 所示；
- 硬点位置输入 0，600，150；
- 单击 Apply，完成参考点创建；
- 右击参考点，选择 Rename，重名为 M2；
- 单击 Bodies > Construction > Construction Geometry：Mark 创建参考点；
- Add to Part;
- Don't Attach;
- 选择部件 body;
- 右击鼠标，弹出硬点位置对话框参考如图 13-2 所示；
- 硬点位置输入 40，-500，550；
- 单击 Apply，完成参考点创建；
- 右击参考点，选择 Rename，重名为 M1；
- 单击 Bodies > Construction > Construction Geometry：Mark 创建参考点；
- Add to Part;
- Don't Attach;
- 选择部件 body;
- 右击鼠标，弹出硬点位置对话框参考如图 13-2 所示；
- 硬点位置输入 40，500，550；
- 单击 Apply，完成参考点创建；
- 右击参考点，选择 Rename，重名为 M2；
- 单击 Forces > Flexible Connections >Spring-Damper;
- K：16;
- C：5;
- 选择点.my_sanlun_car.lca_l.M1 与.my_sanlun_car.body.M1，完成 SPRING_1 的创建；
- 单击 Forces > Flexible Connections >Spring-Damper;
- K：16;
- C：5;
- 选择点.my_sanlun_car.lca_r.M2 与.my_sanlun_car.body.M2，完成 SPRING_2 的创建。

13.2 双 A 臂悬架约束

（1）部件 upright_l 与 uca_l 之间 Spherical 约束。
- 单击 Connecton > Joints > Creat a Fixed Joint;
- Name：uca_to_upright_l;
- First Body：.my_sanlun_car.upright_l;
- Second Body：.my_sanlun_car.uca_l;

- Type：Spherical；
- Force Display：None；
- 单击 OK，完成约束副.my_sanlun_car.uca_to_upright_l 的创建（见图 13-4）。

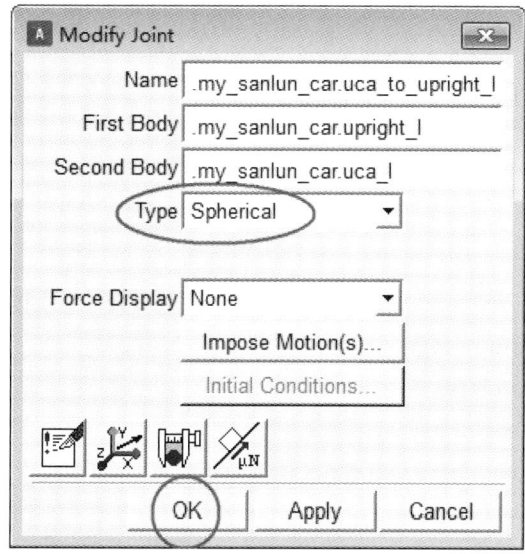

图 13-4　约束

（2）部件 upright_r 与 uca_r 之间 Spherical 约束。
- 单击 Connecton > Joints > Creat a Spherical Joint；
- Name：uca_to_upright_r；
- First Body：.my_sanlun_car.upright_r；
- Second Body：.my_sanlun_car.uca_r；
- Type：Spherical；
- Force Display：None；
- 单击 OK，完成约束副.my_sanlun_car.uca_to_upright_r 的创建。

（3）部件 upright_l 与 lca_l 之间 Spherical 约束。
- 单击 Connecton > Joints > Creat a Spherical Joint；
- Name：lca_to_upright_l；
- First Body：.my_sanlun_car.upright_l；
- Second Body：.my_sanlun_car.lca_l；
- Type：Spherical；
- Force Display：None；
- 单击 OK，完成约束副.my_sanlun_car.lca_to_upright_l 的创建。

（4）部件 upright_r 与 lca_r 之间 Spherical 约束。
- 单击 Connecton > Joints > Creat a Spherical Joint；
- Name：lca_to_upright_r；
- First Body：.my_sanlun_car.upright_r；
- Second Body：.my_sanlun_car.lca_r；

- Type：Spherical；
- Force Display：None；
- 单击 OK，完成约束副.my_sanlun_car.lca_to_upright_r 的创建。

（5）部件 upright_l 与 hub_left 之间 Fixed 约束。
- 单击 Connecton > Joints > Creat a Fixed Joint；
- Name：hub_to_upright_l；
- First Body：.my_sanlun_car.upright_l；
- Second Body：.my_sanlun_car.hub_left；
- Type：Fixed；
- Force Display：None；
- 单击 OK，完成约束副.my_sanlun_car.hub_to_upright_l 的创建。

（6）部件 upright_r 与 hub_right 之间 Fixed 约束。
- 单击 Connecton > Joints > Creat a Fixed Joint；
- Name：hub_to_upright_r；
- First Body：.my_sanlun_car.upright_r；
- Second Body：.my_sanlun_car.hub_right；
- Type：Fixed；
- Force Display：None；
- 单击 OK，完成约束副.my_sanlun_car.hub_to_upright_r 的创建。

（7）部件 upright_l 与 tierod_l 之间 Spherical 约束。
- 单击 Connecton > Joints > Creat a Spherical Joint；
- Name：upright_to_tierod_l；
- First Body：.my_sanlun_car.upright_l；
- Second Body：.my_sanlun_car.tierod_l；
- Type：Spherical；
- Force Display：None；
- 单击 OK，完成约束副.my_sanlun_car.upright_to_tierod_l 的创建。

（8）部件 upright_r 与 tierod_r 之间 Spherical 约束。
- 单击 Connecton > Joints > Creat a Spherical Joint；
- Name：upright_to_tierod_r；
- First Body：.my_sanlun_car.upright_r；
- Second Body：.my_sanlun_car.tierod_r；
- Type：Spherical；
- Force Display：None；
- 单击 OK，完成约束副.my_sanlun_car.upright_to_tierod_r 的创建。

（9）部件 body 与 lca_l 之间 Revolute 约束。
- 单击 Connecton > Joints > Creat a Revolute Joint；
- Name：body_to_lca_l；
- First Body：.my_sanlun_car.lca_l；

- Second Body：.my_sanlun_car.body；
- Type：Revolute；
- Force Display：None；
- 单击 OK，完成约束副.my_sanlun_car.body_to_lca_l 的创建。

（10）部件 body 与 lca_r 之间 Revolute 约束。
- 单击 Connecton > Joints > Creat a Revolute Joint；
- Name：body_to_lca_r；
- First Body：.my_sanlun_car.lca_r；
- Second Body：.my_sanlun_car.body；
- Type：Revolute；
- Force Display：None；
- 单击 OK，完成约束副.my_sanlun_car.body_to_lca_r 的创建。

（11）部件 body 与 uca_l 之间 Revolute 约束。
- 单击 Connecton > Joints > Creat a Revolute Joint；
- Name：body_to_uca_l；
- First Body：.my_sanlun_car.uca_l；
- Second Body：.my_sanlun_car.body；
- Type：Revolute；
- Force Display：None；
- 单击 OK，完成约束副.my_sanlun_car.body_to_uca_l 的创建。

（12）部件 body 与 uca_r 之间 Revolute 约束。
- 单击 Connecton > Joints > Creat a Revolute Joint；
- Name：body_to_uca_r；
- First Body：.my_sanlun_car.uca_r；
- Second Body：.my_sanlun_car.body；
- Type：Revolute；
- Force Display：None；
- 单击 OK，完成约束副.my_sanlun_car.body_to_uca_r 的创建。

（13）部件 body 与 lca_l 之间 Cylindrical 约束。
- 单击 Connecton > Joints > Creat a Cylindrical Joint；
- Name：srping_front_left；
- First Body：.my_sanlun_car.lca_l；
- Second Body：.my_sanlun_car.body；
- Type：Cylindrical；
- Force Display：None；
- 单击 OK，完成约束副.my_sanlun_car.srping_front_left 的创建。

（14）部件 body 与 lca_r 之间 Cylindrical 约束。
- 单击 Connecton > Joints > Creat a Cylindrical Joint；
- Name：srping_front_right；

- First Body：.my_sanlun_car.lca_r；
- Second Body：.my_sanlun_car.body；
- Type：Cylindrical；
- Force Display：None；
- 单击 OK，完成约束副.my_sanlun_car.srping_front_right 的创建。

13.3 后单轮拖拽悬架

- 单击 Bodies > Construction > Geometry Point 创建硬点；
- Add to Ground；
- Don't Attach；
- 右击鼠标，弹出硬点位置对话框如图 13-2 所示；
- 硬点位置输入 2600，-200，300；
- 单击 Apply，完成硬点创建；
- 右击硬点，选择 Rename，重名为 hub_rear_l；
- 重复上述步骤，完成如图 13-5 所示硬点参数的创建。

hub_rear_l	2600.0	-200.0	300.0
hub_rear_r	2600.0	200.0	300.0
rear_arm_r	2100.0	200.0	300.0
rear_arm_l	2100.0	-200.0	300.0

图 13-5 拖拽悬架硬点参数

（1）后轮毂部件 hub_rear。
- 单击 Bodies > Geometry Cylinder 创建圆柱几何体；
- 选择 New Part；
- Radius: 20；
- 选择硬点：hub_rear_l 与 hub_rear_r，完成圆柱形部件创建；
- 右击圆柱体部件，选择 Rename，重名为 hub_rear。

（2）后控制臂部件 rear_arm。
- 单击 Bodies > Geometry Cylinder 创建圆柱几何体；
- 选择 New Part；
- Radius: 20；
- 选择硬点：rear_arm_l 与 rear_arm_r，完成圆柱形部件创建；
- 右击圆柱体部件，选择 Rename，重名为 rear_arm；
- 单击 Bodies > Geometry Cylinder 创建圆柱几何体；
- 选择 Add to Part；
- Radius: 20；
- 选择部件 rear_arm；

- 选择硬点：rear_arm_l 与 hub_rear_l，完成圆柱形几何体创建；
- 单击 Bodies > Geometry Cylinder 创建圆柱几何体；
- 选择 Add to Part；
- Radius：20；
- 选择部件 rear_arm；
- 选择硬点：rear_arm_r 与 hub_rear_r，完成转向节部件创建。

（3）后单轮拖拽臂架弹簧与避震器。
- 单击 Bodies > Construction > Construction Geometry：Mark 创建参考点；
- Add to Part；
- Don't Attach；
- 选择部件 hub_rear；
- 右击鼠标，弹出硬点位置对话框参考如图 13-2 所示；
- 硬点位置输入 2 600，－200，300；
- 单击 Apply，完成参考点创建；
- 右击参考点，选择 Rename，重名为 M1；
- 单击 Bodies > Construction > Construction Geometry：Mark 创建参考点；
- Add to Part；
- Don't Attach；
- 选择部件 hub_rear；
- 右击鼠标，弹出硬点位置对话框参考如图 13-2 所示；
- 硬点位置输入 2 600，200，300；
- 单击 Apply，完成参考点创建；
- 右击参考点，选择 Rename，重名为 M2；
- 单击 Bodies > Construction > Construction Geometry：Mark 创建参考点；
- Add to Part；
- Don't Attach；
- 选择部件 body；
- 右击鼠标，弹出硬点位置对话框参考如图 13-2 所示；
- 硬点位置输入 2 500，－200，600；
- 单击 Apply，完成参考点创建；
- 右击参考点，选择 Rename，重名为 M3；
- 单击 Bodies > Construction > Construction Geometry：Mark 创建参考点；
- Add to Part；
- Don't Attach；
- 选择部件 body；
- 右击鼠标，弹出硬点位置对话框参考如图 13-2 所示；
- 硬点位置输入 2 500，200，600；
- 单击 Apply，完成参考点创建；
- 右击参考点，选择 Rename，重名为 M4；

- 单击 Forces > Flexible Connections >Spring-Damper；
- K：14；
- C：5；
- 选择点.my_sanlun_car.hub_rear.M1 与.my_sanlun_car.body.M3，完成 SPRING_3 的创建；
- 单击 Forces > Flexible Connections >Spring-Damper；
- K：14；
- C：5；
- 选择点.my_sanlun_car. hub_rear.M2 与.my_sanlun_car.body.M4，完成 SPRING_4 的创建。

13.4　后单轮拖拽臂架约束

（1）部件 body 与 rear_arm 之间 Revolute 约束。
- 单击 Connecton > Joints > Creat a Revolute Joint；
- Name：rear_arm_to_body；
- First Body：.my_sanlun_car.rear_arm；
- Second Body：.my_sanlun_car.body；
- Type：Revolute；
- Force Display：None；
- 单击 OK，完成约束副..my_sanlun_car.rear_arm_to_body 的创建。

（2）部件 hub_rear 与 rear_arm 之间 Fixed 约束。
- 单击 Connecton > Joints > Creat a Fixed Joint；
- Name：rear_hub_to_rear_arm；
- First Body：.my_sanlun_car.rear_arm；
- Second Body：.my_sanlun_car.hub_rear；
- Type：Fixed；
- Force Display：None；
- 单击 OK，完成约束副.my_sanlun_car.rear_hub_to_rear_arm 的创建。

（3）部件 body 与 hub_rear 之间 Cylindrical 约束。
- 单击 Connecton > Joints > Creat a Cylindrical Joint；
- Name：spring_rear_left；
- First Body：.my_sanlun_car.hub_rear；
- Second Body：.my_sanlun_car.body；
- Type：Cylindrical；
- Force Display：None；
- 单击 OK，完成约束副.my_sanlun_car.spring_rear_left 的创建。

（4）部件 body 与 lca_r 之间 Cylindrical 约束。
- 单击 Connecton > Joints > Creat a Cylindrical Joint；
- Name：srping_rear_right；

- First Body：.my_sanlun_car.hub_rear；
- Second Body：.my_sanlun_car.body；
- Type：Cylindrical；
- Force Display：None；
- 单击 OK，完成约束副.my_sanlun_car.srping_rear_right 的创建。

13.5 三轮车右舵转向系统

- 单击 Bodies > Construction > Geometry Point 创建硬点；
- Add to Ground；
- Don't Attach；
- 右击鼠标，弹出硬点位置对话框如图 13-2 所示；
- 硬点位置输入 300，400，400；
- 单击 Apply，完成硬点创建；
- 右击硬点，选择 Rename，重名为 steer_axie_low；
- 重复上述步骤，完成如图 13-6 所示硬点参数的创建。

rack_house_mount_l	200.0	-200.0	300.0
rack_house_mount_r	200.0	200.0	300.0
steer_axie_low	300.0	400.0	400.0
steer_axie_mid	450.0	400.0	500.0
steer_axie_up	750.0	400.0	550.0

图 13-6　转向系统硬点参数

（1）齿条部件 tierod_mid。
- 单击 Bodies > Geometry Cylinder 创建圆柱几何体；
- 选择 New Part；
- Radius：10；
- 选择硬点：tierod_inner_l 与 tierod_inner_r，完成圆柱形部件创建；
- 右击圆柱体部件，选择 Rename，重名为.my_sanlun_car.tierod_mid。

（2）齿条箱部件 rack_house。
- 单击 Bodies > Geometry Cylinder 创建圆柱几何体；
- 选择 New Part；
- Radius：25；
- 选择硬点：rack_house_mount_l 与 rack_house_mount_r，完成圆柱形部件创建；
- 右击圆柱体部件，选择 Rename，重名为.my_sanlun_car. rack_house。

（3）转向传动轴部件 axis_1。
- 单击 Bodies > Geometry Cylinder 创建圆柱几何体；
- 选择 New Part；

- Radius：15；
- 选择硬点：tierod_inner_r 与 steer_axie_low，完成圆柱形部件创建；
- 右击圆柱体部件，选择 Rename，重名为.my_sanlun_car.axis_1。

（4）转向传动轴部件 axis_2。
- 单击 Bodies > Geometry Cylinder 创建圆柱几何体；
- 选择 New Part；
- Radius：15；
- 选择硬点：steer_axie_low 与 steer_axie_mid，完成圆柱形部件创建；
- 右击圆柱体部件，选择 Rename，重名为.my_sanlun_car.axis_2。

（5）转向传动轴部件 axis_3。
- 单击 Bodies > Geometry Cylinder 创建圆柱几何体；
- 选择 New Part；
- Radius：15；
- 选择硬点：steer_axie_mid 与 steer_axie_up，完成圆柱形部件创建；
- 右击圆柱体部件，选择 Rename，重名为.my_sanlun_car.axis_3。

（6）转向柱部件 steer_column。
- 单击 Bodies > Geometry Cylinder 创建圆柱几何体；
- 选择 New Part；
- Length：60
- Radius：35；
- 选择参考点：.my_sanlun_car.axis_3.cm；
- 选择方向参考点：steer_axie_mid，完成圆柱形部件的创建；
- 右击圆柱体部件，选择 Rename，重名为 steer_column；

（7）转向柱部件 steering_wheel。
- 单击 Bodies > Geometry Cylinder 创建圆柱几何体；
- 选择 New Part；
- Length：10
- Radius：120；
- 选择参考点：steer_axie_up；
- 选择方向参考点：steer_axie_mid，完成圆柱形部件的创建；
- 右击圆柱体部件，选择 Rename，重名为 steering_wheel。

13.6 三轮车右舵转向系统约束

（1）部件 tierod_l 与 tierod_mid 之间 Constant Velocity 约束。
- 单击 Connecton > Joints > Creat a Constant Velocity Joint；
- Name：tierod_to_mid_l；
- First Body：.my_sanlun_car.tierod_l；

- Second Body：.my_sanlun_car.tierod_mid；
- Type：Constant Velocity；
- Force Display：None；
- 单击 OK，完成约束副.my_sanlun_car.tierod_to_mid_l 的创建；

（2）部件 tierod_r 与 tierod_mid 之间 Constant Velocity 约束。
- 单击 Connecton > Joints > Creat a Constant Velocity Joint；
- Name：tierod_to_mid_r；
- First Body：.my_sanlun_car.tierod_r；
- Second Body：.my_sanlun_car.tierod_mid；
- Type：Constant Velocity；
- Force Display：None；
- 单击 OK，完成约束副.my_sanlun_car.tierod_to_mid_r 的创建。

（3）部件 rack_house 与 body 之间 Fixed 约束。
- 单击 Connecton > Joints > Creat a Fixed Joint；
- Name：rack_house_to_body；
- First Body：.my_sanlun_car.tierod_l；
- Second Body：.my_sanlun_car.body；
- Type：Fixed；
- Force Display：None；
- 单击 OK，完成约束副.my_sanlun_car.rack_house_to_body 的创建。

（4）部件 steering_wheel 与 axis_3 之间 Fixed 约束。
- 单击 Connecton > Joints > Creat a Fixed Joint；
- Name：steer_to_axis_3；
- First Body：.my_sanlun_car.steering_wheel；
- Second Body：.my_sanlun_car.axis_3；
- Type：Fixed；
- Force Display：None；
- 单击 OK，完成约束副.my_sanlun_car.steer_to_axis_3 的创建。

（5）部件 steer_column 与 body 之间 Fixed 约束。
- 单击 Connecton > Joints > Creat a Fixed Joint；
- Name：steer_to_body；
- First Body：.my_sanlun_car.steer_column；
- Second Body：.my_sanlun_car.body；
- Type：Fixed；
- Force Display：None；
- 单击 OK，完成约束副.my_sanlun_car.steer_to_body 的创建。

（6）部件 axis_3 与 steer_column 之间 Revolute 约束。
- 单击 Connecton > Joints > Creat a Revolute Joint；
- Name：axis_3_to_steer_column；

- First Body：.my_sanlun_car.axis_3；
- Second Body：.my_sanlun_car.steer_column；
- Type：Revolute；
- Force Display：None；
- 单击 OK，完成约束副.my_sanlun_car.axis_3_to_steer_column 的创建。

（7）部件 axis_3 与 axis_2 之间 Hooke 约束。
- 单击 Connecton > Joints > Creat a Hooke Joint；
- Name：axis_3_to_axis_2；
- First Body：.my_sanlun_car.axis_3；
- Second Body：.my_sanlun_car.axis_2；
- Type：Hooke；
- Force Display：None；
- 单击 OK，完成约束副.my_sanlun_car.axis_3_to_axis_2 的创建。

（8）部件 axis_2 与 axis_1 之间 Hooke 约束。
- 单击 Connecton > Joints > Creat a Hooke Joint；
- Name：axis_2_to_axis_1；
- First Body：.my_sanlun_car.axis_2；
- Second Body：.my_sanlun_car.axis_1；
- Type：Hooke；
- Force Display：None；
- 单击 OK，完成约束副.my_sanlun_car.axis_2_to_axis_1 的创建。

（9）部件 axis_1 与 rack_house 之间 Revolute 约束。
- 单击 Connecton > Joints > Creat a Revolute Joint；
- Name：axis_1_to_rack_house；
- First Body：.my_sanlun_car.axis_1；
- Second Body：.my_sanlun_car.rack_house；
- Type：Revolute；
- Force Display：None；
- 单击 OK，完成约束副.my_sanlun_car.axis_1_to_rack_house 的创建。

（10）耦合副。
- 单击 Connecton > Couplers > Joint: Coupler；
- Driver: .my_sanlun_car.axis_1_to_rack_house；
- Coupled: .my_sanlun_car.rack_house_to_tierod_mid；
- Scale：0.1，即可用方向盘转动的最大角度与车轮转动的最大角度比值对减速比进行预估；
- 单击 OK，完成耦合副.my_sanlun_car.COUPLER_1 的创建（见图 13-7），此时整车约束关系如图 13-8 所示。

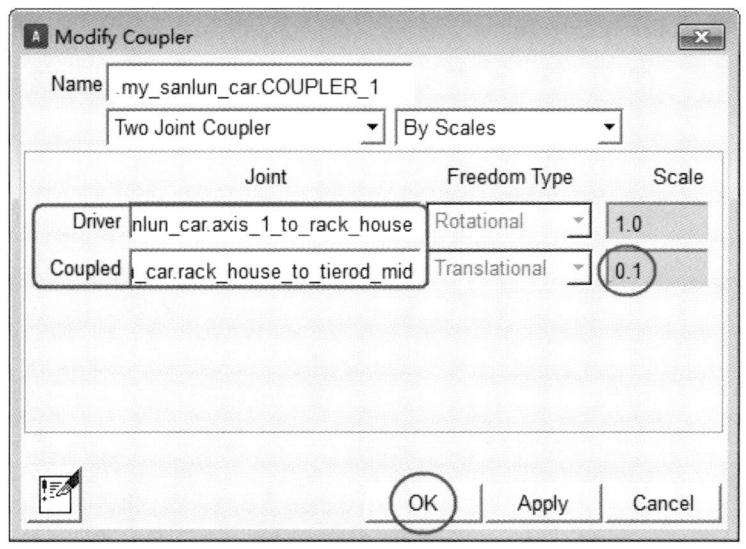

图 13-7　耦合副

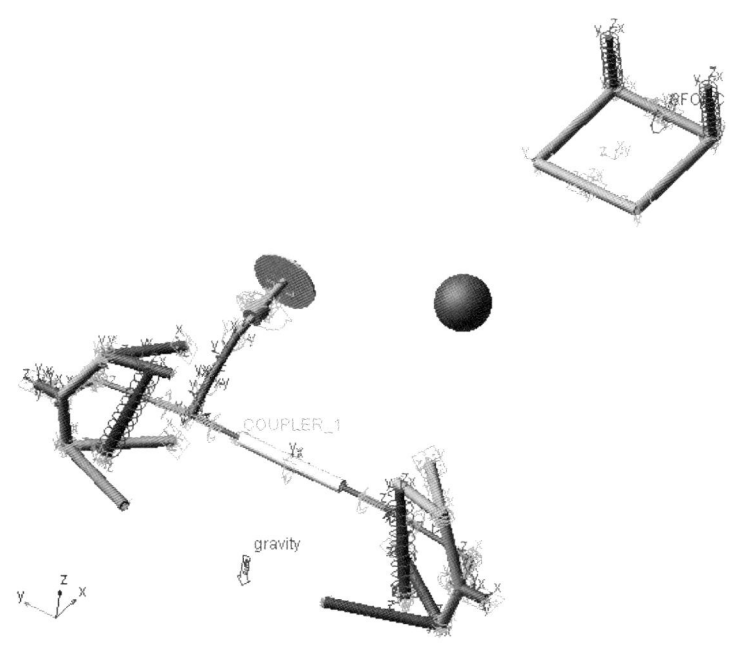

图 13-8　整车约束（轮胎除外）

13.7　三轮车轮胎

"逆"三轮车前后轮胎一般为不同型号，前轮胎一般采用断面宽度较小的轮胎，考虑后轮为驱动轮及整车的稳定性，后轮胎一般采用较大断面宽度的轮胎；此模型前轮胎断面宽度为 225 mm，后轮胎断面宽度为 275 mm，断面宽度通过轮胎属性文件可以修改，具体方法参考第 14 章"摩托车"模型相关章节。

(1)左前轮胎 wheel_left。
- 单击 Forces > Special Forces > Creat a Tire，创建轮胎（包含路面）模型如图 13-9 所示；

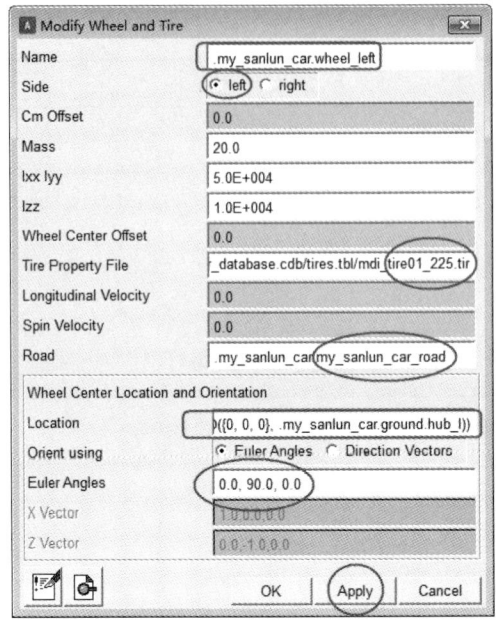

图 13-9　左前轮胎/wheel_left

- Name：wheel_left；
- Side：Left；
- Cm Offset：0；
- Mass：20；
- Ixx Iyy：5e4；
- Izz：1e4；
- Wheel Center Offset：0；
- Tire Property File：D:/MSC.Software/Adams_x64/2015/acar/shared_car_database.cdb/tires.tbl/mdi_tire01_225.tir；
- Longitudinal Velocity：0；
- Spin Velocity：0；
- Road：.my_sanlun_car.my_sanlun_car_road；
① Nam：road；
② Part：.my_sanlunche.ground；
③ Property File：D:/MSC.Software/Adams_x64/2015/acar/shared_car_database.cdb/roads.tbl/2d_sine.rdf，即创建的路面为 2d 正弦路面；
④ Graphics：Off，即显示界面存在路面模型，但不显示；
⑤ Location：0.0, 0.0, 0.0；
⑥ Orient using：Euler Angles；
⑦ Euler Angles：0.0, 0.0, 0.0；

⑧ 单击 OK，完成 .my_sanlun_car.my_sanlun_car_road 路面的创建。
- Location：(LOC_RELATIVE_TO({0, 0, 0}, .my_sanlun_car.ground.hub_l))，通过选取硬点 hub_l 获取，也可以直接输入硬点数据，此处为相对位置函数；
- Orient using：Euler Angles；
- Euler Angles：0.0, 90.0, 0.0；
- 单击 Aplly，完成 wheel_left 轮胎的创建。

（2）右前轮胎 wheel_right。
- 单击 Forces > Special Forces > Creat a Tire，创建轮胎（包含路面）模型如图 13-9 所示；
- Name：wheel_right；
- Side：Left；
- Cm Offset：0；
- Mass：20；
- Ixx Iyy：5e4；
- Izz：1e4；
- Wheel Center Offset：0；
- Tire Property File：D:/MSC.Software/Adams_x64/2015/acar/shared_car_database.cdb/tires.tbl/mdi_tire01_225.tir；
- Longitudinal Velocity：0；
- Spin Velocity：0；
- Road：.my_sanlun_car.my_sanlun_car_road；
- Location：((LOC_RELATIVE_TO({0, 0, 0}, .my_sanlun_car.ground.hub_r))；
- Orient using：Euler Angles；
- Euler Angles：0.0, 90.0, 0.0；
- 单击 Aplly，完成 wheel_right 轮胎的创建。

（3）后轮胎 wheel_rear。
- 单击 Forces > Special Forces > Creat a Tire，创建轮胎（包含路面）模型如图 13-9 所示；
- Name：wheel_rear；
- Side：Left；
- Cm Offset：0；
- Mass：20；
- Ixx Iyy：5e4；
- Izz：1e4；
- Wheel Center Offset：0；
- Tire Property File：D:/MSC.Software/Adams_x64/2015/acar/shared_car_database.cdb/tires.tbl/mdi_tire01_275.tir；
- Longitudinal Velocity：0；
- Spin Velocity：0；
- Road：.my_sanlun_car.my_sanlun_car_road；
- Location：2 600.0, 0.0, 300.0；
- Orient using：Euler Angles；

- Euler Angles：0.0, 90.0, 0.0；
- 单击 OK，完成 wheel_rear 轮胎的创建。

（4）部件 hub_left 与 wheel_left.wheel_part 之间 Revolute 约束。
- 单击 Setting > Working Grid；
- 设置网格方向为 Global XZ；
- 单击 Connecton > Joints > Creat a Revolute Joint；
- Normal To Grid；
- Name：hub_to_wheel_l；
- First Body：.my_sanlun_car.hub_left；
- Second Body：.my_sanlun_car.wheel_left.wheel_part；
- Type：Revolute；
- Force Display：None；
- 单击 OK，完成约束副.my_sanlun_car.hub_to_wheel_l 的创建。

（5）部件 hub_right 与 wheel_right.wheel_part 之间 Revolute 约束。
- 单击 Connecton > Joints > Creat a Revolute Joint；
- Normal To Grid；
- Name：hub_to_wheel_r；
- First Body：.my_sanlun_car.hub_right；
- Second Body：.my_sanlun_car.wheel_right.wheel_part；
- Type：Revolute；
- Force Display：None；
- 单击 OK，完成约束副.my_sanlun_car.hub_to_wheel_r 的创建。

（6）部件 hub_rear 与 wheel_rear.wheel_part 之间 Revolute 约束。
- 单击 Connecton > Joints > Creat a Revolute Joint；
- Normal To Grid；
- Name：rear_hub_to_rear_wheel；
- First Body：.my_sanlun_car.hub_rear；
- Second Body：.my_sanlun_car.wheel_rear.wheel_part；
- Type：Revolute；
- Force Display：None；
- 单击 OK，完成约束副.my_sanlun_car.rear_hub_to_rear_wheel 的创建。

13.8 漂移仿真

（1）方向盘驱动。
- 单击 Motions > Joint Motions；
- Function(time)：修改为 10d * time；
- 选择约束副：.my_sanlun_car.axis_3_to_steer_column，完成.my_sanlun_car.MOTION_1 的创建，创建完成后的约束副修改对话框如图 13-10 所示。

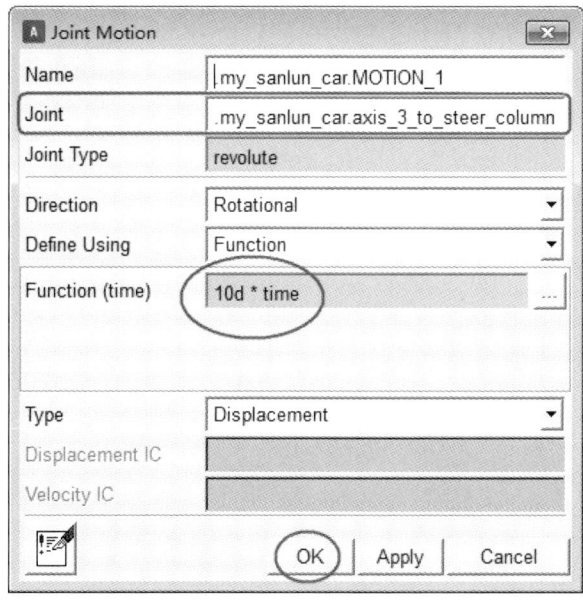

图 13-10 转向驱动副

（2）后轮驱动力矩。

- 单击 Forces > Applied Forces；
- Run-time Direction：Two Bodies；
- Construction：2-Bodies-2-Location；
- Characteristic：Custom；

选择硬点 hub_rear_l 与 hub_rear_r，完成驱动力矩 my_sanlun_car.SFORCE_5 的创建，同时界面弹出驱动力矩修改窗口如图 13-11 所示，特别提示，创建驱动力矩时一定要保证驱动力矩施加在轮胎质心位置，否则会出现轮胎绕其他方向产生旋转；

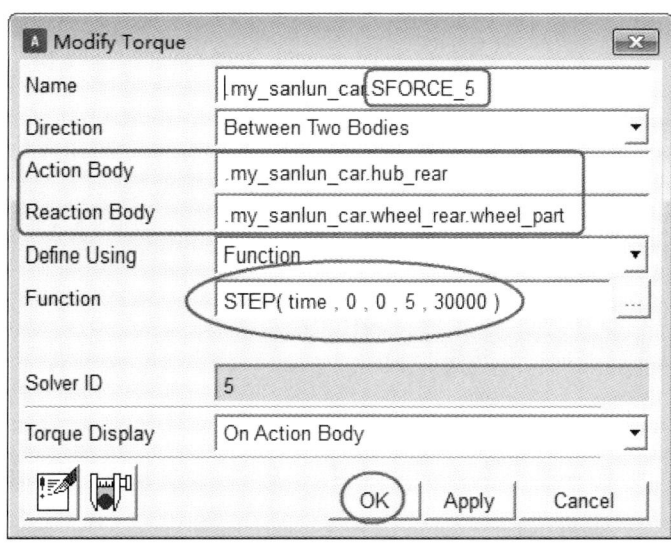

图 13-11 后轮驱动力矩

- Function：STEP(time , 0 , 0 , 5 , 30 000);
- 单击 OK，完成驱动力矩的 SFORCE_5 的创建，此时整车模型完全创建完成，如图 13-1 所示。

（3）漂移仿真。
- 单击 Simulation > Simulate > Run an interative Simulation；
- End Time：30；
- Steps：3 000；
- 勾选 Start at equilibrium，从静平衡开始仿真；
- 单击开始，完成三轮车的漂移仿真，三轮车运行轨迹如图 13-12 所示；整车相关计算参数如图 13-13 ~ 图 13-24 所示。

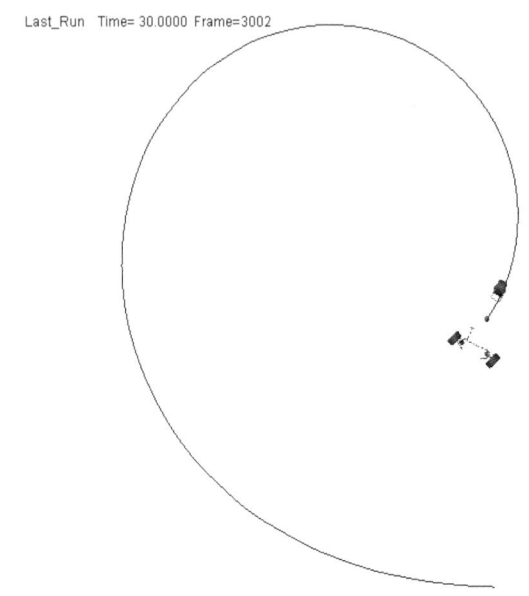

图 13-12　三轮车漂移仿真轨迹

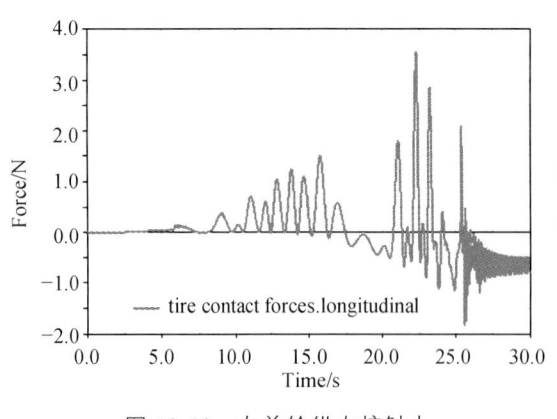

图 13-13　左前轮纵向接触力

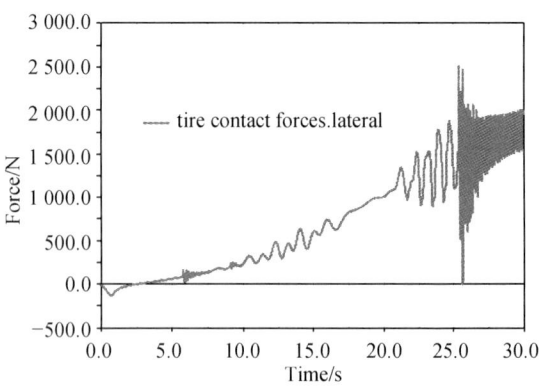

图 13-14　左前轮侧向接触力

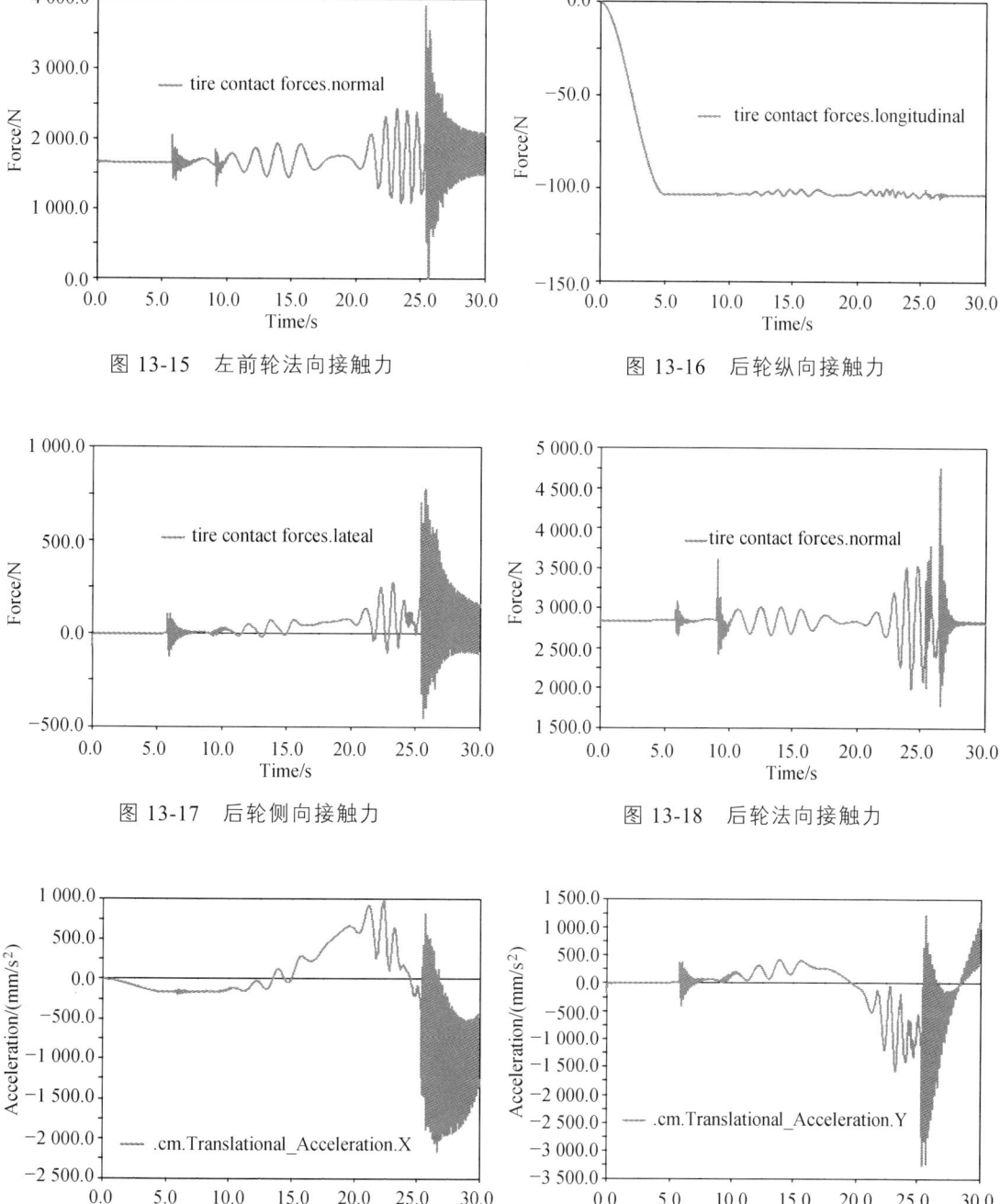

图 13-15　左前轮法向接触力

图 13-16　后轮纵向接触力

图 13-17　后轮侧向接触力

图 13-18　后轮法向接触力

图 13-19　车身 X 方向加速度

图 13-20　车身 Y 方向加速度

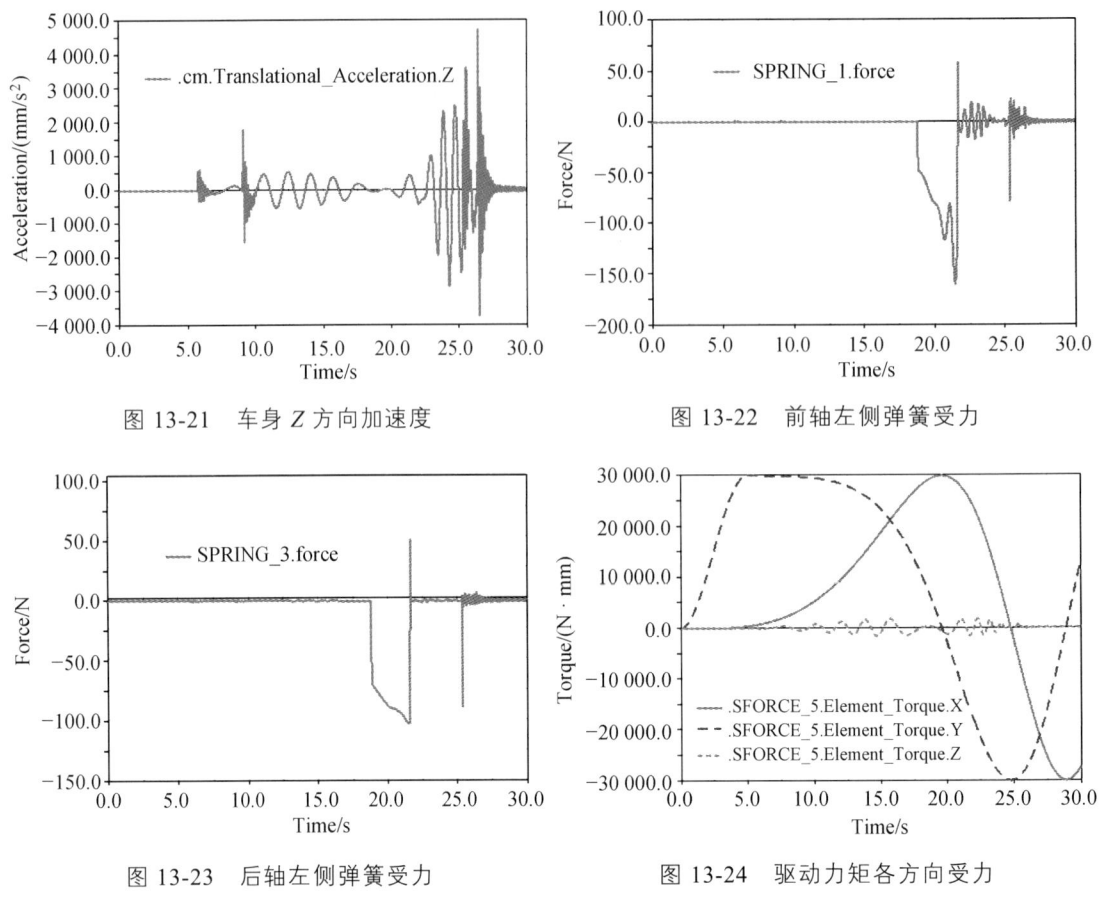

图 13-21 车身 Z 方向加速度

图 13-22 前轴左侧弹簧受力

图 13-23 后轴左侧弹簧受力

图 13-24 驱动力矩各方向受力

13.9 约束关系讨论

上述"逆"三轮车模型建立完成后，整车模型可以完美静平衡，计算结果也符合预期，但是整车模型正确吗？如果不正确，怎么来判定？问题出现在什么地方？

① 约束关系是建立复杂模型的难点，其问题是不同部件之间的约束关系需要仔细琢磨，否则会导致过约束的现实，有些模型出现错误，但并不影响静平衡及仿真的正确进行。

② 力问题，例如弹簧、避震器、力矩等施加位置及参数过大等都会导致收敛问题。

③ 仿真初始时刻整车模型突然出现跳动等问题。

（1）自由度计算。

软件会自动计算模型的自由度，"逆"三轮车模型整车自由度、部件、约束信息如下。

VERIFY MODEL: .my_sanlun_car

-5 Gruebler Count (approximate degrees of freedom) %模型处于过约束状态；

24 Moving Parts (not including ground)

4 Cylindrical Joints
10 Revolute Joints
6 Spherical Joints
1 Translational Joints
2 Convel Joints
7 Fixed Joints
2 Hooke Joints
1 Motions
1 Couplers

9 Degrees of Freedom for .my_sanlun_car

There are 14 redundant constraint equations. %以下为对应的过约束副

This constraint: unnecessarily removes this DOF:

.my_sanlun_car.rear_arm_to_body (Revolute Joint) Rotation Between Zi & Xj
.my_sanlun_car.body_to_lca_l (Revolute Joint) Rotation Between Zi & Xj
.my_sanlun_car.body_to_lca_l (Revolute Joint) Rotation Between Zi & Yj
.my_sanlun_car.body_to_lca_r (Revolute Joint) Rotation Between Zi & Xj
.my_sanlun_car.body_to_lca_r (Revolute Joint) Rotation Between Zi & Yj
.my_sanlun_car.srping_front_right (Cylindrical Joint) Rotation Between Zi & Xj
.my_sanlun_car.srping_front_left (Cylindrical Joint) Rotation Between Zi & Yj
.my_sanlun_car.spring_rear_left (Cylindrical Joint) Translation Along Yj
.my_sanlun_car.spring_rear_left (Cylindrical Joint) Rotation Between Zi & Xj
.my_sanlun_car.spring_rear_left (Cylindrical Joint) Rotation Between Zi & Yj
.my_sanlun_car.srping_rear_right (Cylindrical Joint) Rotation Between Zi & Xj
.my_sanlun_car.srping_rear_right (Cylindrical Joint) Rotation Between Zi & Yj
.my_sanlun_car.rear_hub_to_rear_arm (Fixed Joint) Rotation Between Zi & Yj
.my_sanlun_car.rack_house_to_body (Fixed Joint) Rotation Between Zi & Xj

Model verified successfully %过约束副系统会自动修正，但毫无疑问这修改后的约束就是正确的

从约束信息中可以看出：前双 A 臂悬架左右下控制臂与车身之间的圆柱副、后轮毂与车身之间的圆柱副、转向齿轮箱与车身之间的固定副均为过约束；下控制与车身之间，后轮毂与车身之间安装弹簧与避震器（VIEW 通用模块弹簧与避震器为一个整体），力之间并不需要圆柱副约束其运动（特殊情况也可以施加约束），转向齿轮箱与车身之间应施

加柔性衬套约束。

(2) 删除以下约束副:

① srping_front_right;

② srping_front_left;

③ spring_rear_left;

④ srping_rear_right;

(3) 添加柔性约束。

- 单击 Forces > Applied Connections > Creat a bushing;
- Construction: 2-Bod-1-Loc;
- Pick Feature,即手动定义方向;
- Properties,衬套刚度属性参数设置如下。

① K: 4 500;

② C: 10;

③ KT: 0;

④ CT: 0。

顺序选择 rack_house 与 body,顺序选择点 rack_house_mount_1(定位)与 rack_house_mount_r(定向),完成衬套副 BUSHING_1 的创建;右击衬套副 BUSHING_1 > Modify,显示衬套副信息如图 13-25 所示。

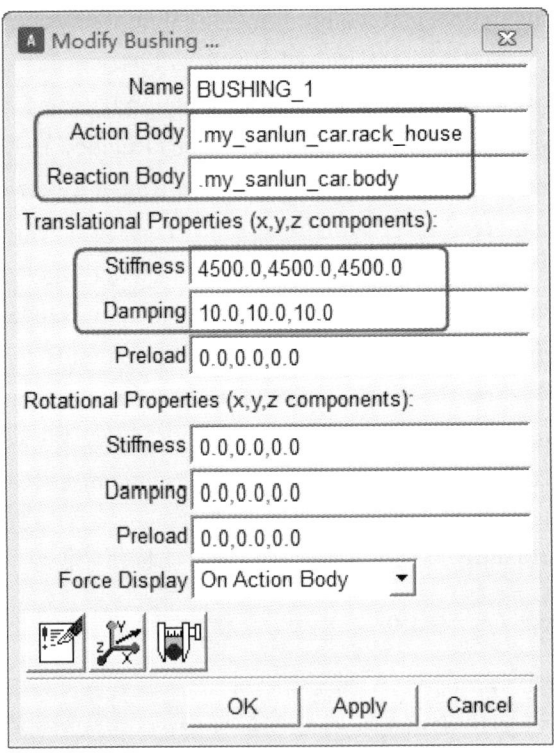

图 13-25　衬套副约束

顺序选择 rack_house 与 body，顺序选择点 rack_house_mount_r（定位）与 rack_house_mount_l（定向），完成衬套副 BUSHING_2 的创建。

模型修改完成后，逆三轮车整车共包含 17 个自由度。

重新仿真，设置参数与上述漂移仿真保持一致；整车模型不能静平衡，但可以完成仿真（不用勾选在静平衡），仿真结束后整车模型如图 13-26 所示，前双 A 臂悬架发生塌陷，从图中可以看出，发生塌陷的原因是弹簧的刚度过小，多次修改弹簧的刚度，最终确定 K：100，C：10。参数修改设置完成后，逆三轮车整车模型能进行静平衡仿真，仿真结束后计算相关参数如图 13-27 ~ 图 13-29 所示。

从弹簧力的变化特性曲线计算结果中看，弹簧力依然过大，原因是因为弹簧的刚度 100 极大，一般轿车的弹簧刚度仅为 23 左右。

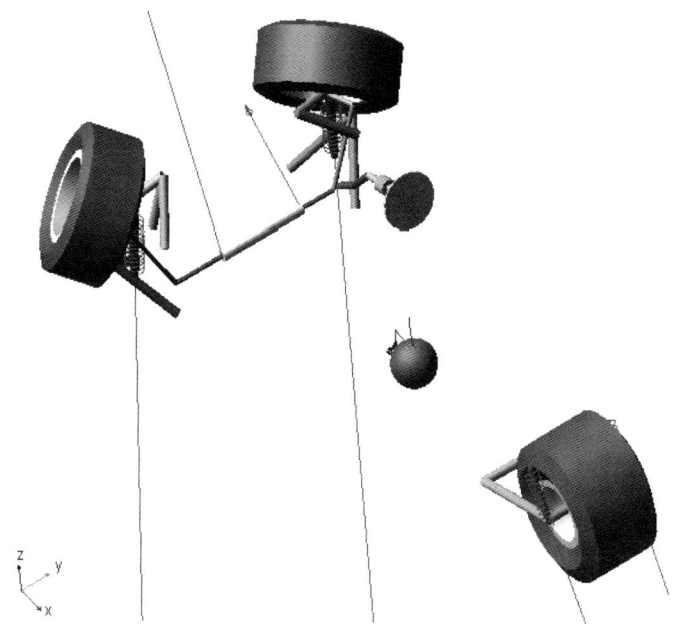

图 13-26　三轮车模型（前轮塌陷）

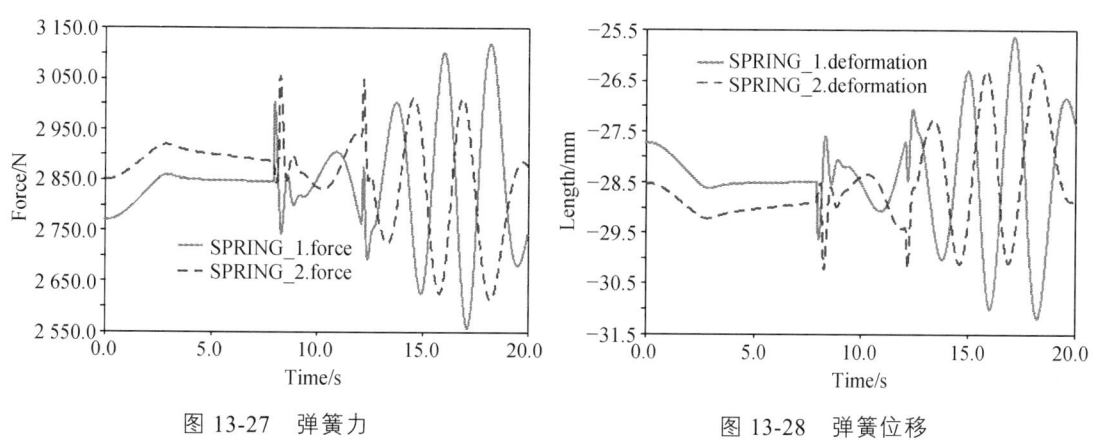

图 13-27　弹簧力　　　　　　　　　　　图 13-28　弹簧位移

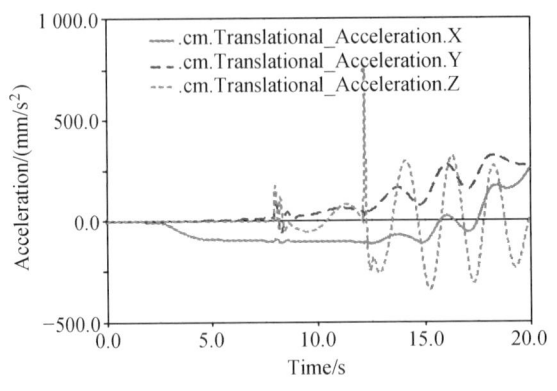

图 13-29　车身 $X/Y/Z$ 方向加速度

13.10 "逆"三轮车衬套约束

真实车辆连杆与车身的连接均为柔性衬套约束，不存在纯刚性约束。柔性约束是通过橡胶衬套把两个不同的部件连接起来，柔性衬套具有刚度和阻尼，刚性衬套没有，因此弹簧刚度不大的话双 A 臂悬架会产生塌陷，柔性衬套在连接中起到了弹簧的作用；因此弹簧刚度可以设置得很小（与真实的弹簧避震器系统参数相同），衬套约束中衬套刚度与阻尼统一设置为 K：4 500，C：10（对此衬套刚度与阻尼参考公版悬架数据参数，具体到某些真实的车型，请读者通过实验获取，也可以通过有限元法获取），创建完成的整车柔性约束模型如图 13-30 所示，模型存储于章节文件中。

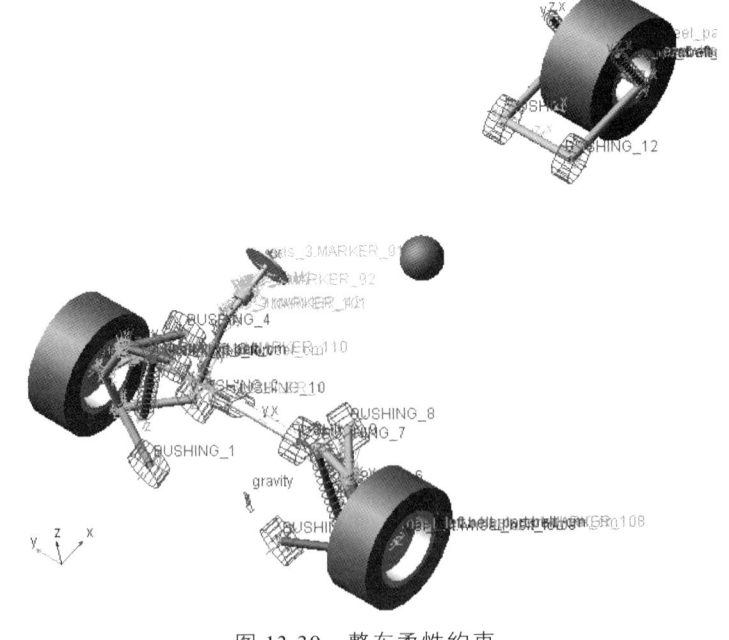

图 13-30　整车柔性约束

(1)部件 lca_r 与 body 之间 BUSHING_1 约束。
- 单击 Forces > Applied Connections > Creat a bushing;
- Construction：2-Bod-1-Loc;
- Pick Feature，即手动定义方向;
- Properties，衬套刚度属性参数设置如下。

K：(4 500.0(newton/mm)),(4 500.0(newton/mm)),(4 500.0(newton/mm));
C：(10(newton-sec/mm)),(10(newton-sec/mm)),(10(newton-sec/mm));
KT：(2(newton-mm/deg)),(2E+004(newton-mm/deg)),(2E+004(newton-mm/deg));
CT：(5 235(newton-mm-sec/deg)),(5 235(newton-mm-sec/deg)),(5 235(newton-mm-sec/deg))。
顺序选择 lca_r 与 body，顺序选择点 lca_front_r（定位）与 lca_rear_r（定向），完成衬套副 BUSHING_1 的创建。

(2)部件 lca_r 与 body 之间 BUSHING_2 约束。
- 单击 Forces > Applied Connections > Creat a bushing;
- Construction：2-Bod-1-Loc;
- Pick Feature，即手动定义方向;
- Properties，衬套刚度属性参数设置如下：

K：(4 500.0(newton/mm)),(4 500.0(newton/mm)),(4 500.0(newton/mm));
C：(10(newton-sec/mm)),(10(newton-sec/mm)),(10(newton-sec/mm));
KT：(2(newton-mm/deg)),(2E+004(newton-mm/deg)),(2E+004(newton-mm/deg));
CT：(5 235(newton-mm-sec/deg)),(5 235(newton-mm-sec/deg)),(5 235(newton-mm-sec/deg))。
顺序选择 lca_r 与 body，顺序选择点 lca_rear_r（定位）与 lca_front_r（定向），完成衬套副 BUSHING_2 的创建。

(3)部件 uca_r 与 body 之间 BUSHING_3 约束。
- 单击 Forces > Applied Connections > Creat a bushing;
- Construction：2-Bod-1-Loc;
- Pick Feature，即手动定义方向;
- Properties，衬套刚度属性参数设置如下。

K：(4 500.0(newton/mm)),(4 500.0(newton/mm)),(4 500.0(newton/mm));
C：(10(newton-sec/mm)),(10(newton-sec/mm)),(10(newton-sec/mm));
KT：(2(newton-mm/deg)),(2E+004(newton-mm/deg)),(2E+004(newton-mm/deg));
CT：(5 235(newton-mm-sec/deg)),(5 235(newton-mm-sec/deg)),(5 235(newton-mm-sec/deg))。
顺序选择 uca_r 与 body，顺序选择点 uca_front_r（定位）与 uca_rear_r（定向），完成衬套副 BUSHING_3 的创建。

(4)部件 uca_r 与 body 之间 BUSHING_4 约束。
- 单击 Forces > Applied Connections > Creat a bushing;
- Construction：2-Bod-1-Loc;
- Pick Feature，即手动定义方向;

- Properties，衬套刚度属性参数设置如下：

K：(4 500.0(newton/mm)),(4 500.0(newton/mm)),(4 500.0(newton/mm))；

C：(10(newton-sec/mm)),(10(newton-sec/mm)),(10(newton-sec/mm))；

KT：(2(newton-mm/deg)),(2E+004(newton-mm/deg)),(2E+004(newton-mm/deg))；

CT：(5235(newton-mm-sec/deg)),(5235(newton-mm-sec/deg)),(5235(newton-mm-sec/deg))。

顺序选择 uca_r 与 body，顺序选择点 uca_rear_r（定位）与 uca_front_r（定向），完成衬套副 BUSHING_4 的创建。

（5）部件 lca_l 与 body 之间 BUSHING_5 约束。

- 单击 Forces > Applied Connections > Creat a bushing；
- Construction：2-Bod-1-Loc；
- Pick Feature，即手动定义方向；
- Properties，衬套刚度属性参数设置如下。

K：(4 500.0(newton/mm)),(4 500.0(newton/mm)),(4 500.0(newton/mm))；

C：(10(newton-sec/mm)),(10(newton-sec/mm)),(10(newton-sec/mm))；

KT：(2(newton-mm/deg)),(2E+004(newton-mm/deg)),(2E+004(newton-mm/deg))；

CT：(5 235(newton-mm-sec/deg)),(5 235(newton-mm-sec/deg)),(5 235(newton-mm-sec/deg))。

顺序选择 lca_l 与 body，顺序选择点 lca_front_l（定位）与 lca_rear_l（定向），完成衬套副 BUSHING_5 的创建。

（6）部件 lca_l 与 body 之间 BUSHING_6 约束。

- 单击 Forces > Applied Connections > Creat a bushing；
- Construction：2-Bod-1-Loc；
- Pick Feature，即手动定义方向；
- Properties，衬套刚度属性参数设置如下：

K：(4500.0(newton/mm)),(4500.0(newton/mm)),(4500.0(newton/mm))；

C：(10(newton-sec/mm)),(10(newton-sec/mm)),(10(newton-sec/mm))；

KT：(2(newton-mm/deg)),(2E+004(newton-mm/deg)),(2E+004(newton-mm/deg))；

CT：(5235(newton-mm-sec/deg)),(5235(newton-mm-sec/deg)),(5235(newton-mm-sec/deg))。

顺序选择 lca_l 与 body，顺序选择点 lca_rear_l（定位）与 lca_front_l（定向），完成衬套副 BUSHING_6 的创建。

（7）部件 uca_l 与 body 之间 BUSHING_7 约束。

- 单击 Forces > Applied Connections > Creat a bushing；
- Construction：2-Bod-1-Loc；
- Pick Feature，即手动定义方向；
- Properties，衬套刚度属性参数设置如下。

K：(4 500.0(newton/mm)),(4 500.0(newton/mm)),(4 500.0(newton/mm))；

C：(10(newton-sec/mm)),(10(newton-sec/mm)),(10(newton-sec/mm))；

KT：(2(newton-mm/deg)),(2E+004(newton-mm/deg)),(2E+004(newton-mm/deg))；

CT：(5 235(newton-mm-sec/deg)),(5 235(newton-mm-sec/deg)),(5 235(newton-mm-sec/deg))。

顺序选择 uca_l 与 body，顺序选择点 uca_front_l（定位）与 uca_rear_l（定向），完成衬套副 BUSHING_3 的创建。

（8）部件 uca_l 与 body 之间 BUSHING_8 约束。
- 单击 Forces > Applied Connections > Creat a bushing；
- Construction：2-Bod-1-Loc；
- Pick Feature，即手动定义方向；
- Properties，衬套刚度属性参数设置如下。

K：(4 500.0(newton/mm)),(4 500.0(newton/mm)),(4 500.0(newton/mm))；

C：(10(newton-sec/mm)),(10(newton-sec/mm)),(10(newton-sec/mm))；

KT：(2(newton-mm/deg)),(2E+004(newton-mm/deg)),(2E+004(newton-mm/deg))；

CT：(5 235(newton-mm-sec/deg)),(5 235(newton-mm-sec/deg)),(5 235(newton-mm-sec/deg))。

顺序选择 uca_l 与 body，顺序选择点 uca_rear_l（定位）与 uca_front_r（定向），完成衬套副 BUSHING_8 的创建。

（9）部件 rack_house 与 body 之间 BUSHING_9 约束。
- 单击 Forces > Applied Connections > Creat a bushing；
- Construction：2-Bod-1-Loc；
- Pick Feature，即手动定义方向；
- Properties，衬套刚度属性参数设置如下。

K：4 500.0，4 500.0，4 500.0；

C：10.0，10.0，10.0；

KT：0.0，0.0，0.0；

CT：0.0，0.0，0.0。

顺序选择 rack_house 与 body，顺序选择点 rack_house_mount_l（定位）与 rack_house_mount_r（定向），完成衬套副 BUSHING_9 的创建。

（10）部件 rack_house 与 body 之间 BUSHING_10 约束。
- 单击 Forces > Applied Connections > Creat a bushing；
- Construction：2-Bod-1-Loc；
- Pick Feature，即手动定义方向；
- Properties，衬套刚度属性参数设置如下。

K：4 500.0，4 500.0，4 500.0；

C：10.0，10.0，10.0；

KT：0.0，0.0，0.0；

CT：0.0，0.0，0.0。

顺序选择 rack_house 与 body，顺序选择点 rack_house_mount_r（定位）与 rack_house_mount_l（定向），完成衬套副 BUSHING_10 的创建。

（11）部件 rear_arm 与 body 之间 BUSHING_11 约束。

- 单击 Forces > Applied Connections > Creat a bushing；
- Construction：2-Bod-1-Loc；
- Pick Feature，即手动定义方向；
- Properties，衬套刚度属性参数设置如下。

K：4 500.0,4 500.0,4 500.0；

C：10.0,10.0,10.0；

KT：0.0,0.0,0.0；

CT：0.0,0.0,0.0。

顺序选择 rear_arm 与 body，顺序选择点 rear_arm_l（定位）与 rear_arm_r（定向），完成衬套副 BUSHING_11 的创建。

（12）部件 rear_arm 与 body 之间 BUSHING_12 约束。

- 单击 Forces > Applied Connections > Creat a bushing；
- Construction：2-Bod-1-Loc；
- Pick Feature，即手动定义方向；
- Properties，衬套刚度属性参数设置如下。

K：4 500.0,4 500.0,4 500.0；

C：10.0,10.0,10.0；

KT：0.0,0.0,0.0；

CT：0.0,0.0,0.0。

顺序选择 rear_arm 与 body，顺序选择点 rear_arm_r（定位）与 rear_arm_l（定向），完成衬套副 BUSHING_12 的创建。

重新仿真，设置参数与上述漂移仿真保持一致。整车静平衡及漂移仿真顺利完成，整车在柔性衬套作用下受力如图 13-31 所示；计算结果如图 13-32 ~ 图 13-39 所示。

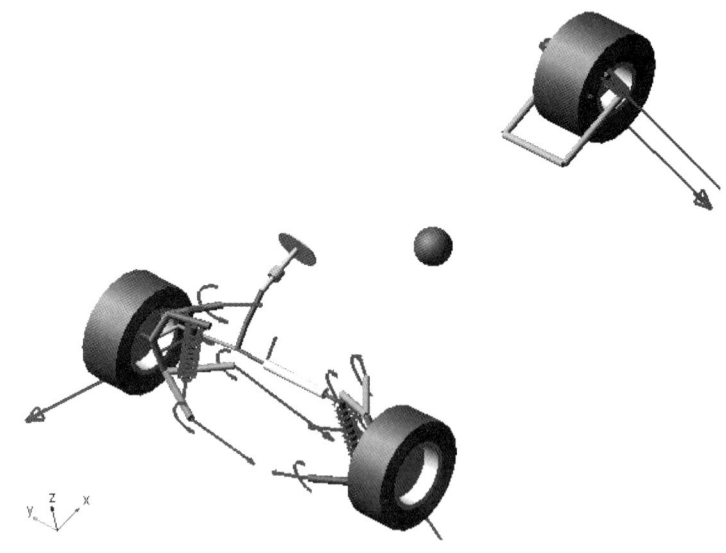

图 13-31　整车柔性衬套受力图

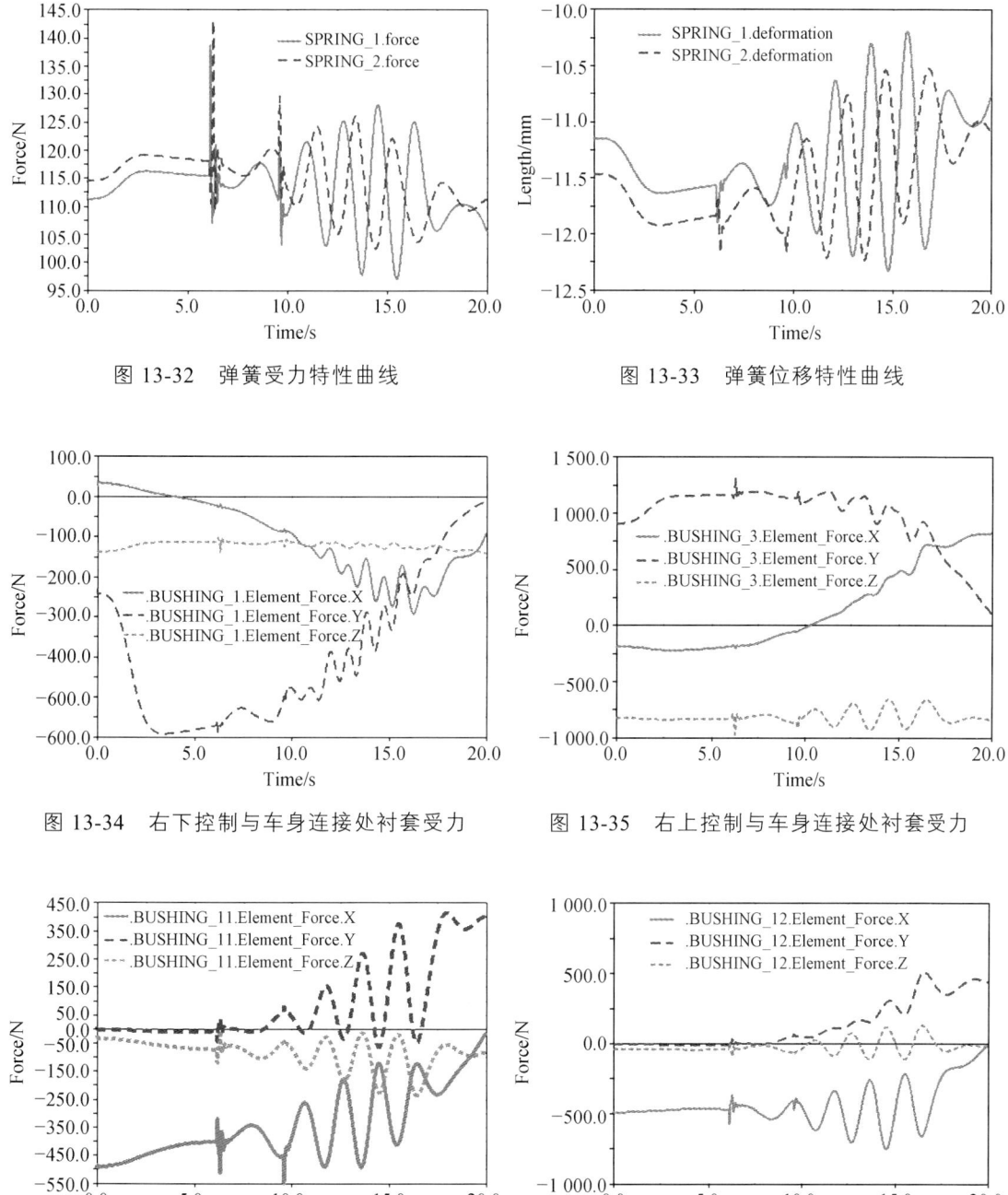

图 13-32 弹簧受力特性曲线

图 13-33 弹簧位移特性曲线

图 13-34 右下控制与车身连接处衬套受力

图 13-35 右上控制与车身连接处衬套受力

图 13-36 后控制臂右侧连接处衬套受力

图 13-37 后控制臂左侧连接处衬套受力

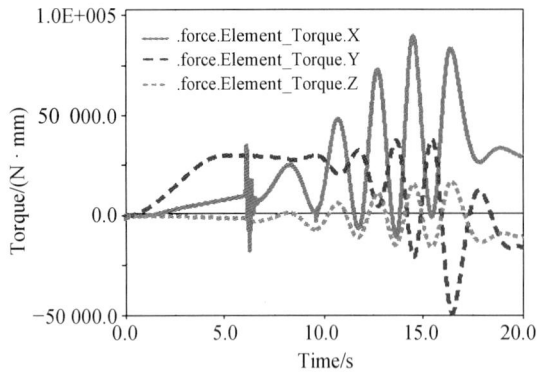 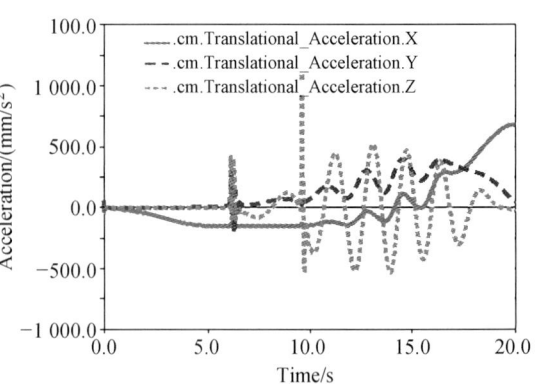

图 13-38　后轮各方向驱动力矩　　　　图 13-39　车身各方向加速度

第 14 章　摩托车

摩托车是生活中常见的交通工具,其结构简单、维修方便、价格便宜,在广大农村、城市有广泛的应用。摩托车结构大都相似,家用摩托车前后轮采用双减震器,重型机车及跑车后轴由于安装空间及轮胎断面宽度较大,因此多采用单个轴向减震器。摩托车传动大多为链条传动,少量高性能车有采用轴传动;小型木兰摩托车多采用发动机与传动系统一体式的整体结构,其变速机构大多为 CVT 无极式,传动多为带传动或同步带传动。本章节通过在 VIEW 模块中建立摩托车模型,分析其运动特性,整车模型建立过程中,考虑链传动及同步皮带传动,驱动采用电动机模型驱动。建立好的电机传动驱动摩托车模型如图 14-1 所示,采用链传动或皮带传动后,由于链条与链轮接触(或皮带同皮带接触),因此整车模型为大型非线性模型,计算速度极为缓慢,有条件的读者建议采用服务器计算。

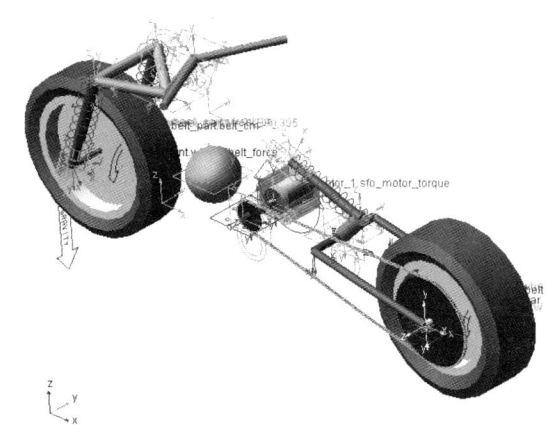

图 14-1　摩托车模型——链传动

学习目标

- ◆ 前双避震器转向轮。
- ◆ 后单避震器驱动轮。
- ◆ 轮胎模型。
- ◆ 路面模型。
- ◆ 链传动。
- ◆ 同步皮带传动。
- ◆ 电动机模型。
- ◆ 转向驱动。

14.1 摩托车身

- 单击 Bodies > Construction > Geometry Point 创建硬点；
- Add to Ground；
- Don't Attach；
- 右击鼠标，弹出硬点位置对话框如图 14-2 所示；
- 硬点位置输入 1 000，0，425；
- 单击 Apply，完成硬点创建；
- 右击硬点，选择 Rename，重名为 body_center；

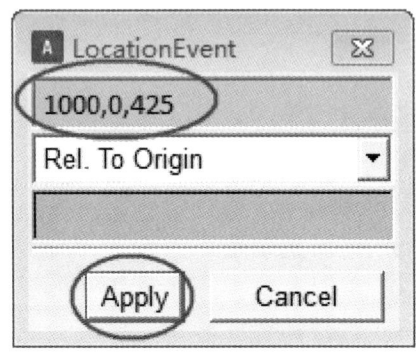

图 14-2　硬点创建对话框

- 单击 Bodies > Geometry Sphere 创建球形几何体；
- 选择 New Part；
- Radius：200；
- 选择硬点：body_center，完成球形部件创建；
- 右击球形部件，选择 Rename，重名为 body。

14.2 前双避震器转向系统

- 单击 Bodies > Construction > Geometry Point 创建硬点；
- Add to Ground；
- Don't Attach；
- 右击鼠标，弹出硬点位置对话框参考如图 14-2 所示；
- 硬点位置输入 250，-150，325；
- 单击 Apply，完成硬点创建；
- 右击硬点，选择 Rename，重名为 hub_front_1；
- 单击 Bodies > Construction > Geometry Point 创建硬点；
- Add to Ground；
- Don't Attach；

- 右击鼠标，弹出硬点位置对话框参考如图 14-2 所示；
- 硬点位置输入 250，150，325；
- 单击 Apply，完成硬点创建；
- 右击硬点，选择 Rename，重名为 hub_front_r；
- 单击 Bodies > Construction > Geometry Point 创建硬点；
- Add to Ground；
- Don't Attach；
- 右击鼠标，弹出硬点位置对话框参考如图 14-2 所示；
- 硬点位置输入 400，−150，725；
- 单击 Apply，完成硬点创建；
- 右击硬点，选择 Rename，重名为 damper_l；
- 单击 Bodies > Construction > Geometry Point 创建硬点；
- Add to Ground；
- Don't Attach；
- 右击鼠标，弹出硬点位置对话框参考如图 14-2 所示；
- 硬点位置输入 400，150，725；
- 单击 Apply，完成硬点创建；
- 右击硬点，选择 Rename，重名为 damper_r；
- 单击 Bodies > Construction > Geometry Point 创建硬点；
- Add to Ground；
- Don't Attach；
- 右击鼠标，弹出硬点位置对话框参考如图 14-2 所示；
- 硬点位置输入 600，0，675；
- 单击 Apply，完成硬点创建；
- 右击硬点，选择 Rename，重名为 steer_wheel_low；
- 单击 Bodies > Geometry Cylinder 创建圆柱几何体；
- 选择 New Part；
- Radius: 10；
- 选择硬点：hub_front_l 与 hub_front_r，完成圆柱形部件创建；
- 右击圆柱体部件，选择 Rename，重名为 hub_front；
- 单击 Bodies > Geometry Cylinder 创建圆柱几何体；
- 选择 New Part；
- Radius: 20；
- 选择硬点：damper_l 与 damper_r 完成圆柱形部件创建；
- 右击圆柱体部件，选择 Rename，重名为：damper_up；
- 单击 Bodies > Geometry Cylinder 创建圆柱几何体；
- 选择 Add to Part；
- Radius: 20；
- 选择部件 damper_up；

- 选择硬点：damper_l 与 steer_wheel_low，完成圆柱形部件创建；
- 单击 Bodies > Geometry Cylinder 创建圆柱几何体；
- 选择 Add to Part；
- Radius: 20；
- 选择部件 damper_up；
- 选择硬点：damper_r 与 steer_wheel_low，完成圆柱形部件创建；
- 单击 Bodies > Construction > Geometry Point 创建硬点，
- Add to Ground；
- Don't Attach；
- 右击鼠标，弹出硬点位置对话框参考如图 14-2 所示；
- 硬点位置输入 750，0，875；
- 单击 Apply，完成硬点创建；
- 右击硬点，选择 Rename，重名为 steer_wheel_up；
- 单击 Bodies > Construction > Geometry Point 创建硬点，
- Add to Ground；
- Don't Attach；
- 右击鼠标，弹出硬点位置对话框参考如图 14-2 所示；
- 硬点位置输入 900，-300，875；
- 单击 Apply，完成硬点创建；
- 右击硬点，选择 Rename，重名为 steer_wheel_left；
- 单击 Bodies > Construction > Geometry Point 创建硬点，
- Add to Ground；
- Don't Attach；
- 右击鼠标，弹出硬点位置对话框参考如图 14-2 所示；
- 硬点位置输入 900，300，875；
- 单击 Apply，完成硬点创建；
- 右击硬点，选择 Rename，重名为 steer_wheel_right；
- 单击 Bodies > Geometry Cylinder 创建圆柱几何体；
- 选择 New Part；
- Radius: 20；
- 选择硬点：steer_wheel_low 与 steer_wheel_up，完成圆柱形部件创建；
- 右击圆柱体部件，选择 Rename，重名为 steer_wheel；
- 单击 Bodies > Geometry Cylinder 创建圆柱几何体；
- 选择 Add to Part；
- Radius: 20；
- 选择部件 steer_wheel；
- 选择硬点：steer_wheel_up 与 steer_wheel_left，完成圆柱形部件创建；
- 单击 Bodies > Geometry Cylinder 创建圆柱几何体；
- 选择 Add to Part；

- Radius：20；
- 选择部件 steer_wheel；
- 选择硬点：steer_wheel_up 与 steer_wheel_right，完成圆柱形部件创建；
- 单击 Bodies > Construction > Construction Geometry：Mark 创建参考点；
- Add to Part；
- Don't Attach；
- 选择部件 hub_front；
- 右击鼠标，弹出硬点位置对话框参考如图 14-2 所示；
- 硬点位置输入 250，–150，325；
- 单击 Apply，完成参考点创建；
- 右击参考点，选择 Rename，重名为 M1；
- 单击 Bodies > Construction > Construction Geometry：Mark 创建参考点；
- Add to Part；
- Don't Attach；
- 选择部件 hub_front；
- 右击鼠标，弹出硬点位置对话框参考如图 14-2 所示；
- 硬点位置输入 250，150，325；
- 单击 Apply，完成参考点创建；
- 右击参考点，选择 Rename，重名为 M2；
- 单击 Bodies > Construction > Construction Geometry：Mark 创建参考点；
- Add to Part；
- Don't Attach；
- 选择部件 damper_up；
- 右击鼠标，弹出硬点位置对话框参考如图 14-2 所示；
- 硬点位置输入 400，–150，725；
- 单击 Apply，完成参考点创建；
- 右击参考点，选择 Rename，重名为 M1；
- 单击 Bodies > Construction > Construction Geometry：Mark 创建参考点；
- Add to Part；
- Don't Attach；
- 选择部件 damper_up；
- 右击鼠标，弹出硬点位置对话框参考如图 14-2 所示；
- 硬点位置输入 400，150，725；
- 单击 Apply，完成参考点创建；
- 右击参考点，选择 Rename，重名为 M2；
- 单击 Forces > Flexible Connections > Spring-Damper；
- K：50；
- C：1 000；
- 选择点 hub_front.M1 与 damper_up.M1，完成 SPRING_1 的创建。

- 单击 Forces > Flexible Connections > Spring-Damper；
- K：50；
- C：1 000；
- 选择点 hub_front.M2 与 damper_up.M2，完成 SPRING_2 的创建。

14.3　后驱动悬架系统

- 单击 Bodies > Construction > Geometry Point 创建硬点；
- Add to Ground；
- Don't Attach；
- 右击鼠标，弹出硬点位置对话框参考如图 14-2 所示；
- 硬点位置输入 2 000，-150，325；
- 单击 Apply，完成硬点创建；
- 右击硬点，选择 Rename，重名为 hub_rear_l；
- 单击 Bodies > Construction > Geometry Point 创建硬点；
- Add to Ground；
- Don't Attach；
- 右击鼠标，弹出硬点位置对话框参考如图 14-2 所示；
- 硬点位置输入 2 000，150，325；
- 单击 Apply，完成硬点创建；
- 右击硬点，选择 Rename，重名为 hub_rear_r；
- 单击 Bodies > Geometry Cylinder 创建圆柱几何体；
- 选择 New Part；
- Radius：15；
- 选择硬点：hub_rear_l 与 hub_rear_r，完成圆柱形部件创建；
- 右击圆柱体部件，选择 Rename，重名为 hub_rear；
- 单击 Bodies > Construction > Geometry Point 创建硬点；
- Add to Ground；
- Don't Attach；
- 右击鼠标，弹出硬点位置对话框参考如图 14-2 所示；
- 硬点位置输入 1 450，－150，425；
- 单击 Apply，完成硬点创建；
- 右击硬点，选择 Rename，重名为 rear_sus_left；
- 单击 Bodies > Construction > Geometry Point 创建硬点；
- Add to Ground；
- Don't Attach；
- 右击鼠标，弹出硬点位置对话框参考如图 14-2 所示；
- 硬点位置输入 1 450，150，425；

- 单击 Apply，完成硬点创建；
- 右击硬点，选择 Rename，重名为 rear_sus_right；
- 单击 Bodies > Construction > Geometry Point 创建硬点；
- Add to Ground；
- Don't Attach；
- 右击鼠标，弹出硬点位置对话框参考如图 14-2 所示；
- 硬点位置输入 1 450，0，425；
- 单击 Apply，完成硬点创建；
- 右击硬点，选择 Rename，重名为 rear_sus_mid；
- 单击 Bodies > Construction > Geometry Point 创建硬点；
- Add to Ground；
- Don't Attach；
- 右击鼠标，弹出硬点位置对话框参考如图 14-2 所示；
- 硬点位置输入 1 550，0，525；
- 单击 Apply，完成硬点创建；
- 右击硬点，选择 Rename，重名为 rear_sus_up；
- 单击 Bodies > Geometry Cylinder 创建圆柱几何体；
- 选择 New Part；
- Radius: 15；
- 选择硬点：rear_sus_left 与 rear_sus_right，完成圆柱形部件创建；
- 右击圆柱体部件，选择 Rename，重名为 control_arm_rear；
- 单击 Bodies > Geometry Cylinder 创建圆柱几何体；
- 选择 Add to Part；
- Radius: 15；
- 选择部件 control_arm_rear；
- 选择硬点：rear_sus_left 与 hub_rear_1，完成圆柱形部件创建；
- 单击 Bodies > Geometry Cylinder 创建圆柱几何体；
- 选择 Add to Part；
- Radius: 15；
- 选择部件 control_arm_rear；
- 选择硬点：rear_sus_right 与 hub_rear_1，完成圆柱形部件创建；
- 单击 Bodies > Geometry Cylinder 创建圆柱几何体；
- 选择 New Part；
- Radius: 30；
- 选择硬点：rear_sus_mid 与 rear_sus_up，完成圆柱形部件创建；
- 右击圆柱体部件，选择 Rename，重名为.damper_down_rear；
- 单击 Bodies > Construction > Construction Geometry：Mark 创建参考点；
- Add to Part；
- Don't Attach；

- 选择部件.damper_down_rear;
- 右击鼠标，弹出硬点位置对话框参考如图 14-2 所示;
- 硬点位置输入 1 550，0，525;
- 单击 Apply，完成参考点创建;
- 右击参考点，选择 Rename，重名为 M1;
- 单击 Bodies > Construction > Construction Geometry：Mark 创建参考点;
- Add to Part;
- Don't Attach;
- 选择部件.body;
- 右击鼠标，弹出硬点位置对话框参考如图 14-2 所示;
- 硬点位置输入 1 200，0，625;
- 单击 Apply，完成参考点创建;
- 右击参考点，选择 Rename，重名为 M1;
- 单击 Forces > Flexible Connections > Spring-Damper;
- K：50;
- C：1 000;
- 选择点 damper_down_rear.M1 与 body.M1，完成 SPRING_3 的创建。

14.4 摩托车约束

（1）部件 hub_front 与 damper_up 之间 Cylindrical 约束。
- 单击 Connecton > Joints > Creat a Cylindrical Joint, 创建圆柱副约束如图 14-3 所示;
- Name：hub_front_and_damper_up_left;
- First Body：hub_front;
- Second Body：damper_up;
- Type：Cylindrical;
- Force Display：None;
- 单击 OK，完成约束副 hub_front_and_damper_up_left 的创建。

（2）部件 hub_front 与 damper_up 之间 Cylindrical 约束。
- 单击 Connecton > Joints > Creat a Cylindrical Joint;
- Name：.hub_front_and_damper_up_right;
- First Body：hub_front;
- Second Body：damper_up;
- Type：Cylindrical;
- Force Display：None;
- 单击 OK，完成约束副.hub_front_and_damper_up_right 的创建。

（3）部件 steer_wheel 与 damper_up 之间 Fixed 约束。
- 单击 Connecton > Joints > Creat a Fixed Joint;

- Name：steer_wheel_and_damper_up；
- First Body：steer_wheel；
- Second Body：damper_up；
- Type：Fixed；
- Force Display：None；
- 单击 OK，完成约束副 steer_wheel_and_damper_up 的创建。

（4）部件 body 与 damper_up 之间 Fixed 约束。
- 单击 Connecton > Joints > Creat a Fixed Joint；
- Name：body_and_damper_up；
- First Body：body；
- Second Body：damper_up；
- Type：Fixed；
- Force Display：None；
- 单击 OK，完成约束副 body_and_damper_up 的创建。

（5）部件 damper_down_rear 与 body 之间 Cylindrical 约束。
- 单击 Connecton > Joints > Creat a Cylindrical Joint；
- Name：damper_down_rear_and_body；
- First Body：damper_down_rear；
- Second Body：body；
- Type：Cylindrical；
- Force Display：None；
- 单击 OK，完成约束副 damper_down_rear_and_body 的创建。

（6）部件 damper_down_rear 与 control_arm_rear 之间 Fixed 约束。
- 单击 Connecton > Joints > Creat a Fixed Joint；
- Name：damper_down_rear_and_control_arm_rear；
- First Body：damper_down_rear；
- Second Body：control_arm_rear；
- Type：Fixed；
- Force Display：None；
- 单击 OK，完成约束副 damper_down_rear_and_control_arm_rear 的创建。

（7）部件 control_arm_rear 与 body 之间 Revolute 约束。
- 单击 Connecton > Joints > Creat a Revolute Joint；
- Name：control_arm_rear_and_body；
- First Body：control_arm_rear；
- Second Body：body；
- Type：Revolute；
- Force Display：None；
- 单击 OK，完成约束副 control_arm_rear_and_body 的创建。

（8）部件 control_arm_rear 与 hub_rear 之间 Fixed 约束。
- 单击 Connecton > Joints > Creat a Revolute Joint；
- Name：control_arm_rear_and_hub_rear；
- First Body：control_arm_rear；
- Second Body：hub_rear；
- Type：Fixed；
- Force Display：None；
- 单击 OK，完成约束副 control_arm_rear_and_hub_rear 的创建。

（9）部件 body 与 ground 之间 Perpendicular 约束。
- 单击 Bodies > Construction > Construction Geometry：Mark 创建参考点；
- Add to Part；
- Don't Attach；
- 选择部件 body；
- 右击鼠标，弹出硬点位置对话框参考如图 14-2 所示；
- 硬点位置输入 1 000，0，675；
- 单击 Apply，完成参考点创建；
- 右击参考点，选择 Rename，重名为 M11；
- 单击 Bodies > Construction > Construction Geometry：Mark 创建参考点；
- Add to Part；
- Don't Attach；
- 选择部件 body；
- 右击鼠标，弹出硬点位置对话框参考如图 14-2 所示；
- 硬点位置输入 1 000，−250，425；
- 单击 Apply，完成参考点创建；
- 右击参考点，选择 Rename，重名为 M22；
- 单击 Connecton > Primitives > Creat a Perpendicular Jiont Primitives，创建垂直虚约束副如图 14-4 所示，虚约束的作用是保证摩托车载运行过程中与地面保持垂直，不会倒地；

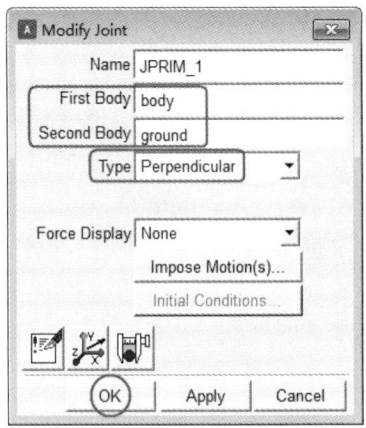

图 14-4　垂直虚约束副

- Name：JPRIM_1；
- First Body：body；
- Second Body：ground；
- Type：Perpendicular；
- Force Display：None；
- 单击 OK，完成约束副 JPRIM_1 的创建。

14.5 摩托车轮胎

在 ADAMS/VIEW 通用模块中，轮胎模型与路面模型是同时创建的，在创建路面模型时，需要注意路面的方向，否则会导致车辆在仿真过程中跌落到空中。

（1）后轮胎。
- 单击 Forces > Special Forces > Creat a Tire，创建轮胎（包含路面）模型如图 14-5 所示；

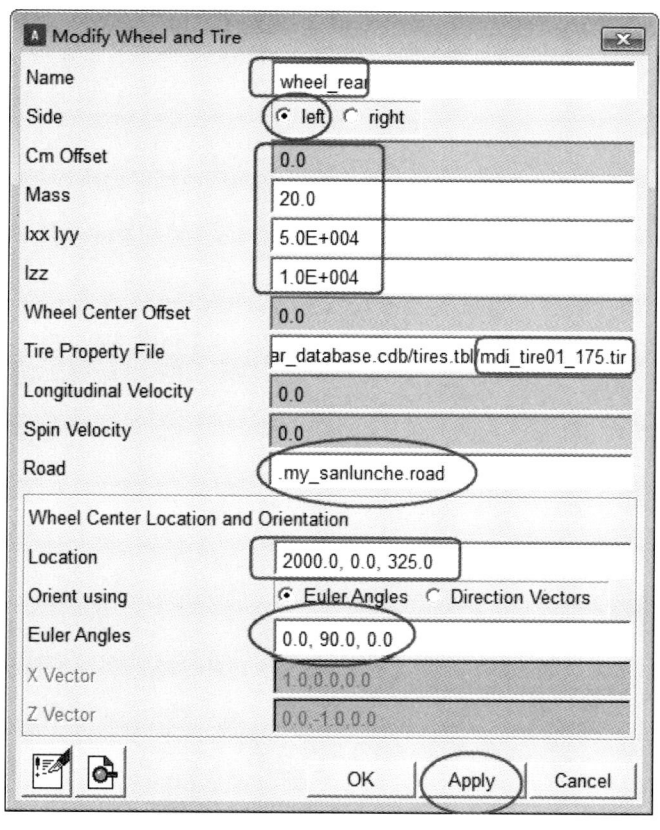

图 14-5 轮胎模型

- Name：wheel_rear；
- Side：Left；
- Cm Offset：0；

- Mass：20；
- Ixx Iyy：5e4；
- Izz：1e4；
- Wheel Center Offset：0.0；
- Tire Property File：D:/MSC.Software/Adams_x64/2015/acar/shared_car_database.cdb/tires.tbl/mdi_tire01_175.tir，轮胎属性文件包含轮胎的一些实验参数及外形参数，轮胎的实验参数获取难度较大，此章节改变轮胎的形状，即横截面的宽度改为 175 mm，其余参数保持不变；
- Longitudinal Velocity：0；
- Spin Velocity：0；
- Road：.my_sanlunche.road；在 Road 框中右击选择创建路面模型，如图 14-6 所示。

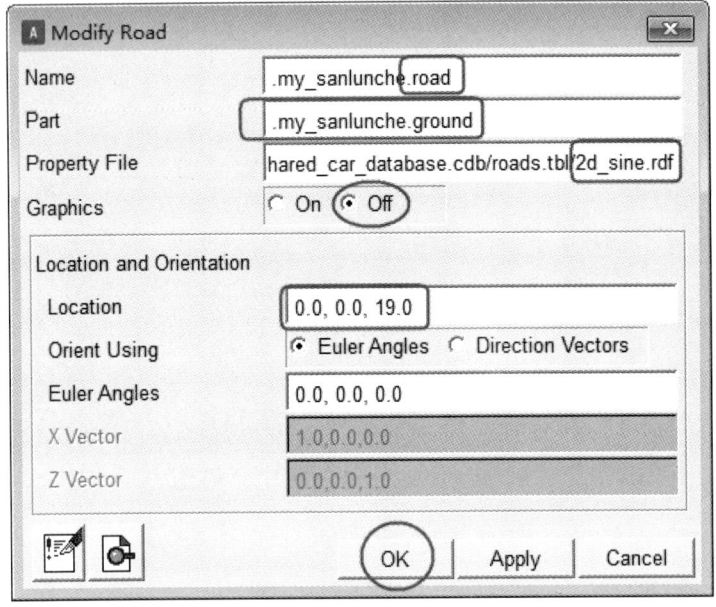

图 14-6　正弦路面模型

① Nam：road；

② Part：.my_sanlunche.ground；

③ Property File：D:/MSC.Software/Adams_x64/2015/acar/shared_car_database.cdb/roads.tbl/2d_sine.rdf，即创建的路面为 2 d 正弦路面；

④ Graphics：Off，即显示界面存在路面模型，但不显示；

⑤ Location：0.0, 0.0, 19.0，即+Z 方向上路面移动 19 mm，路面和摩托车车轮接触，移动距离为轮胎安装位置与轮胎无载荷半径之间的差值；

⑥ Orient using：Euler Angles；

⑦ Euler Angles：0.0, 0.0, 0.0，此处路面角度不用调整，原因在于重力方向在建模初始已经设置为 -Z 方向，如重力方向为系统默认的 -Y 方向，则此处需要调整路面的角度；

⑧ 单击 OK，完成.my_sanlunche.road 路面的创建；

2d 正弦路面信息如下：

```
$------------------------------------------------------------MDI_HEADER
[MDI_HEADER]
FILE_TYPE        = 'rdf'
FILE_VERSION     = 5.00
FILE_FORMAT      = 'ASCII'
(COMMENTS)
{comment_string}
'sine style road description'
$------------------------------------------------------------UNITS
[UNITS]
MASS             = 'kg'
LENGTH           = 'mm'
TIME             = 'sec'
ANGLE            = 'degree'
FORCE            = 'newton'
$------------------------------------------------------------MODEL
[MODEL]
METHOD           = '2D'
FUNCTION_NAME    = 'ARC901'
ROAD_TYPE        = 'sine'
$------------------------------------------------------------GRAPHICS
[GRAPHICS]
LENGTH           = 50000.0
WIDTH            = 20000.0
NUM_LENGTH_GRIDS = 500
NUM_WIDTH_GRIDS  = 50
LENGTH_SHIFT     = 45000.0
WIDTH_SHIFT      = 0.0
$------------------------------------------------------------PARAMETERS
[PARAMETERS]
OFFSET                   =  0
ROTATION_ANGLE_XY_PLANE  =  180
MU                       =  1.0
$
START            = 1000
AMPLITUDE        = 50
WAVE_LENGTH      = 2500
```

- Location：2 000.0, 0.0, 325.0；
- Orient using：Euler Angles；
- Euler Angles：0.0, 90.0, 0.0；
- 单击 Apply，完成 wheel_rear 轮胎的创建。

（2）前轮胎。
- 单击 Forces > Special Forces > Creat a Tire，创建轮胎（包含路面）模型参考如图 14-5 所示；
  - Name：wheel_rear；
  - Side：Left；
  - Cm Offset：0；
  - Mass：20；
  - Ixx Iyy：5e4；
  - Izz：1e4；
  - Wheel Center Offset：0；
  - Tire Property Filc：D:/MSC.Software/Adams_x64/2015/acar/shared_car_database.cdb/tires.tbl/mdi_tire01_145.tir，修改轮胎横截面的宽度为 145 mm，其余参数保持不变；
  - Longitudinal Velocity：0；
  - Spin Velocity：0；
  - Road：.my_sanlunche.road；
  - Location：2 000.0, 0.0, 325.0；
  - Orient using：Euler Angles；
  - Euler Angles：0.0, 90.0, 0.0；
  - 单击 OK，完成 wheel_front 轮胎的创建。

（3）部件 wheel_front.wheel_part 与 hub_front 之间 Revolute 约束。
- 单击 Connecton > Joints > Creat a Revolute Joint；
  - Name：wheel_front_and_hub_front；
  - First Body：wheel_front.wheel_part；
  - Second Body：hub_front；
  - Type：Revolute；
  - Force Display：None；
  - 单击 OK，完成约束副 wheel_front_and_hub_front 的创建。

（4）部件 wheel_rear.wheel_part 与 hub_rear 之间 Revolute 约束。
- 单击 Connecton > Joints > Creat a Revolute Joint；
  - Name：wheel_rear_and_hub_rear；
  - First Body：wheel_rear.wheel_part；
  - Second Body：hub_rear；
  - Type：Revolute；
  - Force Display：None；
  - 单击 OK，完成约束副 wheel_rear_and_hub_rear 的创建。

14.6 摩托车驱动

• 单击 Forces > Applied Forces > Creat a Torque Applied Forces，创建旋转力矩（扭矩）如图 14-7 所示；
• Run-time Directon：Two Bodies；
• Construction：2 Body-2 Locatic，即两个部件与两个位置创建旋转驱动，创建旋转驱动时，显示网格线（调整网格与轴垂直），此时创建出的扭矩与网格面平行；
• Characteristic：Custom，选择 Custom，可以通过编写函数，使驱动力由小到大逐渐增加，此时整车可以静平衡，同时运行过程比较平稳，如果选取 Constant，此时力矩会直接加载在车轮上，摩托车不能平衡，仿真过程开始摩托车会跳动起来；
• 设置完成后根据界面左下角提示，按先后顺序选择部件 hub_rear 与 wheel_rear，接着按先后顺序选择硬点.hub_rear_l 与.hub_rear_r，硬点选择完成后，驱动扭矩 SFORCE_4 创建完成；
• 模型树 Forces 展开，右击 SFORCE_4 > Modify，弹出扭矩修改对话框如图 14-8 所示；

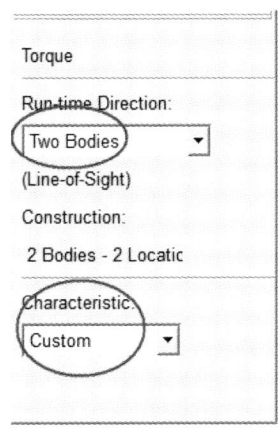 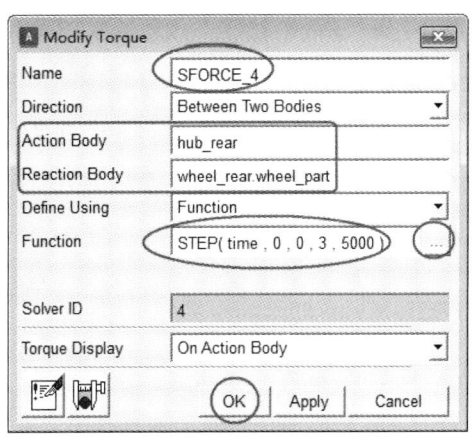

图 14-7 扭矩参数设置　　　图 14-8 扭矩修改对话框

• Function：STEP(time , 0 , 0 , 3 , 5000)，此函数为阶跃函数，在时间 t 等于 0 s 时，力矩为 0，当时间为 3 s 时，力矩为 5 000 N·mm，在 0~3 s，力矩呈线性增加，阶跃函数图形如图 14-9 所示。
• 单击 OK，完成扭矩 SFORCE_4 修改。

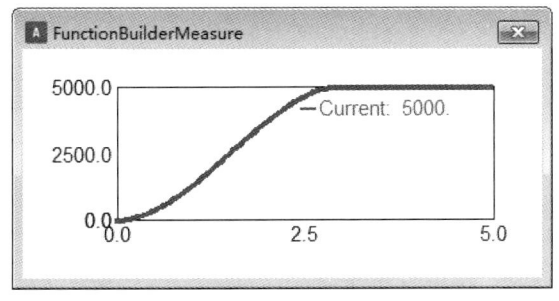

图 14-9 力矩图形

14.7 摩托车加速仿真

（1）仿真设置。

- 单击 Simulation > Simulate > Run an interative Simulation，仿真参数设置如图 14-10 所示；

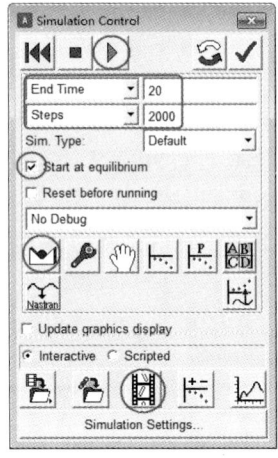

图 14-10 仿真参数设置

- 单击静平衡按钮，检测三轮车整车模型是否能静平衡，静平衡是正确仿真的开始；
- End Time：20；
- Steps：2 000；
- 勾选 Start at equilibrium，从静平衡开始仿真；
- 单击开始，完成摩托车直线仿真，摩托车运行轨迹如图 14-11 所示；

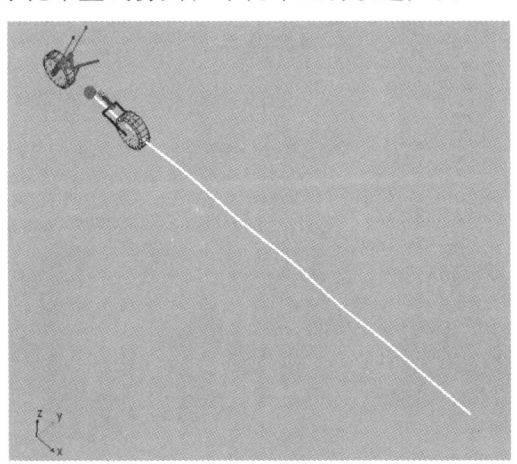

图 14-11 摩托车运动轨迹

- 切换到后处理模块，计算参数如图 14-12～图 14-22 所示，图 14-12 为摩托车速度变化图，从曲线中可以看出，摩托车运行速度一直增加；如图 14-13、图 14-14 分别为车身垂向加速度、垂向加速度功率谱，从频谱图中可以看出，频率在 6.6 Hz 时候，车身的振动幅值最大。

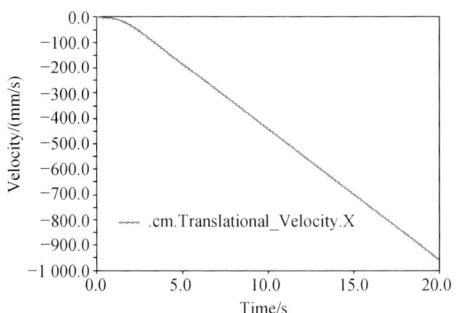

图 14-12 摩托车速度

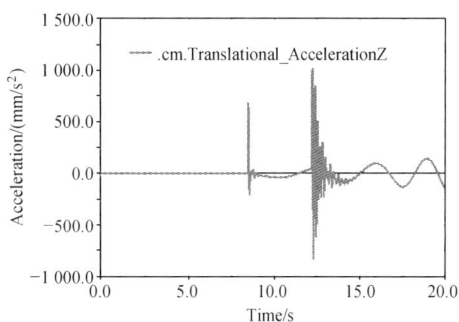

图 14-13 车身垂向加速度/Z

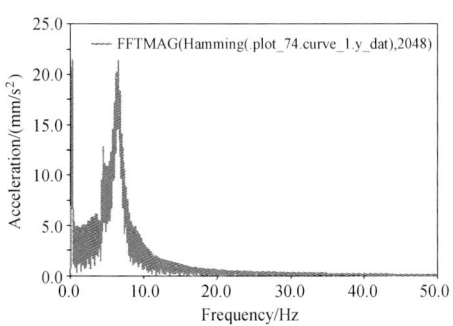

图 14-14 车身垂向加速度功率谱（6.6 Hz）

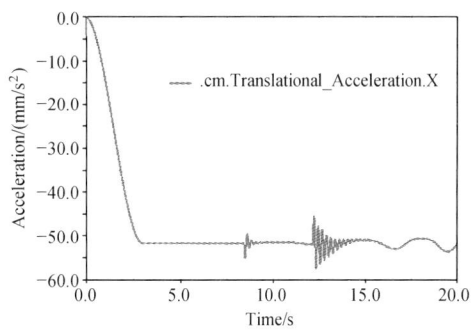

图 14-15 车身垂向加速度/X

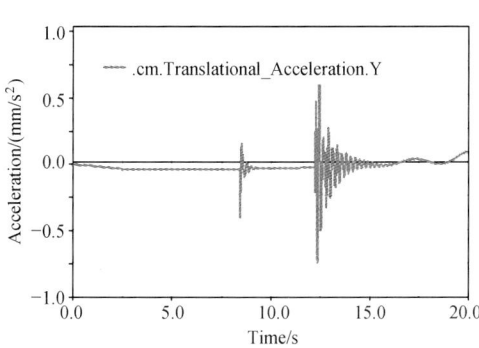

图 14-16 车身垂向加速度/Y

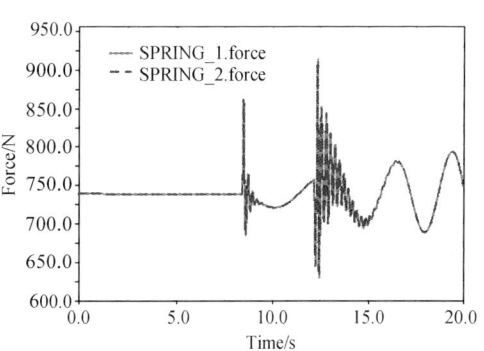

图 14-17 前轴弹簧受力

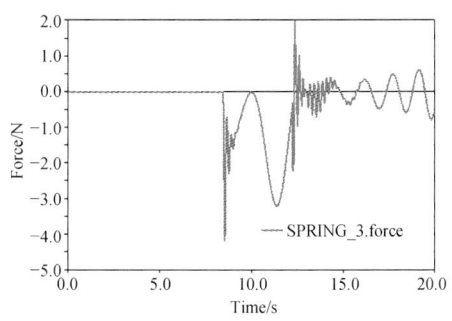

图 14-18 后轴弹簧受力

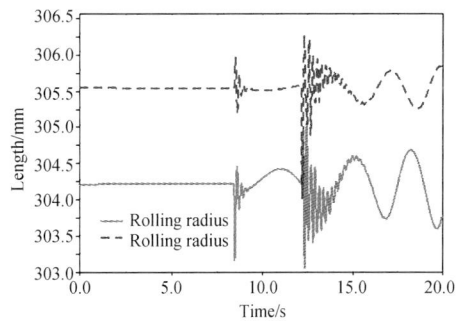

图 14-19 前后轮胎有载滚动半径

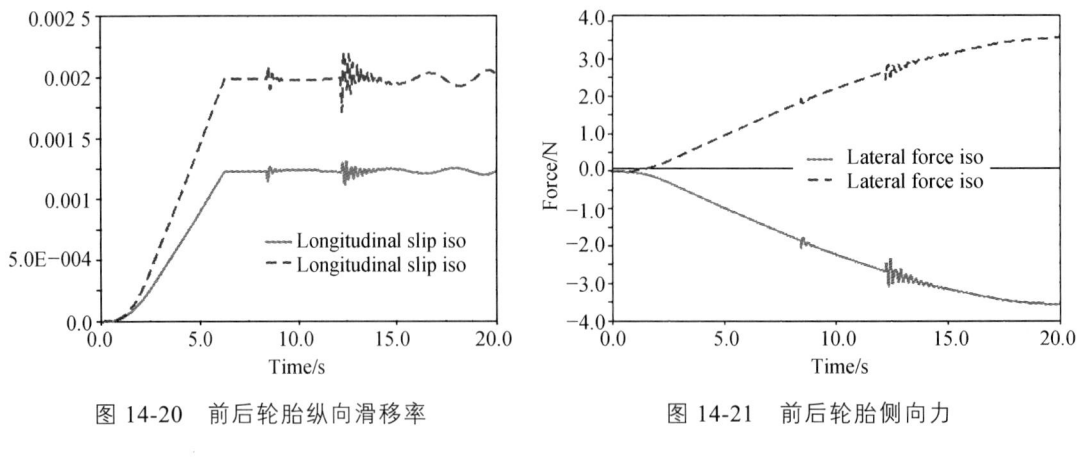

图 14-20　前后轮胎纵向滑移率　　　　　图 14-21　前后轮胎侧向力

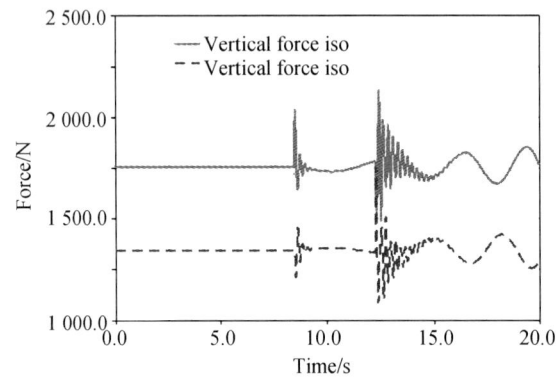

图 14-22　前后轮胎垂向力

14.8　摩托车同步带传动

摩托车大多采用链传动，少数摩托车采用轴传动或同步带传动，相对于链传动，同步带的优势是噪声小，价格便宜，缺点是传动效率相对较低。本节在上述摩托车模型的基础上继续建立同步带传动，在建立皮带传动时，需要对上述摩托车约束进行相应的修改。

（1）修改部件 wheel_rear.wheel_part 与 hub_rear 为 Fixed 约束。
- 模型树单击 Connectors > wheel_rear_and_hub_rear；
- 右击 Modify：wheel_rear_and_hub_rear，弹出修改对话框如图 14-23 所示；
- First Body：wheel_rear.wheel_part；
- Second Body：hub_rear；
- Type：Fixed；
- Force Display：None；
- 单击 OK，完成约束副 wheel_rear_and_hub_rear 的修改。

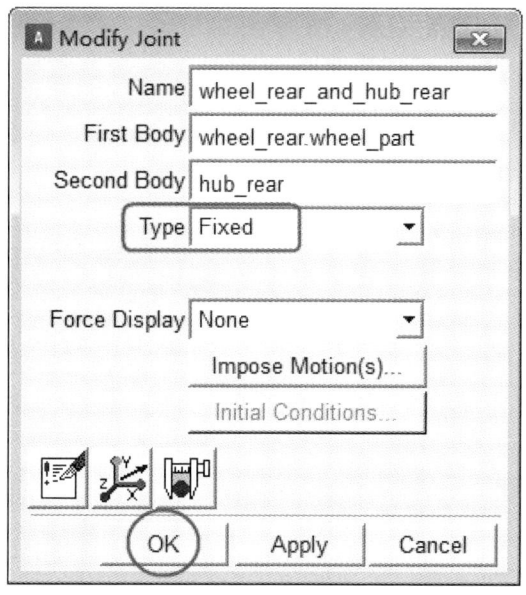

图 14-23 约束副修改——Fixed

（2）修改部件 body 与 damper_up 为 Revolute 约束。
- 模型树单击 Connectors > body_and_damper_up；
- 右击 Modify：body_and_damper_up；
- First Body：body；
- Second Body：damper_up；
- Type：Revolute；
- Force Display：None；
- 单击 OK，完成约束副 body_and_damper_up 的修改。

（3）部件 engine_link。
- 单击 Bodies > Construction > Construction Geometry：Mark 创建参考点；
- Add to Part；
- Don't Attach；
- 选择部件.body；
- 右击鼠标，弹出硬点位置对话框参考如图 14-2 所示；
- 硬点位置输入 1 100.0，−150.0, 425.0；
- 单击 Apply，完成参考点创建；
- 右击参考点，选择 Rename，重名为 M1；
- 单击 Bodies > Construction > Construction Geometry：Mark 创建参考点；
- Add to Part；
- Don't Attach；
- 选择部件.body；
- 右击鼠标，弹出硬点位置对话框参考如图 14-2 所示；
- 硬点位置输入 1 100.0, 0.0, 425.0；

- 单击 Apply，完成参考点创建；
- 右击参考点，选择 Rename，重名为 M2；
- 单击 Bodies > Geometry Cylinder 创建圆柱几何体；
- 选择 New Part；
- Radius: 15；
- 选择参考点 M1 与 M2，完成圆柱形部件创建；
- 右击圆柱体部件，选择 Rename，重名为 engine_link。

(4) 部件 engine_link 与 body 之间 Fixed 约束。
- 单击 Connecton > Joints > Creat a Revolute Joint；
- Name：engine_link_to_body；
- First Body：engine_link；
- Second Body：body；
- Type：Fixed；
- Force Display：None；
- 单击 OK，完成约束副 engine_link_to_body 的创建。

(5) 同步带轮创建。
- 单击 Machinery > Belt > Create Pulley，创建滑轮界面如图 14-24 所示；
- Belt System / Name：beltsys_1，默认皮带传动系统名称，可更改；
- Pully Set / Name：pullyset_1 默认滑轮部件名称，可更改；
- Type： Trapezoidal Toothed，梯形齿或同步带；
- 单击 Next，切换到 Method 界面；
- Method：2D links；

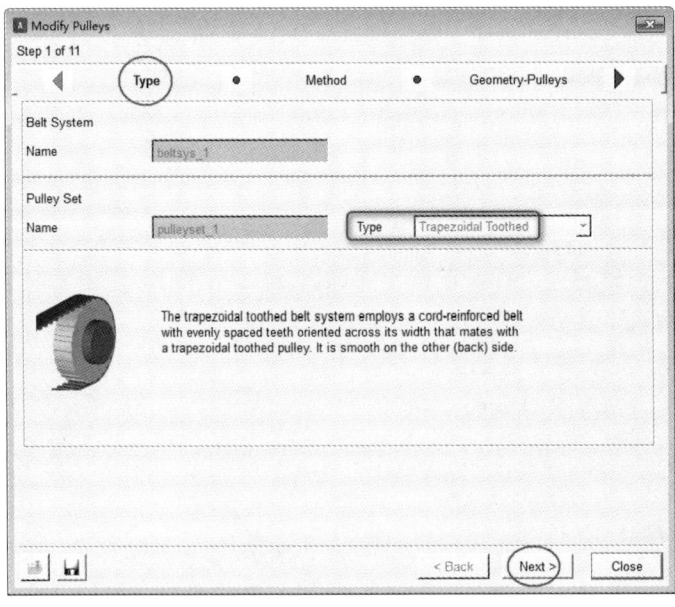

图 14-24　同步皮带轮/Type

- 单击 Next，切换到 Gemetry-Pulleys 滑轮几何参数界面，如图 14-25 所示；

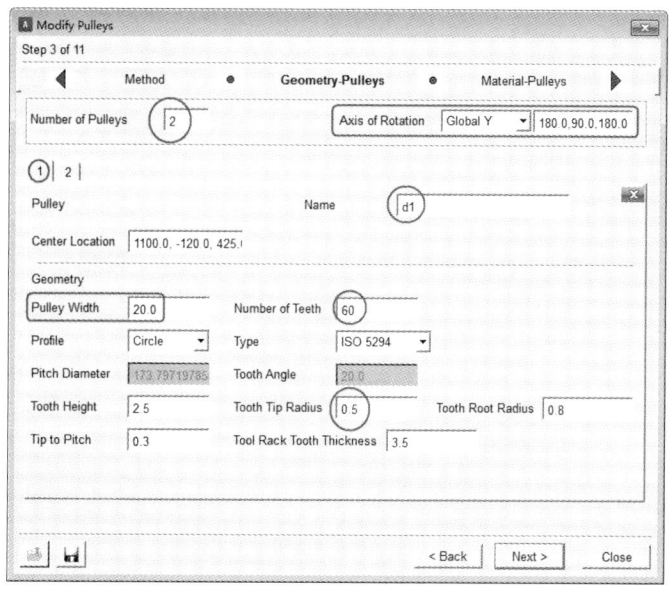

图 14-25（a） 同步皮带轮/d1

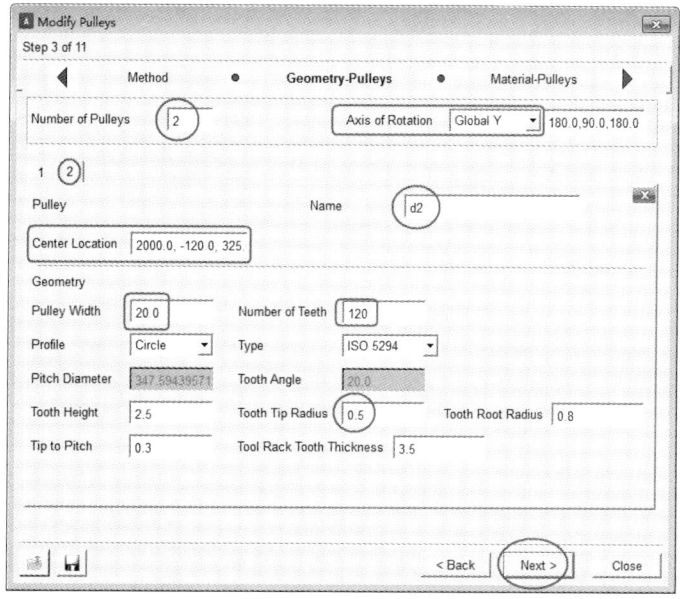

图 14-25（b） 同步皮带轮/d2

- Number of Pulleys（滑轮数量）：2，即皮带轮传动系统中包含两个滑轮，滑轮数量与下面的滑轮几何参数设置保持数量一致；
- Axis of Rotation：Global Y；
- 单击 1；
- Name：d1；
- Center Location：1 100.0，−120.0，425.0，此处可以先建立参考点，然后依次选取；
- Pulley Width（滑轮厚度）：20；
- Number of Teeth：60；

- Profile：Circle；
- Type：ISO 5294；
- Tooth Height：2.5；
- Tooth Tip Radius：0.5；
- Tooth Roof Height：0.8；
- Tip to Pitch：0.3；
- Tool Rack Tooth Thickness：3.5；
- 单击 2；
- Name：d2；
- Center Location：2 000.0，–120.0，325.0，此处可以先建立参考点，然后依次选取；
- Pulley Width（滑轮厚度）：120；
- Number of Teeth：60；
- Profile：Circle；
- Type：ISO 5294；
- Tooth Height：2.5；
- Tooth Tip Radius：0.5；
- Tooth Roof Height：0.8；
- Tip to Pitch：0.3；
- Tool Rack Tooth Thickness：3.5；
- 单击 Next，切换到 Material-Pulleys 滑轮材料参数界面，保持默认设置；
- 单击 Next，切换到 Connection-Pulleys 滑轮约束参数界面；
- 单击 1；
- Type：Rotational；
- Body：.my_sanlunche.engine_link，即滑轮与部件 engine_link 之间采用转动副约束；
- 单击 2；
- Type：Fixed；
- Body：.my_sanlunche.hub_rear，即滑轮与部件.my_sanlunche.hub_rear 之间采用固定副约束；
- 单击 Next，切换到 Output-Pulleys 滑轮输出参数界面，保持默认设置；
- 单击 Next，切换到 Completion-Pulleys 滑轮完成参数界面，保持默认设置；
- 单击 Next，切换到 Gemetry-Tensioners 张紧器参数界；
- Number of Tensioners with Deviation Pulley（带偏差滑轮的张紧器数量）：0，不需要张紧轮；
- 连续单击 Next，界面均保持默认设置；
- 单击 Finish，完成两个同步皮带滑轮的创建。

（6）同步带创建。
- 单击 Machinery > Belt > Create Belt，创建同步皮带界面如图 14-26 所示；
- Pulley Set/Name：.my_sanlunche.beltsys_1.pulleyset_1，通过 Pulley Set > Guesses 选取已经创建好的滑轮；

- Belt System/Name：.my_sanlunche.beltsys_1，系统自动默认命名；

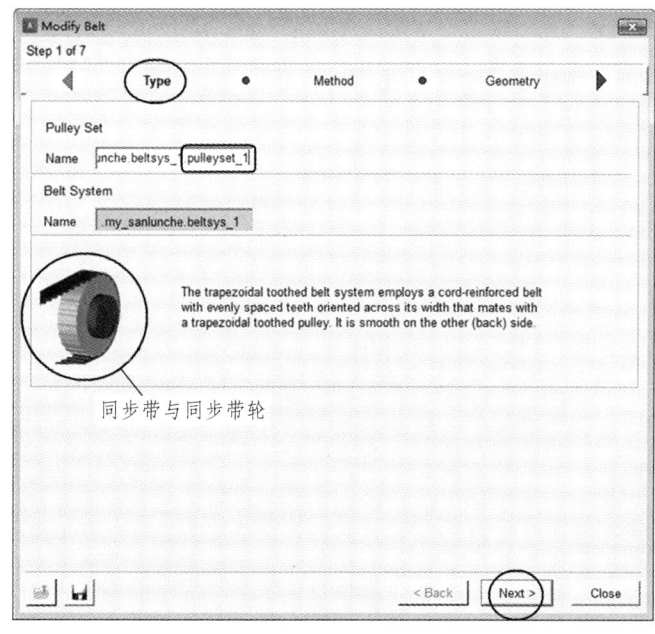

图 14-26　同步皮带（Type）

- 单击 Next，切换到 Method 界面；
- Method：2D links；
- 单击 Next，切换到 Geometry 皮带几何参数界面，如图 14-27 所示；
- Axis of Rotation：Global Y；
- Reference Location：1 100.0，-120.0，425.0；

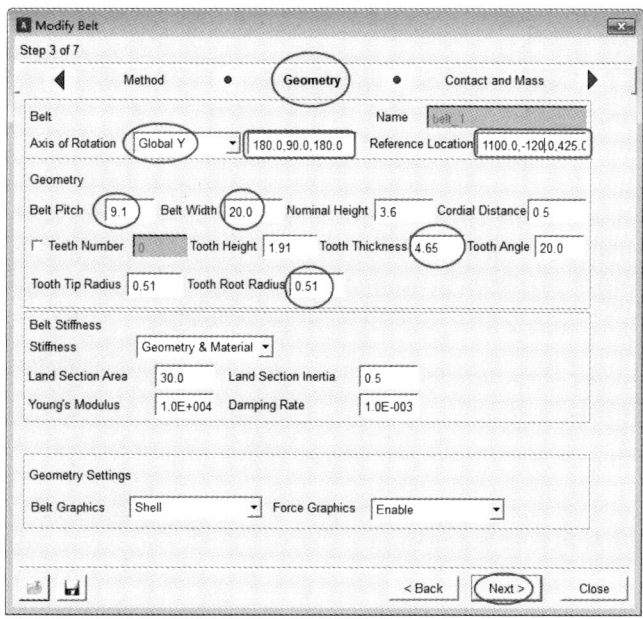

图 14-27　同步皮带（Geometry）

- Belt Pitch（皮带节距）：9.1，皮带节距参数极为重要，需要重复调节此参数保证同步皮带与同步皮带轮齿啮合，在创建皮带传动时此细节是非常容易忽略的因素，虽然忽略此因素也可以创建同步皮带及仿真，但计算结果会有偏差；创建完成后放大同步皮带与皮带轮，观察是否切合，否则退还到 GEOMETRY 界面重新设置相关参数；
- Belt Width（皮带宽度）：20；
- Nominal Height：3.6；
- Cordial Distance：0.5；
- Tooth Height：1.91；
- Tooth Thickness：4.65；
- Tooth Tip Radius：0.51；
- Tooth Root Radius：0.51，其余参数保持默认；
- 单击 Next，切换到 Contant and Mass 皮带接触与质量参数界面，如图 14-28 所示，所有参数保持默认设置；

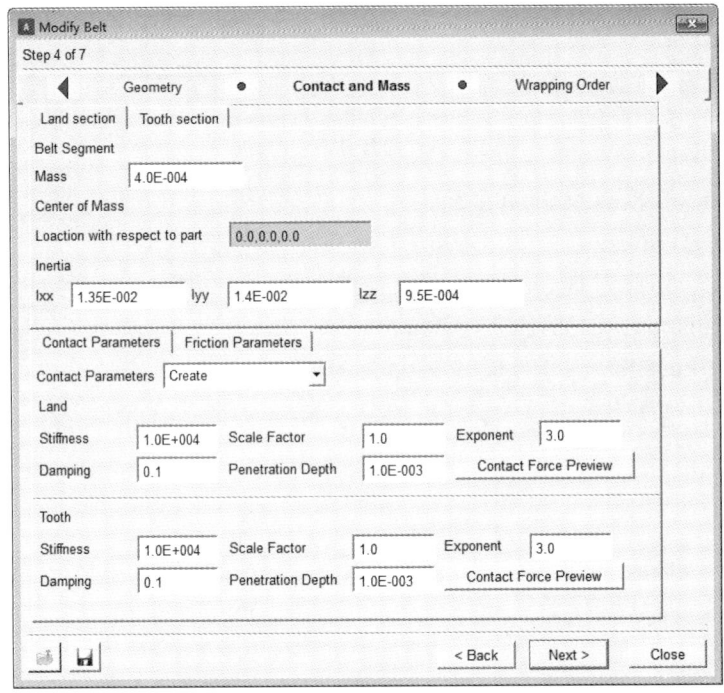

图 14-28　同步皮带/Contant and Mass

- 单击 Next，切换到 Wrapping Order 皮带包裹顺序参数界面如图 14-29 所示；
- Wrapping Order：以下同步皮带轮顺序不能换。
① .my_sanlunche.beltsys_1.pulleyset_1.pulleyset_1_d1；
② .my_sanlunche.beltsys_1.pulleyset_1.pulleyset_1_d2。

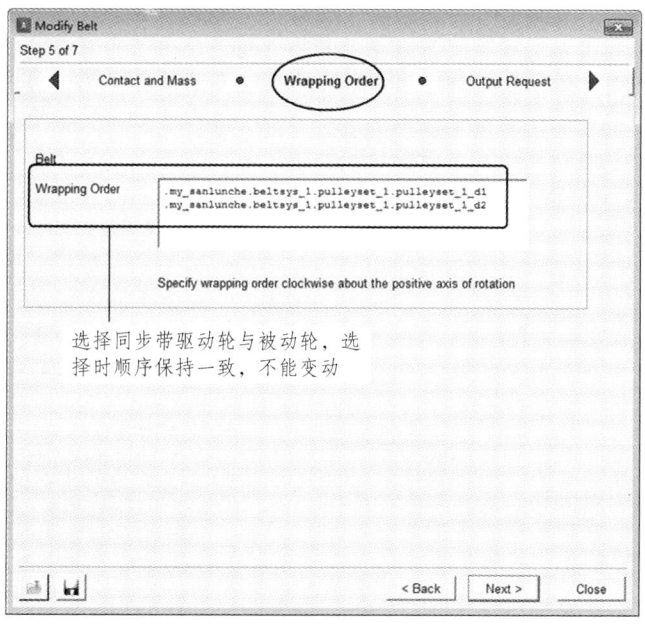

图 14-29　同步皮带（Wrapping Order）

- 单击 Next，弹出问题提示框如图 14-30 所示，皮带共包含 290 个皮带段块，单击 Yes，继续包裹皮带；皮带包裹完成后切换到 Output Request 输出请求界面；需要注意的是同步皮带包裹完成后，误差及皮带张紧力越小越好，对于链传动亦是如此，此处同步带张紧力为 72 N；
- 勾选 Segment Request；
- Link Part(s)：segment_1（皮带中第 1 个段块）；
- 单击 Next，切换到 Completion 参数设置；
- 单击 Finish，完成同步皮带模型建立。

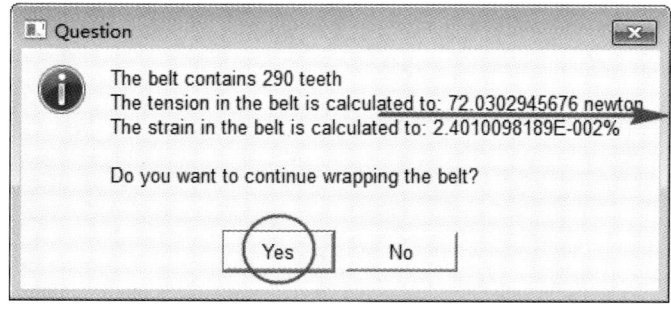

图 14-30　皮带创建问题提示框

（7）驱动力矩。

- 单击 Machinery > Belt > Belt Actuation Input，创建同步带驱动元界面如图 14-31 所示；
- Actuator / Name：.my_sanlunche.beltsys_1.actuator_1；
- Pulley：.my_sanlunche.beltsys_1.pulleyset_1.pulleyset_1_d1；

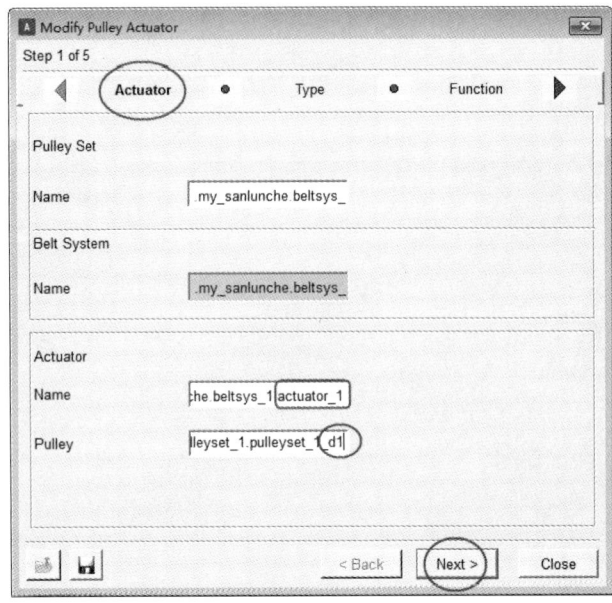

图 14-31　创建驱动元（Actuator）

- 单击 Next，切换到 Type 参数设置界面；
- Type：Torque；
- 单击 Next，切换到 Function 参数设置界面，如图 14-32 所示；
- Function：User Defined；
- User Entered Func.： – STEP(time , 0 , 0 , 3, 5 000)；
- Direction：Clockwise，顺时针方向；
- 单击 Next，切换到 Output 参数设置界面，保持默认设置；

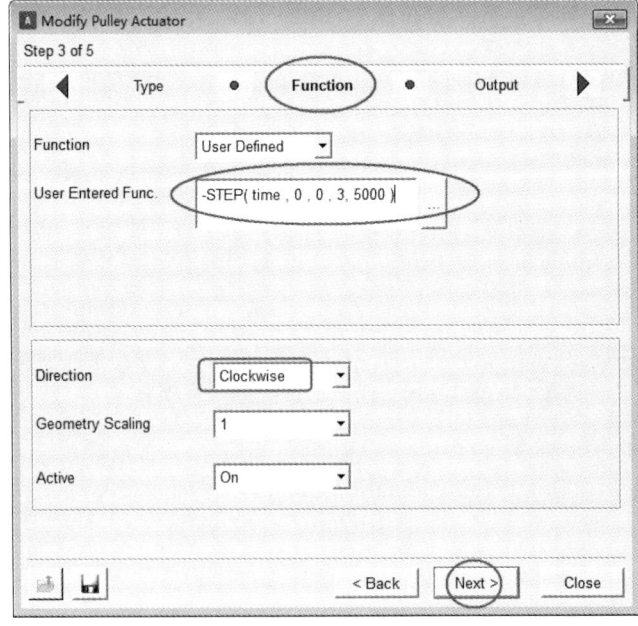

图 14-32　创建驱动元/ Function

- 单击 Next，切换到 Completion 参数设置；
- 单击 Finish，完成驱动元的创建，此时皮带传动摩托车整车模型如图 14-33 所示；

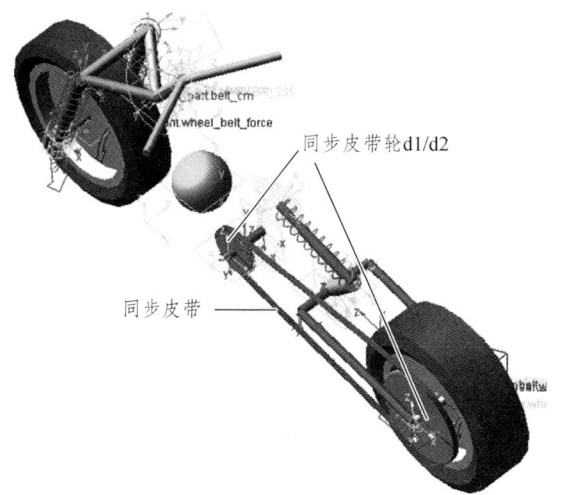

图 14-33　摩托车同步带传动

- 单击 Simulation > Simulate 命令；
- End Time：10；
- Steps：10 000，即步数按仿真时间的 1 000 倍设置，过小的话会导致计算过程出现收敛问题，仿真过程缓慢，有条件的读者建议采用服务器计算；
- 其余保持默认设置，单击 Start simulation；
- 计算完成后，按 F8 切换到后处理模块，驱动函数图形如图 14-34 所示；驱动元转动角度如图 14-35 所示；同步带传动接触力如图 14-36 所示，从计算结果中可以看出，摩托车起步瞬间，同步带接触力瞬间增大，同时伴有高频振动现象，随着时间推移，即摩托车平稳运行后，接触力逐渐减小至常数状态；如图 14-37～图 14-39 为前后轮胎 X、Y、Z 三方向的接触力特性曲线，在起步数据亦有震荡现象；如图 14-40、图 14-41 所示前后弹簧受力转台，前弹簧受力相对于后轴较大，摩托车重型靠近前轴，转向较沉稳，稳定性好；如图 14-42 所示为车身垂向加速度特性曲线。

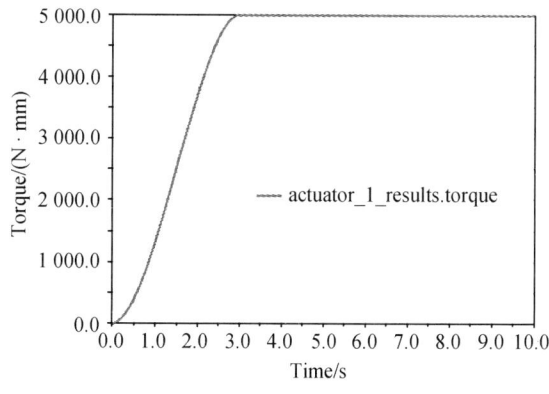

图 14-34　力矩-STEP(time , 0 , 0 , 3 , 5000)图形

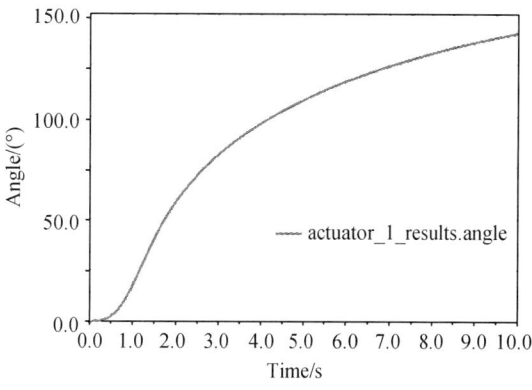

图 14-35　驱动力转动角度

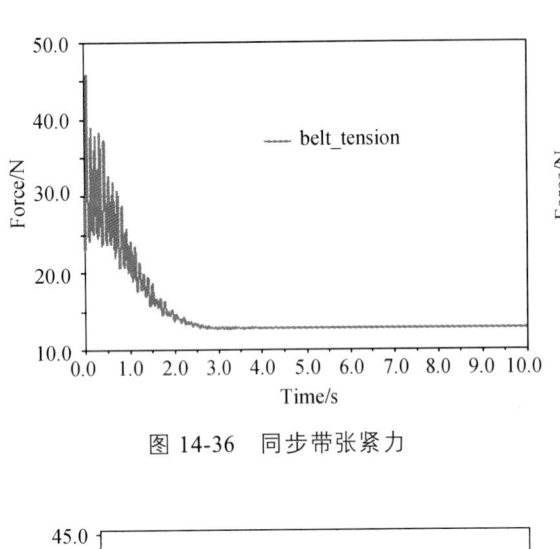

图 14-36 同步带张紧力

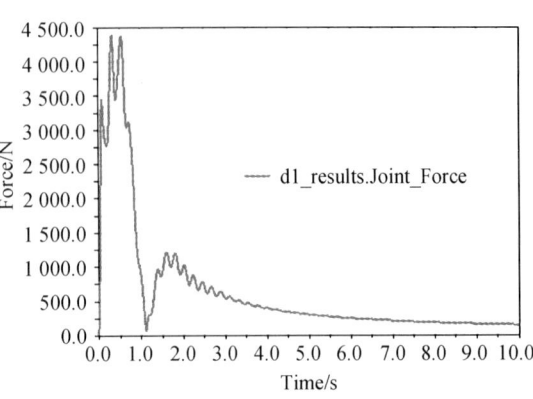

图 14-37 驱动带轮转动力

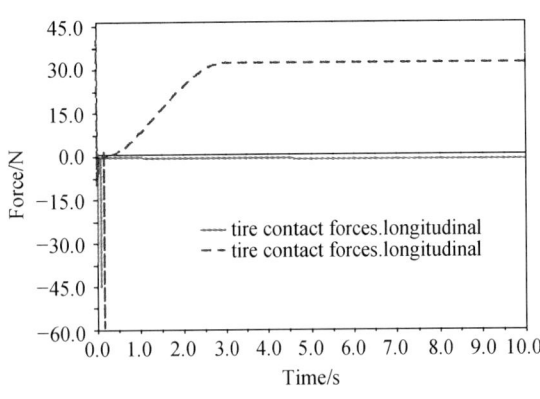

图 14-38 前后轮胎纵向接触力

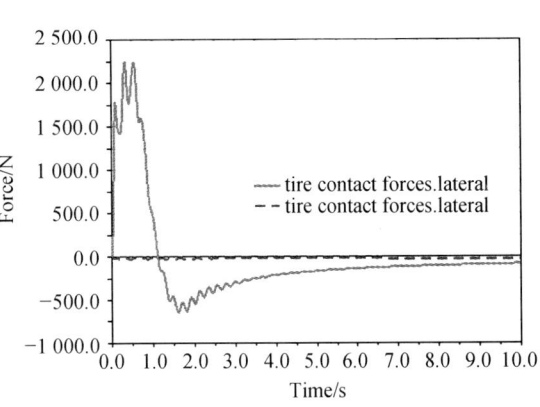

图 14-39 前后轮胎侧向接触力

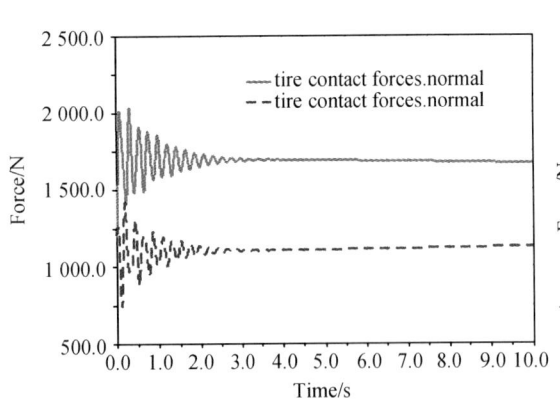

图 14-40 前后轮胎垂向接触力

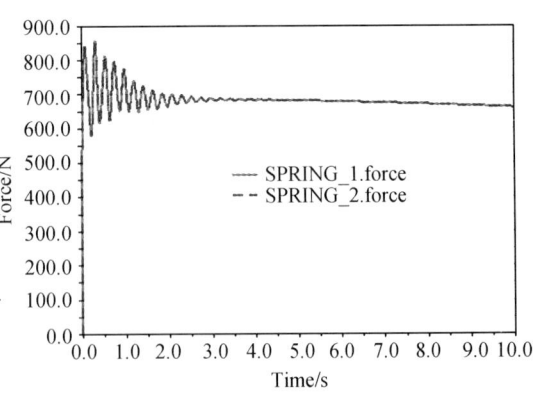

图 14-41 转向轴双减震器受力

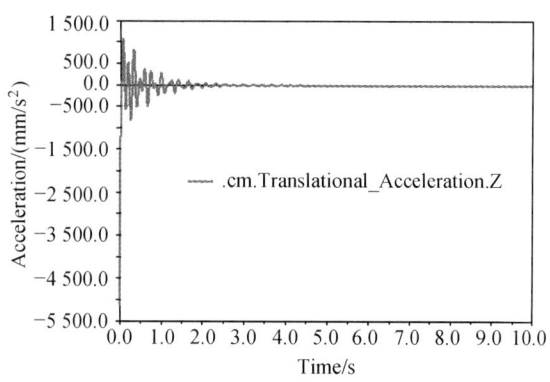

图 14-42　车身垂向加速度

14.9　电动机驱动同步带传动

主动滑轮 d1 需要通过电动来驱动，此时需要删除转动约束副：engine_link_to_body。
（1）删除约束副：engine_link_to_body。
- 模型树单击 Connectors > engine_link_to_body；
- 右击 Delete，完成约束的删除；
- 在驱动皮带轮 d1 附近右击删除驱动力 my_sanlunche.beltsys_1.actuator_1。

（2）电动机。
- 单击 Machinery > Motor > Create Motor 命令，弹出创建电动机对话框；
- Method：Curve Based；
- 单击 Next，切换到 Motor Type 参数界面，保持默认设置；
- 单击 Next，切换到 Motor Connections 参数界面，如图 14-43 所示；
- Motor：New；
- Location：1 100.0,0.0,425.0；
- Axis of Rotation：Global Y；
- Rotor Attach Part ：my_sanlunche.engine_link；
- Stator Attach Part ： my_sanlunche.body；
- 单击 Next，切换到 Motor Geometry 电动机几何参数界面，如图 14-44 所示；
- 勾选 Creat Rotor Stator Parts，创建电动机定子与转子几何体；
- Rotor Length：0.1 m；
- Rotor Radius：0.15 m；
- Stator Length：5.0E－002 m；
- Stator Width：0.15 m；
- Define Mass By：Geometry and Density；

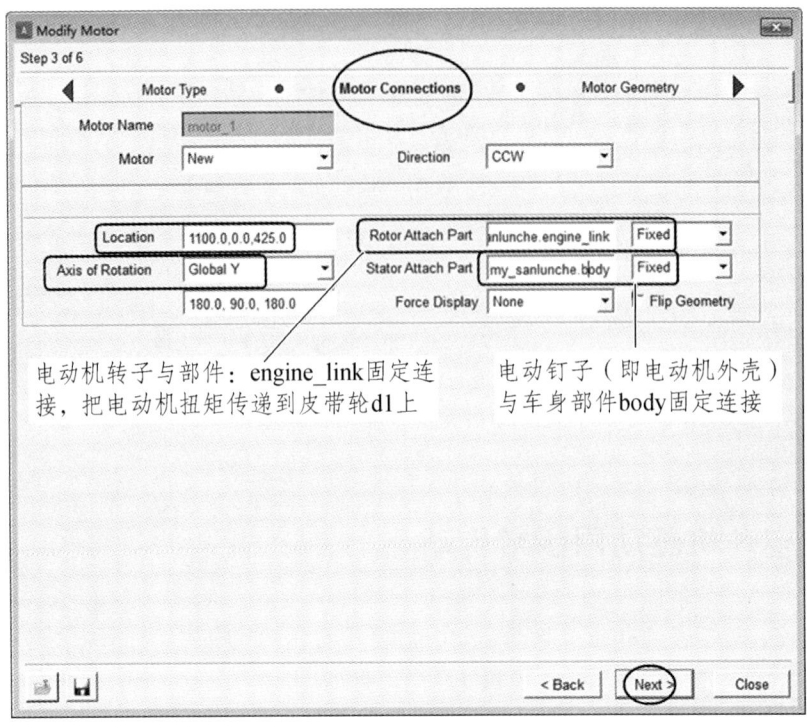

图 14-43 电动机（Motor Connections）

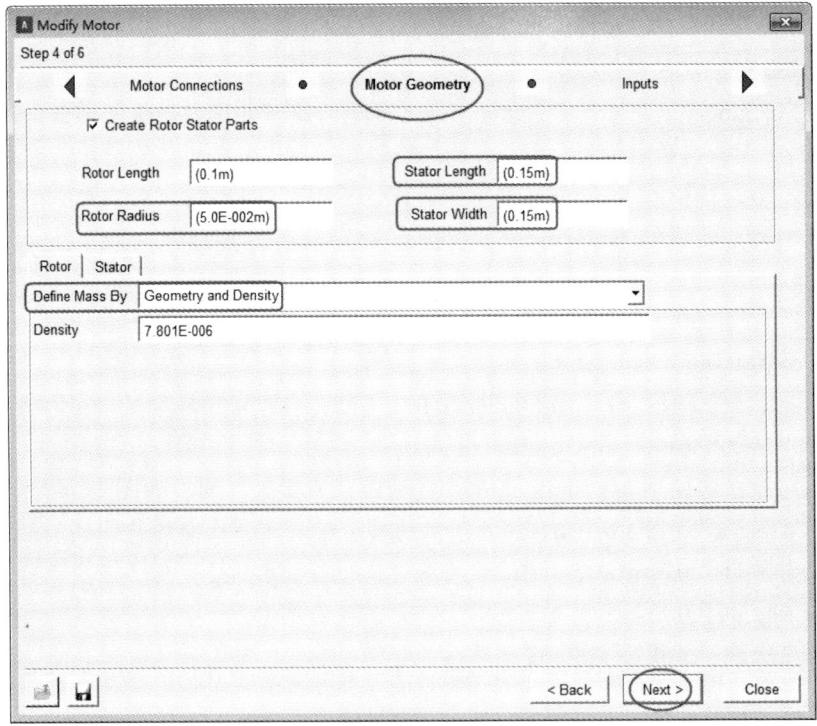

图 14-44 电动机（Motor Geometry）

- 单击 Next，切换到 Inputs 参数界面，如图 14-45 所示；

图 14-45　电动机（Inputs）

- 单击 Next，切换到 Motor Output 参数界面，保持默认设置；
- 单击 Finish，完成电动机创建，此时摩托车整车模型如图 14-46 所示；

图 14-46　摩托车-电动机驱动皮带传动

第 15 章　双轴转向系统

双轴及多轴转向系统在工程及特种车辆上应用得较多，双轴转向一般采用连杆传动，大于两轴系转向的一般采用液压传动；图 15-1 为 6×4 牵引货车右舵双轴转向系统；与单轴转向相比，在转向系统是多了一个摇臂，通过摇臂与车身的旋转拉动后面的传动杆使第二轴车辆产生转动，在此模型上可以继续拓展三轴及多轴连杆传动转向。在摇臂上可以通过增加液压推杆起到转向助力的作用，有关转向助力特性的研究可以通过在此推杆上建立函数，然后与 MATLAB 软件建立联合仿真模型进行研究各种转向助力特性；

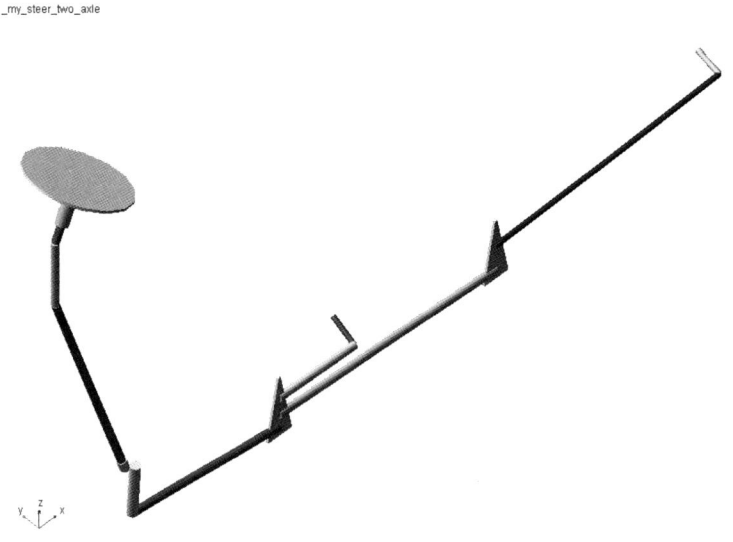

图 15-1　双轴转向系统

学习目标

- ◇ 双轴右舵转向系统。
- ◇ 通信器。
- ◇ 拓展多轴转向模型。
- ◇ TASA 实验。
- ◇ 单轴右舵转向系统。

15.1 双轴转向模型

- 启动 ADAMS/CAR、选择 Template 进入建模界面；
- 单击 File > New 命令，弹出建模对话框如图 15-2 所示；
- Template Name：my_steer_two_axle；
- Major Role：steering；
- 单击 OK，进入到建模界面；

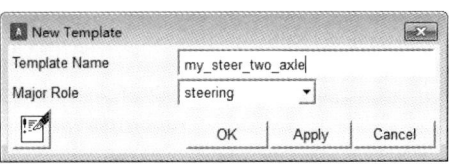

图 15-2 转向模板框

- 单击 Build > Hardpoint > New 命令，弹出 Template 创建硬点对话框如图 15-3 所示；
- 在硬点名称里输入 steering_wheel_center；
- Type：left；
- Location：3 200.0, 800.0, 2 300.0；
- 单击 Apply,完成 steering_wheel_center 硬点的创建；
- 重复上述步骤完成图 15-4 中硬点的创建，创建完成后单击 OK。

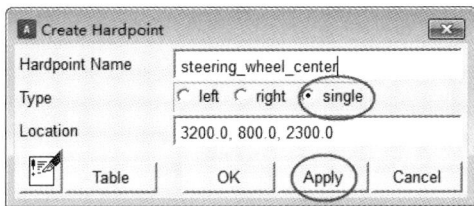

图 15-3 硬点创建

	loc_x	loc_y	loc_z
hps_input_shaft_forward	3400.0	800.0	900.0
hps_intermediate_shaft_forward	3100.0	800.0	1812.5
hps_intermediate_shaft_rearward	3100.0	800.0	2088.6
hps_origin_ref	0.0	0.0	0.0
hps_pitman_arm_aft_front	5050.0	765.0	550.0
hps_pitman_arm_aft_rear	5150.0	765.0	550.0
hps_pitman_arm_aft_upper	5100.0	765.0	800.0
hps_pitman_arm_middle_front	4050.0	765.0	550.0
hps_pitman_arm_middle_rear	4150.0	765.0	550.0
hps_pitman_arm_middle_upper	4100.0	765.0	800.0
hps_pitman_axis	3415.0	750.0	900.0
hps_steer_arm	4450.0	765.0	700.0
hps_steer_link	3415.0	765.0	675.0
hps_steer_link_aft_front	5100.0	765.0	685.0
hps_steer_link_aft_rear	6130.0	765.0	730.0
hps_steer_link_fore_front	4100.0	765.0	710.0
hps_steer_link_middle_front	4100.0	765.0	635.0
hps_steer_link_middle_rear	5100.0	765.0	580.0
hps_steer_link_rear	4100.0	765.0	580.0
hps_steering_arm_attach	4450.0	865.0	760.0
hps_steering_arm_attach_aft	6130.0	865.0	765.0
hps_steering_wheel_center	3200.0	800.0	2300.0

图 15-4 双轴转向系统硬点

(1) 部件 steer_link。
- 单击 Build > Part > General Part > New 命令，弹出创建部件对话框如图 15-5 所示；
- General Part 输入 steer_link；
- Location Dependency：Centered between coordinates；
- Centered between：Two Coordinates；
- Coordinate Reference #1(参考坐标)：._my_steer_two_axle.ground.hps_steer_link；
- Coordinate Reference #2(参考坐标)：._my_steer_two_axle.ground.hps_steer_link_rear；
- Orientation Dependency：Orient axis along line；
- Coordinate Reference #1(参考坐标)：._my_steer_two_axle.ground.hps_steer_link；
- Coordinate Reference #2(参考坐标)：._my_steer_two_axle.ground.hps_steer_link_rear；
- Axis：Z；
- Mass：1；
- Ixx：1；
- Iyy：1；
- Izz：1；
- Density：Material；
- Material Type：.materials.steel；
- 单击 OK，完成部件._my_steer_two_axle.ges_steer_link 创建。

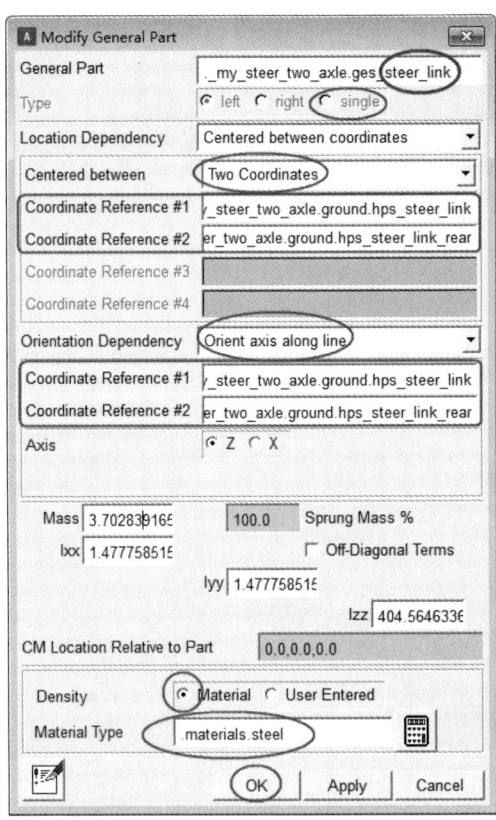

图 15-5　转向连杆部件 steer_link

- 单击 Build > Geometry > Link > New 命令，创建圆柱体如图 15-6 所示；
- Link Name (连杆名称) 输入几何名称：steer_link；
- General Part 输入 ._my_steer_two_axle.ges_steer_link；
- Coordinate Reference #1(参考坐标)：._my_steer_two_axle.ground.hps_steer_link；
- Coordinate Reference #2(参考坐标)：._my_steer_two_axle.ground.hps_steer_link_rear；
- Radius(半径): 15.0；
- Color（杆件几何体颜色）：red；
- 选择 Calculate Mass Properties of General Part 复选框，当几何建立好之后会更新对应部件的质量和惯量参数；
- Density：Material；
- Material Type：steel；
- 单击 OK，完成 ._my_steer_two_axle.ges_steer_link.gralin_steer_link 几何体的创建。

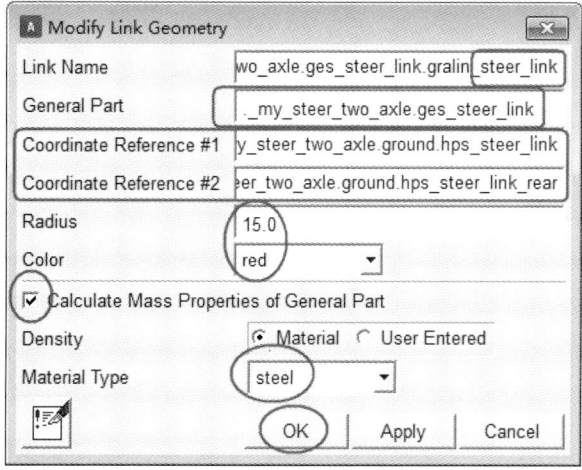

图 15-6　转向连杆几何体 steer_link

（2）部件 pitman_arm_middle。
- 单击 Build > Part > General Part > New 命令，弹出创建部件对话框参考如图 15-5 所示；
- General Part 输入 steer_link；
- Location Dependency：Centered between coordinates；
- Centered between：Three Coordinates；
- Coordinate Reference #1(参考坐标)：._my_steer_two_axle.ground.hps_pitman_arm_middle_upper；
- Coordinate Reference #2(参考坐标)：._my_steer_two_axle.ground.hps_pitman_arm_middle_front；
- Coordinate Reference #3(参考坐标)：._my_steer_two_axle.ground.hps_pitman_arm_middle_rear；
- Orientation Dependency：Oriented in plane；
- Coordinate Reference #1(参考坐标)：._my_steer_two_axle.ground.hps_pitman_arm_middle_upper；
- Coordinate Reference #2(参考坐标)：._my_steer_two_axle.ground.hps_pitman_arm_middle_front；
- Coordinate Reference #3(参考坐标)：._my_steer_two_axle.ground.hps_pitman_arm_middle_rear；
- Axis：Z；

- Mass：1；
- Ixx：1；
- Iyy：1；
- Izz：1；
- Density：Material；
- Material Type：.materials.steel；
- 单击 OK，完成部件._my_steer_two_axle.ges_pitman_arm_middle 创建。
- 单击 Build > Geometry > Arm > New 命令，建立三角臂几何如图 15-7 所示；
- Link Name (连杆名称)输入几何名称：steer_link；
- General Part 输入._my_steer_two_axle.ges_pitman_arm_middle；
- Coordinate Reference #1(参考坐标)：._my_steer_two_axle.ground.hps_pitman_arm_middle_upper；
- Coordinate Reference #2(参考坐标)：._my_steer_two_axle.ground.hps_pitman_arm_middle_front；
- Coordinate Reference #3(参考坐标)：._my_steer_two_axle.ground.hps_pitman_arm_middle_rear；
- Thickness: 10.0；
- Color（杆件几何体颜色）：white；
- 选择 Calculate Mass Properties of General Part 复选框；
- Density：Material；
- Material Type：steel；
- 单击 OK，完成._my_steer_two_axle.ges_pitman_arm_middle.graarm_pitman_arm_middle

几何体的创建。

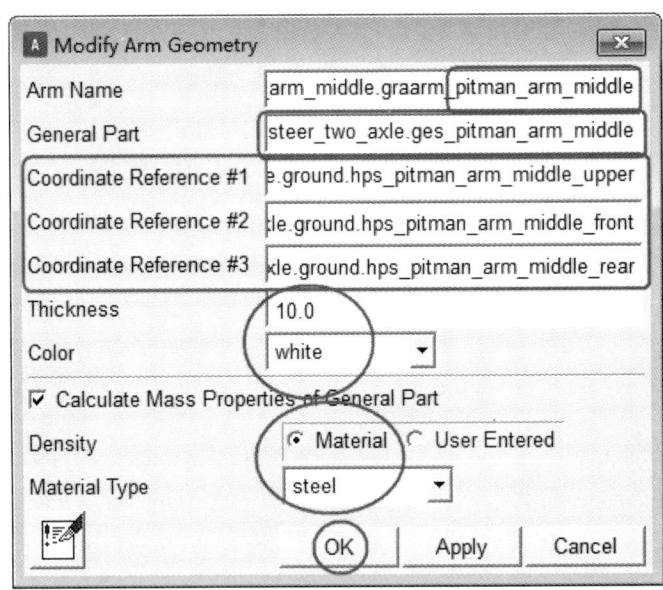

图 15-7　三角臂_arm

（3）部件 steer_input_arm_aft。
- 单击 Build > Part > General Part > New 命令，弹出创建部件对话框如图 15-5 所示；
- General Part 输入 steer_input_arm_aft；

- Location Dependency：Located on a line；
- Coordinate Reference #1(参考坐标)：._my_steer_two_axle.ground.hps_steer_link_aft_rear；
- Coordinate Reference #2(参考坐标)：._my_steer_two_axle.ground.hps_steering_arm_attach_aft；
- Relative location(%)：50；
- Orientation Dependency：User-entered values；
- Orient using：Euler Angles；
- Euler Angles：0,0,0；
- Axis：Z；
- Mass：1；
- Ixx：1；
- Iyy：1；
- Izz：1；
- Density：Material；
- Material Type：.materials.steel；
- 单击 OK，完成部件._my_steer_two_axle.ges_steer_input_arm_aft 创建。
- 单击 Build > Geometry > Link > New 命令，创建圆柱体参考如图 15-6 所示；
- Link Name (连杆名称) 输入几何名称：steer_link；
- General Part 输入._my_steer_two_axle.ges_steer_link；
- Coordinate Reference #1(参考坐标)：._my_steer_two_axle.ground.hps_steer_link；
- Coordinate Reference #2(参考坐标)：._my_steer_two_axle.ground.hps_steer_link_rear；
- Radius(半径): 15.0；
- Color（杆件几何体颜色）：red；
- 选择 Calculate Mass Properties of General Part 复选框，当几何建立好之后会更新对应部件的质量和惯量参数；
- Density：Material；
- Material Type：steel；
- 单击 OK，完成._my_steer_two_axle.ges_steer_link.gralin_steer_link 几何体的创建。

（4）部件 pitman_arm_aft。
- 单击 Build > Part > General Part > New 命令，弹出创建部件对话框如图 15-5 所示；
- General Part 输入 pitman_arm_aft；
- Location Dependency：Delfa location from coordinate；
- Coordinate Reference (参考坐标)：._my_steer_two_axle.ground.hps_steer_link_aft_front；
- Location：0,0,0；
- Location in：Local；
- Orientation Dependency：User-entered values；
- Orient using：Euler Angles；
- Euler Angles：0,0,0；
- Axis：Z；
- Mass：1；

- Ixx：1；
- Iyy：1；
- Izz：1；
- Density：Material；
- Material Type：.materials.steel；
- 单击 OK，完成部件._my_steer_two_axle.ges_pitman_arm_aft 创建。
- 单击 Build > Geometry > Arm > New 命令，建立三角臂几何参考如图 15-7 所示；
- Link Name (连杆名称）输入几何名称：pitman_arm_aft；
- General Part 输入._my_steer_two_axle.ges_pitman_arm_aft；
- Coordinate Reference #1(参考坐标）：._my_steer_two_axle.ground.hps_pitman_arm_aft_upper；
- Coordinate Reference #2(参考坐标）：._my_steer_two_axle.ground.hps_pitman_arm_aft_front；
- Coordinate Reference #3(参考坐标）：._my_steer_two_axle.ground.hps_pitman_arm_aft_rear；
- Thickness: 10.0；
- Color（杆件几何体颜色）：white；
- 选择 Calculate Mass Properties of General Part 复选框；
- Density：Material；
- Material Type：steel；
- 单击 OK,完成._my_steer_two_axle.ges_pitman_arm_aft.graarm_pitman_arm_aft 几何体的创建。

（5）部件 steer_link_aft。
- 单击 Build > Part > General Part > New 命令，弹出创建部件对话框如图 15-5 所示；
- General Part 输入 steer_link_aft；
- Location Dependency：Located on a line；
- Coordinate Reference #1(参考坐标）：._my_steer_two_axle.ground.hps_steer_link_aft_front；
- Coordinate Reference #2(参考坐标）：._my_steer_two_axle.ground.hps_steer_link_aft_rear；
- Relative location(%)：50；
- Orientation Dependency：User-entered values；
- Orient using：Euler Angles；
- Euler Angles：0,0,0；
- Axis：Z；
- Mass：1；
- Ixx：1；
- Iyy：1；
- Izz：1；
- Density：Material；
- Material Type：.materials.steel；
- 单击 OK，完成部件._my_steer_two_axle.ges_steer_link_aft 创建。
- 单击 Build > Geometry > Link > New 命令，创建圆柱体如图 15-6 所示；
- Link Name (连杆名称）输入几何名称：steer_link_aft；

- General Part 输入._my_steer_two_axle.ges_steer_link_aft；
- Coordinate Reference #1(参考坐标)：._my_steer_two_axle.ground.hps_steer_link_aft_front；
- Coordinate Reference #2(参考坐标)：._my_steer_two_axle.ground.hps_steer_link_aft_rear；
- Radius(半径): 10；
- Color（杆件几何体颜色）：blue；
- 选择 Calculate Mass Properties of General Part 复选框；
- Density：Material；
- Material Type：steel；
- 单击 OK，完成._my_steer_two_axle.ges_steer_link_aft.gralin_steer_link_aft 几何体的创建。

（6）部件 steer_link_middle。
- 单击 Build > Part > General Part > New 命令，弹出创建部件对话框如图 15-5 所示；
- General Part 输入 steer_link_middle；
- Location Dependency：Located on a line；
- Coordinate Reference #1(参考坐标)：._my_steer_two_axle.ground.hps_steer_link_middle_front；
- Coordinate Reference #2(参考坐标)：._my_steer_two_axle.ground.hps_steer_link_middle_rear；
- Relative location(%)：50；
- Orientation Dependency：User-entered values；
- Orient using：Euler Angles；
- Euler Angles：0,0,0；
- Axis：Z；
- Mass：1；
- Ixx：1；
- Iyy：1；
- Izz：1；
- Density：Material；
- Material Type：.materials.steel；
- 单击 OK，完成部件._my_steer_two_axle.ges_steer_link_middle 创建。
- 单击 Build > Geometry > Link > New 命令，创建圆柱体如图 15-6 所示；
- Link Name (连杆名称）输入几何名称：steer_link_middle；
- General Part 输入._my_steer_two_axle.ges_steer_link_middle；
- Coordinate Reference #1(参考坐标)：._my_steer_two_axle.ground.hps_steer_link_middle_front；
- Coordinate Reference #2(参考坐标)：._my_steer_two_axle.ground.hps_steer_link_middle_rear；
- Radius(半径): 15；
- Color（杆件几何体颜色）：skyblue；
- 选择 Calculate Mass Properties of General Part 复选框；
- Density：Material；
- Material Type：steel；
- 单击 OK，完成._my_steer_two_axle.ges_steer_link_middle.gralin_steer_link_middle 几何体的创建。

（7）部件 steering_wheel。
- 单击 Build > Construction Frame > New 命令，弹出创建结构框如图 15-8 所示；
- Construction Frame（结构框名称）：steering_whel_center；
- Location Dependency：Delfa location from coordinate；
- Coordinate Reference (参考坐标)：._my_steer_two_axle.ground.hps_steering_wheel_center；
- Location：0,0,0；
- Location in：local；
- Orientation Dependency：Orient axis along line；
- Coordinate Reference #1(参考坐标)：._my_steer_two_axle.ground.hps_steering_wheel_center；
- Coordinate Reference #2(参考坐标)：._my_steer_two_axle.ground.hps_intermediate_shaft_rearward；
- Axis：Z；
- 单击 Apply，完成._my_steer_two_axle.ground.cfs_steering_whel_center 结构框的创建；

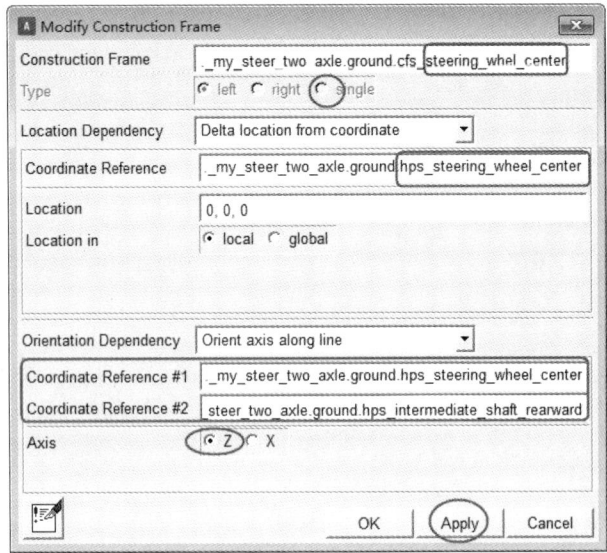

图 15-8　结构框 steering_whel_center

- Construction Frame（结构框名称）：steering_wheel_mcs；
- Location Dependency：Delfa location from coordinate；
- Coordinate Reference (参考坐标)：._my_steer_two_axle.ground.hps_steering_wheel_center；
- Location：0,0,0；
- Location in：local；
- Orientation Dependency：Delfa location from coordinate；
- Construction Frame（结构框名称）：._my_steer_two_axle.ground.cfs_steering_whel_center；
- Orientation：0,0,0；
- 单击 OK，完成._my_steer_two_axle.ground.cfs_steering_wheel_mcs 结构框的创建。
- 单击 Build > Part > General Part > New 命令，弹出创建部件对话框如图 15-5 所示；
- General Part 输入 steering_wheel；

- Location Dependency：Delfa location from coordinate；
- Coordinate Reference (参考坐标)：._my_steer_two_axle.ground.cfs_steering_wheel_mcs；
- Location：0,0,0；
- Location in：Local；
- Orientation Dependency：Delfa location from coordinate；
- Construction Frame (参考坐标)：._my_steer_two_axle.ground.cfs_steering_wheel_mcs；
- Orientation：0,0,0；
- Mass：1；
- Ixx：1；
- Iyy：1；
- Izz：1；
- Density：Material；
- Material Type：.materials.steel；
- 单击 OK，完成部件._my_steer_two_axle.ges_steering_wheel 创建。
- 单击 Build > Geometry > Cylinder (圆柱体) > New 命令，弹出圆柱几何体对话框如图 15-9 所示；
- Cylinder Name (连杆名称) 输入几何名称：steering_wheel；
- General Part 输入._my_steer_two_axle.ges_steering_wheel；
- Construction Frame (参考坐标)：._my_steer_two_axle.ground.cfs_steering_whel_center；
- Radius(半径): 200.0；
- Length In Postive Z（Z 轴正方向长度）：5.0；
- Length In Negative Z（Z 轴负方向长度）：5.0；
- Color（圆柱体几何体颜色）：yellow；
- 选择 Calculate Mass Properties of General Part 复选框；
- 单击 OK，完成转向盘._my_steer_two_axle.ges_steering_wheel.gracyl_steering_wheel 几何体的创建。

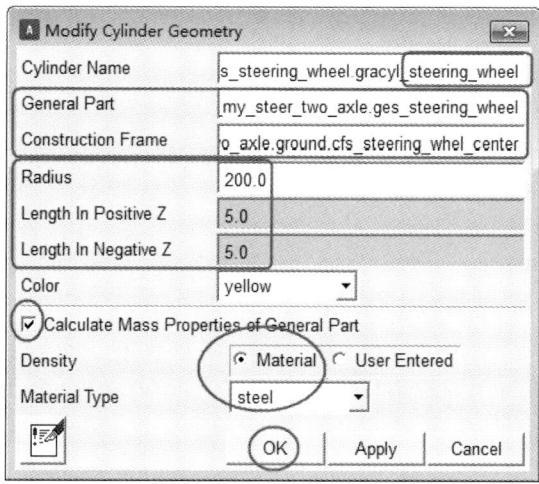

图 15-9　圆柱几何体 steering_wheel

（8）部件 column_housing。
- 单击 Build > Construction Frame > New 命令，弹出创建结构框参考如图 15-8 所示；
- Construction Frame（结构框名称）：column_housing；
- Location Dependency：Centered between coordinates；
- Centered between：Two Coordinates；
- Coordinate Reference #1(参考坐标)：._my_steer_two_axle.ground.hps_intermediate_shaft_rearward；
- Coordinate Reference #2(参考坐标)：._my_steer_two_axle.ground.hps_steering_wheel_center；
- Orientation Dependency：Orient axis along line；
- Coordinate Reference #1(参考坐标)：._my_steer_two_axle.ground.hps_intermediate_shaft_rearward；
- Coordinate Reference #2(参考坐标)：._my_steer_two_axle.ground.hps_steering_wheel_center；
- Axis：Z；
- 单击 OK，完成._my_steer_two_axle.ground.cfs_column_housing 结构框的创建。
- 单击 Build > Part > General Part > New 命令，弹出部件对话框参考如图 15-6 所示；
- General Part 输入 column_housing；
- Location Dependency：Centered between coordinates；
- Centered between：Two Coordinates；
- Coordinate Reference #1(参考坐标)：._my_steer_two_axle.ground.hps_intermediate_shaft_rearward；
- Coordinate Reference #2(参考坐标)：._my_steer_two_axle.ground.hps_steering_wheel_center；
- Orientation Dependency：Orient axis to point；
- Coordinate Reference #1(参考坐标)：._my_steer_two_axle.ground.hps_steering_wheel_center；
- Axis：Z；
- Mass：1；
- Ixx：1；
- Iyy：1；
- Izz：1；
- Density：Material；
- Material Type：.materials.steel；
- 单击 OK，完成部件._my_steer_two_axle.ges_column_housing 创建。
- 单击 Build > Geometry > Cylinder (圆柱体) > New 命令，弹出圆柱体对话框参考如图 15-9 所示；
- Cylinder Name（连杆名称）输入几何名称：column_housing；
- General Part 输入._my_steer_two_axle.ges_column_housing；

- Construction Frame（参考坐标）:._my_steer_two_axle.ground.cfs_column_housing；
- Radius(半径): 25；
- Length In Postive Z（Z轴正方向长度）：50；
- Length In Negative Z（Z轴负方向长度）：50；
- Color（圆柱体几何体颜色）：skyblue；
- 选择 Calculate Mass Properties of General Part 复选框；
- 单击 OK,完成转向盘._my_steer_two_axle.ges_column_housing.gracyl_column_housing 几何体的创建。

（9）部件 steering_column。
- 单击 Build > Part > General Part > New 命令，弹出部件对话框参考如图 15-6 所示；
- General Part 输入 steering_column；
- Location Dependency：Centered between coordinates；
- Centered between：Two Coordinates；
- Coordinate Reference #1(参考坐标)：._my_steer_two_axle.ground.hps_intermediate_shaft_rearward；
- Coordinate Reference #2(参考坐标)：._my_steer_two_axle.ground.hps_steering_wheel_center；
- Orientation Dependency：Orient axis to point；
- Coordinate Reference #1(参考坐标)：._my_steer_two_axle.ground.hps_intermediate_shaft_rearward；
- Axis：Z；
- Mass：1；
- Ixx：1；
- Iyy：1；
- Izz：1；
- Density：Material；
- Material Type：.materials.steel；
- 单击 OK，完成部件._my_steer_two_axle.ges_steering_column 创建。
- 单击 Build > Geometry > Link > New 命令，创建圆柱体参考如图 15-6 所示；
- Link Name (连杆名称) 输入几何名称：steering_column；
- General Part 输入._my_steer_two_axle.ges_steering_column；
- Coordinate Reference #1(参考坐标)：._my_steer_two_axle.ground.hps_intermediate_shaft_rearward；
- Coordinate Reference #2(参考坐标)：._my_steer_two_axle.ground.hps_steering_wheel_center；
- Radius(半径): 15；
- Color（杆件几何体颜色）：red；
- 选择 Calculate Mass Properties of General Part 复选框；
- Density：Material；

- Material Type：steel；
- 单击 OK,完成._my_steer_two_axle.ges_steering_column.gralin_steering_column 几何体的创建。

（10）部件 intermediate_shaft。
- 单击 Build > Part > General Part > New 命令，弹出部件对话框参考如图 15-6 所示；
- General Part 输入 intermediate_shaft；
- Location Dependency：Centered between coordinates；
- Centered between：Two Coordinates；
- Coordinate Reference #1(参考坐标)：._my_steer_two_axle.ground.hps_intermediate_shaft_rearward；
- Coordinate Reference #2(参考坐标)：._my_steer_two_axle.ground.hps_intermediate_shaft_forward；
- Orientation Dependency：Orient axis to point；
- Coordinate Reference #1(参考坐标)：._my_steer_two_axle.ground.hps_intermediate_shaft_rearward；
- Axis：Z；
- Mass：1；
- Ixx：1；
- Iyy：1；
- Izz：1；
- Density：Material；
- Material Type：.materials.steel；
- 单击 OK，完成部件._my_steer_two_axle.ges_intermediate_shaft 创建。
- 单击 Build > Geometry > Link > New 命令，创建圆柱体参考如图 15-6 所示；
- Link Name (连杆名称) 输入几何名称：intermediate_shaft；
- General Part 输入._my_steer_two_axle.ges_intermediate_shaft；
- Coordinate Reference #1(参考坐标)：._my_steer_two_axle.ground.hps_intermediate_shaft_rearward；
- Coordinate Reference #2(参考坐标)：._my_steer_two_axle.ground.hps_intermediate_shaft_forward；
- Radius(半径): 15；
- Color（杆件几何体颜色）：yellow；
- 选择 Calculate Mass Properties of General Part 复选框；
- Density：Material；
- Material Type：steel；
- 单击 OK，完成._my_steer_two_axle.ges_intermediate_shaft.gralin_intermediate_shaft 几何体的创建。

（11）部件 input_shaft。
- 单击 Build > Part > General Part > New 命令，弹出部件对话框参考如图 15-6 所示；

- General Part 输入 input_shaft；
- Location Dependency：Centered between coordinates；
- Centered between：Two Coordinates；
- Coordinate Reference #1(参考坐标)：._my_steer_two_axle.ground.hps_intermediate_shaft_forward；
- Coordinate Reference #2(参考坐标)：._my_steer_two_axle.ground.hps_input_shaft_forward；
- Orientation Dependency：Orient axis to point；
- Coordinate Reference #1(参考坐标)：._my_steer_two_axle.ground.hps_intermediate_shaft_forward；
- Axis：Z；
- Mass：1；
- Ixx：1；
- Iyy：1；
- Izz：1；
- Density：Material；
- Material Type：.materials.steel；
- 单击 OK，完成部件._my_steer_two_axle.ges_input_shaft 创建。
- 单击 Build > Geometry > Link > New 命令，创建圆柱体参考如图 15-6 所示；
- Link Name（连杆名称）输入几何名称：input_shaft；
- General Part 输入._my_steer_two_axle.ges_input_shaft；
- Coordinate Reference #1(参考坐标)：._my_steer_two_axle.ground.hps_intermediate_shaft_forward；
- Coordinate Reference #2(参考坐标)：._my_steer_two_axle.ground.hps_input_shaft_forward；
- Radius(半径): 15；
- Color（杆件几何体颜色）：red；
- 选择 Calculate Mass Properties of General Part 复选框；
- Density：Material；
- Material Type：steel；
- 单击 OK，完成._my_steer_two_axle.ges_input_shaft.gralin_input_shaft 几何体的创建。

（12）部件 ball_screw。
- 单击 Build > Construction Frame > New 命令，弹出创建结构框参考如图 15-8 所示；
- Construction Frame（结构框名称）：ball_screw_rearward；
- Location Dependency：Delta lacation from coordinate；
- Coordinate Reference (参考坐标)：._my_steer_two_axle.ground.hps_input_shaft_forward；
- Orientation Dependency：Delta lacation from coordinate；
- Construction Frame(参考坐标)：._my_steer_two_axle.ground.cfs_input_shaft_forward；
- Orientation：0,0,0；

- 单击 Apply，完成._my_steer_two_axle.ground.cfs_ball_screw_rearward 结构框的创建；
- 单击 Build > Construction Frame > New 命令，弹出创建结构框参考如图 15-8 所示；
- Construction Frame（结构框名称）：input_shaft_forward；
- Location Dependency：Delta lacation from coordinate；
- Coordinate Reference（参考坐标）：._my_steer_two_axle.ground.hps_input_shaft_forward；
- Location：0,0,0；
- Location in: local；
- Orientation Dependency：Oriented in plane；
- Coordinate Reference #1(参考坐标)：._my_steer_two_axle.ground.hps_input_shaft_forward；
- Coordinate Reference #2(参考坐标)：._my_steer_two_axle.ground.hps_intermediate_shaft_forward；
- Coordinate Reference #3(参考坐标)：._my_steer_two_axle.ground.hps_intermediate_shaft_rearward；
- Axes：ZX；
- 单击 Apply，完成._my_steer_two_axle.ground.cfs_input_shaft_forward 结构框的创建；
- 单击 Build > Construction Frame > New 命令，弹出创建结构框参考如图 15-8 所示；
- Construction Frame（结构框名称）：screw_rearward；
- Location Dependency：Delta lacation from coordinate；
- Coordinate Reference（参考坐标）：._my_steer_two_axle.ground.hps_input_shaft_forward；
- Location：0,0,0；
- Location in: local；
- Orientation Dependency：Delta lacation from coordinate；
- Construction Frame(参考坐标)：._my_steer_two_axle.ground.cfs_input_shaft_forward；
- Orientation：0,0,0；
- 单击 OK，完成._my_steer_two_axle.ground.cfs_ball_screw_rearward 结构框的创建。
- 单击 Build > Part > General Part > New 命令，弹出部件对话框参考如图 15-6 所示；
- General Part 输入 ball_screw；
- Location Dependency：Centered between coordinates；
- Centered between：Two Coordinates；
- Coordinate Reference #1(参考坐标)：._my_steer_two_axle.ground.cfs_ball_screw_rearward；
- Coordinate Reference #2(参考坐标)：._my_steer_two_axle.ground.cfs_ball_screw_forward；
- Orientation Dependency：Orient axis to point；
- Coordinate Reference #1(参考坐标)：._my_steer_two_axle.ground.cfs_ball_screw_rearward；
- Axis：Z；

- Mass：1；
- Ixx：1；
- Iyy：1；
- Izz：1；
- Density：Material；
- Material Type：.materials.steel；
- 单击 OK，完成部件._my_steer_two_axle.ges_ball_screw 创建。
- 单击 Build > Geometry > Link > New 命令，创建圆柱体参考如图 15-6 所示；
- Link Name (连杆名称) 输入几何名称：ball_screw；
- General Part 输入._my_steer_two_axle.ges_ball_screw；
- Coordinate Reference #1(参考坐标)：._my_steer_two_axle.ground.cfs_ball_ screw_rearward；
- Coordinate Reference #2(参考坐标)：._my_steer_two_axle.ground.cfs_ball_ screw_forward；
- Radius(半径): 15；
- Color（杆件几何体颜色）：red；
- 选择 Calculate Mass Properties of General Part 复选框；
- Density：Material；
- Material Type：steel；
- 单击 OK，完成._my_steer_two_axle.ges_ball_screw.gralin_ball_screw 几何体的创建。

（13）部件 rack：
- 单击 Build > Part > General Part > New 命令，弹出创建部件对话框如图 15-5 所示；
- General Part 输入 rack；
- Location Dependency：Located on a line；
- Coordinate Reference #1(参考坐标)：._my_steer_two_axle.ground.cfs_ball_ screw_rearward；
- Coordinate Reference #2(参考坐标)：._my_steer_two_axle.ground.cfs_ball_ screw_ forward；
- Relative location(%)：50；
- Orientation Dependency：Orien axis to point；
- Coordinate Reference (参考坐标)：._my_steer_two_axle.ground.cfs_ball_ screw_ rearward；
- Axis：Z；
- Mass：1；
- Ixx：1；
- Iyy：1；
- Izz：1；
- Density：Material；
- Material Type：.materials.steel；
- 单击 OK，完成部件._my_steer_two_axle.ges_rack 创建。

- 单击 Build > Geometry > Link > New 命令，创建圆柱体如图 15-6 所示；
- Link Name (连杆名称）输入几何名称：rack；
- General Part 输入._my_steer_two_axle.ges_rack；
- Coordinate Reference #1(参考坐标）：._my_steer_two_axle.ground.cfs_ball_screw_rearward；
- Coordinate Reference #2(参考坐标）：._my_steer_two_axle.ground.cfs_ball_screw_forward；
- Radius(半径): 18；
- Color（杆件几何体颜色）：white；
- 选择 Calculate Mass Properties of General Part 复选框；
- Density：Material；
- Material Type：steel；
- 单击 OK，完成._my_steer_two_axle.ges_rack.gralin_rack 几何体的创建。

（14）部件 steer_input_arm_fore。
- 单击 Build > Part > General Part > New 命令，弹出部件对话框参考如图 15-6 所示；
- General Part 输入 steer_input_arm_fore；
- Location Dependency：Centered between coordinates；
- Centered between：Two Coordinates；
- Coordinate Reference #1(参考坐标）：._my_steer_two_axle.ground.hps_steering_arm_attach；
- Coordinate Reference #2(参考坐标）：._my_steer_two_axle.ground.hps_steer_arm；
- Orientation Dependency：User-entered values；
- Orient using：Euler Angles；
- Euler Angles：0,0,0；
- Mass：1；
- Ixx：1；
- Iyy：1；
- Izz：1；
- Density：Material；
- Material Type：.materials.steel；
- 单击 OK，完成部件._my_steer_two_axle.ges_steer_input_arm_fore 创建。
- 单击 Build > Geometry > Link > New 命令，创建圆柱体参考如图 15-6 所示；
- Link Name (连杆名称）输入几何名称：steer_input_arm；
- General Part 输入._my_steer_two_axle.ges_steer_input_arm_fore；
- Coordinate Reference #1(参考坐标）：._my_steer_two_axle.ground.hps_steering_arm_attach；
- Coordinate Reference #2(参考坐标）：._my_steer_two_axle.ground.hps_steer_arm；
- Radius(半径): 10；

- Color（杆件几何体颜色）：red；
- 选择 Calculate Mass Properties of General Part 复选框；
- Density：Material；
- Material Type：steel；
- 单击 OK，完成._my_steer_two_axle.ges_steer_input_arm_fore.gralin_steer_input_arm 几何体的创建。

（15）部件 steer_link_fore。
- 单击 Build > Part > General Part > New 命令，弹出部件对话框参考如图 15-6 所示；
- General Part 输入 steer_link_fore；
- Location Dependency：Centered between coordinates；
- Centered between：Two Coordinates；
- Coordinate Reference #1(参考坐标)：._my_steer_two_axle.ground.hps_steer_link_fore_front；
- Coordinate Reference #2(参考坐标)：._my_steer_two_axle.ground.hps_steer_arm；
- Orientation Dependency：User-entered values；
- Orient using：Euler Angles；
- Euler Angles：0,0,0；
- Mass：1；
- Ixx：1；
- Iyy：1；
- Izz：1；
- Density：Material；
- Material Type：.materials.steel；
- 单击 OK，完成部件._my_steer_two_axle.ges_steer_link_fore 创建。
- 单击 Build > Geometry > Link > New 命令，创建圆柱体参考如图 15-6 所示；
- Link Name (连杆名称) 输入几何名称：steer_link_fore；
- General Part 输入._my_steer_two_axle.ges_steer_link_fore；
- Coordinate Reference #1(参考坐标)：._my_steer_two_axle.ground.hps_steer_arm；
- Coordinate Reference #2(参考坐标)：._my_steer_two_axle.ground.hps_steer_link_fore_front；
- Radius(半径): 15；
- Color（杆件几何体颜色）：yellow；
- 选择 Calculate Mass Properties of General Part 复选框；
- Density：Material；
- Material Type：steel；
- 单击 OK，完成._my_steer_two_axle.ges_steer_link_fore.gralin_steer_link_fore 几何体的创建。

（16）部件 pitman_arm。

- 单击 Build > Part > General Part > New 命令，弹出部件对话框参考如图 15-6 所示；
- General Part 输入 pitman_arm；
- Location Dependency：Centered between coordinates；
- Centered between：Two Coordinates；
- Coordinate Reference #1(参考坐标)：._my_steer_two_axle.ground.hps_pitman_axis；
- Coordinate Reference #2(参考坐标)：._my_steer_two_axle.ground.hps_steer_link；
- Orientation Dependency：User-entered values；
- Orient using：Euler Angles；
- Euler Angles：0,0,0；
- Mass：1；
- Ixx：1；
- Iyy：1；
- Izz：1；
- Density：Material；
- Material Type：.materials.steel；
- 单击 OK，完成部件._my_steer_two_axle.ges_pitman_arm 创建。
- 单击 Build > Geometry > Link > New 命令，创建圆柱体参考如图 15-6 所示；
- Link Name (连杆名称) 输入几何名称：pitman；
- General Part 输入._my_steer_two_axle.ges_pitman_arm；
- Coordinate Reference #1(参考坐标)：._my_steer_two_axle.ground.hps_pitman_axis；
- Coordinate Reference #2(参考坐标)：._my_steer_two_axle.ground.hps_steer_link；
- Radius(半径):20；
- Color（杆件几何体颜色）：yellow；
- 选择 Calculate Mass Properties of General Part 复选框；
- Density：Material；
- Material Type：steel；
- 单击 OK,完成._my_steer_two_axle.ges_pitman_arm.gralin_pitman 几何体的创建。

（17）安装部件 pitman_mount。

- 单击 Build > Part > Mount > New 命令，弹出创建部件对话框如图 15-10 所示；

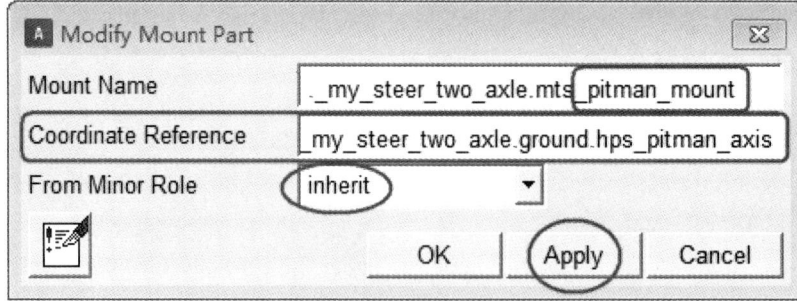

图 15-10　安装部件

- Mount name（安装件名称）：pitman_mount；
- Coordinate Reference （参考坐标）：._my_steer_two_axle.ground.hps_pitman_axis；
- 安装件此特征选择 inherit（继承特性）；
- 单击 OK，完成._my_steer_two_axle.mts_pitman_mount 安装部件的创建。

（18）安装部件 strarm_to_spindle_fore。
- 单击 Build > Part > Mount > New 命令，弹出创建部件对话框如图 15-10 所示；
- Mount name（安装件名称）：strarm_to_spindle_fore；
- Coordinate Reference （参考坐标）：._my_steer_two_axle.ground.hps_steering_arm_attach；
- 安装件此特征选择 inherit（继承特性）；
- 单击 OK，完成._my_steer_two_axle.mts_strarm_to_spindle_fore 安装部件的创建。

（19）安装部件 column_to_body。
- 单击 Build > Part > Mount > New 命令，弹出创建部件对话框如图 15-10 所示；
- Mount name（安装件名称）：column_to_body；
- Coordinate Reference （参考坐标）：._my_steer_two_axle.ground.cfs_column_housing；
- 安装件此特征选择 inherit；
- 单击 OK，完成._my_steer_two_axle.mts_steering_column_to_body 安装部件的创建。

（20）安装部件 pitman_arm_aft_to_body。
- 单击 Build > Part > Mount > New 命令，弹出创建部件对话框如图 15-10 所示；
- Mount name（安装件名称）：pitman_arm_aft_to_body；
- Coordinate Reference （参考坐标）：._my_steer_two_axle.ground.hps_pitman_arm_aft_upper；
- 安装件此特征选择 inherit；
- 单击 OK，完成._my_steer_two_axle.mts_pitman_arm_aft_to_body 安装部件的创建。

（21）安装部件 strarm_to_spindle_aft。
- 单击 Build > Part > Mount > New 命令，弹出创建部件对话框如图 15-10 所示；
- Mount name（安装件名称）：strarm_to_spindle_aft；
- Coordinate Reference （参考坐标）：._my_steer_two_axle.ground.hps_steering_arm_attach_aft；
- 安装件此特征选择 inherit；
- 单击 OK，完成._my_steer_two_axle.mts_strarm_to_spindle_aft 安装部件的创建。

（22）安装部件 pitman_arm_middle_to_body。
- 单击 Build > Part > Mount > New 命令，弹出创建部件对话框如图 15-10 所示；
- Mount name（安装件名称）：pitman_arm_middle_to_body；
- Coordinate Reference （参考坐标）：._my_steer_two_axle.ground.hps_pitman_arm_middle_upper；
- 安装件此特征选择 inherit；
- 单击 OK，完成._my_steer_two_axle.mts_pitman_arm_middle_to_body 安装部件的创建。

15.2 双轴转向系统约束

（1）部件 pitman_arm 与安装件 pitman_mount 之间 revolute 约束。
- 单击 Build > Construction Frame > New 命令，弹出创建结构框参考如图 15-8 所示；
- Construction Frame（结构框名称）：pitman_axis；
- Location Dependency：Delta lacation from coordinate；
- Coordinate Reference（参考坐标）：._my_steer_two_axle.ground.hps_pitman_axis；
- Location：0,0,0；
- Location in: local；
- Orientation Dependency：User-entered values；
- Orient using：Euler Angles；
- Euler Angles：-90，0，0；
- 单击 OK，完成._my_steer_two_axle.ground.cfs_pitman_axis 结构框的创建。
- 单击 Build > Attachments > Joint > New 命令，弹出创建约束件对话框如图 15-11 所示；

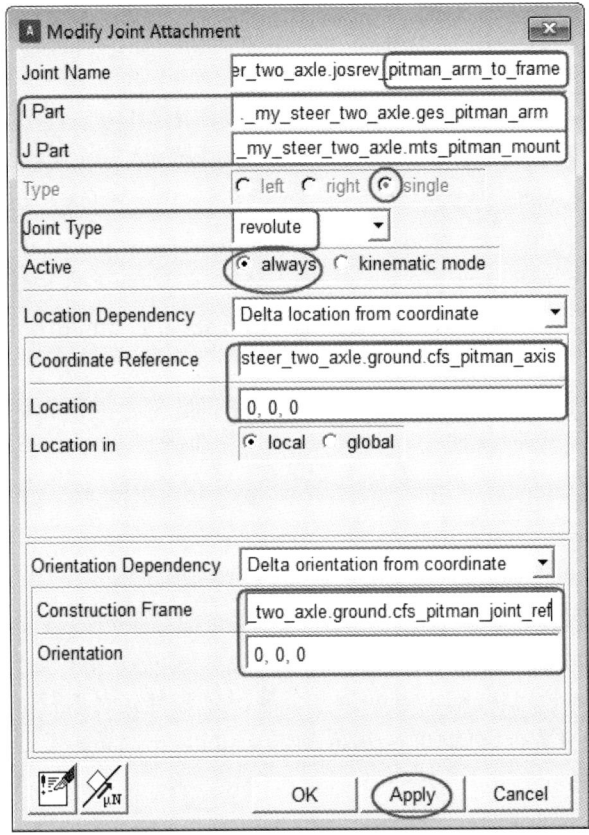

图 15-11　约束副——revolute

- Joint Name（约束副名称）：pitman_arm_to_frame；
- I Part：._my_steer_two_axle.ges_pitman_arm；

- J Part：._my_steer_two_axle.mts_pitman_mount；
- Joint Type（约束副类型）：revolute，即转动副，约束 5 个自由度；
- Active（激活）：always；
- Location Dependency：Delta location from coordinate；
- Coordinate Reference（参考坐标）：._my_steer_two_axle.ground.cfs_pitman_axis；
- Location：0,0,0；
- Location in：local；
- Orientation Dependency：Delta location from coordinate；
- Construction Frame（参考坐标）：._my_steer_two_axle.ground.cfs_pitman_joint_ref；
- Orientation：0,0,0；
- 单击 Apply，完成 ._my_steer_two_axle.josrev_pitman_arm_to_frame 转动副的创建。

（2）部件 steer_input_arm_fore 与 steer_link_fore 之间 convel 约束。
- Joint Name（约束副名称）：input_steering_arm_to_axle；
- I Part：._my_steer_two_axle.ges_steer_input_arm_fore；
- J Part：._my_steer_two_axle.ges_steer_link_fore；
- Joint Type（约束副类型）：convel；
- Active（激活）：always；
- Location Dependency：Delta location from coordinate；
- Coordinate Reference（参考坐标）：._my_steer_two_axle.ground.hps_steer_arm；
- Location：0,0,0；
- Location in：local；
- I-Part Axis：._my_steer_two_axle.ground.hps_steering_arm_attach；
- J-Part Axis：._my_steer_two_axle.ground.hps_steer_link_fore_front；
- 单击 Apply，完成 ._my_steer_two_axle.joscon_input_steering_arm_to_axle 恒速副的创建。

（3）部件 pitman_arm 与 steer_link 之间 spherical 约束。
- Joint Name（约束副名称）：pitman_to_draglink；
- I Part：._my_steer_two_axle.ges_pitman_arm；
- J Part：._my_steer_two_axle.ges_steer_link；
- Joint Type（约束副类型）：spherical；
- Active（激活）：always；
- Location Dependency：Delta location from coordinate；
- Coordinate Reference（参考坐标）：._my_steer_two_axle.ground.hps_steer_link；
- Location：0,0,0；
- Location in：local；
- 单击 Apply，完成 ._my_steer_two_axle.jossph_pitman_to_draglink 球副的创建。

（4）部件 steer_input_arm_fore 与 strarm_to_spindle_fore 之间 fixed 约束：
- Joint Name（约束副名称）：strarm_to_spindle；
- I Part：._my_steer_two_axle.ges_steer_input_arm_fore；
- J Part：._my_steer_two_axle.mts_strarm_to_spindle_fore；

- Joint Type（约束副类型）：fixed；
- Active（激活）：always；
- Location Dependency：Delta location from coordinate；
- Coordinate Reference（参考坐标）：._my_steer_two_axle.ground.hps_steer_link；
- Location：0,0,0；
- Location in：local；
- 单击 Apply，完成._my_steer_two_axle.josfix_strarm_to_spindle 固定副的创建。

（5）部件 rack 与 pitman_mount 之间 translational 约束。
- Joint Name（约束副名称）：rack_steering_gear；
- I Part：._my_steer_two_axle.ges_rack；
- J Part：._my_steer_two_axle.mts_pitman_mount；
- Joint Type（约束副类型）：translational；
- Active（激活）：always；
- Location Dependency：Delta location from coordinate；
- Coordinate Reference（参考坐标）：._my_steer_two_axle.ground.cfs_ball_screw_forward；
- Location：0,0,0；
- Location in：local；
- Orientation Dependency：Delta location from coordinate；
- Construction Frame（参考坐标）：._my_steer_two_axle.ground.cfs_ball_screw_forward；
- Orientation：0,0,0；
- 单击 Apply，完成._my_steer_two_axle.jostra_rack_steering_gear 移动副的创建。

（6）部件 ball_screw 与 pitman_mount 之间 revolute 约束。
- Joint Name（约束副名称）：ball_screw_steering_gear；
- I Part：._my_steer_two_axle.ges_ball_screw；
- J Part：._my_steer_two_axle.mts_pitman_mount；
- Joint Type（约束副类型）：revolute；
- Active（激活）：always；
- Location Dependency：Delta location from coordinate；
- Coordinate Reference（参考坐标）：._my_steer_two_axle.ground.cfs_ball_screw_forward；
- Location：0,0,0；
- Location in：local；
- Orientation Dependency：Delta location from coordinate；
- Construction Frame（参考坐标）：._my_steer_two_axle.ground.cfs_ball_screw_forward；
- Orientation：0,0,0；
- 单击 Apply，完成._my_steer_two_axle.josrev_ball_screw_steering_gear 转动副的创建。

（7）部件 input_shaft 与 pitman_mount 之间 revolute 约束。
- Joint Name（约束副名称）：input_shaft_steering_gear；
- I Part：._my_steer_two_axle.ges_input_shaft；
- J Part：._my_steer_two_axle.mts_pitman_mount；

- Joint Type（约束副类型）：revolute；
- Active（激活）：always；
- Location Dependency：Delta location from coordinate；
- Coordinate Reference（参考坐标）：._my_steer_two_axle.ground.hps_input_shaft_forward；
- Location：0,0,0；
- Location in：local；
- Orientation Dependency：Orient to zpoint-xpoint；
- Coordinate Reference #1(参考坐标)：._my_steer_two_axle.ground.hps_intermediate_shaft_forward；
- Coordinate Reference #2(参考坐标)：._my_steer_two_axle.ground.hps_intermediate_shaft_rearward；
- Axes：ZX；
- 单击 Apply，完成._my_steer_two_axle.josrev_input_shaft_steering_gear 转动副的创建。

（8）部件 intermediate_shaft 与 input_shaft 之间 hooke 约束。
- Joint Name（约束副名称）：intermediate_shaftinput；
- I Part：._my_steer_two_axle.ges_intermediate_shaft；
- J Part：._my_steer_two_axle.ges_input_shaft；
- Joint Type（约束副类型）：hooke；
- Active（激活）：always；
- Location Dependency：Delta location from coordinate；
- Coordinate Reference（参考坐标）：._my_steer_two_axle.ground.hps_intermediate_shaft_forward；
- Location：0,0,0；
- Location in：local；
- I-Part Axis：._my_steer_two_axle.ground.hps_intermediate_shaft_rearward；
- J-Part Axis：._my_steer_two_axle.ground.hps_input_shaft_forward；
- 单击 Apply，完成._my_steer_two_axle.joshoo_intermediate_shaftinput 胡克副的创建。

（9）部件 steering_column 与 intermediate_shaft 之间 hooke 约束。
- Joint Name（约束副名称）：column_intermediate；
- I Part：._my_steer_two_axle.ges_steering_column；
- J Part：._my_steer_two_axle.ges_intermediate_shaft；
- Joint Type（约束副类型）：hooke；
- Active（激活）：always；
- Location Dependency：Delta location from coordinate；
- Coordinate Reference（参考坐标）：._my_steer_two_axle.ground.hps_intermediate_shaft_rearward；
- Location：0，0，0；
- Location in：local；
- I-Part Axis：._my_steer_two_axle.ground.hps_steering_wheel_center；

- J-Part Axis：._my_steer_two_axle.ground.hps_intermediate_shaft_forward；
- 单击 Apply，完成._my_steer_two_axle.joshoo_column_intermediate 胡克副的创建。

（10）部件 steering_wheel 与 column_housing 之间 revolute 约束。
- Joint Name（约束副名称）：steering_wheel；
- I Part：._my_steer_two_axle.ges_steering_wheel；
- J Part：._my_steer_two_axle.ges_column_housing；
- Joint Type（约束副类型）：revolute；
- Active（激活）：always；
- Location Dependency：Delta location from coordinate；
- Coordinate Reference（参考坐标）：._my_steer_two_axle.ground.hps_steering_wheel_center；
- Location：0,0,0；
- Location in：local；
- Orientation Dependency：Delta location from coordinate；
- Construction Frame(参考坐标)：._my_steer_two_axle.ground.cfs_steering_whel_center；
- Orientation：0,0,0；
- 单击 Apply，完成._my_steer_two_axle.josrev_steering_wheel 转动副的创建。

（11）部件 column_housing 与 steering_column_to_body 之间 fixed 约束。
- Joint Name（约束副名称）：column_housing_to_housing_mount；
- I Part：._my_steer_two_axle.ges_column_housing；
- J Part：._my_steer_two_axle.mts_steering_column_to_body；
- Joint Type（约束副类型）：fixed；
- Active（激活）：always；
- Location Dependency：Delta location from coordinate；
- Coordinate Reference（参考坐标）：._my_steer_two_axle.ground.cfs_column_housing；
- Location：0,0,0；
- Location in：local；
- 单击 Apply，完成._my_steer_two_axle.josfix_column_housing_to_housing_mount 固定副的创建。

（12）部件 steering_column 与 column_housing 之间 cylindrical 约束。
- Joint Name（约束副名称）：steering_column；
- I Part：._my_steer_two_axle.ges_steering_column；
- J Part：._my_steer_two_axle.ges_column_housing；
- Joint Type（约束副类型）：cylindrical；
- Active（激活）：always；
- Location Dependency：Delta location from coordinate；
- Coordinate Reference（参考坐标）：._my_steer_two_axle.ground.cfs_column_housing；
- Location：0,0,0；
- Location in：local；

- Orientation Dependency：Orient axis to point；
- Coordinate Reference #1（参考坐标）：._my_steer_two_axle.ground.hps_intermediate_shaft_rearward；
- Axis：Z；
- 单击 Apply，完成._my_steer_two_axle.joscyl_steering_column 转动副的创建。

（13）部件 pitman_arm_middle 与 steer_link_middle 之间 spherical 约束。
- Joint Name（约束副名称）：pitman_middle_to_steer_link_middle；
- I Part：._my_steer_two_axle.ges_pitman_arm_middle；
- J Part：._my_steer_two_axle.ges_steer_link_middle；
- Joint Type（约束副类型）：spherical；
- Active（激活）：always；
- Location Dependency：Delta location from coordinate；
- Coordinate Reference（参考坐标）：._my_steer_two_axle.ground.hps_steer_link_middle_front；
- Location：0,0,0；
- Location in：local；
- 单击 Apply，完成._my_steer_two_axle.jossph_pitman_middle_to_steer_link_middle 球副的创建。

（14）部件 pitman_arm_aft 与 pitman_arm_aft_to_body 之间 revolute 约束。
- Joint Name（约束副名称）：pitman_arm_aft_to_body；
- I Part：._my_steer_two_axle.ges_pitman_arm_aft；
- J Part：._my_steer_two_axle.mts_pitman_arm_aft_to_body；
- Joint Type（约束副类型）：revolute；
- Active（激活）：always；
- Location Dependency：Delta location from coordinate；
- Coordinate Reference（参考坐标）：._my_steer_two_axle.ground.hps_pitman_arm_aft_upper；
- Location：0,0,0；
- Location in：local；
- Orientation Dependency：User-entered values；
- Orient using：Euler Angles；
- Euler Angles：0，90，0；
- 单击 Apply，完成._my_steer_two_axle.josrev_pitman_arm_aft_to_body 球副的创建。

（15）部件 steer_link_middle 与 pitman_arm_aft 之间 convel 约束。
- Joint Name（约束副名称）：steer_link_aft_to_pitman_arm_aft；
- I Part：._my_steer_two_axle.ges_steer_link_middle；
- J Part：._my_steer_two_axle.ges_pitman_arm_aft；
- Joint Type（约束副类型）：convel；
- Active（激活）：always；

- Location Dependency：Delta location from coordinate；
- Coordinate Reference（参考坐标）：._my_steer_two_axle.ground.hps_steer_link_middle_rear；
- Location：0,0,0；
- Location in：local；
- I-Part Axis：._my_steer_two_axle.ground.hps_pitman_arm_aft_upper；
- J-Part Axis：._my_steer_two_axle.ground.hps_steer_link_middle_front；
- 单击 Apply，完成._my_steer_two_axle.joscon_steer_link_aft_to_pitman_arm_aft 恒速副的创建。

（16）部件 pitman_arm_aft 与 steer_link_aft 之间 spherical 约束。
- Joint Name（约束副名称）：pitman_arm_aft_to_steer_link_aft；
- I Part：._my_steer_two_axle.ges_pitman_arm_aft；
- J Part：._my_steer_two_axle.ges_steer_link_aft；
- Joint Type（约束副类型）：spherical；
- Active（激活）：always；
- Location Dependency：Delta location from coordinate；
- Coordinate Reference（参考坐标）：._my_steer_two_axle.ground.hps_steer_link_aft_front；
- Location：0,0,0；
- Location in：local；
- 单击 Apply，完成._my_steer_two_axle.jossph_pitman_arm_aft_to_steer_link_aft 球副的创建。

（17）部件 steer_link_aft 与 steer_input_arm_aft 之间 convel 约束。
- Joint Name（约束副名称）：steering_arm_aft_to_axle；
- I Part：._my_steer_two_axle.ges_steer_link_aft；
- J Part：._my_steer_two_axle.ges_steer_input_arm_aft；
- Joint Type（约束副类型）：convel；
- Active（激活）：always；
- Location Dependency：Delta location from coordinate；
- Coordinate Reference(参考坐标)：._my_steer_two_axle.ground.hps_steer_link_aft_rear；
- Location：0,0,0；
- Location in：local；
- I-Part Axis：._my_steer_two_axle.ground.hps_steering_arm_attach_aft；
- J-Part Axis：._my_steer_two_axle.ground.hps_steer_link_aft_front；
- 单击 Apply，完成._my_steer_two_axle.joscon_steering_arm_aft_to_axle 恒速副的创建。

（18）部件 steer_input_arm_aft 与 strarm_to_spindle_aft 之间 fixed 约束。
- Joint Name（约束副名称）：strarm_to_spindle_aft；
- I Part：._my_steer_two_axle.ges_steer_input_arm_aft；
- J Part：._my_steer_two_axle.mts_strarm_to_spindle_aft；

- Joint Type（约束副类型）：fixed；
- Active（激活）：always；
- Location Dependency：Delta location from coordinate；
- Coordinate Reference（参考坐标）：._my_steer_two_axle.ground.hps_steering_arm_attach_aft；
- Location：0,0,0；
- Location in：local；
- 单击 Apply，完成._my_steer_two_axle.josfix_strarm_to_spindle_aft 固定副的创建。

（19）部件 steer_link 与 pitman_arm_middle 之间 convel 约束：
- Joint Name（约束副名称）：steering_link_to_pitman_arm_middle；
- I Part：._my_steer_two_axle.ges_steer_link；
- J Part：._my_steer_two_axle.ges_pitman_arm_middle；
- Joint Type（约束副类型）：convel；
- Active（激活）：always；
- Location Dependency：Delta location from coordinate；
- Coordinate Reference（参考坐标）：._my_steer_two_axle.ground.hps_steer_link_rear；
- Location：0,0,0；
- Location in：local；
- I-Part Axis：._my_steer_two_axle.ground.hps_pitman_arm_middle_upper；
- J-Part Axis：._my_steer_two_axle.ground.hps_steer_link；
- 单击 Apply，完成._my_steer_two_axle.joscon_steering_link_to_pitman_arm_middle 恒速副的创建；

（20）部件 steer_link_fore 与 pitman_arm_middle 之间 spherical 约束。
- Joint Name（约束副名称）：pitman_arm_middle_to_steer_link_fore；
- I Part：._my_steer_two_axle.ges_steer_link_fore；
- J Part：._my_steer_two_axle.ges_pitman_arm_middle；
- Joint Type（约束副类型）：spherical；
- Active（激活）：always；
- Location Dependency：Delta location from coordinate；
- Coordinate Reference（参考坐标）：._my_steer_two_axle.ground.hps_steer_link_fore_front；
- Location：0,0,0；
- Location in：local；
- 单击 Apply，完成._my_steer_two_axle.jossph_pitman_arm_middle_to_steer_link_fore 球副的创建；

（21）部件 pitman_arm_middle 与 pitman_arm_middle_to_body 之间 revolute 约束。
- Joint Name（约束副名称）：pitman_arm_middle_to_body；
- I Part：._my_steer_two_axle.ges_pitman_arm_middle；
- J Part：._my_steer_two_axle.mts_pitman_arm_middle_to_body；

- Joint Type（约束副类型）：revolute；
- Active（激活）：always；
- Location Dependency：Delta location from coordinate；
- Coordinate Reference（参考坐标）：._my_steer_two_axle.ground.hps_pitman_arm_middle_upper；
- Location：0,0,0；
- Location in：local；
- Orientation Dependency：User-entered values；
- Orient using：Euler Angles；
- Euler Angles：0，90，0；
- 单击 OK，完成._my_steer_two_axle.josrev_pitman_arm_middle_to_body 球副的创建。

15.3 减速齿轮

- 单击 Build > Gear > Reduction Gear > New 命令，弹出创建齿轮对话框如图 15-12 所示，减速齿轮本质上是一对耦合副，需要指定输入输出约束及传动比；

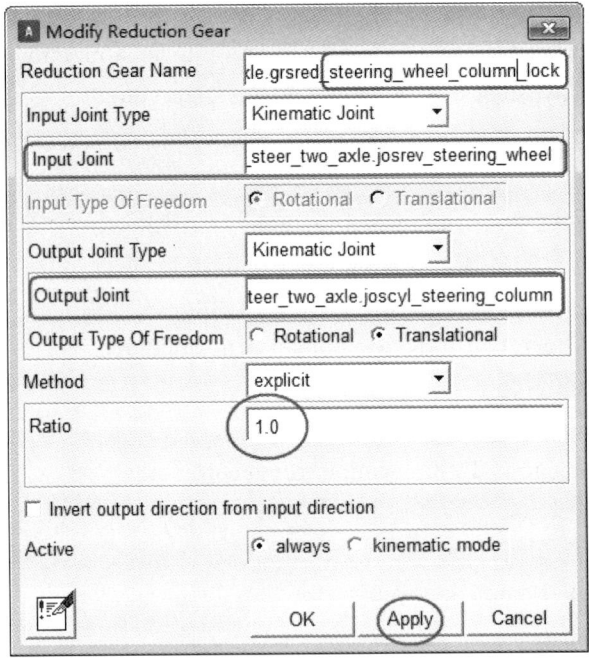

图 15-12 减速齿轮

- Reduction Gear Name(减速器齿轮名称)：steering_wheel_column_lock；
- Input Joint (输入约束名称)：._my_steer_two_axle.josrev_steering_wheel；
- Output Joint (输出约束名称)：._my_steer_two_axle.joscyl_steering_column；
- Reduction Ratio(减速比)：1.0；

- Active(激活)：always；
- 单击 Apply，完成._my_steer_two_axle.grsred_steering_wheel_column_lock 减速齿轮的创建；
- Reduction Gear Name(减速器齿轮名称)：ball_screw_rack；
- Input Joint (输入约束名称)：._my_steer_two_axle.josrev_ball_screw_steering_gear；
- Output Joint (输出约束名称)：._my_steer_two_axle.jostra_rack_steering_gear；
- Reduction Ratio(减速比)：18；
- Active(激活)：always；
- 单击 Apply，完成._my_steer_two_axle.grsred_ball_screw_rack 减速齿轮的创建；
- Reduction Gear Name(减速器齿轮名称)：pitman_arm_rack；
- Input Joint (输入约束名称)：._my_steer_two_axle.josrev_pitman_arm_to_frame；
- Output Joint (输出约束名称)：._my_steer_two_axle.jostra_rack_steering_gear；
- Reduction Ratio(减速比)：1；
- Active(激活)：always；
- 单击 Apply，完成._my_steer_two_axle.grsred_pitman_arm_rack 减速齿轮的创建；
- Reduction Gear Name(减速器齿轮名称)：ball_screw_input_shaft_lock；
- Input Joint (输入约束名称)：._my_steer_two_axle.josrev_input_shaft_steering_gear；
- Output Joint (输出约束名称)：._my_steer_two_axle.josrev_ball_screw_steering_gear；
- Reduction Ratio(减速比)：1；
- Active(激活)：always；
- 单击 OK，完成._my_steer_two_axle.grsred_ball_screw_input_shaft_lock 减速齿轮的创建。

15.4 双轴转向变量参数

- 单击 Build > Parameter Variable > New 命令，弹出参数变量对话框如图 15-13 所示；
- Parameter Variable Name：max_rack_displacement；
- Real Value（实数值）：100.0；
- Units：length；
- Hide from standard user（是否从标准界面隐藏）：no；
- 单击 Apply，完成变量._my_steer_two_axle.pvs_max_rack_displacement 的创建；
- Parameter Variable Name：kinematic_flag；
- Integer Value：0；
- Units：length；
- Hide from standard user（是否从标准界面隐藏）：yes；
- 单击 Apply，完成变量._my_steer_two_axle.phs_kinematic_flag 的创建；
- Parameter Variable Name：max_rack_force；
- Real Value（实数值）：500；

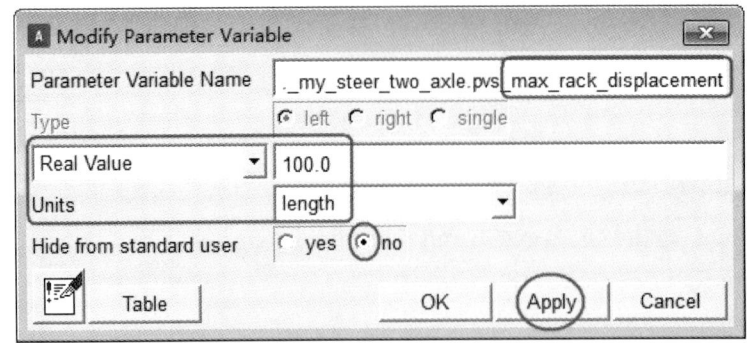

图 15-13 参数变量

- Units：force；
- Hide from standard user（是否从标准界面隐藏）：no；
- 单击 Apply，完成变量._my_steer_two_axle.pvs_max_rack_force 的创建；
- Parameter Variable Name：max_steering_angle；
- Real Valuc（实数值）：720；
- Units：angle；
- Hide from standard user（是否从标准界面隐藏）：no；
- 单击 Apply，完成变量._my_steer_two_axle.pvs_max_steering_angle 的创建；
- Parameter Variable Name：max_steering_torque；
- Real Value（实数值）：720；
- Units：torque；
- Hide from standard user（是否从标准界面隐藏）：no；
- 单击 Apply，完成变量._my_steer_two_axle.pvs_max_steering_torque 的创建；
- Parameter Variable Name：steering_assist_active；
- Integer Value（实数值）：1；
- Units：torque；
- Hide from standard user（是否从标准界面隐藏）：yes；
- 单击 OK，完成变量._my_steer_two_axle.phs_steering_assist_active 的创建。

15.5 双轴转向通信器

- 单击 Build > Communicator > Output >New 命令，弹出输出通信器对话框如图 15-14 所示；
  - Output Communicator Name（输出通信器名称）：steering_wheel_joint；
  - Matching Name(s)：steering_wheel_joint；
  - Type：single；
  - Entity：joint for motion；
  - To Minor Role：inherit；

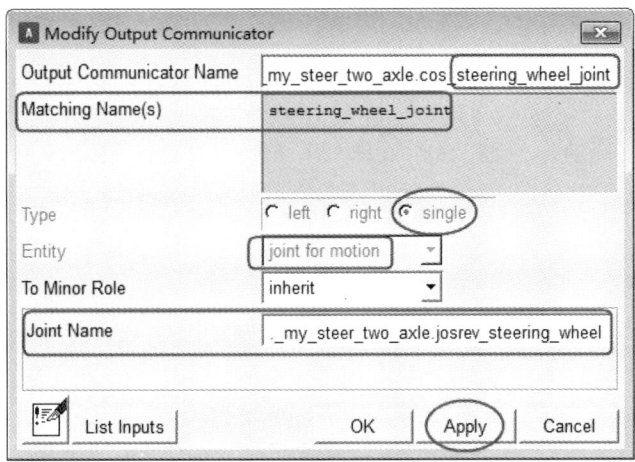

图 15-14　输出通信器

- Joint Name：._my_steer_two_axle.josrev_steering_wheel；
- 单击 Apply，完成通信器._my_steer_two_axle.cos_steering_wheel_joint 的创建；
- Output Communicator Name（输出通信器名称）：max_rack_displacement；
- Matching Name(s)：max_rack_displacement；
- Type：single；
- Entity：parameter real；
- To Minor Role：inherit；
- Parameter Variable Name：._my_steer_two_axle.pvs_max_rack_displacement；
- 单击 Apply，完成通信器._my_steer_two_axle.cos_max_rack_displacement 的创建；
- Output Communicator Name（输出通信器名称）：max_rack_force；
- Matching Name(s)：max_rack_force；
- Type：single；
- Entity：parameter real；
- To Minor Role：inherit；
- Parameter Variable Name：._my_steer_two_axle.pvs_max_rack_force；
- 单击 Apply，完成通信器._my_steer_two_axle.cos_max_rack_force 的创建；
- Output Communicator Name（输出通信器名称）：max_steering_angle；
- Matching Name(s)：max_steering_angle；
- Type：single；
- Entity：parameter real；
- To Minor Role：inherit；
- Parameter Variable Name：._my_steer_two_axle.pvs_max_steering_angle；
- 单击 Apply，完成通信器._my_steer_two_axle.cos_max_steering_angle 的创建；
- Output Communicator Name（输出通信器名称）：max_steering_torque；
- Matching Name(s)：max_steering_torque；
- Type：single；

- Entity：parameter real；
- To Minor Role：inherit；
- Parameter Variable Name：._my_steer_two_axle.pvs_max_steering_torque；
- 单击 Apply，完成通信器._my_steer_two_axle.cos_max_steering_torque 的创建；
- Output Communicator Name（输出通信器名称）：steering_rack_joint；
- Matching Name(s)：steering_rack_joint；
- Type：single；
- Entity：joint for motion；
- To Minor Role：inherit；
- Joint Name：._my_steer_two_axle.jostra_rack_steering_gear；
- 单击 OK，完成通信器._my_steer_two_axle.cos_steering_rack_joint 的创建。
- 单击 File > Save As 命令，弹出保存模板对话框如图 15-15 所示；

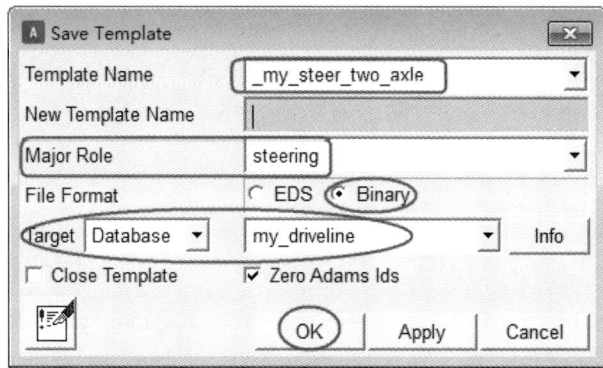

图 15-15 双轴转向模型保存

- Major Role(主特征)：steering；
- File Format：Binary；
- Target：Database，my_driveline；
- 单击 OK，完成双轴转向模型模板._my_steer_two_axle 的保存。
- 按 F9，把专家模板转换到标准模式，单击 File > New > Suspension 命令，弹出子系统对话框如图 15-16 所示；

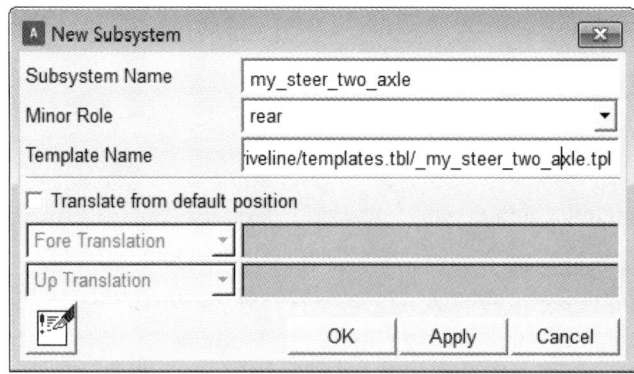

图 15-16 双轴转向子系统创建

- Subsystem Name(系统名称)：my_steer_two_axle；
- Minor Role（副特征）：rear（指悬架为后悬架）；
- Template Name（模板路径）：mdids://my_driveline/templates.tbl/_my_steer_two_axle.tpl；
- 单击 OK，完成推杆式悬架子系统 my_steer_two_axle 的创建。

15.6 TASA 转向仿真

（1）双轴转向子系统。
- 按 F9，把专家模板转换到标准模式，单击 File > New > Suspension 命令，弹出子系统对话框如图 15-17 所示；
- Subsystem Name(系统名称)：my_steer_two_axle；
- Minor Role（副特征）:rear（指悬架为后悬架），此处副特征必须为 rear，方可与双轴转向桥进行匹配；
- Template Name（模板路径）：mdids://my_driveline/templates.tbl/_my_steer_two_axle.tpl；
- 单击 OK，完成双轴转向子系统 my_steer_two_axle 的创建。

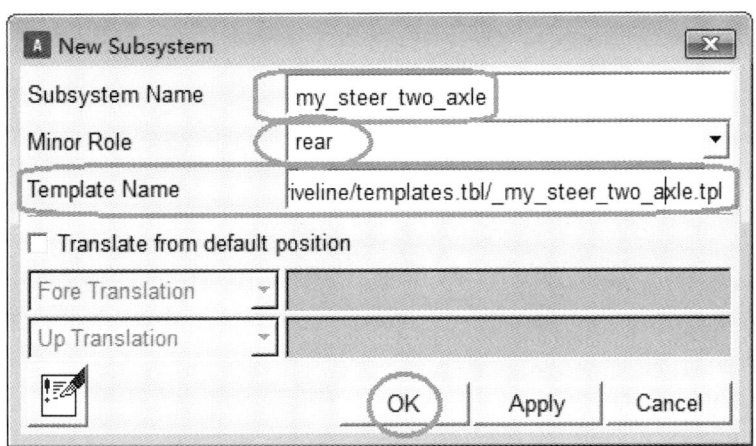

图 15-17 双轴转向子系统创建对话框

（2）Tasa 试验台。
- 单击 File > Open > Assembly 命令；
- Assembly Name（系统名称）：mdids://atruck_shared/assemblies.tbl/tasa_truck_leaf_tandem_susp.asy；
- 单击 OK，打开公版数据库中双轴试验台如图 15-18 所示。
- 单击 File > Manage Assembly > Replace Subsystem 命令；
- Subsystem(s) to remove：msc_truck_twin_axle_steering
- Subsystem(s) to add：mdids://my_driveline/subsystems.tbl/my_steer_two_axle.sub；

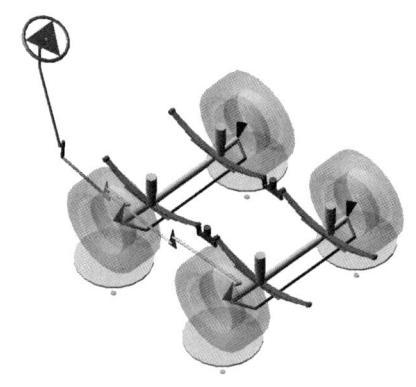

图 15-18　TASA 试验台（附带左舵转向系统）

- 单击 OK，完成转向系统的替换，如图 15-19 所示。

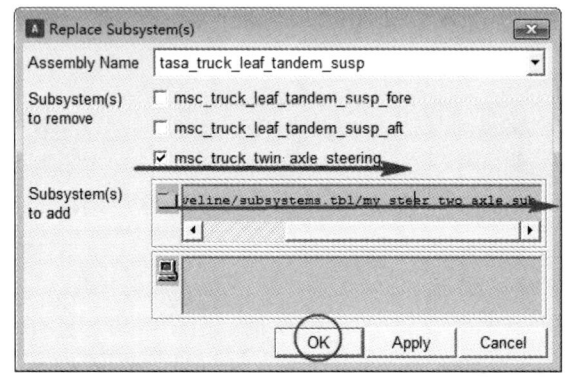

图 15-19　替换 TASA 试验台转向子系统

（3）Tasa 试验台修正。

替换完成后的 Tasa 试验台如图 15-20 所示，此时试验台并不能正确仿真，原因在于把左舵转向替换成右舵转向系统后，转向系统与转向轮毂的连接也需要修改，修改前后车桥与转向系统连接的输出通信器，把左轮毂部件替换为右轮毂部件，此时 Tasa 试验台修改成功，可以进行各种工况特性的仿真。

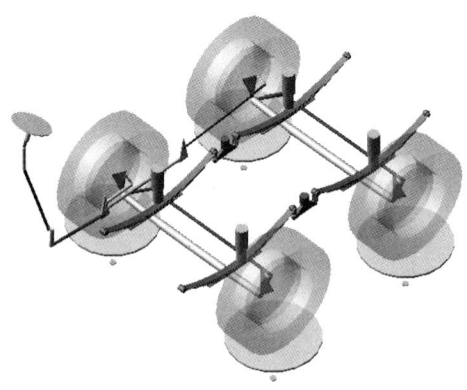

图 15-20　TASA 试验台（右舵转向系统）

(4) 双轴转向仿真。

• 单击 Simulate > Suspension Analysis > Steering 命令，弹出转向仿真对话框如图 15-21 所示；

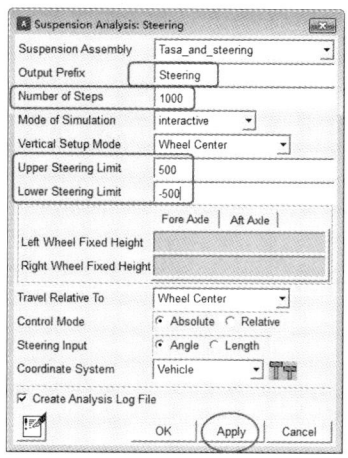

图 15-21　双轴转向仿真设置

- Output Prefix：Steering；
- Number of Steps（仿真步数）：1 000；
- Mode of Simulation：interactive；
- Vertical Setup Mode：Wheel Center；
- Upper Steering Limit：500；
- Lower Steering Limit：-500；
- Travel Relative To：Wheel Center；
- Control Mode：Absolute；
- Coordinate System：Vehicle；
- 单击 OK，完成双轴转向仿真如图 15-22、图 15-23 所示；

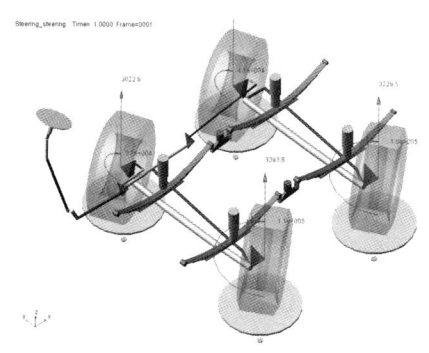

图 15-22　转向盘左转 500°

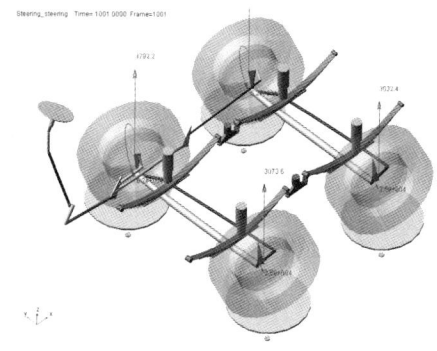

图 15-23　转向盘右转 500°

- 按 F8，界面转换到后处理模块；
- 设置横坐标为方向盘转动的角度，即转向范围为 -500°~500°，计算前后车桥的四轮定位参数如图 15-24 ~ 图 15-27 所示，车辆侧向偏移量如图 15-28 所示。

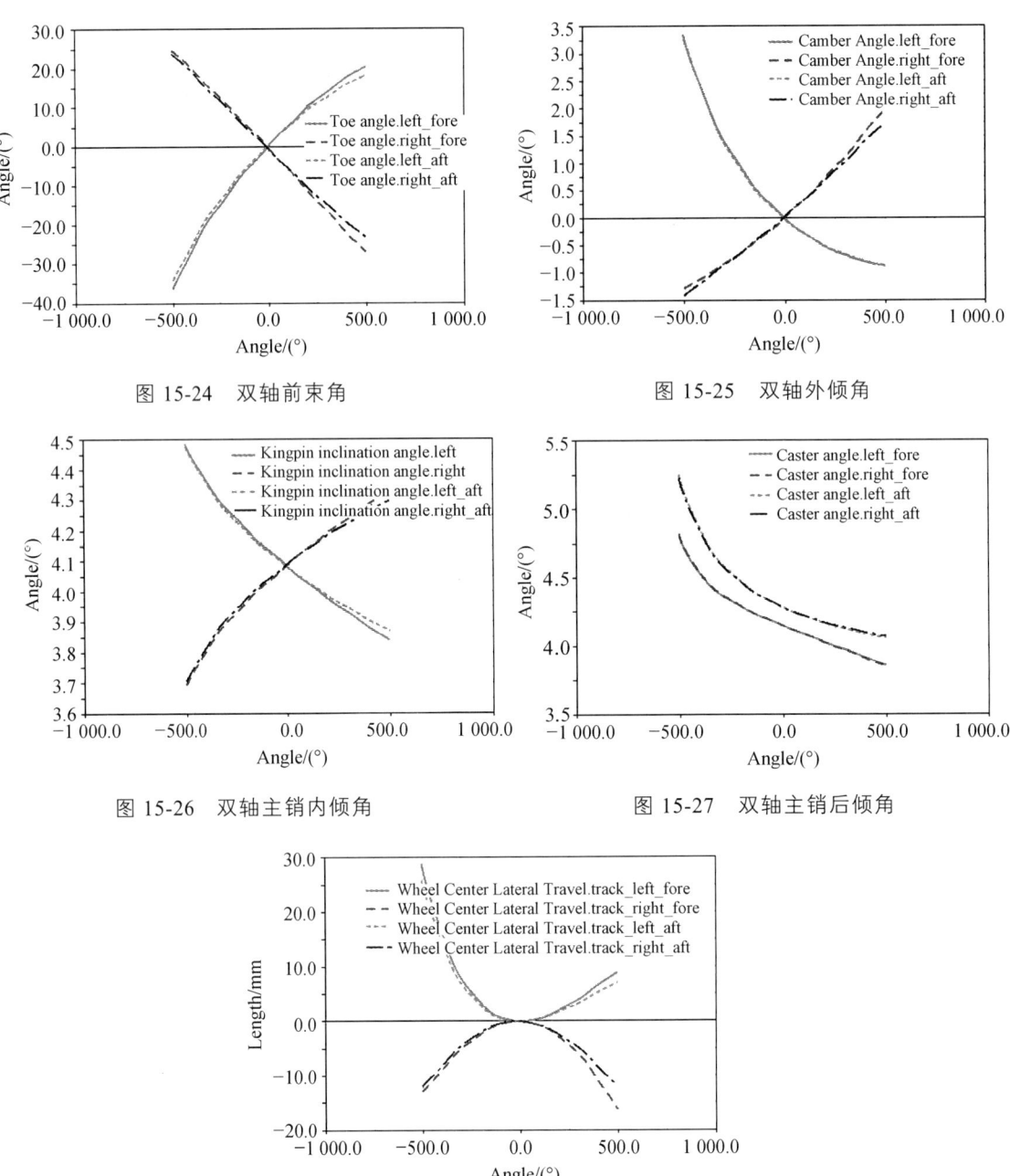

图 15-24 双轴前束角

图 15-25 双轴外倾角

图 15-26 双轴主销内倾角

图 15-27 双轴主销后倾角

图 15-28 双轴车辆侧向偏移量

（5）双轴跳动仿真。

- 单击 Simulate > Suspension Analysis > Parallel Wheel Travel 命令，弹出双轴激振对话框如图 15-29 所示；
- Output Prefix：PT；
- Number of Steps（仿真步数）：1 000；
- Mode of Simulation：interactive；

- Vertical Setup Mode：Wheel Center；
- 单击 Fore Axle：
① Bump Travel：100；
② Rebound Travel：-100。
- 单击 Aft Axle：
① Bump Travel：100；
② Rebound Travel：-100。
- Travel Relative To：Wheel Center；
- Control Mode：Absolute；
- Coordinate System：Vehicle；
- 单击 OK，完成双轴转向仿真。
- 按 F8，界面转换到后处理模块；
- 设置横坐标为车轮跳动位移，即跳动范围为 -100~100 mm，计算前后车桥的四轮定位参数如图 15-30~图 15-33 所示，车辆侧向偏移量如图 15-34 所示。

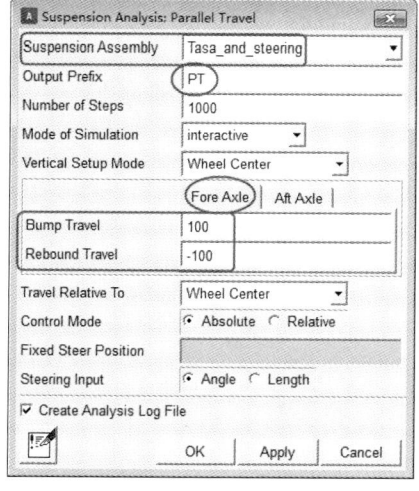

（a）Fore Axle 设置

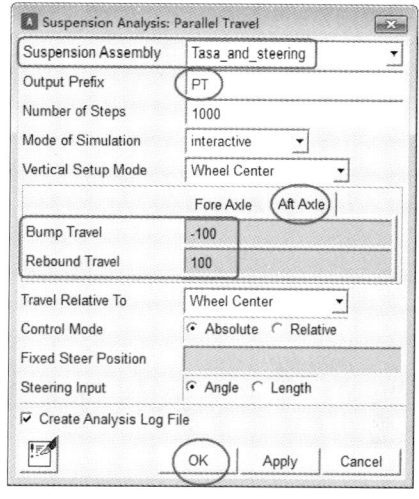

（b）Alt Axle 设置

图 15-29 双轴同向激振仿真

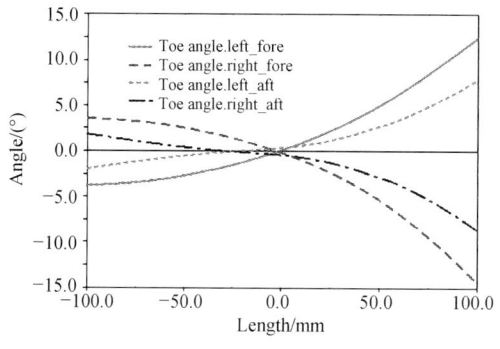

图 15-30 双轴前束角

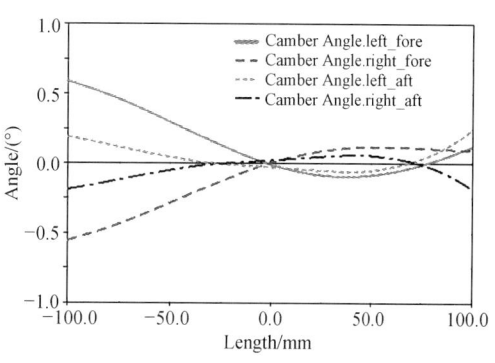

图 15-31 双轴外倾角

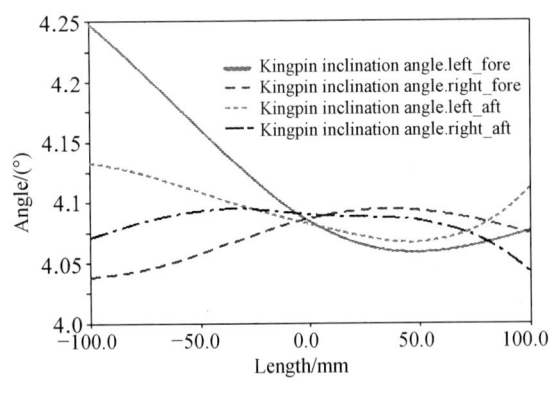

图 15-32　双轴主销内倾角

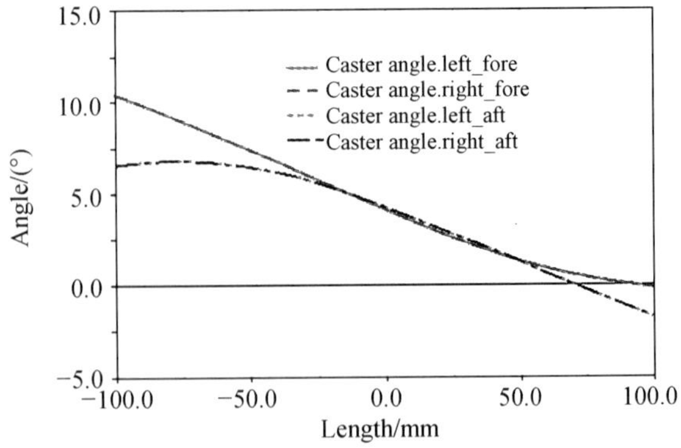

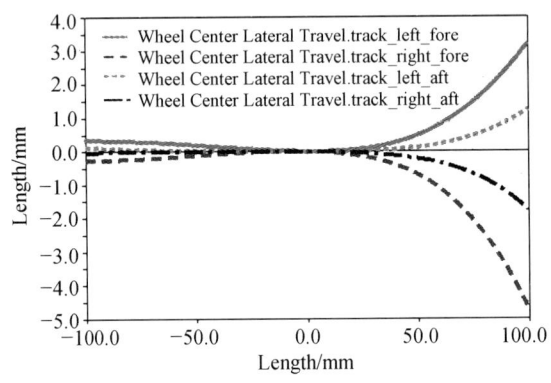

图 15-33　双轴主销后倾角

图 15-34　双轴车辆侧向偏移量

15.7　单轴右舵转向系统

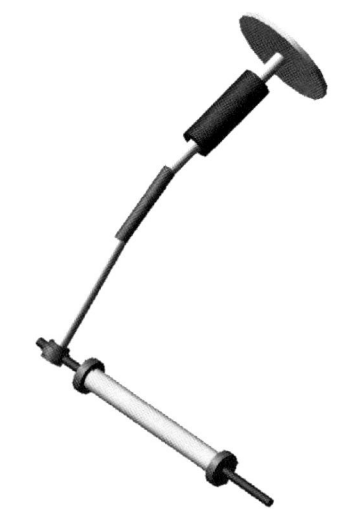

图 15-35　单轴右舵转向系统

- 394 -

右舵转向系统在英联邦国家地区应用较多，国内香港、澳门地区的车辆均采用的是右舵转向系统，单轴右舵转向系统（见图15-35）建模过程在此不再重复，其模型的硬点、部件、刚性约束、柔性约束、参数变量、通信器等信息如下：

Info for subsystem: my_steering_right

File Name   : <my_driveline>/subsystems.tbl/my_steering_right.sub
Template   : mdids://FASE/templates.tbl/_my_steering_right.tpl
Comments   : *no comments found*
Major Role   : steering
Minor Role   : front

HARDPOINTS:

hardpoint name	symmetry	x_value	y_value	z_value
intermediate_shaft_forward	single	500.0	300.0	525.0
intermediate_shaft_rearwar	single	650.0	300.0	625.0
pinion_pivot	single	300.0	300.0	325.0
steering_wheel_center	single	1000.0	300.0	725.0
rack_house_mount	left/right	300.0	−200.0	325.0
tierod_inner	left/right	300.0	−350.0	325.0

PARTS:
intermediate_shaft
symmetry   : single
mass   : 0.9652705135
sprung_percentage   : 100.0
location (dependent)   : 575.0, 300.0, 575.0
orientation (dependent)   : zp_vector=0.8320502943, 0.0, 0.5547001962
                          : xp_vector=0.5547001962, 0.0, −0.8320502943
cm_location_from_part   : 0.0, 0.0, 0.0
Ixx, Iyy, Izz   : 2667.0060484366 , 2667.0060484366 , 105.4634820018
Ixy, Izx, Iyz   : 0.0 , 0.0 , 0.0

intermediate_shaft link geometry
name   : intermediate_shaft
symmetry   : single
radius   : 15.0

pinion
    symmetry : single
    mass : 0.5949286036
    sprung_percentage : 100.0
    location (dependent) : 300.0, 300.0, 325.0
    orientation (dependent) : zp_vector=0.7071067812, 0.0, 0.7071067812
    : xp_vector=0.7071067812, 0.0, −0.7071067812
    cm_location_from_part : 0.0, 0.0, 0.0
    Ixx, Iyy, Izz : 169.6025393729, 169.6025393729, 180.5574511141
    Ixy, Izx, Iyz : 0.0, 0.0, 0.0

rack
    symmetry : single
    mass : 2.0227572523
    sprung_percentage : 100.0
    location (dependent) : 300.0, 0.0, 325.0
    orientation (dependent) : zp_vector=0.0, −1.0, 0.0
    : xp_vector=1.0, 0.0, 0.0
    cm_location_from_part : 0.0, 0.0, 0.0
    Ixx, Iyy, Izz : 1.2183595453E+005, 1.2183595453E+005, 98.2232534061
    Ixy, Izx, Iyz : 0.0, 5.3065426719E−011, −3.2847982369E−011

rack link geometry
    name : rack
    symmetry : single
    radius : 10.0

rack_housing
    symmetry : single
    mass : 4.2834859461
    sprung_percentage : 100.0
    location (dependent) : 300.0, 0.0, 325.0
    orientation (dependent) : zp_vector=0.0, −1.0, 0.0
    : xp_vector=1.0, 0.0, 0.0
    cm_location_from_part : 0.0, 0.0, 0.0
    Ixx, Iyy, Izz : 2.2868658625E+005, 2.2868658625E+005, 468.0049132878
    Ixy, Izx, Iyz : 0.0, 1.2265100081E−011, −4.6711159673E−011

rack_housing link geometry
  name   : rack_housing
  symmetry   : single
  radius   : 25.0

steering_column
  symmetry   : single
  mass   : 1.9490155248
  sprung_percentage   : 100.0
  location (dependent)   : 825.0, 300.0, 675.0
  orientation (dependent) : zp_vector= $-$ 0.9615239476, 0.0, $-$ 0.2747211279
                                : xp_vector= $-$ 0.2747211279, 0.0, 0.9615239476
  cm_location_from_part : 0.0, 0.0, 0.0
  Ixx, Iyy, Izz   : 2.1626852478E+004 , 2.1626852478E+004 , 212.9454498412
  Ixy, Izx, Iyz   : 0.0 , 0.0 , 0.0

steering_column link geometry
  name   : steering_column
  symmetry   : single
  radius   : 15.0

steering_column_to_body
  symmetry   : single
  mass   : 5.8303003155
  sprung_percentage   : 100.0
  location (dependent)   : 825.0, 300.0, 675.0
  orientation (dependent) : zp_vector= $-$ 0.9615239476, 0.0, $-$ 0.2747211279
                                : xp_vector= $-$ 0.2747211279, 0.0, 0.9615239476
  cm_location_from_part : 0.0, 0.0, 0.0
  Ixx, Iyy, Izz   : 2.1168408145E+004 , 2.1168408145E+004 , 3468.1475210001
  Ixy, Izx, Iyz   : 0.0 , 0.0 , 0.0

steering_shaft
  symmetry   : single
  mass   : 1.5144409798
  sprung_percentage   : 100.0
  location (dependent)   : 400.0, 300.0, 425.0
  orientation (dependent) : zp_vector=0.7071067812, 0.0, 0.7071067812

	:	xp_vector=0.7071067812, 0.0, − 0.7071067812
cm_location_from_part	:	0.0, 0.0, 0.0
Ixx, Iyy, Izz	:	1.0179005561E+004 , 1.0179005561E+004 , 165.4647239072
Ixy, Izx, Iyz	:	0.0 , 0.0 , 0.0

steering_shaft link geometry
   name   :   steering_shaft
   symmetry   :   single
   radius   :   15.0

steering_wheel
   symmetry   :   single
   mass   :   3.9483989067
   sprung percentage   :   100.0
   location (dependent)   :   1000.0, 300.0, 725.0
   orientation (dependent) :   zp_vector= − 0.9615239476, 0.0, − 0.2747211279
                                        :   xp_vector= − 0.2747211279, 0.0, 0.9615239476
   cm_location_from_part   :   0.0, 0.0, 0.0
   Ixx, Iyy, Izz   :   1.2577386331E+004 , 1.2577386331E+004 , 2.5048633119E+004
   Ixy, Izx, Iyz   :   0.0 , 0.0 , 0.0

SWITCH PARTS:
   rack_house_mount
   symmetry   :   single
   switched to   :   rack_to_body (mount part)
   part list   :   rack_to_body (mount part)
                     :   rack_housing_to_suspension_subframe (mount part)

BUSHINGS:
   torsion_bar
   definition   :   .ACAR.attachments.ac_bushing
   symmetry   :   single
   orientation (dependent) :   zp_vector=0.7071067812, 0.0, 0.7071067812
                                        :   xp_vector=0.7071067812, 0.0, − 0.7071067812
   t preload x   :   0.0
   t preload y   :   0.0
   t preload z   :   0.0
   r preload x   :   0.0

r preload y	:	0.0
r preload z	:	0.0
t offset x	:	0.0
t offset y	:	0.0
t offset z	:	0.0
r offset x	:	0.0
r offset y	:	0.0
r offset z	:	0.0
fx scaling factor	:	1.0
fy scaling factor	:	1.0
fz scaling factor	:	1.0
tx scaling factor	:	1.0
ty scaling factor	:	1.0
tz scaling factor	:	1.0
tx damping force scale	:	1.0
ty damping force scale	:	1.0
tz damping force scale	:	1.0
rx damping force scale	:	1.0
ry damping force scale	:	1.0
rz damping force scale	:	1.0
property file	:	mdids://acar_shared/bushings.tbl/mdi_0001.bus

rack_housing_bushing

definition	:	.ACAR.attachments.ac_bushing
symmetry	:	left/right
orientation (dependent)	:	zp_vector=0.0, 1.0, 0.0
	:	xp_vector=1.0, 0.0, 0.0
t preload x	:	0.0
t preload y	:	0.0
t preload z	:	0.0
r preload x	:	0.0
r preload y	:	0.0
r preload z	:	0.0
t offset x	:	0.0
t offset y	:	0.0
t offset z	:	0.0
r offset x	:	0.0
r offset y	:	0.0

r offset z	:	0.0
fx scaling factor	:	1.0
fy scaling factor	:	1.0
fz scaling factor	:	1.0
tx scaling factor	:	1.0
ty scaling factor	:	1.0
tz scaling factor	:	1.0
tx damping force scale	:	1.0
ty damping force scale	:	1.0
tz damping force scale	:	1.0
rx damping force scale	:	1.0
ry damping force scale	:	1.0
rz damping force scale	:	1.0
property file	:	mdids://acar_shared/bushings.tbl/mdi_0001.bus

GEARS:
  pinion_to_rack
  symmetry   : single
  reduction ratio : 0.1745
  invert input   : no

PARAMETERS:

parameter name	symmetry	type	value
--------------	--------	----	-----
kinematic_flag	single	integer	0
steering_assist_active	single	integer	1
max_rack_displacement	single	real	0.0
max_rack_force	single	real	500.0
max_steering_angle	single	real	540.0
max_steering_torque	single	real	500.0

第 16 章　麦弗逊悬架联合仿真

麦弗逊悬架应用较多，几乎所有乘用车前悬架系统均采用麦弗逊悬架，其结构简单，占用空间小；在 VIEW 模块中建立好的麦弗逊悬架模型如图 16-1 所示。麦弗逊悬架通常由两个基本部分组成：支柱式减震器和 A 字形托臂。减震器除了减震功能外还有支撑整个车身的作用，结构很紧凑，把减震器和减震弹簧集成在一起，组成一个可以上下运动的滑柱；下托臂通常是 A 字形的设计，用于给车轮提供部分横向支撑力，以及承受全部的前后方向冲击力。整车重力和汽车在运动时车轮承受的所有冲击靠这两个部件承担；占用空间小带来的直接好处就是设计师能在发动机舱布置下更大的发动机，而且发动机的放置方式也能随心所欲。在中型车上能放下大型发动机，在小型车上也能放下中型发动机，让各种发动机的匹配更灵活。经典的 PID 控制算法较为简单，PID 控制器（比例-积分-微分控制器）是工业控制应用中常见的反馈回路部件，由比例单元 P、积分单元 I 和微分单元 D 组成。PID 控制的基础是比例控制；积分控制可消除稳态误差，但可能增加超调；微分控制可加快大惯性系统响应速度以及减弱超调趋势。

图 16-1　麦弗逊悬架模型

学习目标

- ✧ 麦弗逊悬架模型建立。
- ✧ 路面模型。
- ✧ PID 控制理论算法。
- ✧ 半主动悬架联合仿真。
- ✧ 时频域、功率谱密度变换程序。

16.1 麦弗逊悬架模型建立

麦弗逊悬架模型在 ADAMS/VIEW 模块中建立，悬架的硬点参数参考 CAR 模块共享数据库中麦弗逊悬架的硬点参数。通用模块与专业模块建模稍有不同。
- 启动 ADAMS/VIEW，选择 New Model；
- Model Name（模型名称）：adams_view_zhengche；
- 单击 OK 完成新模型名称创建，如图 16-2 所示，接下来可以在窗口中完成模型任务；
- 单击硬点快捷方式，右击鼠标，在弹出的方框中输入 –200，150，–450；
- 选中硬点，右击鼠标选择 Rename，修改硬点名称为 rca_front；
- 单击 OK，完成硬点重命名；
- 重复以上步骤，完成如图 16-3 所示硬点的建立。

> 单击硬点快捷方式，在左侧命令窗口选择硬点表格 Point Table 创建如图 16-3 所示硬点，推荐采用硬点表格方式批量创建硬点，速度较快；悬架模型建立过程中，可以边建立硬点，边建立部件、约束等，也可以批量完成硬点建立，接下来批量完成部件建立，最后建立约束。建模方法多样可行，总之模型准确无误是前提条件。

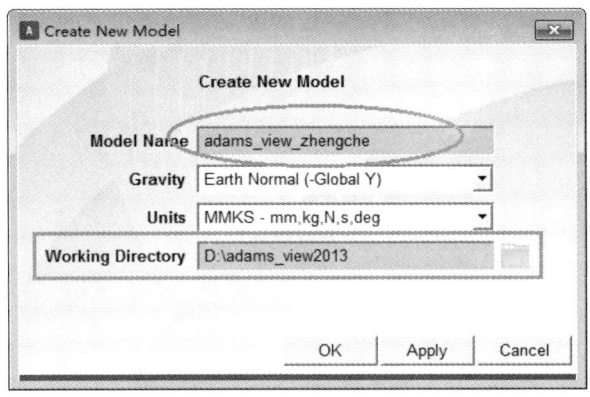

图 16-2　模型创建对话框

	Loc X	Loc Y	Loc Z
rca_front	-200.0	150.0	-450.0
rca_outer	0.0	150.0	-750.0
rca_rear	200.0	150.0	-450.0
r_tierod_outer	200.0	300.0	-400.0
r_tierod_inner	150.0	300.0	-750.0
r_wheel_center	0.0	300.0	-800.0
r_spring_lower	40.0	600.0	-650.0
r_spring_up	57.5	900.0	-603.8

图 16-3　硬点参数

16.1.1 下控制臂部件

- 单击 Cylinder（圆柱体）；选择 Radius，在对应方框中输入 20，单位为 mm；
- 选择硬点 rca_front 与 rca_outer，创建 PART_2；
- 重复上述步骤，选择硬点 rca_rear 与 rca_outer，创建 PART_3；
- 单击 Booleans，分别选择 PART_2 与 PART_3，完成部件的布尔合并，PART_2 与 PART_3 两个部件合并一个独立的部件 PART_2；
- 选中部件 PART_2，右击鼠标选择 Rename，在弹出的修改名称对话框输入 lca_arm；
- 单击 OK，完成部件名称的修改。

16.1.2 转向主销部件

- 单击 Cylinder（圆柱体），选择 New Part，勾选 Radius，在对应方框中输入 20；
- 选择硬点 r_wheel_center 与 rca_outer，创建 PART_3；
- 选中部件 PART_3，右击鼠标选择 Rename，在弹出的修改名称对话框输入 up_right；
- 单击 OK，完成转向节部件名称的修改。
- 单击 Cylinder（圆柱体），选择 Add to Part，勾选 Radius，在对应方框中输入 20；
- 选择硬点 r_wheel_center 与 r_spring_lower，完成几何体 up_right.CYLINDER_33 创建；
- 选择硬点 r_wheel_center 与 r_tierod_inner，完成几何体 up_right.CYLINDER_32 创建，至此完成转向节部件的建立。

> 转向节部件的创建也可采用在四个硬点之间建立三个部件，最后采用布尔操纵合并三个部件为一个部件。不推荐采用此种方法，原因在于通过布尔合并后几何体的参数化失败，不能通过快捷方式调节部件几何的形状。

16.1.3 转向横拉杆部件

- 单击 Cylinder（圆柱体），选择 New Part，勾选 Radius，在对应方框中输入 15；
- 选择硬点 r_tierod_outer 与 r_tierod_inner，创建 PART_4；
- 选中部件 PART_4，右击鼠标选择 Rename，在弹出的修改名称对话框输入 tierod_right；
- 单击 OK，完成转向横拉杆部件名称的修改。

16.1.4 转向节部件

- 菜单栏单击 Setting，选择 Working Grid，弹出 Working Grid Setting 对话框；
- 单击 Set Location，选择 Pick，在屏幕中选择硬点 r_wheel_center，此时主窗口中的坐标原点位于硬点 r_wheel_center；
- 单击 Set Orientation，选择 Global YZ 方向，设置网格对话对话框如图 16-4 所示；
- 单击 Cylinder（圆柱体），选择 New Part，勾选 Radius，在对应方框中输入 15，勾选

Length，在对应方框中输入 250；

- 在主窗口选择硬点 r_wheel_center 单击，保持圆柱体部件与 -Z 轴平行，单击鼠标左键完成部件 PART_5 的创建；
- 选中部件 PART_5，右击鼠标选择 Rename，在弹出的修改名称对话框输入 knuckle_right；
- 单击 OK，完成转向节部件名称的修改。

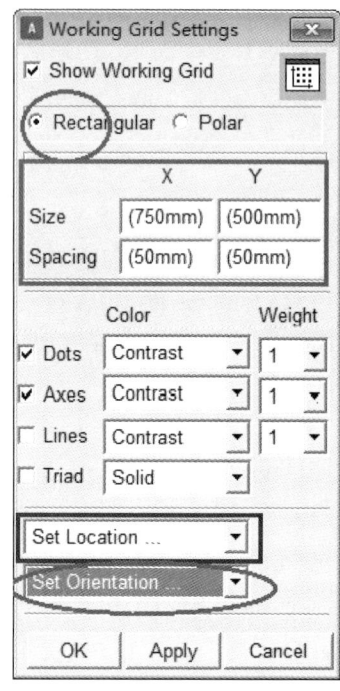

图 16-4　网格设置对话框

16.1.5　车轮部件创建

- 单击 Cylinder（圆柱体），选择 New Part，勾选 Radius，在对应方框中输入 350，勾选 Length，在对应方框中输入 215；
- 在主窗口选择方向点 MARKER_22 单击，保持圆柱体部件与 Z 轴平行，单击鼠标左键完成部件 PART_6 的创建；
- 选中部件 PART_6，右击鼠标选择 Rename，在弹出的修改名称对话框输入 wheel_right；
- 单击 OK，完成车轮部件名称的修改。
- 菜单栏单击 Setting，选择 Working Grid，弹出 Working Grid Setting 对话框；
- 单击 Set Location，选择 Pick，在屏幕中选择硬点 r_wheel_center，此时主窗口中的坐标原点位于硬点 r_wheel_center；
- 单击 Set Orientation，选择 Global XY 方向；
- 单击 OK，完成网格位置与方向设置。
- 单击菜单栏快捷方式 Add a hole，左侧 Radius 输入 325，勾选 Depth，输入 215，选

择轮胎部件 wheel_right 的侧面，接着选择方向点 MARKER_22，完成车轮部件的掏空。

16.1.6 弹簧底座部件创建

- 单击 Cylinder（圆柱体），选择 New Part，勾选 Radius，在对应方框中输入 50；
- 选择硬点 r_spring_lower 与 r_spring_up，创建 PART_7；
- 选中部件 PART_7 下的几何体 CYLINDER_34，右击选择 Modify；
- 在弹出的 Geometry Modify Shape Cylinder 对话框中修改 Length 值为 10；
- 单击 OK，完成弹簧底座部件 PART_7 的创建。
- 选中部件 PART_7，右击鼠标选择 Rename，在弹出的修改名称对话框输入 srping_down；
- 单击 OK，完成弹簧底座部件名称的修改。
- 单击 Cylinder（圆柱体），选择 New Part，勾选 Radius，在对应方框中输入 50；
- 选择硬点 r_spring_up 与 r_spring_lower，创建 PART_8，在此注意选择硬点的顺序；
- 选中部件 PART_8 下的几何体 CYLINDER_35，右击选择 Modify；
- 在弹出的 Geometry Modify Shape Cylinder 对话框中修改 Length 值为 10；
- 单击 OK，完成弹簧底座部件 PART_8 的创建。
- 选中部件 PART_8，右击鼠标选择 Rename，在弹出的修改名称对话框输入 srping_up；
- 单击 OK，完成弹簧顶座部件名称的修改。

16.1.7 车身部件

1/4 悬架模型也需要建立简化车身模型，悬架系统包含车身部件模型较为精准。

- 单击 Sphere（球体），选择 New Part，勾选 Radius，在对应方框中输入 30；
- 选择硬点 r_spring_up，创建 PART_9；
- 选中部件 PART_9，右击鼠标选择 Rename，在弹出的修改名称对话框输入 body；
- 单击 OK，完成车身简化部件名称的修改。
- 选中部件 body，右击选择 Modify 弹出部件修改对话框；
- Define Mass By:在下拉菜单中选择 User Input，手动输入 1/4 车身的质量及惯量；
- Mass：250；
- Ixx：5.0E+007；
- yy：1.5E+008；
- Izz：1.25E+008；
- 单击 OK，完成车身部件参数的修改。

16.1.8 弹簧与减震器

- 单击菜单栏 Force，选择 Flexibile Connections（柔性连接）框的 Spring（创建弹簧与减震器）；

- Properties 栏中勾选 K&C，在 K 栏中输入 17.0，在 C 栏中输入 1.3；
- 选择 spring_up.cm 与 srping_down.cm 两个参考点，完成弹簧与减震器的创建，弹簧创建需要选择两个不同部件对应的点或者参考点，选择时可以右击部件在弹出的快捷 Select 对话中选择相应点；
- 选中 SPRING_1，右击选择 Modify，弹出部件修改对话框如图 16-5 所示；

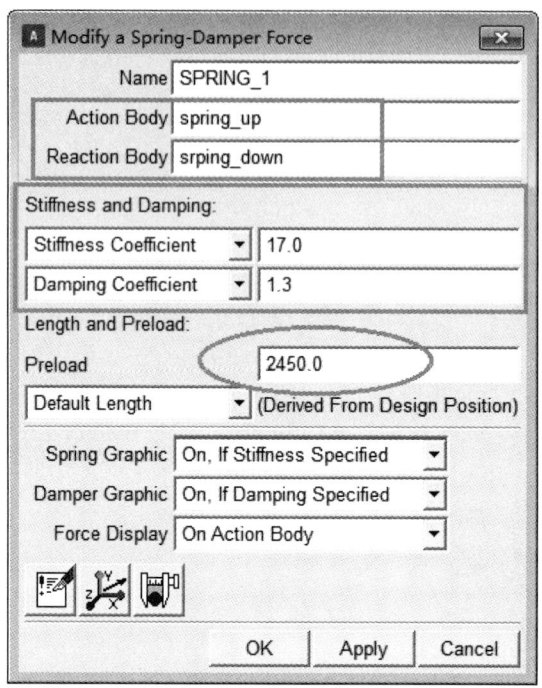

图 16-5　弹簧与减震器参数对话框

- 在 Preload（预载荷，输入 1/4 车身的重力）：2 450，其余保持默认；
- 单击 OK，完成弹簧与减震器参数的设置。

16.1.9　振动台

- 单击 Box（六面体）；选择 New Part，勾选 Length、Height 、Depth，分别输入 400、45、500；
- 选择位置 0.0，-50.0，0.0 单击，创建六面体部件 PART_10；
- 选中部件 PART_10 下的 MARKER_23，右击选择 Modify；
- Location：-200.0，-120.0，-1 200.0；
- 单击 OK，完成 PART_10 的位置修改。
- 选中部件 PART_10，右击鼠标选择 Rename,在弹出的修改名称对话框输入 test_patch；
- 单击 OK，完成振动台部件名称的修改。
- 菜单栏单击 Setting，选择 Working Grid，弹出 Working Grid Setting 对话框；
- 单击 Set Location，选择 Pick，在屏幕中选择参考点 test_patch.cm，此时主窗口中的坐标原点位于参考点 test_patch.cm 处；
- 单击 OK，完成网格位置与方向设置。
- 单击 Cylinder（圆柱体），选择 Add to Part，勾选 Length、Radius，在对应方框中输入 350、50；
- 选择参考点 test_patch.cm 处，方向与 –Y 轴平行重合单击，完成圆柱体 CYLINDER_25 的创建。

悬架建模探讨。

（1）在建模过程中忽略车身部件，直接把弹簧和减震器与大地连接，这种模型对于研究车轮的运动学（狭义指车轮的运动空间）是可以满足要求的。

（2）对于研究悬架的动力学车身部件不可忽略（实际整车在运行过程中，车轮与车身部件存在相对运动，绝对不可以忽略）。

（3）对于主动悬架的研究，必学考虑车身部件；有些文献即使考虑了车身，但仍存在以下错误：下控制及转向横拉杆与大地连接而非与车身连接，这样的模型虽然能正确进行仿真，但是其运动特性与真实悬架不符。

（4）从学术上讲，对于以上建立的麦弗逊悬架模型符合研究要求，但对于汽车工程研究院中真实的整车及悬架模型来说依然存在缺陷，原因在于整车的振动和簧载质量与非簧载质量有关，以上建立的麦弗逊悬架模型控制臂等部件采用简化的杆件而非真实的冲压件。除此之外，在研发过程中，对应载荷的提取结果会应用零部件的有限元、疲劳特性等研究，因此模型与实际越接近，结果越精确。

16.1.10 悬架部件约束

- 菜单栏单击 Setting，选择 Working Grid，弹出 Working Grid Setting 对话框；
- 单击 Set Orientation，选择 Global YZ 方向；
- 单击 OK，完成网格位置与方向设置。
- 单击菜单栏 Connector，选择 Joint 框中的 Revolute Joint（铰接副）；
- 设置 Construction：2 Bodies -1 Location、Normal To Grid；
- 顺序选择两部件 lca_arm、body，再选择硬点 rca_rear，完成铰接副 JOINT_1 的创建，铰接副约束 2 个旋转自由度，3 个移动自由度，两个部件之间存在一个旋转自由度，同时需要注意下控制臂与车身之间只建立一个铰接副，而非在控制臂前后硬点之间建立两个铰接副，实际部件的约束与理论模型之间存在差异，铰接副的创建如图 16-6 所示；
- 选中铰接副 JOINT_1，右击鼠标选择 Rename，在弹出的修改名称对话框输入 rca_rear；

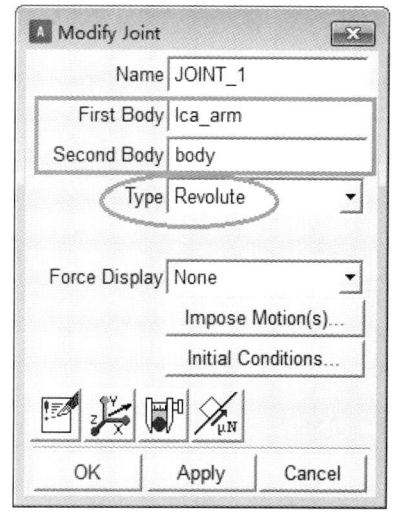

图 16-6 铰接副对话框

- 单击 OK，完成铰接副重命名为 rca_rear 的修改。
- 单击菜单栏 Connector，选择 Joint 框中的 Spherical Joint（球形副）；
- 设置 Construction：2 Bodies -1 Location、Normal To Grid；
- 顺序选择两部件 lca_arm、up_right，再选择硬点 rca_outer，完成铰接副 JOINT_2 的创建，球形副约；
- 3 个移动自由度，部件之间存在 3 个旋转自由度；
- 选中铰接副 JOINT_2，右击鼠标选择 Rename，在弹出的修改名称对话框输入 rca_outer；
- 单击 OK，完成球形副重命名为 rca_outer 的修改。
- 单击菜单栏 Connector，选择 Joint 框中的 Spherical Joint（球形副）；
- 设置 Construction：2 Bodies -1 Location、Normal To Grid；
- 顺序选择两部件 lca_arm、up_right，再选择硬点 rca_outer，完成铰接副 JOINT_2 的创建，球形副约 3 个移动自由度，部件之间存在 3 个旋转自由度；
- 选中铰接副 JOINT_2，右击鼠标选择 Rename，在弹出的修改名称对话框输入 rca_outer；
- 单击 OK，完成球形副重命名为 rca_outer 的修改。
- 单击菜单栏 Connector，选择 Joint 框中的 Fix Joint（固定副）；
- 设置 Construction：2 Bodies -1 Location、Normal To Grid；
- 顺序选择两部件 up_right、knuckle_right 再选择硬点 r_wheel_center，完成铰接副 JOINT_3 的创建，固定副约束两个部件之间的 6 个自由度；
- 选中铰接副 JOINT_3，右击鼠标选择 Rename，在弹出的修改名称对话框输入 r_wheel_center；
- 单击 OK，完成固定副重命名为 r_wheel_center 的修改。
- 单击菜单栏 Connector，选择 Joint 框中的 Spherical Joint（球形副）；
- 设置 Construction：2 Bodies -1 Location、Normal To Grid；
- 顺序选择两部件 tierod_right、body，再选择硬点 r_tierod_outer，完成铰接副 JOINT_4 的创建；
- 选中铰接副 JOINT_4，右击鼠标选择 Rename，在弹出的修改名称对话框输入 r_tierod_outer；
- 单击 OK，完成球形副重命名为 r_tierod_outer 的修改。
- 单击菜单栏 Connector，选择 Joint 框中的 Spherical Joint（球形副）；
- 设置 Construction：2 Bodies -1 Location、Normal To Grid；
- 顺序选择两部件 tierod_right、body，再选择硬点 r_tierod_outer，完成铰接副 JOINT_4 的创建；
- 选中铰接副 JOINT_4，右击鼠标选择 Rename，在弹出的修改名称对话框输入 r_tierod_outer；
- 单击 OK，完成球形副重命名为 r_tierod_outer 的修改。
- 单击菜单栏 Connector，选择 Joint 框中的 Spherical Joint（球形副）；
- 设置 Construction：2 Bodies -1 Location、Normal To Grid；

- 顺序选择两部件 up_right、tierod_right，再选择硬点 r_tierod_inner，完成铰接副 JOINT_5 的创建；
- 选中铰接副 JOINT_5，右击鼠标选择 Rename，在弹出的修改名称对话框输入 r_tierod_inner；
- 单击 OK，完成球形副重命名为 r_tierod_inner 的修改。
- 单击菜单栏 Connector，选择 Joint 框中的 Fix Joint（固定副）；
- 设置 Construction：2 Bodies -1 Location、Normal To Grid；
- 顺序选择两部件 wheel_right、knuckle_right，再选择参考点 MARKER_38，完成铰接副 JOINT_6 的创建；
- 选中铰接副 JOINT_6，右击鼠标选择 Rename，在弹出的修改名称对话框输入 knuckle_right_fix；
- 单击 OK，完成固定副重命名为 knuckle_right_fix 的修改。
- 单击菜单栏 Connector，选择 Joint 框中的 Fix Joint（固定副）；
- 设置 Construction：2 Bodies -1 Location、Normal To Grid；
- 顺序选择两部件 srping_down、up_right，再选择硬点 r_spring_lower，完成铰接副 JOINT_7 的创建；
- 选中铰接副 JOINT_7，右击鼠标选择 Rename，在弹出的修改名称对话框输入 r_spring_lower；
- 单击 OK，完成固定副重命名为 r_spring_lower 的修改。
- 单击菜单栏 Connector，选择 Joint 框中的 Cylindrical Joint（圆柱副）；
- 设置 Construction：2 Bodies -1 Location、Pick Geometry Feature；
- 顺序选择两部件 srping_down、srping_up，顺序选择硬点 r_spring_lower、r_spring_up 完成圆柱副 JOINT_8 的创建，圆柱副约束两部件之间的 3 个旋转自由度，2 个移动自由度；
- 选中铰接副 JOINT_8，右击鼠标选择 Rename，在弹出的修改名称对话框输入 r_spring_lower_cylindrical；
- 单击 OK，完成圆柱固定副重命名为 r_spring_lower_cylindrical 的修改。
- 单击硬点快捷方式，右击鼠标，在弹出的方框中输入 57.5，950，−603.8；
- 选中硬点，右击鼠标选择 Rename，修改硬点名称为 r_spring_up_ref；
- 单击 OK，完成硬点重命名。
- 单击菜单栏 Connector，选择 Joint 框中的 Hook Joint（胡克副）；
- 设置 Construction：2 Bodies -1 Location、Pick Geometry Feature；
- 顺序选择两部件 spring_up、body，顺序选择硬点 r_spring_up、r_spring_lower、r_spring_up_ref 完成胡克副 JOINT_9 的创建，胡克副约束两部件之间的 1 个旋转自由度，3 个移动自由度；
- 选中铰接副 JOINT_9，右击鼠标选择 Rename，在弹出的修改名称对话框输入 r_spring_up；
- 单击 OK，完成胡克副重命名为 r_spring_up 的修改。
- 单击菜单栏 Connector，选择 Joint 框中的 Translational Joint（移动副）；
- 设置 Construction：2 Bodies -1 Location、Pick Geometry Feature；

- 顺序选择两部件 body、.adams_view_zhengche.ground，再选择硬点 r_spring_up、r_spring_up_ref，完成铰接副 JOINT_10 的创建；
- 选中铰接副 JOINT_10，右击鼠标选择 Rename，在弹出的修改名称对话框输入 r_spring_up_Translational；
- 单击 OK，完成固定副重命名为 r_spring_up_Translational 的修改。
- 单击菜单栏 Connector，选择 Joint 框中的 Translational Joint（移动副）；
- 设置 Construction：2 Bodies -1 Location、Pick Geometry Feature；
- 顺序选择两部件 test_patch、.adams_view_zhengche.ground，选择参考点 MARKER_24，然后移动鼠标，保持箭头方向与 Y 轴平行单击，完成铰接副 JOINT_11 的创建；
- 选中铰接副 JOINT_11，右击鼠标选择 Rename，在弹出的修改名称对话框输入 test_patch_Translational；
- 单击 OK，完成固定副重命名为 test_patch_Translational 的修改。
- 单击菜单栏 Connector，选择基本约束栏 Primitives 框中的 In-Plane（点面副），点面副限制一个部件在另一个部件的某个平面内运动，减少一个自由度；
- 设置 Construction：2 Bodies -1 Location、Pick Geometry Feature；
- 顺序选择两部件 wheel_right、test_patch，选择参考点 MARKER_24，然后移动鼠标，保持箭头方向与 Y 轴平行单击，完成基本点面副 JPRIM_1 的创建。

至此麦弗逊悬架模型与振动试验台模型建立完成，接下来的工作需要把路面的振动数据添加到振动试验台上，当然也可以用简单的正余弦驱动验证模型的正确性。

通过工具菜单栏 Tool 下的 Model Topology Map 可以显示不同部件之间的连接关系，在参考共享数据库模型建模时经常需要判定部件之间的连接关系，除此之外，还可在命令窗口中用图形的方式显示部件之间的连接关系，用图形显示拓扑关系更加直观。

```
Topology of model: adams_view_zhengche

Ground Part: ground

Part ground
Is connected to:
test_patch      via   test_patch_Translational    (Translational Joint)
body            via   r_spring_up_Translational   (Translational Joint)

Part lca_arm
Is connected to:
up_right        via   rca_outer                   (Spherical Joint)
body            via   rca_rear                    (Revolute Joint)

Part knuckle_right
Is connected to:
```

up_right	via	r_wheel_center	(Fixed Joint)
wheel_right	via	knuckle_right_fix	(Fixed Joint)

Part wheel_right
Is connected to:
test_patch	via	JPRIM_1	(Inplane Primitive_Joint)
knuckle_right	via	knuckle_right_fix	(Fixed Joint)

Part srping_down
Is connected to:
spring_up	via	SPRING_1.sforce	(Single_Component_Force)
up_right	via	r_spring_lower	(Fixed Joint)
spring_up	via	r_spring_lower_cylindrical	(Cylindrical Joint)
spring_up	via	zhudongli	(Single_Component_Force)

Part test_patch
Is connected to:
ground	via	test_patch_Translational	(Translational Joint)
wheel_right	via	JPRIM_1	(Inplane Primitive_Joint)

Part tierod_right
Is connected to:
up_right	via	r_tierod_inner	(Spherical Joint)
body	via	r_tierod_outer	(Spherical Joint)

Part up_right
Is connected to:
knuckle_right	via	r_wheel_center	(Fixed Joint)
lca_arm	via	rca_outer	(Spherical Joint)
tierod_right	via	r_tierod_inner	(Spherical Joint)
srping_down	via	r_spring_lower	(Fixed Joint)

Part spring_up
Is connected to:
srping_down	via	SPRING_1.sforce	(Single_Component_Force)
srping_down	via	r_spring_lower_cylindrical	(Cylindrical Joint)
body	via	r_spring_up	(Hooke Joint)
srping_down	via	zhudongli	(Single_Component_Force)

```
Part body
Is connected to:
lca_arm          via   rca_rear                  (Revolute Joint)
tierod_right     via   r_tierod_outer            (Spherical Joint)
spring_up        via   r_spring_up               (Hooke Joint)
ground           via   r_spring_up_Translational (Translational Joint)
```

16.2 路面模型

对悬架性能分析时需要输入路面模型。根据国家标准将公路等级分为 8 种，在不同的路段测量，很难得到两个完全相同的路面轮廓曲线。通常是把测量得到的大量路面不平度随机数据，经数据处理得到路面功率谱密度。产生随机路面不平度时间轮廓有两种方法，由白噪声通过一个积分器产生或者由白噪声通过一个成形滤波器产生。路面时域模型可用公式（16-1）描述；根据公式在 MATLAB\SIMULINK 中建立 B 级路面不同车速的仿真模型如图 16-7 所示，B 级路面不同车速的垂直位移计算结果如图 16-8 所示。

$$\dot{q}(t) = -2\pi f_0 q(t) + 2\pi \sqrt{G_q V} w(t) \tag{16-1}$$

式中，$q(t)$ 为路面随激励；$w(t)$ 为积分白噪声；f_0 为时间频率；G_q 为路面不平度系数；V 为汽车行驶速度。不同级别及对不同的车速路面参数请查看相关资料。

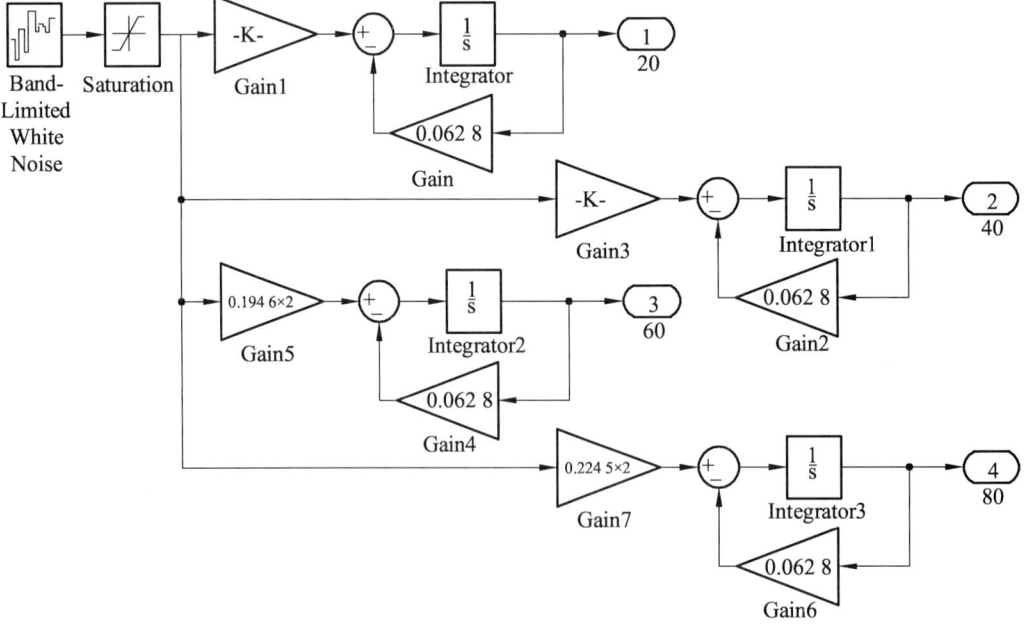

图 16-7 B 级路面不同车速时域仿真模型

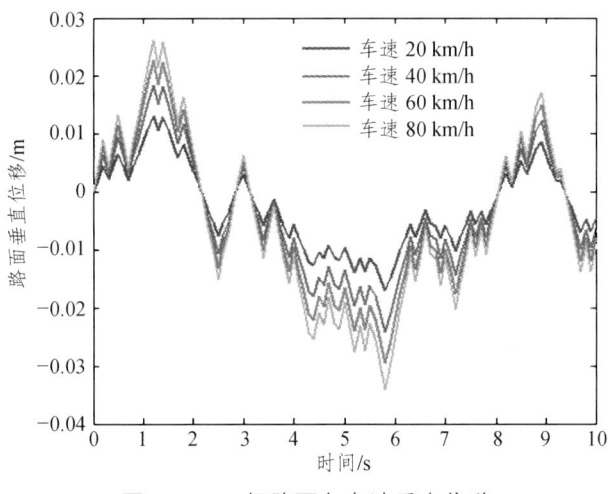

图 16-8 B 级路面各车速垂向位移

路面模型需要添加到振动试验台上,路面模型驱动添加有两种方式,在进行联合仿真时推荐采用方案 B。

> A. 直接把 B 级路面的仿真数据通过函数 AKISPL( )添加到振动试验台上,在 ADAMS 软件中可以仿真在路面条件下麦弗逊悬架运动的真实状态,当更换路面时需要重复计算路面参数及重复添加驱动函数,尤其是在进行联合仿真时,过程较为烦琐。
>
> B. 在 ADAMS 中建立状态变量函数,把此状态函数通过 ADAMS\CONTROL 模块设置为系统的输入接口,路面模型在 MATLAB\SIMULINK 模型中搭建如图 16-7 所示,输出结果直接与 ADAMS_SYS 的路面输入接口对接,此种方式的优点是可以预先建立好仿真需要的各种路面,联合仿真模型建立好后可以方便快速地更换不同路面,推荐采用此种方法。

16.3 路面驱动方案 A

针对在 MATLAB\SIMULINK 中建立 B 级路面不同车速的仿真模型,仿真时间设置为 10 s,运行仿真后在 MATLAB 的工作空间 Workspace 会得到两组数据 tout,yout;在 D 盘中新建一个文本文件,命名为 road.txt;将 tout 作为第一列,yout 中的第一列复制到文本文件 road.txt 中保存。此处提供一个路面文件 road.txt 在光盘中,仅供参考。

- 打开 ADAMS/VIEW 中建立的麦弗逊悬架模型,在主菜单选 File>Import,弹出对话框如图 16-9 所示;
- File Type:Test Data;
- 点选 Create Spline;
- File To Read:D:\road.txt;
- 其余保持默认,单击 OK,完成仿真路面数据导入。如果要更换其他路面模型,需要重复以上仿真过程及以上步骤的重新导入,相对较为烦琐。

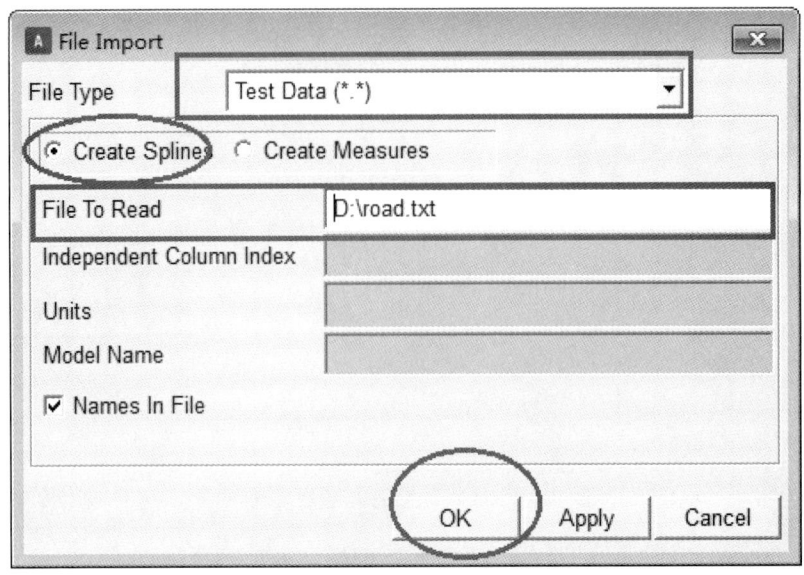

图 16-9 路面数据导入对话框

打开 ADAMS 的数据库浏览器如图 16-10 所示，SPLINE_2 为生成的样条曲线数据。双击打开 SPLINE_2，在弹出的 Information 窗口中显示如下信息，此信息包含的数据与路面文件 road.txt 中的数据相同。对于有多个试验振动台的整车模型，可以依次导入不同的路面模型，设置在同一个模型中不同的振动试验台有不同的振动效果。

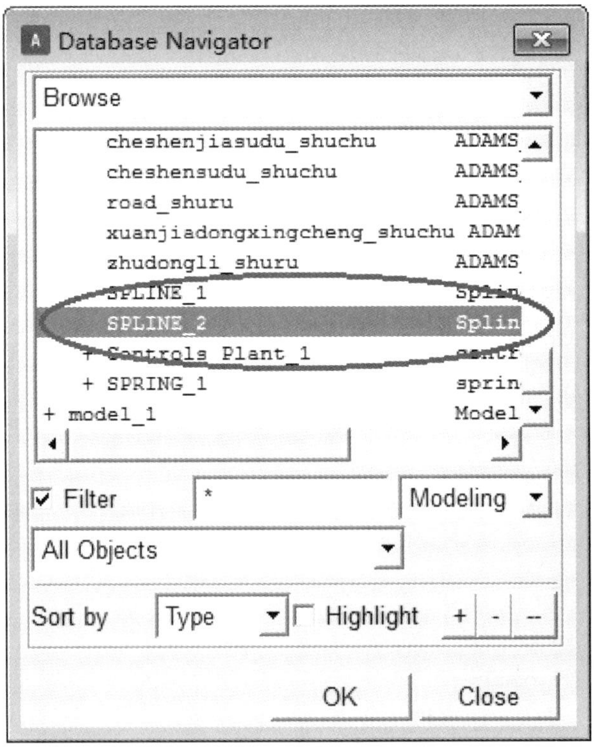

图 16-10 数据库浏览器对话框

SPLINE_2 样条数据。

Object Name   : .adams_view_zhengche.SPLINE_2
Object Type   : Spline
Parent Type   : Model
Adams ID   : 0
Active   : NO_OPINION
X Units   : NO UNITS
Y Units   : NO UNITS
Spline Points:

(X = 1.0,   Y = 0.2008942924)
(X = 2.0,   Y = 1.2036690038)
(X = 3.0,   Y = 2.2319211241)
(X = 4.0,   Y = 17.1592158991)
(X = 5.0,   Y = 11.6840101222)
(X = 6.0,   Y = 19.6574141868)
(X = 7.0,   Y = 20.7626001622)
(X = 8.0,   Y = 18.2043021902)
(X = 9.0,   Y = 12.3320688983)
(X = 10.0, Y = 13.1176331434)
(X = 11.0, Y = 16.6482607299)
(X = 12.0, Y = 18.1223665756)
(X = 13.0, Y = 21.2087067783)
(X = 14.0, Y = 24.1851909962)
(X = 15.0, Y = 23.165983258)
(X = 16.0, Y = 30.8669520711)
(X = 17.0, Y = 27.4372350815)
(X = 18.0, Y = 13.9764209914)
(X = 19.0, Y = 4.2068003494)
(X = 20.0, Y = 15.5260556619)
(X = 21.0, Y = 12.7388426178)
(X = 22.0, Y = 6.6497175466)
(X = 23.0, Y = 1.3583780206)
(X = 24.0, Y = – 3.3223270142)
(X = 25.0, Y = – 6.3246530621)
(X = 26.0, Y = – 9.3619599109)
(X = 27.0, Y = – 10.6419856681)
(X = 28.0, Y = – 1.241284351)

(X = 29.0,   Y = − 0.7729604272)
(X = 30.0,   Y = 7.2391497849)
(X = 31.0,   Y = 12.0138478618)
(X = 32.0,   Y = 14.0406498922)
(X = 33.0,   Y = 10.2822107278)
(X = 34.0,   Y = 7.3400461246)
(X = 35.0,   Y = 5.822534108)
(X = 36.0,   Y = − 2.1005830571)
(X = 37.0,   Y = 11.3482505873)
(X = 38.0,   Y = 17.4644483624)
(X = 39.0,   Y = 13.1119102857)
(X = 40.0,   Y = 6.9110780294)
(X = 41.0,   Y = 5.9189550731)
(X = 42.0,   Y = 10.6042550475)
(X = 43.0,   Y = 8.8497533756)
(X = 44.0,   Y = 0.7340467417)
(X = 45.0,   Y = − 4.9846087554)
(X = 46.0,   Y = − 5.1291263)
(X = 47.0,   Y = 2.1813242014)
(X = 48.0,   Y = 1.8578747187)
(X = 49.0,   Y = 7.6197835954)
(X = 50.0,   Y = 4.3011814626)
(X = 51.0,   Y = 4.1085670937)
(X = 52.0,   Y = 4.9545937392)
(X = 53.0,   Y = − 5.3379970314)
(X = 54.0,   Y = − 19.5222166417)
(X = 55.0,   Y = − 16.8979451067)
(X = 56.0,   Y = − 17.751622188)
(X = 57.0,   Y = − 10.3357422219)
(X = 58.0,   Y = − 10.6740149358)
(X = 59.0,   Y = − 13.090919801)
(X = 60.0,   Y = − 16.3579177288)
(X = 61.0,   Y = − 12.1750299942)
(X = 62.0,   Y = − 8.9585917002)
(X = 63.0,   Y = − 3.5191306676)
(X = 64.0,   Y = 8.7584919584)
(X = 65.0,   Y = 12.5213179179)
(X = 66.0,   Y = 1.7283436916)

(X = 67.0, Y = 2.5545743641)
(X = 68.0, Y = 11.9302113598)
(X = 69.0, Y = 5.6161232304)
(X = 70.0, Y = 5.4291102585)
(X = 71.0, Y = − 3.9851221492)
(X = 72.0, Y = − 1.6101060218)
(X = 73.0, Y = − 4.6170343759)
(X = 74.0, Y = − 14.3337974285)
(X = 75.0, Y = − 10.7385528551)
(X = 76.0, Y = 2.6601640362)
(X = 77.0, Y = 6.6761759735)
(X = 78.0, Y = 5.538095211)
(X = 79.0, Y = 24.859606528)
(X = 80.0, Y = 20.5153212318)
(X = 81.0, Y = 27.3536586215)
(X = 82.0, Y = 31.9759557217)
(X = 83.0, Y = 36.5164598195)
(X = 84.0, Y = 36.7784670709)
(X = 85.0, Y = 28.0611391681)
(X = 86.0, Y = 32.1177054177)
(X = 87.0, Y = 33.3570934985)
(X = 88.0, Y = 24.3426326995)
(X = 89.0, Y = 41.814734247)
(X = 90.0, Y = 51.4731759113)
(X = 91.0, Y = 51.5084722166)
(X = 92.0, Y = 44.1394257716)
(X = 93.0, Y = 40.0990967222)
(X = 94.0, Y = 38.0502028171)
(X = 95.0, Y = 37.87671055)
(X = 96.0, Y = 32.4000817014)
(X = 97.0, Y = 26.7647784662)
(X = 98.0, Y = 23.5445126387)
(X = 99.0, Y = 17.9074381032)
(X = 100.0, Y = 25.2181669987)
(X = 101.0, Y = 19.5024043564)
(X = 102.0, Y = 23.4432401045)

- 单击菜单栏 Motions，选择系统单元 Joint Motions 框中的创建移动约束副驱动快捷方式图标：Translations Joint Motions；
- 选择移动副 test_patch_Translational，完成移动副驱动 MOTION_1 的创建；
- 右击 MOTION_1，选择 Modify；在弹出的 Joint Motion 对话框中选择 Fuction(time)：100*AKISPL(time,0,SPLINE_2, 0)。AKISPL（）是 ADAMS 的一个函数，表示按 Akima 插值方法将样条数据"SPLINE_2"拟合成以时间为横轴的函数曲线。
- 单击单击 OK，完成 MOTION_1 的修改。
- 点击 Simulaton，仿真时间设置为 10 s，仿真步数设置为 1 000，先计算悬架系统静平衡，计算完成后测量车身 Body 部件在 Y 方向的加速度，计算结果如图 16-11 所示，从计算结果中看，车身在垂向的加速度在 100 mm/s^2，效果极好。

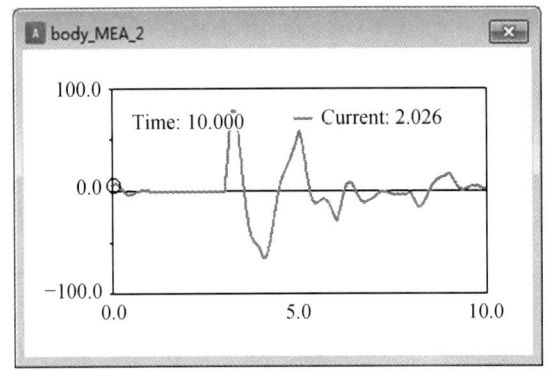

图 16-11　车身垂向加速度

检查模型麦弗逊悬架模型自由度，系统显示信息如下：所建立的悬架模型的部件数量、约束副等具体信息会显示出来，软件根据系统自由度计算公式，计算出所建立的麦弗逊悬架有 2 个自由度，模型正确无误。

VERIFY MODEL: .adams_view_zhengche

2 Gruebler Count (approximate degrees of freedom)
9 Moving Parts (not including ground)
1 Cylindrical Joints
1 Revolute Joints
3 Spherical Joints
2 Translational Joints
3 Fixed Joints
1 Hooke Joints
1 Inplane Primitive_Joints
1 Motions

2 Degrees of Freedom for .adams_view_zhengche

There are no redundant constraint equations.

Model verified successfully

16.4 路面驱动方案 B

- 单击菜单栏 Elements，选择系统单元 System Elements 框中的创建状态变量快捷方式图标：Create a State Variable defined by an Algebraic Equation；
- Name (状态变量名称)：road_shuru；
- Definition: Run-Time Expression；
- F(time，…)=：0；
- 单击单击 OK，完成状态变量 road_shuru 的创建，如图 16-12 所示。

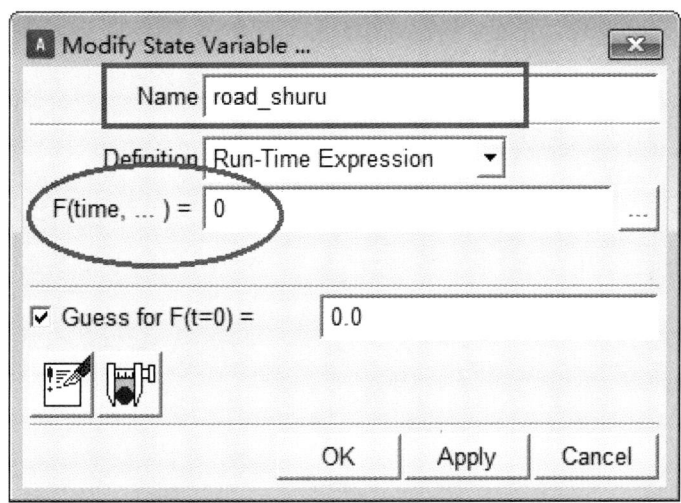

图 16-12　路面输入状态变量创建

- 单击菜单栏 Motions，选择系统单元 Joint Motions 框中的创建移动约束副驱动快捷方式图标：Translations Joint Motions；
- 选择移动副 test_patch_Translational，完成移动副驱动 MOTION_1 的创建；
- 右击 MOTION_1，选择 Modify；
- 在弹出的 Joint Motion 对话框中选择 Fuction(time)：VARVAL(.adams_view_zhengche.road_shuru)；
- 单击单击 OK，完成 MOTION_1 的修改，如图 16-13 所示。

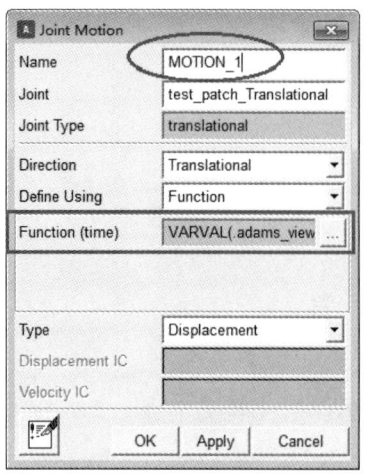

图 16-13　约束副驱动对话框

16.5　PID 控制器设计

PID 控制具有调节原理简单、参数容易整定和实用性强等优点，其控制规律如公式（16-2）所示：

$$u(t) = K_p e(t) + K_I' \int_0^t e(t)dt + K_d \frac{\mathrm{d}}{\mathrm{d}t}e(t) \quad (16\text{-}2)$$

式中，K_p 为比例系数；K_I 为时间极品常数，K_d 为微分时间常数，$e(t)$ 为实时误差，即车身速度与理想值之间差值；$u(t)$ 为实时主动控制力。根据公式（16-2）建立好的 PID 控制器模型如图 16-14 所示。

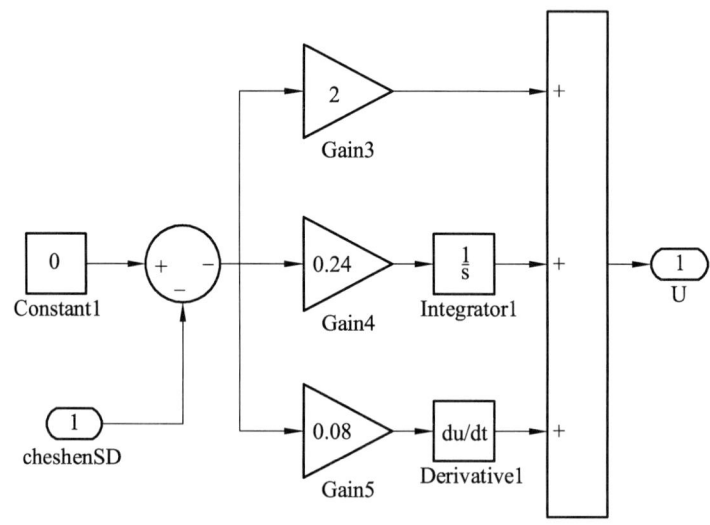

图 16-14　PID 控制器

16.6 半主动悬架联合仿真

上述建立的麦弗逊多体悬架模型为被动悬架模型,要想进行半主动悬架或者主动悬架联合仿真,首先需要在被动悬架模型的基础上构造或者建立主动悬架模型。

16.6.1 半主动悬架模型

半主动悬架模型构建首先需要添加主动力,主动力主要根据控制算法计算得出。主动悬架模型可采用不同算法:模糊控制算法、PID 模糊、神经网络、自适应模糊等。
- 单击菜单栏 Elements,选择系统单元 System Elements 框中的创建状态变量快捷方式图标:Create a State Variable defined by an Algebraic Equation;
- Name (状态变量名称):zhudongli_shuru;
- Definition: Run-Time Expression;
- F(time,…)=: 0;
- 单击 OK,完成状态变量 zhudongli_shuru 的创建,参考如图 16-12 所示。
- 单击菜单栏 Force,选择 Applied Forces 框的 Force 快捷方式,在两部件 srping_down、srping_up 之间建单向主动力;
- Run-time Direction (主动力运行时方向):Two Bodies;
- Construction:2 Bodies -2 Location;
- Characteristic:Custom;
- 根据命令窗口提示顺序选择两部件 srping_down、srping_up,顺序选择参考点 spring_down.cm、spring_up.cm,完成主动力 SFORCE_1 的创建;
- 选中主动力 SFORCE_1 右击鼠标选择 Rename:修改名称为 zhudongli;
- 单击 OK,完成硬主动力的重命名。
- 右击 zhudongli,选择 Modify;
- 在弹出的 Modify Force 对话框中修改 Fuction:输入 VARVAL(.adams_view_zhengche.zhudongli_shuru),其余参数保持默认;
- 单击单击 OK,完成主动力 zhudongli 的修改函数,如图 16-15 所示。

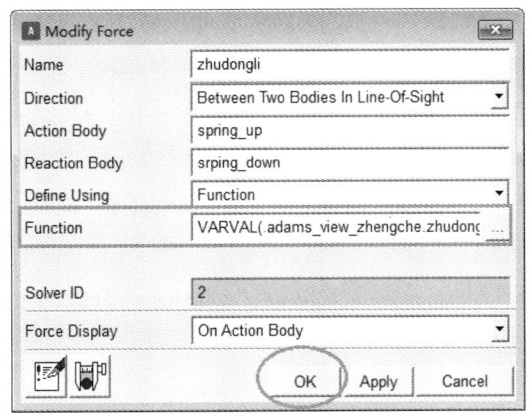

图 16-15 主动力修改对话框

建立车身速度、加速度、悬架动行程及车轮侧向滑移量状态输出函数，首先需要建立车身速度、加速度、悬架动行程及车轮侧向滑移量的测量函数。

- 单击菜单栏 Design Exploration，选择系统单元 Measures 框中的创建状态变量快捷方式图标：Create a new Function Measures，弹出函数构建对话框如图 16-16 所示；

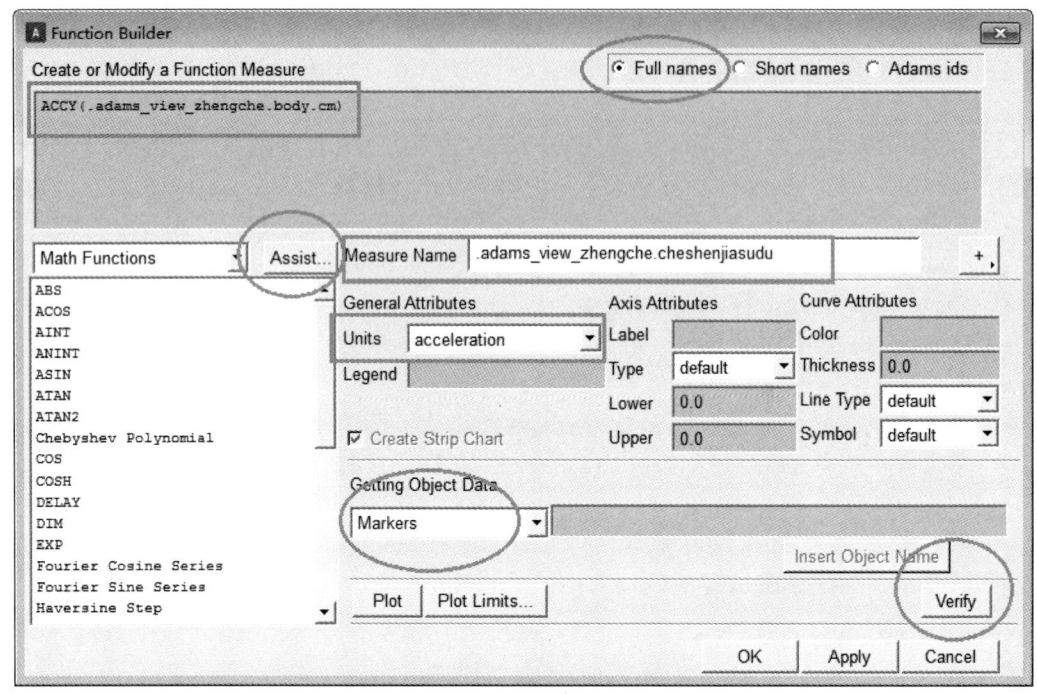

图 16-16　函数构建对话框

- Measures Name: cheshenjiasudu；
- Units：accelaeration；
- 选择 Accelaeration along Y；
- 点击 Assist 弹出 Accelaeration along Y 对话框；

To_Marker 框中输入 body.cm，其余 From_Marker，Along_Marker，Ref_Frame 框保持默认不用输入，辅助对话框如图 16-17 所示，单击 OK，完成加速度函数 ACCY(.adams_view_zhengche.body.cm)输入。

- 单击 Verify，检查函数 ACCY(.adams_view_zhengche.body.cm)正确无误；
- 单击 OK，完成函数构建。
- 重复以上步骤，建立以下测量函数，分别为车身速度、悬架动行程、车辆侧向滑移量：
① *VY(.adams_view_zhengche.body.cm)*；
② *DY(body.cm, wheel_right.cm) − DY(body_cm, ground.wheel_cm)+11.4*；
③ *DZ(MARKER_76, test_patch.cm)+0.3674*。

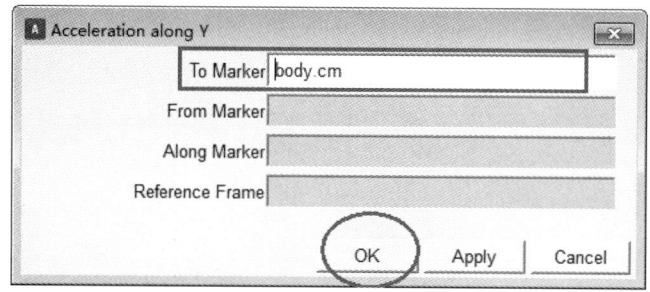

图 16-17　辅助对话框

- 单击菜单栏 Elements，选择系统单元 System Elements 框中的创建状态变量快捷方式图标：Create a State Variable defined by an Algebraic Equation；
- Name (状态变量名称)：cheshenjiasudu_shuchu；
- Definition: Run-Time Expression；
- F(time，…)=：ACCY(.adams_view_zhengche.body.cm)；
- 单击 OK，完成状态变量 cheshenjiasudu_shuchu 的创建，如图 16-18 所示。

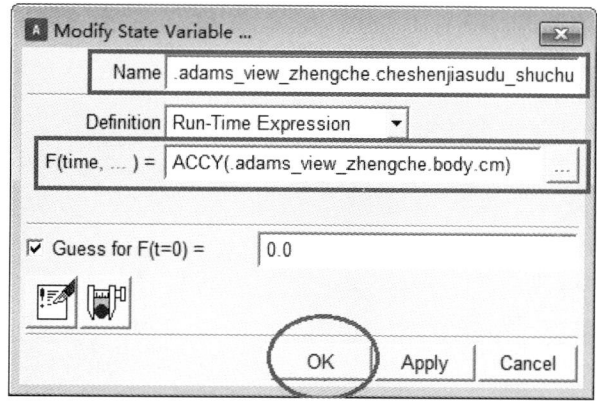

图 16-18　状态变量对话框

- 重复以上步骤，分别建立状态变量 cheshensudu_shuchu、xuanjiadongxingcheng_shuchu、cexianghuayiliang_shuchu；
- 单击菜单栏 Elements，选择数据块单元 Date Elements 框中的创建输入集快捷方式图标：Create an ADAMS plant input；
- Variable Name(变量名称，输入之前建立好的输入状态变量)：.adams_view_zhengche.zhudongli_shuru,.adams_view_zhengche.road_shuru；
- 单击 OK，完成输入集.adams_view_zhengche.PINPUT_1 的创建；输入集如图 16-19 所示。
- 单击菜单栏 Elements，选择数据块单元 Date Elements 框中的创建输入集快捷方式图标：Create an ADAMS plant output；
- Variable Name(变量名称，输入之前建立好的输出状态变量)：.adams_view_zhengche.cexianghuayiliang_shuchu,.adams_view_zhengche.cheshenjiasudu_shuchu,.adams_view_zhengche.cheshensudu_shuchu,.adams_view_zhengche.xuanjiadongxingcheng_shuchu；

- 单击 OK，完成输出集 .adams_view_zhengche.POUTPUT_1 的创建；输出集如图 16-20 所示。

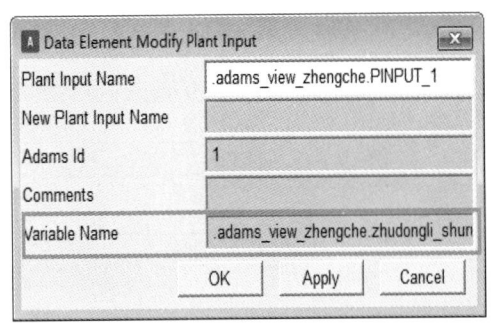 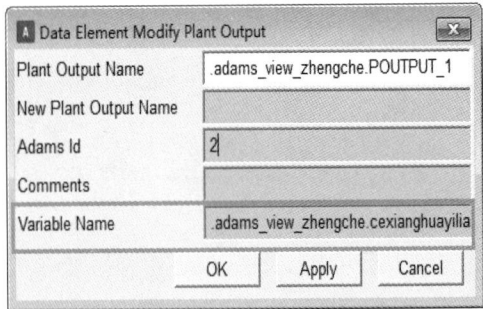

图 16-19　输入集对话框　　　　　　　　图 16-20　输出集对话框

至此，完成麦弗逊悬架被动模型到主动悬架模型的转变，建立好的主动悬架模型如图 16-21 所示，不加控制系统，主动悬架模型依然可以在方案 A 下进行仿真，仿真结果准确无误；在方案 B 下也可进行仿真，但结果不正确，原因在于振动台架不动，悬架只是在重力作用下进行的静平衡计算。

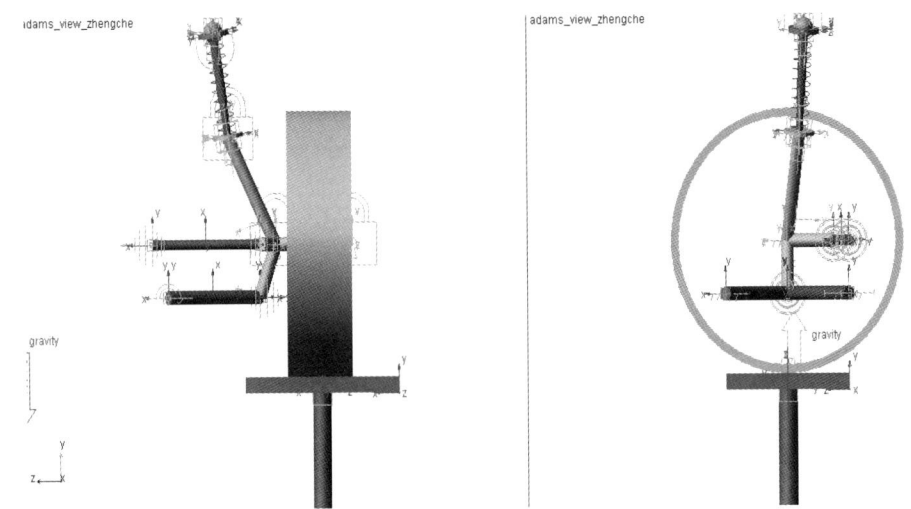

图 16-21　主动悬架模型

16.6.2　机控协同模型

通过 ADAMS\CONTROL 模块系统机械模型与控制模型，ADAMS 与 MATLAB 软件路径统一设置为 D:\adams_view2013\adams_matlab。

- 单击菜单栏插件 Plugins，选择 Controls 单击，出现下拉列表选择 **Plant Export** 命令，弹出控制接口输出对话框如图 16-22 所示；

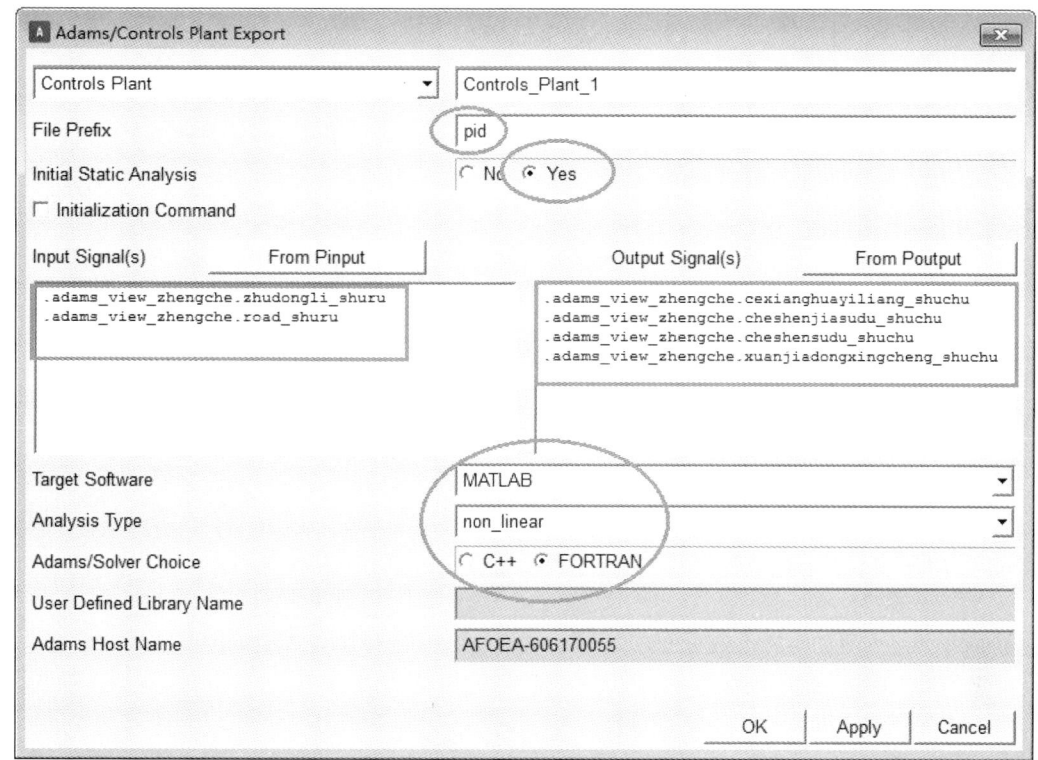

图 16-22 控制接口输出对话框

- File Prefix（输出文件别名）：pid；
- Initial Static Analysis(初始静态分析）：Yes，此处需要进行静平衡，静平衡完成之后再进行计算；
- 单击 From Pinput，在弹出的数据命令窗口中选择子系统双击 adams_view_zhengche 下的 PINPUT1；
- 单击 From Poutput，在弹出的数据命令窗口中选择子系统双击 adams_view_zhengche 下的 POUTPUT1；
- Target Software（目标软件或者对接软件）：MATLAB；
- Analysis Type(分析类型）：选择非线性 non_linear；
- Adams/Solver Choice：选择 FORTRAN；
- 其余保持默认，单击 OK 完成 ADAMS\CONTROLS 模块下的输入输出集的创建。
- MATLAB 软件中命令窗口中输入 Controls_Plant_1；
- 单击键盘 Enter 键，此时命令窗口显示出输入输出集信息；
- 命令窗口中输入 adams_sys，单击键盘 Enter 键调出 adams_plant 对话框，如图 16-23 所示。

导通 ADAMS 与 MATLAB 软件之间通信，对路面及 PID 控制器进行封装，建立 ADAMS 主动悬架联合仿真模型如图 16-24 所示。在 B 级路面上车辆分别以 20 km/h、40 km/h、60 km/h、80 km/h 的速度直线行驶，计算主被动悬架的车身加速度、悬架动行程、车轮侧向滑移量。主被动悬架计算结果如图 16-25 ~ 图 16-29 所示，仿真步长为 0.005 s，仿真时间为 10 s。

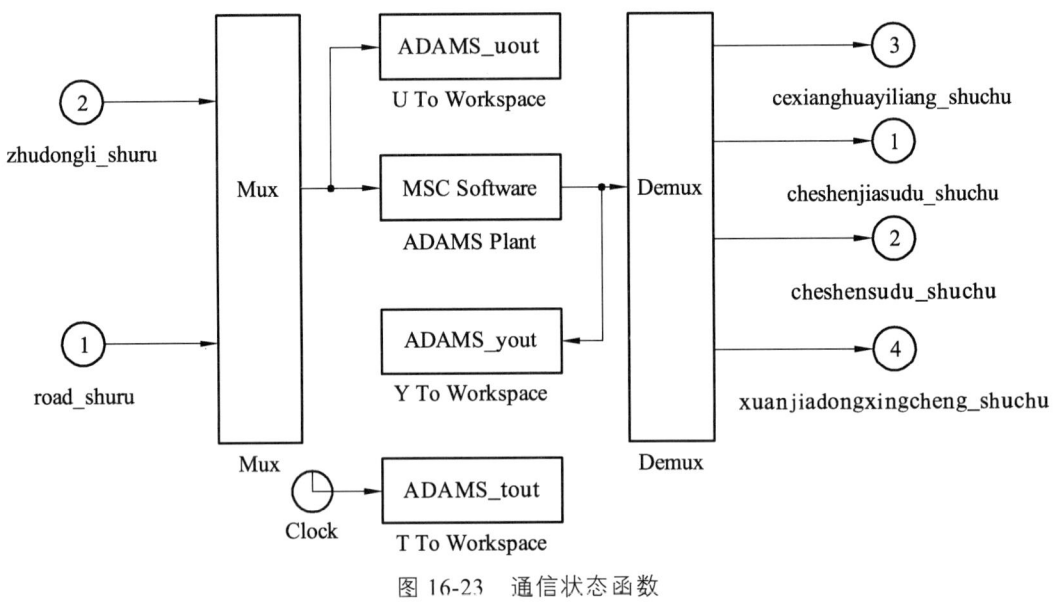

图 16-23 通信状态函数

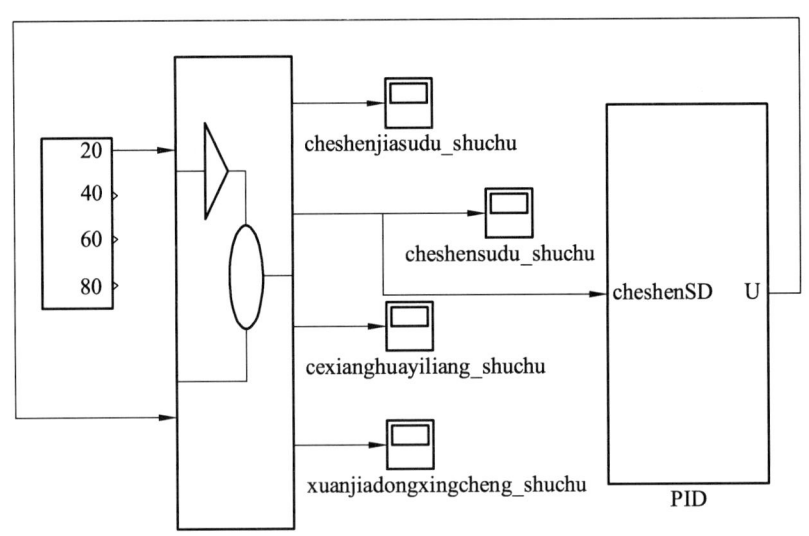

图 16-24 联合仿真模型

从计算结果中可以看出,主动悬架相对于被动悬架在性能上整体都有所提升。在各不同车速阶段,车身垂直加速度、悬架动行程、轮胎动位移性能均有改善,其中车身垂向加速度改善尤为突出,在全速范围内改善车辆行驶的乘坐舒适性。随着车速的增加,悬架动行程及侧向滑移量稍有改善,增加整车行驶过程中的操作稳定性。各个速度段的悬架性能参数变化如表16-1所示。

表 16-1　性能均方根值对比表

均方根值	车速/(km/h)	主动悬架	被动悬架	优化比
垂直加速度/(m/s²)	20	2.33E−1	4.52E−1	48.5
悬架动行程/m		3.90E−2	4.10E−2	4.9
侧向滑移量/m		2.80E−5	4.39E−5	36.2
垂直加速度/(m/s²)	40	3.30E−1	6.40E−1	48.4
悬架动行程/m		4.02E−2	4.27E−2	5.9
侧向滑移量/m		3.85E−5	6.11E−5	37.0
垂直加速度/(m/s²)	60	4.04E−1	7.84E−1	48.5
悬架动行程/m		4.11E−2	4.41E−2	6.8
侧向滑移量/m		4.67E−5	7.43E−5	37.1
垂直加速度/(m/s²)	80	4.66E−1	9.04E−1	48.5
悬架动行程/m		4.18E−2	4.53E−2	7.7
侧向滑移量/m		5.35E−5	8.53E−5	37.3

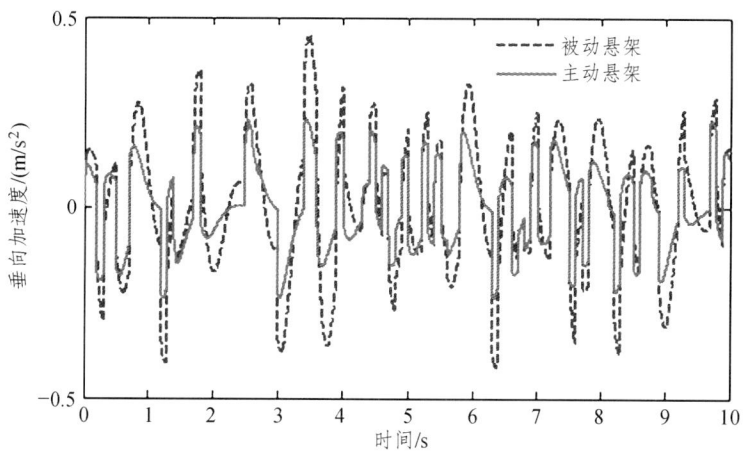

图 16-25　车身垂向加速度

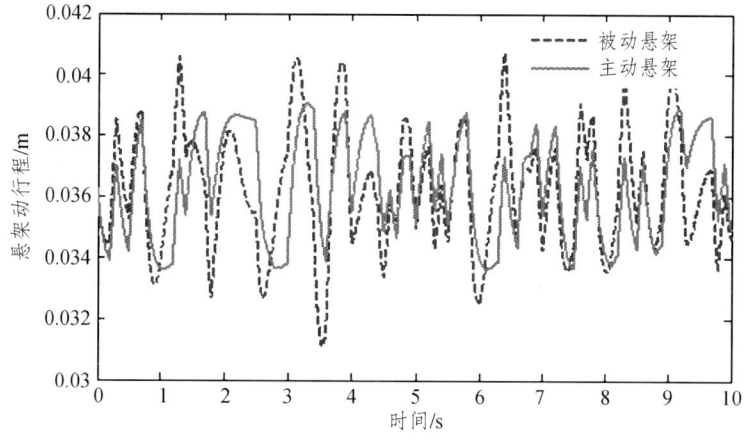

图 16-26　悬架动行程

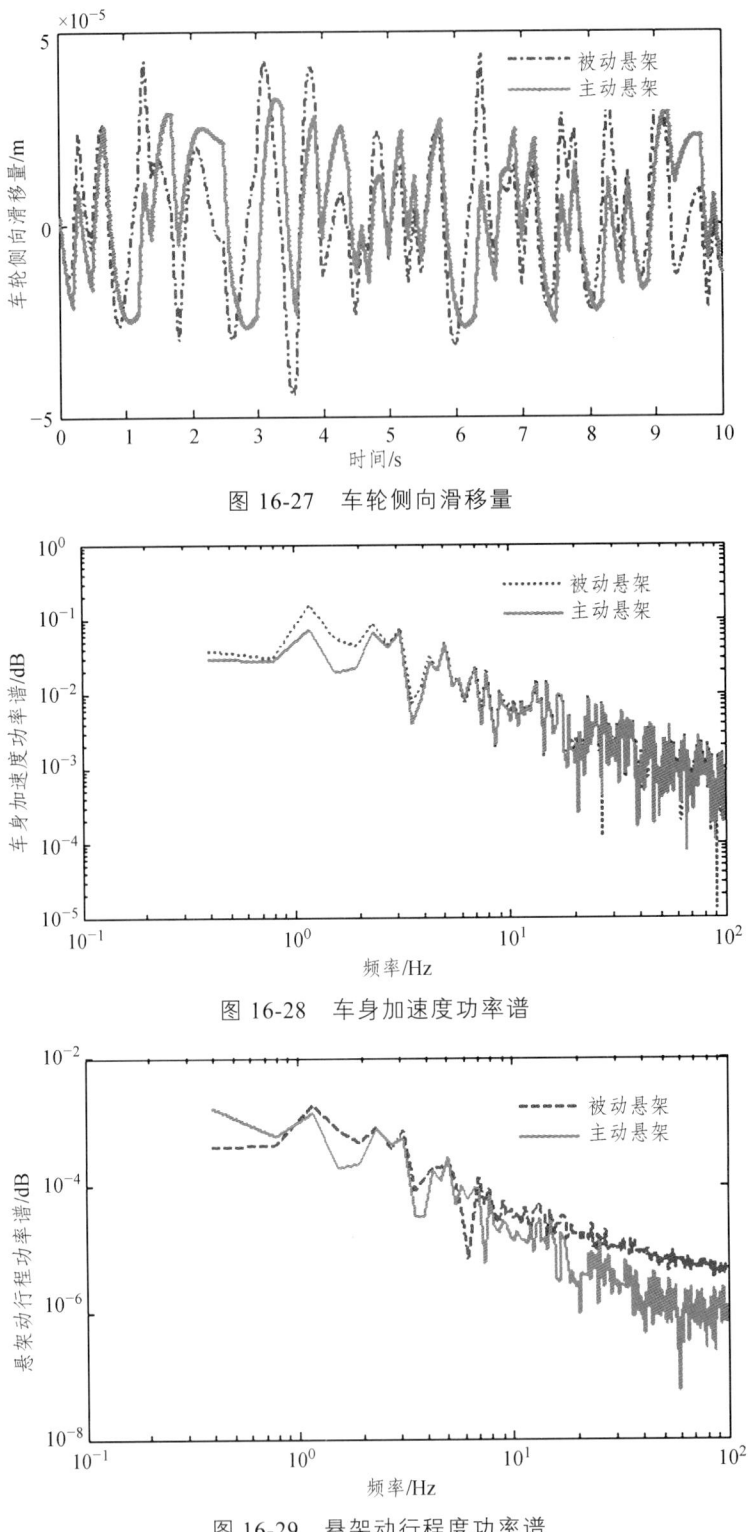

图 16-27 车轮侧向滑移量

图 16-28 车身加速度功率谱

图 16-29 悬架动行程度功率谱

如图 16-28、图 16-29 所示为车身加速度、悬架动行程的功率谱曲线。从功率谱曲线中可以看出，整车运行过程中，主动悬架的幅值相对被动悬架都较小，同时可以看出，振幅最大值都出现在频率较小处，低频路面输入信息对整车的振动特性较大，悬架动行程在高频路面激励下车轮的振动得到较好的抑制。

16.7 时频域、功率谱密度变换程序

程序一：

```
k=yout(:,1);
Fs=100; %采样频率(Hz)
N=500; %采样点数
t=[0:1/Fs:N/Fs]; %采样时刻
S=k;%信号
Y = fft(S,N); %做 FFT 变换
Ayy = abs(Y); %取模
Ayy=Ayy/(N/2);    %换算成实际的幅度
F=([1:N] – 1)*Fs/N; %换算成实际的频率值，Fn=(n – 1)*Fs/N
plot(F(1:N/2),Ayy(1:N/2)); %显示换算后的 FFT 模值结果 title('幅度-频率曲线图')。
```

程序二：

```
k=yout(:,1); k1=yout(:,2);
Fs=100; %采样频率(Hz)
N=500; %采样点数
t=[0:1/Fs:N/Fs]; %采样时刻
S=k;S1=k1;%信号
Y= fft(S,N); %做 FFT 变换
Y1 = fft(S1,N); %做 FFT 变换
Ayy = abs(Y); %取模
Ayy=Ayy/(N/2);    %换算成实际的幅度
Ayy1= abs(Y1); %取模
Ayy1=Ayy1/(N/2);    %换算成实际的幅度
F=([1:N] – 1)*Fs/N; %换算成实际的频率值，Fn=(n – 1)*Fs/N
plot(F(1:N/2),Ayy(1:N/2),F(1:N/2),Ayy1(1:N/2)); %显示换算后的 FFT 模值结果 title('幅度-频率曲线图')。
```

程序三：

```
Nfft=2048;
Fs=200;
n=0:N – 1;
t=n/Fs;
window=hanning(Nfft);
```

```
overlap=128;
dflag='none';
xn=yout(:,1);
Pxx=psd(xn,Nfft,Fs,window,overlap,dflag);%Create frequency vector
f=(0:Nfft/2)*Fs/Nfft;
plot(f,10*log10(Pxx));
set(gca,'XScale','log');set(gca,'YScale','log');
xlabel('Frequency (Hz)');ylabel('Power Spectrum (dB)');
```
%此部分中 f 的创建方法：它与函数 psd 的输出 Pxx 的长度有关。若 x 为实序列，当 Nfft 为奇数时 f=(0:(Nfft+1)/2 − 1)/Nfft；%当 Nfft 为偶数时 f=(0:Nfft/2)/Nfft。

程序四：

```
Nfft=2048;
Fs=200;
n=0:N − 1;
t=n/Fs;
window=hanning(Nfft);
overlap=128;
dflag='none';
xn=yout(:,1); xn1=yout(:,2);
Pxx=psd(xn,Nfft,Fs,window,overlap,dflag);%Create frequency vector
Pxx1=psd(xn1,Nfft,Fs,window,overlap,dflag);
f=(0:Nfft/2)*Fs/Nfft;
plot(f,10*log10(Pxx),f,10*log10(Pxx1));
set(gca,'XScale','log');set(gca,'YScale','log');
xlabel('频率(Hz)');ylabel('车身加速度功率谱 (dB)');
```
%此部分中 f 的创建方法：它与函数 psd 的输出 Pxx 的长度有关。若 x 为实序列，当 Nfft 为奇数时 f=(0:(Nfft+1)/2 − 1)/Nfft；%当 Nfft 为偶数时 f=(0:Nfft/2)/Nfft。

第 17 章 驾驶室隔振联合仿真

驾驶室悬置系统的优劣关系到驾乘人员的乘坐品质感受。国内商用货车驾驶室多采用四点全浮支撑,即驾驶室前后端分别采用对称的弹簧与阻尼器进行支撑。以 6×4 底盘为基础的商用牵运引货车及工程车辆常在国、省、乡道路面(减速带较多,即为阶跃或者正弦路面信号输入)及极差的工地路面运行,舒适性差,主动驾驶室悬置系统可以有效改善垂向振动特性,提升乘坐舒适感。针对驾驶室振动特性,本章节基于商用牵引车整车平台建立主动驾驶室模型,此模型更能反映驾驶室真实运行状态,同时又可以进行系统间参数的匹配;主动驾驶室采用模糊 PID-D 耦合算法,用车身加速度判别路面状态,对 PID 算法中的微分系数进行在线自适应实时调节,避免在较差路面及减速带路面造成的定点冲击,适合多工况路面输入特性,提升驾驶室乘坐品质感,建立好的主动驾驶室模型如图 17-1 所示。

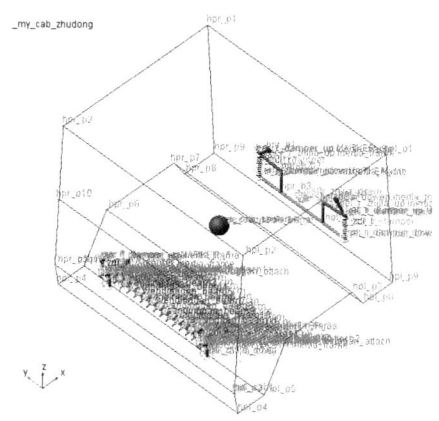

图 17-1 驾驶室模型

学习目标

- ✧ 驾驶模型。
- ✧ 横向稳定杆(离散梁)。
- ✧ 驾驶室约束关系。
- ✧ 主动驾驶室函数设定。
- ✧ 整车平台。
- ✧ ADAMS\CONTROLS 设置。
- ✧ ADAMS 与 MATLAB 软件协同。
- ✧ PID-D 耦合算法。

◆ 悬架辅助系统。

17.1 驾驶模型

- 启动 ADAMS/CAR；
- 单击 File > New 命令，弹出建模对话框如图 17-2 所示；
- Template Name：my_cab_zhudong；
- Major Role：cab；
- 单击 OK，完成驾驶室模板建立。

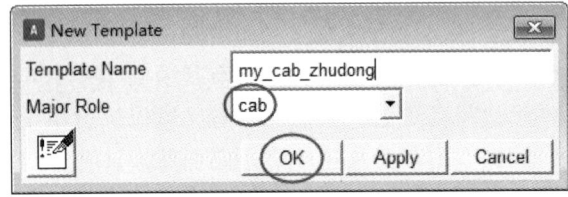

图 17-2　驾驶模板

- 单击 Build > Hardpoint > New 命令，弹出创建硬点对话框如图 17-3 所示；
- Hardpoint Name：cab_center；
- Type：single；
- Location：1 900.0, 0.0, 1 900.0；
- 单击 OK，完成 .my_cab_zhudong.ground.hps_cab_center 硬点的创建。
- 重复上述步骤，完成如表 17-1 所示硬点参数的创建，创建过程中请注意左右对称的情况，具体请参考已经建立好的驾驶室模型，该模型存储于章节文件中；

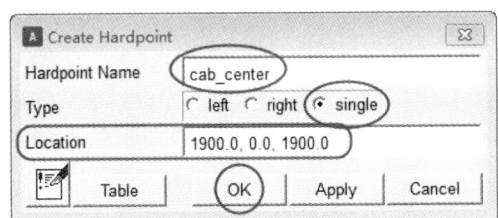

图 17-3　驾驶室硬点

表 17-1　驾驶室硬点参数

硬点名称	X 方向	Y 方向	Z 方向
r_damper_down	3 028.0	−591.5	1 352.0
r_damper_up	3 028.0	−591.5	1 657.0
weidinggan	1 010.0	−456.0	1 326.0
zhijia_down	1 085.0	−665.0	1 180.0
zhijia_front	1 085.0	−665.0	1 340.0
cab_center	1 900.0	0.0	1 900.0
cab1	900.0	−1 225.0	1 200.0

续表

硬点名称	X方向	Y方向	Z方向
f_damper_down	985.0	-665.0	1 390.0
f_damper_up	985.0	-665.0	1 590.0
f_spring_down	1 040.0	-552.5	1 375.0
f_spring_up	1 040.0	-552.5	1 534.5
fzb_front	1 085.0	-665.0	1 340.0
fzb_rear	1 324.0	-665.0	1 340.0
b1	3 028.0	-470.0	1 792.6
b2	3 028.0	-288.5	1 635.0
b3	3 028.0	-288.5	1 352.0
b4	985.0	-665.0	1 390.0
p1	2 950.0	-1 225.0	3 000.0
p2	1 000.0	-1 225.0	3 000.0
p3	900.0	-1 225.0	1 200.0
p4	950.0	-1 225.0	900.0
p5	1 300.0	-1 225.0	900.0
p6	1 600.0	-1 225.0	1 450.0
p7	2 500.0	-1 225.0	1 450.0
p8	2 650.0	-1 225.0	1 200.0
p9	3 050.0	-1 225.0	1 200.0
p10	950.0	-1 225.0	2 050.0

（1）驾驶室质心部件

- 单击 Build > Part > General Part > New 命令（见图 17-4）；

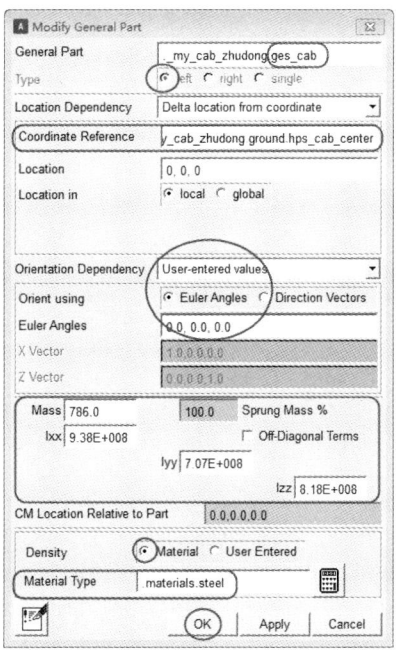

图 17-4 驾驶室简化质心部件

- General Part：ges_cab；
- Type: left；
- Location Dependency: Delta location from coordinate；
- Coordinate Reference: ._my_cab_zhudong.ground.hps_cab_center；
- Location: 0, 0, 0 ；
- Orientation Dependency: User-entered values；
- Orient using: Euler Angles；
- Euler Angles: 0, 0, 0；
- Mass: 786.0；
- Ixx: 9.38E+008；
- Iyy: 7.07E+008；
- Izz: 8.18E+008；
- Density：Material；
- Material Type：.materials.steel；
- 单击 OK，完成部件._my_cab_zhudong.ges_cab 创建。
- 单击 Build > Geometry > Ellipsoid > New 命令如图 17-5 所示；

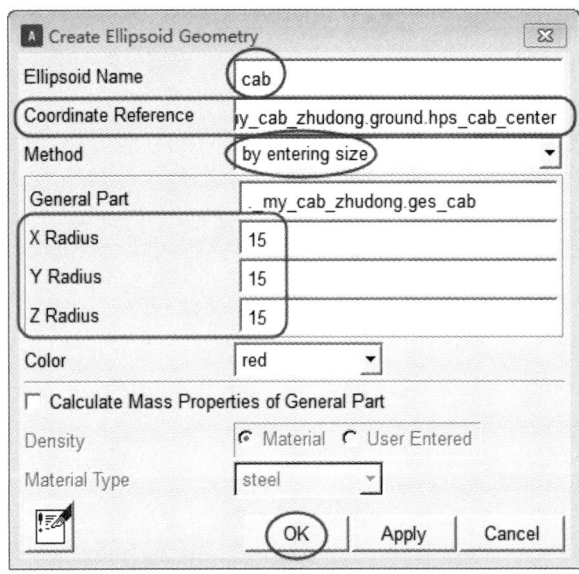

图 17-5 球形几何体

- Ellipsoid Name（连杆名称）输入几何名称：cab；
- Coordinate Reference：._my_cab_zhudong.ground.hps_cab_center；
- Method: by entering size；
- General Part 输入._my_cab_zhudong.ges_cab；
- X Radius（半径）: 15；
- Y Radius（半径）: 15；
- Z Radius（半径）: 15；

- Color（杆件几何体颜色）：red；
- 不勾选：Calculate Mass Properties of General Part；
- Density：Material；
- Material Type：steel；
- 单击 OK，完成驾驶室几何体 cab 的创建。

（2）后避震器上连接处部件。
- 单击 Build > Part > General Part > New 命令参考如图 17-4 所示；
- General Part：r_damper_up；
- Type: left；
- Location Dependency: Delta location from coordinate；
- Coordinate Reference: ._my_cab_zhudong.ground.hpl_r_damper_up；
- Location: 0, 0, 0；
- Location in: local；
- Orientation Dependency: Orient axis along line；
- Coordinate Reference #1（参考坐标）:._my_cab_zhudong.ground.hpl_r_damper_down；
- Coordinate Reference #2（参考坐标）:._my_cab_zhudong.ground.hpl_r_damper_up；
- Axis：Z；
- Mass: 1；
- Ixx:1；
- Iyy: 1；
- Izz: 1；
- Density：Material；
- Material Type：.materials.steel；
- 单击 OK，完成部件._my_cab_zhudong.gel_r_damper_up 创建。

（3）后避震器下连接处部件。
- 单击 Build > Part > General Part > New 命令参考如图 17-4 所示；
- General Part：r_damper_down；
- Type: left；
- Location Dependency: Delta location from coordinate；
- Coordinate Reference: ._my_cab_zhudong.ground.hpl_r_damper_down；
- Location: 0, 0, 0 ；
- Location in: local；
- Orientation Dependency: Orient axis along line；
- Coordinate Reference #1（参考坐标）:._my_cab_zhudong.ground.hpl_r_damper_down；
- Coordinate Reference #2（参考坐标）:._my_cab_zhudong.ground.hpl_r_damper_up；
- Axis：Z；
- Mass: 1；
- Ixx:1；
- Iyy: 1；

- Izz: 1;
- Density：Material；
- Material Type：.materials.steel；
- 单击 OK，完成部件._my_cab_zhudong.gel_r_damper_down 创建。

（4）前避震器上连接处部件。
- 单击 Build > Part > General Part > New 命令参考如图 17-4 所示；
- General Part：f_damper_up；
- Type: left；
- Location Dependency: Delta location from coordinate；
- Coordinate Reference: ._my_cab_zhudong.ground.hpl_f_damper_up；
- Location: 0, 0, 0；
- Orientation Dependency: User-entered values；
- Orient using: Euler Angles；
- Euler Angles: 0, 0, 0；
- Mass: 1；
- Ixx: 1；
- Iyy: 1；
- Izz: 1；
- Density：Material；
- Material Type：.materials.steel；
- 单击 OK，完成部件._my_cab_zhudong.gel_f_damper_up 创建。

（5）前避震器下连接处部件。
- 单击 Build > Part > General Part > New 命令参考如图 17-4 所示；
- General Part：f_damper_down；
- Type: left；
- Location Dependency: Delta location from coordinate；
- Coordinate Reference: ._my_cab_zhudong.ground.hpl_f_damper_down；
- Location: 0, 0, 0 ；
- Orientation Dependency: User-entered values；
- Orient using: Euler Angles；
- Euler Angles: 0, 0, 0；
- Mass: 1；
- Ixx: 1；
- Iyy: 1；
- Izz: 1；
- Density：Material；
- Material Type：.materials.steel；
- 单击 OK，完成部件._my_cab_zhudong.gel_f_damper_down 创建。

（6）驾驶室前上支架部件。
- 单击 Build > Part > General Part > New 命令参考如图 17-4 所示；
- General Part：zhijia_UP；
- Type: left；
- Location Dependency: Centered between coordinates；
- Centered between：Two coordinates；
- Coordinate Reference #1（参考坐标）：._my_cab_zhudong.ground.hpl_fzb_rear；
- Coordinate Reference #2（参考坐标）：._my_cab_zhudong.ground.hpl_zhijia_up_front；
- Orientation Dependency: User-entered values；
- Orient using: Euler Angles；
- Euler Angles: 0, 0, 0；
- Mass: 1；
- Ixx: 1；
- Iyy: 1；
- Izz: 1；
- Density：Material；
- Material Type：.materials.steel；
- 单击 OK，完成部件._my_cab_zhudong.gel_zhijia_UP 创建。

（7）驾驶室前上支架几何体。
- 单击 Build > Geometry > Link > New 命令，弹出创建连杆对话框如图 17-6 所示；

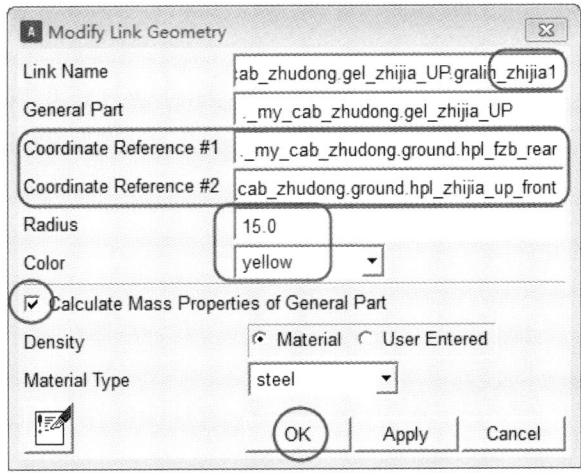

图 17-6　连杆几何体_zhijia1

- Link Name (连杆名称）输入几何名称：zhijia1；
- General Part 输入._my_cab_zhudong.gel_zhijia_UP；
- Coordinate Reference #1(参考坐标）：._my_cab_zhudong.ground.hpl_fzb_rear；
- Coordinate Reference #2(参考坐标）：._my_cab_zhudong.ground.hpl_zhijia_up_front；
- Radius(半径): 15；

- 437 -

- Color：yellow；
- 选择 Calculate Mass Properties of General Part 复选框，当几何体建立好之后会更新对应部件的质量和惯量参数；
- Density：Material；
- Material Type：steel；
- 单击 Apply，完成 ._my_cab_zhudong.gel_zhijia_UP.gralin_zhijia1 几何体的创建；
- Link Name（连杆名称）输入几何名称：zhijia2；
- General Part 输入 ._my_cab_zhudong.gel_zhijia_UP；
- Coordinate Reference #1(参考坐标)：._my_cab_zhudong.ground.hpl_zhijia_up_front；
- Coordinate Reference #2(参考坐标)：._my_cab_zhudong.ground.hpl_b4；
- Radius(半径): 15；
- Color：yellow；
- 选择 Calculate Mass Properties of General Part 复选框；
- Density：Material；
- Material Type：steel；
- 单击 Apply，完成 ._my_cab_zhudong.gel_zhijia_UP.gralin_zhijia_2 几何体的创建。

（8）驾驶室前下支架部件。
- 单击 Build > Part > General Part > New 命令参考如图 17-4 所示；
- General Part：zhijia_DOWN；
- Type: left；
- Location Dependency: Centered between coordinates；
- Centered between：Two coordinates；
- Coordinate Reference #1（参考坐标）：._my_cab_zhudong.ground.hpl_fzb_front；
- Coordinate Reference #2（参考坐标）：._my_cab_zhudong.ground.hpl_zhijia_down；
- Orientation Dependency: User-entered values；
- Orient using: Euler Angles；
- Euler Angles: 0, 0, 0；
- Mass: 1；
- Ixx: 1；
- Iyy: 1；
- Izz: 1；
- Density：Material；
- Material Type：.materials.steel；
- 单击 OK，完成部件 ._my_cab_zhudong.gel_zhijia_DOWN 创建。

（9）驾驶室前下支架几何体。
- 单击 Build > Geometry > Link > New 命令，弹出创建连杆对话框参考如图 17-6 所示；
- Link Name（连杆名称）输入几何名称：zhijia_A；
- General Part 输入 ._my_cab_zhudong.gel_zhijia_DOWN；
- Coordinate Reference #1（参考坐标）：._my_cab_zhudong.ground.hpl_fzb_front；

- Coordinate Reference #2（参考坐标）：._my_cab_zhudong.ground.hpl_zhijia_down；
- Radius（半径）：15；
- Color：skyblue；
- 选择 Calculate Mass Properties of General Part 复选框，当几何体建立好之后会更新对应部件的质量和惯量参数；
- Density：Material；
- Material Type：steel；
- 单击 OK，完成._my_cab_zhudong.gel_zhijia_DOWN.gralin_zhijia_A 几何体的创建。

（10）驾驶室后下支架部件。
- 单击 Build > Part > General Part > New 命令参考如图 17-4 所示；
- General Part：r_zhijia_dowen；
- Type: single；
- Location Dependency: Centered between coordinates；
- Centered between：Four coordinates；
- Coordinate Reference #1（参考坐标）：._my_cab_zhudong.ground.hpl_r_damper_down；
- Coordinate Reference #2（参考坐标）：._my_cab_zhudong.ground.hpr_r_damper_down；
- Coordinate Reference #3（参考坐标）：._my_cab_zhudong.ground.hpr_b2；
- Coordinate Reference #4（参考坐标）：._my_cab_zhudong.ground.hpl_b2；
- Orientation Dependency: User-entered values；
- Orient using: Euler Angles；
- Euler Angles: 0, 0, 0；
- Mass: 1；
- Ixx: 1；
- Iyy: 1；
- Izz: 1；
- Density：Material；
- Material Type：.materials.steel；
- 单击 OK，完成部件._my_cab_zhudong.ges_r_zhijia_dowen 创建。

（11）驾驶室后下支架几何体。
- 单击 Build > Geometry > Link > New 命令，弹出创建连杆对话框参考如图 17-6 所示；
- Link Name（连杆名称）输入几何名称：zhijia_a；
- General Part 输入：._my_cab_zhudong.ges_r_zhijia_dowen；
- Coordinate Reference #1（参考坐标）：._my_cab_zhudong.ground.hpl_r_damper_down；
- Coordinate Reference #2（参考坐标）：._my_cab_zhudong.ground.hpr_r_damper_down；
- Radius（半径）：15；
- Color：green；
- 选择 Calculate Mass Properties of General Part；
- Density：Material；
- Material Type：steel；

- 单击 Apply,完成._my_cab_zhudong.ges_r_zhijia_dowen.gralin_zhijia_a 几何体的创建；
- Link Name (连杆名称）输入几何名称：zhijia_b；
- General Part 输入._my_cab_zhudong.ges_r_zhijia_dowen；
- Coordinate Reference #1(参考坐标)：._my_cab_zhudong.ground.hpl_b2；
- Coordinate Reference #2(参考坐标)：._my_cab_zhudong.ground.hpl_b3；
- Radius(半径): 15；
- Color：green；
- 选择 Calculate Mass Properties of General Part；
- Density：Material；
- Material Type：steel；
- 单击 Apply,完成._my_cab_zhudong.ges_r_zhijia_dowen.gralin_zhijia_b 几何体的创建；
- Link Name (连杆名称）输入几何名称：zhijia_c；
- General Part 输入._my_cab_zhudong.ges_r_zhijia_dowen；
- Coordinate Reference #1(参考坐标)：._my_cab_zhudong.ground.hpr_b2；
- Coordinate Reference #2(参考坐标)：._my_cab_zhudong.ground.hpr_b3；
- Radius(半径): 15；
- Color：green；
- 选择 Calculate Mass Properties of General Part；
- Density：Material；
- Material Type：steel；
- 单击 OK，完成._my_cab_zhudong.ges_r_zhijia_dowen.gralin_zhijia_c 几何体的创建。

（12）驾驶室后上支架部件。

- 单击 Build > Part > General Part > New 命令参考如图 17-4 所示；
- General Part：r_zhijia_up；
- Type: left；
- Location Dependency: Centered between coordinates；
- Centered between：Two coordinates；
- Coordinate Reference #1（参考坐标）:._my_cab_zhudong.ground.hpl_b2；
- Coordinate Reference #2（参考坐标）:._my_cab_zhudong.ground.hpl_r_damper_up；
- Orientation Dependency: User-entered values；
- Orient using: Euler Angles；
- Euler Angles: 0, 0, 0；
- Mass: 1；
- Ixx: 1；
- Iyy: 1；
- Izz: 1；
- Density：Material；

- Material Type：.materials.steel；
- 单击 OK，完成部件._my_cab_zhudong.gel_r_zhijia_up 创建。

（13）驾驶室后上支架几何体。
- 单击 Build > Geometry > Link > New 命令，弹出创建连杆对话框参考如图 17-6 所示；
- Link Name（连杆名称）输入几何名称：zhijia_a；
- General Part 输入._my_cab_zhudong.gel_r_zhijia_up；
- Coordinate Reference #1（参考坐标）：._my_cab_zhudong.ground.hpl_b2；
- Coordinate Reference #2（参考坐标）：._my_cab_zhudong.ground.hpl_r_damper_up；
- Radius（半径): 15；
- Color：red；
- 选择 Calculate Mass Properties of General Part；
- Density：Material；
- Material Type：steel；
- 单击 Apply,完成._my_cab_zhudong.gel_r_zhijia_up.gralin_zhijia_a 几何体的创建；
- Link Name（连杆名称）输入几何名称：zhijia_b；
- General Part 输入._my_cab_zhudong.gel_r_zhijia_up；
- Coordinate Reference #1（参考坐标）：._my_cab_zhudong.ground.hpl_r_damper_up；
- Coordinate Reference #2（参考坐标）：._my_cab_zhudong.ground.hpl_b1；
- Radius(半径): 15；
- Color：red；
- 选择 Calculate Mass Properties of General Part；
- Density：Material；
- Material Type：steel；
- 单击 OK，完成._my_cab_zhudong.gel_r_zhijia_up.gralin_zhijia_b 几何体的创建。

（14）安装部件 cab_to_body。
- 单击 Build > Part > Mount > New 命令，弹出创建部件对话框如图 17-7 所示；
- Mount name（安装件名称）：cab_to_body；
- Coordinate Reference （参考坐标）：._my_cab_zhudong.ground.hps_cab_center；
- 安装件此特征选择 inherit（继承特性）；
- 单击 OK，完成._my_cab_zhudong.mts_cab_to_body 安装部件的创建。

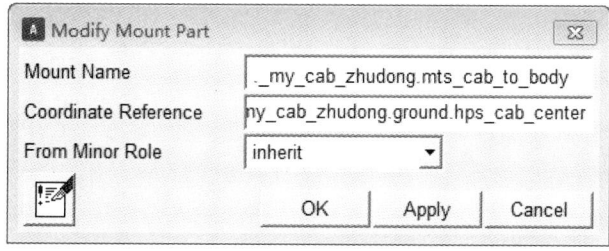

图 17-7　安装部件

17.2 前横向稳定杆

- 单击 Tools > ADAMS/VIEW interface 命令，建模界面切换 VIEW 通用模块；
- 单击 Bodies > Flexible Bodies > Discrete Flexible Link 命令，弹簧离散量建模界面如图 17-8 所示

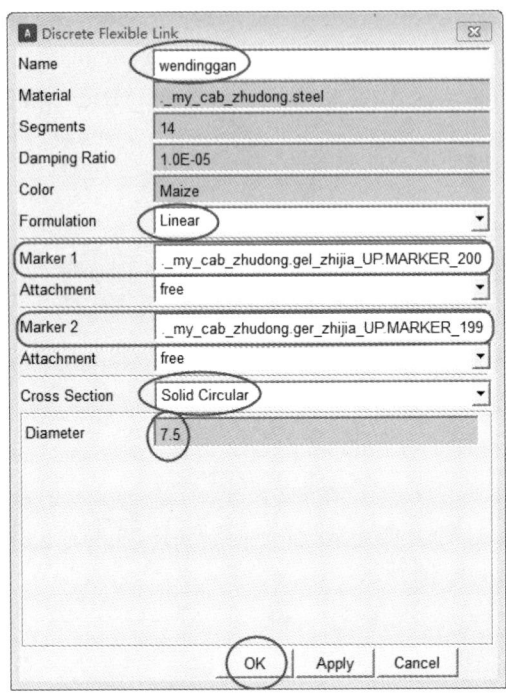

图 17-8　横向稳定杆（离散梁）

- Name：wendinggan；
- Material：._my_cab_zhudong.steel；
- Segments：14；
- Damping Ratio：1.0E – 05；
- Formulation：Linear；
- Marker 1：._my_cab_zhudong.gel_zhijia_UP.MARKER_200；
- Attachment：free；
- Marker 2：._my_cab_zhudong.gel_zhijia_UP.MARKER_199；
- Attachment：free；
- Cross Section：Solid Circular；
- Diameter：7.5；
- 单击 OK，完成前横向稳定杆离散梁的创建。
- 单击 Tools > Select Mode > Switch to A/Car Template Builder 命令，切换到 ADAMS/CAR 模块。

17.3 驾驶室弹簧与避震器

（1）弹簧。

- 击 Build > Force > Spring > New 命令，弹出创建部件对话框如图 17-9 所示；
- Spring Name（减震器名称）：r_spring；

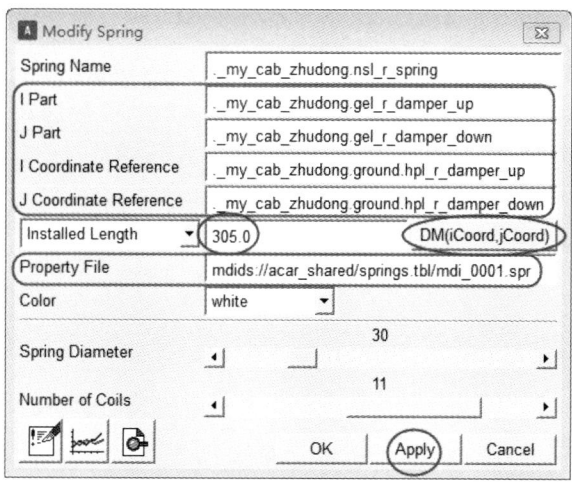

图 17-9 spring 弹簧创建对话框

- I Part：._my_cab_zhudong.gel_r_damper_up；
- J Part：._my_cab_zhudong.gel_r_damper_down；
- I Coordinate Reference（参考坐标）：._my_cab_zhudong.ground.hpl_r_damper_up；
- J Coordinate Reference（参考坐标）：._my_cab_zhudong.ground.hpl_r_damper_down；
- Installed Length（安装长度）：单击 DM（iCoord, jCoord)自动计算弹簧的安装长度并填入到方框中，此模型的安装长度为 305.0；
- Property File（属性文件）：mdids://acar_shared/springs.tbl/mdi_0001.spr，弹簧刚度曲线如图 17-10 所示；

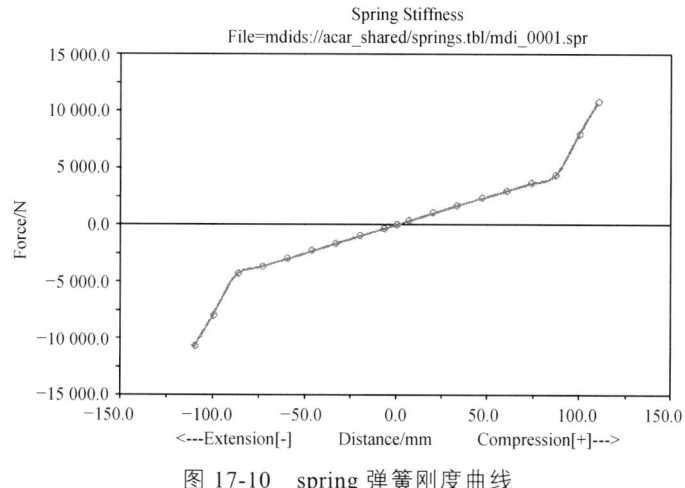

图 17-10 spring 弹簧刚度曲线

- Spring Diameter（弹簧直径）：拖动滑块选择 30 mm；
- Spring of Coils （弹簧圈数）：拖动滑块选择 11；
- 单击 Apply，完成弹簧._my_cab_zhudong.nsl_r_spring 的创建；
- Spring Name（减震器名称）：f_spring ；
- I Part：._my_cab_zhudong.gel_f_damper_up；
- J Part：._my_cab_zhudong.gel_f_damper_down；
- I Coordinate Reference（参考坐标）：._my_cab_zhudong.ground.hpl_f_damper_up；
- J Coordinate Reference（参考坐标）：._my_cab_zhudong.ground.hpl_f_damper_down；
- Installed Length（安装长度）：单击 DM（iCoord, jCoord)自动计算弹簧的安装长度并填入到方框中，此模型的安装长度为 310；
- Property File（属性文件）：mdids://acar_shared/springs.tbl/mdi_0001.spr；
- Spring Diameter（弹簧直径）：拖动滑块选择 26 mm；
- Spring of Coils （弹簧圈数）：拖动滑块选择 8；
- 单击 OK，完成弹簧 my_cab_zhudong.nsl_f_spring 的创建。

（2）避震器。
- 击 Build > Force > Damper > New 命令，弹出避震器创建对话框如图 17-11 所示；

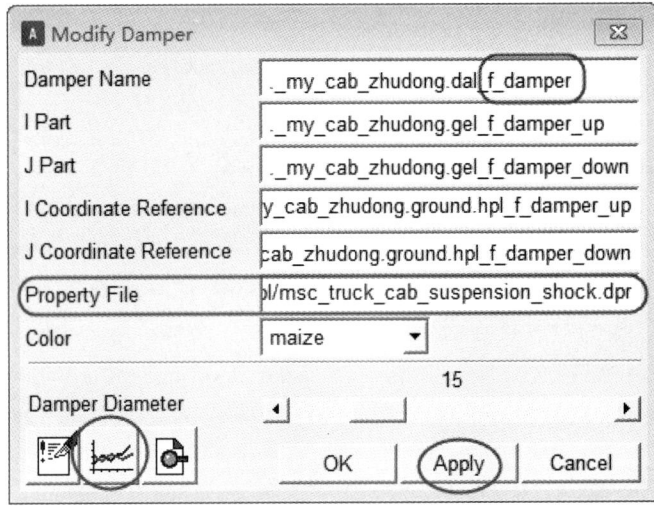

图 17-11 damper 避震器创建对话框

- Damper Name（减震器名称）：f_damper；
- I Part：._my_cab_zhudong.gel_f_damper_up；
- J Part：._my_cab_zhudong.gel_f_damper_down；
- I Coordinate Reference（参考坐标）：._my_cab_zhudong.ground.hpl_f_damper_up；
- J Coordinate Reference（参考坐标）：._my_cab_zhudong.ground.hpl_f_damper_down；
- Property File（属性文件）： mdids://atruck_shared/dampers.tbl/msc_truck_cab_suspension_shock.dpr，阻尼器属性特性曲线如图 17-12 所示；
- Damper Diameter（避震器直径)：拖动滑块选择 15mm；
- Color：maize；

- 单击 Apply，完成避震器 ._my_cab_zhudong.dal_f_damper 的创建；

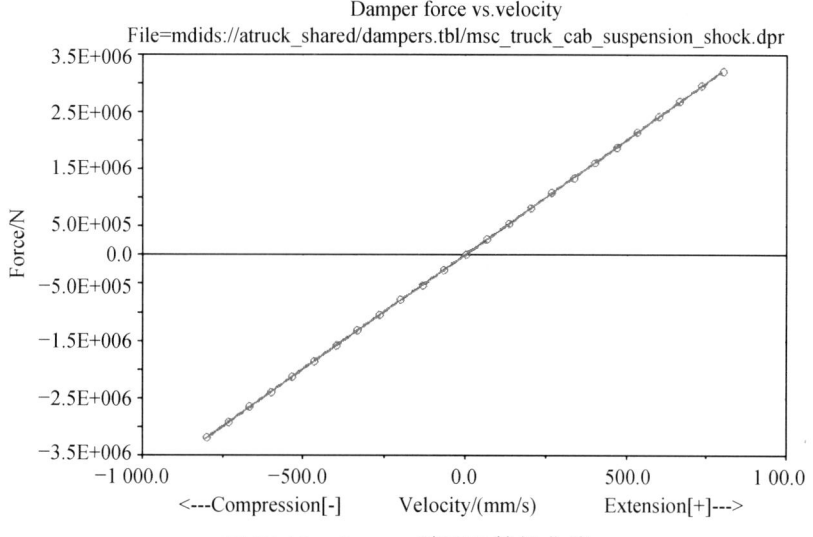

图 17-12 damper 避震器特性曲线

- Damper Name（减震器名称）：r_damper ；
- I Part：._my_cab_zhudong.gel_r_damper_up；
- J Part：._my_cab_zhudong.gel_r_damper_down；
- I Coordinate Reference（参考坐标）：._my_cab_zhudong.ground.hpl_r_damper_up；
- J Coordinate Reference（参考坐标）：._my_cab_zhudong.ground.hpl_r_damper_down；
- Property File（属性文件）：mdids://atruck_shared/dampers.tbl/msc_truck_cab_suspension_shock.dpr；
- Damper Diameter（避震器直径）：拖动滑块选择 15 mm；
- Color：maize；
- 单击 OK，完成避震器 ._my_cab_zhudong.dal_r_damper 的创建。

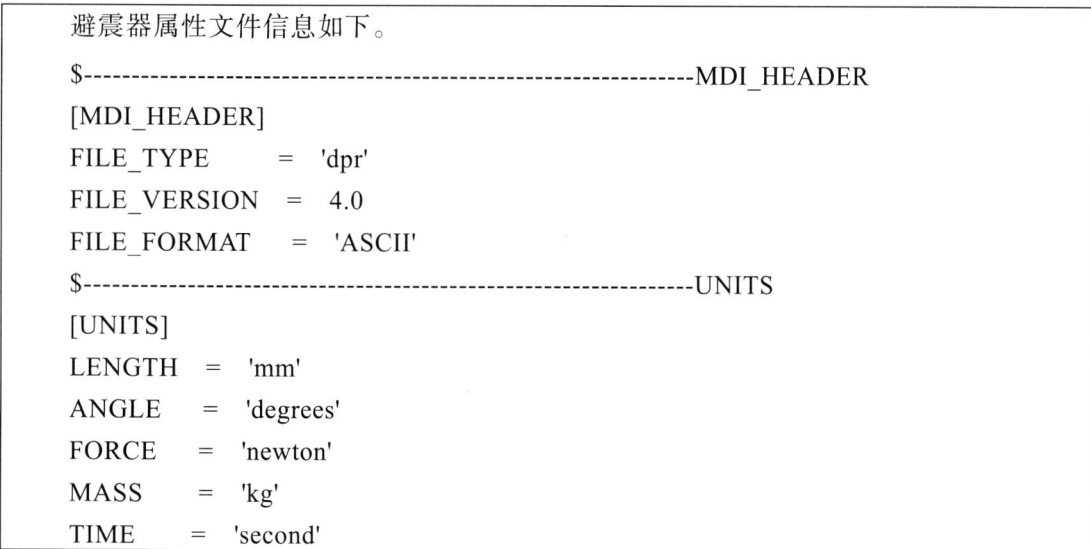

```
$------------------------------------------------------------CURVE
```
% 以下为避震器参数，即力和速度之间的关系，对于不同车型的使用过的避震器，可以通过实验获取以下参数

```
[CURVE]
{    vel         force}
-800.0          -3200000.0
-733.3333       -2933333.3333
-666.6667       -2666666.6667
-600.0          -2400000.0
-533.3333       -2133333.3333
-466.6667       -1866666.6667
-400.0          -1600000.0
-333.3333       -1333333.3333
-266.6667       -1066666.6667
-200.0          -800000.0
-133.3333       -533333.3333
-66.6667        -266666.6667
0.0             0.0
66.6667         266666.6667
133.3333        533333.3333
200.0           800000.0
266.6667        1066666.6667
333.3333        1333333.3333
400.0           1600000.0
466.6667        1866666.6667
533.3333        2133333.3333
600.0           2400000.0
666.6667        2666666.6667
733.3333        2933333.3333
800.0           3200000.0
```

17.4 驾驶室约束关系

17.4.1 刚性约束

单击 Build > Attachments > Joint > New 命令，弹出创约束件对话框如图 17-13 所示。

（1）部件 r_damper_down 与 r_damper_up 之间 cylindrical 约束。
- Joint Name（约束副名称）：r_damper；

- I Part：._my_cab_zhudong.gel_r_damper_down；
- J Part：._my_cab_zhudong.gel_r_damper_up；
- Type：left；
- Joint Type（约束副类型）：cylindrical，圆柱副，约束 4 个自由度；
- Active（激活）：always；
- Location Dependency：Centered between coordinates；
- Centered between：Two Coordinates；
- Coordinate Reference #1（参考坐标）：._my_cab_zhudong.ground.hpl_r_damper_down；
- Coordinate Reference #2（参考坐标）：._my_cab_zhudong.ground.hpl_r_damper_up；
- Orientation Dependency：Orient axis along line；
- Coordinate Reference #1（参考坐标）：._my_cab_zhudong.ground.hpl_r_damper_down；
- Coordinate Reference #2（参考坐标）：._my_cab_zhudong.ground.hpl_r_damper_up；
- 单击 Apply，完成 ._my_cab_zhudong.jolcyl_r_damper 圆柱副的创建。

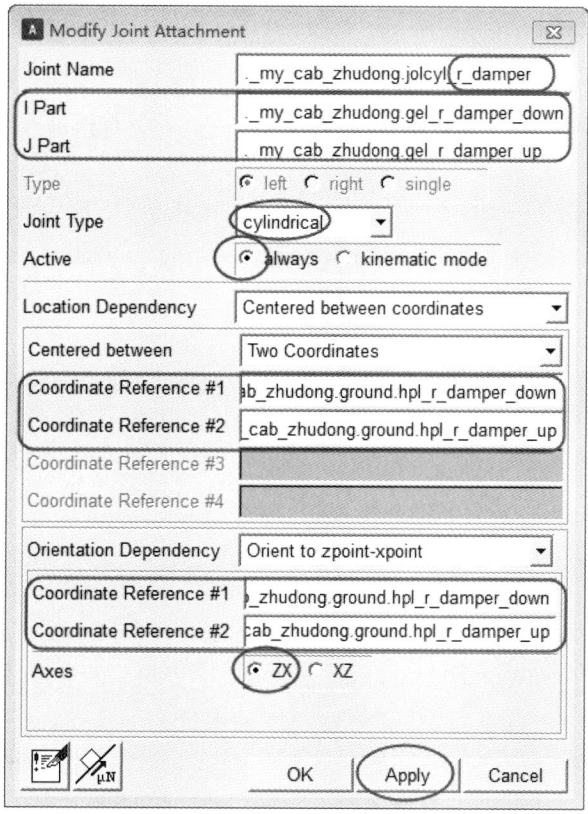

图 17-13 圆柱约束

（2）部件 f_damper_down 与 f_damper_up 之间 cylindrical 约束。

- Joint Name（约束副名称）：f_damper；
- I Part：._my_cab_zhudong.gel_f_damper_down；
- J Part：._my_cab_zhudong.gel_f_damper_up；

- Type：left；
- Joint Type（约束副类型）：cylindrical，圆柱副，约束 4 个自由度；
- Active（激活）：always；
- Location Dependency：Centered between coordinates；
- Centered between：Two Coordinates；
- Coordinate Reference #1（参考坐标）：._my_cab_zhudong.ground.hpl_f_damper_down；
- Coordinate Reference #2（参考坐标）：._my_cab_zhudong.ground.hpl_f_damper_up；
- Orientation Dependency：Orient axis along line；
- Coordinate Reference #1（参考坐标）：._my_cab_zhudong.ground.hpl_f_damper_down；
- Coordinate Reference #2（参考坐标）：._my_cab_zhudong.ground.hpl_f_damper_up；
- 单击 Apply，完成._my_cab_zhudong.jolcyl_f_damper 圆柱副的创建。

（3）部件 zhijia_DOWN 与 cab_to_body 之间 fixed 约束。
- Joint Name（约束副名称）：zhijia_body；
- I Part：._my_cab_zhudong.gel_zhijia_DOWN；
- J Part：._my_cab_zhudong.mts_cab_to_body；
- Type：left；
- Joint Type（约束副类型）：fixed，固定副，约束 6 个自由度；
- Active（激活）：always；
- Location Dependency: Delta location from coordinate；
- Coordinate Reference：._my_cab_zhudong.ground.hpl_f_damper_down；
- Location: 0, 0, 0；
- Location in : local；
- 单击 Apply，完成._my_cab_zhudong.jolfix_zhijia_body 固定副的创建。

（4）部件 r_zhijia_dowen 与 cab_to_body 之间 fixed 约束。
- Joint Name（约束副名称）：zhijia_down；
- I Part：._my_cab_zhudong.ges_r_zhijia_dowen；
- J Part：._my_cab_zhudong.mts_cab_to_body；
- Type：single；
- Joint Type（约束副类型）：fixed，固定副，约束 6 个自由度；
- Active（激活）：always；
- Location Dependency: Centered between coordinates；
- Centered between：Four coordinates；
- Coordinate Reference #1（参考坐标）：._my_cab_zhudong.ground.hpl_r_damper_down；
- Coordinate Reference #2（参考坐标）：._my_cab_zhudong.ground.hpr_r_damper_down；
- Coordinate Reference #3（参考坐标）：._my_cab_zhudong.ground.hpl_b2；
- Coordinate Reference #4（参考坐标）：._my_cab_zhudong.ground.hpr_b2；
- 单击 Apply，完成._my_cab_zhudong.josfix_zhijia_down 固定副的创建。

（5）部件 r_zhijia_dowen 与 r_zhijia_up 之间 revolute 约束。
- Joint Name（约束副名称）：b2；

- I Part：._my_cab_zhudong.ges_r_zhijia_dowen；
- J Part：._my_cab_zhudong.gel_r_zhijia_up；
- Type：left；
- Joint Type（约束副类型）：revolute，铰接副，约束 5 个自由度；
- Active（激活）：always；
- Location Dependency: Delta location from coordinate；
- Coordinate Reference: ._my_cab_zhudong.ground.hpl_b2；
- Location: 0, 0, 0；
- Location in : local；
- Orientation Dependency：User entered values；
- Orient using：Euler Angles；
- Euler Angles：90, 90, 0；
- 单击 Apply，完成._my_cab_zhudong.jolrev_b2 转动副的创建。

（6）部件 zhijia_UP 与 zhijia_DOWN 间 revolute 约束。
- Joint Name（约束副名称）：zhijia_up_to_down；
- I Part：._my_cab_zhudong.gel_zhijia_UP；
- J Part：._my_cab_zhudong.gel_zhijia_DOWN；
- Type：left；
- Joint Type（约束副类型）：revolute，铰接副，约束 5 个自由度；
- Active（激活）：always；
- Location Dependency: Delta location from coordinate；
- Coordinate Reference: ._my_cab_zhudong.ground.hpl_fzb_front；
- Location: 0, 0, 0；
- Location in : local；
- Orientation Dependency：Orient axis to point；
- Coordinate Reference: ._my_cab_zhudong.ground.hpl_fzb_front；
- Axis：Z；
- 单击 Apply，完成._my_cab_zhudong.jolrev_zhijia_up_to_down 转动副的创建。

（7）部件 zhijia_UP 与 wendinggan_elem1 之间 fixed 约束。
- Joint Name（约束副名称）：f_wendinggan_right；
- I Part：._my_cab_zhudong.ger_zhijia_UP；
- J Part：._my_cab_zhudong.wendinggan_elem1；
- Type：single；
- Joint Type（约束副类型）：fixed，固定副，约束 6 个自由度；
- Active（激活）：always；
- Location Dependency: Delta location from coordinate；
- Coordinate Reference: ._my_cab_zhudong.ground.hpr_fzb_front；
- Location: 0, 0, 0；
- Location in : local；

- 单击 Apply，完成._my_cab_zhudong.josfix_f_wendinggan_right 固定副的创建。

（8）部件 zhijia_UP 与 wendinggan_elem15 之间 fixed 约束。
- Joint Name（约束副名称）：f_wendinggan_left；
- I Part：._my_cab_zhudong.wendinggan_elem15；
- J Part：._my_cab_zhudong.gel_zhijia_UP；
- Type：single；
- Joint Type（约束副类型）：fixed，固定副，约束 6 个自由度；
- Active（激活）：always；
- Location Dependency: Delta location from coordinate；
- Coordinate Reference: ._my_cab_zhudong.ground.hpl_fzb_front；
- Location: 0, 0, 0；
- Location in：local；
- 单击 OK，完成._my_cab_zhudong.josfix_f_wendinggan_left 固定副的创建。

17.4.2 柔性约束

单击 Build > Attachments > Bushing > New 命令，弹出创衬套件对话框如图 17-14 所示；
（1）部件 r_zhijia_up 与 r_damper_up 之间 bushing 约束。
- Bushing Name（约束副名称）：r_damper_up；
- I Part：._my_cab_zhudong.gel_r_zhijia_up；
- J Part：._my_cab_zhudong.gel_r_damper_up；
- Inactive（抑制）：never；
- Preload：0，0，0；
- Tpreload:0，0，0；
- Offset：0，0，0；
- Roffset：0，0，0；
- Geometry Length：20.0；
- Geometry Radius：30.0；
- Property File：mdids:/atruck_shared/bushings.tbl/msc_truck_cab_suspension_shock.bus，用记事本文件打开衬套属性文件信息；
- Location Dependency：Delta location from coordinate；
- Coordinate Reference（参考坐标）：._my_cab_zhudong.ground.hpl_r_damper_up；
- Location: 0，0，0；
- Location in：local；
- Orientation Dependency：User entered values；
- Orient using：Euler Angles；
- Euler Angles：90, 90, 0；
- 单击 Apply，完成轴套._my_cab_zhudong.bgl_r_damper_up 的创建。

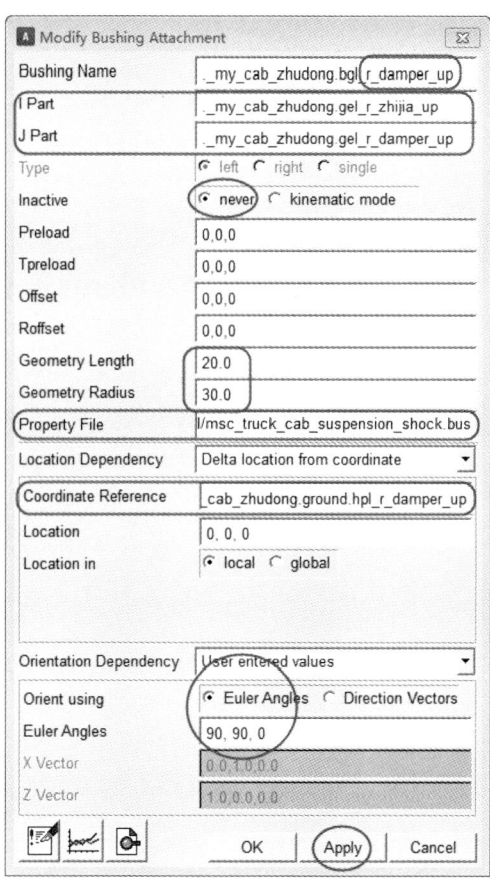

图 17-14 衬套连接——r_damper_up

衬套信息如下：
$--MDI_HEADER
[MDI_HEADER]
FILE_TYPE   =   'bus'
FILE_VERSION =   4.0
FILE_FORMAT   =   'ASCII'
$--UNITS
[UNITS]
LENGTH   =   'mm'
ANGLE   =   'degrees'
FORCE   =   'newton'
MASS   =   'kg'
TIME   =   'second'
$--DAMPING
[DAMPING]
FX_DAMPING   =   22.0

```
        FY_DAMPING    =    22.0
        FZ_DAMPING    =    22.0
        TX_DAMPING    =    100.0
        TY_DAMPING    =    100.0
        TZ_DAMPING    =    0.0
$------------------------------------------------------------FX_CURVE
```
%衬套实验数据，可以通过有限元方法或者实验方法测出衬套在 X\Y\Z 三个方向的刚度与扭转刚度

```
        [FX_CURVE]
        {      x                 fx}
        -500.0                -1100000.0
        -458.3333             -1008333.3333
        -416.6667             -916666.6667
        -375.0                -825000.0
        -333.3333             -733333.3333
        -291.6667             -641666.6667
        -250.0                -550000.0
        -208.3333             -458333.3333
        -166.6667             -366666.6667
        -125.0                -275000.0
        -83.3333              -183333.3333
        -41.6667              -91666.6667
        0.0                   0.0
        41.6667               91666.6667
        83.3333               183333.3333
        125.0                 275000.0
        166.6667              366666.6667
        208.3333              458333.3333
        250.0                 550000.0
        291.6667              641666.6667
        333.3333              733333.3333
        375.0                 825000.0
        416.6667              916666.6667
        458.3333              1008333.3333
        500.0                 1100000.0
$------------------------------------------------------------FY_CURVE
        [FY_CURVE]
        {      y                 fy}
```

−500.0	−1100000.0
−458.3333	−1008333.3333
−416.6667	−916666.6667
−375.0	−825000.0
−333.3333	−733333.3333
−291.6667	−641666.6667
−250.0	−550000.0
−208.3333	−458333.3333
−166.6667	−366666.6667
−125.0	−275000.0
−83.3333	−183333.3333
−41.6667	−91666.6667
0.0	0.0
41.6667	91666.6667
83.3333	183333.3333
125.0	275000.0
166.6667	366666.6667
208.3333	458333.3333
250.0	550000.0
291.6667	641666.6667
333.3333	733333.3333
375.0	825000.0
416.6667	916666.6667
458.3333	1008333.3333
500.0	1100000.0

$--FZ_CURVE

[FZ_CURVE]

{ z	fz}
−500.0	−1100000.0
−458.3333	−1008333.3333
−416.6667	−916666.6667
−375.0	−825000.0
−333.3333	−733333.3333
−291.6667	−641666.6667
−250.0	−550000.0
−208.3333	−458333.3333
−166.6667	−366666.6667
−125.0	−275000.0

−83.3333	−183333.3333
−41.6667	−91666.6667
0.0	0.0
41.6667	91666.6667
83.3333	183333.3333
125.0	275000.0
166.6667	366666.6667
208.3333	458333.3333
250.0	550000.0
291.6667	641666.6667
333.3333	733333.3333
375.0	825000.0
416.6667	916666.6667
458.3333	1008333.3333
500.0	1100000.0

$--TX_CURVE

[TX_CURVE]

{ ax	tx}
−500.0	−5000000.0
−458.3333	−4583333.3333
−416.6667	−4166666.6667
−375.0	−3750000.0
−333.3333	−3333333.3333
−291.6667	−2916666.6667
−250.0	−2500000.0
−208.3333	−2083333.3333
−166.6667	−1666666.6667
−125.0	−1250000.0
−83.3333	−833333.3333
−41.6667	−416666.6667
0.0	0.0
41.6667	416666.6667
83.3333	833333.3333
125.0	1250000.0
166.6667	1666666.6667
208.3333	2083333.3333
250.0	2500000.0
291.6667	2916666.6667

333.3333	3333333.3333
375.0	3750000.0
416.6667	4166666.6667
458.3333	4583333.3333
500.0	5000000.0

$--TY_CURVE

[TY_CURVE]

{ ay	ty }
− 500.0	− 5000000.0
− 458.3333	− 4583333.3333
− 416.6667	− 4166666.6667
− 375.0	− 3750000.0
− 333.3333	− 3333333.3333
− 291.6667	− 2916666.6667
− 250.0	− 2500000.0
− 208.3333	− 2083333.3333
− 166.6667	− 1666666.6667
− 125.0	− 1250000.0
− 83.3333	− 833333.3333
− 41.6667	− 416666.6667
0.0	0.0
41.6667	416666.6667
83.3333	833333.3333
125.0	1250000.0
166.6667	1666666.6667
208.3333	2083333.3333
250.0	2500000.0
291.6667	2916666.6667
333.3333	3333333.3333
375.0	3750000.0
416.6667	4166666.6667
458.3333	4583333.3333
500.0	5000000.0

$--TZ_CURVE

[TZ_CURVE]

{ az	tz }
− 500.0	0.0
− 458.3333	0.0

−416.6667	0.0
−375.0	0.0
−333.3333	0.0
−291.6667	0.0
−250.0	0.0
−208.3333	0.0
−166.6667	0.0
−125.0	0.0
−83.3333	0.0
−41.6667	0.0
0.0	0.0
41.6667	0.0
83.3333	0.0
125.0	0.0
166.6667	0.0
208.3333	0.0
250.0	0.0
291.6667	0.0
333.3333	0.0
375.0	0.0
416.6667	0.0
458.3333	0.0
500.0	0.0

（2）部件 r_zhijia_dowen 与 r_damper_down 之间 bushing 约束。
- Bushing Name（约束副名称）：r_damper_down；
- I　Part：._my_cab_zhudong.ges_r_zhijia_dowen；
- J　Part：._my_cab_zhudong.gel_r_damper_down；
- Inactive（抑制）：never；
- Preload：0，0，0；
- Tpreload:0，0，0；
- Offset：0，0，0；
- Roffset：0，0，0；
- Geometry Length：20；
- Geometry Radius：30；
- Property File：mdids://atruck_shared/bushings.tbl/msc_truck_cab_suspension_shock.bus；
- Location Dependency：Delta location from coordinate；
- Coordinate Reference（参考坐标）：._my_cab_zhudong.ground.hpl_r_damper_down；

- Location: 0, 0, 0;
- Location in: local;
- Orientation Dependency: User entered values;
- Orient using: Euler Angles;
- Euler Angles: 90, 90, 0;
- 单击 Apply, 完成轴套._my_cab_zhudong.bgl_r_damper_down 的创建。

（3）部件 zhijia_UP 与 cab 之间 bushing 约束。
- Bushing Name (约束副名称): zhijia_UP_rear;
- I Part: ._my_cab_zhudong.gel_zhijia_UP;
- J Part: ._my_cab_zhudong.ges_cab;
- Inactive (抑制): never;
- Preload: 0, 0, 0;
- Tpreload: 0, 0, 0;
- Offset: 0, 0, 0;
- Roffset: 0, 0, 0;
- Geometry Length: 20;
- Geometry Radius: 30;
- Property File: mdids://acar_shared/bushings.tbl/mdi_0001.bus;
- Location Dependency: Delta location from coordinate;
- Coordinate Reference (参考坐标): ._my_cab_zhudong.ground.hpl_fzb_rear;
- Location: 0, 0, 0;
- Location in: local;
- Orientation Dependency: Orient axis to point;
- Coordinate Reference (参考坐标): ._my_cab_zhudong.ground.hpr_fzb_rear;
- Axis: Z;
- 单击 Apply, 完成轴套._my_cab_zhudong.bgl_zhijia_UP_rear 的创建。

（4）部件 r_zhijia_up 与 cab 之间 bushing 约束。
- Bushing Name (约束副名称): b1;
- I Part: ._my_cab_zhudong.gel_r_zhijia_up;
- J Part: ._my_cab_zhudong.ges_cab;
- Inactive (抑制): never;
- Preload: 0, 0, 0;
- Tpreload: 0, 0, 0;
- Offset: 0, 0, 0;
- Roffset: 0, 0, 0;
- Geometry Length: 20;
- Geometry Radius: 30;
- Property File: mdids://atruck_shared/bushings.tbl/msc_truck_cab_suspension_lateral_bar.bus;
- Location Dependency: Delta location from coordinate;

- Coordinate Reference（参考坐标）：._my_cab_zhudong.ground.hpl_b1；
- Location：0，0，0；
- Location in：local；
- Orientation Dependency：User entered values；
- Orient using：Euler Angles；
- Euler Angles：90，90，0；
- 单击 Apply，完成轴套._my_cab_zhudong.bgl_b1 的创建。

（5）部件 f_damper_up 与 cab 之间 bushing 约束。
- Bushing Name（约束副名称）：f_damper_up；
- I Part：._my_cab_zhudong.gel_f_damper_up；
- J Part：._my_cab_zhudong.ges_cab；
- Inactive（抑制）：never；
- Preload：0，0，0；
- Tpreload：0，0，0；
- Offset：0，0，0；
- Roffset：0，0，0；
- Geometry Length：20；
- Geometry Radius：30；
- Property File：mdids://acar_shared/bushings.tbl/mdi_0001.bus；
- Location Dependency：Delta location from coordinate；
- Coordinate Reference（参考坐标）：._my_cab_zhudong.ground.hpl_f_damper_up；
- Location：0，0，0；
- Location in：local；
- Orientation Dependency：Orient axis to point；
- Coordinate Reference（参考坐标）：._my_cab_zhudong.ground.hpr_f_damper_up；
- Axis：Z；
- 单击 Apply，完成轴套._my_cab_zhudong.bgl_f_damper_up 的创建。

（6）部件 f_damper_down 与 zhijia_UP 之间 bushing 约束。
- Bushing Name（约束副名称）：f_damper_down；
- I Part：._my_cab_zhudong.gel_f_damper_down；
- J Part：._my_cab_zhudong.gel_zhijia_UP；
- Inactive（抑制）：never；
- Preload：0，0，0；
- Tpreload：0，0，0；
- Offset：0，0，0；
- Roffset：0，0，0；
- Geometry Length：20；
- Geometry Radius：30；
- Property File：mdids://acar_shared/bushings.tbl/mdi_0001.bus；

- Location Dependency：Delta location from coordinate；
- Coordinate Reference（参考坐标）：._my_cab_zhudong.ground.hpl_f_damper_down；
- Location：0，0，0；
- Location in：local；
- Orientation Dependency：Orient axis to point；
- Coordinate Reference（参考坐标）：._my_cab_zhudong.ground.hpr_f_damper_down；
- Axis：Z；
- 单击 Apply，完成轴套 ._my_cab_zhudong.bgl_f_damper_down 的创建。

17.5 主动驾驶室函数设定

（1）状态变量。
- 单击 Build >System Elements > State variable > New 命令，弹出创建状态变量对话框如图 17-15 所示；
- Name (状态变量名称)：frot_left；
- Definition: Run-Time Expression；
- F(time=0)：0；
- 单击 Apply 完成状态变量 ._my_cab_zhudong.frot_left 的创建；
- 重复上述步骤，完成以下状态变量的建立：
① ._my_cab_zhudong.front_right；
② ._my_cab_zhudong.rear_left；
③ ._my_cab_zhudong.rear_right。

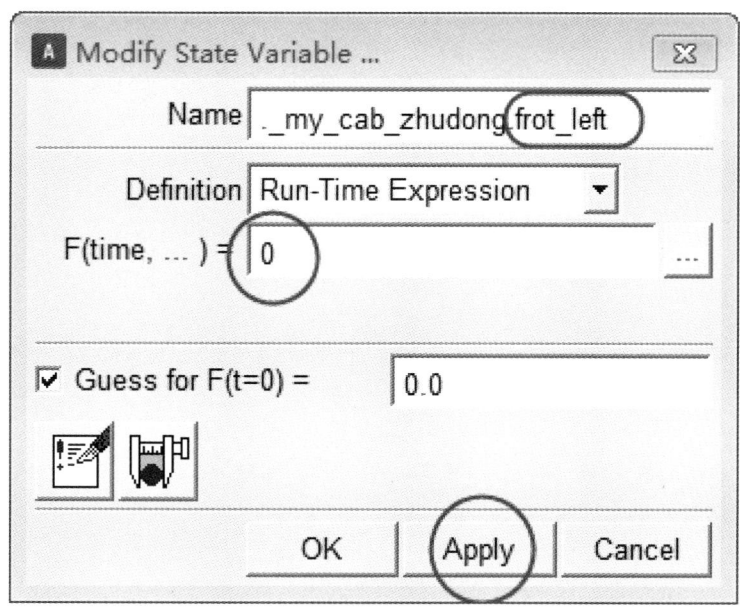

图 17-15 状态变量——frot_left

(2)主动力。
- 切换到 ADAMS/VIEW 模块；
- 单击菜单栏 Force，选择 Applied Forces 框的 Force 快捷方式，在两部件 srping_down、srping_up 之间建单向主动力；
- Run-time Direction（主动力运行时方向）：Two Bodies；
- Construction：2 Bodies -2 Location；
- Characteristic：Custom；
- 根据命令窗口提示顺序选择两部件._my_cab_zhudong.gel_f_damper_up、._my_cab_zhudong.gel_f_damper_down，顺序选择参考点 spring_down.cm、spring_up.cm，完成主动力 SFORCE_1 的创建；
- 选中主动力 SFORCE_1 右击鼠标选择 Rename：修改名称为 f_zdl_l；
- 单击 OK，完成硬主动力的重命名。
- 右击 zhudongli，选择 Modify；
- 在弹出的 Modify Force 对话框中修改 Fuction：输入 VARVAL(._my_cab_zhudong.frot_left)，其余参数保持默认；
- 单击 OK，完成主动力 f_zdl_l 的修改函数，如图 17-16 所示。

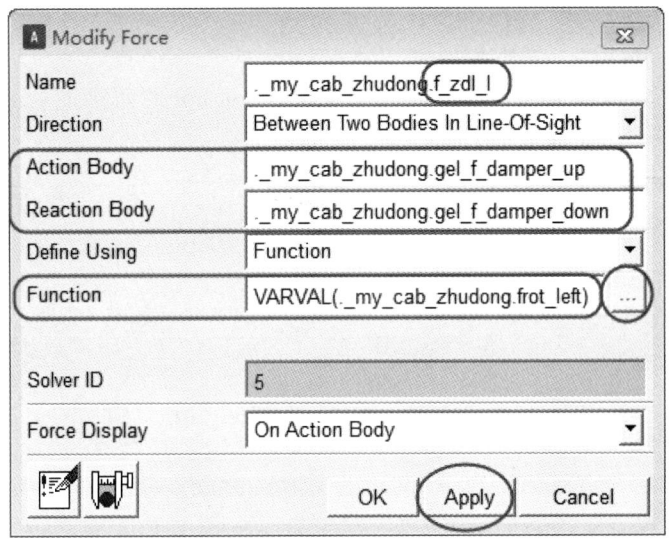

图 17-16　主动力修改对话框

- 重复上述步骤，完成以下主动力的创建：
① ._my_cab_zhudong.f_zdl_r；
② ._my_cab_zhudong.r_zdl_l；
③ ._my_cab_zhudong.r_zdl_r。

(3)测量函数。

构建主动驾驶室模型，需要输出驾驶与支撑悬置连接处的速度及其他参数。测量函数的建立如图 17-17 所示。

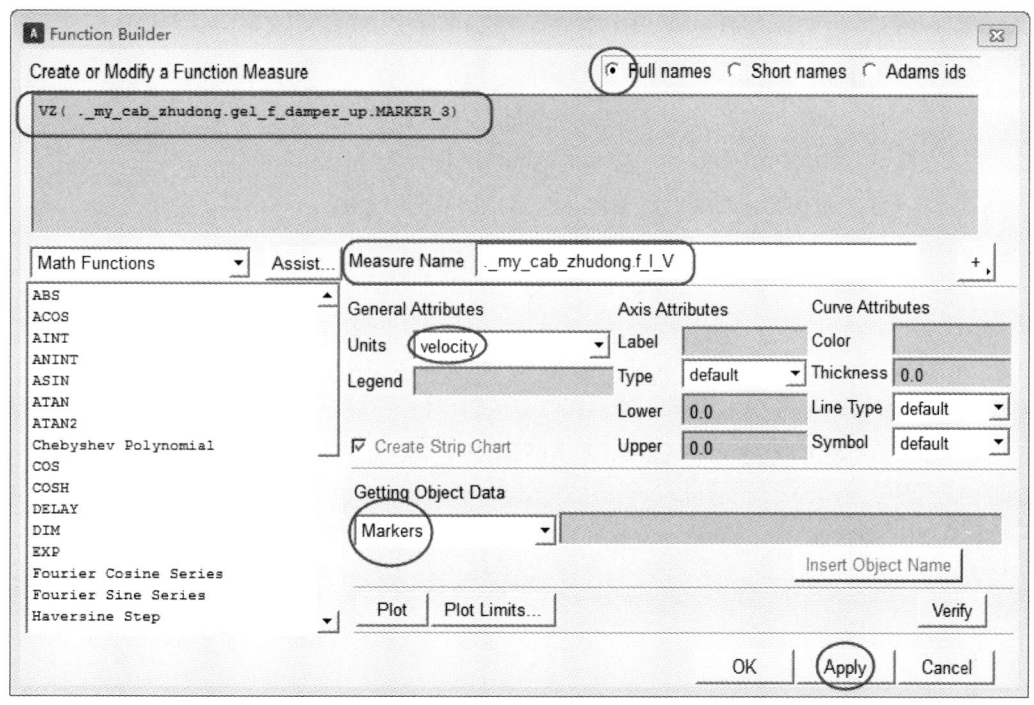

图 17-17 测量函数构建

- 单击菜单栏 Design Exploration，选择系统单元 Measures 框中的创建状态变量快捷方式图标：Create a new Function Measures，弹出函数构建对话框；
- Measures Name: f_l_V；
- Units：velocity；
- 选择 Velocity along Y；
- 点击 Assist 弹出 Velocity along Y 对话框；
- To_Marker 框中输入 gel_f_damper_up.MARKER_3，其余 From_Marker，Along_Marker，Ref_Frame 框保持默认不用输入，辅助对话框如图 17-18 所示，单击 OK，完成加速度函数 VZ(._my_cab_zhudong.gel_f_damper_up.MARKER_3)输入。

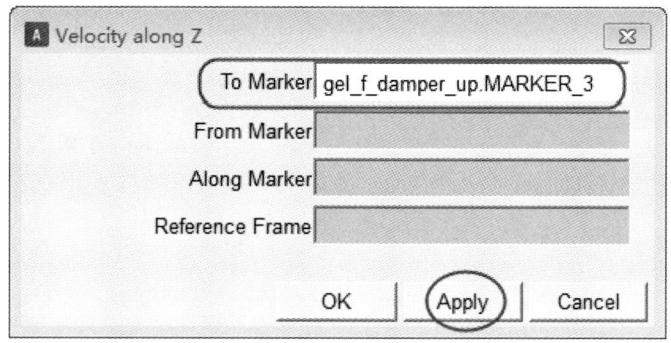

图 17-18 辅助对话框

- 单击 Verify，检查函数 VZ(._my_cab_zhudong.gel_f_damper_up.MARKER_3)正确无误；

- 单击 OK，完成函数构建。
- 重复以上步骤，完成以下测量函数的建立：
① VZ(._my_cab_zhudong.ger_f_damper_up.MARKER_5);
② VZ(._my_cab_zhudong.gel_r_damper_up.MARKER_7);
③ VZ(._my_cab_zhudong.ger_r_damper_up.MARKER_9);
④ ACCZ(._my_cab_zhudong.gel_f_damper_up.MARKER_3);
⑤ ACCZ(._my_cab_zhudong.ger_f_damper_up.MARKER_5);
⑥ ACCZ(._my_cab_zhudong.gel_r_damper_up.MARKER_7);
⑦ ACCZ(._my_cab_zhudong.ger_r_damper_up.MARKER_9);
⑧ ACCX(._my_cab_zhudong.ges_cab.MARKER_1);
⑨ ACCY(._my_cab_zhudong.ges_cab.MARKER_1);
⑩ ACCZ(._my_cab_zhudong.ges_cab.MARKER_1);
11) WX(._my_cab_zhudong.ges_cab.MARKER_1);
12) WY(._my_cab_zhudong.ges_cab.MARKER_1);
13) WZ(._my_cab_zhudong.ges_cab.MARKER_1);

（4）输入输出集。
- 切换到 ADAMS/CAR 专家模块；
- 单击 Build >Date Elements > Plant Input > New 命令，弹出创建状态变量对话框如图 17-19 所示；
- Variable Name（变量名称，输入之前建立好的状态变量）：._my_cab_zhudong.frot_left,._my_cab_zhudong.front_right,._my_cab_zhudong.rear_left,._my_cab_zhudong.rear_right；
- 单击 OK，完成输入集._my_cab_zhudong.PINPUT_1 的创建。
- 单击 Build >Date Elements > Plant Output > New 命令，弹出创建状态变量对话框如图 17-20 所示；

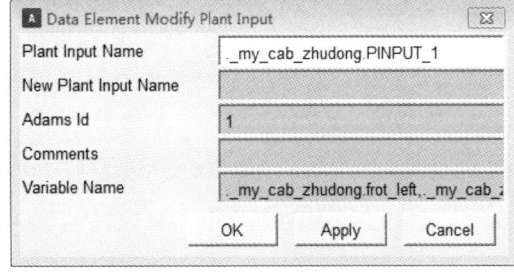 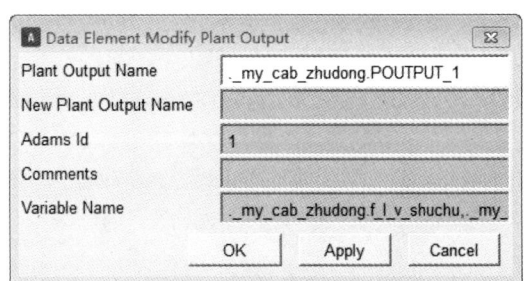

图 17-19　输入集　　　　　　　　图 17-20　输出集

- Variable Name(变量名称，输入之前建立好的状态变量)：._my_cab_zhudong.f_l_v_shuchu,._my_cab_zhudong.f_r_v_shuchu,._my_cab_zhudong.r_l_v_shuchu,._my_cab_zhudong.r_r_v_shuchu,._my_cab_zhudong.f_l_av_shuchu,._my_cab_zhudong.f_r_av_shuchu,._my_cab_zhudong.r_l_av_shuchu,._my_cab_zhudong.r_r_av_shuchu,._my_cab_zhudong.cab_wx_shuchu,._my_cab_zhudong.cab_wy_shuchu,._my_cab_zhudong.cab_wz_shuchu,._my_cab_zhudong.cab_AX_shuchu,._my_cab_zhudong.cab_AY_shuchu,._my_cab_zhudong.cab_AZ_shuchu；

- 单击 OK，完成输出集._my_cab_zhudong.POUTPUT_1 的创建。

至此，主动驾驶室模型建立完成，保存主动驾驶室模型，切换到 ADAMS/CAR 标准模块，建立主动驾驶室子系统，并在 6×2 整车上添加主动驾驶室子系统。6×2 整车模型建立请参考《车辆系统动力学仿真》，由于 6×2 整车模型极为复杂，在此处不再详细叙述其建模过程。

17.6 整车平台

相对于独立的驾驶室模型，整车平台环境下研究驾驶室的动态特性更符合驾驶室真实的工作状态。整车平台下可以详细考虑驾驶室与其他系统的匹配特性，同时可以考虑不同的路面特性；整车平台下的缺点是建模工作量较大，系统的匹配与调试较为复杂，计算量大。整车平台如图 17-21 所示，包含车架、推杆式平衡悬架、前转向悬架、右舵转向系统、制动、动力传动及轮胎多个系统。整车共包含 977 个自由度。

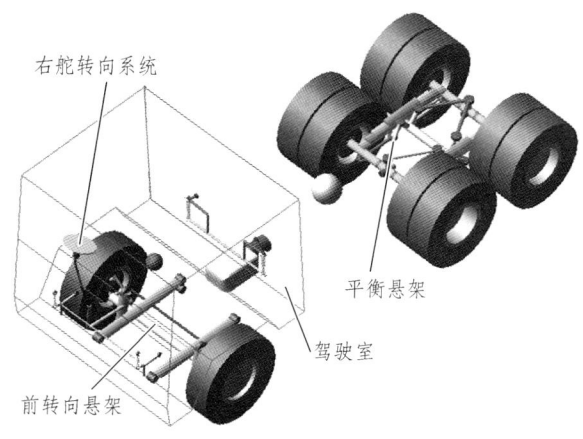

图 17-21 整车平台

包含主动驾驶室系统的 6×2 整车模型打开信息如下，可以从打开信息中看出整车包含的系统及通信器匹配情况，如果熟悉 ADAMS/CAR 通信器的特性，可以凭经验判断整车装配是否存在小的缺陷，如果整车装配不正确，装配信息会有适当的提示；若用高版本的软件，装配过程会自动更新或转换为适用于高版本软件的模型。

Opening the assembly: 'my_truck_full_DX_496_cab'...
Opening the rear wheel subsystem: 'msc_truck_drive_wheels'...
Opening the rear_2 wheel subsystem: 'msc_truck_drive_wheels_2'...
Opening the front wheel subsystem: 'msc_truck_steer_wheels'...
Opening the body subsystem: 'my_truck_body'...
Opening the front steering subsystem: 'my_truck_steering'...
Converting template from version 2014.0 to 2015.0 ...

Template has been converted to version 2015.0.

Opening the front suspension subsystem: 'my_truck_sus_f'...
Converting template from version 2014.0 to 2015.0 ...

 - Converting bushing: bgl_damper_down...
 - Converting bushing: bgr_damper_down...
 - Converting bushing: bgl_damper_up...
 - Converting bushing: bgr_damper_up...
 - Converting bushing: bkl_p1...
 - Converting bushing: bkr_p1...
 - Converting bushing: bkl_p15...
 - Converting bushing: bkr_p15...
 - Converting bushing: bkl_p16...
 - Converting bushing: bkr_p16...
 - Converting damper: dal_damper...
 - Converting damper: dar_damper...

Template has been converted to version 2015.0.
Opening the powertrain subsystem: 'my_truck_powertrain'...
Opening the brake_system subsystem: 'my_truck_brake'...
Converting template from version 2014.0 to 2015.0 ...

Template has been converted to version 2015.0.
Opening the rear suspension subsystem: 'my_truck_driveaxle_DX_496'...
Opening the cab subsystem: 'my_cab_zhudong'...
Converting template from version 2014.0 to 2015.0 ...

 - Converting bushing: bgl_b1...
 - Converting bushing: bgr_b1...
 - Converting bushing: bgl_f_damper_down...
 - Converting bushing: bgr_f_damper_down...
 - Converting bushing: bgl_f_damper_up...
 - Converting bushing: bgr_f_damper_up...
 - Converting bushing: bgl_r_damper_down...
 - Converting bushing: bgr_r_damper_down...
 - Converting bushing: bgl_r_damper_up...
 - Converting bushing: bgr_r_damper_up...
 - Converting bushing: bgl_zhijia_UP_rear...
 - Converting bushing: bgr_zhijia_UP_rear...

```
- Converting damper: dal_f_damper...
- Converting damper: dar_f_damper...
- Converting damper: dal_r_damper...
- Converting damper: dar_r_damper...
--------------------------------------------------------
Template has been converted to version 2015.0.
Assembling subsystems...
Assigning communicators...
WARNING: The following input communicators were not assigned during assembly:
%以下为不匹配的输入通信器，但不影响整车的正常仿真
testrig.cis_downforce_coefficient
testrig.cis_crankshaft_ratio
testrig.cis_transmission_efficiency
testrig.cis_drive_torque_bias_front
testrig.cil_svs_ride_height_front
testrig.cir_svs_ride_height_front
testrig.cil_svs_ride_height_rear
testrig.cir_svs_ride_height_rear
testrig.cis_svs_trim_part
testrig.cis_engine_idle_speed
Assignment of communicators completed.
Assembly of subsystems completed.
Full vehicle assembly ready.
```

17.7 ADAMS\CONTROLS 设置

通过 ADAMS\CONTROL 模块系统机械模型与控制模型，ADAMS 与 MATLAB 软件路径统一设置为 D:\cab_cosimulation。

- 单击菜单栏插件 Plugins，选择 Controls 单击，出现下拉列表选择 Plant Export 命令，弹出控制接口输出对话框如图 17-22 所示；
- File Prefix（输出文件别名）：Controls_Plant_1；
- Initial Static Analysis（初始静态分析）：No；
- 单击 From Pinput，从输入集中快速输入以下变量：
① .my_truck_full_DX_496_cab.my_cab_zhudong.frot_left；
② .my_truck_full_DX_496_cab.my_cab_zhudong.front_right；
③ .my_truck_full_DX_496_cab.my_cab_zhudong.rear_left；

④ .my_truck_full_DX_496_cab.my_cab_zhudong.rear_right。
- 单击 From Poutput，从输出集中快速输入以下变量（可以删除输出集中不必要的变量，此处只保留主动驾驶室连接的速度变量）：
① .my_truck_full_DX_496_cab.my_cab_zhudong.f_l_v_shuchu；
② .my_truck_full_DX_496_cab.my_cab_zhudong.f_r_v_shuchu；
③ .my_truck_full_DX_496_cab.my_cab_zhudong.r_l_v_shuchu；
④ .my_truck_full_DX_496_cab.my_cab_zhudong.r_r_v_shuchu。
- Target Software（目标软件或者对接软件）：MATLAB；
- Analysis Type(分析类型)：选择非线性 non_linear；
- ADAMS/Solver Choice：选择 FORTRAN；
- 其余保持默认，单击单击 OK 完成 ADAMS\CONTROLS 模块下的输入输出集的创建。

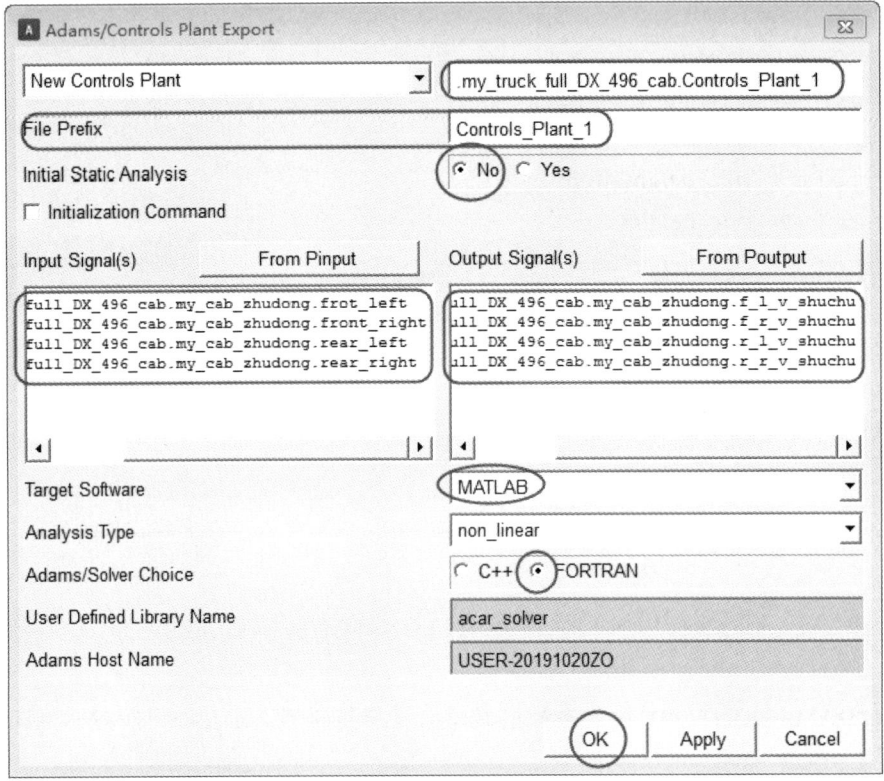

图 17-22　控制接口输出对话框

17.8　匀速直线仿真

- 单击 Simulate > Full-Vehicle Analysis > Straight Line Events > Acceleration 命令，弹出整车匀速仿真对话框如图 17-23 所示；
- Output Prefix（输出别名）：slme；

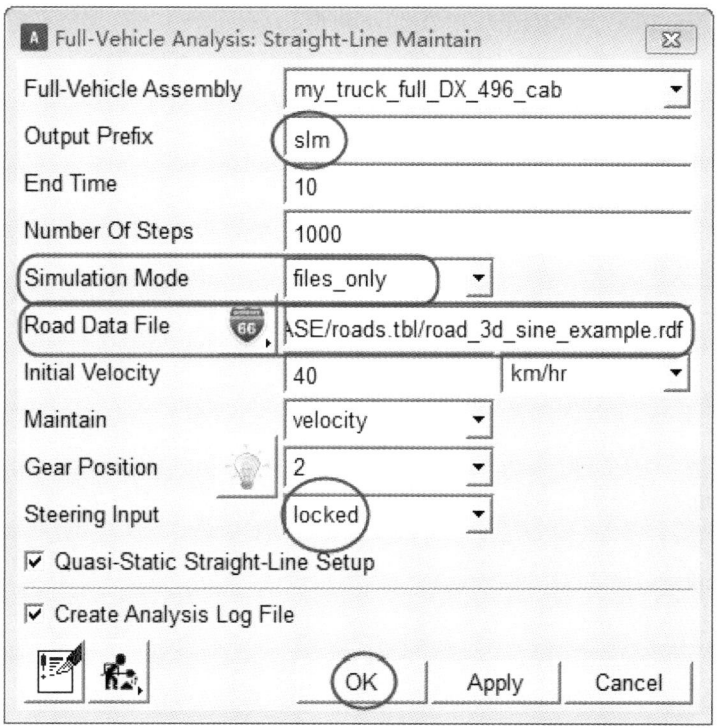

图 17-23 匀速仿真设定

- End Time：10；
- Number of Steps（仿真步数）：1 000；
- Simulation Mode：files_only；
- Road Date File：mdids://FASE/roads.tbl/road_3d_sine_example.rdf；
- Initial Velocity：40 km/hr；
- Maintain：velocity；
- Gear Position：2；
- Steering Input：locked；
- 勾选 Quasi-Static Straight-Line Setup；
- 单击 OK，完成匀速直线行驶仿真设置并提交运算。

17.9　ADAMS 与 MATLAB 协同

17.9.1　协同方案 A

用记事本打开文件 Controls_Plant_1.m：
A. 修改 ADAMS_prefix = 'slm_maintain'；
B. 修改 ADAMS_init = 'file/command=Controls_Plant_1_controls.acf'为 ADAMS_init='file/command=file/command=slm_maintain_controls.acf；

C. 具体操作过程如下，程序修改部分用下划线斜体区别：

```
% Adams / MATLAB Interface - Release 2015.0.0
system('taskkill /IM scontrols.exe /F >NUL');clc;
global ADAMS_sysdir; % used by setup_rtw_for_adams.m
global ADAMS_host; % used by start_adams_daemon.m
machine=computer;
datestr(now)
if strcmp(machine, 'SOL2')
   arch = 'solaris32';
elseif strcmp(machine, 'SOL64')
   arch = 'solaris32';
elseif strcmp(machine, 'GLNX86')
   arch = 'linux32';
elseif strcmp(machine, 'GLNXA64')
   arch = 'linux64';
elseif strcmp(machine, 'PCWIN')
   arch = 'win32';
elseif strcmp(machine, 'PCWIN64')
   arch = 'win64';
else
   disp( '%%% Error : Platform unknown or unsupported by Adams/Controls.' ) ;
   arch = 'unknown_or_unsupported';
   return
end
   if strcmp(arch,'win64')
   [flag, topdir]=system('adams2015_x64 -top');
else
[flag, topdir]=system('adams2015 -top');
end
if flag == 0
   temp_str=strcat(topdir, '/controls/', arch);
   addpath(temp_str)
   temp_str=strcat(topdir, '/controls/', 'matlab');
   addpath(temp_str)
   temp_str=strcat(topdir, '/controls/', 'utils');
   addpath(temp_str)
ADAMS_sysdir = strcat(topdir, '');
   else
```

```
        addpath( 'D:\MSC~1.SOF\ADAMS_~1\2015\controls/win64' ) ;
        addpath( 'D:\MSC~1.SOF\ADAMS_~1\2015\controls/win32' ) ;
        addpath( 'D:\MSC~1.SOF\ADAMS_~1\2015\controls/matlab' ) ;
        addpath( 'D:\MSC~1.SOF\ADAMS_~1\2015\controls/utils' ) ;
        ADAMS_sysdir = 'D:\MSC~1.SOF\ADAMS_~1\2015\' ;
    end
    ADAMS_exec = 'acar_solver' ;
    ADAMS_host = 'USER-20191020ZO' ;
    ADAMS_cwd ='D:\cab_cosimulation' ;
    ADAMS_prefix = 'slm_maintain ' ;
    ADAMS_static = 'no' ;
    ADAMS_solver_type = 'Fortran' ;
    if exist([ADAMS_prefix,'.adm']) == 0
        disp( ' ' ) ;
        disp( '%%% Warning : missing ADAMS plant model file(.adm) for Co-simulation or Function Evaluation.' ) ;
        disp( '%%% If necessary, please re-export model files or copy the exported plant model files into the' ) ;
        disp( '%%% working directory.  You may disregard this warning if the Co-simulation/Function Evaluation' ) ;
        disp( '%%% is TCP/IP-based (running Adams on another machine), or if setting up MATLAB/Real-Time Workshop' ) ;
        disp( '%%% for generation of an External System Library.' ) ;
        disp( ' ' ) ;
    end
    ADAMS_init = 'file/command= slm_maintain _controls.acf' ;
    ADAMS_inputs ='my_cab_zhudong.frot_left!my_cab_zhudong.front_right!my_cab_zhudong.rear_left!my_cab_zhudong. rear_right' ;
    ADAMS_outputs = 'my_cab_zhudong.f_l_v_shuchu!my_cab_zhudong.f_r_v_shuchu!my_cab_zhudong.r_l_v_shuchu!my_cab_zhudong.r_r_v_shuchu' ;
    ADAMS_pinput = 'Controls_Plant_1.ctrl_pinput' ;
    ADAMS_poutput = 'Controls_Plant_1.ctrl_poutput' ;
    ADAMS_uy_ids   = [
                      532
                      533
                      534
                      535
                      547
```

```
                            548
                            549
                            550
                          ] ;
ADAMS_mode    = 'non-linear' ;
tmp_in    = decode( ADAMS_inputs   ) ;
tmp_out = decode( ADAMS_outputs ) ;
disp( ' ' ) ;
disp( '%%% INFO : ADAMS plant actuators names :' ) ;
disp( [int2str([1:size(tmp_in,1)]'),blanks(size(tmp_in,1))',tmp_in] ) ;
disp( '%%% INFO : ADAMS plant sensors     names :' ) ;
disp( [int2str([1:size(tmp_out,1)]'),blanks(size(tmp_out,1))',tmp_out] ) ;
disp( ' ' ) ;
clear tmp_in tmp_out ;
% Adams / MATLAB Interface - Release 2015.0.0
```

17.9.2 协同方案 B

用记事本打开文件 slm_maintain.m，如下参数与 Controls_Plant_1.m 文件对应的参数相同，可以把 Controls_Plant_1.m 中对应的参数复制粘贴过来保存即可。

A. 修改 ADAMS_outputs = '……' ;
B. 修改 ADAMS_poutput = '……';
C. 修改 ADAMS_uy_ids='……';

```
具体操作过程如下，程序修改部分用斜体区别：斜体与 Controls_Plant_1.m 文件对应的
参数相同。
% Adams / MATLAB Interface - Release 2015.0.0
system('taskkill /IM scontrols.exe /F >NUL');clc;
global ADAMS_sysdir; % used by setup_rtw_for_adams.m
global ADAMS_host; % used by start_adams_daemon.m
machine=computer;
datestr(now)
if strcmp(machine, 'SOL2')
   arch = 'solaris32';
elseif strcmp(machine, 'SOL64')
   arch = 'solaris32';
elseif strcmp(machine, 'GLNX86')
   arch = 'linux32';
elseif strcmp(machine, 'GLNXA64')
```

```
    arch = 'linux64';
  elseif strcmp(machine, 'PCWIN')
    arch = 'win32';
  elseif strcmp(machine, 'PCWIN64')
    arch = 'win64';
  else
    disp( '%%% Error : Platform unknown or unsupported by Adams/Controls.' ) ;
    arch = 'unknown_or_unsupported';
    return
  end
  if strcmp(arch,'win64')
    [flag, topdir]=system('adams2015_x64 -top');
  else
    [flag, topdir]=system('adams2015 -top');
  end
  if flag == 0
    temp_str=strcat(topdir, '/controls/', arch);
    addpath(temp_str)
    temp_str=strcat(topdir, '/controls/', 'matlab');
    addpath(temp_str)
    temp_str=strcat(topdir, '/controls/', 'utils');
    addpath(temp_str)
    ADAMS_sysdir = strcat(topdir, '');
  else
    addpath( 'D:\MSC~1.SOF\ADAMS_~1\2015\controls/win64' ) ;
    addpath( 'D:\MSC~1.SOF\ADAMS_~1\2015\controls/win32' ) ;
    addpath( 'D:\MSC~1.SOF\ADAMS_~1\2015\controls/matlab' ) ;
    addpath( 'D:\MSC~1.SOF\ADAMS_~1\2015\controls/utils' ) ;
    ADAMS_sysdir = 'D:\MSC~1.SOF\ADAMS_~1\2015\' ;
  end
    ADAMS_exec = 'acar_solver' ;
    ADAMS_host = '' ;
    ADAMS_cwd ='D:\cab_cosimulation' ;
    ADAMS_prefix = 'slm_maintain' ;
    ADAMS_static = 'no' ;
    ADAMS_solver_type = 'Fortran' ;
  if exist([ADAMS_prefix,'.adm']) == 0
  disp( ' ' ) ;
```

```
    disp( '%%% Warning : missing ADAMS plant model file(.adm) for Co-simulation or
Function Evaluation.' ) ;
    disp( '%%% If necessary, please re-export model files or copy the exported plant model files
into the' ) ;
    disp( '%%% working directory.   You may disregard this warning if the Co-simulation/
Function Evaluation' ) ;
    disp( '%%% is TCP/IP-based (running Adams on another machine), or if setting up
MATLAB/Real-Time Workshop' ) ;
    disp( '%%% for generation of an External System Library.' ) ;
    disp( ' ' ) ;
    end
    ADAMS_init = 'file/command=slm_maintain_controls.acf' ;
    ADAMS_inputs  = 'my_truck_brake.front_left_INPUT!my_truck_brake.front_right_INPUT!
my_truck_brake.mid_left_INPUT!my_truck_brake.mid_right_INPUT!my_truck_brake.rear_left_
INPUT!my_truck_brake.rear_right_INPUT!my_cab_zhudong.frot_left!my_cab_zhudong.
front_right!my_cab_zhudong.rear_left!my_cab_zhudong.rear_right' ;
    ADAMS_outputs  =  'my_cab_zhudong.f_l_v_shuchu!my_cab_zhudong.f_r_v_shuchu!my_
cab_zhudong.
    r_l_v_shuchu!my_cab_zhudong.r_r_v_shuchu' ;
    ADAMS_pinput = 'Controls_Plant_1.ctrl_pinput' ;
    ADAMS_poutput = 'Controls_Plant_1.ctrl_poutput' ;
    ADAMS_uy_ids   = [
                    532
                    533
                    534
                    535
                    547
                    548
                    549
                    550
                ] ;
    ADAMS_mode    = 'non-linear' ;
    tmp_in  = decode( ADAMS_inputs  ) ;
    tmp_out = decode( ADAMS_outputs ) ;
    disp( ' ' ) ;
    disp( '%%% INFO : ADAMS plant actuators names :' ) ;
    disp( [int2str([1:size(tmp_in,1)]'),blanks(size(tmp_in,1))',tmp_in] ) ;
    disp( '%%% INFO : ADAMS plant sensors     names :' ) ;
```

```
disp( [int2str([1:size(tmp_out,1)]'),blanks(size(tmp_out,1))',tmp_out] ) ;
disp( ' ' ) ;
clear tmp_in tmp_out ;
% Adams / MATLAB Interface - Release 2015.0.0
```

- MATLAB 软件中命令窗口中输入 Controls_Plant_1；
- 单击键盘 Enter 键；此时命令窗口显示出如下信息，信息包含输入输出集信息。

```
Matlab 窗口界面显示如下信息。
Controls_Plant_1

%%% INFO : ADAMS plant actuators names :
1 my_cab_zhudong.frot_left
2 my_cab_zhudong.front_right
3 my_cab_zhudong.rear_left
4 my_cab_zhudong.rear_right
%%% INFO : ADAMS plant sensors    names :
1 my_cab_zhudong.f_l_v_shuchu
2 my_cab_zhudong.f_r_v_shuchu
3 my_cab_zhudong.r_l_v_shuchu
4 my_cab_zhudong.r_r_v_shuchu
```

- 运行 adams_sys，调出 adams_plant 对话框，如图 17-24 所示。

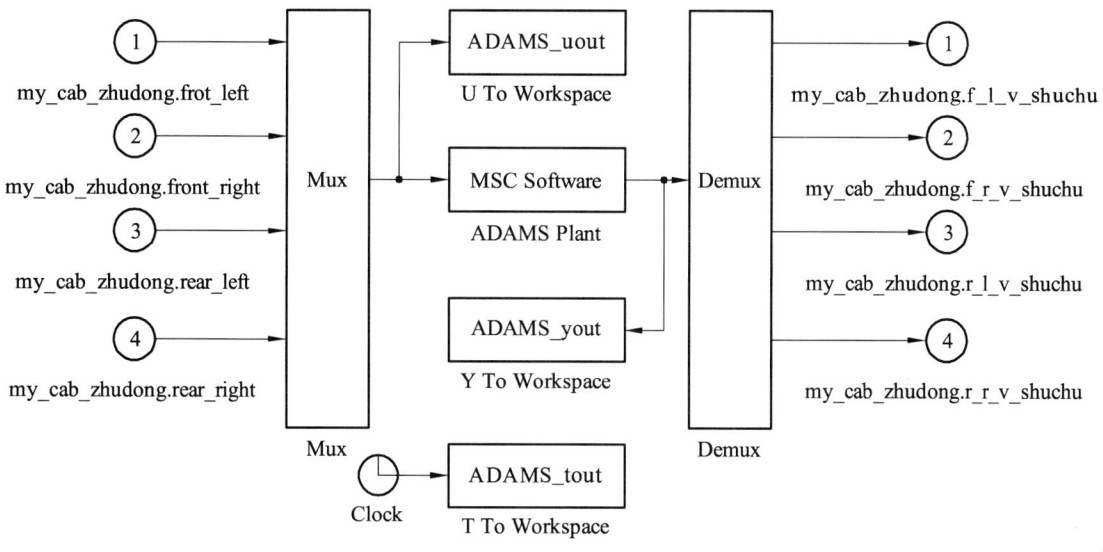

图 17-24　adams_plant 对话框

17.10 模糊 PID-D 耦合算法

6×4 驱动底盘形式主要用于工程车辆和商用牵引车,牵引车多在国道路面运输,一般工作路面较差。对于不同的路面工作状态,驾驶室输出的振动特性不同。当工作路面较差且整车运行速度较小时,输入信号等同阶跃信号,在驾驶室主动悬置系统控制过程中会造成定点冲击,增加驾驶室的瞬间振动。对于固定的路面信号输入,微分先行 PID 控制可以有效地改善瞬时定点冲击现象,但当路面输入改变时,已调整好的系统调节参数已不适用,针对此问题提出模糊 PID-D 耦合算法,通过车身加速度判定路面的输入状态,然后通过模糊算法在线自适应调节 PID-D 微分系数,使整车在各状态运行时都可以适度地减小及避免定点冲击,改善驾驶室的舒适性。

磁流变阻尼器实验请参考文献《磁流变式驾驶室悬置系统隔振研究》。

以左前磁流变阻尼器为例,模糊 PID-D 耦合算法公式推导如下。

$$u(t) = K_p e(t) + K_I \int_0^t e(t) \mathrm{d}t + K_{d1} F_1 \frac{\mathrm{d}}{\mathrm{d}t} e(t) - K_{d2} F_2 \frac{\mathrm{d}}{\mathrm{d}t} y(t) \tag{17-1}$$

$$e(t) = 0 - y(t) \tag{17-2}$$

$$F_1 = \Omega(V_z) \tag{17-3}$$

$$F_2 = 1 - \Omega(V_z) \tag{17-4}$$

将公式(17-2)~公式(17-4)带入到公式(17-1)中整理得

$$u(t) = -K_p y(t) - K_I \int_0^t y(t) \mathrm{d}t - \frac{\mathrm{d}}{\mathrm{d}t} y(t) - \Omega(V_z) \left[K_{d1} \frac{\mathrm{d}}{\mathrm{d}t} y(t) - K_{d2} \frac{\mathrm{d}}{\mathrm{d}t} y(t) \right] \tag{17-5}$$

式中,$e(t)$ 为输入输出之间误差;$y(t)$ 为驾驶室与阻尼器连接处垂向速度;K_p 为缩放系数;K_I 为积分系数;K_{d1} 为误差反馈预设微分系数;K_{d2} 为输出反馈预设微分系数;F_1、F_2 为微分在线调节系数,由模糊算法根据路面状态输出;$u(t)$ 为磁流变阻尼器输出控制力;$\Omega(V_z)$ 为模糊控制规则。

微分在线调节系数由模糊算法输出,输入为车身垂向加速度,系统模糊控制规则如表 17-2 所示。建立好的模糊 PID-D 控制系统如图 17-25 所示。

表 17-2 微分系数调节模糊规则

$\dot{y}(t)$	-3	-2	-1	0	1	2	3
F_1	0.1	0.2	0.5	0.8	0.5	0.2	0.1
F_2	0.9	0.8	0.5	0.2	0.5	0.8	0.9

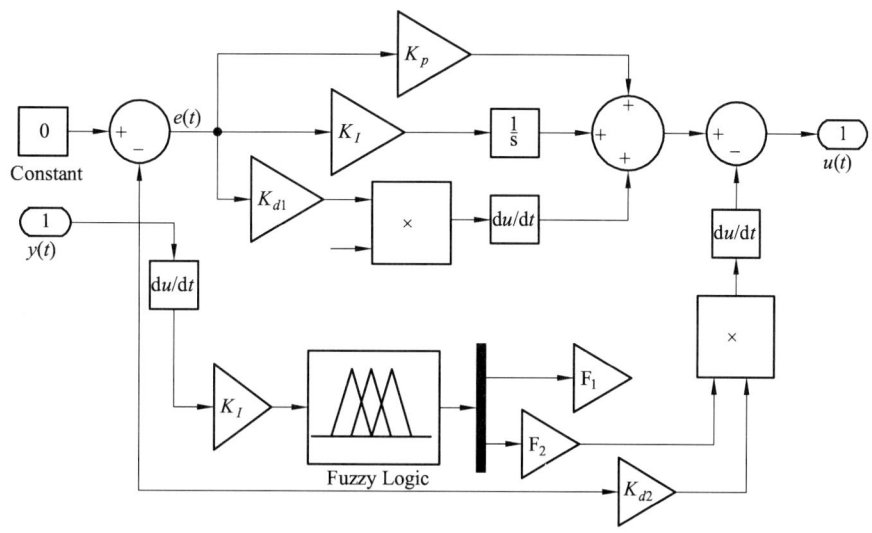

图 17-25 模糊 PID-D 系统

车身垂向加速度论域为

$$E = [-1\,500,\ 1\,500] \tag{17-6}$$

量化因子为

$$K = 3/E = 0.002 \tag{17-7}$$

17.11 驾驶室机控联合仿真

（1）路面模型。

按要求编制连续正弦波路面文件谱，波纹路面宽 2 m，路面摩擦系数为 0.9，路面垂向峰值为 10 mm，波长 8 m，路面特征为 sine 函数，波纹路面无偏移，编制好的正弦波路面如图 17-26 所示。

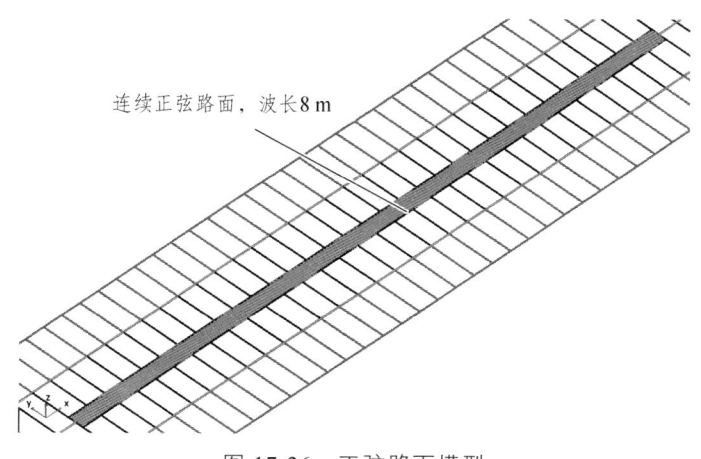

图 17-26 正弦路面模型

（2）速度保持仿真。

整车保持匀速直线行驶状态，速度为 40 km/h，方向盘锁定，仿真计算时间为 10 s。计算结果如图 17-27 ~ 图 17-29 所示，图中 passive 为常规阻尼器仿真结果曲线，active 为磁流变阻尼器仿真结果曲线。驾驶室垂向加速度改善明显，极值从 1 026.98 降低为 403.50，均方根值从 415.65 降低为 107.47，垂向加速度极值与均方根性能分别提升 60.71%、74.14%；驾驶室横摆角速度极值从 0.022 4 降低为 0.017 3，均方根值从 0.007 4 降低为 0.005 0，横摆角速度极值与均方根性能分别提升 22.77%、32.43%；驾驶室侧倾角速度极值从 1.466 2 降低为 0.772 0，均方根值从 0.319 5 降低为 0.272 0，侧倾角速度极值与均方根性能分别提升 47.35%，14.87%；

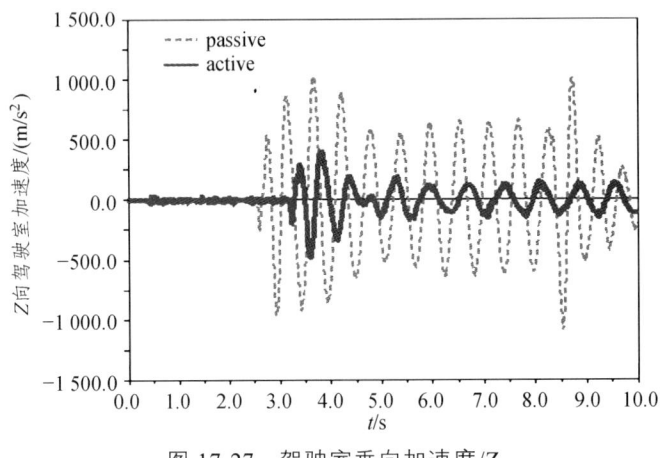

图 17-27　驾驶室垂向加速度/Z

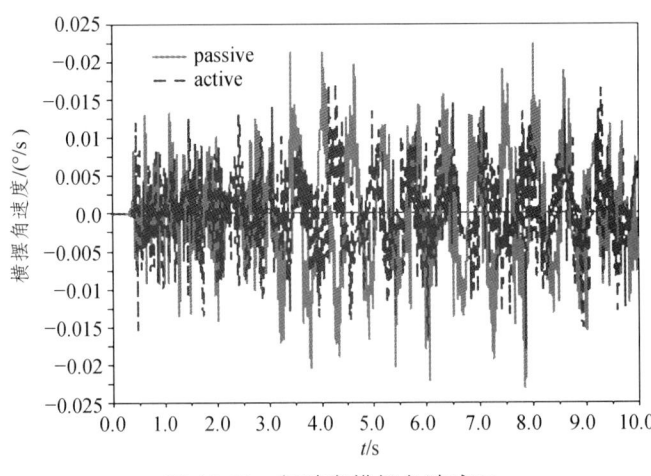

图 17-28　驾驶室横摆角速度/Z

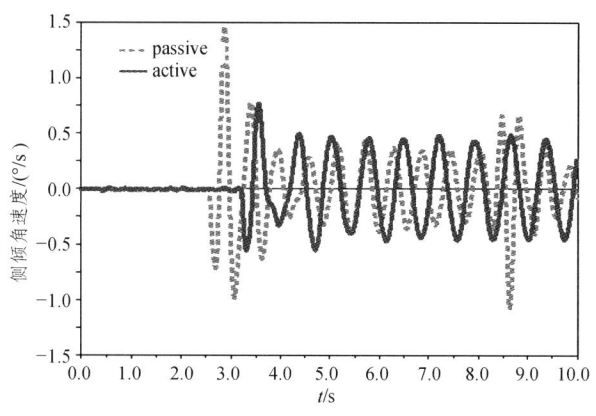

图 17-29 驾驶室侧倾角速度/X

（3）转向桥避震器。

牵引车轴距较长，同时转向桥板簧刚度相对后轴平衡悬架刚度要小很多，在经过坑洼路面时整车的俯仰角过大，因而导致安装在车架上的驾驶振动过大。针对此问题，提出在转向桥加装阻尼器，阻尼器安装位置如图 17-30 所示。更换驾驶室阻尼器特性文件为如图 17-5 所示变频率实验数据。按同工况进行速度保持仿真，车身垂向加速度计算结果如图 17-31、图 17-32 所示，auxiliary 为转向桥加装阻尼器仿真结果曲线。驾驶室垂向加速度极值为 243.57，均方根值为 37.54，驾驶室在磁流变主动阻尼器的基础上极值与均方根性能继续提升 39.64%、65.07%；功率谱显示在全频域范围内，驾驶室性能均提升，低频段改善明显。

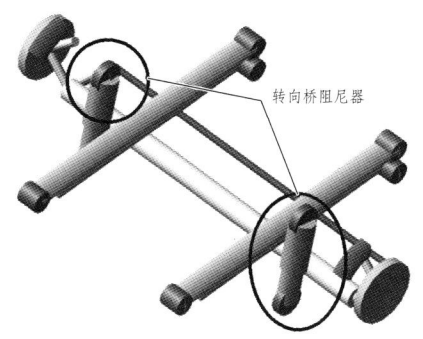

图 17-30 转向桥阻尼器

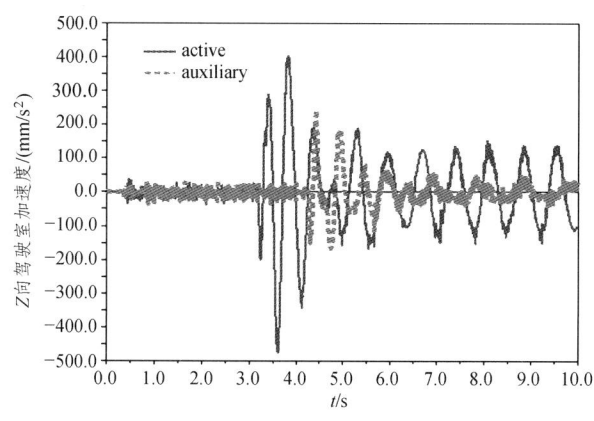

图 17-31 驾驶室垂向加速度/阻尼器

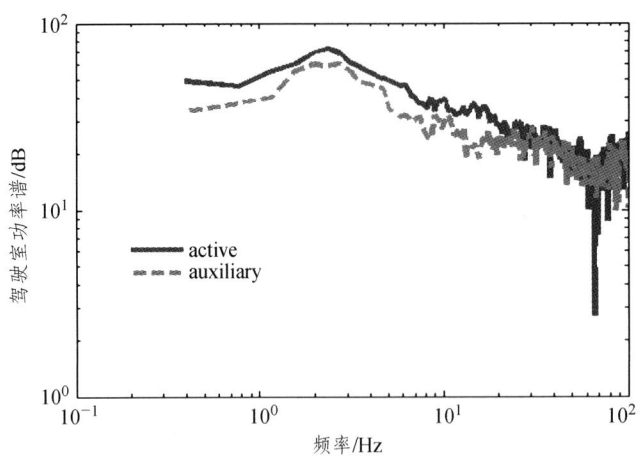

图 17-32　驾驶室垂向加速度功率谱

（4）结论。

① 磁流变阻尼器变电流实验表明，随着电流的增加，阻尼力增加，阻尼特性为非重合曲线。变频率实验表明，随着频率的增加，阻尼力亦增加，同时阻尼器有效工作区域范围增加，适当提升阻尼器工作频率对系统有益。

② 采用模糊 PID-D 耦合算法后，驾驶室垂向加速度、横摆角速度、侧倾角速度指标参数均有改善，其中驾驶室垂向加速度改善较为明显，垂向加速度极值与均方根性能分别提升 60.71%、74.14%。

③ 转向桥加装阻尼器后，驾驶室在磁流变主动阻尼器的基础上极值与均方根性能继续提升 39.64%、65.07%；功率谱显示在全频域范围内提升，低频段改善明显。

④ 整车平台下研究驾驶室与其他系统匹配、优化等特性对于车辆理论及工程研究均具有指导意义。

第 18 章　FSAE 整车变刚度悬架特性研究

通过变刚度横置板簧悬架模型设计，板簧刚度可实现 9 倍范围变化，FSAE 赛车可实现 16 种变刚度底盘特性组合。弯道仿真实验表明，FSAE 赛车前后悬架不同刚度组合均可降低整车质心高度，提升稳定性，其中 BB 刚度组合性能改善最为明显，车身高度降低 81.18 mm，整车横摆角速度指标提升 35.39%，侧向加速度指标提升 57.50%；横置板簧与车身及下控制连接处添加衬套后，可有效改善实验初期振荡现象；板簧结构优化后，质量减少 24.00%，稳定性指标微幅提升，但实验过程伴有较小的振荡现象，建立好的整车模型如图 18-1 所示。

图 18-1　FSAE 整车

学习目标

- ◆ 板簧有限元前处理。
- ◆ 板簧模态。
- ◆ 板簧刚度。
- ◆ FSAE 整车。
- ◆ 定常半径转向转弯。
- ◆ 板簧结构优化。

18.1 横置板簧悬架

FSAE 赛车设计关注的重点是整车的操控稳定性，操稳性对整车的底盘要求较高。纵观国内近些年赛事，绝大多数 FSAE 赛车前后悬架均采用推杆式双横臂悬架，有少数车辆采用双横臂悬架。推杆式悬架与双横臂悬架对于整车稳定的提升均有改善作用，但推杆式悬架最大的缺点是安装时需要占用较大的车身空间。FSAE 赛车驱动采用中置后驱模式，发动机、传动系统、车身附属装置及悬架系统均布置在后轮附近空间，集成度较高，同时导致整车质心后移，稳定性变差。针对此问题提出横置板簧悬架模型设计，旨在去掉推杆及螺旋弹簧部件，减少空间占用，同时车轮及非簧载质量减轻，固有频率提升，车辆振动减小，横置板簧既起到螺旋弹簧作用同时又起到横向拉杆作用。在横置板簧悬架模型的基础上，改变板簧与车身的固定位置即可以改变板簧横向力臂，最终可以分段调节板簧的刚度特性。板簧两端与下控制臂连接，安装在悬架最底部，不占用空间，可以进一步降低整车质心高度，对于提升操控稳定性极为有利。

国内 FSAE 赛车前后悬架均为推杆式双 A 臂悬架模型，此悬架的优点是悬架空气动力学性能较好，阻尼效率高；缺点是悬架的整体质量增幅较大，占用较多的安装空间。FSAE 赛车为中后置后轮驱动，后悬架附近需要安装发动机、变速器、传动机构及悬架等附属装置，系统部件布置空间小且后轴系偏中。针对此问题提出一种横置板簧悬架模型设计，增大后轴布置空间，降低车身质心，进一步提升整车稳定性。

18.1.1 变刚度板簧模型

变刚度板簧模型如图 18-2 所示。钢板宽度为 20 mm，厚度为 5 mm，长度为 730 mm；板簧长度中心线上设计出 9 个孔，孔直径为 5 mm。此板簧有 4 种刚度：RP-5 为板簧长度的中心，固定 RP-5 时，单侧臂 RP-5 与 RP-1 之间的刚度为 A，单侧臂 RP-5 与 RP-9 之间的刚度为 A；RP-4 与 RP-6 关于 RP-5 对称，固定 RP-4 与 RP-6 时，单侧臂 RP-4 与 RP-1 之间的刚度为 B，单侧臂 RP-6 与 RP-9 之间的刚度为 B；RP-3 与 RP-7 关于 RP-5 对称，固定 RP-4 与 RP-6 时，单侧臂 RP-3 与 RP-1 之间的刚度为 C，单侧臂 RP-7 与 RP-9 之间的刚度为 C；RP-2 与 RP-8 关于 RP-5 对称，固定 RP-2 与 RP-8 时，单侧臂 RP-2 与 RP-1 之间的刚度为 D，单侧臂 RP-8 与 RP-9 之间的刚度为 D；RP-1、RP-9 与下控制臂刚性固定连接。

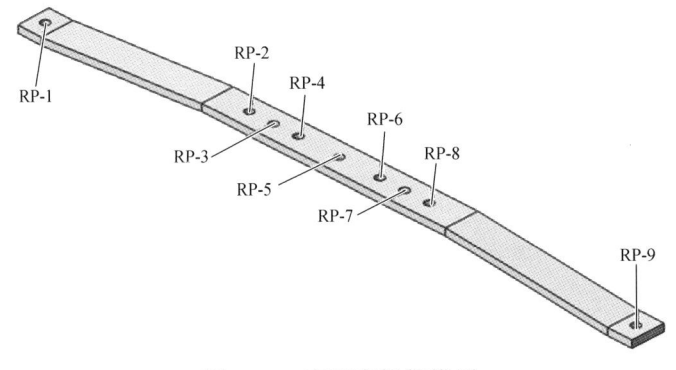

图 18-2 变刚度板簧模型

18.1.2 板簧模态

在 ABAQUS 软件中计算板簧前 20 阶模态并输出板簧中性模态文件 MNF 到 ADAMS 软件总构建横置板簧悬架模型。在 RP-1 至 RP-9 孔中分别建立 MPC 多点约束，输出模态中固定约束 RP-1、RP-5、RP-9。网格划分为六面体，共 2 808 个单元，单元类型 C3D8R。计算并生成子数据块，其中 5、6、7 阶模态如图 18-3 所示。

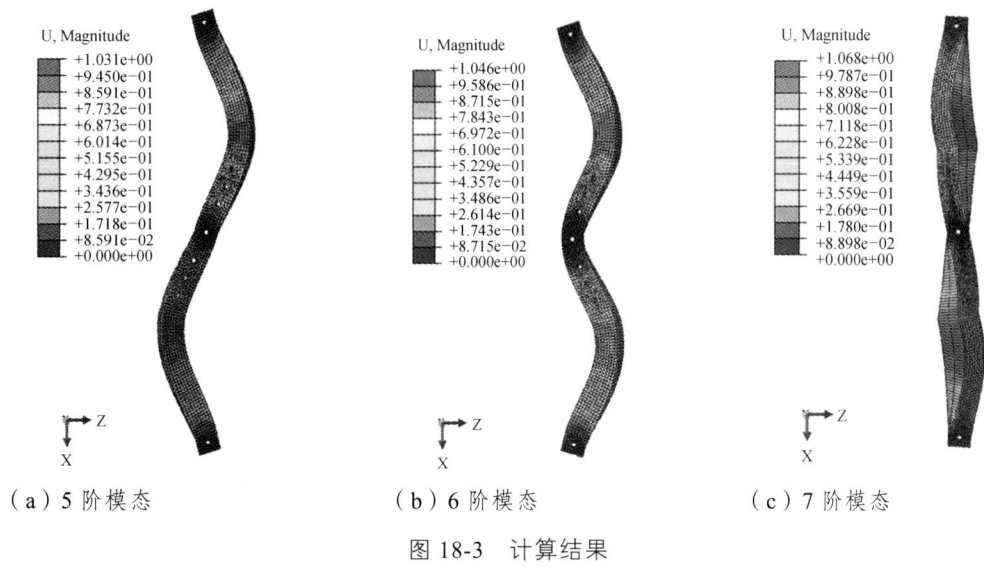

（a）5 阶模态　　　　（b）6 阶模态　　　　（c）7 阶模态

图 18-3　计算结果

18.1.3 板簧刚度

板簧子数据块完成计算后通过转换命令生成板簧中性文件 MNF，在 ADAMS 中导入中性文件添加约束、驱动计算板簧刚度。单侧臂刚度测试过程如下：RP-9 处添加与 Y 轴平行的移动副，在移动副上添加驱动位移，速度为 20 mm/s，分别固定约束 RP-5、RP-6、RP-7、RP-8 计算出刚度 A、B、C、D，如图 18-4 所示。刚度 A 为 26.10 N/mm，刚度 B 为 56.04 N/mm，刚度 C 为 107.54 N/mm，刚度 D 为 232.55 N/mm。从计算结果中可以看出，同一片钢板弹簧，通过改变力臂大小，刚度实现了 9 倍范围内变化。

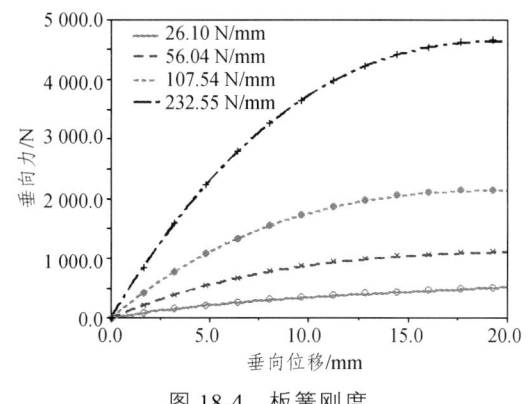

图 18-4　板簧刚度

18.1.4 参数测试

前横置板簧悬架模型前束角设置为1°，车轮外倾设置为-5°，外倾角为负且角度较大有利于提升整车稳定性。对前横置板簧悬架模型进行同向车轮激振实验，车轮跳动距离为50 mm，计算出推杆式双横臂悬架与横置板簧悬架的前束角变化范围分别为-1.17°～2.85°、-1.30°～2.75°；车轮外倾角变化范围分别为-2.53°～-7.83°、-2.57°～-7.90°；主销内倾角变化范围分别为12.66°～17.97°、12.70°～18.04°；主销后倾角变化范围分别为0.0049～0.0843、-0.01～6.8e-5。从计算结果中可以看出，前束角、外倾角、内倾角曲线重合度较高，主销后倾角变化角度小，但相对变化范围较大，变化趋势如图18-5所示。横置板簧悬架模型后倾角在车轮跳动中变化范围不大，性能相对推杆式双横臂悬架有所提升。

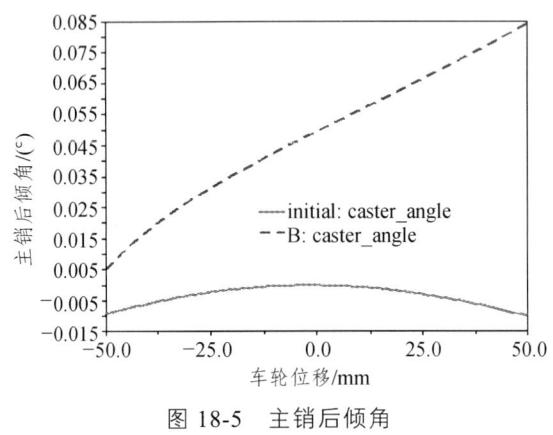

图 18-5　主销后倾角

18.2　定常半径弯道仿真

用前后横置板簧悬架模型完成FSAE整车模型建立，如图18-1所示，整车共196个自由度。前后横置板簧均有A、B、C、D四种刚度，通过前后悬架刚度组合共有16组刚度可调，刚度组合如表18-1所示，表中G_1表示前轴悬架板簧刚度，G_2表示后轴板簧刚度。板簧刚度C、D相对于刚度A大很多，接近于刚性连接，同时由于后悬架刚度相对于前悬架刚度一般会略大或者相同，在如表18-1所示刚度组合中，具有实际研究意义的刚度组合为AA、BA、BB、CC、DD。如果变刚度板簧的刚度增量变化较小，中刚度组合均具有研究意义。AA、BA、BB、CC、DD五种刚度组合中，AA组合整车静平衡发散，原因在于后悬架板簧刚度为A时变形量过大导致，BA、BB两种刚度组合计算结果相近，说明后轴刚度对整车稳定性具有主导作用，因此选取BB、CC、DD三种刚度组合与采用推杆式悬架FSAE整车进行对比分析。对整车进行定常半径转弯仿真，相同工况下测试整车横摆角速度、侧向加速度稳定性参数，车辆转向半径为15 m，初始速度为10 km/h，最终速度为50 km/h，发动机变速器均为3挡工况，运行时间10 s。

表 18-1 刚度组合表

G_2	G_1			
	A	B	C	D
A	AA	AB	AC	AD
B	BA	BB	BC	BD
C	CA	CB	CC	CD
D	DA	DB	DC	DD

图形中 initial 曲线表示推杆式双横臂悬架 FSAE 整车模型计算结果。从图 18-6 中可以看出，推杆式双横臂悬架整车模型车身高度为 348.17 mm，采用横置板簧悬架后整车的车身高均有降低。BB 刚度组合后车身高度为 302.75 mm，降低 45.42 mm；CC 组合后车身高度为 310.88 mm，降低 37.29 mm；采用 DD 组合后车身高度为 314.37 mm，降低 33.8 毫米；如图 18-7 所示为横摆角速度变化曲线，initial 为 29.39°/s；BB 刚度组合最大值为 24.50°/s，性能提升 16.64%；CC 刚度组合最大值为 26.65°/s，性能提升 9.32%；DD 刚度组合最大值为 27.48°/s，性能提升 6.50%。如图 18-8 所示为侧向加速度，initial 为 -0.40 mm/s^2；BB 刚度组合最大值为 -0.28 mm/s^2，性能提升 30.00%；CC 刚度组合最大值为 -0.33 mm/s^2，性能提升 17.50%；DD 刚度组合最大值为 -0.35 mm/s^2，性能提升 12.50%。

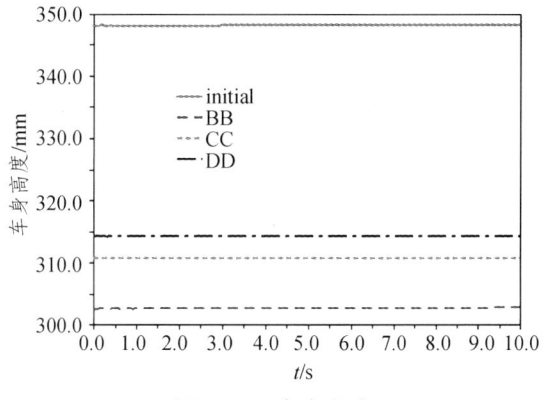

图 18-6 车身高度

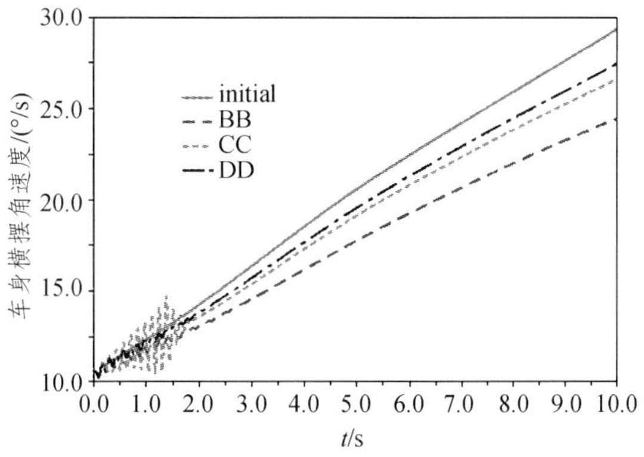

图 18-7 横摆角速度

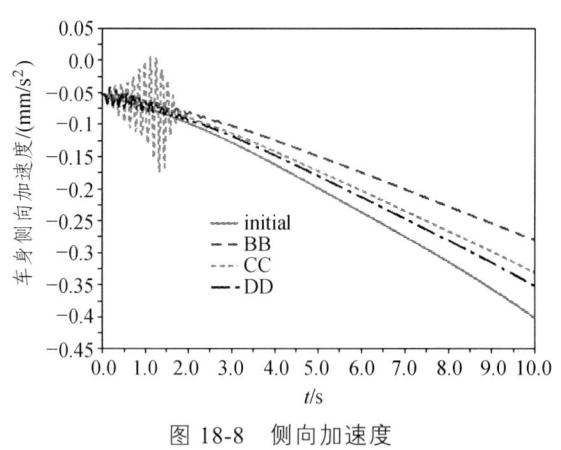

图 18-8 侧向加速度

18.3 板簧优化

通过定值半径转弯计算，采用横置板簧悬架的整车稳定性均具有提升，其中 BB 刚度组合的整车性能最佳。但 BB、CC 刚度组合在实验初始都伴有较大的振荡现象，针对此问题对板簧进行继续优化。

18.3.1 板簧衬套

针对实验初期存在的振荡现象，当刚度组合为 BB 时，在板簧孔 RP-4、RP-6 与 RP-1、RP-9 处添加柔性衬套；当刚度组合为 CC 时，在板簧孔 RP-3、RP-7 与 RP-1、RP-9 处添加柔性衬套；刚度组合为 CC 时添加衬套如图 18-9 所示。

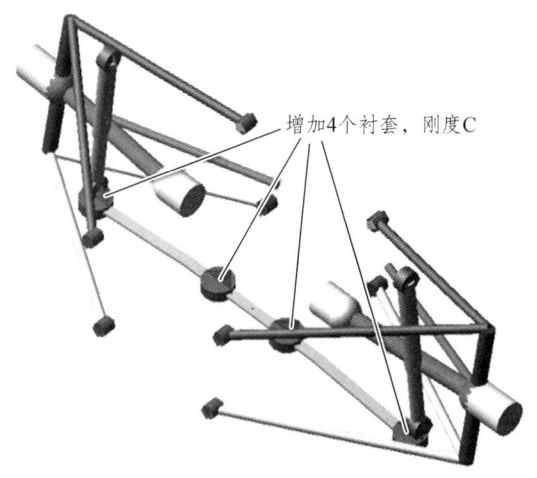

图 18-9 横置板簧衬套

对优化后的横置板簧悬架整车模型进行计算，当刚度组合为 CC 时，如图 18-10 所示整车实验初期振荡现象改善明显，同时稳定性指标参数进一步提升，其中横摆角度最大值降低为 25.44°/s，性能相对添加衬套前提升 4.54%，相对于推杆式双横臂悬架提升 13.44%；侧向加速度最大降低为 −0.30 mm/s²，性能相对添加衬套前提升 9.10%，相对于推杆式双横臂悬架提升 25.00%。

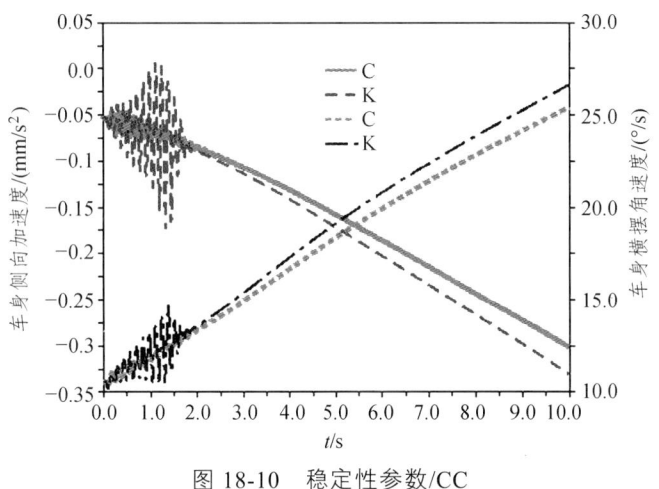

图 18-10　稳定性参数/CC

当刚度组合为 BB 时，如图 18-11 所示整车稳定性指标参数进一步提升，其中横摆角度最大值降低为 18.99°/s，性能相对添加衬套前提升 22.49%，相对于推杆式双横臂悬架提升 35.39%；侧向加速度最大降低为 −0.17 mm/s²，性能相对添加衬套前提升 39.29%，相对于推杆式双横臂悬架提升 57.50%；车身高度降低为 266.99 mm，相对于推杆式悬架整车模型整车降低 81.18 mm。

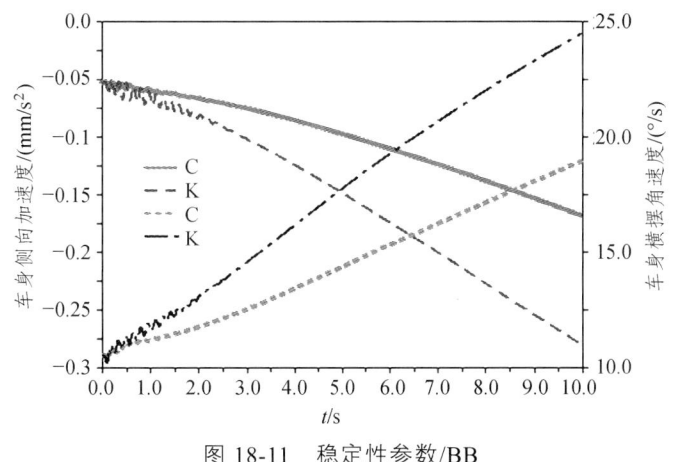

图 18-11　稳定性参数/BB

18.3.2　板簧轻量化

对 FSAE 赛车右后轮处板簧与下控制臂连接点测量受力如图 18-12 所示，其中侧向力最大为 4 650 N，垂向力为 183 N；板簧纵向力微小可以忽略，从计算结果中可以看出横置板簧主要承受侧向力与垂向力，其作用相当于悬架上增加了一根横向拉杆同时起到弹簧作用，这也是采用横置板簧悬架整车模型弯道模式下侧向加速度参数大幅降低的最主要原因，整车纵向力主要由悬架上下控制臂承受。

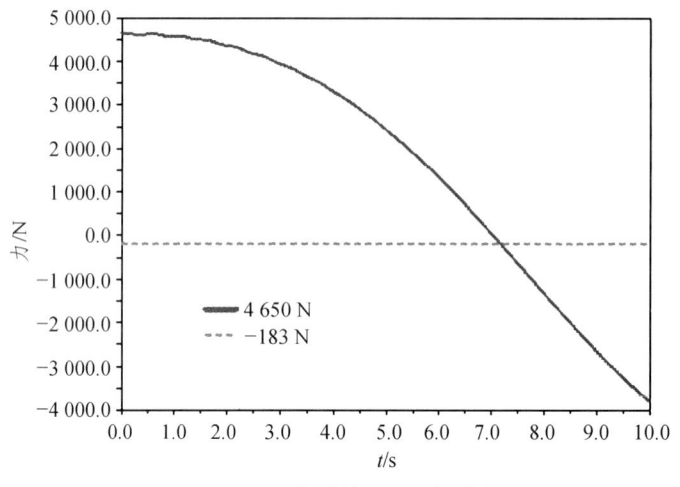

图 18-12　右后轮 RP-1 点受力

横置板簧材料：60Si2Mn，弹性模量：2.06E5 MPa，泊桑比：0.29，密度：7.74×10^3 kg/m³；抗拉强度 1 270 MPa。对板簧进行有限元分析，单侧臂应力变化如图 18-13 所示，最大应力为 449.7 MPa，最大应变为 28.3 mm。图中优化区域承受应力较小，远小于抗拉强度，对此区域进行拓扑优化，循环计算 30 次，在拓扑优化的基础上输出板簧几何图形并对其进行形貌与尺寸修正，最终板簧单侧几何体如图 18-14 所示；对优化后的板簧再次进行分析，约束与载荷条件相同，计算结果显示最大应力为 555.90 MPa，最大应变为 28.10 mm，与优化之前对比最大应力增加，最大应变减小，最大应力依然小于抗拉强度，符合设计要求。

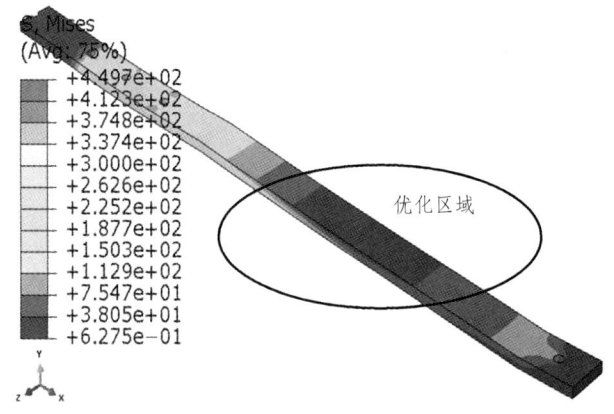

图 18-13　单侧板簧应力

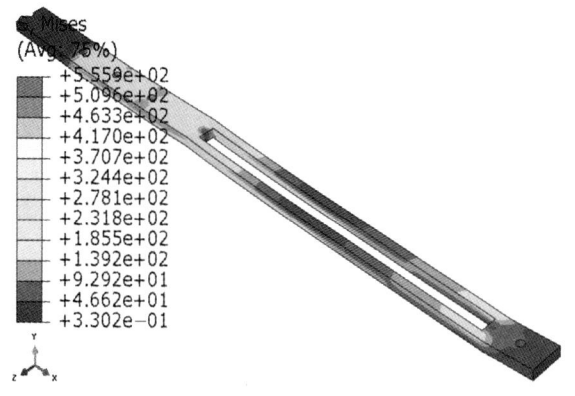

图 18-14 优化后单侧板簧应力

优化前横置板簧质量为 0.595 7 kg，优化后质量为 0.452 7 kg，质量减少 24.0%，优化效果较明显。对优化后的板簧进行刚度测试，计算显示优化后的板簧刚度为 50.65 N/mm，如图 18-15 所示，相对优化前刚度 56.04 N/mm 有所减小；横置板簧替换后通过仿真实验计算整车稳定性参数如图 18-16 所示，整车侧向加速度与横摆角速度分别为 0.1577 mm/s^2、18.32°/s，性能相对优化前整车 BB 刚度组合提升 8.05%、4.58%，但运行过程中伴有微小振荡现象。

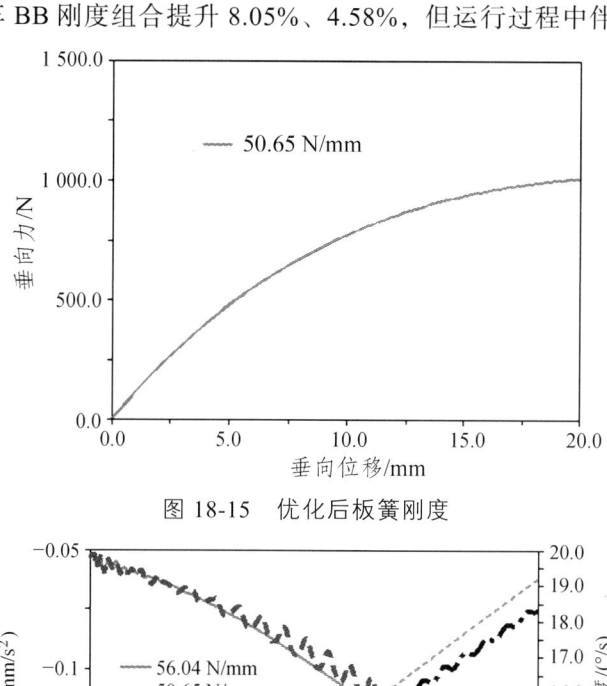

图 18-15 优化后板簧刚度

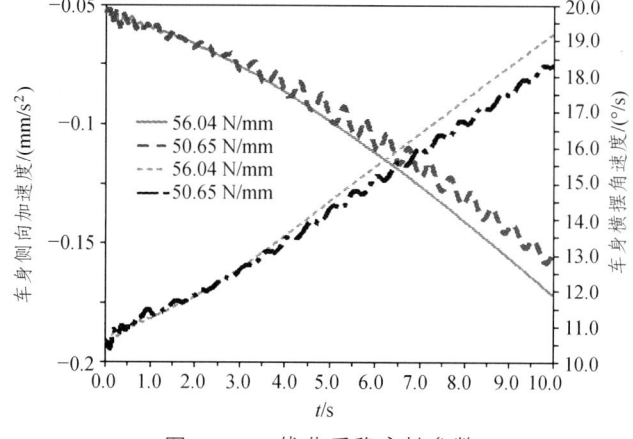

图 18-16 优化后稳定性参数

18.4 总　结

（1）变刚度横置板簧可以实现弹簧刚度 9 倍范围内变化，最小刚度为 26.10 N/mm，最大刚度为 232.55 N/mm，FSAE 整车模型可以实现 16 种可变刚度组合底盘模型。

（2）FSAE 采用横置板簧后，相对于推杆式双横臂悬架整车车身高度均有所降低，侧向加速度、横摆角速度等稳定性参数均提升，其中 BB 刚度组合性能提升最为明显，分别为 16.64%、30.00%。

（3）横置板簧与下控制臂、车身连接处添加柔性衬套后，仿真实验初期振荡现象改善明显，同时整车稳定性指标进一步提升，车身高度总降低 81.18 mm。

（4）板簧结构优化后，质量减少 24%，FSAE 整车稳定性继续改善，但伴有振荡现象。

（5）本章研究对 FSAE 赛车悬架设计、底盘参数匹配及进一步整车其他系统优化具有重要指导意义。

第 19 章　FSAE 赛车后轮随动转向

理论分析建立后轮瞬态随动转向系统数学模型，分析得出摆臂旋转角度及摆臂与车身连接衬套刚度是影响随动转向的主要因素。为验证理论模型的正确性，用 ADAMS 软件建立包含后轮随动转向特性的 FSAE 整车模型，后轮随动悬架模型设计为扭力梁悬架，衬套刚度通过动静刚度试验机获取，柔性扭转梁通过 ABAQUS 输出模态中性文件获取。反向车轮激振仿真表明，左右车轮中心可以获取随动转向位移，与理论数模模型对比，误差仅为 1.7%；整车弯道仿真表明，车辆入弯时为过渡转向，出弯时为不足转向，整车兼顾平顺与操稳性；扭力梁安装位置 C 值变动时，随着 C 值的增加，不足转向特性趋势减小，整车稳定性能变差；衬套安装角度 θ 增加时不足转向特性趋势减小，整车稳定性能提升。后轮随动转向 FSAE 整车模型如图 19-1 所示。

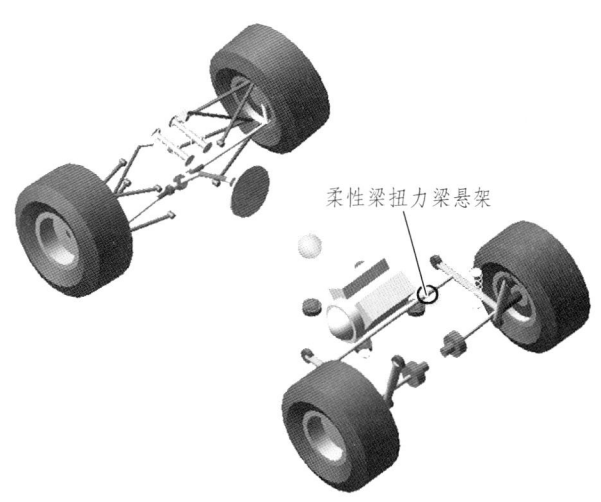

图 19-1　后轮随动转向 FSAE 模型

学习目标

- ◆ 随动转向数学模型。
- ◆ 随动转向物理模型。
- ◆ 衬套实验。
- ◆ 扭转梁 MNF。
- ◆ 反向激振仿真。
- ◆ 扭力梁位置因素。
- ◆ 衬套安装角度。

19.1 随动转向数学模型

后轮随动转向特性在一定程度上可以改善整车行驶平顺性并兼顾稳定性，主要体现在低速模式下转弯半径小，高速模式下入弯半径小，出弯半径大。后轮随动转向特性相关文献较少，检索相关文献主要集中在两方面：① 商用车后轮随动转向特性设计，商用车后驱动轮及挂车随动转向以减小整车及汽车转向半径为目的，不考虑整车瞬时转向特性及整车稳定性；② 采用控制算法设计控制后轮转向，文献研究的重心主要在于验证算法，并没有从理论上及结构模型特性上对随动转向特性进行系统分析，此类文献研究本质上为四轮转向。FSAE 赛车属于小型赛车，设计定位的方向以操控稳定性为主导，适宜的后轮随动转向特性对于提升 FSAE 赛车稳定性具有促进作用。要实现后轮随动转向特性，后悬架须设计成半独立式扭转梁悬架或独立式扭转梁悬架。从设计效果上看，独立式扭转梁悬架瞬时转向特性效果更好，但两根独立的扭转梁在车身底部占用较大空间，扭转梁的作用是替代了螺旋弹簧，同时独立式扭转梁悬架与车身之间需要安装四个不同刚度的柔性衬套才能实现较好的转向特性，因此选择较为简单半独立式扭转梁较为适宜，占用空间小，结构简单，成本低，同时半独立式扭转梁悬架存在旋转臂（拖拽臂），在整车长度一定的前提下可以进一步减少车身的长度，降低车身质量，提升稳定性。

FSAE 赛车向左转向时，车身向右侧倾斜，右侧车身向下压缩，即右侧轮胎向上跳动，左侧车轮向下跳动，后悬架车轮跳动模型简化如图 19-2 所示。FSAE 赛车在静止状态时后悬架摆臂与车身之间的安装位置高于车轮中心时摆臂角为正，反之为负，当摆臂角为正时，转向瞬间整车为过渡转向状态，后轮转向与前轮方向相反，FSAE 整车模型简化如图 19-3 所示。

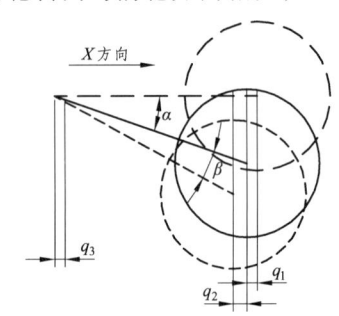

图 19-2 后悬架车轮跳动模型

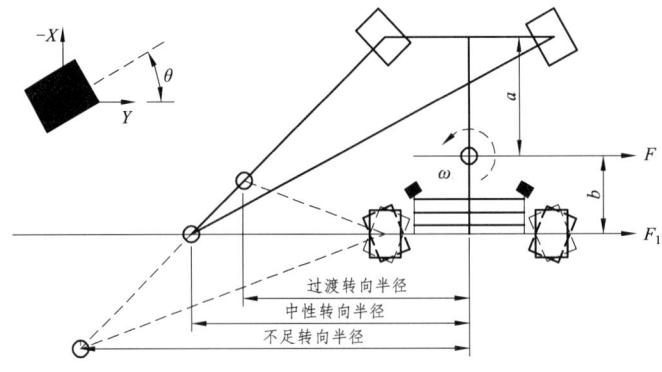

图 19-3 FSAE 整车瞬态转向模型

后轮瞬态转向数学模型如下。

右后车轮正 X 方向运动位移:

$$l - l\cos\alpha = q_1 \tag{19-1}$$

左后车负 X 方向运动位移:

$$l - l\cos\beta = q_2 \tag{19-2}$$

FSAE 赛车离心力:

$$F = mrw^2 \tag{19-3}$$

忽略轮胎侧偏力及轮胎本身的迟滞特性,后左右轮胎侧向受力总和为

$$F_1 = F\frac{a}{a+b} \tag{19-4}$$

右后车轮摆臂衬套 X 方向的位移量为

$$F_1 \sin\theta = 2k\frac{q_3}{\cos\theta} \tag{19-5}$$

衬套有增加过渡转向的趋势,后悬架左右车轮在 X 方向之间的总位移为

$$q_1 + q_2 + q_3 = q \tag{19-6}$$

将公式(19-1)~公式(19-5)代入公式(19-6)并整理得

$$l(2 - \cos\alpha - \cos\beta) + \frac{mrw^2 a\sin\theta}{2k(a+b)}\cos\theta = q \tag{19-7}$$

摆臂角为负时,后轮转向与前轮保持同方向,整车弯道转向为不足转向状态,同时衬套有减小不足转向趋势:

$$q_1 + q_2 - q_3 = q \tag{19-8}$$

将公式(19-1)~公式(19-5)代入公式(19-8)并整理得

$$l(2 - \cos\alpha - \cos\beta) - \frac{mrw^2 a\sin\theta}{2k(a+b)}\cos\theta = q \tag{19-9}$$

式中,l 为摆臂长度;α 为右侧车轮摆臂旋转角度;β 为左侧车轮摆臂旋转角度;q_1 为右侧车轮中心移动距离;q_2 为左侧车轮中心移动距离;q_3 为摆臂衬套 X 方向的位移量;q 为左右车轮中心偏移总距离;m 为整车质量;r 为车辆转向半径;w 为车身横摆角速度;a 为车辆质心距前轴距离;b 为车辆质心距前轴距离;θ 为摆臂与车身连接衬套安装角度;k 为衬套径向刚度。

从公式中可以看出,影响瞬态转向的因素很多,其中摆臂旋转角度及摆臂与车身连接衬套刚度是影响随动转向的主要因素。当摆臂角为正时,即后轮与前轮转向相反,较小的衬套刚度会加大转向的力度,此时整车舒适性变好但稳定性变差;当摆臂角为负时,即后轮与前

轮转向相同，较小的衬套刚度会抵消车轮的同向偏转，因此必须增加衬套刚度，增大不足转向特性，提升整车稳定性。

19.2 随动转向物理模型

由于赛车稳定性要求较高，应选择摆臂角为负，此时在结构上存在如下问题：悬架与车身之间没有空间安装减震器与螺旋弹簧。借鉴雪铁龙系列车型的特点，螺旋弹簧可以改为双横置扭杆弹簧，减震器为大角度斜置，但由于 FSAE 赛车的中置后驱底盘布置形式依然不能实现，因此选择半独立式扭力梁悬架设计后轮随动转向特性。

衬套刚度采用衬套动静刚度试验机获取，实验前需要将衬套嵌套在夹具内，然后把夹具安装在丝杠上。实验之前要确保接线准确并进行预热 15 min，以保证传感器稳定性；实验过程中，上下限位块的位移需要合理设定，防止过大位移导致夹具和试样损坏。X 方向的位移设定为 9 mm，扭转角度设定为 10°；Y 方向的位移设定为 6 mm，扭转角度设定为 10°；Z 方向的位移设定为 15 mm，扭转角度设定为 15°；衬套实验如图 19-4 所示，各方向刚度如图 19-5、图 19-6 所示。

图 19-4 衬套刚度实验

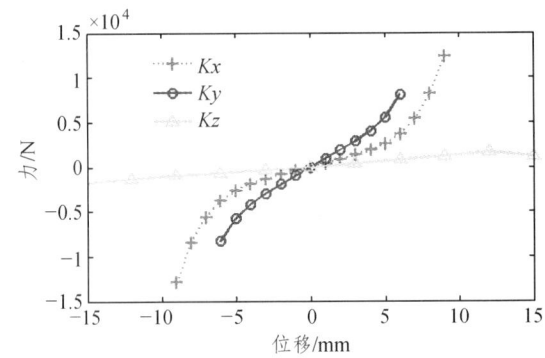

图 19-5 衬套 $X/Y/Z$ 垂向刚度

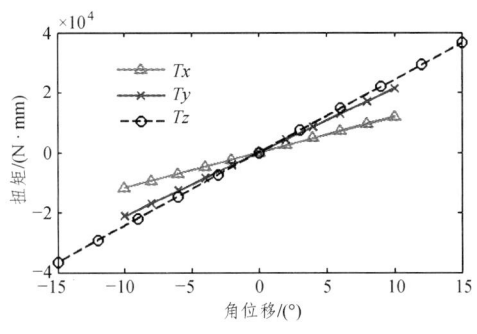

图 19-6 衬套 X/Y/Z 扭转刚度

19.3 柔性扭转梁

扭力梁物理模型建立过程的核心是扭转梁柔性化处理,采用 ABAQUS 软件输出扭转杆模态中性文件,将文件导入 ADAMS 中建立扭力梁悬架模型,建模过程中要保证悬架通信器与发动机总成及车身正确匹配。ABAQUS 创建扭力梁模态中性文件程序如下。

子结构数据块生成程序:
Substructure Generate, overwrite, type=Z1, recovery matrix=YES,MASS MATRIX=YES
柔性体转换程序:
FLEXIBLE BODY, TYPE=ADAMS
应力应变输出程序:
ELEMENT RECOVERY MATRIX, POSITION=AVERAGED AT NODES
S,
E,
模态中性文件 MNF 生成程序:
abaqus adams job=torsion_beam substructure_sim= torsion_beam _Z1 model_odb= torsion_beam length=mm mass=tonne time=sec force=N

扭转梁模态中性文件转换完后共 20 阶,其中 4 阶、6 阶、8 阶位移变化如图 19-7 所示。

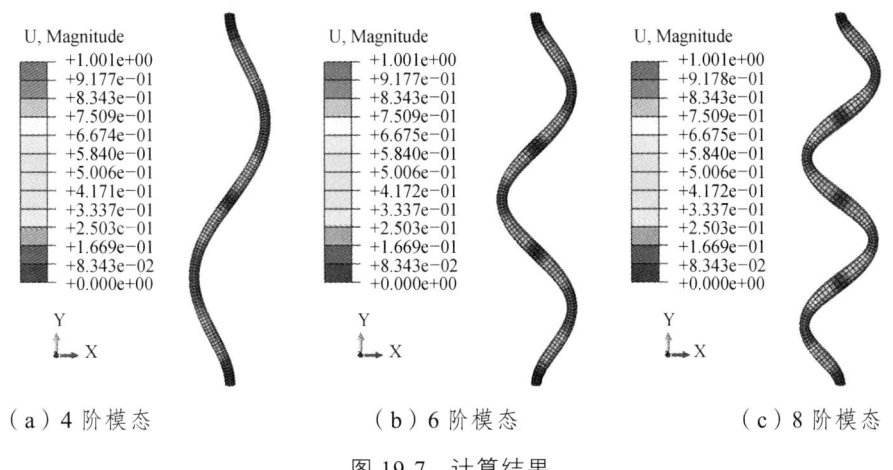

(a) 4 阶模态　　　　　　(b) 6 阶模态　　　　　　(c) 8 阶模态

图 19-7 计算结果

19.4 反向激振仿真

扭力梁物理悬架模型建立好后对其进行车轮反向激振仿真如图 19-8 所示。车轮反向激振实验的目的是为了获取车轮上下跳动过程中车轮中心在纵向位移偏移量，计算结果如图 19-9 所示；左侧车轮下跳最大位移为 10.60 mm，平衡状态位移为 0.89 mm，上跳最大位移为 13.45 mm；右侧车轮位移变化量与左侧数值大小相反。左转向过程中，左侧车轮跳动量较小，测试左右车辆之间最大偏移量为 12.56 mm，可以实现后轮瞬态转向特性。

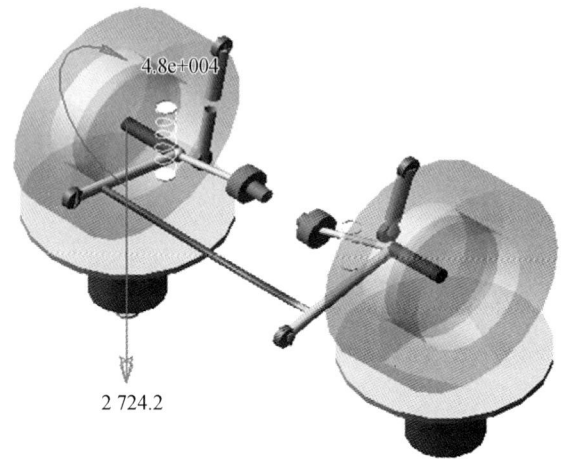

图 19-8　车轮反向激振实验

悬架摆臂的长度为 375.63 mm，车轮上跳 100 mm，实测车轮上调角度为 14.907°，车轮反向激振实验不考虑衬套安装角度，把参数代入公式（19-1）、公式（19-2），计算出左右车辆之间最大偏移量为 12.77 mm，误差仅为 1.7%。

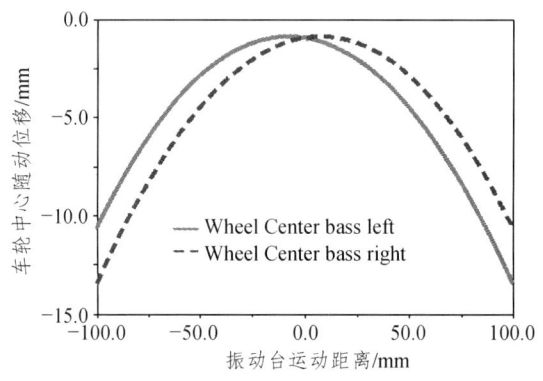

图 19-9　车轮中心运动偏移量

19.5 弯道仿真

构建包含扭力梁悬架的整车模型，当扭力悬架中的扭转梁为刚体时，整车模型为 58 个自由度；把刚性扭转梁替换为柔性扭转梁时，整车为 84 个自由度。通过阶跃转向弯道仿真，对比后扭力梁悬架在整车环境模式下瞬时随动转向特性对整车性能的影响。仿真时间为 5 s，方向盘向左转 180°，转向时刻在 0 s，即仿真初始状态已经开始转向，转向时间持续 2 s，初始速度为 50 km/h，挡位为 2 挡。整车模型如图 19-1 所示。

如图 19-10 所示实线为整车在刚性扭转梁悬架模式下的运动轨迹，虚线为把刚性梁替换为柔扭转梁后整车的运动轨迹。通过提取 0 s 时刻数据，刚性扭力梁整车模型初始位移为 0 mm，柔性扭力梁整车模型初始位移为 5.5e – 15 mm，说明仿真开始时后轮随动转向已经起作用。从图中可以看出，柔性扭力梁在的运动轨迹整体比刚性梁略大，在 4 s 之前，重合度较高，即整车在入弯时进入到瞬时过渡转向，转向半径减小，4 s 之后整车在出弯道时进入不足转向状态，转向半径增大，整车稳定性能提升。

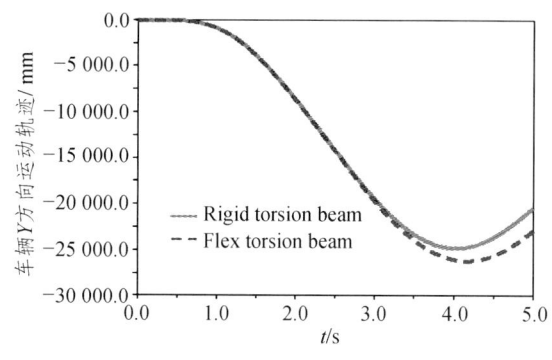

图 19-10 车辆质心 Y 方向运动轨迹

为进一步验证整车的稳定性是否提升，通过计算车身质心处的横摆角与侧向速度速度（见图 19-11、图 19-12）可以看出，柔性梁悬架模式下整车的侧向速度及横摆角速度变化范围均比刚性扭转梁小，横摆角速度 RMS 值分别为 54.29、50.95，性能提升 6.15%；车身侧向速度最大值分别为 1.24、1.06，性能提升 14.52%；

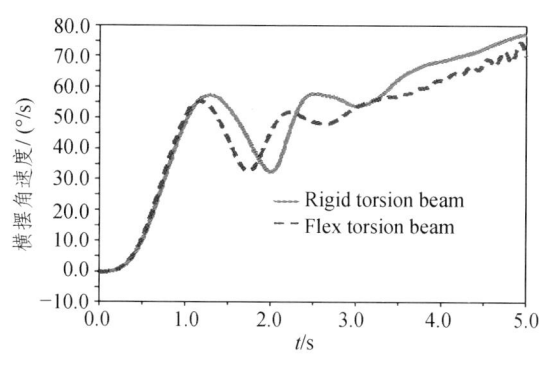

图 19-11 车身横摆角速度

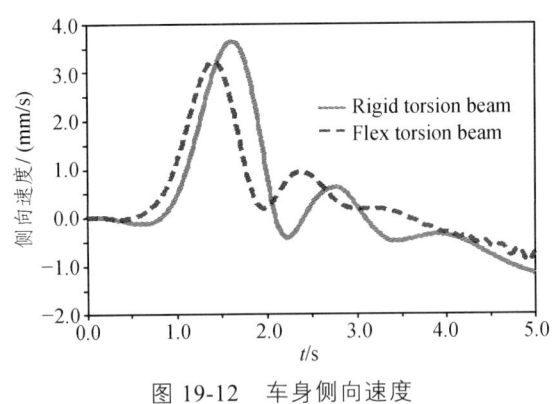

图 19-12　车身侧向速度

19.6　扭力梁位置因素

扭力梁悬架中扭转梁的安装位置不同会导致车轮中心随动位移人小产生变化。为系统研究此问题，分别把柔性扭转梁安装在摆臂上 3 个位置：C_0 指原有柔性梁安装位置；C_150 指在原有位置上向正 X 方向移动 150 mm；C_250 指在原有位置上向正 X 方向移动 250 mm。如图 9-13 所示柔性扭转梁安装的位置为 C_150；计算结果如图 19-14 所示，随着柔性梁偏移距离的增加，后轮随动转向特性逐渐减小；C_0 的 RMS 值为 24 591.33，C_150 的 RMS 值为 24 423.17，C_250 的 RMS 值为 24 257.48。从图 19-15、图 19-16 中可以出，随着柔性梁偏移距离的增加，车身侧向速度、横摆角速度幅值逐渐增加，车辆稳定性变差。车身侧向速度：C_0 的 RMS 值为 1.06，C_150 的 RMS 值为 1.00，C,250 的 RMS 值为 1.07。车身横摆角速度：C_0 的 RMS 值为 64.99，C_150 的 RMS 值为 65.62，C,250 的 RMS 值为 66.07。

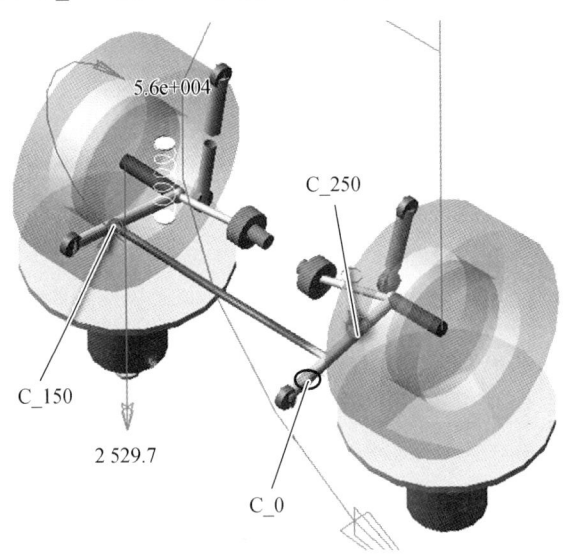

图 19-13　扭转梁安装位置

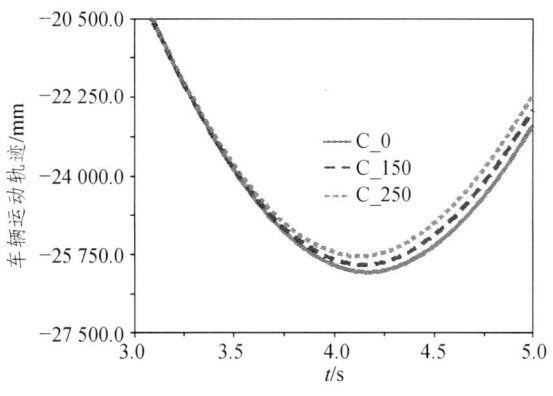

图 19-14 车辆质心 Y 方向运动轨迹/C

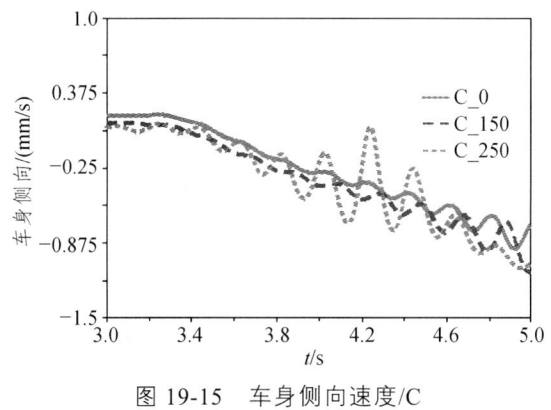

图 19-15 车身侧向速度/C

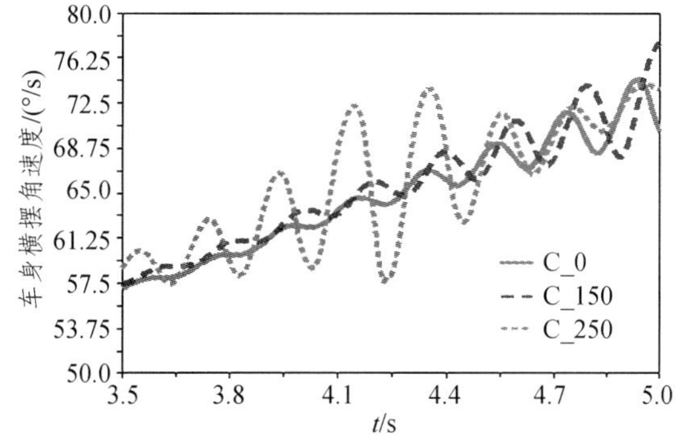

图 19-16 车身横摆角速度/C

19.7 衬套安装角度

柔性衬套安装角度会影响整车的稳定性，如果采用与扭转梁轴向平行布置会导致后悬架整体横向偏移量过大，此时需要添加横向连杆保证侧向位移，这对于 FSAE 赛车后悬架安装空间来说不可行。由于衬套的各方向刚度不同，采用不同安装角度会抑制侧向偏移，但衬套受力较大，如图 19-17 为衬套安装角度为 45°。

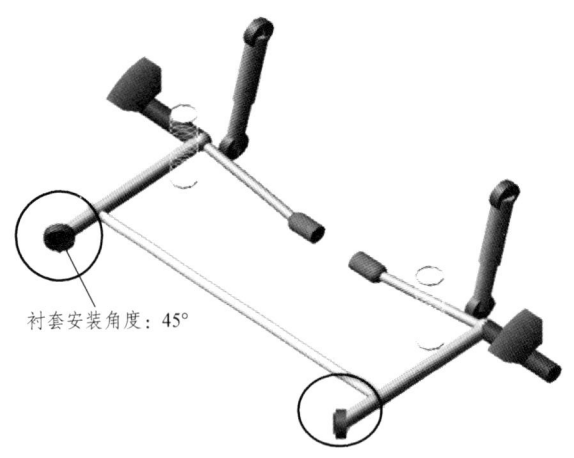

图 19-17 衬套安装角度

如图 19-18 所示为不同安装角度衬套力，从图中可以看出，45°安装衬套受力最大，最大值为 760.78 N，RMS 值为 626.10；30°安装衬套受力其次，最大值为 703.76 N，RMS 值为 593.18；0°安装衬套受力最小，最大值为 531.0 N，RMS 值为 538.88。

从图 19-19 中可以看出，随着衬套安装角度的逐步增加，整车不足转向有减小的趋势，衬套 0°安装时 RMS 值为 25 597.84；衬套 30°安装时 RMS 值为 25 479.06；衬套 45°安装时 RMS 值为 25 369.80；从图 19-20 中可以看出，随着衬套安装角度的逐步增加，整车身横摆角速度逐步减小，整车稳定性能提升。

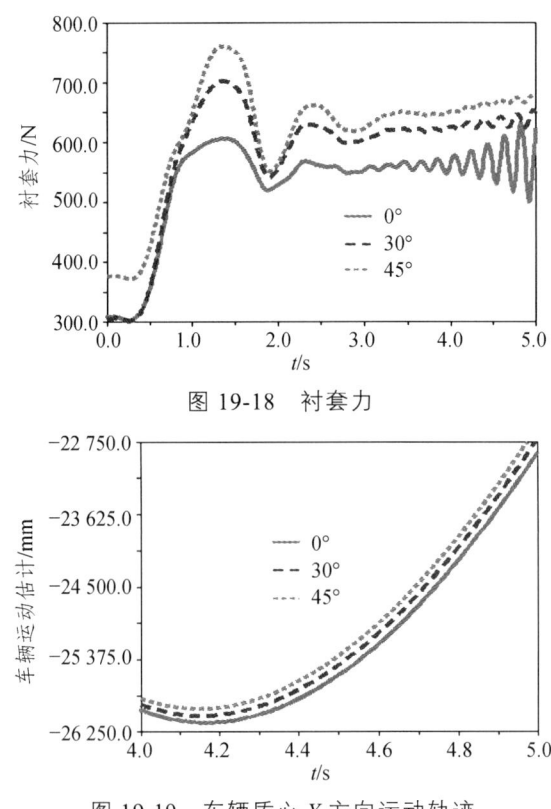

图 19-18 衬套力

图 19-19 车辆质心 Y 方向运动轨迹

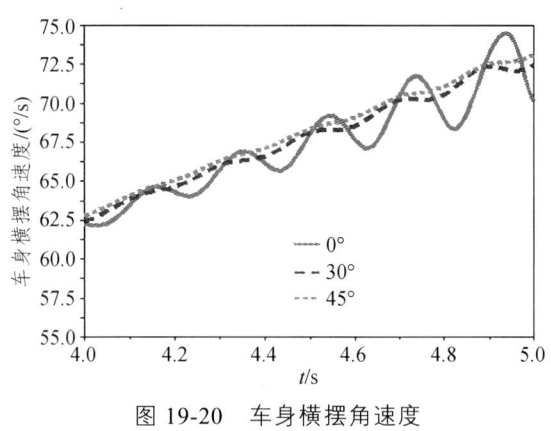

图 19-20 车身横摆角速度

19.8 总　结

（1）摆臂旋转角度及摆臂与车身连接处的衬套刚度是影响瞬态转向的两个最主要因素。

（2）与刚性扭力梁悬架对比，柔性扭力梁悬架入弯半径小，出弯半径大，兼顾平顺性与操纵稳定性。

（3）扭转梁位置影响随动转向特性，随着安装位置距离的增加，不足转向趋势减小，整车稳定性变差。

（4）衬套安装角度逐步增加时，整车不足转向特性趋势减小，整车稳定性能提升。

第 20 章 平衡悬架与推杆特性研究

通过 CAR 模块编写白驱动轴状态参数程序及 BEAM 离散梁方法建立平行式推杆与 V 型推杆平衡悬架模型,采用 VIEW 模块自建四柱振动试验台测试出平衡悬架垂向与扭转总刚度分别为 5 515.2 N/mm、2 677.8 N/mm。推力杆传力模型表明随着推杆角度的增加,推杆抵消侧向平衡力增加,传递到车架上的侧向力减小;连续减速带制动极限工况仿真表明 V 型推杆随着开口角度的增加,商用整车稳定性指标参数持续提升,同时验证了推力杆传递模型的正确性,但 V 型推杆安装受到车架宽度物理空间限制,只能安装在车架边梁上;建立好的平衡悬架与振动台耦合模型如图 20-1 所示。

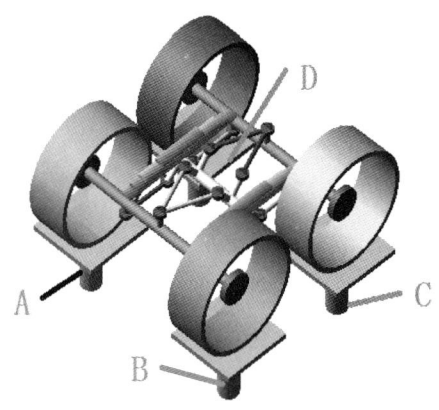

图 20-1 平衡悬架与振动台架

学习目标

 ◇ 平衡悬架模型。
 ◇ 横振动台模型。
 ◇ 垂向刚度。
 ◇ 扭转刚度。
 ◇ 推力杆传力模型。
 ◇ 稳定性仿真。

20.1 平衡悬架模型

国内商用牵引车与国外同类型车辆设计及执行标准不同,主要体现在国外商用牵引车底盘全部采用拖拽式非独立单驱动桥或者双轴系及多轴系车桥,弹性元件多采用空气弹簧;国内商用货运牵引车、水泥搅拌车、消防车,以及特殊工程车辆后悬架多采用推杆式平衡悬架。平衡式悬架物理动力学模型难点主要体现在① 板簧精确模型建立;② 双轴系及多轴系集成参数的建立。文献中平衡悬架模型建模主要采用3种方法:① 采用弹簧质量系统建立双轴系及多轴系,此模型只考虑悬架的系统的垂向振动特性;② 在VIEW模块中建立平衡悬架模型,此模型为物理动力学悬架模型,与真实的平衡悬架模型贴近,缺点是平衡悬架模型缺少集成参数,只能作为单一的系统部件进行研究,基于VIEW模块商用整车模型建立及匹配复杂程度高;③ 平衡悬架装配体有限元模型,此模型主要对悬架的总刚度、零部件进行分析,并不能较好地考虑悬架的动力学特性。有些文献主要对平衡悬架板簧间的摩擦粗糙问题进行了二次开发并提出了一种动刚度公式定义方法,提升板簧模型的准确性;还有些文献采用弹簧质量模型建立牵引车及挂车的数模并采用MATLAB计算模型的垂向特性,但它们并没有系统考虑平衡悬架的侧向特性及物理结构因素;另有些文献采用有限元法对装配体平衡悬架对称模型进行模态分析,从疲劳和耐久特性角度找出平衡悬架系统及零部件损伤与破坏的原因,针对此问题提出CAR模块中通过编写白驱动轴状态参数程序,采用与钢板弹簧模型合并特性可以把驱动轴悬架模型任意拓展的 N 轴系,用此种方法建立的平衡悬架可以快速与组装整车以及其他子系统进行匹配,在整车架构下研究平衡悬架推杆结构特性变化对整车稳定性的影响。

平衡悬架建模的核心是钢板弹簧模型与悬架集成参数,双轴及多轴模型参数需要采用通用模块合并功能实现,CAR模块并不支持多轴集成参数;钢板弹簧采用非线性梁建模,完成平衡悬架模型建立,如图20-2所示,平衡悬架共包含476个自由度。

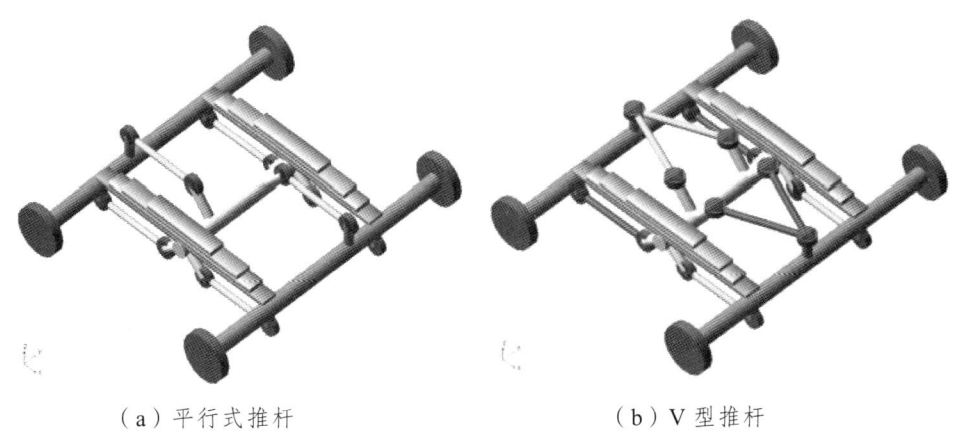

(a)平行式推杆　　　　　　　　(b)V型推杆

图 20-2　平衡悬架模型

20.2 白双驱动轴程序

白双驱动轴指驱动轴模型仅包含描述动力传递的方程及车辆定位主销参数等，并不考虑其物理结构。平衡悬架的双驱动轴参数需要通过单驱动轴合并功能实现，单驱动轴状态参数程序如下。

左半轴转速程序 halfshaft_omega_left：1004.0,(._my_bus_drive_axle.gel_hub.jxl_joint_i_7.adams_id),(._my_bus_drive_axle.gel_drive_axle.jxl_joint_j_7.adams_id),(._my_bus_drive_axle.gel_drive_axle.jxl_joint_j_7.adams_id),(._my_bus_drive_axle.cil_tire_force_adams_id)。

右半轴转速程序 halfshaft_omega_right：1004.0,(._my_bus_drive_axle.ger_hub.jxr_joint_i_7.adams_id),(._my_bus_drive_axle.ger_drive_axle.jxr_joint_j_7.adams_id),(._my_bus_drive_axle.ger_drive_axle.jxr_joint_j_7.adams_id),(._my_bus_drive_axle.cir_tire_force_adams_id)。

左右半轴转速差程序 delta_halfshaft_omega：(varval(._my_bus_drive_axle.halfshaft_omega_left)-varval(._my_bus_drive_axle.halfshaft_omega_right))*9.5493。

差速器力矩程序 diffcrential_torque:sign(AKISPL(ABS (varval(._my_bus_drive_axle.delta_halfshaft_omega)),0, ._my_bus_drive_axle.gss_differential),varval(._my_bus_drive_axle.delta_halfshaft_omega))。

白双驱动轴通过两个单轴系驱动轴合并建立，合并过程包含单驱动轴程序，合并完成后白双驱动轴模型如图 20-3 所示。

图 20-3 白双驱动轴模型

20.3 振动台模型

采用 Beam 梁建立 4 片装配体钢板弹簧对称模型如图 20-4 所示，板簧对应 Beam 块之间采用接触属性模拟簧片之间的摩擦特性，点面副约束限制 Beam 块之间的运动方向，起到弹簧夹的作用。板簧在 X 方向对称中心的上下 Beam 块之间采用 3 个固定副约束，此固定副起到板簧无效长度作用，即板簧通过骑马螺栓与车轴固定后，骑马螺栓固定长度范围对板簧的刚度并没有影响。Beam 块的参数为 30×100，单位：mm。

构建平衡悬架刚度仿真测试台架如图 20-1 所示。在轮毂处建立四个刚性轮胎，轮胎与轮毂采用固定副约束；修改轮毂与白驱动轴之间的旋转约束副为固定约束副；四个垂向振动试验台与大地采用移动副约束；刚性轮胎与振动台采用点面虚约束，此约束副的主要作用是保证刚性轮胎在振动台架的平面上进行移动。

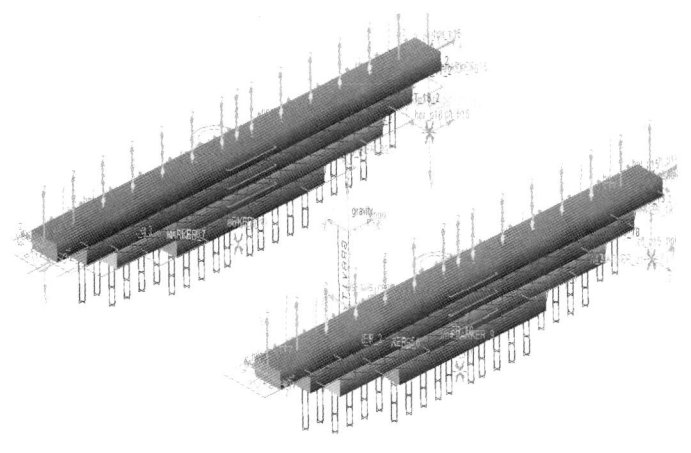

图 20-4　对称板簧模型

20.4　垂向刚度测试

A 振动台与 B 振动台在移动副上分别施加驱动位移函数：$50.0 \times \sin(180 \times d \times time)$，运行仿真时间 1 s，A、B 试验台垂向运动 50 mm 后返回初始位置，经计算平衡悬架垂向总刚度如图 20-5 所示，平衡悬架垂向刚度曲线为闭合非重合曲线，由于板簧前端与白车轴之间的移动副存在间隙，接触瞬间产生撞击导致力较大，接触间隙抵消后板簧力回复到整车状态。

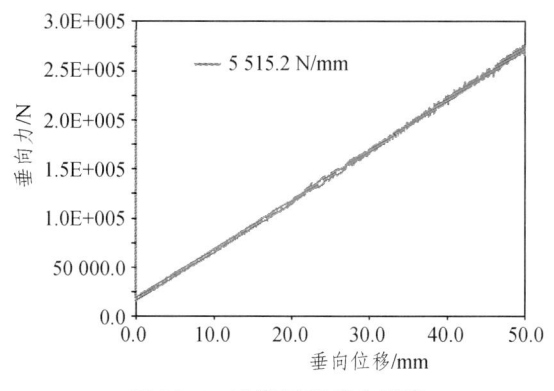

图 20-5　平衡悬架垂向刚度

20.5 扭转刚度测试

平衡悬架在经过坑洼路面时整车车桥会产生扭转刚度，测试时，A 振动台施加驱动位移函数：$50.0 \times \sin(180 \times d \times time)$，其余三个试验振动台放空保持静止，运行仿真时间 1 s，经计算平衡悬架扭转刚度如图 20-6 所示，扭转刚度曲线同样为闭合非重合曲线。

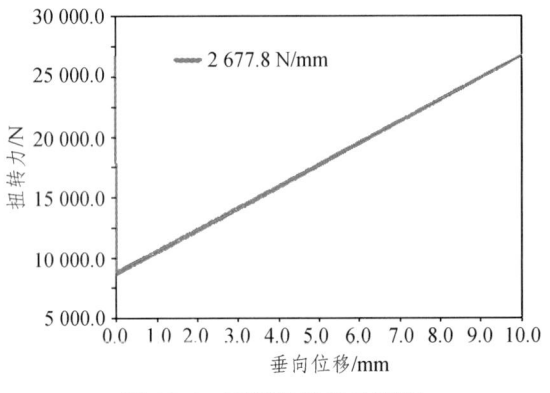

图 20-6 平衡悬架扭转刚度

20.6 推杆传力模型

推杆开口角度大小会影响到平衡悬架的侧向力，侧向力大小是影响整车稳定性最关键的参数。整车动力传动路径如图 20-7 所示，由传动轴同时驱动前后驱动桥，前后驱动桥通过推杆与车架连接处 B、C、B'、C' 点传递纵向驱动力带动整车行驶。推杆受力模型如图 20-8 所示。

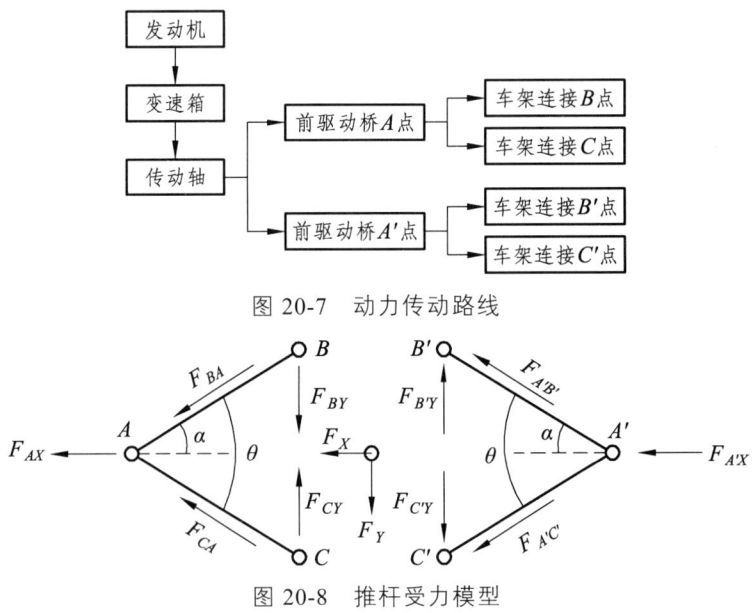

图 20-7 动力传动路线

图 20-8 推杆受力模型

推杆受力公式如下：

$$F_X = (F_{AX} + F_{A'X}) \tag{20-1}$$

$$F_{AX} = F_{BA} + F_{CA} \tag{20-2}$$

$$F_{A'X} = F_{A'B'} + F_{A'C'} \tag{20-3}$$

$$F_{BY} = F_{BA} \sin \alpha \tag{20-4}$$

$$F_{CY} = F_{CA} \sin \alpha \tag{20-5}$$

$$F_{B'Y} = F_{A'B'} \sin \alpha \tag{20-6}$$

$$F_{C'Y} = F_{A'C'} \sin \alpha \tag{20-7}$$

$$\theta = 2\alpha \tag{20-8}$$

将公式（20-2）~公式（20-7）代入到公式（20-1）中整理得

$$F_X \sin \alpha = (F_{BY} + F_{CY} + F_{B'Y} + F_{C'Y}) = F_Y \tag{20-9}$$

式中，F_X 为 X 方向驱动力；F_Y 为平衡悬架平衡力；F_{AX} 为连接 A 点 X 方向驱动力；$F_{A'X}$ 为连接 A' 点 X 方向驱动力；F_{BA} 为前推力杆 BA 方向传递力；F_{CA} 为前推力杆 CA 方向传递力；$F_{A'B'}$ 为后推力杆 $A'B'$ 方向传递力；$F_{A'C'}$ 为后推力杆 $A'C'$ 方向传递力；F_{BY} 为连接 B 点 Y 方向驱动力；F_{CY} 为连接 C 点 Y 方向驱动力；$F_{B'Y}$ 为连接 B' 点 Y 方向驱动力；$F_{C'Y}$ 为连接 C' 点 Y 方向驱动力；θ 为推杆夹角。

公式（20-4）与公式（20-5）为前推杆在 Y 方向上的平衡力，大小相等，方向相反；公式（20-6）与公式（20-7）为后推杆在 Y 方向上的平衡力，大小相等，方向相反；从公式（20-9）中可以看出，随着推杆夹角 θ 增加，推杆侧向平衡力 F_Y 增加，即驱动力 F_X 通过平衡悬架推杆平衡抵消掉的力增加，因而传递车架上的力减少，整车稳定性提升。

20.7 稳定性仿真

考虑三种 V 型推杆安装方式：① V 型推杆角度为 17.4°，此时 V 型推杆开口与中轴中心部位连接；② V 型推杆角度为 35.2°，此时 V 型推杆开口与中轴左右侧中心部位连接；③ V 型推杆角度为 49.6°，此时 V 型推杆开口与车架连接；车架宽度限制 V 型推杆开口的最大角度。为检验推杆对平衡悬架的稳定特性的影响，需要整车在特殊路面下进行极限工况测试。构造连续减速带路面模型如图 20-9 所示，路面包含 3 个等间距分别为 10 m 的减速带，路面宽度为 12 m，路面摩擦系数为 0.9，减速带断面宽度为 0.35 m，高度为 0.05 m。整车模型的难点是平衡悬架模型建立及系统之间的匹配,构建 6×4 整车模型如图 20-10 所示,整车模型包含后平衡悬架、前转向桥、右舵转向系统、发动机、简化刚性车型、盘式制动系统、前后轮胎模型、整车模型包含 841 个自由度。整车在制动过程中通过减速度,更能检验平衡悬架的稳定特性,同时更能体现不同推杆位置与角度对稳定性的影响。整车制动参数设置如下:初始制动速度为 50 km/h,制动开始时间为第 4 s,制动减速度设置为 0.6 g,制动过程中方向盘角度锁定,制动过程为闭环控制。

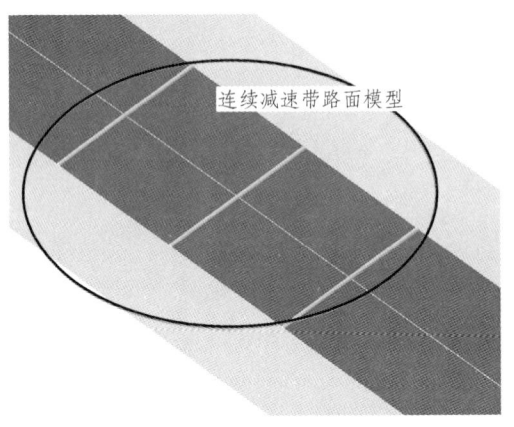

图 20-9 连续减速带路面模型

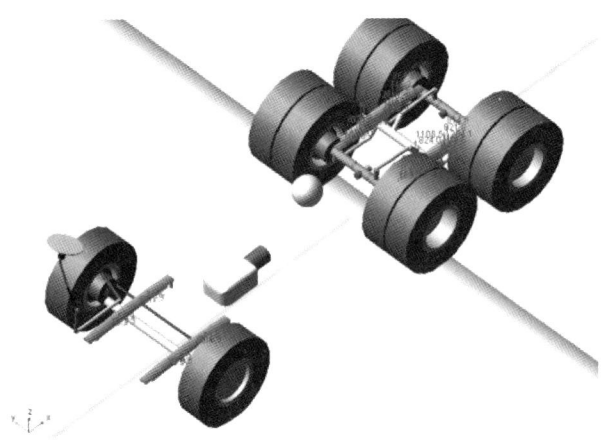

图 20-10 6×4 整车模型

计算结果如图 20-11 ~ 图 20-14 所示,图中 B1 为基于平行式推杆平衡悬架整车参数变化曲线,B2 为基于 V 型推杆(35.2°)平衡悬架整车参数变化曲线。侧向加速度 B1 的 RMS 值为 33.61,幅值最大绝对值为 307.72;B2 的 RMS 值为 8.69,幅值最大绝对值为 60.74,有效值 RMS 提升 74.14%,最大振荡幅值改善 80.26%;侧倾角速度 B1 的 RMS 值为 0.33,幅值最大绝对值为 2.92;B2 的 RMS 值为 0.16,幅值最大绝对值为 0.87,有效值 RMS 提升 51.52%,最大震荡幅值改善 70.21%;俯仰角速度 B1 的 RMS 值为 5.37,幅值最大绝对值为 20.50;B2 的 RMS 值为 4.91,幅值最大绝对值为 17.92,有效值 RMS 提升 8.57%,最大振荡幅值改善 12.59%;横摆角速度 B1 的 RMS 值为 0.081,幅值最大绝对值为 0.57;B2 的 RMS 值为 0.037,幅值最大绝对值为 0.14,有效值 RMS 提升 54.32%,最大振荡幅值改善 75.44%;

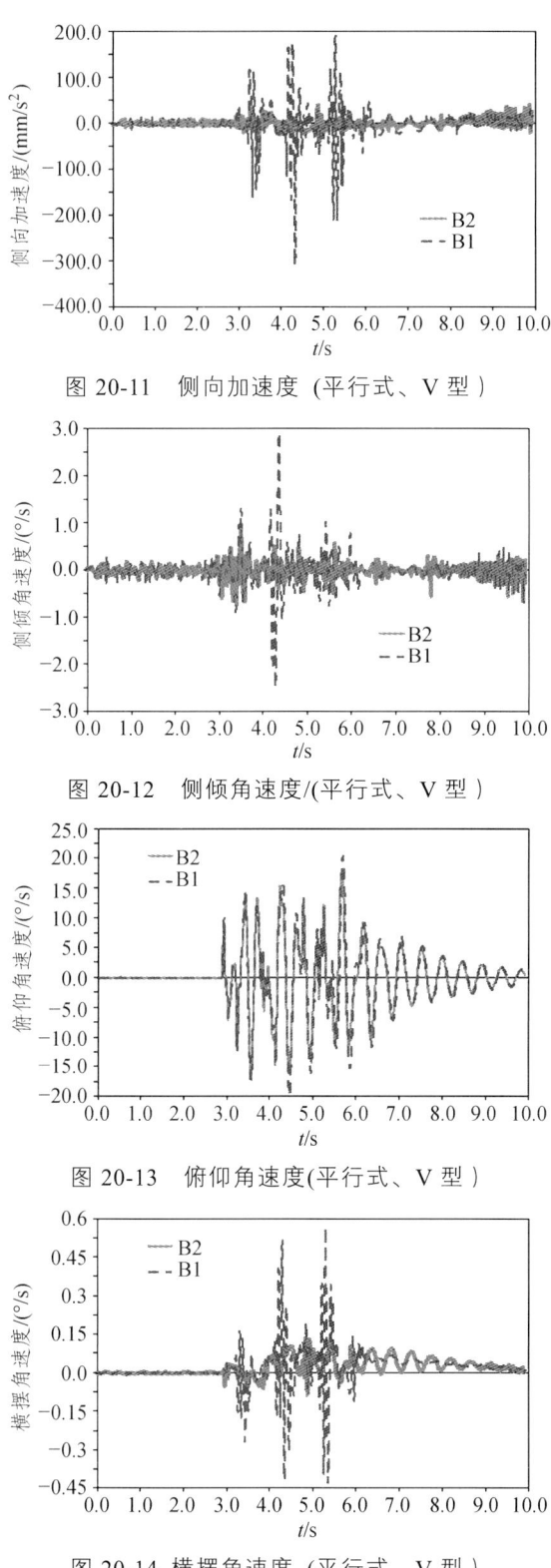

图 20-11 侧向加速度（平行式、V 型）

图 20-12 侧倾角速度/(平行式、V 型)

图 20-13 俯仰角速度(平行式、V 型）

图 20-14 横摆角速度（平行式、V 型）

当 V 型推杆角度为 17.4° 与 49.6° 时，整车稳定性参数如表 20-1 所示。从表中数据可以看出,随着推杆角度的增加整车稳定参数指标都明显地提升。

表 20-1 稳定性指标参数

稳定性参数	推杆角度 θ/(°)	RMS	最大幅值/(°/s)
侧倾角速度	17.4	0.48	5.23
	49.6	0.14	0.65
俯仰角速度	17.4	5.02	17.56
	49.6	4.87	17.58
横摆角速度	17.4	0.054	0.33
	49.6	0.036	0.17

20.8 总　结

（1）通过编写白驱动轴状态参数程序及 BEAM 梁法建立平行杆式与 V 型推杆式平衡悬架精准模型,振动台架仿真计算出平衡悬架总垂向刚度与弯曲刚度分别为 5 515.2 N/mm、2 677.8 N/mm。

（2）推杆传力模型表明随着 V 型推杆开口角度的增加,推杆 Y 方向抵消平衡力增加,通过推杆传递到车身上的侧向力减少,稳定性提升。

（3）整车连续减速带制动仿真表明,相对于平行式推杆平衡悬架,V 型推杆平衡悬架在提升整车稳定性方面优势明显,且随着 V 型推杆开口角度增加,稳定性能持续提升,同时验证了推力杆模型的正确性。

（4）平衡悬架模型对于商用整车模型建立及系统分析具有理论与工程上的指导意义。

第 21 章　复杂耦合式悬架模型

耦合式悬架较为少见，常用于高等级方程式赛车及高性能跑车，此种悬架结构较为复杂。耦合式悬架结构一般在双 A 臂悬架的基础上通过增加推杆及耦合扭转（旋转）杆完成设计，耦合式悬架包含对立悬架与非独立悬架的特性，左右两车轮可以通过扭转（旋转）杆配合减震器联动，左右车轮的上下跳动范围一般在 2 cm 内，采用此种悬架，可以极大程度地提升车辆高速过弯时整车的稳定特性，同时可以通过调节阻尼器的特性精确控制四个车轮与地面的接触力。如图 21-1 所示为一级方程式赛车前悬架采用的耦合式悬架。不同的赛车类型器左右车轮通过扭杆耦合的方式（结构）完全不同，但其最终的作用相同，请读者自行查阅其他类型的耦合悬架。

图 21-1　耦合悬架

学习目标

- ◆ 耦合悬架模型。
- ◆ 耦合悬架变量参数。
- ◆ 耦合悬架通信器。
- ◆ 反向跳动仿真。

21.1 耦合悬架模型

- 启动 ADAMS/CAR，选择专家模块进入建模界面；
- 单击 File > Open 命令，弹出建模对话框如图 21-2 所示；

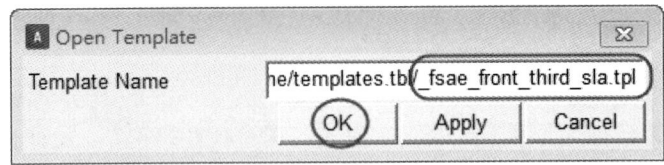

图 21-2 模板界面

- Template Name：mdids://my_driveline/templates.tbl/_fsae_front_third_sla.tpl；
- 单击 OK，打开耦合式悬架模型如图 21-3 所示；
- 按 F9，把专家模板转换到标准模块；
- 单击 File > New > Suspension 命令，弹出子系统对话框如图 21-4 所示；
- Subsystem Name（系统名称）：fsae_front_third_；
- Minor Role（副特征）：front（指悬架为前悬架）；
- Template Name（模板路径）：mdids://my_driveline/templates.tbl/_fsae_front_third_sla.tpl；
- 单击 OK，完成推杆式耦合悬架的创建。

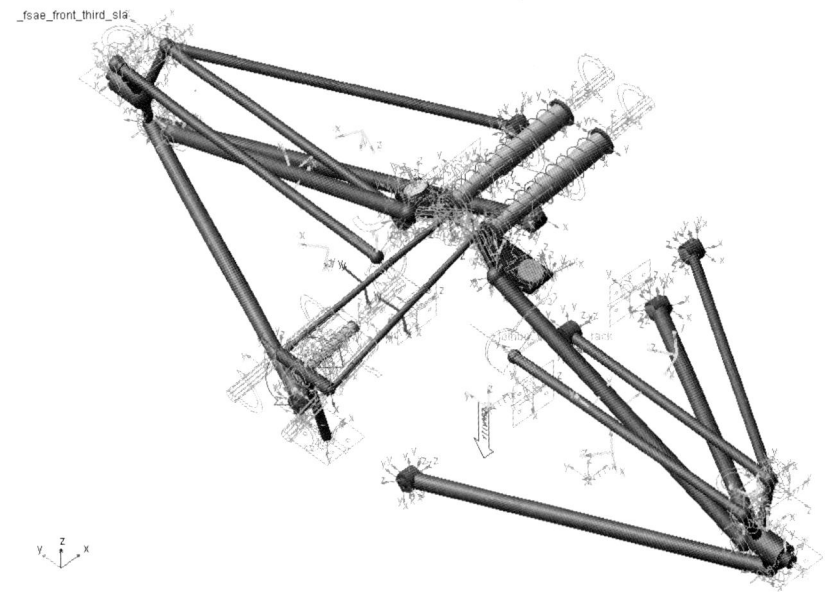

图 21-3 推杆耦合式悬架模型

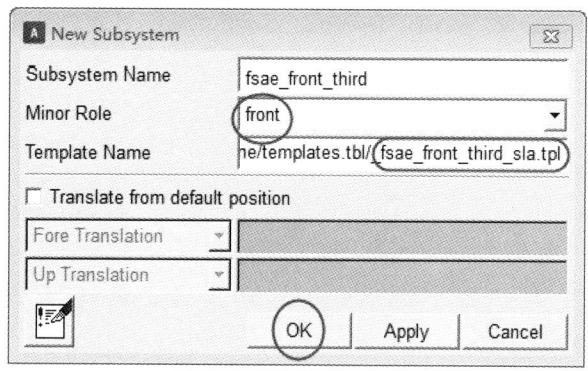

图 21-4　耦合悬架子系统

推杆式耦合悬架建模过程不再详细叙述，推杆式耦合悬架模型存储在章节文件中，读者可自行查阅，具体建模过程读者可参考本书第 2 章；读者可以通过子系统信息查阅推杆式悬架其结构、部件、约束、属性及变量参数等详细内容，本章提供推杆式悬架子系统信息，查阅方法如下。

- 单击 File > Info 命令，弹出子系统信息查阅对话框如图 21-5 所示；
- Subsystem Name：通过下拉菜单选择子系统 fsae_front_third_sus；

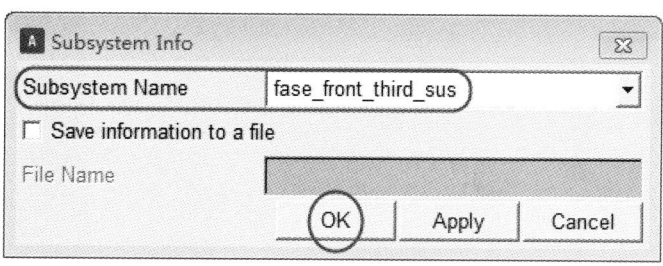

图 21-5　系统信息

- 单击 OK，显示具体信息如下。

推杆式耦合悬架详细信息如下（包含硬点、部件、几何、约束、柔性约束、变量参数等）。

Info for subsystem:　fsae_front_third

File Name　　　　:　*subsystem has not been saved*
Template　　　　:　mdids://my_driveline/templates.tbl/_fsae_front_third_sla.tpl
Comments　　　　:
Template　　　　:　Standard Pushrod Actuated Double Wishbone w/ Third Spring
Subsystem　　　　:　*no subsystem comments found*
Major Role　　　　:　suspension
Minor Role　　　　:　front

HARDPOINTS:

hardpoint name	symmetry	x_value	y_value	z_value
arb_blade_pivot_at_T	single	−473.075	0.0	427.8122
arb_T_pivot	single	−419.1	0.0	226.9998
arb_T_pivot_axis	single	−439.099	0.0	226.9998
global	single	0.0	0.0	0.0
third_spring_at_arb	single	−473.075	0.0	427.8122
third_spring_at_chassis	single	−346.6338	0.0	452.3994
arb_link_at_blade	left/right	−473.075	−63.5	427.8122
arb_link_at_rocker	left/right	−67.8942	−35.7124	507.7206
damper_at_chassis	left/right	240.8936	−50.8	531.6474
damper_at_rocker	left/right	−40.386	−50.8	504.571
lca_front	left/right	−342.9	−139.7	165.1
lca_outer	left/right	−78.2828	−795.7312	212.6742
lca_rear	left/right	276.225	−158.75	165.1
pushrod_inner	left/right	−90.424	−112.522	475.1324
pushrod_outer	left/right	−79.0702	−730.6818	234.8992
ride_height_reference	left/right	0.0	−254.0	0.0
rocker_pivot	left/right	−35.814	−145.2372	467.3346
rocker_pivot_axis	left/right	−37.5666	−152.5016	485.5464
trackrod_inner	left/right	−108.331	−177.8	331.7748
trackrod_outer	left/right	−154.94	−806.2468	407.67
uca_front	left/right	−1.3208	−209.3976	334.9498
uca_outer	left/right	−54.864	−773.938	403.1234
uca_rear	left/right	298.45	−221.1578	334.9498
wheel_center	left/right	−101.6	−856.7928	299.72

PARTS:

  arb_blade
    symmetry : single
    mass : 0.45359237
    sprung_percentage : 100.0
    location (dependent) : −473.075, 0.0, 427.8122
    orientation (dependent) : zp_vector=0.0, −1.0, 0.0
    : xp_vector=1.0, 0.0, 0.0
    cm_location_from_part : 0.0, 0.0, 0.0
    Ixx, Iyy, Izz : 292.6396534292 , 292.6396534292 , 292.6396534292

    Ixy, Izx, Iyz   :   0.0 , 0.0 , 0.0

arb_blade link geometry
    name   :   arb_blade
    symmetry   :   single
    radius   :   12.7

arb_T
    symmetry   :   single
    mass   :   0.45359237
    sprung_percentage   :   100.0
    location (dependent)   :   − 446.0875, 0.0, 327.406
    orientation (dependent) :   zp_vector= − 0.2595704374, 0.0, 0.965724178
                                :   xp_vector=0.965724178, 0.0, 0.2595704374
    cm_location_from_part   :   0.0, 0.0, 0.0
    Ixx, Iyy, Izz   :   292.6396534292 , 292.6396534292 , 292.6396534292
    Ixy, Izx, Iyz   :   0.0 , 0.0 , 0.0

arb_T link geometry
    name   :   arb_T
    symmetry   :   single
    radius   :   9.525

third_damper_arb
    symmetry   :   single
    mass   :   0.45359237
    sprung_percentage   :   100.0
    location (dependent)   :   − 431.349404, 0.0, 435.925976
    orientation (dependent) :   zp_vector=0.9816133371, 0.0, 0.190880215
                                :   xp_vector=0.190880215, 0.0, − 0.9816133371
    cm_location_from_part   :   0.0, 0.0, 0.0
    Ixx, Iyy, Izz   :   292.6396534292 , 292.6396534292 , 292.6396534292
    Ixy, Izx, Iyz   :   0.0 , 0.0 , 0.0

third_damper_chassis
    symmetry   :   single
    mass   :   0.45359237
    sprung_percentage   :   100.0

location (dependent) : − 389.623808, 0.0, 444.039752
orientation (dependent) : zp_vector=0.9816133371, 0.0, 0.190880215
: xp_vector=0.190880215, 0.0, − 0.9816133371
cm_location_from_part : 0.0, 0.0, 0.0
Ixx, Iyy, Izz : 292.6396534292 , 292.6396534292 , 292.6396534292
Ixy, Izx, Iyz : 0.0 , 0.0 , 0.0

arb_link
  symmetry : left/right
  mass : 0.45359237
  sprung_percentage : 100.0
  location (dependent) : − 270.4846, − 49.6062, 467.7664
  orientation (dependent): zp_vector=0.9788889771, 6.7132932607E − 002, 0.1930532047
  : xp_vector=0.1934897098, 0.0, − 0.9811023047
  cm_location_from_part : 0.0, 0.0, 0.0
  Ixx, Iyy, Izz : 292.6396534292 , 292.6396534292 , 292.6396534292
  Ixy, Izx, Iyz : 0.0 , 0.0 , 0.0

arb_link link geometry
  name : arb_link
  symmetry : left/right
  radius : 6.35

damper_chassis
  symmetry : left/right
  mass : 0.45359237
  sprung_percentage : 100.0
  location (dependent) : 148.071332, − 50.8, 522.712188
  orientation (dependent) : zp_vector=0.9953988128, 0.0, 9.5818596216E − 002
  : xp_vector=9.5818596216E − 002, 0.0, − 0.9953988128
  cm_location_from_part : 0.0, 0.0, 0.0
  Ixx, Iyy, Izz : 292.6396534292 , 292.6396534292 , 292.6396534292
  Ixy, Izx, Iyz : 0.0 , 0.0 , 0.0

damper_rocker
  symmetry : left/right
  mass : 0.45359237
  sprung_percentage : 100.0

location (dependent)	:	55.249064, − 50.8, 513.776976
orientation (dependent)	:	zp_vector=0.9953988128, 0.0, 9.5818596216E − 002
	:	xp_vector=9.5818596216E − 002, 0.0, − 0.9953988128
cm_location_from_part	:	0.0, 0.0, 0.0
Ixx, Iyy, Izz	:	292.6396534292 , 292.6396534292 , 292.6396534292
Ixy, Izx, Iyz	:	0.0 , 0.0 , 0.0

hub

symmetry	:	left/right
mass	:	0.45359237
sprung_percentage	:	100.0
location (dependent)	:	− 101.6, − 856.7928, 299.72
orientation (dependent)	:	zp_vector=0.0, − 1.0, 0.0
	:	xp_vector=1.0, 0.0, 0.0
cm_location_from_part	:	0.0, 0.0, 0.0
Ixx, Iyy, Izz	:	292.6396534292 , 292.6396534292 , 292.6396534292
Ixy, Izx, Iyz	:	0.0 , 0.0 , 0.0

hub link geometry

name	:	hub
symmetry	:	left/right
radius	:	24.9999999999

lca

symmetry	:	left/right
mass	:	0.45359237
sprung_percentage	:	100.0
location (dependent)	:	− 48.3192666667, − 364.7270666667, 180.9580666667
orientation (dependent):		zp_vector= − 0.7939447015, 0.6064858528, − 4.2740161121E − 002
	:	xp_vector= − 0.6079858005, − 0.791714568, 5.9508900499E − 002
cm_location_from_part	:	0.0, 0.0, 0.0
Ixx, Iyy, Izz	:	292.6396534292 , 292.6396534292 , 292.6396534292
Ixy, Izx, Iyz	:	0.0 , 0.0 , 0.0

lca link geometry

name	:	lca1
symmetry	:	left/right
radius	:	15.24

lca link geometry
    name   : lca2
    symmetry   : left/right
    radius   : 15.24

pushrod
    symmetry   : left/right
    mass   : 0.45359237
    sprung_percentage   : 100.0
    location (dependent) : $-84.7471, -421.6019, 355.0158$
    orientation (dependent): zp_vector= $-1.7117228179E-002, 0.9319507432, 0.3621806356$
                                 : xp_vector=$0.9988850391, 0.0, 4.7208882691E-002$
    cm_location_from_part : 0.0, 0.0, 0.0
    Ixx, Iyy, Izz   : 292.6396534292 , 292.6396534292 , 292.6396534292
    Ixy, Izx, Iyz   : 0.0 , 0.0 , 0.0

pushrod link geometry
    name   : pushrod
    symmetry   : left/right
    radius   : 15.24

rocker
    symmetry   : left/right
    mass   : 0.45359237
    sprung_percentage   : 100.0
    location (dependent) : $-58.62955, -86.0679, 488.68965$
    orientation (dependent) : zp_vector=$0.4265972313, 0.8246853542, 0.3713608338$
                                  : xp_vector= $-0.9005388133, 0.4254035558, 8.9786749958E-002$
    cm_location_from_part : 0.0, 0.0, 0.0
    Ixx, Iyy, Izz   : 292.6396534292 , 292.6396534292 , 292.6396534292
    Ixy, Izx, Iyz   : 0.0 , 0.0 , 0.0

rocker link geometry
    name   : rocker1
    symmetry   : left/right
    radius   : 6.35

rocker link geometry
    name   : rocker2
    symmetry   : left/right
    radius   : 6.35

rocker link geometry
    name   : rocker3
    symmetry   : left/right
    radius   : 6.35

rocker link geometry
    name   : rocker4
    symmetry   : left/right
    radius   : 6.35

rocker link geometry
    name   : rocker5
    symmetry   : left/right
    radius   : 6.35

steer_arm
    symmetry   : left/right
    mass   : 1.6122963556
    sprung_percentage   : 100.0
    location (dependent)   : $-$104.902, $-$790.0924, 405.3967
    orientation (dependent): zp_vector=$-$0.9507475919, $-$0.3069418622, 4.3193862677E$-$002
                                   : xp_vector=4.5384658833E$-$002, 0.0, 0.9989695855
    cm_location_from_part : 0.0, 0.0, 0.0
    Ixx, Iyy, Izz   : 1740.5727905923 , 1740.5727905923 , 503.8426111084
    Ixy, Izx, Iyz   : 0.0 , 0.0 , 0.0

trackrod
    symmetry   : left/right
    mass   : 0.45359237
    sprung_percentage   : 100.0
    location (dependent)   : $-$123.71197, $-$385.187444, 356.820216
    orientation (dependent): zp_vector=$-$7.3431615709E$-$002, $-$0.9901062866, 0.1195714811
                                   : xp_vector=0.8521377588, 0.0, 0.5233175326

cm_location_from_part   :   0.0, 0.0, 0.0
  Ixx, Iyy, Izz   :   292.6396534292 , 292.6396534292 , 292.6396534292
  Ixy, Izx, Iyz   :   0.0 , 0.0 , 0.0

trackrod link geometry
  name   :   trackrod
  symmetry   :   left/right
  radius   :   10.16

uca
  symmetry   :   left/right
  mass   :   0.45359237
  sprung_percentage   :   100.0
  location (dependent)   :   80.7550666667, − 401.4978, 357.6743333333
  orientation (dependent)   :   zp_vector= − 0.3905924685, 0.914189449, − 0.1081442321
                              :   xp_vector= − 0.9205517717, − 0.3872848637, 5.0939866393E − 002
  cm_location_from_part   :   0.0, 0.0, 0.0
  Ixx, Iyy, Izz   :   292.6396534292 , 292.6396534292 , 292.6396534292
  Ixy, Izx, Iyz   :   0.0 , 0.0 , 0.0

uca link geometry
  name   :   uca1
  symmetry   :   left/right
  radius   :   10.16

uca link geometry
  name   :   uca2
  symmetry   :   left/right
  radius   :   10.16

upright
  symmetry   :   left/right
  mass   :   0.45359237
  sprung_percentage   :   100.0
  location (dependent)   :   − 97.4217, − 808.1772, 330.7969
  orientation   :   zp_vector=0.0, 0.0, 1.0
                              :   xp_vector=1.0, 0.0, 0.0
  cm_location_from_part   :   0.0, 0.0, 0.0

Ixx, Iyy, Izz	:	292.6396534292 , 292.6396534292 , 292.6396534292
Ixy, Izx, Iyz	:	0.0 , 0.0 , 0.0

upright link geometry
  name   : lca_spar
  symmetry   : left/right
  radius   : 10.0

upright link geometry
  name   : spindle
  symmetry   : left/right
  radius   : 12.7

upright link geometry
  name   : tierod_spar
  symmetry   : left/right
  radius   : 10.0

upright link geometry
  name   : uca_spar
  symmetry   : left/right
  radius   : 10.0

SWITCH PARTS:
  pushrod_pickup
  symmetry   : left/right
  switched to : lca (general part)
  part list   : lca (general part)
                : upright (general part)

BUSHINGS:
  lca_front
  definition   : .ACAR.attachments.ac_bushing
  symmetry   : left/right
  orientation (dependent) : zp_vector=0.9995269631, $-3.0754675787E-002$, 0.0
                              : xp_vector=0.0, 0.0, -1.0
  t preload x   : 0.0
  t preload y   : 0.0

t preload z	:	0.0
r preload x	:	0.0
r preload y	:	0.0
r preload z	:	0.0
t offset x	:	0.0
t offset y	:	0.0
t offset z	:	0.0
r offset x	:	0.0
r offset y	:	0.0
r offset z	:	0.0
fx scaling factor	:	1.0
fy scaling factor	:	1.0
fz scaling factor	:	1.0
tx scaling factor	:	1.0
ty scaling factor	:	1.0
tz scaling factor	:	1.0
tx damping force scale	:	1.0
ty damping force scale	:	1.0
tz damping force scale	:	1.0
rx damping force scale	:	1.0
ry damping force scale	:	1.0
rz damping force scale	:	1.0
property file	:	mdids://FASE/bushings.tbl/fsae_control_arm_bushing.bus

lca_rear

definition	:	.ACAR.attachments.ac_bushing
symmetry	:	left/right
orientation (dependent)	:	zp_vector= − 0.9995269631, 3.0754675787E − 002, 0.0
	:	xp_vector=0.0, 0.0, 1.0
t preload x	:	0.0
t preload y	:	0.0
t preload z	:	0.0
r preload x	:	0.0
r preload y	:	0.0
r preload z	:	0.0
t offset x	:	0.0
t offset y	:	0.0
t offset z	:	0.0

r offset x	:	0.0
r offset y	:	0.0
r offset z	:	0.0
fx scaling factor	:	1.0
fy scaling factor	:	1.0
fz scaling factor	:	1.0
tx scaling factor	:	1.0
ty scaling factor	:	1.0
tz scaling factor	:	1.0
tx damping force scale	:	1.0
ty damping force scale	:	1.0
tz damping force scale	:	1.0
rx damping force scale	:	1.0
ry damping force scale	:	1.0
rz damping force scale	:	1.0
property file	:	mdids://FASE/bushings.tbl/fsae_control_arm_bushing.bus

uca_front

definition	:	.ACAR.attachments.ac_bushing
symmetry	:	left/right
orientation (dependent)	:	zp_vector=0.9992313656, $-3.9200484856E-002$, 0.0
	:	xp_vector=0.0, 0.0, -1.0
t preload x	:	0.0
t preload y	:	0.0
t preload z	:	0.0
r preload x	:	0.0
r preload y	:	0.0
r preload z	:	0.0
t offset x	:	0.0
t offset y	:	0.0
t offset z	:	0.0
r offset x	:	0.0
r offset y	:	0.0
r offset z	:	0.0
fx scaling factor	:	1.0
fy scaling factor	:	1.0
fz scaling factor	:	1.0
tx scaling factor	:	1.0

ty scaling factor	:	1.0
tz scaling factor	:	1.0
tx damping force scale	:	1.0
ty damping force scale	:	1.0
tz damping force scale	:	1.0
rx damping force scale	:	1.0
ry damping force scale	:	1.0
rz damping force scale	:	1.0
property file	:	mdids://FASE/bushings.tbl/fsae_control_arm_bushing.bus

uca_rear

definition	:	.ACAR.attachments.ac_bushing
symmetry	:	left/right
orientation (dependent)	:	zp_vector= − 0.9992313656, 3.9200484856E − 002, 0.0
	:	xp_vector=0.0, 0.0, 1.0
t preload x	:	0.0
t preload y	:	0.0
t preload z	:	0.0
r preload x	:	0.0
r preload y	:	0.0
r preload z	:	0.0
t offset x	:	0.0
t offset y	:	0.0
t offset z	:	0.0
r offset x	:	0.0
r offset y	:	0.0
r offset z	:	0.0
fx scaling factor	:	1.0
fy scaling factor	:	1.0
fz scaling factor	:	1.0
tx scaling factor	:	1.0
ty scaling factor	:	1.0
tz scaling factor	:	1.0
tx damping force scale	:	1.0
ty damping force scale	:	1.0
tz damping force scale	:	1.0
rx damping force scale	:	1.0
ry damping force scale	:	1.0

```
        rz damping force scale :    1.0
        property file              :    mdids://FASE/bushings.tbl/fsae_control_arm_bushing.bus

    NSPRINGS:
      third_spring
        definition        :   .ACAR.forces.ac_spring
        symmetry          :   single
        property file :   *unable to locate file mdids://fsae_2007r1_MDR2/springs.tbl/msc_0001.spr
        value type        :   'installed_length'
        user value        :   128.8095782985

      main_coil
        definition        :   .ACAR.forces.ac_spring
        symmetry          :   left/right
        property file :   mdids://FASE/springs.tbl/test.spr
        value type        :   'installed_length'
        user value        :   282.5798025569

    DAMPERS:
      third_damper
        definition        :   .ACAR.forces.ac_damper
        symmetry          :   single
        property file :   *unable to locate file mdids://fsae_2007r1_MDR2/dampers.tbl/msc_0001.dpr

      ride_damper
        definition        :   .ACAR.forces.ac_damper
        symmetry          :   left/right
        property file :   mdids://FASE/dampers.tbl/MSC_default.dpr
```

21.2 耦合悬架变量参数

推杆式耦合悬架变量参数如表 21-1 所示。

表 21-1　耦合悬架变量参数

Parameter name	symmetry	type	value
cross_weight	single	real	0.0
driveline_active	single	integer	0
drive_torque_bias_front	single	real	0.0
kinematic_flag	single	integer	0
odatum	single	real	−25.4
slider_activity	single	integer	0
torsion_bar_active	single	integer	0
wheel_bearing_flag	single	integer	0
arb_rate	single	real	0.0
front_ride_height	left/right	real	25.4
pin_height	left/right	real	284.999 999 998 9
pushrod_stiffness	left/right	real	5 999.999 999 93
camber_angle	left/right	real	0.0
toe_angle	left/right	real	0.0

21.3　耦合悬架通信器

推杆式耦合悬架输入通信器如表 21-2 所示。

表 21-2　耦合悬架输入通信器

Communicator Name	Entity Class	From Minor Role	Matching Name
ci[lr]_tierod_to_steering	mount	inherit	tierod_to_steering
cis_simulation_type	parameter_integer	inherit	simulation_type
cis_std_tire_ref_location	location	inherit	std_tire_ref_location
cis_suspension_to_chassis	mount	inherit	suspension_to_chassis

推杆式耦合悬架输出通信器如表 21-3 所示。

表 21-3　耦合悬架输出通信器

CommunicatorName	Entity Class	To Minor Role	Matching Name
co[lr]_camber_angle	parameter_real	inherit	camber_angle
co[lr]_hub_mount	mount	inherit	hub_mount
co[lr]_inboard_steering_location	location	inherit	inboard_steering_location
co[lr]_suspension_mount	mount	inherit	suspension_mount
co[lr]_suspension_upright	mount	inherit	suspension_upright
co[lr]_toe_angle	parameter_real	inherit	toe_angle
co[lr]_wheel_center	location	inherit	wheel_center
co[lr]_wheel_hub	mount	inherit	wheel_hub
co[lr]_wheel_joint	joint_for_motion	inherit	wheel_joint

续表

CommunicatorName	Entity Class	To Minor Role	Matching Name
cos_arb_stiffness	parameter_real	inherit	arb_stiffness
cos_driveline_active	parameter_integer	inherit	driveline_active
cos_drive_torque_bias_front	parameter_real	inherit	drive_torque_bias_front
cos_suspension_parameters_ARRAY	array	inherit	suspension_parameters_array
cos_suspension_wheel_bearing_flag	parameter_integer	inherit	suspension_wheel_bearing
cos_torsion_spring_active	parameter_integer	inherit	torsion_spring_active

21.4 耦合悬架车轮反向激振仿真

（1）悬架装配。
- 单击 File > New > Suspension Assembly 命令，弹出耦合悬架装配对话框如图 21-6 所示；
- Assembly Name(系统名称)：fsae_sus_third_asm；
- Suspension Subsystem（模板路径）:fsae_front_third；
- 单击 OK，完成耦合悬架的装配如图 21-7 所示。

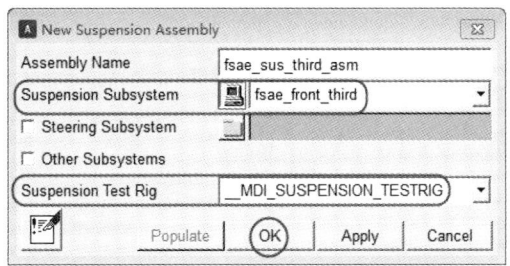

图 21-6 耦合悬架台架仿真装配

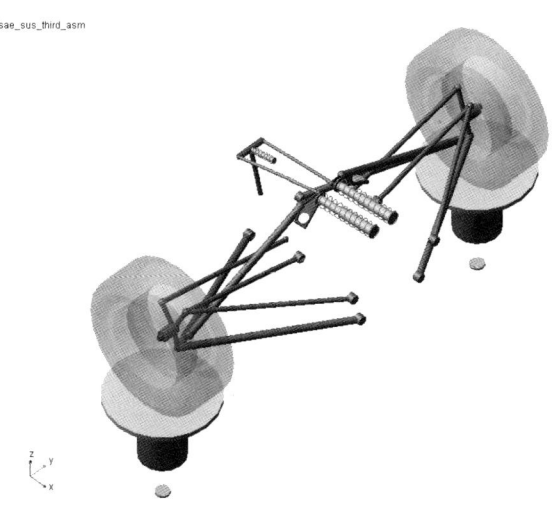

图 21-7 耦合悬架装配模型

(2)仿真设置。
- 单击 Simulate > Suspension Analysis > Opposite Travel 命令,弹出双轮反向激振对话框如图 21-8 所示;
  - Output Prefix:OT;
  - Number of Steps(仿真步数):100;
  - Mode of Simulation:interactive;
  - Vertical Setup Mode:Wheel Center;
  - Bump Travel:30;
  - Rebound Travel: -30;
  - Travel Relative To:Wheel Center;
  - Control Mode:Absolute;
  - Coordinate System:Vehicle;
- 单击 OK,完成耦合悬架在 C 模式下的仿真。
- 按 F8,界面转换到后处理模块,观看仿真动画如图 21-9 所示,此时为仿真结束左右车轮的位置,从图中可以看出,耦合式(三推杆式)悬架左右车轮的位置变化极小,设计允许车轮的变化范围为 2 cm;因此在高速弯道的稳定性极好。计算结果如图 21-10 ~ 图 21-16 所示。

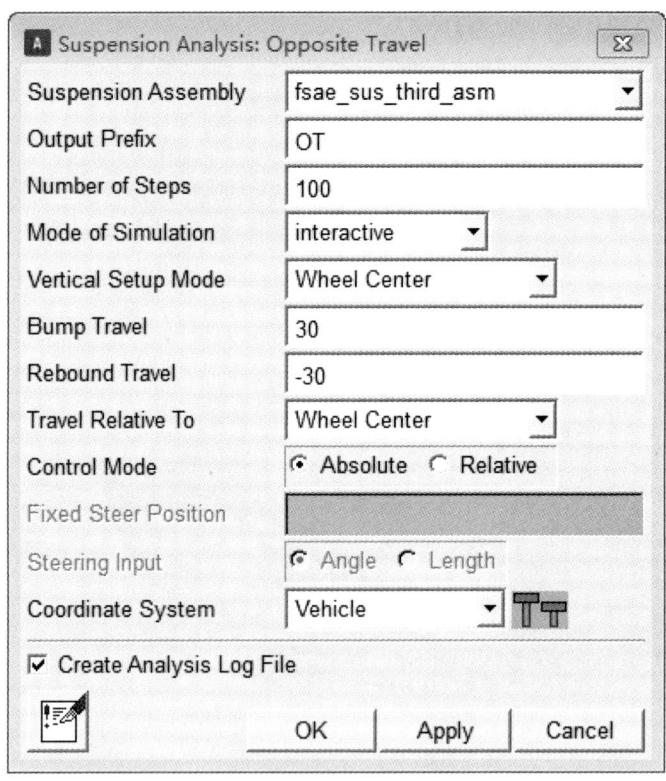

图 21-8 车轮反向激振参数设置

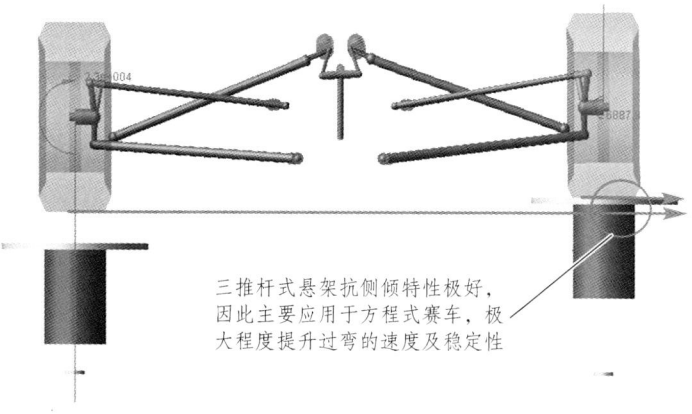

三推杆式悬架抗侧倾特性极好，因此主要应用于方程式赛车，极大程度提升过弯的速度及稳定性

图 21-9　仿真视图

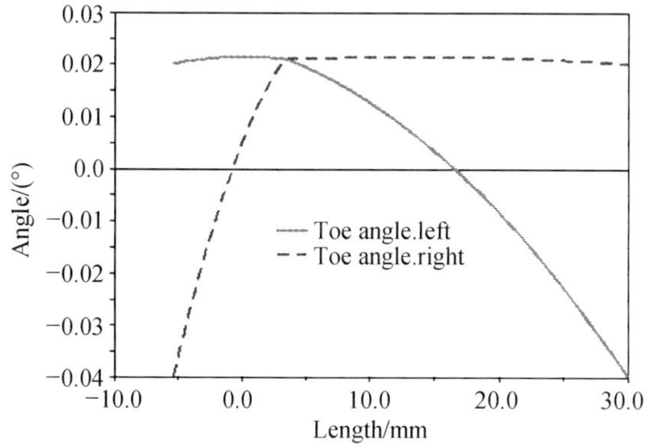

图 21-10　前轮前束

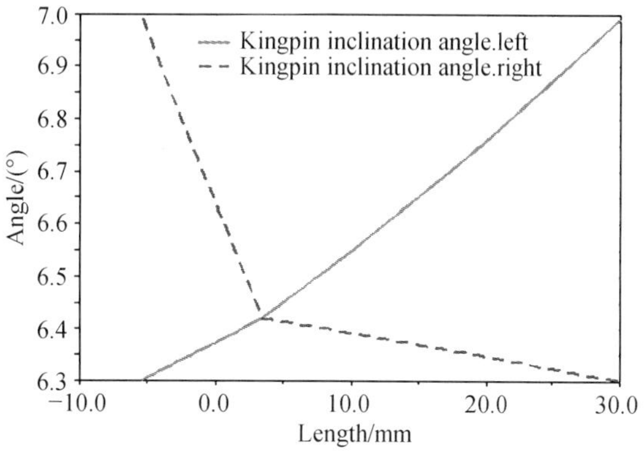

图 21-11　主销内倾

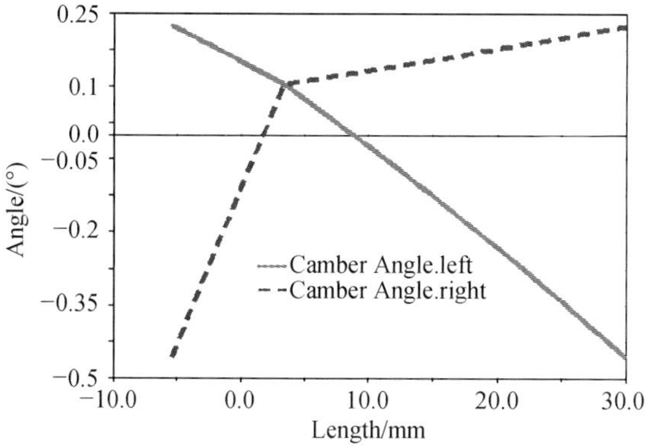

图 21-12　前轮外倾

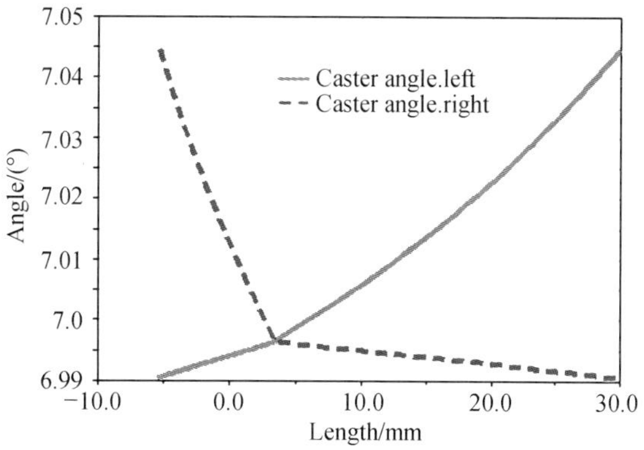

图 21-13　主销后倾

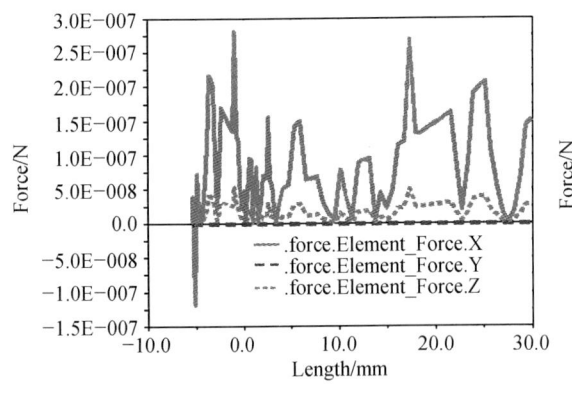
图 21-14 左侧阻尼力

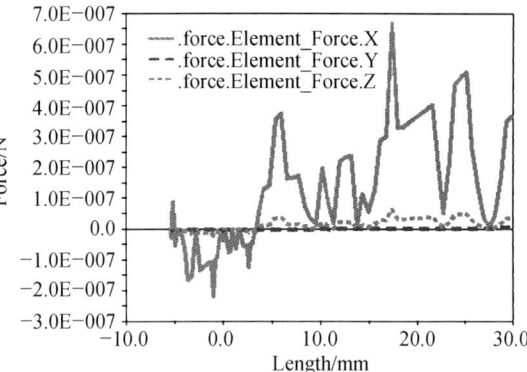
图 21-15 第三阻尼力

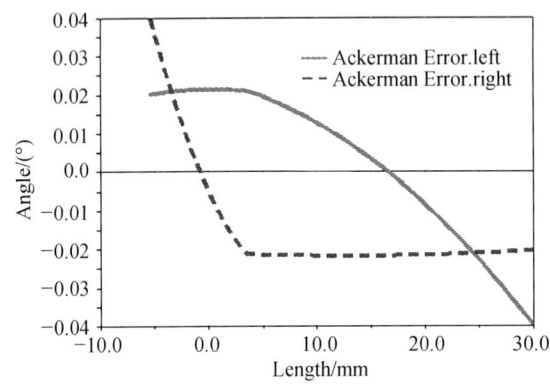
图 21-16 阿克曼角误差

第 22 章 优化设计实验——INSIGHT

对于一个动力学模型，设计越复杂，影响设计的因素也就越多。由于各个参数之间是相互影响的，所以每次改变一个参数很难提高设计的性能。如果同时改变多个参数，需要大量的仿真计算，并产生庞大的仿真数据，这样很难判断到底哪个参数是主要的，哪个是次要的。利用 ADAMS/INSIGHT，工程师们可以对虚拟样机和物理样机进行系统的研究、深入的分析，并可以与整个团队分享自己的成果；研究策略可以应用于部件或子系统，或者扩展到评估多层次问题中，实现跨部门的设计方案优化；ADAMS/INSIGHT 可以通过网页或者数据表格实现数据交换，从而使设计人员、研究人员以及项目管理人员能够直接参与到"如果?—怎样?"的研究中，而不需要接触到实际的仿真模型。

ADAMS/INSIGHT 特点如下：① 研究策略有设计研究、蒙特卡罗法研究、设计实验、扫描研究、周期研究、单目标和多目标优化；② 支持用户自定义策略或将已有策略应用于其他模型；③ 响应曲面法（Response Surface Methods）是通过对试验数据进行数学回归分析的方法，帮助工程师更好地理解产品的性能和系统内部各个参数之间的相互关系；④ 可综合考虑各种制造因素的影响（例如:公差、装配误差、加工精度等）；⑤ 对拥有共同输入的不同域的实验进行综合分析；⑥ 将实验结果与解算结果进行综合比较，以便更深入地研究；⑦ 网络发布实验结果；⑧ 可输出为 Excel、MATLAB 以及 Visual Basic 文件格式；⑨ 既可与其他 MSC.ADAMS 模块联合使用，也可脱离 MSC.ADAMS 环境单独使用。

学习目标

- ◆ 双 A 臂悬架前束角优化。
- ◆ 运载火箭模型优化。
- ◆ 推杆式悬架模型外倾角优化。

22.1 双 A 臂悬架前束角优化——AVIEW

（1）数据库导入模型。

- 启动 ADAMS/VIEW，保持界面默认设置；
- 单击 File > Import...，弹出导入模型界面如图 22-1 所示；

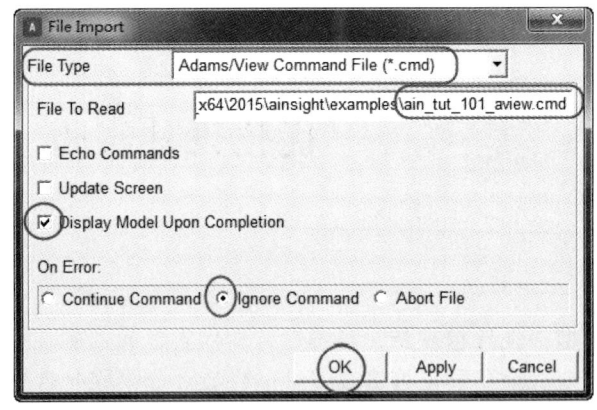

图 22-1 导入 CMD 模型

- File Type：Adams/View Command File（*.cmd）;
- File To Read：D:\MSC.Software\Adams_x64\2015\ainsight\examples\ain_tut_101_aview.cmd;
- 勾选 Display Model Upon Completion;
- 单击 OK，完成模型导入如图 22-2 所示，此时为双 A 臂悬架概念化模型，模型中的部件特性、约束、驱动等参数请读者自行查看学习，此处不做详细的叙述。

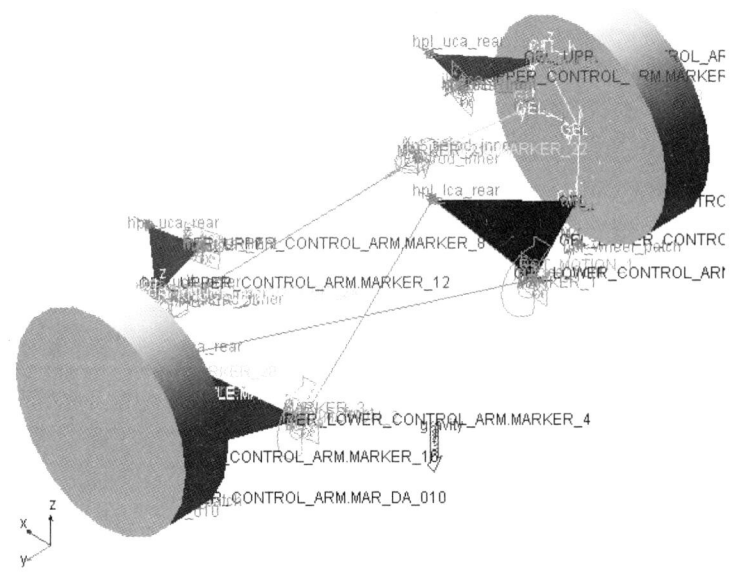

图 22-2 双 A 臂悬架概念模型

（2）运行仿真设定。

- 单击 Simulation > Simulate 命令;
- End Time：5;
- Steps：500;
- 其余保持默认设置（见图 22-3）;

- 单击 Start simulation，运行完成仿真；

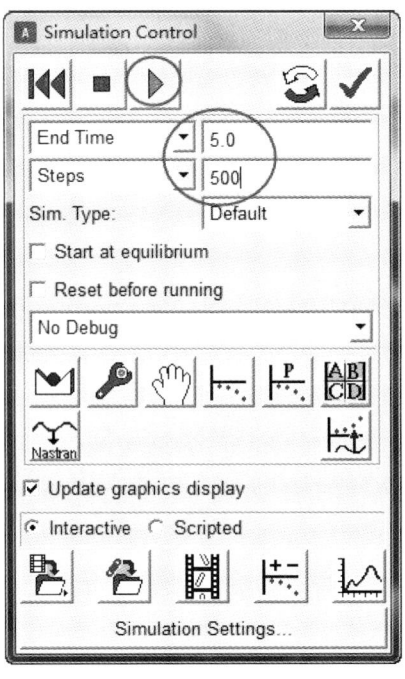

图 22-3　仿真设定

（3）优化设计实验。

- 单击 Design Exploration > Adams/Insight Export Dialog box 命令，弹出优化输出界面如图 22-4 所示；
- Experiment: suspension_insight_experiment；
- Model：tut_101_aview；
- Simulation Script: .tut_101_aview.Last_Sim；
- 单击 OK，完成输出接口的设置，此时 ADAMS/VIEW 消失，弹出 ADAMS/INSIGHT，其界面较为简单，包含菜单栏、工具条、模型树及显示窗口四部分；实验矩阵的设置、分析等将在此界面完成。

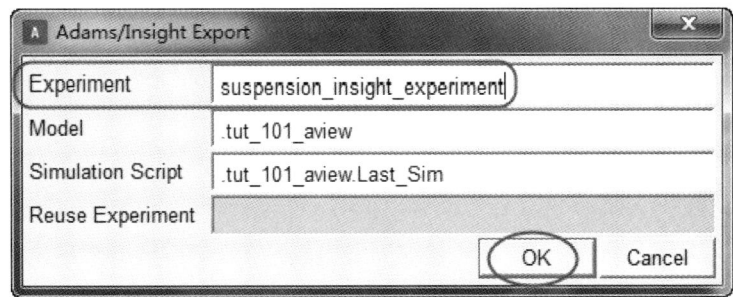

图 22-4　ADAMS/INSIGHT 输出界面

（4）创建设计矩阵（优化变量选取）。

- 选取优化变量，按如下顺序依次展开模型树：Factors > Candidates > tut_101_aview >

ground > hpl_tierod_outer；
- 选择 ground.hpl_tierod_outer.x，此时视窗显示如图 22-5 所示；

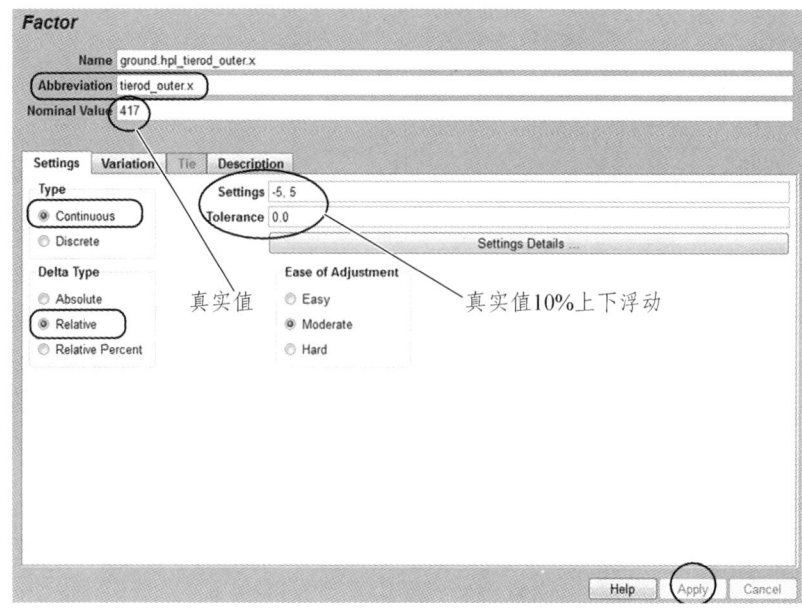

图 22-5　设计变量因素

- 单击 Promote to inclusion，将设计因素 ground.hpl_tierod_outer.x 提升为设计变量；
- Abbreviation（简称）：ground.hpl_tierod_outer.x；
- Nominal Value：417，即此数值为转向横拉杆在 x 方向的真实值；
- Type：Continuous；
- Delta Type：Relative，即相对值，一般允许其变化范围为 Nominal Value 的 10%；
- Settings：–5,5；在 Nominal Value 的基础减少/增加 5，即允许数值的变化范围为 [412,422]；
- 切换到 Description 菜单；
- Units：mm；
- 单击 Apply，完成 ground.hpl_tierod_outer.x 参数的设定；
- 重复上述步骤，完成以下设计因素的设定：
① ground.hpl_tierod_outer.y；
② ground.hpl_tierod_outer.z。

（5）优化目标。
- 选取优化目标，按如下顺序依次展开模型树：Responses > Candidates > tut_101_aview > toe_left_REQ，此优化目标模型导入之前已经创建好，因此不需要创建，如果是自建模型，则需要根据优化的任务创建自己所希望的优化目标；
- 选择 toe_left_REQ，此时视窗显示如图 22-6 所示；

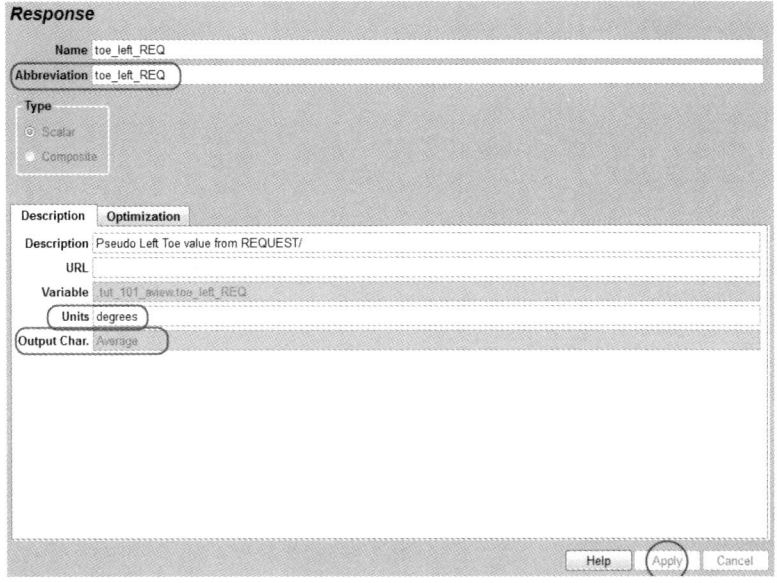

图 22-6　优化目标

- 单击 Promote to inclusion，将响应因素 ground.hpl_tierod_outer.x 提升为响应目标（优化目标）；
  - Abbreviation（简称）：toe_left_REQ；
  - Units：degrees；
  - 单击 Apply，完成 toe_left_REQ 优化目标的设定；
  - 重复上述步骤，完成 toe_right_REQ 优化目标的设定。

（6）设置设计规范。

- 单击 Define > Experiment Design > Set Design Specification，弹出设计规范界面如图 22-7 所示；

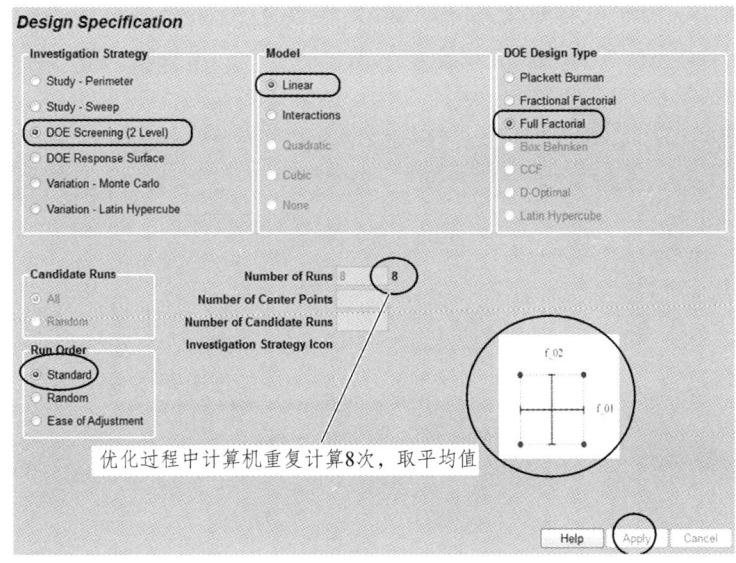

图 22-7　设计规范

- Investigation Strategy: DOE Screening (2 Level);
- Model: Linear;
- DOE Design Type: Full Factorial;
- 单击 Apply，完成设计规范中参数设定。

（7）创建设计与工作空间。
- 单击 Define > Experiment Design > Create Design Space;
- 单击 Define > Experiment Design > Create Work Space;
- 模型树上单击 Work Space，视图窗口如图 22-8 所示，从图中可以看到上述选取的优化变量及优化目标参数，优化变量通过不同的组合（共有 8 种不同的组合），提交后需要重复计算 8 次。

Work Space						
	Trial	tierod_outer.y	tierod_outer.z	tierod_outer.x	toe_right_REQ	toe_left_REQ
1	Trial 1	-755	325	412		
2	Trial 2	-755	325	422		
3	Trial 3	-755	335	412		
4	Trial 4	-755	335	422		
5	Trial 5	-745	325	412		
6	Trial 6	-745	325	422		
7	Trial 7	-745	335	412		
8	Trial 8	-745	335	422		

图 22-8　工作空间

（8）提交计算。
- 单击 Simulation > Build-Run-Load > All;
- ADAMS/VIEW 打开并运行由实验定义的仿真。ADAMS/VIEW 状态栏显示模拟进度的消息，消息窗口也会出现并显示有关关键位置的警告，在本教程中可以忽略这些警告;
- 计算完成后，界面显示如图 22-9、图 22-10 所示。如图 22-9 所示参数保持恒定值并没有变化，原因在于左右车轮为独立悬架并不相互影响，同时优化变量选取的是右侧横向拉杆外侧点 X、Y、Z 三个方向的参数，因此优化目标输出变化仅为左侧车轮的前束角。

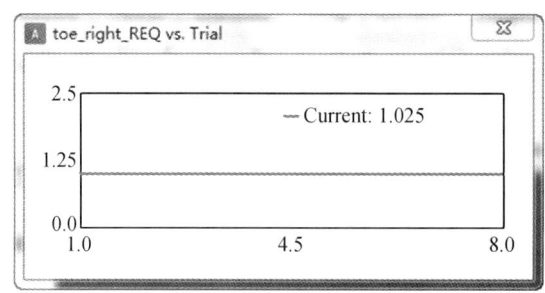

图 22-9　右轮前束角

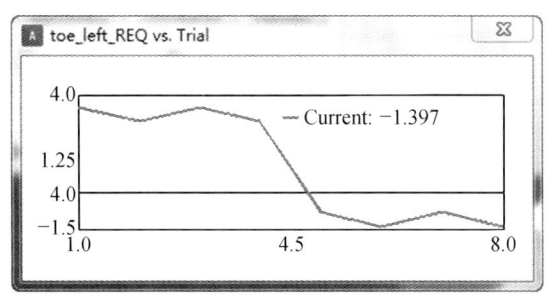

图 22-10 左轮前束角

（9）优化结果。

- 单击 Simulation > Adams/Insight > Display 命令，显示如图 22-11 所示界面；

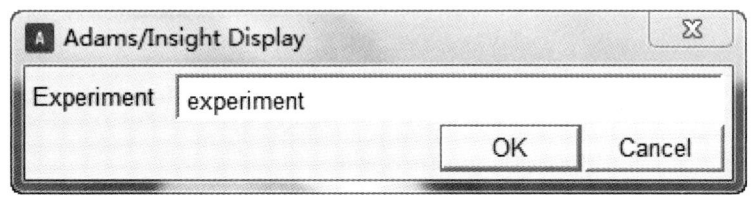

图 22-11 优化结果输出界面

- 模型树下单击 Work Space，计算优化出的结果如图 22-12 所示，从结果中可以看出，每种不同的组合左侧车轮前束角的值完全不同，根据设计要求，可以选取最符合目标的一组值。

Trial	tierod_outer.y	tierod_outer.z	tierod_outer.x	toe_right_REQ	toe_left_REQ
Trial 1	-755	325	412	1.02452	3.5103
Trial 2	-755	325	422	1.02452	2.90266
Trial 3	-755	335	412	1.02452	3.5103
Trial 4	-755	335	422	1.02452	2.90266
Trial 5	-745	325	412	1.02452	-0.777356
Trial 6	-745	325	422	1.02452	-1.39724
Trial 7	-745	335	412	1.02452	-0.777356
Trial 8	-745	335	422	1.02452	-1.39724

图 22-12 优化结果

（10）拟合结果。

ADAMS/VIEW 已经完成了工作空间矩阵中定义的测试，接下来可以使用 ADAMS/INSIGHT 将结果拟合到多项式或响应曲面。

- 单击 Tools > Fit New Model 命令；
- 单击 Regression > toe_left_REQ 命令；
- Display 界面可以选择需要显示的参数，此处选择 Fit，显示结果如图 22-13 所示；

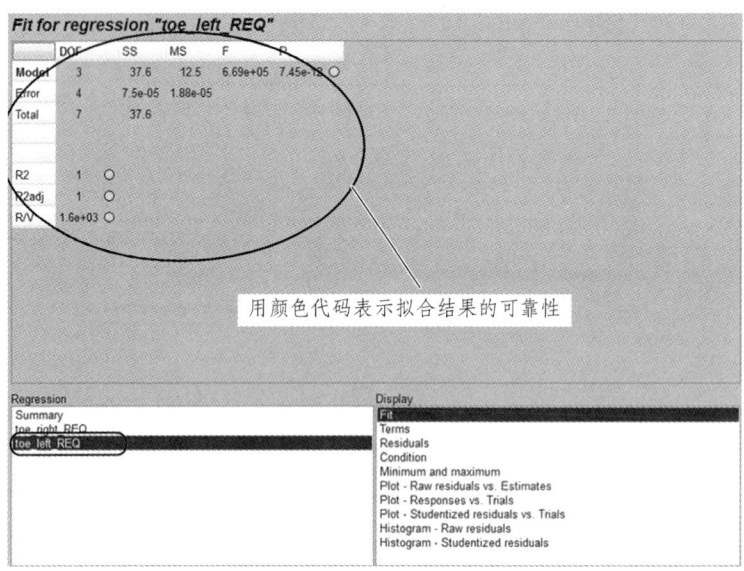

图 22-13　左侧车轮前束角回归拟合分析

① 绿色表示所有拟合标准均满足或超过最高拟合阈值；
② 黄色表示适合标准可能需要调查；
③ 红色表示应调查拟合标准。

- Display 界面可以选择 Plot—Responses vs.Trials，显示结果如图 22-14 所示，其中的数值与和图 22-12 所示的数值相同。

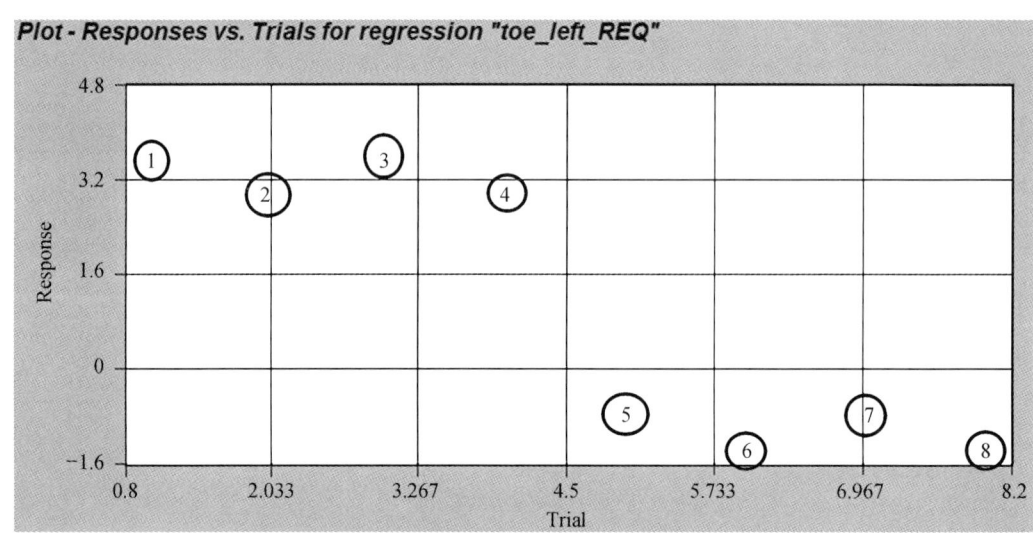

图 22-14　响应（Responses vs Trials）

（11）刷新因素设定。

可以使用 ADAMS / INSIGHT 执行单目标和多目标优化。单目标优化旨在标量响应；多目标优化涉及多个标量响应。

- 单击 Tools > Optimize Model 命令，显示如图 22-15 所示界面；

- 在优化模型界面中，可以通过滑动条幅修改参数 tierod_outer.x\ tierod_outer.y\ tierod_outer.z 的值，修改完成后，下列的设计目标值会通过刷新按钮更新；

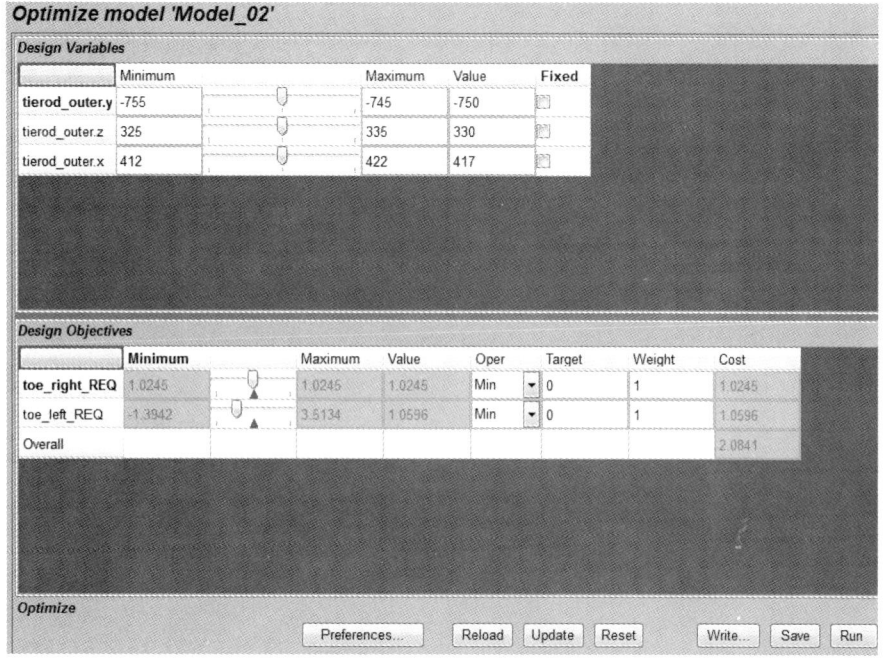

图 22-15　优化模型界面

- 单击 Analysis > Model_01 > Export to Web > Model_01 命令，显示图 22-16 所示界面；

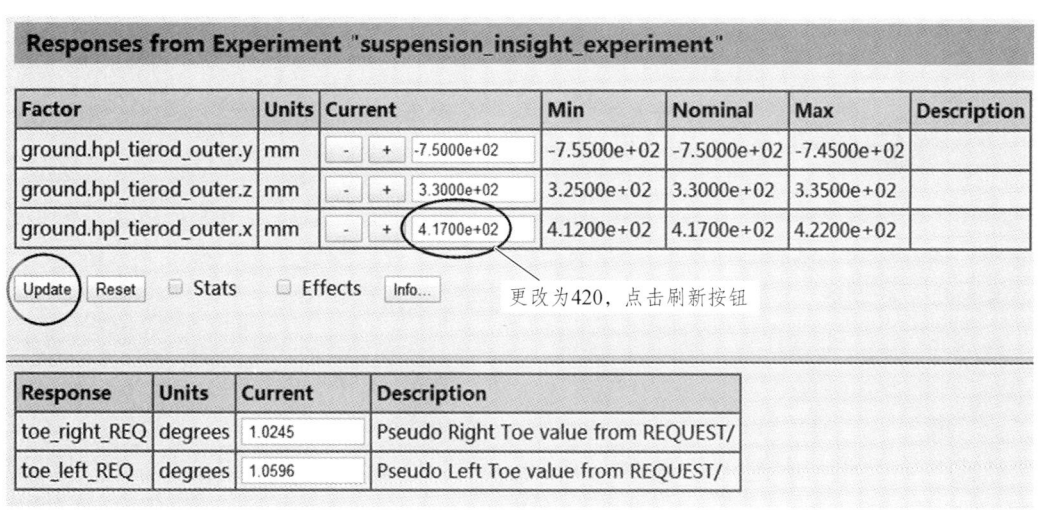

图 22-16　响应输出（网页模式）

- 将第一个因子 hpl_tierod_outer.x 的值从 417 更改为 420，然后选择 Update。目标响应会进行调整以反映新的因子值。注意，只有一个的值响应中的 toe_left_REQ 反映了变化，因为模型是一个独立的悬架，其中右拉杆未与左拉杆相连，因子值更改仅影响悬架的左侧。左车轮前束角变化如图 22-17 所示。

- 537 -

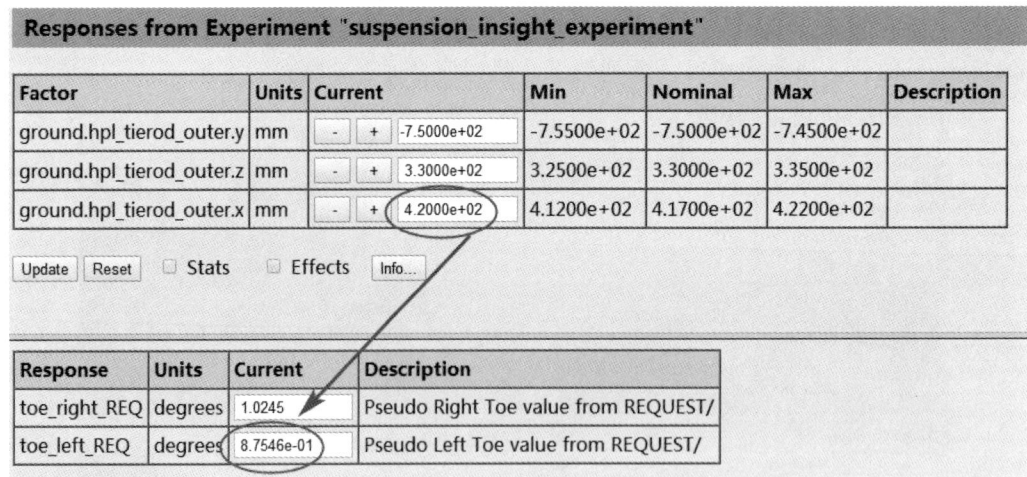

图 22-17 响应输出（网页模式，改变数值为 420）

- 勾选 Effects，优化变量灵敏度显示如图 22-18 所示，可以看出，Y 方向的数值对前束角的影响最大。

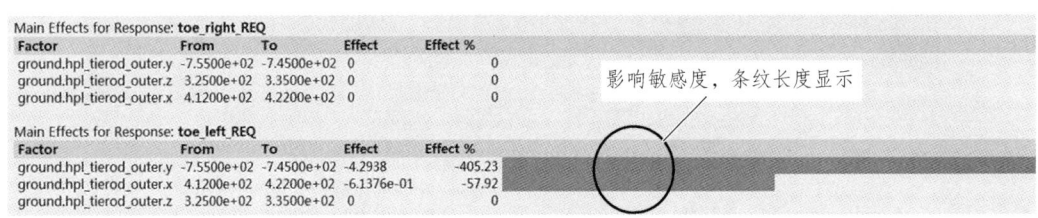

图 22-18 响应参数灵敏度分析

22.2 运载火箭模型优化

应用于机械系统的蒙特卡罗分析方法涉及多次运行参数，目的是为预测机构性能提供统计依据。该方法的基础涉及使用概率密度函数（PDF）表征参数，必须为将在分析中变化的每个参数指定此功能，例如弹簧刚度、阻尼率和初始旋转率等。

- 启动 ADAMS/VIEW，保持默认设置；
- 单击 File > Import...，弹出导入模型界面参考如图 22-1 所示；
- File Type：ADAMS/View Command File（*.cmd）；
- File To Read：D:\MSC.Software\Adams_x64\2015\ainsight\examples\ain_tut_141_aview.cmd；
- 勾选 Display Model Upon Completion；
- 单击 OK，完成运载火箭模型的导入，如图 22-19 所示。

（1）火箭运行仿真设定。
- 单击 Simulation > Simulate 命令；
- End Time：5；

- Steps：500；
- 其余保持默认设置；
- 单击 Start simulation，运行完成仿真，仿真完成观看动画效果如图 22-20 所示，航天器与接口分离；

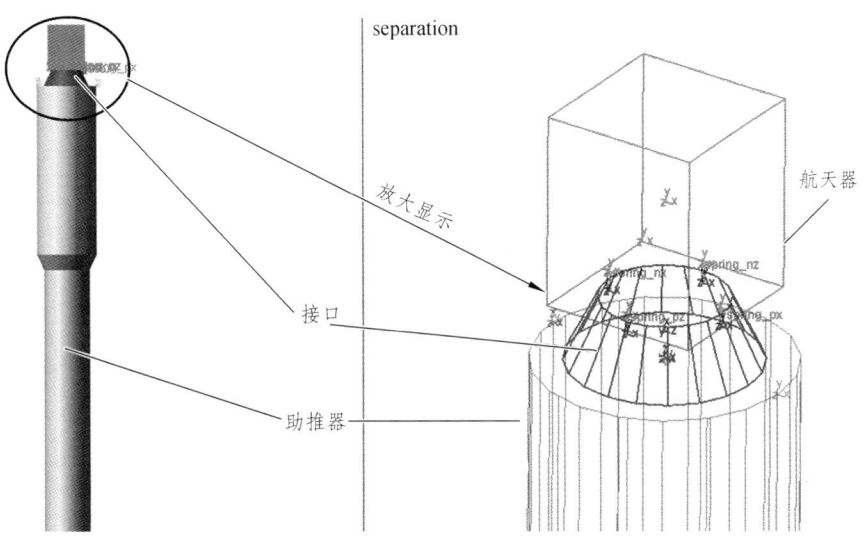

图 22-19　运载火箭模型

图 22-20　航天器发射

（2）优化设计实验。
- 单击 Design Exploration > Adams/Insight Export Dialog box 命令，弹出优化输出界面如图 22-21 所示；

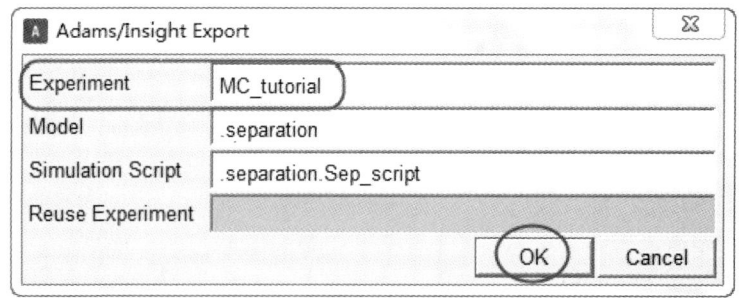

图 22-21 ADAMS/INSIGHT 输出接口

- Experiment:MC_tutorial；
- Model：separation；
- Simulation Script: . separation.Sep_script；
- 单击 OK，完成输出接口的设置，此时 ADAMS/VIEW 消失，弹出 ADAMS/INSIGHT；
- 参考双 A 臂悬架设定优化变量与优化目标，设定完成后的运载火箭模型树如图 22-22 所示，设置过程中需要修改的参数如图 22-23 所示；

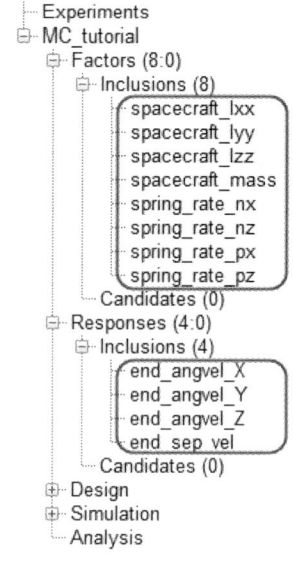

图 22-22 运载火箭优化界面模型树

Factor:	Variation Distribution:	Tolerance:
spacecraft_lyy	Normal	30
spacecraft_lzz	Normal	35
spacecraft_mass	Uniform	23
spring_rate_nx	Normal	200
spring_rate_nz	Normal	200
spring_rate_px	Normal	200
spring_rate_pz	Normal	200

图 22-23 优化变量参数修订值

（3）设置设计规范。
- 单击 Define > Experiment Design > Set Design Specification，弹出设计规范界面如图 22-24 所示。
- Investigation Strategy: Variation-Monte Carlo；
- Model: Linear；
- Number of Runs：100；
- Number of Center Points：0；
- 单击 Apply，完成设计规范中参数设定。

（4）提交计算。
- 单击 Simulation > Build-Run-Load > All；
- ADAMS/VIEW 打开并运行由实验定义的仿真。ADAMS/VIEWW 状态栏显示模拟进度的消息，消息窗口也会出现并显示有关关键位置的警告，在本教程中可以忽略这些警告；

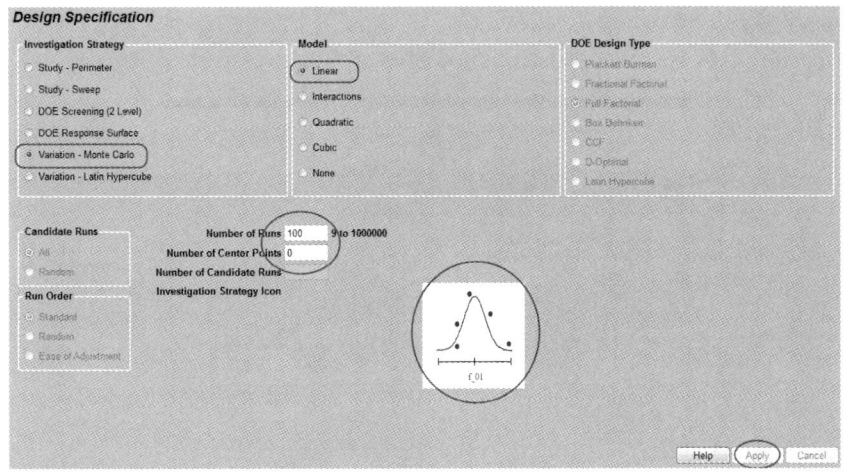

图 22-24 运载火箭设计规范

- 运载火箭模型计算较为缓慢，计算机需要重复计算 128 次；计算完成后界面显示如图 22-25 ~ 图 22-28 所示。

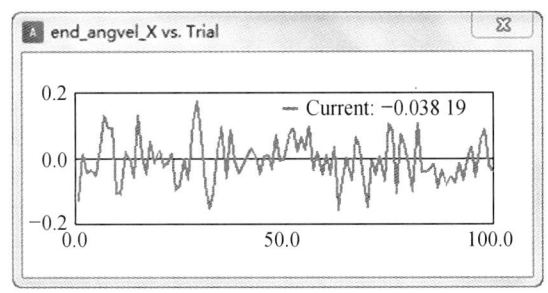

图 22-25 航天器终点时 X 方向角速度

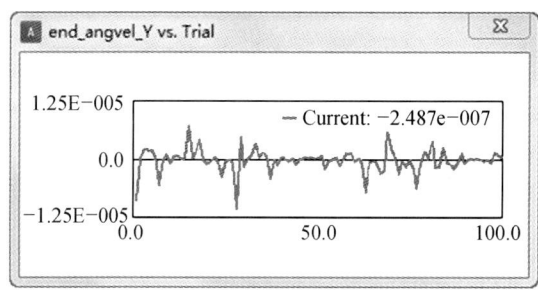

图 22-26　航天器终点时 Y 方向角速度

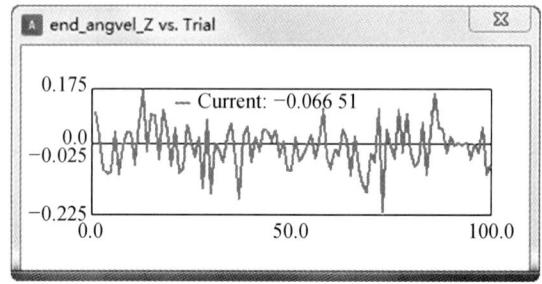

图 22-27　航天器终点时 Z 方向角速度

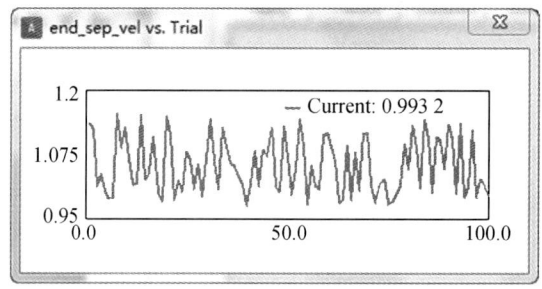

图 22-28　助推器速度

（5）优化结果。

单击 Simulation > Adams/Insight > Display 命令，显示如图 22-29 所示界面。

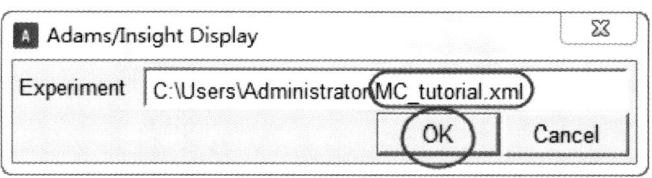

图 22-29　优化结果输出界面

（6）刷新因素设定。

可以使用 ADAMS / INSIGHT 执行单目标和多目标优化。单目标优化旨在标量响应；多目标优化涉及多个标量响应。

- 单击 Tools > Optimize Model 命令，显示如图 22-30 所示界面；
- 在优化模型界面中，可以通过滑动条幅修改参数值，修改完成后，相应的设计目标值会通过刷新按钮更新。

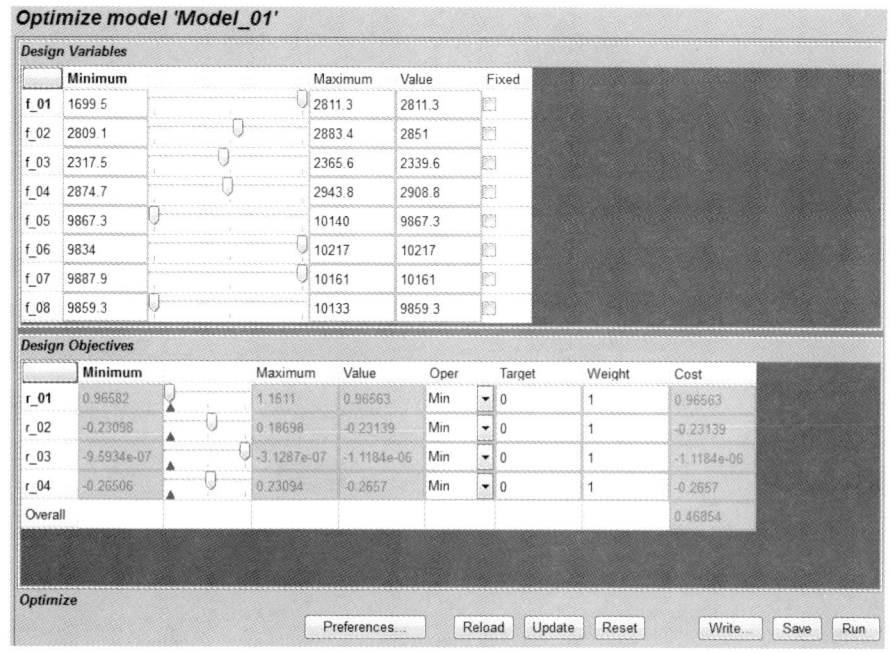

图 22-30 优化模型界面

22.3 推杆式悬架外倾角优化——ACAR

（1）悬架装配。
- 单击 File > New > Suspension Assembly 命令，弹出推杆式悬架装配对话框如图 22-31 所示；

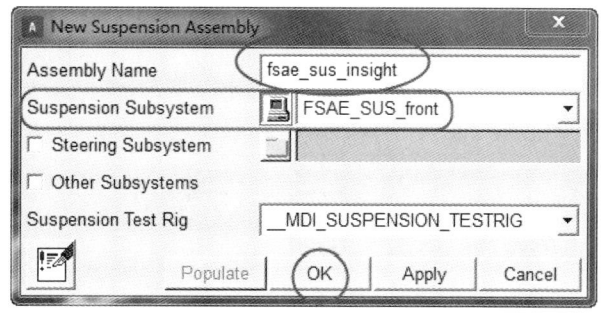

图 22-31 推杆式悬架装配

- Assembly Name(系统名称)：fsae_sus_insight；
- Suspension Subsystem（模板路径）：FSAE_SUS_front；
- 单击 OK，完成推杆式悬架的装配如图 22-32 所示。

（2）仿真设置。
- 单击 Simulate > Suspension Analysis > Opposite Travel 命令，弹出双轮同向激振对话框如图 22-33 所示；

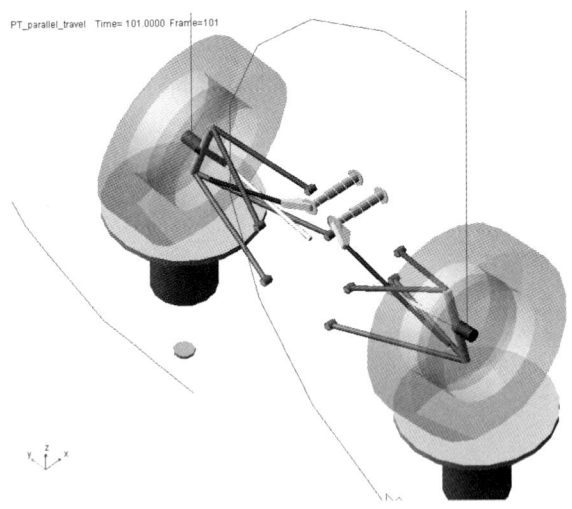

图 22-32 推杆式悬架车轮同向激振仿真

- Output Prefix：PT；
- Number of Steps（仿真步数）：100；
- Mode of Simulation：interactive；
- Vertical Setup Mode：Wheel Center；
- Bump Travel：50；
- Rebound Travel：-50；
- Travel Relative To：Wheel Center；
- Control Mode：Absolute；
- Coordinate System：Vehicle；
- 单击 OK，完成耦合悬架在 C 模式下的仿真如图 22-32 所示。

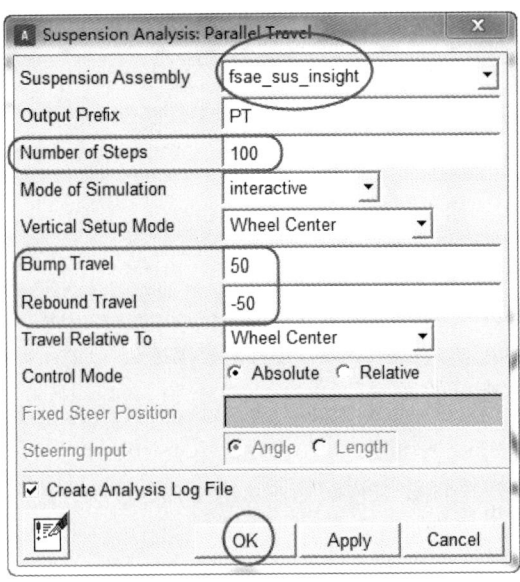

图 22-33 车轮同向激振仿真

（3）创建优化目标。

• 单击 Simulate > DOE Interface > Design Objective > New 命令，弹出设计目标对话框如图 22-34 所示；

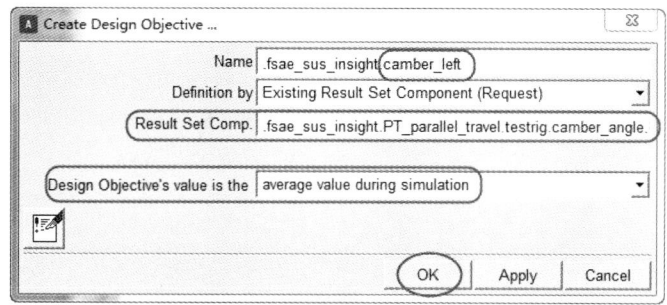

图 22-34　设计目标对话框——Camber_left

- Definition by：Existing Result Set Component(Request)；
- Result Set Comp：.fsae_sus_insight.PT_parallel_travel.testrig.camber_angle.left；
- Design Objective's value is the：average value duringsimulation；
- 单击 Apply，完成 camber_angle.left 优化目标的创建；
- Result Set Comp：.fsae_sus_insight.PT_parallel_travel.testrig.camber_angle.right；
- Design Objective's value is the：average value duringsimulation；
- 单击 OK，完成 camber_angle.right 优化目标的创建。

（4）优化设计实验。

• 单击 Simulate > DOE Interface > Adams/Insight > Export 命令弹出优化输出界面如图 35 所示；

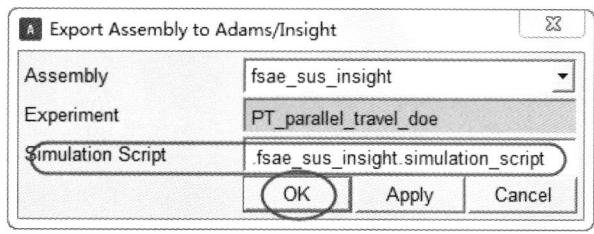

图 22-35　Adams/Insight 输出接口

- Assembly：fsae_sus_insight；
- Experiment：PT_parallel_travel_doe；
- Simulation Script: fsae_sus_insight.simulation_script；
- 单击 OK，完成输出接口的设置，此时 ADAMS/VIEW 消失，弹出 ADAMS/INSIGHT 界面；

（5）优化结果。

后续具体操作请参考前束角优化，此处不再详细叙述，计算机共运行 64 次，优化结果如图 22-36 所示；优化变量敏感度如图 22-37 所示。

Work Space

Trial	hpl uca outer.x	hpl uca outer.y	hpl uca outer.z	hpr uca outer.x	hpr uca outer.y	hpr uca outer.z	camber angle left	camber angle right
Trial 1	-5	-487.6	350.6	-5	477.6	350.6	-7.64193	-7.71144
Trial 2	-5	-487.6	350.6	-5	477.6	360.6	-7.64193	-7.94597
Trial 3	-5	-487.6	350.6	-5	487.6	350.6	-7.64193	-7.64193
Trial 4	-5	-487.6	350.6	-5	487.6	360.6	-7.64193	-7.87602
Trial 5	-5	-487.6	350.6	5	477.6	350.6	-7.64193	-7.7873
Trial 6	-5	-487.6	350.6	5	477.6	360.6	-7.64193	-8.0239
Trial 7	-5	-487.6	350.6	5	487.6	350.6	-7.64193	-7.7165
Trial 8	-5	-487.6	350.6	5	487.6	360.6	-7.64193	-7.95269
Trial 9	-5	-487.6	360.6	-5	477.6	350.6	-7.87602	-7.71144
Trial 10	-5	-487.6	360.6	-5	477.6	360.6	-7.87602	-7.94597
Trial 11	-5	-487.6	360.6	-5	487.6	350.6	-7.87602	-7.64193
Trial 12	-5	-487.6	360.6	-5	487.6	360.6	-7.87602	-7.87602
Trial 13	-5	-487.6	360.6	5	477.6	350.6	-7.87602	-7.7873
Trial 14	-5	-487.6	360.6	5	477.6	360.6	-7.87602	-8.0239
Trial 15	-5	-487.6	360.6	5	487.6	350.6	-7.87602	-7.7165
Trial 16	-5	-487.6	360.6	5	487.6	360.6	-7.87602	-7.95269
Trial 17	-5	-477.6	350.6	-5	477.6	350.6	-7.71144	-7.71144
Trial 18	-5	-477.6	350.6	-5	477.6	360.6	-7.71144	-7.94597
Trial 19	-5	-477.6	350.6	-5	487.6	350.6	-7.71144	-7.64193
Trial 20	-5	-477.6	350.6	-5	487.6	360.6	-7.71144	-7.87602
Trial 21	-5	-477.6	350.6	5	477.6	350.6	-7.71144	-7.7873
Trial 22	-5	-477.6	350.6	5	477.6	360.6	-7.71144	-8.0239
Trial 23	-5	-477.6	350.6	5	487.6	350.6	-7.71144	-7.7165
Trial 24	-5	-477.6	350.6	5	487.6	360.6	-7.71144	-7.95269
Trial 25	-5	-477.6	360.6	-5	477.6	350.6	-7.94597	-7.71144
Trial 26	-5	-477.6	360.6	-5	477.6	360.6	-7.94597	-7.94597
Trial 27	-5	-477.6	360.6	-5	487.6	350.6	-7.94597	-7.64193
Trial 28	-5	-477.6	360.6	-5	487.6	360.6	-7.94597	-7.87602
Trial 29	-5	-477.6	360.6	5	477.6	350.6	-7.94597	-7.7873
Trial 30	-5	-477.6	360.6	5	477.6	360.6	-7.94597	-8.0239
Trial 31	-5	-477.6	360.6	5	487.6	350.6	-7.94597	-7.7165
Trial 32	-5	-477.6	360.6	5	487.6	360.6	-7.94597	-7.95269
Trial 33	5	-487.6	350.6	-5	477.6	350.6	-7.7165	-7.71144
Trial 34	5	-487.6	350.6	-5	477.6	360.6	-7.7165	-7.94597
Trial 35	5	-487.6	350.6	-5	487.6	350.6	-7.7165	-7.64193
Trial 36	5	-487.6	350.6	-5	487.6	360.6	-7.7165	-7.87602
Trial 37	5	-487.6	350.6	5	477.6	350.6	-7.7165	-7.7873
Trial 38	5	-487.6	350.6	5	477.6	360.6	-7.7165	-8.0239
Trial 39	5	-487.6	350.6	5	487.6	350.6	-7.7165	-7.7165
Trial 40	5	-487.6	350.6	5	487.6	360.6	-7.7165	-7.95269
Trial 41	5	-487.6	360.6	-5	477.6	350.6	-7.95269	-7.71144
Trial 42	5	-487.6	360.6	-5	477.6	360.6	-7.95269	-7.94597
Trial 43	5	-487.6	360.6	-5	487.6	350.6	-7.95269	-7.64193
Trial 44	5	-487.6	360.6	-5	487.6	360.6	-7.95269	-7.87602
Trial 45	5	-487.6	360.6	5	477.6	350.6	-7.95269	-7.7873
Trial 46	5	-487.6	360.6	5	477.6	360.6	-7.95269	-8.0239
Trial 47	5	-487.6	360.6	5	487.6	350.6	-7.95269	-7.7165
Trial 48	5	-487.6	360.6	5	487.6	360.6	-7.95269	-7.95269
Trial 49	5	-477.6	350.6	-5	477.6	350.6	-7.7873	-7.71144
Trial 50	5	-477.6	350.6	-5	477.6	360.6	-7.7873	-7.94597
Trial 51	5	-477.6	350.6	-5	487.6	350.6	-7.7873	-7.64193
Trial 52	5	-477.6	350.6	-5	487.6	360.6	-7.7873	-7.87602
Trial 53	5	-477.6	350.6	5	477.6	350.6	-7.7873	-7.7873
Trial 54	5	-477.6	350.6	5	477.6	360.6	-7.7873	-8.0239
Trial 55	5	-477.6	350.6	5	487.6	350.6	-7.7873	-7.7165
Trial 56	5	-477.6	350.6	5	487.6	360.6	-7.7873	-7.95269
Trial 57	5	-477.6	360.6	-5	477.6	350.6	-8.0239	-7.71144
Trial 58	5	-477.6	360.6	-5	477.6	360.6	-8.0239	-7.94597
Trial 59	5	-477.6	360.6	-5	487.6	350.6	-8.0239	-7.64193
Trial 60	5	-477.6	360.6	-5	487.6	360.6	-8.0239	-7.87602
Trial 61	5	-477.6	360.6	5	477.6	350.6	-8.0239	-7.7873
Trial 62	5	-477.6	360.6	5	477.6	360.6	-8.0239	-8.0239
Trial 63	5	-477.6	360.6	5	487.6	350.6	-8.0239	-7.7165
Trial 64	5	-477.6	360.6	5	487.6	360.6	-8.0239	-7.95269

图 22-36 优化结果

Main Effects for Response: **camber_angle_left**

Factor	From	To	Effect	Effect %
FSAE_SUS_front.ground.hpl_uca_outer.z	3.5060e+02	3.6060e+02	-2.3535e-01	-3.01
FSAE_SUS_front.ground.hpl_uca_outer.x	-5.0000	5.0000	-7.6259e-02	-0.97
FSAE_SUS_front.ground.hpl_uca_outer.y	-4.8760e+02	-4.7760e+02	-7.0366e-02	-0.9
FSAE_SUS_front.ground.hpr_uca_outer.z	3.5060e+02	3.6060e+02	8.8818e-16	0
FSAE_SUS_front.ground.hpr_uca_outer.x	-5.0000	5.0000	0	0
FSAE_SUS_front.ground.hpr_uca_outer.y	4.7760e+02	4.8760e+02	0	0

Main Effects for Response: **camber_angle_right**

Factor	From	To	Effect	Effect %
FSAE_SUS_front.ground.hpr_uca_outer.z	3.5060e+02	3.6060e+02	-2.3535e-01	-3.01
FSAE_SUS_front.ground.hpr_uca_outer.x	-5.0000	5.0000	-7.6259e-02	-0.97
FSAE_SUS_front.ground.hpr_uca_outer.y	4.7760e+02	4.8760e+02	7.0366e-02	0.9
FSAE_SUS_front.ground.hpl_uca_outer.z	3.5060e+02	3.6060e+02	-4.4409e-15	0
FSAE_SUS_front.ground.hpl_uca_outer.x	-5.0000	5.0000	1.7764e-15	0
FSAE_SUS_front.ground.hpl_uca_outer.y	-4.8760e+02	-4.7760e+02	1.7764e-15	0

图 22-37 外倾角优化变量敏感度分析

参考文献

[1] 游雄杰，干年妃，程超. 两片变刚度全啮合钢板弹簧粒子群优化设计[J]. 机械设计与制造，2018（03）：205-208.

[2] 陈丽，常勇. 后钢板弹簧悬架布置对不足转向性能的影响[J]. 重型汽车，2018（04）：15-16.

[3] 韩莉，李雪梅，陈综艺，刘夫云. 少片变截面钢板弹簧动刚度计算方法研究[J]. 机械设计与制造，2018（10）：55-58.

[4] 张洁，卢剑伟，王翔宇，李海波. 等寿命曲线的变截面钢板弹簧可靠性分析方法[J]. 汽车工程学报，2019，9（01）：36-42.

[5] 李舜酩，张凯成，闻静. 某钢板弹簧结构优化设计[J]. 机械设计与制造，2019（01）：111-117.

[6] 杨凯，王海艳，王兴平，王海燕. 钢板弹簧支架轻量化优化设计[J]. 汽车工艺与材料，2017（10）：27-31.

[7] 吴伟斌，李泽艺，洪添胜，刘文超，黄家曦，余耀烽. 基于山地果园路谱的轮式运输车钢板弹簧悬架优化设计[J]. 华中农业大学学报，2018，37（04）：7-14.

[8] 唐应时，付建朝，姚汉波，胡远宏. 两片变截面变刚度钢板弹簧遗传优化设计[J]. 湖南大学学报（自然科学版），2011，38（10）：39-43.

[9] 田晋跃，陈治领，韩顺，王新成. 随动转向半挂汽车列车机动性分析[J]. 机械设计与制造， 2018（02）：13-15.

[10] 刘春辉，关志伟，申荣卫，严英. 四轮转向半挂汽车列车鲁棒最优保性能控制[J]. 现代制造工程，2016（04）：69-73.

[11] 刘春辉，关志伟，杜峰，严英. 四轮转向半挂汽车列车横向稳定性的模糊 PID 控制[J]. 现代制造工程，2016（07）：47-50.

[12] 徐晓美，陈宁，H P Lee. 后轮随动转向技术应用研究综述[J]. 汽车技术，2016（07）：1-6.

[13] 宋作军. 基于中心流形理论的四轮转向汽车 Hopf 分岔分析[J]. 振动与冲击，2016，35（13）：219-223.

[14] 刘启佳，陈思忠. 基于 LQR 的四轮转向汽车控制方法[J]. 北京理工大学学报，2014，

34（11）：1135-1139.

[15] 刘刚，陈思忠，郑凯锋，王文竹. 四轮转向车辆的操纵稳定性分析[J]. 中国机械工程，2015，26（09）：1250-1254.

[16] 赵立军，邓宁宁，罗念宁，刘昕晖. 基于直接横摆力矩的四轮转向/驱动滑模控制[J]. 华南理工大学学报（自然科学版），2015，43（08）：69-74.

[17] 宋宇，陈无畏，陈黎卿. 四轮转向车辆横摆角速度反馈与神经网络自适应混合控制的研究[J]. 汽车工程，2013，35（01）：66-71.

[18] 来飞，黄超群. 汽车四轮转向变增益跟踪控制的研究[J]. 汽车工程，2012，34（06）：517-522.

[19] 段亮，杨树凯，宋传学，范士琦，卢炳武. 平衡悬架钢板弹簧动态特性的研究[J]. 机械工程学报，2016，52（06）：153-158.

[20] 段亮，杨树凯，宋传学，范士琦，卢炳武. 某多轴商用车平衡悬架高精度建模与分析[J]. 汽车工程，2016，38（02）：229-233.

[21] 苏继龙，连兴峰. 载重汽车 3 种结构形式平衡悬架模态分析[J]. 计算机辅助工程，2012，21（02）：21-24.